BASEBALLHQ.COM'S **2015**

MINOR LEAGUE BASEBALL ANALYST

ROB GORDON AND JEREMY DELONEY | BRENT HERSHEY, EDITOR | TENTH EDITION

TRIUMPH
BOOKS

This book is available in quantity at special discounts for your group or organization. For further information, contact:

Triumph Books LLC
814 North Franklin Street
Chicago, Illinois 60610
(312) 337-0747
www.triumphbooks.com

Printed in U.S.A.
ISBN: 978-1-62937-014-9

Data provided by TheBaseballCube.com and Baseball Info Solutions

Cover design by Brent Hershey
Front cover photograph by Jerry Lai/USA TODAY Sports Images

Acknowledgments

Jeremy Deloney:

It is never difficult to express gratitude and thanks to those who deserve such praise, though many of those individuals prefer to deflect the positive attention. The challenge is finding new and creative ways to convey my appreciation. This is my sixth year with the *Minor League Baseball Analyst* and the hard work and dedication devoted to this project remains.

I am forever grateful to the fine folks at BaseballHQ.com who provided me with such an opportunity, especially as a young aspiring writer who had little industry experience. What began as a hobby evolved into something greater and this experience wouldn't be possible without the support of several individuals. Thank you to Deric McKamey, Ron Shandler, Brent Hershey, Ray Murphy, and Rob Gordon for their leadership, expertise, and encouragement.

My wife Amy continues to be my main source of support and inspiration. I believe luck is evident in everyday life and I certainly am fortunate that our paths crossed at the University of Dayton way back in the early- to mid-1990s. Sure, we've aged (somewhat) and my hair continues to thin, but her love and support is a constant. I'm not one to resort to clichés, but she is the best person ever.

My terrific kids, Owen, Ethan, and Madeline, who may be partially responsible for my thinning hair, also are equally accountable for the joy I encounter on a daily basis. They are all unique, yet seem to share a love and zest of life. My advice to them: be passionate, laugh, and play/work hard.

My parents, Bill and Nancy, and my brothers BJ and Andy. have known me the longest, yet continue to allow me to keep the Deloney name. I use it proudly.

Lastly, I want to thank the readers of the MLBA and BaseballHQ.com. I will always appreciate your support and feedback, whether positive or negative. Perhaps I'll see you again next year.

Rob Gordon:

In 2003 Ron Shandler gave me the opportunity to do something I'd wanted to do all of my life—write about baseball. Ron is one of the smartest baseball people I've had the pleasure of meeting, and I owe him a huge thank you.

Deric McKamey took me under his wing and spent countless hours explaining what scouts look for. Deric's total recall of the most obscure minor league players still amazes me. Deric has moved on to bigger and better things in professional baseball, but his imprint on the structure and content of this book lives.

Jeremy Deloney and I are now in our sixth edition of the *Minor League Baseball Analyst* and each year I'm more and more impressed with his comprehensive and astute knowledge of the minor leagues. Jeremy sees tons of games in the Midwest League and elsewhere and is able to quickly and concisely analyze a player's potential. Over the past couple of years Jeremy and I have gotten invaluable help from the rest of the HQ minor league team: Colby Garrapy, Brent Hershey, and Chris Mallonee.

I would especially like to thank Brent Hershey. Brent served as our editor at BaseballHQ.com throughout the year and throughout the production of this book. Brent and partner Ray Murphy have always been the glue that has held this project together. Thank you Brent and Ray!

Many other baseball people provided invaluable support and encouragement over the years. They include Jeff Barton, Jim Callis, John Sickels, Rick Wilton, Patrick Davitt, Todd Zola, Jason Grey, Joe Sheehan, Jeff Erickson, Lawr Michaels, Mark Murray, Brian Walton, Jason Collette, Kimball Crossley, Steve Moyer, Phil Hertz, Jock Thompson, and Doug Dennis.

Some day, someone will write a story about Baseball Unlimited. Until then, I'll just have to thank the boys—Michael Hartman, Steve Hartman, Keegan Hartman, Michael Cooney, Bob Hathaway, Doug Hathaway, Raj Patel, Derald Cook, Todd Hooper, Dave Dannemiller, Ted Maizes, Nick Gleckman, Greg Murrey, Randy Jones, and John Mundelius. You guys rock and may BU live forever!

My oldest son Bobby started high school this year and is going into his 4th year of travel baseball. His head coach Rob Stockman and the rest of the coaching staff, John Schneider and Steve Farkas, took the boys travel team to another level in 2014. All of the boys improved and learned good sportsmanship along the way. Also a big shout-out to rest of the Dearborn baseball gang, Greg McKae, Matt McKae, Danny McKae, Kevin Barkoff, Rob Fay, and Craig Cotter.

I would especially like to thank my family. My two boys— Bobby and Jimmy—make the sky bluer, the sun brighter, and the crack of the bat all the more sweet. My mother Sandra Gordon took me on an annual birthday trip to see the Cubs play and drove me to countless baseball practices, and my father Robert W. Gordon III took me to Chicago to see the great Roberto Clemente play in his last season and has shared my passion for the game. My sister Susan Arntson helped raise me and tried to keep me out of trouble. Thank you! Her husband Jeff and kids Rachael, Josh, Marrisa, and Jake seem like more than "just" family.

Finally—a huge thank you to my amazing and beautiful wife Paula Gordon. This may sound like a cliché, but I really would not have been able to do this without her in my life.

TABLE OF CONTENTS

by Jeremy Deloney

Now in its tenth edition in 2015, the *Minor League Baseball Analyst* has shown to have staying power within the prospect universe. It all started in 2005 with Deric McKamey, now a scout with the St. Louis Cardinals. His unique and expert insights added a lot of color to the ambiguous world of minor league prospects and the tradition continues today. Deric passed the torch to Rob Gordon and me six years ago and we've done our best to maintain the consistent, objective perspective that Deric brought to the table. While we've added several names to the mix, the goal remains the same: to bring readers fresh ideas in an inimitable format while adding our own personal assessments. Brent Hershey, the editor of the MLBA and General Manager of Content for BaseballHQ. com, continues to bring out the best in all of us, while Colby Garrapy and Chris Mallonee have proven they have gifted eyes for all things minor leagues.

The space for prospect coverage has gotten awfully crowded, and that is a good thing. Not only does it give all of us plenty of resources and insight, it also forces us at BHQ to remain the standard-bearers by finding new ways to keep our readers informed and entertained. We do that in the MLBA and with our coverage at BaseballHQ.com. You'll see some new features in this book and at our site in 2015, and we're excited to take you along for the ride.

There is little doubt the MLBA attracts fantasy baseball players with its statistical focus and valuable compilation of lists and rankings. However, the MLBA also is an important resource for any minor league baseball fan. With assessments on over 1,000 prospects, most minor league games will have at least a few players featured in this book. I've actually seen the MLBA at a few games myself.

We truly appreciate the thirst for prospect information and we enjoy bringing our assessments to you. While we also understand there are several other qualified prospect sites and outlets available to you, we encourage you to make the MLBA a staple of your annual routine, whether it be taking it with you to a minor league game or enjoying the daily and weekly analysis via BaseballHQ. com. Rob and I have done this for a long time and have several connections within the game. We don't simply regurgitate information from other outlets and present it as our own. We spend a lot of time at minor league ballparks and in contact with organizational personnel so you get the benefit of both observations and analysis.

While the general format of the book remains the same with valuable statistical information, impactful essays, and a multitude of lists, you'll see some slight tweaks to our coverage. The player commentaries are more structured and will tell you more of the hows and whys behind the statistical outputs of the various prospects. The essays are written from different perspectives and will shine a different kind of light on the topics.

With our expanded lineup of more contributors to the MLBA, we have greater coverage all across the U.S. Most of us have contacts within the game who can provide us with scouting tips and valuable information on various prospects and organizations. All of us attend games and like to chat with the scouts in

attendance. While we all have our own personal biases and likes/dislikes, the collaboration on this project is even more evident.

This year, our team engaged in several conference calls to discuss each organization in detail. This exercise was extremely helpful as it allowed us to share viewpoints with each other. So while I may have an opinion on a player in an organization I cover, one of my collegues may have seen this player several times and had a different perspective. I'd like to think I have a strong mastery of the prospect universe, but the calls allowed me to take a different approach and provide—and receive—assessments on players I don't necessarily cover. This will likely be a staple going forward.

The organizational coverage continues to be diverse and well-rounded, as we each take responsibility for covering prospects in terms of the 30 farm systems. I took the entire American League again while the National League was split up between Rob (ATL, MIA, PIT, STL, CHC, MIL, LA, SD, COL, ARI), Chris (NYM, CIN), Brent (PHI, WAS), and Colby (SF). Because of our year-round sharing of information, there is definitely more of a collaborative feel for the coverage. After all, the competition in this industry forces us to be at the top of our games. I think that is evident in the 2015 *Minor League Baseball Analyst*.

The BaseballHQ rating system (detailed at the beginning of the Batters and Pitchers sections) continues to be a source of debate, but also an effective way to evaluate minor league prospects. The Potential Ratings are a two-part system in which a player is assigned a number rating based on his upside potential (1-10) and a letter rating based on the probability of reaching that potential (A-E). A 10 implies Hall of Fame potential, whereas a 1 is minor league roster filler. Given our coverage of 1,000+ prospects, you won't find any player with less than a 6 in this book. The letter/probability ratings, on the other hand, are all across the board and for good reason.

Rating minor league baseball players can be a difficult exercise, just like any assessment system dealing with 17-to-24-year-olds. Some prospects improve. Some prospects regress. That's just the nature of the business. That's why this system wasn't designed to be your only way to assess prospects. We rate players first by the upside potential, and conduct internal debates on whether this five-tool player should be a 9 or an 8, for example. The letter/probably rating comes next, and we have just as much debate over that. We consider all kinds of factors and variables including, but not limited to: athleticism, tools, ability to improve, and historical performance. Ratings can and will change, though not typically in a drastic fashion from year to year. Our goal is to give you a snapshot of a player's ultimate upside and likelihood of success. AA player's final rating—made by the team author—can be a difficult decision. But in the end, it is just a rating. The more valuable information is in the player boxes and commentary.

As mentioned previously, the outline of the book will look and feel similar to previous editions of the MLBA. The Insights section is filled with premium essays designed to shine a spotlight on more free-form assessments. Some of the essays are topics from previous years—this is, in large part, by design as we've gotten positive feedback from our readers—Sleepers Outside the HQ100, Top 20 International Prospects, 2015 College Baseball Names to Know, and a team-by-team 2014 Draft Recap. And this year, a new voice, BHQ contributor Nick Richards, adds his thoughts on using stats to discover minor league breakout stars. We hope you find the different perspectives valuable.

One of the more difficult exercises this year was the Organizational Ratings/Rankings section. As most of you know, the player movement during—and after—the Winter Meetings was unprecedented and we had to continually revise the rankings. For instance, seven of the original top 15 prospects of the Padres were traded in a very short time frame. Clearly, the team ratings and rankings changed dramatically as a result of the trade-happy nature of new GM A.J. Preller. Regardless, there are some plentiful farm systems in baseball (Cubs, Astros) and some thin ones (Tigers, Angels).

The bulk of the book continues to be made up of the hitter and pitcher profiles. We bring you expanded stats, tool assessments, expected arrival dates, draft info, potential roles, and the BaseballHQ rating. While a player's skills may improve or regress from year to year, our goal is to quantify and measure a player at one certain point in time. A player's tool analysis is equally as important as the statistical tables. Over-analysis of statistics in the minor leagues can be a dangerous proposition. Not only are there severe hitting/pitching environments, but these are mostly still young players who are developing their bodies and their games. Don't get too caught up in a hitter's BA or a pitcher's ERA—look deeper at their skills and how their tools project. That's where the BHQ team comes into play. It's one thing to look at an OBP and draw conclusions. It's another thing to provide reasons why the OBP is at a certain level and why it may get better or get worse.

As I mentioned previously, the player commentaries have become more consistent and provide more information on how a prospect's tools and skills project rather than just a regurgitation of their statistical outputs from previous seasons. While stats are certainly important, they don't tell the full story. There has to be some consideration for hitting/pitching environments as well as age-to-level analysis. A powerful position player prospect in the spacious ballparks of the Florida State League may not hit many HR while a so-so prospect in the hitter-friendly California League may hit 25 HR. The player commentaries are meant to provide insights into this type of situation.

Major League Equivalents remain a staple of the MLBA and provides MLEs on several prospects. Used correctly, MLEs are excellent indicators of potential. But just as we cannot take traditional major league statistics at face value, the same goes for

MLEs. Compare what you see in that space versus what you see in the batter/pitcher profiles and commentaries. You'll often notice eerie similarities. Fun stuff.

The section that always generates constructive debate is the Mega-Lists. Here you will find lists such as the HQ100, Top Prospects by Organization, Top Positional Prospects, Top Prospects by Category, Best Fantasy Prospects, and the Top 100 Archives. Everybody loves lists—we do as well—and this section brings all of the assessments and analytics together. Let the debates begin.

The HQ100 is a combination of five individual contributor Top 100 lists. All five of our writers submitted their own Top 100 lists—without consulting or reviewing any other list—and the HQ100 is the end result. This continues to be an interesting exercise. Sixty-five prospects who are listed in the HQ100 appeared on all five ballots—that's remarkably consistent given the large universe of minor league players.

One important caveat with the HQ100—you will notice that a prospect's placement on this list may run contrary to their placement on the organizational rankings. This is because the top prospects by organization lists were constructed by one individual contributor. For example, I ranked the Top 15 prospects in each organization in the American League. My opinion will obviously differ from the four other writers when submitting a Top 100 list. The HQ100 shows Mark Appel is the second best Astros prospect. However, I ranked Appel as the fourth best Astros prospect behind Carlos Correa, Mike Foltynewicz, and Vince Velasquez. The HQ100 was designed to be a combination of all contributor lists.

This is also evident in the lists of Top Prospects by Position. These lists were generated and formulated directly from the HQ100 as opposed to from an individual writer's opinion. Some prospects play multiple positions currently or may change positions in the future. This was captured in these lists. Take the case of Kyle Schwarber. He was drafted as a catcher and played some there in his pro debut. However, he also saw time in the outfield and that is where he will likely play going forward. Thus, he's listed as an outfielder.

We hope you enjoy the tenth edition of the MLBA. This is a result of year-round hard work and constant communication with each other. We are always open to your feedback on what we can do to make your reading experience more enjoyable. It is OK to disagree with some of our assessments and ratings—we welcome it. Let us know what you think. We look forward to the 2015 baseball season and hope you do as well. Enjoy!

Early Discovery of Prospects: Stats-Based Approach

by Nick Richards

It is commonly understood that when evaluating minor league talent, we should pay more attention to scouting reports than to results on the field. That is absolutely true. After all, perhaps that highly touted Double-A pitcher has been told to throw nothing but curve balls for a few innings so he can get a better mastery of the pitch. The fact that he gave up a lot of hits in the process tells us little about his actual talent level. If the scouts say he is a great prospect, we can ignore that ugly ERA and WHIP and wait for better days. Or maybe there is a corner outfielder who is smashing the ball left and right, but the scouts say he's a tweener, and he's doing this in the very hitter-friendly Pacific Coast League. Not a top prospect after all.

So how can we stay ahead of our leaguemates, especially in dynasty leagues where other owners read what the scouts say and all jump on the hot new minor league prospects at the same time?

Scouting comes first, but stats still count

Very simply, we use stats. Scouts find the next great prospects from watching the players on the field. We can do something similar. We may not have the scout's eye, and we may not have the opportunity to see the players in real life very often, but we have all the stats we can handle at our fingertips. If we know what to look for, we can find the next wave of emerging talent before the articles get written.

Filters to find the best batters

Other than the standard measurements we use (strikeout rate, walk rate, etc.), what can we use to search for the next good minor leaguers? A simple method is to break things down to these basic metrics:

- OBP—An On-Base Percentage of .340 or more shows a batter who knows how to get on base at a good rate.
- ISO—Isolated Power is simply slugging percentage – batting average, and it serves as a nice view of the raw power of a batter in isolation. A measure of .200 or greater is a sign of a big-league power hitter.
- SB/Game—Stolen Bases per Game is a very simple measurement that is designed to filter through different levels and playing time considerations to do an apples-to-apples comparison: In how many games did that batter appear? And in those games, how many stolen bases did he get? An index of 0.20 or higher reveals a speedster getting a SB every five games, which results in about 30 at the end of a 150-game season. Higher is better, but a 30-SB guy is nice to have.
- K%—Strikeout percentage is the number of strikeouts divided by Plate Appearances (not ABs). It asks, of the times that batter came to the plate, how many times did he strike out? Anything over 25% is a warning sign, and ideally we want to see a rate under 20%.
- BB%—Walk percentage is similar: Walks divided by Plate Appearances. Of the times that batter came to the plate, how many times did he walk? 10% or better should be the target.

These filters will find either a power guy or a speed guy (both is great, of course) who has an excellent batting eye and thus gets on base. Using those filters early in 2014, a discerning owner would have discovered Mookie Betts tearing up Double-A pitching before he was called up to Triple-A and then the majors. Betts was not on most top prospect lists going into 2014, so to discover him before anyone else would mean monitoring the statistics.

Filters to find the best pitchers

Use a similar approach for pitchers with these metrics:

- WHIP—Less than 1.200 shows a pitcher who isn't walking too many and is proving effective at keeping batters off the bases.
- BF/IP—Batters Faced per Innings Pitched is designed to look for pitchers who cannot seem to put a team away inning after inning. Look for under 4.10 to show dominance. The best pitchers will have rates under 4.00.
- K%—Strikeout rate for pitchers is simply Strikeouts divided by Batters Faced. How many batters did he face, and of those, how many did he strike out? Unlike K/9, this is inning independent, and it protects against those pitchers who put up great K/9 numbers because they simply face more batters. K% is short and to the point and works for both starters and relievers. 20% or higher is what to look for, and 25% is exceptional.
- BB%—Walks divided by Batters Faced. Similar to K%, this simplifies things to how many batters did he face, and of those how many did he walk? 8% or less is what to look for.
- K%-BB%—As Cmd combines both Dom and Ctl, this measurement protects against extreme pitchers who don't strike out enough batters but whose walk rate is so low we tend to overlook it. We want both a good strikeout rate and a good walk rate. K%-BB% should be at least 15%.

Using these filters back in 2013 would have discovered Matt Wisler putting up great numbers in Double-A before he was on the radar—or tout's lists—for most owners.

Who looks good now?

Using end-of-season stats for Double-A players from Baseball-Reference.com (they provide a handy list of top performing minor leaguers by clicking Minors | Leaders | the three Double-A leagues | 2014 | Batting Leaders / Pitching Leaders), and applying the metrics listed above (plus filtering out older prospects or guys already called up in 2014), we find the following batters:

BATTER	Age	TM	LV	OBP	ISO	SB/G	K%	BB%
Micah Johnson	23	CHW	AA	.414	.137	.27	16%	12%
Tony Kemp	22	HOU	AA	.381	.133	.22	12%	10%
Francisco Lindor	20	CLE	AA	.352	.111	.28	16%	10%

Obviously, Lindor is already well known. Johnson and Kemp are less so, but both are showing quite good bat control, drawing walks, and showing speed on the base paths. None of them shows much power, but they get on base at a rate that should help them transition to the big leagues while still putting up decent numbers for infielders. In early December 2014, Lindor wass already owned by 18% of CBSsports.com owners, Johnson is only owned by 3% and Tony Kemp wasn't even in their database yet. Those owners looking toward 2015 might keep an eye on Micah Johnson, while those in deep dynasty leagues might note Tony Kemp.

Using the pitching metrics yielded the following pitchers:

PITCHER	Age	TM	LV	WHIP	BF/IP	K%	BB%	K%-BB%
Daniel Winkler	24	COL	AA	0.714	3.74	27%	6%	21%
Tyler Cravy	24	MIL	AA	0.845	3.84	23%	5%	18%
Steven Matz	23	NYM	AA	1.121	4.01	24%	5%	19%
Brian Johnson	23	BOS	AA	0.932	3.83	22%	7%	15%
Christian Binford	21	KC	AA	1.062	4.04	20%	3%	17%

Winkler has been in the news for both his Tommy John surgery that will keep him out for a good chunk of 2015, as well being an Atlanta Braves Rule 5 draftee. Steven Matz and Christian Binford both made several hot prospects lists in 2014 and are already probably on owner's radars. But Cravy and Johnson also put up great numbers in Double-A, yet Johnson is only owned by 1% of CBSsports.com owners and Cravy is not even in their database yet.

Conclusion

This method works best in-season, such as in June or July when prospects in Single-A or Double-A are first putting themselves on our radars. Doing this at the end of the season turns up prospects who already made headlines and got picked up. Plus most leagues do not allow offseason pickups of free agents, so to notice a guy in the offseason just means waiting until spring to get him, by which time he might be on several prospect lists. Still, even in the offseason the method can help us focus on some unheralded players who are putting up solid numbers across the board. This article focused on Double-A, but the same method can be used for Single-A players too, and these are usually even less known (and are more speculative).

Will all of these players make it to the major leagues? Not necessarily, they could stumble along the way through the minor leagues. It's not until they dominate Double-A that we should really sit up and notice, and even then some will fail as they reach Triple-A or the major leagues. Some of these players are too young to know for sure how they will ultimately pan out.

However, the idea of this article is that we can find players who put up good numbers in 2014. Some of them will show up on top prospect lists going into 2015. Those who wait for such lists will get them the same time as their fellow owners. But those who explore the statistics ahead of time can find these players before the lists get published. In deeper or dynasty leagues, these are the sorts of players to speculate on. If they fall by the wayside before reaching the major leagues, it's a gamble that did not pay off. However, every time one of these prospects makes it, it's like hitting the jackpot that is all the sweeter because of finding them before anyone else. Yet all it took was statistics and common sense.

Sleepers Outside the HQ100

by Rob Gordon

Each year the BaseballHQ.com minors team spends countless hours scouting, watching video, researching, and debating which players will end up on HQ100 list of top prospects. Yet the reality is that each year there are dozens of talented prospects who fail to make the cut. Their exclusion can be justified for all sorts of reasons: too old, too young, too one dimensional, too flawed, or not enough of a track record to warrant inclusion. Yet for those who play in deep keeper formats or just have a strong affinity for scouting prospects, top 100 lists just aren't deep enough.

Below we take a look at some sleeper prospects who didn't make the cut, but have a good chance of being on the list in 2016 or beyond. We opted to focus on sleepers outside the top 100 and decided to focus our attention—and yours—on younger, lesser known players,

Michael Gettys (OF, SD) was one of the more athletic players available in the 2014 draft. He's strong and runs well, but his swing can get long and scouts were mixed on his ability to make contact and hit for average. Gettys fell all the way to draft pick #51 as teams opted for safer, more signable players. That should be a boon to the Padres, as Gettys quickly established himself as one of the better prospects in the Arizona Rookie League. Although he cooled off after a blistering start, he hit over .300 in every month and ended the season slashing .310/.353/.437 with eight doubles, five triples, three home runs, and 14 SB.

Gettys shows a combination of speed and power. He plays hard and aggressively at all times, and has 4.0 speed to first. Defensively, he covers ground well in CF and flashed a mid-90s arm as a pitcher in high school. He has easy bat speed, quick hands and should develop above-average power down the road. He can be overly aggressive at the plate, as he fanned 66 times in 213 AB. Strike zone judgment is a teachable skill, and if Gettys can improve his pitch recognition without sacrificing his power, he has the tools to be a 20/20 player upon reaching the majors.

Jose De Leon (RHP, LA) is a little bit of a late bloomer. The 22-year-old from Southern University took a huge step forward in 2014, going 7-0 with a 2.22 ERA and 21 BB/119 K in 77 innings between rookie ball and Low-A. His velocity was a couple of ticks better than in the past as he started to fill out his 6'2", 185 frame. His fastball now sits at 92-94 mph with good late movement, topping out at 96, and he mixes in a plus low-80s slurve and an improved change-up.

Improved conditioning and a mechanical adjustment fueled the breakout and he had an attention-grabbing strikeout-to-walk ratio of 42:2 while limiting opposing hitters to a .171 BA after being moved up to the Midwest League. The 24th-round pick will need to prove that 2014 was no fluke, but the uptick in velocity, improved breaking ball, and solid command all bode well for the future.

Kevin Padlo (3B, COL) didn't really garner much attention until he impressed scouts in the California Area Code Games in the summer before his senior year at Murrietta Valley High School, where he was a two-sport standout. Padlo jumped up draft boards heading into June and was taken by the Rockies in the 5th round. They signed him for an over-slot $650,000 to lure him away from a college commitment to San Diego.

Although he hit only two home runs as a high school senior, Padlo flashes a quick bat and above-average power and hit 15 doubles and eight home runs in his Pioneer League debut. He also showed an advanced understanding of the strike zone, walking 31 times in 160 AB. He moves well defensively with good hands and a strong arm and should be able to stick at 3B over the long term, though with the presence of Nolan Arenado the club will be in no hurry to rush Padlo to the majors.

Ozhaino Albies (SS, ATL) came out of nowhere to establish himself as one of the most exciting young prospects in the National League. The 18-year-old from Curacao showed a plus feel for the game despite being one of the youngest players in both the GCL and the APPY. He is a quick-twitch athlete with plus speed and an advanced feel for hitting. The switch-hitter rakes from both sides of the plate with a short, compact stroke and across two levels he hit .364/.446/.444 with 22 SB in 198 AB.

Albies uses the entire field, makes consistent contact, and has an excellent understanding of the strike zone, walking more than he struck out. He doesn't project to develop much if any power, but that is his only obvious shortcoming. Defensively he moves well to both sides of the ball, has soft hands, good footwork, and a strong, accurate arm. Albies will move up to full-season ball in 2015 and if he can duplicate these results, he will rise to the top of the Braves list next year.

Mallex Smith (OF, ATL) has some of the best pure speed in the minors. The Padres 5th-round pick out of junior college in Florida is short, but he had a monster breakout season in 2014, hitting .310 with 69 BB and 111 runs scored. Smith also led the minors with 92 SB, 20 more than the next highest total.

Smith has a quick bat and a balanced approach at the plate. He works the count well and has an advanced understanding of the strike zone that should allow him to continue to hit for average as he moves up. His plus-plus speed is his best asset, but he is also an accomplished bunter and knows how to put the ball into play to take advantage of his legs. Defensively Smith reads the ball well and covers ground in CF with an average, but accurate, arm. Power is the one area where Smith is going to be well below average. He did hit five home runs in the CAL, but that isn't going to be part of his game once he reaches the majors. At the end

of the year, Smith was traded to the Braves as part of the Justin Upton deal and the ATL system is thin on position players.

Francellis Montas (RHP, CHW) had an impressive breakout season for the Sox, going 5-0 with a 1.44 ERA and 22 BB/80 K in 81 IP between rookie ball and Low-A. The 21-year-old righty from the Dominican Republic showed improved command of his hard, plus 91-98 mph fastball that has excellent late movement. Montas also has an average slider that he threw more consistently for strikes.

Montas missed significant time with two knee injuries, but when he was on the mound he dominated and showed improved command of all three offerings. His change-up remains a work in progress and will be key going forward. If that doesn't develop, he has the control and arm strength to grow into an elite level closer, though for now the Sox continue to see him as a starter.

Gabby Guerrero (OF, SEA) is the nephew of former major leaguer Vladimir Guerrero, and was signed out of the Dominican Republic in 2010. Just like his uncle, the younger Guerrero is a very aggressive free-swinger who can hit anything around the plate with authority. He makes contact and covers the plate well with amazing hand-eye coordination.

On the year, the 21-year-old Guerrero hit .307/.347.467 with 28 doubles, 18 home runs, and 18 SB in 538 AB in the California League. Guerrero has emerging power that should develop into his best tool down the road, but needs to prove that his outburst in 2014 was not simply a product of the hitter-friendly CAL. Defensively Guerrero runs well and covers ground with a cannon for an arm and will likely end up in RF.

Nomar Mazara (OF, TEX) made a splash when the Rangers signed the Dominican OF to a record-breaking $4.95M bonus in 2011. In his first two seasons, he showed solid power, but struck out too much and struggled in 2013. He made some critical adjustments in his approach at the plate, namely shelving a high leg kick and working on better strike zone judgment. The 6'4" left-handed hitter belted 19 home runs in 398 AB in the South Atlantic League and then smacked another three round-trippers in a brief stint at Double-A.

For the year, the 19-year-old RF hit .271/.362/.478 with 28 doubles and 21 home runs. Mazara still struggles with LHP, hitting just .214 with three home runs in 112 AB, and will need to make an adjustment as he moves up. He is also a fringy defender with below-average speed, so his bat will be his ticket to the majors. But his power and athleticism are legit and worth owning.

2014 First-Year Player Draft Recap
by Rob Gordon (NL) and Jeremy Deloney (AL)

NATIONAL LEAGUE

ARIZONA DIAMONDBACKS

The Diamondbacks' top three prospects (Bradley, Shipley, and Aaron Blair) are all right-handed pitchers and they added to that depth, taking high school RHP Touki Toussaint with the 13th overall pick. Toussaint drew mixed reviews from scouts, some of who raved about his athleticism, upside, and 97 mph fastball, but others worried about his size, durability, and lack of polish. The Snakes followed up with three second round picks—all high school players—and high school OF Matt Railey (3rd) before finally taking a college player (Brent Jones) in the 4th round. This high school draft class has good long-term potential but is unlikely to yield any major league ready player in the next several years.

Sleeper: 1B Kevin Cron (14th) is the younger brother of the Angels C.J. Cron and had a solid pro debut, hitting .291 with 12 home runs in 261 AB. Like his brother, he has a good understanding of the strike zone and was a 3rd round pick out of high school in 2011 before deciding to attend TCU.

Grade: B

ATLANTA BRAVES

The Braves have focused on high school players for at least the past decade and 2014 was no different. The Braves didn't pick until near the end of round one and selected high school OF Braxton Davidson. The 6-2, 210 OF projects to develop above-average power, though he failed to homer in his pro debut, and should be able to hit for average. He profiles best in LF where his power and athleticism should play well. The Braves took two well-regarded arms in high school RHP Garrett Fulenchek (2nd) and UNC-Greensboro RHP Max Povse (3rd). They also drafted 2B Luke Dykstra (7th), son of former major leaguer Lenny Dykstra. None of the Braves top 10 picks in the draft did much to stand out in their first pro summer, though Davidson, Fulenchek, and Povse all have good long-term potential.

Sleeper: RHP Caleb Dirks (15th) was a closer at California Baptist and features a good 90-94 mph fastball. He had a solid debut, going 1-0 with a 2.23 ERA, 5 saves, and 37 strikeouts in 32.1 IP.

Grade: C

CHICAGO CUBS

The Cubs continued to stockpile advanced college bats when they surprised many by selecting Indiana C/OF Kyle Schwarber with the 4th pick in the draft. Most analysts agreed that Schwarber was the top collegiate hitter available, but concerns about his ability to stick behind the plate caused many to project him to go in the 10-20 range. The early results justify the Cubs optimism as he hit .341/.427/.636 at three different levels. The Cubs also added Maryland RHP Jake Stinnett (2nd) and Virginia Tech C Mark Zagunis (3rd). High school LHP Carson Sands (4th) had a solid debut and could be a steal. He features a good low-90s fastball and has an advanced three-pitch mix. The Cubs went college-heavy

through their first 11 picks, signing only high school LHPs Sands and Justin Steele (5th).

Sleeper: RHP James Farris (9th) doesn't overpower hitters—his fastball rarely breaks 90 mph—but he's a polished college starter with four solid offerings including a plus change-up. Farris posted a 2.57 ERA in his debut, with a K:BB ratio of 21:3 in 14 IP.

Grade: A

CINCINNATI REDS

Coming into the draft, many teams agreed that Virginia closer RHP Nick Howard (1st) had some of the best raw stuff. His fastball was in the 93-95 mph range, topping out at 97 mph and at 6-3, 215, he already had the size and CWS experience many teams value. The Reds, as they have done numerous times in the past, rolled the dice and drafted Howard as a starter. He made a decent debut in that role, but needs to refine his change-up and breaking ball. His progress over the next several years will make or break this draft class and at this point, that transition is far from a sure thing. The Reds had two picks in round one and selected Stanford SS Alex Blandino at #29. He has a good approach at the plate with solid plate discipline and the ability to make consistent, hard contact. 3B Taylor Sparks (2nd) is physically imposing, but struggled in his debut and needs to prove he can hit. Outside of Howard and Blandino, the Reds didn't add a lot of impact talent.

Sleeper: RHP Brian Hunter (9th) is a polished collegiate right-hander from Hartford. His fastball sits at 88-92 mph and can go as high as 94 mph. He also has an average slider and a good, low-80s slider. He worked exclusively in relief in his debut, going 2-0 with a 1.95 ERA with 9 BB/31 K in 27.2 IP.

Grade: C–

COLORADO ROCKIES

The Rockies, in their long and frustrating quest to develop home-grown pitching, have taken a pitcher in the first round of the draft in every year since 2004. In 2014 the Rockies grabbed Evansville LHP Kyle Freeland with the 8th overall pick. He has good low-to-mid-90s velocity and showed excellent command in his debut, walking 6 while striking out 33 in 39 innings. The Rockies also added prep RHP Ryan Castellani (2nd) and LHP Sam Howard (3rd) from Georgia Southern. Despite the emphasis on arms, the Rockies biggest impacts seem likely to come from the position players. They landed three impact bats in 2B Forrest Wall (supplemental 1st), OF Wes Rogers (4th), and SS Max George (6th). George hit .301 with an .896 OPS and Wall hit .318/.416/.490 with 18 SB in 157 AB.

Sleeper: 3B Kevin Padlo (5th) was a two-sport star in high school in California, but looked very impressive in his pro debut, hitting .300/.421/.594 with 31 BB/38 K in 160 AB. The Rockies moved him from SS to 3B and at 6-2, 200 he should be able to develop enough power to have value going forward.

Grade: A–

LOS ANGELES DODGERS

The Dodgers have never been shy about drafting high school players and their top two picks in 2014 were prepsters. They landed RHP Grant Holmes (1st) with the 22nd overall pick and OF Alex Verdugo (2nd). Holmes has excellent stuff that is highlighted by a plus 93-96 mph fastball that can hit triple digits with a plus power curve and a change-up that shows potential. He immediately becomes the best RHP in the system and he whiffed 58 in 48.1 innings. Verdugo was one of the better two-way players in the draft and looked very impressive in his debut, hitting .353/.421/.511 with 11 SB in 190 AB.

Sleeper: RHP Matt Campbell (9th) looks to be a fast-rising reliever. He served as Clemson's closer, posting an ERA of 0.84 in 25 games. His fastball sits in the low 90s and tops out at 94 mph with a good, hard slider. He was lights out after signing with the Dodgers, going 0-1 with a 2.00 ERA and 10 BB/45 K in 36 innings.
Grade: B+

MIAMI MARLINS

The Marlins surprised many when they selected high school RHP Tyler Kolek with the 2nd pick. There was little doubt Kolek had the best velocity in the draft class, featuring a fastball that sits in the upper-90s, topping out at 102 mph. He also has a decent slider, curve, and an under-utilized change-up. The only concern with him is that at 6-5, 260 he is already fully developed and will need to watch his weight as he progresses, though he does have good athleticism. The Marlins also added prep C Blake Anderson (supplemental 1st) and SS Justin Twine (2nd)—though both struggled in their initial exposure to pro ball. 2B Brian Anderson (3rd) is the best hitter in this group and hit .300/.363/.496 in 230 AB. The Marlins most advanced arm may be juco LHP Michael Mader (supplemental 3rd) who showed surprising velocity and a plus curve in posting a 2.00 ERA in the NYPL.

Sleeper: OF Zach Sullivan (14th), from a New York high school, is quite raw and toolsy. He has plus speed and at 6-3, 180 he projects to develop plus raw power. He had a solid debut, hitting .280/.389/.398, showing surprising patience at the plate.
Grade: B–

MILWAUKEE BREWERS

Heading into the draft, the Brewers had one of the weaker farm systems in the NL. Taking the long-term view, the Brewers late scouting director, Bruce Seid, went after high-upside high school players early in the draft. With their 1st round pick the Brewers rolled the dice on high school LHP Kodi Medeiros. The athletic Medeiros has a good low-90s fastball that tops out at 95 mph and a plus slider. His mechanics are very unorthodox, causing some teams to project him as a reliever in the majors. He struggled with control in a brief stint in the Arizona League, posting a 7.13 ERA, but also had a 13.3 K/9. The Brewers also added high school SS Jake Gatewood (supplemental 1st) and speedy OF Monte Harrison (2nd). Harrison had the best debut of any player in this draft class, hitting .261 with 32 SB in 34 attempts. Harrison, Gatewood, and Medeiros immediately moved into the Brewers Top 15 prospects, but that is as much of an indictment of a thin farm system as it is a testament to their future potential.

Sleeper: 3B Dustin DeMuth (5th) is a strong-bodied collegiate teammate of the Cubs Kyle Schwarber, and was a key piece of the Hoosiers CWS run this past summer. He doesn't project to hit for power, but he has a nice approach at the plate and should hit for average.
Grade: B

NEW YORK METS

While the Mets have developed and traded for some of the best young arms in the NL, they have failed to duplicate those results with position players. The team took strides to address that problem, and for the first time in several years drafted an advanced collegiate hitter in Oregon State OF Michael Conforto (1st). Conforto was one of the better all-around players in this year's draft and had an impressive debut, hitting .331/.403/.448. He has plus raw power, but currently focuses on a line-drive approach in game action. He's a heady player and could be in the majors by mid-2016. The club took two more position players in rounds three and four with SS Milton Ramos (3rd) and 3B Eudor Garcia (4th). The Mets didn't draft a pitcher until the 5th round when they rolled the dice on 6'8", 225 pound RHP Josh Prevost. Prevost played basketball and baseball at Seton Hall and is fairly raw on the mound. Conforto is the only sure thing in this group, but the Mets did well to address an organizational weakness.

Sleeper: LHP Brad Wieck (7th) is even taller than Prevost. He is from NAIA Oklahoma City where he struck out 118 in 69.2 IP. He replicated those results in a brief stint in the NYPL, going 1-1 with a 1.40 ERA and 6 BB/39 K in 25.2 IP. Wieck shows surprising control for such a large pitcher and has a good 92-94 mph fastball, a plus breaking ball, and a change-up.
Grade: B

PHILADELPHIA PHILLIES

For years the Phillies have targeted toolsy, high-upside high school prospects—a strategy that has produced mixed results at best. In 2014 the club moved in a different direction, drafting college players with their first seven picks. The Phillies nabbed LSU RHP Aaron Nola with the 8th overall pick. The 21-year-old was arguably the most polished pitcher in the draft class and it showed in his debut, as he compiled a 4-3 record with a 2.93 ERA, and 10 BB/45 K in 55.1 innings. Nola reached Double-A and should be in the majors at some point in 2015. The Phillies added Cal Poly LHP Matt Imhof (2nd) and Pepperdine OF Aaron Brown (3rd). The 6'5" Imhof has a good low-90s fastball, a decent curve, and a seldom used change-up. Brown has good athleticism, but struck out an alarming 60 times in 235 BA. The club also added 1B Rhys Hoskins (5th) who proved a reliable hitter at Sacramento State, though he struggled in the NYPL.

Sleeper: LHP Brandon Leibrandt (6th) is the son of former major leaguer Charlie Leibrandt. He isn't overpowering, but has an advanced understanding of how to keep hitters off balance. In 10 pro starts, he was 3-5 with a 2.82 ERA and 10 BB/67 K in 60.2 IP and could develop into a nice command and control lefty.
Grade: C+

PITTSBURGH PIRATES

The Pirates found themselves in unfamiliar territory in 2014, and for the first time since 2000, the team did not have a pick in the first 15 slots. When they finally selected at #24, the Pirates surprised almost everyone in the industry by taking unheralded high school SS Cole Tucker (1st). He was one of the youngest players available in the draft and didn't turn 18 until a month after being selected. Scouts like his range, work ethic, and baseball savvy, but are not convinced he'll be able to stick at SS. He had a solid debut in the GCL, but is far from a Top 100 prospect. The Pirates also added San Diego OF Connor Joe (supplemental 1st) and high school RHPs Mitch Keller (2nd) and Trey Supak (supplemental 2nd). Joe suffered a back injury and will make his pro debut in 2015, while Keller and Supak had solid starts and both made the Pirates Top 15 prospect list. If Tucker develops into a legitimate first round talent, this draft will have done the job of keeping the Pirates farm system stocked with excellent talent.

Sleeper: C Kevin Krause (9th) gives the Pirates yet another in a long list of catching prospects. The Stony Brook grad missed most of his sophomore season due to a broken leg and so remains a bit raw behind the plate. He does have a good bat and hit .276/.363/.560 with 7 HR and 16 BB/28 K in 134 AB. Given the organizational depth at the position, it isn't likely Krause will stick behind the plate, but his bat and athleticism gives him a chance to make it in the OF.

Grade: B+

ST. LOUIS CARDINALS

Over the years, the Cardinals have done an excellent job of building through the draft despite not having picked higher than #13 since 1998. Their 2014 draft looks like more of the same. In round one the Cardinals took Florida State RHP Luke Weaver. At 6'2", 170, he isn't overpowering, and his fastball sits at 88-92, but had been topping out at 96 mph in his sophomore season. He mixes in a good change-up and an average slider. They also landed high school RHP Jack Flaherty (supplemental 1st). The 6'3" righty sits at the same 88-92 mph with a good slider and a change-up that has nice potential. The team picked up RHPs Ronnie Williams and Andrew Morales with their two 2nd round picks. Both profile as back-end starters or relievers. The club didn't draft a position player until selecting Miami Dade JC 2B Darren Seferina (5th), who had a solid debut, hitting .291 with 20 SB in the NYPL. They did a good job of securing potential major league talent, though none of the players has elite level upside.

Sleeper: RHP Daniel Poncedeleon (9th) was drafted for the fourth time and finally signed for just $5,000. The NAIA Embry-Riddle grad has a good idea of how to pitch. His low-90s fastball has good movement and he keeps hitters honest with a nice four-pitch mix. He showed better than anticipated results in the NYPL, going 3-3 with a 2.44 ERA and 14 BB/52 K in 44.1 IP.

Grade: A-

SAN DIEGO PADRES

The Padres came into the 2014 draft with one of the deeper farm systems in baseball and added some nice pieces. With the 13th overall pick the Padres took NC State SS Trea Turner. At one point he was considered a possible 1st overall pick, but concerns about an ankle injury and struggles with wood bats for USA Baseball caused him to slide out of the top 10. Turner has plus speed and projects as a prototypical leadoff hitter who draws walks and has excellent bat control. The Padres had been interested in prep OF Michael Gettys (2nd) at #13 and were surprised he was still available at #51. Gettys is a vastly underrated prospect. Gettys impressed in his stint in the AZL, leading the league in hits while slashing .310/.353/.437 with 3 HR and 14 SB. The Padres also

added Rice closer RHP Zech Lemond (3rd) and are giving him a shot as a starter. Lemond walked just 5 in 40 IP while posting a 3.60 ERA. OF Auston Bousfield (5th) has a nice bat and good power and was one of the top offensive prospects in short-season ball, hitting .296 with a .512 Slg%. The Padres leveraged their organizational depth during the off-season, trading Turner and numerous other prospects to add Matt Kemp, Justin Upton, and Wil Myers.

Sleeper: LHP Thomas Dorminy (10th) was a standout at NAIA Faulkner. He has a good 90-93 mph fastball with some feel for a curve and change-up. He struck out 131 in 109 IP in college and then whiffed 11.2 per nine in short-season ball.

Grade: A

SAN FRANCISCO GIANTS

While the World Series champs don't have the deepest or most talented farm system in the NL, they have done an excellent job of stocking the big league club with both elite level talent and serviceable parts. The player most likely to make an impact from the 2014 draft class is RHP Tyler Beede (1st). He was a 1st round pick in 2011, but failed to sign with the Blue Jays and instead pitched at Vanderbilt. Beede has big time stuff highlighted by a 92-95 mph fastball that tops out at 97 mph. He also has an above-average change-up and a power curve. Beede struggled with control throughout his collegiate career and did so in his brief pro debut, but he has excellent potential. The Giants also landed Florida International C Aramis Garcia (2nd) and Oregon State OF Dylan Davis (3rd)—neither of whom fared well in their initial exposure to pro ball, but Garcia should hit eventually. The Giants didn't take a high school player until nabbing prep RHP Logan Webb (4th). Webb has plus velocity and good athleticism and could be a steal. Southern Illinois RHP Sam Coonrod (5th) also has premium velocity and worked primarily in relief where he features a good 93-97 mph heater. Rice 1B Skyler Ewing (6th) has the best power in this group and smacked 9 HR in 220 AB.

Sleeper: OF Austin Slater (8th) was Stanford's most consistent hitter in 2014 and racked the ball in his pro debut, hitting .346/.411/.457 between rookie ball and short-season ball. At 6'2", 195 he has good size, above-average speed, and projectable power. Not an elite level talent, but he fits the Giants approach and could emerge as a solid big league OF.

Grade: B

WASHINGTON NATIONALS

The Nationals have been one of the most aggressive teams in baseball since the new CBA went into effect. Realizing they can't just throw money at players, the Nationals have instead targeted risky/injured players, landing both Anthony Rendon and Lucas Giolito after other teams balked. That strategy worked so successfully in the past the club stayed the course in 2014 drafting UNLV RHP Erick Fedde with the 18th overall pick. After a standout college career and as part of Team USA, Fedde suffered an elbow injury in May and that required Tommy John surgery and will miss all of 2015. Prior to the injury, Fedde showed a 91-94 mph fastball that topped out at 96 mph, an above-average slider, and an inconsistent change-up. The fastball/slider combination give him the potential to be an impact arm in the majors. The Nats failed to sign LHP Andrew Suarez (2nd), who will return to Miami for his senior season. They did land high school C Jackson Reetz (3rd) who has solid offensive potential and should be able to stick behind the plate. The inability to sign Suarez means that Fedde has to pan out for this draft to have impact down the road.

Sleeper: RHP Domenick Mancini (12th) is a reliever out of Miami Dade JC. He has a good sinking fastball that peaks at 96 mph. He only got into 12 games as a pro, going 1-2 with a 2.45 ERA, but he could move up quickly.

Grade: C+

AMERICAN LEAGUE

BALTIMORE ORIOLES

The Orioles did not have a selection until the 3rd round (90th pick) and thus missed out on several high-upside players. They like their first pick, LHP Brian Gonzalez (3rd), who may not have a high ceiling, but is a fairly polished high school arm. They focused on pitchers for their first five picks, mostly from the collegiate ranks. RHP Pat Connaughton (4th) is better known for his exploits on the basketball court, but he has good potential, particularly if he focuses on baseball full-time. There are high hopes for LHP Tanner Scott (6th), who signed for a large bonus ($650,000) and has an outstanding fastball. However, he has a lot of development time ahead of him as he rarely repeats his complicated delivery and doesn't throw consistent strikes. There aren't many position players to get too excited about, though several selections offer at least one intriguing tool.

Sleeper: LHP John Means (11th) certainly knows how to throw strikes (0.5 Ctl in 39 innings in pro debut) and has the pitchability to move up quickly. He lacks premium velocity and doesn't have a true swing and miss pitch, but he has a solid-average curveball and deceives hitters with his delivery and arm slot.

Grade: D

BOSTON RED SOX

The focus on high-upside prep players could pay dividends down the line for the Red Sox, but they had a few relatively safe picks. They had two selections in the first round and opted for two high school prospects: SS Michael Chavis and RHP Michael Kopech, both of whom have high ceilings. One of the better pure hitters in the draft, 1B Sam Travis (2nd), could move quickly because of his advanced approach. While Kopech is the headliner among drafted pitchers in this class, RHP Jake Cosart (3rd) also provides upside. He is a terrific athlete who may just need some tweaks to his delivery to become a standout as a pro. RHP Karsten Whitson (11th) was the ninth overall pick in 2010, but chose not to sign and attended the University of Florida. His stock has obviously dropped, but he has the potential to recapture his wipeout slider. Boston added to the intrigue with its selections by handing a few high school players over-slot bonuses.

Sleeper: OF Trenton Kemp (15th) signed for $250,000 and is all about athleticism and projection. He has impressive tools in his arsenal, particularly speed and power, and will be brought along slowly as a high school draftee.

Grade: B+

CHICAGO WHITE SOX

The early focus was on pitching as their top three selections were all power arms. The White Sox later loaded up on position players, some of whom had solid pro debuts. Without question, the top pick was LHP Carlos Rodon (1st) who already is among the top pitching prospects in the game. With his plus fastball and plus-plus power slider, he could pitch in the majors right now. The drafting and signing of high school RHP Spencer Adams (2nd) gives the White Sox two arms that project to sit atop the rotation for years to come. LHP Jace Fry (3rd) may not have the same upside, but he has a good sinker/slider combination and could pitch out of the bullpen if necessary. The White Sox selected eight college players with their first nine picks and the best position prospect could be 2B Jake Peter (7th) who lacks tools, but knows how to play the game.

Sleeper: RHP Matt Cooper (16th) doesn't possess an intimidating frame, but he has impeccable fastball location and command and has the stuff and deception to project as a #4-5 starter in the near-term.

Grade: B+

CLEVELAND INDIANS

Few teams can match the upside of the players the Indians selected. With three of the top 38 picks and five of the top 97, Cleveland got a nice haul of players. Included in the first four rounds were three high school arms. LHP Justus Sheffield (1st) has great athleticism and a good feel for pitching. LHP Sam Hentges (4th) and RHP Grant Hockin (2nd) give the Indians two more young arms that could be nice options in the middle of the rotation. All three of them signed for at least $700,000. The top pick, OF Bradley Zimmer (1st), will likely appear on many Top 100 lists due to his well-rounded game. High school 1B Bobby Bradley (3rd) had as good a debut as any position player in the draft, leading the rookie-level Arizona League in HR and BA. The Indians are also very high on OF Mike Papi (supplemental 1st) who signed for a seven-figure bonus.

Sleeper: RHP Micah Miniard (8th) has a long, angular frame that allows him to throw downhill and induce groundballs. He doesn't throw hard now, but has plenty of projection and should be able to hit the mid-90s very soon.

Grade: A-

DETROIT TIGERS

Rarely do the Tigers have a first round pick due to free agent signings, but they opted for a high school position player with their top selection. OF Derek Hill (1st) struggled in his pro debut and will take some time to develop, but he has a chance at evolving into a leadoff hitter who patrols CF with above average defense. After that, the Tigers went back to their usual routine and selected collegiate players. Overall, all but two draftees were from the college ranks. Two of the top five selections were college catchers, led by Grayson Greiner (3rd) who could become a solid big league backstop if he can continue to hit. He was terrific in his pro debut in Low-A. College pitchers were also in abundance as RHP Spencer Turnbull (2nd) and RHP Adam Ravenelle (4th) give them some depth.

Sleeper: OF Mike Gerber (15th) was a senior sign, but performed well in his pro debut, showing the ability to hit for both BA and power (.298-7 HR in 248 at bats) despite an aggressive approach. He also is a solid defender at all outfield positions.
Grade: C+

HOUSTON ASTROS

The Astros draft may unfortunately may be most known for their inability to sign their top pick, LHP Brady Aiken (1st) and their settlement of a grievance with RHP Jacob Nix (5th). If they had signed both players, their draft would've likely been the best in baseball. There were still a number of quality selections, particularly with collegiate position players in OF Derek Fisher (supplemental 1st), 1B A.J. Reed (2nd) and 3B J.D. Davis (3rd). All three had standout pro debuts with both Reed and Davis achieving success at Low-A. The Astros signed only one high school player and that was C Ruben Castro (19th). They also focused a lot on intriguing junior college players, led by RHP Brock Dykxhoorn (6th). Ultimately this draft may be judged on the Aiken/Nix debacles, but there is enough here to suggest success in the future.
Sleeper: RHP Derick Velazquez (7th) could become a dynamic late-innings reliever with an arm that generates a sneaky-quick, low- to mid-90s fastball. If he can develop a true breaking ball, he could wipe out hitters from both sides of the plate.
Grade: B

KANSAS CITY ROYALS

The Royals spent a ton of money in the draft, as they had five picks in the first 92 selections, including three first-rounders. They also selected four high school players with their first six picks and gave four players signing bonuses of over $1 million. After pitching in the World Series, LHP Brandon Finnegan (1st) has already made a name for himself and a lot will be expected of him in 2015. Kansas City is enthralled with its top three prep picks. LHP Foster Griffin (1st) and RHP Scott Blewett (2nd) both have high ceilings and have the type of arms that could eventually turn into top prospects. Griffin is more advanced at present while Blewett needs to build strength. C Chase Vallot (supplemental 1st) has all the ingredients to become a standout backstop. He has massive power potential while showing enough to stick behind the plate.
Sleeper: OF Brandon Downes (7th) didn't have a very productive college season at the University of Virginia, but played very well in short-season ball upon signing. He hit .308/.358/.485 with 3 HR in 169 AB while showing good speed and athleticism.
Grade: A–

LOS ANGELES ANGELS

With one of the worst farm systems in baseball, the Angels hoped to stockpile pitching early in the draft and they did just that, selecting five hurlers with their first five picks. College LHP Sean Newcomb (1st) and prep RHP Joe Gatto (2nd) headline the draft and both immediately become two of the best prospects in the organization despite pitching in the northern states. Newcomb throws hard and owns a big, durable frame. Gatto has a way to go, but has the makings of two plus pitches. RHPs Chris Ellis (3rd), Jeremy Rhoades (4th), and Jake Jewell (5th) round out the first five rounds. It was mostly a college-heavy draft and the position players selected look more like organizational depth than true prospects. OF Bo Way (7th) had a nice pro debut and much will be expected of him in 2015.
Sleeper: LHP Greg Mahle (15th) is a college reliever with a big, durable frame and plenty of stamina. He throws in the low-90s and varies his release point to add deception. He could become a nice situational reliever fairly quickly.
Grade: C

MINNESOTA TWINS

With several power-armed relievers selected in the first ten rounds, the Twins continued to focus on building a stable of arms that complements the organization's abundance of command-oriented pitchers. After selecting gifted SS Nick Gordon (1st), the Twins then turned their attention to college pitchers as their next seven picks were from the collegiate ranks. Excitement abounds for RHPs Nick Burdi (2nd) and Michael Cederoth (3rd) who have plus fastballs that can touch triple-digits. Burdi already reached High-A and struck out 38 hitters in only 20.1 innings as a pro. RHP Jake Reed (5th) also found the pros to his liking and he could advance quickly based upon his dominant performance in Low-A (0.36 ERA, 1.1 Ctl, 11.2 Dom in 25 innings). The Twins selected several position players in the later rounds and OF Max Murphy (9th) was among the better ones.
Sleeper: OF Tanner English (11th) is a highlight athlete with plus defensive skills and amazing speed. He doesn't have much size or strength, but can be an impact player when focusing on contact.
Grade: B+

NEW YORK YANKEES

Without a first round pick, the Yankees opted for pitchers with their first five selections, four of them from the collegiate ranks. Overall, it was a college-heavy draft with only one high school player signed. LHP Jacob Lindgren (2nd) should get to the majors very quickly out of the bullpen on the basis of his solid fastball/slider combination. LHP Jordan Montgomery (4th) could also advance rapidly because of his feel for pitching and plus command. The highest upside belongs to the only prepster who signed with the Yankees, RHP Austin DeCarr (3rd). He has projectable arm strength and the potential for a plus fastball if he cleans up his mechanics. Despite not selecting many position players, the Yankees hope that OF Mark Payton (7th) can blossom as a pro and power-hitters 1B Chris Gittens (12th) and 1B Bo Thompson (13th) grow into other parts of their games.
Sleeper: OF Dominic Jose (24th) is a solid athlete who never amounted to much at Stanford, but has very intriguing tools with excellent speed and some power potential.
Grade: C

OAKLAND ATHLETICS

The Athletics chose relatively safe picks in this draft, mostly headlined by collegiate players. They focused early on pitching before adding a handful of middle infielders. With their first pick, Oakland selected 3B Matt Chapman (1st) who should progress quickly because he has advanced skills with both the bat and glove. He doesn't project as a superstar, but he has solid-average tools at his disposal. High school SS Trace Loehr (6th) is an interesting middle infield prospect who received a hefty signing bonus. In rounds two through four, the Athletics feasted on college right-handed pitchers. Daniel Gossett (2nd), Brett Graves (3rd), and Jordan Schwartz (4th) project as more of #4 starters down the line, but have tangible tools that could be cultivated whether in the rotation or in the bullpen.

Sleeper: RHP Branden Kelliher (8th) lacks ideal size, but he has a quick arm and can hit the mid-90s with his fastball. He misses bats with it while his curveball shows flashes of becoming a solid-average offering.

Grade: C

SEATTLE MARINERS

There was interest in adding raw power to the organization and the Mariners got two good ones with their top two picks. OF Alex Jackson (1st) was the sixth overall pick and brings a powerful bat to the middle of the lineup. He has an advanced approach and a very quick stroke. High school OF Gareth Morgan (supplemental 2nd) received a hefty signing bonus ($2 million), due to his huge frame and the ability to give the ball a ride. He is quite crude when it comes to his approach, however, and makes minimal contact at present. Seattle also picked another outfielder in the 3rd round, this time from the college ranks. OF Austin Cousino (3rd) is the polar opposite of Jackson and Morgan. He is more of a speedy, defensive player who makes contact, though can reach the seats. The Mariners signed their first 30 picks and focused on pitching from rounds four through nine. They also drafted and signed four catchers, addressing an organizational weakness.

Sleeper: RHP Trey Cochran-Gill (17th) relies on a solid-average sinker to induce groundballs, but he also has a good enough slider to register strikeouts. He may only be a reliever, but he can succeed with two effective offerings.

Grade: B+

TAMPA BAY RAYS

The Rays made good use of their bonus pool by signing their first 25 selections. They did a nice job of mixing high school and college talent as well as position players and pitchers. Their top pick, 1B Casey Gillaspie (1st), fits a need for a power-hitting corner infielder while they opted for arms with their next two picks. RHP Brent Honeywell (supplemental 2nd) had an outstanding pro debut after signing out of junior college and he has high upside as a 19-year-old with plenty of projection. RHP Cameron Varga (2nd) was a prep arm who will take time to develop, but he has good arm strength and an impressive curveball for his age. Two high school pitchers, LHP Brock Burke (3rd) and Blake Bivens (4th), are opposites of one another, but give the Rays some versatility. Outside of Gillaspie, the position players are relatively thin, though there is some power and speed selected in the later rounds.

Sleeper: RHP Spencer Moran (11th) is tall and lean at 6'6" 180 pounds and he oozes projection. He got knocked around in rookie ball in his pro debut, but he should be able to throw harder and master his breaking ball in due time.

Grade: B

TEXAS RANGERS

The intial focus on high upside players brought the Rangers high school prospects with their first three selections. They did a nice job of balancing pitchers and position players with their first ten picks before selecting mostly pitchers in the later rounds. RHP Luis Ortiz (1st) headlines the power arms and is quite advanced for a prep pitcher. He has good command and feel while possessing a fastball that flashes plus. Next came high school shortstops in Ti'quan Forbes (2nd) and Josh Morgan (3rd). Both may not stay at the position as Forbes saw extensive action at 3B upon signing and Morgan split time between SS and 2B. Of the two, Forbes has a significantly higher ceiling. Another position player the Rangers like is C/3B Jose Trevino (6th). They are converting him to a full-time catcher and he has plenty of power in his profile.

Sleeper: RHP John Fasola (31st) was among the best pitchers in the short-season Northwest League with his power arsenal in late relief. He sits in the low- to mid-90s and wipes out hitters with his hard slider. He also throws consistent strikes.

Grade: A–

TORONTO BLUE JAYS

The Blue Jays draft was highlighted by two first round selections and two others who could've easily been selected in the top round. Overall, Toronto spent at least $300,000 on six draftees, including three with seven-figure bonuses. With the 9th overall pick, the Blue Jays opted for RHP Jeff Hoffman (1st), though he'll start his pro debut near mid-season as he recovers from Tommy John surgery in May 2014. He has top-of-the-rotation stuff, but will need time to regain his arm strength. RHP Sean Reid-Foley (2nd) has a high ceiling predicated on his big, durable frame and ability to mix his pitches despite his youth. He has #2 starter stuff. LHP Nick Wells (3rd), a high school pitcher, didn't get the accolades of Hoffman or Reid-Foley, but he is very projectable with a quick arm and potential for a plus breaking ball. C Max Pentecost (1st) already is one of the better catching prospects in baseball due to his athleticism and advanced hitting ability.

Sleeper: LHP Grayson Huffman (6th) doesn't have the best fastball among the draftees, but he has a very deceptive change-up and a repeatable delivery. He's only 19, but could be among the quicker movers in the class.

Grade: A–

Top 20 International Prospects for 2015

by Jeremy Deloney

Major League Baseball has implemented changes to the signing of international players over the past few years. Given the potential changes in the U.S. relationship with Cuba, there may be more Cuban players entering the U.S. in the next few years. Listed below are the top international prospects who inked contracts during the international signing period in 2014 and players who could make the jump to the U.S. in the next two seasons.

Christopher Acosta (RHP, BOS)

Long and lean, he will play 2015 as a 17-year-old, but is considered an advanced pitcher for his age. He throws strikes with three pitches, and can set up hitters. Acosta has plenty of room to add muscle, and doing so could add a few ticks to his low-90s fastball. While he does a nice job of repeating his delivery and throwing strikes, a few mechanical adjustments could add more effectiveness to his below-average curveball. Acosta throws from a low ¾ slot and has a very good change-up.
Signing bonus/status: Signed for $1.5 million
MLB Debut: 2019

Roberto Baldoquin (2B, LAA)

At 20 years old, the short and strong infielder has a fairly mature game. Baldoquin can play either middle infield spot, though there are indications LAA will keep him at SS for the time being. There are questions about his ability to impact the game with his bat, but he understands the strike zone and can lace doubles to both gaps. An instinctual player, he relies more on fundamentals than flashy tools.
Signing bonus/status: Signed for $8 million
MLB Debut: 2016

Juan De Leon (OF, NYY)

One of the more acclaimed prospects on the international scene, the 17-year-old has the potential to showcase five tools. De Leon already owns significant bat speed and very projectable power. Once he adds more strength, he could become a middle-of-the-order run producer. He has good speed and possesses ideal arm strength for a RF. He'll need to tweak his swing and polish his pitch recognition, but the upside is huge.
Signing bonus/status: Signed for $2 million
MLB Debut: 2019

Anderson Espinoza (RHP, BOS)

A high-profile sign from Venezuela, he impressed the Red Sox with his pure arm strength and smooth delivery. He can already touch 95 mph, but generally sits in the 88-94 mph range. As he has a very loose arm, the expectation is that he'll eventually work in the mid-90s consistently. Espinoza exhibits good feel for pitching and can sequence pitches well. The only knocks on him are his size (6'0", 175) and a tendency to throw across his body.
Signing bonus/status: Signed for $1.8 million
MLB Debut: 2020

Dermis Garcia (SS, NYY)

He has the best raw power of any prospect in this international class. He swings aggressively and has the strength, bat speed, and loft in his stroke to reach the seats consistently. Though he can overswing and cam get himself out by flailing at pitches outside of the zone, the hope is that he'll harness his strength and learn to be patient. Garcia has a very strong arm and will likely move to 3B as a pro.
Signing bonus/status: Signed for $3 million
MLB Debut: 2020

Wilkerman Garcia (SS, NYY)

The 16-year-old might be the most polished of the Yankees' impressive international haul from 2014. He maximizes his average tools due to his intelligence, and has the hitting potential to be a solid contributor. He has current strength, but focuses on hitting the gaps and getting on base with his patient approach. He lacks the ideal quickness and range for SS, but could eventually move to 2B or 3B where his hands and feet work fine.
Signing bonus/status: Signed for $1.35 million
MLB Debut: 2020

Nelson Gomez (3B, NYY)

The tall and powerful right-handed hitter is presently all about bat speed and strength. Though he swings and misses quite frequently, he has the acumen to recognize pitches and use his advanced batting eye to get on base. Gomez has the arm strength for 3B, but may eventually have to move to 1B or an outfield corner as he grows into his frame and slows down some. Few international prospects can match his raw power.
Signing bonus/status: Signed for $2.25 million
MLB Debut: 2020

Pedro Gonzalez (SS, COL)

The 17-year-old has a long and wiry frame (6'4", 160 pounds) with room to add muscle and strength. Gonzalez currently has an exploitable swing due to his long arms, but has a fluid stroke and sound strike zone judgment. Defensively, he can play a legitimate SS as he possesses quick hands and average arm strength. He has a very high ceiling, but patience is warranted.
Signing bonus/status: Signed for $1.3 million
MLB Debut: 2020

Brayan Hernandez (OF, SEA)

The tall and lean switch-hitter brings a lot to the table. Not only does he exhibit excellent tools, but he has a solid work ethic and instinctual nature. Hernandez has fluid swing mechanics and enough jolt in his bat to eventually produce 20+ HR annually. He runs well enough to play CF in a pinch, but his reads, routes and strong arm may be more ideal for an OF corner.
Signing bonus/status: Signed for $1.85 million
MLB Debut: 2019

Kenny Hernandez (SS, NYM)

With textbook swing mechanics and natural bat speed, the 16-year-old offers exciting offensive upside. He has a feel for contact with gap power at present, and should grow into more long ball pop as he learns to read pitches and add loft to his swing. Hernandez will most likely have to move off SS; 2B maybe a better fit due to lack of arm strength. Though not fast, he is a sound baserunner who knows how to take the extra base.
Signing bonus/status: Signed for $1 million
MLB Debut: 2020

Raisel Iglesias (RHP, CIN)

The Reds inked the short 23-year-old to a major league contract and watched him have great success during his limited action in the Arizona Fall League. Though he pitched in relief in Cuba, the Reds insist he has the goods to make it as a starter. Iglesias has a deep repertoire; he works with a 90-94 mph fastball that features explosive movement, two breaking balls, and an improving change-up. With a deceptive delivery and varying arm slots, he's tough to make hard contact against.

Signing bonus/status: Signed 7-year contract worth $27 million
MLB Debut: 2015

Jung-Ho Kang (SS, South Korea)

Already 27, he is ready to contribute immediately in the major leagues, though to what extent is still in question. He led the Korea Baseball organization in slugging percentage and finished second in HR while winning the league's equivalent to a Gold Glove. He has useful tools, though none stand out as plus. At the plate he can sell out for power, and his lack of quickness and arm strength will likely lead to a utility role.

Signing bonus/status: His Korean team accepted bid of $5M from Pirates for rights to negotiate, but he had not signed as of press date.
MLB Debut: 2015

Gilbert Lara (SS, MIL)

Has an impressive frame (6'3", 210) with natural strength, and makes loud contact with a complicated and max-effort stroke. The length in his swing will lead to strikeouts, but he puts a charge into the ball with plus bat speed. The right-handed hitter can also be too pull-conscious, and is at his best when using the whole field. Defensively, he'll likely move to 3B or 1B down the line, as he doesn't have the feet or hands to play in the middle infield.

Signing bonus/status: Signed for $3.1 million
MLB Debut: 2019

Kenta Maeda (RHP, Japan)

There was excitement over the potential arrival of the 27-year-old, though his big league debut will have to wait another year. Maeda re-upped with Hiroshima for two years, but he could still head to the majors in 2016. With three solid-average offerings in his arsenal, he fits the profile of a #3-4 starter with a moderate strikeout rate. He commands his 90-95 mph fastball to both sides of the plate and can mix in a slider and change-up. Maeda has a durable frame and plenty of stamina to eat innings.

Signing bonus/status: Remains in Japan and will be eligible for international free agency in 2017
MLB Debut: 2017

Juan Meza (RHP, TOR)

At 6'3", 190 pounds, he projects to one day throw consistently in the mid-to-high 90s. At present, he sits 87-91 mph, but his fastball features late life. Meza throws on a downhill angle with little effort. He also has decent command for his age; he'll play 2015 at 17 years old. Meza needs to work on his curveball, as it lacks consistency, though his change-up can be a go-to pitch in any count. He will take some time, but the payoff could be huge.

Signing bonus/status: Signed for $1.6 million
MLB Debut: 2020

Yoan Moncada (3B, Cuba)

One of the most gifted players to come out of Cuba, the 19-year-old has been declared a free agent, but has yet to be cleared by OFAC at press time. When available, Mondaca will command a premium contract. He has significant upside and is already close to being ready for the big leagues. He has a strong frame with explosive power and speed tools. While there are questions as to his ultimate defensive home, he has shown the ability to play any infield position. At his peak, Mondaca could become a .300 hitter with 30 HR and 25 SB.

Signing bonus/status: International free agent; expected to sign
MLB Debut: 2016

Franklin Perez (RHP, HOU)

Projectable at 18 years old, Perez stands 6'4" and currently throws 87-90 mph. With more experience and mechanical tweaks, he could eventually hit the mid-90s. He uses his height to throw downhill, but has difficulty repeating his delivery and arm slot. Once he becomes a pitcher rather than a thrower, his rudimentary curveball and change-up should improve. Still needs significant polish, but the Astros will be patient.

Signing bonus/status: Signed for $1 million
MLB Debut: 2020

Adrian Rondon (SS, TAM)

Though just 16 years old, he plays a very mature game with both the bat and glove. The tall and athletic infielder is a consistent performer who combines bat speed with a short stroke to make excellent contact. He possesses ideal hand-eye coordination to hit for BA, and has strength to project to moderate pop. Rondon should be able to stick at SS with fine quickness and clean feet and hands, but could grow out of SS and be a solid 3B or RF.

Signing bonus/status: Signed for $2.95 million
MLB Debut: 2020

Yasmany Tomas (OF, ARI)

He should compete for a starting job in spring training due to his brute, raw power from the right side. He has elite bat speed and loft in his stroke to project to 30+ HR, but there are doubts about his ability to hit big league pitching. His vicious uppercut stroke will likely lead to strikeouts, and he also has a tendency to chase pitches. Tomas is a fine outfielder with a very strong arm, though he doesn't often take good routes to flyballs.

Signing bonus/status: Signed 6-year contract worth $68.5 million
MLB Debut: 2015

Huascar Ynoa (RHP, MIN)

The younger brother of Michael (RHP, OAK) doesn't have the same build or arm strength. Huascar has a power pitcher's frame, but mostly sits in the 87-93 mph range at present. He can dominate at times by using a deep repertoire of offerings, including a solid cutter, and a curveball that is a true out pitch. He shows impressive arm speed on his change-up, though he can be guilty of pitching up too frequently.

Signing bonus/status: Signed for $800,000
MLB Debut: 2020

2015 College Names to Know

by Chris Lee

In past years when we've looked at the collegiate class, usually there's a can't-miss bat like Kris Bryant, or a number of polished collegiate hitters like Kyle Schwarber (C, CHC) and Michael Conforto (OF, NYM). Sometimes, there's even a Trea Turner (SS, SD/WAS) who has one tool that could easily make him a $30 fantasy stud if things pan out. As for pitchers, at times there is a Carlos Rodon (LHP, CHW), who might be simply too good not to stash somewhere on a roster in keeper leagues.

Unfortunately, this is not that kind of year.

It's not that the 2015 collegiate class is poor; it's just that names don't jump off the page as they have in past years. It's a strong class of collegiate pitchers, but there's not even a sure-fire, low-risk, elite command guy like an Aaron Nola (RHP, PHI) out there. It's quite weak as far as top-notch bats, though there are certainly some players who could wind up being 20/20 players down the road.

Normally, we rank 10 or so players, but in this iteration, here are some quick reports on 10 collegiate players to watch closely this spring. Players are listed in alphabetical order.

Phil Bickford, RHP
Southern Nevada JC, R/R, So., 6-4, 208

In case this name sounds familiar, it should: Toronto drafted Bickford 10th overall in 2013, but failed to sign him and he went to Cal State Fullerton. Bickford had a nice year at UCF (2.13 ERA, 76 Ks, 74 IP) but wasn't throwing as hard as he had been before. Bickford left for Southern Nevada so that he could be drafted again for 2015. (JUCO players, unlike their counterparts at four-year schools, can be selected after each season.) Last summer in the Cape Cod League, that velocity returned as Bickford was hitting 97 and 98 out of the bullpen, and he's added an excellent slider and improved his change-up. His Cmd (5.7) and Dom (8.8) as a freshman show a pitcher with elite ability.

The bottom line: Bickford is clearly a better pitcher than when he was picked two years ago. If he can maintain his fastball velocity, he'll go in the top 10 again, and his control at such a young age makes him an elite talent.

Alex Bregman, SS
LSU, R/R, Jr., 6-0, 190

The 2013 National Freshman of the Year dipped from .369/.417/.546 in that season to .316/.397/.455 in 2014, but that's not stopping anyone from including him in mock first rounds as the season approaches—a 1.10 batting eye and a 91.3 ct% will do that. Bregman may or may not stick at shortstop (he would shift to second if not), because he doesn't have elite defensive tools, but he's reasonably athletic, can run a bit and has enough pop to be a double-digit home run hitter.

The bottom line: Bregman has one of the highest floors of any player in the draft due to his ability to do everything well, plus he has a reputation for high character and a tremendous work ethic.

Bregman could be a middle infielder who provides a handful of homers and steals along with a good batting average.

Walker Buehler, RHP
Vanderbilt, R/R, Jr., 6-1, 160

The slightly-built Buehler doesn't look like much, but when you put a baseball in his hand, Vanderbilt's version of Clark Kent can become Superman in any given outing. Buehler consistently sits at 95-96 with his fastball and throws two breaking balls and a change-up, all of which move considerably, and all of which he can command. The results (9.7 Dom, 3.6 Cmd) prove it. Buehler tends to leave a ball or two up every start and they often get hit hard, but he gave up just four homers in 102 1/3 innings a year ago. That could change with the new flatter-seamed baseballs, which are going to travel a couple dozen feet further than last year if struck well. Despite the slight build, Buehler has shown the ability to throw 120-plus pitches in games. *Baseball America* named Buehler its top prospect in the Cape Cod League.

The bottom line: An exceptionally poised and polished pitcher from a school with a track record of producing them, Buehler could be one of the top five picks off the board. There is some risk if he can't stay down in the zone, but he also is a pitcher with considerable stuff.

Carson Fulmer, RHP
Vanderbilt, R/R, Jr., 5-11, 195

There are a lot of questions about Fulmer, starting with his size and his quick, violent delivery, which leave many doubting his ability to start. Fulmer dialed down his velocity a bit last season to operate in the low-to-mid-90s with his fastball, but he can touch 98 if needed and he offsets it with a wicked 12-to-6 curve and a change-up. Fulmer excelled as a closer for the first half of last season (10 saves) before moving in to anchor Vanderbilt's rotation in mid-season, and he certainly has the stuff (9.4 Dom, .195 average against) for either gig in the big leagues. Throwing strikes (4.1 BB/9 in 2014) has been a big issue at times.

The bottom line: The things that scouts love about Fulmer—and the questions they have about him—sound almost exactly like ones they had with another Vanderbilt pitcher, Sonny Gray, four years ago. Both are fearless, and despite their size, both showed the ability to go 120-plus pitches before as collegians and maintain velocity. The big issue will be command, and maybe health given his delivery, but the latter has not been an issue yet. Like Gray, reports on Fullmer's makeup are off the charts.

Ian Happ, 2B
Cincinnati, S/R, Jr., 6-0, 205

After hitting .322/.451/.483 as a freshman, Happ followed up with a nearly identical .322/.443/.497 campaign, and has totaled 11 homers and 44 steals (in 53 tries) through 107 collegiate games. To make matters better, Happ slashed 293/.359/.469 over 39 games in the Cape Cod League in 2013, followed by a .329, four-homer, 12-double summer in 149 at-bats, which suggests he's a legitimate wooden-bat hitter.

The bottom line: Happ is a bit difficult to project, because he may not have a natural defensive position (some see him as a left fielder). Also, he plays in the American Athletic Conference, which has some good baseball schools like Louisville and Houston, but doesn't have the overall balance of an ACC or SEC, and it makes the stats a little harder to interpret against the others on this list. Still, Happ can flat-out hit and did well in summer ball, so there's certainly reason to think he could become a fantasy asset. Some have made comparisons to Chase Utley.

James Kaprielian, RHP
UCLA, R/R, Jr., 6-4, 200
Following a great freshman season out of the bullpen, Kaprielian moved into the rotation and the results (9.2 Dom, 3.0 Ctl) were outstanding, as he led the Pac-12 in strikeouts. He has a mid-90s fastball, a curve, a slider, and a change that sometimes resembles a splitter. What makes him special is that he can throw his breaking balls for strikes and with different breaks.
The bottom line: Kaprielian may not be as consistently highly regarded as others on this list—some see him as a late first-rounder—but 38 Ks to 6 BBs in 26 Cape Cod innings may have changed that. It's rare to see someone throw as many pitches as effectively as he does, and that's what will give him a chance to be an MLB star.

Nathan Kirby, LHP
Virginia, L/L, Jr., 6-2, 185
One of college baseball's best lefties in 2014, Kirby showed all the tools (8.9 Dom, 2.6 Ctl, 3.4 Cmd) in leading the Cavaliers to the College World Series. He throws a fastball that sits at 91-94 with movement, a terrific curve and a change-up. When he was on, the results were second-to-none, as he no-hit Pittsburgh in an 18-strikeout, one-walk game. Few have his polish or feel for pitching.
The bottom line: Kirby has the potential to be a Cy Young Award winner one day, though there could be a few durability concerns; after pitching just 32 2/3 innings in 2013, Kirby's command absolutely abandoned him during the third inning of a CWS start against Vanderbilt and he gave up eight runs in that one frame alone while absorbing the loss. It's worth keeping any eye on in 2015; otherwise, there's a whole lot to like.

Mike Matuella, RHP
Duke, R/R, Jr., 6-7, 220
If you could build a starting pitcher from scratch, chances are, you'd make him look a whole lot like Matuella, a big-bodied right-hander with a smooth delivery, a fastball that sits at 93-97, a nice-breaking curve and a change-up. Matuella threw only 58 1/3 innings last year, but struck out 68 and limited opponents to a .190 average in one of college baseball's premier leagues.
The bottom line: Matuella burst upon the scene last spring after fanning just 28 in 57 2/3 innings as a freshman, thanks to a velocity bump. However, that also came with some arm soreness. There's not much of a track record, but there is enough talent to warrant the whispers that Matuella could go No. 1 overall in June depending on his 2015 season. A definite high-risk, high-reward prospect.

D.J. Stewart, OF
Florida State, L/R, Jr., 6-0, 230
Stewart attended The Bolles School, the same high school that produced Chipper Jones, and looks more like a linebacker than he does a baseball player. After hitting .351/.452/.557 as a sophomore—numbers almost identical to what he put up as a freshman—he won ACC Player of the Year honors and established himself as one of the better pure collegiate bats for 2015. He's not going to steal a lot of bases as a major leaguer (4-for-5 last year), but as seven homers and 19 doubles in 2014 attest, the pop is there, and a 1.30 Eye and 84.5 ct% show plate discipline, too.
The bottom line: Though lack of stolen base prowess and positional certainty limit Stewart's fantasy upside, he'll be a fundamentally good hitter with big-time power potential.

Dansby Swanson, SS
Vanderbilt, R/R, Jr., 6-0, 190
Last year's College World Series MVP posted a stat line of .333/.411/.475 with three homers, and while Swanson is mostly a line-drive hitter, don't get too concerned with that home run total; he plays in a pitcher's park and the high-seam baseballs of the 2014 season greatly deflated home runs. Perhaps a better indicator as to what is to come is the fact that Swanson tied a school record with 27 doubles and smacked a pair of homers in one of Vanderbilt's three fall scrimmage games, and he's even got some pop the opposite way. Swanson does strike out some (82 ct% as a junior) but he's also quite patient (13.1 bb%) and can really run, too (22-27 SB). He played second last year because the team had some positional flexibility issues and he was the team's best option at second; in 2015, he'll be at shortstop, where his instincts and athleticism should make him one of college baseball's most spectacular shortstops. He did spend almost all of his freshman year sidelined with various injuries, so durability could be a question.
The bottom line: In a weak crop of college hitters, few have Swanson's all-around gifts. The defense ensures he'll get a shot, and if the bat continues to develop, you might be looking at a 15-homer, 25-steal shortstop who won't hurt the batting average.

Five more to watch: Gio Brusa, OF, Pacific; Kyle Cody, RHP, Kentucky; Thomas Eshelman, RHP, Cal State Fullerton; Kyle Funkhouser, RHP, Louisville; Riley Ferrell, RHP, TCU. (And, of course, last year's No. 1 overall pick, LHP Brady Aiken, should he decide to attend a junior college in the spring.)

ORGANIZATION RATINGS/RANKINGS

Each organization is graded on a standard A-F scale in four separate categories, and then after weighing the categories and adding some subjectivity, a final grade and ranking are determined. The four categories are the following:

Hitting: The quality and quantity of hitting prospects, the balance between athleticism, power, speed, and defense, and the quality of player development.

Pitching: The quality and quantity of pitching prospects and the quality of player development.

Top-End Talent: The quality of the top players within the organization. Successful teams are ones that have the most star-quality players. These are the players who are a teams' above average regulars, front-end starters, and closers.

Depth: The depth of both hitting and pitching prospects within the organization.

Overall Grade: The four categories are weighted, with top-end talent being the most important and depth being the least.

TEAM	Hitting	Pitching	Top-End Talent	Depth	Overall
Chicago (N)	A+	B	A+	A	A
Boston	B+	A-	A-	A-	A-
Houston	B+	A-	A-	A-	A-
Pittsburgh	B	A-	A-	A-	A-
Texas	A	B+	A-	A	A-
Kansas City	B+	B	A-	B+	B+
Los Angeles (N)	A-	B	A-	B+	B+
Minnesota	B	B+	A	B	B+
San Francisco	B	A	B+	B+	B+
New York (N)	B-	B+	B	A-	B+
Toronto	C+	A-	B+	B	B
Washington	B-	A	B+	B	B
Colorado	B+	C+	B	B	B
St. Louis	C	A-	B	B	B
Tampa Bay	B	B-	B	B+	B
Cincinnati	C-	A-	B	B-	B-
Cleveland	B	C	B	B	B-
Seattle	B	C	B	B-	B-
Arizona	C	A-	B-	B-	B-
Atlanta	B-	B-	C	B	B-
Oakland	B	C	B	C+	C+
New York (A)	B-	C-	C	C+	C+
San Diego	C+	C	C+	B	C+
Chicago (A)	C-	C	B-	C-	C
Miami	C	C	C+	C-	C
Baltimore	C-	C	C-	C-	C-
Milwaukee	C	C-	D	C	C-
Philadelphia	C-	C	D	C-	C-
Detroit	D+	C-	D	D	D
Los Angeles (A)	D	C+	D	D	D

POSITIONS: Up to four positions are listed for each batter and represent those for which he appeared (in order) the most games at in 2011. Positions are shown with their numeric designation (2=CA, 3=1B, 7=LF, 0=DH, etc.)

BATS: Shows which side of the plate he bats from—right (R), left (L) or switch-hitter (S).

AGE: Player's age, as of April 1, 2015.

DRAFTED: The year, round, and school that the player performed at as an amateur if drafted, or where the player was signed from, if a free agent.

EXP MLB DEBUT: The year a player is expected to debut in the major leagues.

H/W: The player's height and weight.

FUT: The role that the batter is expected to have for the majority of his major league career, not necessarily his greatest upside.

SKILLS: Each skill a player possesses is graded and designated with a "+", indicating the quality of the skills, taking into context the batter's age and level played. An average skill will receive three "+" marks.

- **PWR:** Measures the player's ability to drive the ball and hit for power.
- **BAVG:** Measures the player's ability to hit for batting average and judge the strike zone.
- **SPD:** Measures the player's raw speed and base-running ability.
- **DEF:** Measures the player's overall defense, which includes arm strength, arm accuracy, range, agility, hands, and defensive instincts.

PLAYER STAT LINES: Player statistics for the last five teams that he played for (if applicable), including college and the major leagues.

TEAM DESIGNATIONS: Each team that the player performed for during a given year is included.

LEVEL DESIGNATIONS: The level for each team a player performed is included. "AAA" means Triple-A, "AA" means Double-A, "A+" means high Class-A, "A-" means low Class-A, and "Rk" means rookie level.

SABERMETRIC CATEGORIES: Descriptions of all the sabermetric categories appear in the glossary.

CAPSULE COMMENTARIES: For each player, a brief analysis of their skills/statistics, and their future potential is provided.

ELIGIBILITY: Eligibility for inclusion is the standard for which Major League Baseball adheres to; 130 at-bats or 45 days on the 25-man roster, not including the month of September.

POTENTIAL RATINGS: The Potential Ratings are a two-part system in which a player is assigned a number rating based on his upside potential (1-10) and a letter rating based on the probability of reaching that potential (A-E).

Potential

10:	Hall of Famer	5:	MLB reserve
9:	Elite player	4:	Top minor leaguer
8:	Solid regular	3:	Average minor leaguer
7:	Average regular	2:	Minor league reserve
6:	Platoon player	1:	Minor league roster filler

Probability Rating

A: 90% probability of reaching potential
B: 70% probability of reaching potential
C: 50% probability of reaching potential
D: 30% probability of reaching potential
E: 10% probability of reaching potential

SKILLS: Scouts usually grade a player's skills on the 20-80 scale, and while most of the grades are subjective, there are grades that can be given to represent a certain hitting statistic or running speed. These are indicated on this chart:

Scout Grade	HR	BA	Speed (L)	Speed (R)
80	39+	.320+	3.9	4.0
70	32-38	.300-.319	4.0	4.1
60	25-31	.286-.299	4.1	4.2
50 (avg)	17-24	.270-.285	4.2	4.3
40	11-16	.250-.269	4.3	4.4
30	6-10	.220-.249	4.4	4.5
20	0-5	.219-	4.5	4.6

CATCHER POP TIMES: Catchers are timed (in seconds) from the moment the pitch reaches the catcher's mitt until the time that the middle infielder receives the baseball at second base. This number assists both teams in assessing whether a base-runner should steal second base or not.

1.85	+
1.95	MLB average
2.05	−

Adames,Cristhian

456 | Colorado | EXP MLB DEBUT: 2014 | H/W: 6-0 180 | FUT: Utility INF | 7D

Bats B Age 23
2007 FA (DR)
Pwr ++
BAvg +++
Spd +++
Def ++++

Year	Lev	Team	AB	R	H	HR	RBI	Avg	OB	Slg	OPS	bb%	ct%	Eye	SB	CS	x/h%	Iso	RC/G
2012	A+	Modesto	418	59	117	2	54	280	353	378	731	10	80	0.57	4	2	26	98	4.75
2013	AA	Tulsa	389	45	104	3	36	267	326	350	676	8	80	0.44	13	7	23	82	3.89
2014	AA	Tulsa	330	42	88	2	38	267	326	336	662	8	82	0.50	7	9	17	70	3.76
2014	AAA	ColoradoSprgs	145	19	49	1	14	338	392	441	834	8	83	0.52	5	1	27	103	5.88
2014	MLB	Colorado	15	1	1	0	0	67	67	67	133	0	67	0.00	0	0	0	0	-4.22

Switch-hitting SS got a taste of the big leagues filling in for Tulo. Slap hitter makes consistent contact and puts the ball into play, but without any authority. Excellent fielder with sure hands and a strong arm. Speed is not a part of his game, giving him limited fantasy appeal.

Adames,Willy

6 | Tampa Bay | EXP MLB DEBUT: 2017 | H/W: 6-1 180 | FUT: Starting SS/3B | 9D

Bats R Age 19
2012 FA (DR)
Pwr ++
BAvg ++++
Spd +++
Def +++

Year	Lev	Team	AB	R	H	HR	RBI	Avg	OB	Slg	OPS	bb%	ct%	Eye	SB	CS	x/h%	Iso	RC/G
2013	Rk	DSL Tigers	200	48	49	1	21	245	410	370	780	22	78	1.27	9	12	37	125	6.03
2014	A	West Michigan	353	40	95	6	50	269	342	428	770	10	73	0.41	3	6	34	159	5.31
2014	A	Bowling Green	97	15	27	2	11	278	375	433	808	13	69	0.50	3	0	33	155	6.08

Athletic INF who bypassed short-season. Advanced approach and emerging bat give him very high upside. Can struggle to put bat to ball, but has fast stroke and room to add strength. Gap power evolving into HR pop. Exhibits average speed and arm and range may work better at 3B.

Adams,Lane

8 | Kansas City | EXP MLB DEBUT: 2014 | H/W: 6-4 190 | FUT: Starting OF | 7D

Bats R Age 25
2009 (13) HS (OK)
Pwr +++
BAvg ++
Spd ++++
Def +++

Year	Lev	Team	AB	R	H	HR	RBI	Avg	OB	Slg	OPS	bb%	ct%	Eye	SB	CS	x/h%	Iso	RC/G
2013	A+	Wilmington	323	56	89	7	39	276	361	424	785	12	80	0.65	23	6	36	149	5.45
2013	AA	NW Arkansas	156	30	38	5	26	244	322	397	719	10	71	0.40	15	0	34	154	4.50
2014	Rk	Burlington	10	3	5	0	4	500	643	1100	1743	29	90	4.00	0	0	80	600	18.67
2014	AA	NW Arkansas	405	65	109	11	36	269	342	427	769	10	79	0.52	38	9	36	158	5.13
2014	MLB	Kansas City	3	1	0	0	0	0	0	0	0	0	33	0.00	0	0		0	-9.58

Tall, athletic OF who was 3rd in TL in SB. Got off to slow start, but tied career high in SB while cutting K rate. Has plus raw power, but likes to use whole field and put ball in play. Speed is best tool and enhances CF play, where he is solid. Ranges well and has accurate, average arm.

Adolfo,Micker

9 | Chicago (A) | EXP MLB DEBUT: 2018 | H/W: 6-3 200 | FUT: Starting OF | 8E

Bats R Age 18
2013 FA (DR)
Pwr +++
BAvg ++
Spd ++
Def ++

Year	Lev	Team	AB	R	H	HR	RBI	Avg	OB	Slg	OPS	bb%	ct%	Eye	SB	CS	x/h%	Iso	RC/G
2014	Rk	AZL White Sox	179	27	39	5	21	218	275	380	654	7	53	0.16	0	0	44	162	4.47

Tall, wiry strong OF who possesses terrific raw power that could emerge to plus status. Fits RF profile with power and strong arm. A long way from majors, and needs to make more contact to hit for BA. Long swing can be exploited, and is very raw. Doesn't run well and won't steal bases.

Aguilar,Angel

6 | New York (A) | EXP MLB DEBUT: 2018 | H/W: 6-0 170 | FUT: Starting SS | 8E

Bats R Age 19
2012 FA (Venezuela)
Pwr +++
BAvg +++
Spd ++
Def ++

Year	Lev	Team	AB	R	H	HR	RBI	Avg	OB	Slg	OPS	bb%	ct%	Eye	SB	CS	x/h%	Iso	RC/G
2013	Rk	DSL Yankees	229	35	60	3	37	262	313	406	719	7	81	0.39	2	1	40	144	4.43
2014	Rk	GCL Yankees 2	151	34	47	7	31	311	370	536	906	8	81	0.50	8	2	40	225	6.64

Smooth INF who projects well with nice tools. May not have range to stay at SS long-term, but has plenty of arm strength and quickness for 3B or 2B. Hits for power to pull side and should grow into more in time. Has consistent approach and makes contact with level swing path.

Aguilar,Jesus

3 | Cleveland | EXP MLB DEBUT: 2014 | H/W: 6-3 250 | FUT: Starting 1B | 7C

Bats R Age 24
2007 FA (Venezuela)
Pwr ++++
BAvg ++
Spd +
Def ++

Year	Lev	Team	AB	R	H	HR	RBI	Avg	OB	Slg	OPS	bb%	ct%	Eye	SB	CS	x/h%	Iso	RC/G
2012	A+	Carolina	368	63	102	12	58	277	356	454	810	11	75	0.49	0	1	38	177	5.72
2012	AA	Akron	72	12	21	3	13	292	400	500	900	15	67	0.54	0	0	43	208	7.53
2013	AA	Akron	499	66	137	16	105	275	348	427	775	10	79	0.52	0	1	32	152	5.14
2014	AAA	Columbus	427	69	130	19	77	304	395	511	906	13	78	0.67	0	0	38	206	6.98
2014	MLB	Cleveland	33	2	4	0	3	121	216	121	337	11	61	0.31	0	0	0	0	-1.35

Large-framed 1B who produces consistent power with bat speed and natural strength. Can get pull-happy and expand strike zone, but has turned into better hitter with hard contact and disciplined eye. Has become passable defender with soft hands, but is very poor runner on base.

Ahmed,Nick

6 | Arizona | EXP MLB DEBUT: 2014 | H/W: 6-3 205 | FUT: Starting SS | 7C

Bats R Age 25
2011 (2) Connecticut
Pwr ++
BAvg +++
Spd ++++
Def +++

Year	Lev	Team	AB	R	H	HR	RBI	Avg	OB	Slg	OPS	bb%	ct%	Eye	SB	CS	x/h%	Iso	RC/G
2011	Rk	Danville	248	46	65	4	24	262	342	379	721	11	81	0.65	18	6	29	117	4.60
2012	A+	Lynchburg	506	84	136	6	49	269	333	391	725	9	80	0.48	40	10	34	123	4.58
2013	AA	Mobile	487	58	115	4	46	236	285	324	609	6	85	0.46	26	7	26	88	3.11
2014	AAA	Reno	407	57	127	4	47	312	369	425	794	8	86	0.67	14	6	27	113	5.42
2014	MLB	Arizona	70	9	14	1	4	200	233	271	504	4	86	0.30	0	1	21	71	1.72

Has a solid approach at the plate with gap power; improved contact rate sparked the turnaround. Has above-average speed that results in good range, plus soft hands and a quick, strong throwing motion. Has solid tools across the board with plus speed and good defense.

Albies,Ozhaino

6 | Atlanta | EXP MLB DEBUT: 2018 | H/W: 5-9 150 | FUT: Starting SS | 9D

Bats B Age 18
2013 FA (Venezuela)
Pwr ++
BAvg ++++
Spd ++++
Def +++

Year	Lev	Team	AB	R	H	HR	RBI	Avg	OB	Slg	OPS	bb%	ct%	Eye	SB	CS	x/h%	Iso	RC/G
2014	Rk	Danville	135	25	48	1	14	356	428	452	879	11	87	1.00	15	3	17	96	6.60
2014	Rk	GCL Braves	63	16	24	0	5	381	473	429	902	15	90	1.83	7	2	13	48	7.14

Switch-hitter rakes from both sides of the plate with a short, compact stroke. Uses the entire field, makes consistent contact, and walked more than he struck out. Swiped 22 bags in 27 attempts. Doesn't project to develop much if any power, but that is his only obvious shortcoming.

Alcantara,Sergio

6 | Arizona | EXP MLB DEBUT: 2017 | H/W: 5-10 150 | FUT: Starting SS | 7C

Bats B Age 18
2012 FA (DR)
Pwr +
BAvg +++
Spd ++
Def ++++

Year	Lev	Team	AB	R	H	HR	RBI	Avg	OB	Slg	OPS	bb%	ct%	Eye	SB	CS	x/h%	Iso	RC/G
2013	Rk	AZL Dbacks	169	31	41	0	16	243	399	320	719	21	79	1.22	3	2	22	77	5.15
2014	Rk	Missoula	266	48	65	1	18	244	360	297	657	15	77	0.77	8	4	18	53	3.98

Quick, agile fielder with soft hands and a cannon for an arm. Doesn't project to have much power, but makes good contact. His hit tool could still develop as he played most of 2014 as a 17-year-old. Has only average speed, but has the glove and arm strength to stick at SS.

Alfaro,Jorge

23 | Texas | EXP MLB DEBUT: 2016 | H/W: 6-2 185 | FUT: Starting C | 8C

Bats R Age 21
2010 FA (Colombia)
Pwr ++++
BAvg ++
Spd ++
Def ++

Year	Lev	Team	AB	R	H	HR	RBI	Avg	OB	Slg	OPS	bb%	ct%	Eye	SB	CS	x/h%	Iso	RC/G
2013	Rk	AZL Rangers	21	5	9	2	8	429	478	810	1288	9	71	0.33	2	0	44	381	12.11
2013	A	Hickory	372	63	96	16	53	258	310	452	762	7	70	0.25	16	3	41	194	4.94
2013	A+	Myrtle Beach	11	4	2	0	0	182	308	182	490	15	55	0.40	0	0	0	0	1.23
2014	A+	Myrtle Beach	398	63	104	13	73	261	302	440	741	5	75	0.23	6	5	38	178	4.55
2014	AA	Frisco	88	12	23	4	14	261	309	443	752	6	74	0.26	0	0	35	182	4.62

Athletic backstop who continues to struggle with glove, but stands out with the bat. Generates plus power with bat speed and natural strength. Can be too aggressive at plate and flail at pitches out of zone. Footwork has improved and arm strength exceptional. Runs well for position.

Aliotti,Anthony

3 | Oakland | EXP MLB DEBUT: 2015 | H/W: 6-0 205 | FUT: Reserve 1B | 6B

Bats L Age 27
2009 (15) St. Mary's
Pwr ++
BAvg +++
Spd +
Def +++

Year	Lev	Team	AB	R	H	HR	RBI	Avg	OB	Slg	OPS	bb%	ct%	Eye	SB	CS	x/h%	Iso	RC/G
2012	AA	Midland	455	72	133	10	76	292	384	426	811	13	72	0.53	0	0	30	134	5.96
2013	AA	Midland	340	49	119	12	51	350	456	541	997	16	76	0.80	3	2	34	191	8.53
2013	AAA	Sacramento	154	17	41	2	20	266	331	344	676	9	71	0.34	0	0	17	78	3.87
2014	AA	Midland	166	26	46	7	27	277	381	482	863	14	61	0.44	0	0	41	205	7.31
2014	AAA	Sacramento	243	30	63	2	21	259	345	354	699	12	69	0.42	1	1	30	95	4.45

Strong 1B who has spent most of last 3 yrs in AA. Owns patient, selective approach, but can't seem to solve LHP. Struck out at least 177 times in each full season and has added more loft to add more pop. Has well below average wheels, but is solid defensive 1B with good hands.

Allie,Stetson — 3 — Pittsburgh

EXP MLB DEBUT: 2015 | H/W: 6-2 240 | FUT: Backup 1B | 6C

Bats R Age 24 — 2010 (2) HS (OH)

Pwr ++++ · BAvg ++ · Spd ++ · Def ++

Year	Lev	Team	AB	R	H	HR	RBI	Avg	OB	Slg	OPS	bb%	ct%	Eye	SB	CS	x/h%	Iso	RC/G
2012	Rk	GCL Pirates	150	23	32	3	19	213	310	340	650	12	67	0.42	2	0	34	127	3.71
2013	A	West Virginia	244	42	79	17	61	324	411	607	1017	13	68	0.46	6	1	43	283	8.95
2013	A+	Bradenton	236	28	54	4	25	229	343	356	699	15	65	0.50	2	3	41	127	4.60
2014	AA	Altoona	407	60	100	21	62	246	358	440	798	15	69	0.56	9	6	37	194	5.72

Has a grip-it-and-rip-it approach with good power, but lots of swings and misses. Value is tied up in power as he brings little else to the table. Below avg runner with limited range though he does have a plus arm. Likely nothing more than backup 1B/4th OF with good power.

Almonte,Jose — 79 — Texas

EXP MLB DEBUT: 2019 | H/W: 6-3 205 | FUT: Starting OF | 8E

Bats R Age 18 — 2013 FA (DR)

Pwr +++ · BAvg ++ · Spd ++ · Def +++

Year	Lev	Team	AB	R	H	HR	RBI	Avg	OB	Slg	OPS	bb%	ct%	Eye	SB	CS	x/h%	Iso	RC/G
2014	Rk	DSL Rangers	41	3	13	0	5	317	364	366	729	7	80	0.38	0	0	15	49	4.49
2014	Rk	AZL Rangers	171	16	28	2	18	164	210	222	432	6	70	0.20	5	3	18	58	0.31

Tall, athletic OF who had poor performance, but has intriguing upside with plus power potential. Swings hard early in count and needs to make better contact. Has room to add more strength to lean frame. Has strong arm ideal for RF, though isn't a burner on base and lacks range.

Almora,Albert — 8 — Chicago (N)

EXP MLB DEBUT: 2016 | H/W: 6-2 180 | FUT: Starting CF | 8C

Bats R Age 20 — 2012 (1) HS (FL)

Pwr +++ · BAvg +++ · Spd +++ · Def +++

Year	Lev	Team	AB	R	H	HR	RBI	Avg	OB	Slg	OPS	bb%	ct%	Eye	SB	CS	x/h%	Iso	RC/G
2012	Rk	AZL Cubs	75	18	26	1	13	347	364	480	844	3	89	0.25	5	1	27	133	5.57
2012	A-	Boise	65	9	19	1	6	292	292	446	738	0	92	0.00	0	1	42	154	4.32
2013	A	Kane County	249	39	82	3	23	329	372	466	838	6	88	0.57	4	4	29	137	5.81
2014	A+	Daytona	367	55	104	7	50	283	306	406	712	3	87	0.26	6	3	28	123	4.09
2014	AA	Tennessee	141	20	33	2	10	234	245	355	599	1	84	0.09	0	1	33	121	2.67

Athletic OF has not advanced. Has quick hands and a smooth line-drive stroke. Sprays balls to all fields and makes consistent contact. Still needs to be more patient and work deeper into counts. Scouts remain convinced that he will add power once he fills out.

Altherr,Aaron — 8 — Philadelphia

EXP MLB DEBUT: 2014 | H/W: 6-5 220 | FUT: Starting CF | 7C

Bats R Age 24 — 2009 (9) HS (AZ)

Pwr +++ · BAvg ++ · Spd ++++ · Def +++

Year	Lev	Team	AB	R	H	HR	RBI	Avg	OB	Slg	OPS	bb%	ct%	Eye	SB	CS	x/h%	Iso	RC/G
2012	A	Lakewood	420	65	106	8	50	252	314	402	717	8	76	0.37	25	8	39	150	4.44
2013	A+	Clearwater	466	57	128	12	69	275	339	455	793	9	70	0.32	23	5	42	180	5.63
2014	A+	Clearwater	28	6	7	0	2	250	364	429	792	15	71	0.63	1	0	43	179	6.11
2014	AA	Reading	449	54	106	14	57	236	278	399	677	5	76	0.24	12	6	41	163	3.68
2014	MLB	Philadelphia	5	0	0	0	0	0	0	0	0	0	60	0.00	0	0		0	-6.81

Toolsy physical specimen whose long arms are both blessing and curse. When extended and on-time, power comes easy. But swing can get long, contact on breaking stuff still a challenge and impatience an issue. Plus runner with long strides and very good defender in CF. Needs consistency to excel.

Alvarez,Dariel — 89 — Baltimore

EXP MLB DEBUT: 2015 | H/W: 6-2 180 | FUT: Starting OF | 7C

Bats R Age 26 — 2013 FA (Cuba)

Pwr +++ · BAvg +++ · Spd ++ · Def ++

Year	Lev	Team	AB	R	H	HR	RBI	Avg	OB	Slg	OPS	bb%	ct%	Eye	SB	CS	x/h%	Iso	RC/G
2013	Rk	GCL Orioles	9	2	4	1	2	444	500	1222	1722	10	89	1.00	0	0	100	778	16.17
2013	A+	Frederick	39	5	17	2	7	436	463	641	1104	5	97	2.00	1	2	24	205	8.29
2013	AA	Bowie	31	2	6	1	1	194	219	290	509	3	71	0.11	0	0	17	97	1.17
2014	AA	Bowie	359	52	111	14	68	309	333	487	821	3	90	0.37	7	4	32	178	5.27
2014	AAA	Norfolk	173	23	52	1	19	301	331	439	771	4	84	0.30	1	1	38	139	4.95

Natural-hitting OF who makes extreme contact with ideal plate coverage and bat control. Uses entire field and exhibits moderate pop. Pitch recognition is a little short and only has fringy speed. Has enough arm for any OF spot, though range and instincts best suited for corner position.

Amaya,Gioskar — 4 — Chicago (N)

EXP MLB DEBUT: 2015 | H/W: 5-11 175 | FUT: Starting 2B | 7C

Bats R Age 22 — 2009 FA (Venezuela)

Pwr ++ · BAvg ++++ · Spd ++ · Def ++

Year	Lev	Team	AB	R	H	HR	RBI	Avg	OB	Slg	OPS	bb%	ct%	Eye	SB	CS	x/h%	Iso	RC/G
2011	Rk	AZL Cubs	204	37	77	0	36	377	415	510	925	6	81	0.33	13	8	25	132	6.96
2012	A-	Boise	272	61	81	8	33	298	374	496	870	11	76	0.51	15	5	32	199	6.57
2012	AAA	Iowa	1	1	1	0	0	1000	1000	2000	3000	0	100		0	0	100	1000	27.71
2013	A	Kane County	453	65	114	5	28	252	315	369	684	8	76	0.39	13	6	32	117	4.03
2014	A+	Daytona	369	56	102	4	35	276	367	369	736	13	76	0.59	14	7	23	92	4.89

Short, athletic 2B has a quick bat and makes consistent contact, but doesn't have much power. Speed and range are avg, but he does have soft hands and good instincts. Did make the FSL All-Star team, but the Cubs left him exposed in the Rule 5 draft where he went unpicked.

Anderson,Blake — 2 — Miami

EXP MLB DEBUT: 2019 | H/W: 6-3 180 | FUT: Starting C | 7D

Bats R Age 19 — 2014 (S-1) HS (MS)

Pwr ++ · BAvg ++ · Spd ++ · Def +++

Year	Lev	Team	AB	R	H	HR	RBI	Avg	OB	Slg	OPS	bb%	ct%	Eye	SB	CS	x/h%	Iso	RC/G
2014	Rk	GCL Marlins	74	6	8	0	5	108	233	135	368	14	55	0.36	0	1	25	27	-0.96

Has good blocking and receiving skills with a plus arm and should be able to stick behind the dish. Has a balanced approach at the plate, but lacks bat speed or the ability to square up the ball and scouts aren't convinced he will hit. Struggled to make contact in his debut.

Anderson,Brian — 45 — Miami

EXP MLB DEBUT: 2018 | H/W: 6-3 175 | FUT: Starting 2B | 7C

Bats R Age 21 — 2014 (3) Arkansas

Pwr ++ · BAvg +++ · Spd ++ · Def +++

Year	Lev	Team	AB	R	H	HR	RBI	Avg	OB	Slg	OPS	bb%	ct%	Eye	SB	CS	x/h%	Iso	RC/G
2012	NCAA	Arkansas	120	23	34	2	11	283	363	367	730	11	70	0.42	2	3	18	83	4.73
2013	NCAA	Arkansas	209	47	68	4	36	325	436	488	924	16	84	1.24	6	1	31	163	7.49
2014	NCAA	Arkansas	241	39	79	7	51	328	379	498	877	8	83	0.50	9	2	30	170	6.27
2014	A-	Batavia	77	11	21	3	12	273	325	455	780	7	86	0.55	1	1	33	182	5.04
2014	A	Greensboro	153	27	48	8	37	314	367	516	884	8	82	0.46	0	0	31	203	6.23

Scrappy infielder has a good approach at the plate and makes consistent contact. Has good power and slugged 11 HR. Was moved to 3B, where he profiles better due to his size, power, and arm strength. He has good speed and played CF his first year in college.

Anderson,Tim — 6 — Chicago (A)

EXP MLB DEBUT: 2016 | H/W: 6-1 180 | FUT: Starting SS | 8B

Bats R Age 21 — 2013 (1) E Central (MS) CC

Pwr +++ · BAvg +++ · Spd +++ · Def +++

Year	Lev	Team	AB	R	H	HR	RBI	Avg	OB	Slg	OPS	bb%	ct%	Eye	SB	CS	x/h%	Iso	RC/G
2013	NCAA	East Central CC	182	63	90	10	45	495	538	879	1417	9	93	1.42	41	4	43	385	12.21
2013	A	Kannapolis	267	45	74	1	21	277	334	363	698	8	71	0.29	24	4	22	86	4.26
2014	Rk	AZL White Sox	15	2	3	2	2	200	294	600	894	12	67	0.40	0	1	67	400	6.63
2014	A+	Winston-Salem	286	48	85	6	31	297	314	472	786	2	76	0.10	10	3	36	175	5.03
2014	AA	Birmingham	44	7	16	1	7	364	364	500	864	0	80	0.00	0	1	25	136	5.63

Smooth, instinctual INF who missed time with fractured wrist. Swings very fast bat and laces line drives to all fields. Pitch recognition is a little short and at times rarely draws walks, but offers some power projection along with BA. Plus speed and quickness enhance package, but could move to CF.

Andujar,Miguel — 5 — New York (A)

EXP MLB DEBUT: 2018 | H/W: 6-0 175 | FUT: Starting 3B | 8D

Bats R Age 20 — 2011 FA (DR)

Pwr +++ · BAvg +++ · Spd ++ · Def ++

Year	Lev	Team	AB	R	H	HR	RBI	Avg	OB	Slg	OPS	bb%	ct%	Eye	SB	CS	x/h%	Iso	RC/G
2012	Rk	GCL Yankees	177	21	41	1	19	232	284	299	584	7	79	0.35	1	3	24	68	2.66
2013	Rk	GCL Yankees 2	133	18	43	4	25	323	357	496	853	5	84	0.33	4	1	35	173	5.80
2014	A	CharlestonSC	484	75	129	10	70	267	316	397	713	7	83	0.42	5	1	30	130	4.26

Pure-hitting INF who finished hot in first full season. Owns fluid swing and bat-to-ball ability to project to high BA. Possesses plus raw power and will need to tame aggressive approach to realize pop. Isn't the fleetest afoot, though isn't a slouch and brings good defensive tools to table.

Aplin,Andrew — 89 — Houston

EXP MLB DEBUT: 2015 | H/W: 6-0 205 | FUT: Reserve OF | 6B

Bats L Age 24 — 2012 (5) Arizona State

Pwr ++ · BAvg ++ · Spd +++ · Def +++

Year	Lev	Team	AB	R	H	HR	RBI	Avg	OB	Slg	OPS	bb%	ct%	Eye	SB	CS	x/h%	Iso	RC/G
2012	A-	Tri City	164	38	57	4	25	348	431	537	967	13	87	1.09	20	7	32	189	7.73
2012	A+	Lancaster	104	19	27	3	13	260	287	423	710	4	85	0.25	4	3	33	163	4.06
2013	A+	Lancaster	500	102	139	9	107	278	381	424	805	14	87	1.32	24	6	35	146	5.92
2014	AA	Corpus Christi	356	49	95	6	50	267	380	354	734	15	84	1.16	21	8	19	87	5.03
2014	AAA	Oklahoma City	96	14	25	0	15	260	360	313	673	14	84	1.00	5	3	16	52	4.28

Instinctual OF who maximizes limited tools and is on verge of big leagues. Doesn't provide much offensive punch in unorthodox swing, but controls bat well to make easy contact. Draws walks to get on base and use average speed. Mostly plays CF with good reads and owns average arm.

Aquino,Aristides

9 | Cincinnati | EXP MLB DEBUT: 2018 | H/W: 6-4 190 | FUT: Starting RF | 8E

Bats R Age 20
2011 FA (DR)
Pwr ++++
BAvg +++
Spd +++
Def +++

Year	Lev	Team	AB	R	H	HR	RBI	Avg	OB	Slg	OPS	bb%	ct%	Eye	SB	CS	x/h%	Iso	RC/G
2013	Rk	AZL Reds	194	37	54	4	38	278	314	479	793	5	79	0.25	4	3	46	201	5.27
2013	Rk	Billings	69	13	14	3	10	203	225	377	602	3	67	0.09	1	1	36	174	2.55
2014	Rk	Billings	284	48	83	16	64	292	328	577	905	5	77	0.23	21	5	53	285	6.57

Finally turned plus tools into production in '14. Pioneer League leader in nearly every offensive category. Still projects more strength and athleticism. Plus raw power, quick bat, and leveraged swing should generate HR at any level. Knows how to steal bases and defends RF well. Very high upside.

Arcia,Orlando

46 | Milwaukee | EXP MLB DEBUT: 2016 | H/W: 6-0 165 | FUT: Starting SS | 7C

Bats R Age 20
2010 FA (Venezuela)
Pwr ++
BAvg +++
Spd +++
Def ++++

Year	Lev	Team	AB	R	H	HR	RBI	Avg	OB	Slg	OPS	bb%	ct%	Eye	SB	CS	x/h%	Iso	RC/G
2013	A	Wisconsin	442	67	111	4	39	251	306	333	639	7	91	0.88	20	9	21	81	3.67
2014	A+	Brevard Cnty	498	65	144	4	50	289	344	392	736	8	87	0.65	31	11	26	102	4.72

Rarely strikes out and makes consistent contact. Power is not a part of his game now, but has raw strength that should allow more as he matures. In the field, he is a plus SS, showing good range, footwork, and a strong arm. He is not a burner, but his speed plays a tick above avg.

Arias,Junior

8 | Cincinnati | EXP MLB DEBUT: 2018 | H/W: 6-1 200 | FUT: Backup OF | 6D

Bats R Age 23
2008 FA (DR)
Pwr ++
BAvg +
Spd ++++
Def ++

Year	Lev	Team	AB	R	H	HR	RBI	Avg	OB	Slg	OPS	bb%	ct%	Eye	SB	CS	x/h%	Iso	RC/G
2012	A	Dayton	361	52	75	7	35	208	249	313	562	5	73	0.21	28	7	28	105	2.16
2013	A	Dayton	271	45	77	10	33	284	317	469	786	5	73	0.18	40	10	34	185	5.08
2013	A+	Bakersfield	222	30	57	5	20	257	273	396	670	2	73	0.08	19	10	33	140	3.48
2014	Rk	AZL Reds	36	4	6	0	0	167	333	194	528	20	61	0.64	6	0	17	28	1.96
2014	A+	Bakersfield	70	15	19	3	10	271	320	429	749	7	74	0.28	9	3	26	157	4.56

Missed time with injury; repeated level from '13. Excellent athlete who utilizes plus speed to steal bases with ease but is still learning to play OF. Extreme groundball hitter. Aggressive approach and poor pitch recognition a bad combo, but makes hard contact when he connects.

Arroyo,Christian

6 | San Francisco | EXP MLB DEBUT: 2016 | H/W: 6-1 180 | FUT: Starting SS | 8D

Bats R Age 19
2013 (1) HS (FL)
Pwr ++
BAvg ++++
Spd +++
Def ++

Year	Lev	Team	AB	R	H	HR	RBI	Avg	OB	Slg	OPS	bb%	ct%	Eye	SB	CS	x/h%	Iso	RC/G
2013	Rk	AZL Giants	184	47	60	2	39	326	389	511	900	9	83	0.59	3	2	42	185	6.86
2014	A-	Salem-Kaizer	243	39	81	5	48	333	379	469	848	7	87	0.58	6	1	26	136	5.88
2014	A	Augusta	118	10	24	1	14	203	230	271	501	3	81	0.18	1	2	21	68	1.51

Instinctual SS had an up-and-down, injury-plagued year across two levels in '14. BA ceiling is promising with good ct% and bat speed. Gap power now, but raw power should translate to average production in his prime. Tick below avg speed raise questions about his future at SS, but with a strong arm and athleticism, he'll have every chance to stick.

Arruebarrena,Erisbel

6 | Los Angeles (N) | EXP MLB DEBUT: 2014 | H/W: 6-0 200 | FUT: Starting SS | 7D

Bats R Age 25
2014 FA (Cuba)
Pwr +++
BAvg ++
Spd +++
Def +++

Year	Lev	Team	AB	R	H	HR	RBI	Avg	OB	Slg	OPS	bb%	ct%	Eye	SB	CS	x/h%	Iso	RC/G
2014	Rk	AZL Dodgers	18	3	4	2	4	222	222	667	889	0	44	0.00	0	0	100	444	10.55
2014	A+	Rancho Cuca	49	8	12	2	11	245	275	490	764	4	51	0.08	1	0	58	245	6.81
2014	AA	Chattanooga	96	10	20	1	6	208	240	302	542	4	68	0.13	0	0	30	94	1.88
2014	AAA	Albuquerque	84	7	28	1	11	333	404	452	857	11	69	0.38	1	1	21	119	6.70
2014	MLB	LA Dodgers	41	4	8	0	4	195	250	220	470	7	59	0.18	0	0	13	24	0.85

24-year-old Cuban SS signed a 5-year, $25M deal, though the Dodgers removed him from the 40-man roster in Dec. Physically strong frame with good footwork and range with a chance to be a plus defender in the majors. Shows good bat speed with 15-20 HR power, but can be overly aggressive and struck out 108 times.

Arteaga,Humberto

46 | Kansas City | EXP MLB DEBUT: 2017 | H/W: 6-1 160 | FUT: Utility INF | 6B

Bats R Age 21
2010 FA (Venezuela)
Pwr +
BAvg ++
Spd ++
Def ++++

Year	Lev	Team	AB	R	H	HR	RBI	Avg	OB	Slg	OPS	bb%	ct%	Eye	SB	CS	x/h%	Iso	RC/G
2011	Rk	AZL Royals	213	30	54	0	28	254	284	324	608	4	82	0.23	8	2	24	70	2.91
2012	Rk	Burlington	234	40	64	2	29	274	300	380	681	4	87	0.29	7	3	28	107	3.82
2013	Rk	Idaho Falls	300	56	84	3	58	280	337	393	731	8	83	0.50	11	7	27	113	4.62
2013	A	Lexington	240	17	45	0	13	188	207	225	432	2	82	0.14	0	4	16	38	0.70
2014	A	Lexington	450	33	89	2	31	198	227	249	476	4	75	0.15	7	6	19	51	1.03

Defensive specialist with first-step quickness and ideal range for middle infield. Exhibits smooth actions and quick hands to turn DP. Does not provide much value with bat. Has quick compact stroke, but fans frequently and lacks the strength for power. Does not run well for profile.

Asencio,Yeison

79 | San Diego | EXP MLB DEBUT: 2016 | H/W: 6-1 225 | FUT: Backup RF | 6C

Bats R Age 25
2009 FA (DR)
Pwr +++
BAvg ++
Spd ++
Def ++

Year	Lev	Team	AB	R	H	HR	RBI	Avg	OB	Slg	OPS	bb%	ct%	Eye	SB	CS	x/h%	Iso	RC/G
2012	A	Fort Wayne	350	47	113	8	61	323	352	474	827	4	89	0.42	7	6	29	151	5.47
2013	A+	Lake Elsinore	243	34	72	5	44	296	324	457	781	4	88	0.34	1	1	38	160	4.97
2013	AA	San Antonio	291	25	76	2	32	261	293	354	647	4	90	0.45	3	2	26	93	3.56
2014	AA	San Antonio	455	51	129	10	44	284	319	409	728	5	87	0.42	8	4	26	125	4.37
2014	AAA	El Paso	81	16	27	5	15	333	365	568	933	5	89	0.44	0	1	33	235	6.48

Notched career high in HR while maintaining a consistent contact rate, but walks infrequently. Avg speed and a below-avg defender means his value is tied up bat. Hit well in a brief stint at Triple-A, but the recent influx of major league OF talent pushes him well down the org depth chart.

Asuaje,Carlos

457 | Boston | EXP MLB DEBUT: 2016 | H/W: 5-9 160 | FUT: Utility player | 6B

Bats R Age 23
2013 (11) NovaSoutheastern
Pwr ++
BAvg +++
Spd +++
Def ++

Year	Lev	Team	AB	R	H	HR	RBI	Avg	OB	Slg	OPS	bb%	ct%	Eye	SB	CS	x/h%	Iso	RC/G
2012	NCAA	Nova SthEstrn	190	49	74	5	29	389	473	611	1083	14	91	1.67	15	3	41	221	9.10
2013	NCAA	Nova SthEstrn	178	40	57	2	33	320	440	449	889	18	93	2.92	32	3	30	129	7.24
2013	A-	Lowell	171	19	46	1	21	269	369	368	737	14	81	0.82	4	3	30	99	5.03
2014	A	Greenville	325	59	99	11	73	305	383	542	924	11	83	0.73	7	4	45	237	7.15
2014	A+	Salem	155	27	50	4	28	323	393	516	909	10	78	0.53	1	3	40	194	7.02

Short, versatile player who had big rise in first full season. Led SAL in SLG and 3rd in OBP. Plays multiple positions, though not polished at any. Controls bat with level swing path. Can hit HR, but will lace more doubles to gaps. Ideal #2 hitter who can put balls in play. Limited upside, but one to keep eye on.

Austin,Tyler

359 | New York (A) | EXP MLB DEBUT: 2015 | H/W: 6-1 220 | FUT: Starting OF | 7C

Bats R Age 23
2010 (13) HS (GA)
Pwr ++
BAvg +++
Spd ++
Def ++

Year	Lev	Team	AB	R	H	HR	RBI	Avg	OB	Slg	OPS	bb%	ct%	Eye	SB	CS	x/h%	Iso	RC/G
2012	A+	Tampa	134	20	43	2	23	321	377	478	854	8	79	0.43	6	0	37	157	6.20
2012	AA	Trenton	7	2	2	0	1	286	375	286	661	13	86	1.00	0	0	0	0	4.04
2013	Rk	GCL Yankees 2	6	1	4	0	0	667	714	667	1381	14	100		0	0	0	0	12.11
2013	AA	Trenton	319	43	82	6	40	257	342	373	715	11	75	0.52	4	0	29	116	4.51
2014	AA	Trenton	396	56	109	9	47	275	336	419	755	8	80	0.45	3	2	31	144	4.86

Sweet-swinging OF who repeated AA and was slightly better. Needs to find defensive home and will need to hit for more pop for 1B or OF corner. Swings a quick bat and makes easy contact while using entire field. Has some power potential, but seems content to use opposite field.

Avelino,Abiatal

6 | New York (A) | EXP MLB DEBUT: 2018 | H/W: 5-11 185 | FUT: Starting SS | 7D

Bats R Age 20
2011 FA (DR)
Pwr +
BAvg +++
Spd +++
Def ++++

Year	Lev	Team	AB	R	H	HR	RBI	Avg	OB	Slg	OPS	bb%	ct%	Eye	SB	CS	x/h%	Iso	RC/G
2013	Rk	GCL Yankees 2	70	21	28	0	13	400	468	586	1054	11	94	2.25	17	1	32	186	8.73
2013	Rk	GCL Yankees	58	14	15	0	4	259	338	328	666	11	88	1.00	9	3	20	69	4.16
2013	A-	Staten Island	70	10	17	0	6	243	284	271	555	5	91	0.67	2	0	12	29	2.65
2014	Rk	GCL Yankees	31	7	11	0	3	355	394	548	942	6	87	0.50	0	0	55	194	7.16
2014	A	CharlestonSC	220	31	51	2	12	232	287	323	610	7	80	0.39	11	5	29	91	3.03

Quick INF who missed time with injury and is solid defender with plus arm and ideal quickness for SS. Packs some strength in frame but focuses on contact and hitting to all fields. Owns solid-average speed and possesses honed instincts on base. Aggressive free-swinger early in count.

Avery,Xavier

789 | Detroit | EXP MLB DEBUT: 2012 | H/W: 6-0 190 | FUT: Starting OF | 7E

Bats L Age 25
2008 (2) HS (GA)
Pwr ++
BAvg ++
Spd ++++
Def +++

Year	Lev	Team	AB	R	H	HR	RBI	Avg	OB	Slg	OPS	bb%	ct%	Eye	SB	CS	x/h%	Iso	RC/G
2012	MLB	Baltimore	94	14	21	1	6	223	305	340	645	10	76	0.48	6	3	38	117	3.62
2013	AA	Bowie	160	34	48	1	12	300	388	406	794	13	73	0.52	12	3	27	106	5.80
2013	AAA	Norfolk	295	36	70	2	23	237	310	312	622	10	75	0.42	17	5	23	75	3.22
2013	AAA	Tacoma	12	5	6	1	3	500	538	833	1372	8	92	1.00	1	0	33	333	11.42
2014	AAA	Tacoma	400	70	110	10	38	275	344	413	756	10	77	0.46	31	8	30	138	4.92

Premium athlete who consistently steals 30+ bases, but has trouble hitting and making contact. Hit career high in HR, but at best when hitting ball on ground and using speed. Pitch recognition is issue and struggles with LHP. Lacks arm strength, but is solid defender with plus range.

Baez,Jeffrey — 89 — Chicago (N)

EXP MLB DEBUT: 2018 | H/W: 6-0 180 | FUT: Starting OF | 8E

Bats R Age 21 — 2010 FA (Venezuela) — Pwr +++ | BAvg ++ | Spd ++++ | Def +++

Year	Lev	Team	AB	R	H	HR	RBI	Avg	OB	Slg	OPS	bb%	ct%	Eye	SB	CS	x/h%	Iso	RC/G
2012	Rk	AZL Cubs	18	0	4	0	2	222	263	222	485	5	72	0.20	1	0	0	0	1.08
2013	Rk	AZL Cubs	164	31	47	1	12	287	350	384	734	9	76	0.41	25	3	26	98	4.72
2013	A-	Boise	13	2	2	0	2	154	267	462	728	13	54	0.33	1	0	100	308	6.45
2014	A-	Boise	161	31	43	7	30	267	326	460	785	8	75	0.35	15	6	35	193	5.17
2014	A	Kane County	106	14	25	6	15	236	302	491	792	9	64	0.26	2	2	56	255	5.73

Venezuelan OF struggled when moved up. Does have moderate bat speed and hit 13 HR, but overly aggressive approach results in poor contact and he hit .255 for the year. Does have decent speed in the OF and is an average defender. Future value is tied up in his power.

Bandy,Jett — 2 — Los Angeles (A)

EXP MLB DEBUT: 2016 | H/W: 6-4 235 | FUT: Backup C | 6B

Bats R Age 25 — 2011 (31) Arizona — Pwr +++ | BAvg ++ | Spd + | Def ++

Year	Lev	Team	AB	R	H	HR	RBI	Avg	OB	Slg	OPS	bb%	ct%	Eye	SB	CS	x/h%	Iso	RC/G
2011	AA	Arkansas	2	1	1	1	1	500	500	2000	2500	0	100		0	0	100	1500	20.12
2011	AAA	Salt Lake	1	0	0	0	0	0	0	0	0	0	100		0	0		0	-2.66
2012	A+	Inland Empire	324	42	80	7	46	247	291	386	677	6	84	0.39	1	1	38	139	3.81
2013	AA	Arkansas	245	26	59	4	28	241	282	376	657	5	84	0.36	0	1	39	135	3.60
2014	AA	Arkansas	312	38	78	13	40	250	322	413	735	10	80	0.52	2	4	32	163	4.54

Tall, strong C who repeated AA and had career high in HR. Huge frame sets up easy target and handles pitchers well. Has average arm, but footwork hampers release. Lacks frontline bat speed, but has strength for emerging pull power. Will always strike out and doesn't run well.

Barnes,Austin — 245 — Los Angeles (N)

EXP MLB DEBUT: 2015 | H/W: 5-9 185 | FUT: Starting C | 7D

Bats R Age 25 — 2011 (9) Arizona State — Pwr ++ | BAvg +++ | Spd ++ | Def +++

Year	Lev	Team	AB	R	H	HR	RBI	Avg	OB	Slg	OPS	bb%	ct%	Eye	SB	CS	x/h%	Iso	RC/G
2012	A	Greensboro	478	76	152	12	65	318	393	481	874	11	87	0.97	9	2	34	163	6.47
2013	A+	Jupiter	350	42	91	4	38	260	356	343	699	13	83	0.88	5	2	22	83	4.47
2013	AA	Jacksonville	62	10	21	1	7	339	446	484	930	16	84	1.20	0	0	24	145	7.56
2014	A+	Jupiter	180	24	57	1	14	317	382	417	799	10	86	0.76	3	3	25	100	5.57
2014	AA	Jacksonville	284	56	84	12	43	296	401	507	908	15	87	1.39	8	0	40	211	7.06

Small, athletic backstop with contact-oriented swing. Shows great patience at the plate, and makes hard contact going gap-to-gap. Power and speed will never be a big part of his game. Behind the plate his arm works with good hands and receiving skills that will keep him there.

Barnes,Barrett — 8 — Pittsburgh

EXP MLB DEBUT: 2017 | H/W: 6-1 195 | FUT: Starting CF | 8E

Bats R Age 23 — 2012 (S-1) Texas Tech — Pwr +++ | BAvg +++ | Spd +++ | Def +++

Year	Lev	Team	AB	R	H	HR	RBI	Avg	OB	Slg	OPS	bb%	ct%	Eye	SB	CS	x/h%	Iso	RC/G
2012	A-	State College	125	16	36	5	24	288	373	456	829	12	83	0.81	10	6	31	168	5.87
2013	A	West Virginia	183	26	49	5	24	268	330	399	729	9	74	0.35	10	3	29	131	4.51
2014	Rk	GCL Pirates	16	5	5	2	5	313	500	813	1313	27	81	2.00	1	0	80	500	12.57
2014	A	West Virginia	13	1	2	0	2	154	267	154	421	13	85	1.00	2	0	0	0	1.17
2014	A+	Bradenton	21	3	5	0	1	238	333	333	667	13	76	0.60	1	0	40	95	4.07

Injuries have slowed his development. Has good bat speed, solid plate discipline, and plus raw power. Has above-average speed, covers ground well, and should be able to stick in CF as he moves up. Loads of potential, but checkered injury history makes him unreliable.

Barnhart,Tucker — 2 — Cincinnati

EXP MLB DEBUT: 2014 | H/W: 5-11 195 | FUT: Starting C | 7C

Bats B Age 24 — 2009 (10) HS (IN) — Pwr + | BAvg ++ | Spd ++ | Def ++++

Year	Lev	Team	AB	R	H	HR	RBI	Avg	OB	Slg	OPS	bb%	ct%	Eye	SB	CS	x/h%	Iso	RC/G
2012	A+	Bakersfield	198	26	55	4	22	278	370	409	779	13	77	0.64	0	2	31	131	5.43
2012	AA	Pensacola	130	10	26	2	12	200	262	292	555	8	83	0.50	1	1	27	92	2.43
2013	AA	Pensacola	339	31	88	3	44	260	346	348	694	12	83	0.79	1	0	26	88	4.38
2014	AAA	Louisville	256	18	63	1	29	246	320	316	637	10	87	0.82	0	1	21	70	3.70
2014	MLB	Cincinnati	54	3	10	1	1	185	241	241	482	7	81	0.40	0	0	10	56	1.36

Superb defensive catcher. Possesses athletic frame and solid blocking skills with plus arm. Posts respectable bb%/ ct% thanks to patient approach, but boasts few notable other offensive skills.

Barnum,Keon — 3 — Chicago (A)

EXP MLB DEBUT: 2017 | H/W: 6-5 225 | FUT: Starting 1B | 8E

Bats L Age 22 — 2012 (1-S) HS (FL) — Pwr ++++ | BAvg ++ | Spd + | Def ++

Year	Lev	Team	AB	R	H	HR	RBI	Avg	OB	Slg	OPS	bb%	ct%	Eye	SB	CS	x/h%	Iso	RC/G
2012	Rk	Bristol	43	6	12	3	8	279	354	512	866	10	70	0.38	0	0	33	233	6.37
2013	A	Kannapolis	201	22	51	5	26	254	318	403	721	9	68	0.29	0	0	37	149	4.61
2014	A+	Winston-Salem	491	49	124	8	60	253	305	365	669	7	67	0.23	3	0	31	112	3.83

Hulking 1B who got off to very slow start, but got better as season progressed. Led CAR in Ks and had struggles with LHP. BA in question as he has large holes in long swing. Can drive ball long way upon contact. Can be OK defender with soft hands, but doesn't cover much ground.

Barreto,Franklin — 6 — Oakland

EXP MLB DEBUT: 2018 | H/W: 5-9 175 | FUT: Starting INF | 8D

Bats R Age 19 — 2012 FA (Venezuela) — Pwr ++ | BAvg ++++ | Spd ++++ | Def +++

Year	Lev	Team	AB	R	H	HR	RBI	Avg	OB	Slg	OPS	bb%	ct%	Eye	SB	CS	x/h%	Iso	RC/G
2013	Rk	GCL Blue Jays	174	30	52	4	19	299	348	529	876	7	76	0.31	10	4	50	230	6.56
2013	Rk	Bluefield	54	4	11	0	7	204	232	333	565	4	74	0.14	0	2	55	130	2.39
2014	A-	Vancouver	289	65	90	6	61	311	368	481	849	8	78	0.41	29	5	37	170	6.13

Exciting INF with feel for bat despite youth. Hits hard line drives to gaps and has bat speed and strength to project to at least average power. Swings aggressively early in count and uses above average speed efficiently. Could improve footwork at SS, but owns soft hands and plus arm.

Bauers,Jake — 3 — Tampa Bay

EXP MLB DEBUT: 2018 | H/W: 6-1 195 | FUT: Starting 1B | 7D

Bats L Age 19 — 2013 (7) HS (CA) — Pwr +++ | BAvg ++ | Spd ++ | Def +

Year	Lev	Team	AB	R	H	HR	RBI	Avg	OB	Slg	OPS	bb%	ct%	Eye	SB	CS	x/h%	Iso	RC/G
2013	Rk	AZL Padres	163	22	46	1	25	282	339	374	713	8	81	0.45	2	0	24	92	4.39
2014	A	Fort Wayne	406	59	120	8	64	296	374	414	788	11	80	0.64	5	6	24	118	5.42

Has plus raw power and a good bat. Uses a short, compact LH stroke to put the ball into play with authorit—26 2B and 8 HR in the MWL. Well below-average speed and defense limits him to 1B so he will need to hit to have value.

Bautista,Rafael — 8 — Washington

EXP MLB DEBUT: 2017 | H/W: 6-2 165 | FUT: Starting CF | 8C

Bats R Age 22 — 2012 FA (DR) — Pwr + | BAvg +++ | Spd ++++ | Def +++

Year	Lev	Team	AB	R	H	HR	RBI	Avg	OB	Slg	OPS	bb%	ct%	Eye	SB	CS	x/h%	Iso	RC/G
2013	Rk	GCL Nationals	202	44	65	1	27	322	377	391	768	8	83	0.53	26	7	15	69	5.05
2014	A	Hagerstown	487	97	141	5	54	290	335	382	717	6	85	0.46	69	15	21	92	4.34

Steals make you take notice, but there's more below the surface. Though could stand to be more selective, he makes very good contact and has enough bat speed to sting line drives into the gaps. Top-shelf speed aids his overall plus defensive profile, where he gets great jumps with natural instincts and has a strong arm.

Beckham,Tim — 46 — Tampa Bay

EXP MLB DEBUT: 2013 | H/W: 6-0 195 | FUT: Starting SS/2B | 7C

Bats R Age 25 — 2008 (1) HS (GA) — Pwr ++ | BAvg +++ | Spd +++ | Def +++

Year	Lev	Team	AB	R	H	HR	RBI	Avg	OB	Slg	OPS	bb%	ct%	Eye	SB	CS	x/h%	Iso	RC/G
2013	AAA	Durham	460	71	127	4	51	276	339	387	726	9	77	0.41	17	7	28	111	4.61
2013	MLB	Tampa Bay	7	1	3	0	1	429	429	429	857	0	100		0	0	0	0	5.47
2014	Rk	GCL Devil Rays	21	5	10	1	4	476	542	810	1351	13	81	0.75	1	0	40	333	12.62
2014	A+	Charlotte	12	2	2	0	0	167	231	167	397	8	67	0.25	0	0	0	0	-0.24
2014	AAA	Durham	62	8	16	0	4	258	281	290	572	3	77	0.14	0	2	13	32	2.26

Athletic INF who returned in July after tearing ACL in '13. Looks part of standout propsect with solid tools, but struggling to put all together. Owns bat speed and has raw power, but overswings and displays poor selectivity. Ks have been issue. Runs well and has range best suited for 2B.

Bell,Josh — 79 — Pittsburgh

EXP MLB DEBUT: 2016 | H/W: 6-2 235 | FUT: Starting RF | 9D

Bats B Age 22 — 2011 (2) HS (TX) — Pwr ++++ | BAvg +++ | Spd ++ | Def +++

Year	Lev	Team	AB	R	H	HR	RBI	Avg	OB	Slg	OPS	bb%	ct%	Eye	SB	CS	x/h%	Iso	RC/G
2012	A	West Virginia	62	6	17	1	11	274	297	403	700	3	66	0.10	1	0	35	129	4.19
2013	A	West Virginia	459	75	128	13	76	279	352	453	805	10	80	0.58	1	2	41	174	5.60
2014	A+	Bradenton	331	45	111	9	53	335	382	502	884	7	87	0.58	5	4	30	166	6.28
2014	AA	Altoona	94	13	27	0	7	287	343	309	652	8	87	0.67	4	1	7	21	3.70

Switch-hitting OF has plus bat speed and plus raw power. Struggles to make hard contact on breaking balls and can be a bit stiff at the plate. Shows decent range in the OF, but doesn't take great routes. Avg arm allows him to play RF, but LF or 1B is more likely. Makes consistent contact.

Bellinger,Cody — 3 — Los Angeles (N)

EXP MLB DEBUT: 2018 | H/W: 6-4 180 | FUT: Starting 1B | 8D

Bats L Age 19 — 2013 (6) HS (CA)

Pwr + + + / BAvg + + + / Spd + + / Def + + + +

Year	Lev	Team	AB	R	H	HR	RBI	Avg	OB	Slg	OPS	bb%	ct%	Eye	SB	CS	x/h%	Iso	RC/G
2013	Rk	AZL Dodgers	162	25	34	1	30	210	337	358	695	16	72	0.67	3	3	47	148	4.63
2014	Rk	AZL Dodgers	20	2	3	0	0	150	190	200	390	5	75	0.20	0	0	33	50	0.01
2014	Rk	Ogden	195	49	64	3	34	328	373	503	876	7	82	0.40	8	0	34	174	6.34

Tall 1B put up impressive offensive numbers in rookie ball. Plus defender with Gold Glove potential. Moves well around the bag with soft hands and good instincts. Nice LH swing results in good contact and a line-drive approach. Should be able to hit for avg but not much power.

Beras,Jairo — 79 — Texas

EXP MLB DEBUT: 2018 | H/W: 6-5 178 | FUT: Starting OF | 8D

Bats R Age 19 — 2012 FA (DR)

Pwr + + + / BAvg + + / Spd + + / Def + +

Year	Lev	Team	AB	R	H	HR	RBI	Avg	OB	Slg	OPS	bb%	ct%	Eye	SB	CS	x/h%	Iso	RC/G
2013	Rk	AZL Rangers	64	11	16	2	15	250	304	438	742	7	70	0.26	1	0	38	188	4.78
2014	A	Hickory	389	38	94	7	33	242	301	342	643	8	66	0.25	5	4	27	100	3.45

Tall, lanky OF with impressive credentials and upside, but needs to perform. Pitch selection is subpar while impatient approach leads to low OBP. Natural power is plus and has swing path to hit for BA. Runs OK and can cover ground at all OF positions. Classic high risk/high reward.

Betancourt,Javier — 46 — Detroit

EXP MLB DEBUT: 2017 | H/W: 6-0 180 | FUT: Starting 2B/SS | 7C

Bats R Age 19 — 2011 FA (Venezuela)

Pwr + + / BAvg + + + / Spd + + + / Def + + +

Year	Lev	Team	AB	R	H	HR	RBI	Avg	OB	Slg	OPS	bb%	ct%	Eye	SB	CS	x/h%	Iso	RC/G
2013	Rk	GCL Tigers	177	28	59	2	22	333	376	441	816	6	92	0.86	5	3	22	107	5.56
2014	A	West Michigan	558	67	150	6	54	269	301	344	645	4	85	0.32	9	6	18	75	3.37

Instinctual, spry INF who ran out of steam late in first full year. Has positive attributes and some polish with bat and glove. Doesn't walk much, but has feel for contact with level swing path. Doesn't project to much pop, but has room to add strength. Range works better at 2B than SS.

Bethancourt,Christian — 2 — Atlanta

EXP MLB DEBUT: 2013 | H/W: 6-2 205 | FUT: Starting C | 7A

Bats R Age 23 — 2008 FA (Panama)

Pwr + + / BAvg + + / Spd + + / Def + + + +

Year	Lev	Team	AB	R	H	HR	RBI	Avg	OB	Slg	OPS	bb%	ct%	Eye	SB	CS	x/h%	Iso	RC/G
2012	AA	Mississippi	268	30	65	2	26	243	272	291	563	4	83	0.24	8	6	12	49	2.31
2013	AA	Mississippi	358	42	99	12	45	277	307	436	743	4	84	0.28	11	7	33	159	4.42
2013	MLB	Atlanta	1	0	0	0	0	0	0	0	0	0	0	0.00	0	0		0	
2014	AAA	Gwinnett	343	33	97	8	48	283	309	408	717	4	82	0.21	7	1	27	125	4.08
2014	MLB	Atlanta	113	7	28	0	9	248	267	274	542	3	77	0.12	1	1	11	27	1.84

Remains one of the better defensive backstops in the minors with good actions, a quick release, and a strong arm. Makes consistent contact, but can be overly aggressive and has yet to show much power. Average bat speed and poor strike zone judgment limit his offensive potential

Bird,Greg — 3 — New York (A)

EXP MLB DEBUT: 2016 | H/W: 6-3 215 | FUT: Starting 1B | 7B

Bats L Age 22 — 2011 (5) HS (CO)

Pwr + + + / BAvg + + + / Spd + / Def + +

Year	Lev	Team	AB	R	H	HR	RBI	Avg	OB	Slg	OPS	bb%	ct%	Eye	SB	CS	x/h%	Iso	RC/G
2012	Rk	GCL Yankees	49	9	14	0	5	286	417	367	784	18	73	0.85	0	0	21	82	5.95
2012	A-	Staten Island	40	4	16	2	8	400	478	650	1128	13	75	0.60	0	0	38	250	10.09
2013	A	CharlestonSC	458	84	132	20	84	288	423	511	934	19	71	0.81	1	1	45	223	7.94
2014	A+	Tampa	274	36	76	7	32	277	379	442	821	14	74	0.64	1	0	39	164	6.10
2014	AA	Trenton	95	16	24	7	11	253	372	558	930	16	72	0.67	0	0	63	305	7.52

Patient hitter who was AFL MVP after second productive season. Can be too patient at plate and lacks athleticism and speed, but owns terrific bat. Puts charge into ball and drives to all fields while recognizing and hitting spin. Moved to 1B from C in 2013 and lacks range and hands.

Blandino,Alex — 645 — Cincinnati

EXP MLB DEBUT: 2017 | H/W: 6-0 190 | FUT: Starting INF | 8C

Bats R Age 22 — 2014 (1) Stanford

Pwr + + + / BAvg + + + / Spd + + / Def + +

Year	Lev	Team	AB	R	H	HR	RBI	Avg	OB	Slg	OPS	bb%	ct%	Eye	SB	CS	x/h%	Iso	RC/G
2012	NCAA	Stanford	153	26	45	8	40	294	345	523	868	7	80	0.39	4	1	40	229	6.08
2013	NCAA	Stanford	179	31	48	7	32	268	332	453	784	9	82	0.52	2	0	38	184	5.16
2014	NCAA	Stanford	226	49	70	12	44	310	391	531	922	12	85	0.91	2	1	37	221	6.92
2014	Rk	Billings	110	20	34	4	16	309	397	527	924	13	84	0.89	6	3	44	218	7.18
2014	A	Dayton	134	20	35	4	16	261	327	440	767	9	69	0.31	1	2	43	179	5.26

Experienced IF with solid bat. Could end up at any of 2B/SS/3B depending how power numbers play out. Has added loft to swing in pros. Disciplined approach and pitch recognition makes up for average bat speed. Average range and plus arm defensively. Should move through system quickly.

Blash,Jabari — 79 — Seattle

EXP MLB DEBUT: 2014 | H/W: 6-5 225 | FUT: Starting OF | 7D

Bats R Age 25 — 2010 (8) Miami Dade CC

Pwr + + + + / BAvg + + / Spd + + / Def + + +

Year	Lev	Team	AB	R	H	HR	RBI	Avg	OB	Slg	OPS	bb%	ct%	Eye	SB	CS	x/h%	Iso	RC/G
2012	A	Clinton	400	71	98	15	50	245	343	433	776	13	67	0.45	13	7	41	188	5.57
2013	A+	High Desert	283	42	73	16	53	258	350	505	855	12	70	0.47	14	8	48	247	6.47
2013	AA	Jackson	97	13	30	9	21	309	427	619	1046	17	71	0.71	1	1	40	309	9.09
2014	AA	Jackson	127	27	30	6	22	236	374	449	823	18	72	0.80	4	1	47	213	6.19
2014	AAA	Tacoma	162	23	34	12	37	210	285	481	766	9	65	0.30	2	2	59	272	5.14

Tall, strong OF who served 50 game suspension for drug of abuse. Hits for plus power with fast bat and quick wrists. Has ideal profile for RF with plus arm strength. Not a sound baserunner despite fringy speed and will have trouble hitting for BA due to inconsistent swing path and eye.

Bonifacio,Jorge — 9 — Kansas City

EXP MLB DEBUT: 2016 | H/W: 6-1 195 | FUT: Starting OF | 8E

Bats R Age 21 — 2009 FA (DR)

Pwr + + / BAvg + + + / Spd + + + / Def + + +

Year	Lev	Team	AB	R	H	HR	RBI	Avg	OB	Slg	OPS	bb%	ct%	Eye	SB	CS	x/h%	Iso	RC/G
2012	A	Kane County	412	54	116	10	61	282	330	432	762	7	80	0.36	6	3	31	150	4.86
2013	Rk	AZL Royals	30	4	9	0	6	300	382	533	916	12	80	0.67	1	0	56	233	7.45
2013	A+	Wilmington	206	32	61	2	29	296	367	408	775	10	81	0.58	0	2	26	112	5.27
2013	AA	NW Arkansas	93	15	28	2	19	301	375	441	816	11	75	0.48	2	1	32	140	5.83
2014	AA	NW Arkansas	505	49	116	4	51	230	299	309	608	9	75	0.39	8	3	24	79	3.01

Pure-hitting OF who has seen stock drop with disappointing power development. Saw decline in BA despite patient eye, though has compact stroke to use whole field. Bat speed and strength good for potential pop. Limited speed hinders OF range, though has strong arm suitable for RF.

Borenstein,Zach — 7 — Arizona

EXP MLB DEBUT: 2015 | H/W: 6-0 225 | FUT: Starting LF | 7C

Bats L Age 24 — 2011 (23) Eastern Illinois

Pwr + + + / BAvg + + + / Spd + + / Def + +

Year	Lev	Team	AB	R	H	HR	RBI	Avg	OB	Slg	OPS	bb%	ct%	Eye	SB	CS	x/h%	Iso	RC/G
2013	A+	Inland Empire	407	76	137	28	95	337	400	631	1031	10	78	0.49	5	5	42	295	8.28
2014	AA	Arkansas	184	23	49	5	28	266	341	440	782	10	71	0.40	6	4	41	174	5.46
2014	AA	Mobile	87	13	21	3	14	241	333	437	770	12	80	0.71	3	0	43	195	5.24
2014	AAA	Salt Lake	117	11	30	2	22	256	275	342	617	3	72	0.09	0	2	20	85	2.74
2014	AAA	Reno	73	12	19	5	15	260	325	548	873	9	70	0.32	0	1	53	288	6.52

Short, strong-bodied LF took a step back after an impressive breakout in '13. Sold plate discipline, and ability to hit LHP. Likes to attack FB, but has learned to lay off breaking pitches. Bat speed may not lead to same success at upper levels. Lacks plus tool and athleticism.

Bostick,Chris — 4 — Washington

EXP MLB DEBUT: 2016 | H/W: 5-11 185 | FUT: Starting 2B | 7C

Bats R Age 22 — 2011 (44) HS (NY)

Pwr + + / BAvg + + + / Spd + + + / Def + +

Year	Lev	Team	AB	R	H	HR	RBI	Avg	OB	Slg	OPS	bb%	ct%	Eye	SB	CS	x/h%	Iso	RC/G
2011	Rk	AZL Athletics	52	13	23	1	5	442	473	654	1127	5	77	0.25	4	0	35	212	9.61
2012	A-	Vermont	279	41	70	3	29	251	317	369	686	9	76	0.41	12	5	33	118	4.09
2013	A	Beloit	489	75	138	14	89	282	350	452	802	9	75	0.42	25	8	34	170	5.57
2014	A+	Myrtle Beach	495	81	124	11	62	251	315	412	728	9	77	0.41	24	11	40	162	4.59

Short, instinctual INF who covers plate well and focuses on hard line drives. Limited power profile, but draws walks and makes most of average bat speed. Will pile up Ks when selling out for power. Good athlete with sufficient arm and range to stick at 2B, though will make errors.

Bour,Justin — 3 — Miami

EXP MLB DEBUT: 2014 | H/W: 6-4 250 | FUT: Backup 1B | 6C

Bats L Age 26 — 2009 (25) George Mason

Pwr + + + + / BAvg + + / Spd + / Def + +

Year	Lev	Team	AB	R	H	HR	RBI	Avg	OB	Slg	OPS	bb%	ct%	Eye	SB	CS	x/h%	Iso	RC/G
2011	A+	Daytona	502	65	139	23	85	277	338	478	816	8	79	0.44	3	2	39	201	5.51
2012	AA	Tennessee	506	64	143	17	110	283	361	455	815	11	77	0.54	4	1	37	172	5.74
2013	AA	Tennessee	317	48	75	18	64	237	314	461	775	10	80	0.57	0	2	47	224	5.04
2014	AAA	New Orleans	385	59	118	18	72	306	370	517	887	9	85	0.68	3	1	38	210	6.39
2014	MLB	Miami	74	10	21	1	11	284	361	365	726	11	74	0.47	0	0	19	81	4.63

Tall, thick-bodied 1B has a good approach at the plate and above-avg power. Hit .306 in the PCL with 18 HR. Solid defender at 1B with good hands and solid range for his size. Improved contact rate makes him a viable big league hitter, though it is likely to be in a bench role.

Bousfield,Auston | 8 | San Diego

Bats R Age 21 — 2014 (5) Mississippi

EXP MLB DEBUT: 2018 | H/W: 5-11 185 | FUT: Starting CF | 7D

Pwr ++ | BAvg +++ | Spd ++++ | Def +++

Year	Lev	Team	AB	R	H	HR	RBI	Avg	OB	Slg	OPS	bb%	ct%	Eye	SB	CS	x/h%	Iso	RC/G
2012	NCAA	Mississippi	221	38	62	2	22	281	348	362	710	9	87	0.82	6	2	21	81	4.50
2013	NCAA	Mississippi	242	45	61	2	25	252	335	343	678	11	84	0.77	9	4	25	91	4.16
2014	NCAA	Mississippi	286	61	96	6	50	336	379	476	855	7	91	0.74	19	1	27	140	5.95
2014	A-	Eugene	166	36	50	3	13	301	389	512	902	13	78	0.65	12	4	48	211	7.17

A solid pro debut. plus speed should allow him to stick in CF as he moves up. Good approach at the plate with a short, compact stroke and projects to have at least moderate power, but speed and the ability to hit for average will be his carrying tools.

Boyd,B.J. | 78 | Oakland

Bats L Age 21 — 2012 (4) HS (CA)

EXP MLB DEBUT: 2017 | H/W: 5-11 230 | FUT: Starting OF | 7D

Pwr ++ | BAvg ++ | Spd +++ | Def +++

Year	Lev	Team	AB	R	H	HR	RBI	Avg	OB	Slg	OPS	bb%	ct%	Eye	SB	CS	x/h%	Iso	RC/G
2012	Rk	AZL Athletics	143	37	43	1	20	301	398	434	831	14	75	0.64	16	4	30	133	6.36
2013	A-	Vermont	260	39	74	8	32	285	369	442	812	12	75	0.53	8	6	31	158	5.80
2014	A	Beloit	464	57	105	6	38	226	299	319	618	9	80	0.51	15	9	25	93	3.21

Raw, athletic OF who is still learning art of hitting. Has trouble with LHP and can get too pull-conscious, resulting in Ks. Could hit for more power with more leveraged stroke. Willing to work counts, but is poor baserunner despite solid-average speed. Ranges well in OF with good arm.

Boyd,Jayce | 3 | New York (N)

Bats R Age 24 — 2012 (6) Florida State

EXP MLB DEBUT: 2016 | H/W: 6-3 185 | FUT: Starting 1B | 7C

Pwr ++ | BAvg +++ | Spd + | Def ++++

Year	Lev	Team	AB	R	H	HR	RBI	Avg	OB	Slg	OPS	bb%	ct%	Eye	SB	CS	x/h%	Iso	RC/G
2012	NCAA	Florida State	255	47	96	4	61	376	455	506	961	13	90	1.42	8	1	26	129	7.62
2012	A-	Brooklyn	201	18	48	5	19	239	323	368	691	11	85	0.83	1	3	31	129	4.27
2013	A	Savannah	249	40	90	5	46	361	440	494	934	12	87	1.09	0	4	24	133	7.26
2013	A+	St. Lucie	209	28	61	4	37	292	370	421	791	11	86	0.90	2	0	30	129	5.51
2014	AA	Binghamton	413	60	121	8	59	293	372	414	786	11	84	0.78	2	1	26	121	5.42

Has displayed excellent plate discipline, ct%, and OBP skills at each stop. Very polished hitter. Power has been slow to develop but strong enough and young enough that it could still come. Above-average defender with plus range and hands but hampered by shoulder injury in '14.

Bradley,Bobby | 3 | Cleveland

Bats L Age 18 — 2014 (3) HS (MS)

EXP MLB DEBUT: 2018 | H/W: 6-1 225 | FUT: Starting 1B | 9E

Pwr ++++ | BAvg +++ | Spd ++ | Def ++

Year	Lev	Team	AB	R	H	HR	RBI	Avg	OB	Slg	OPS	bb%	ct%	Eye	SB	CS	x/h%	Iso	RC/G
2014	Rk	AZL Indians	155	39	56	8	50	361	421	652	1073	9	77	0.44	3	0	45	290	9.04

Powerful hitter who led AZL in HR and BA. All about offense; plus bat speed generated from compact stroke. Has good feel for contact and drives ball with authority to all fields. LHH give him fits, but can read spin well. Secondary skills need work as he is sloppy defender with poor speed.

Brentz,Bryce | 79 | Boston

Bats R Age 26 — 2010 (1-S) Middle TN St

EXP MLB DEBUT: 2014 | H/W: 6-0 210 | FUT: Starting OF | 7D

Pwr ++++ | BAvg ++ | Spd ++ | Def ++

Year	Lev	Team	AB	R	H	HR	RBI	Avg	OB	Slg	OPS	bb%	ct%	Eye	SB	CS	x/h%	Iso	RC/G
2013	AAA	Pawtucket	326	36	86	17	56	264	306	475	782	6	74	0.23	1	0	40	212	5.00
2014	Rk	GCL Red Sox	18	1	1	0	0	56	190	111	302	14	72	0.60	0	0	100	56	-1.09
2014	A-	Lowell	8	2	1	0	1	125	222	125	347	11	75	0.50	0	0	0	0	-0.45
2014	AAA	Pawtucket	230	42	56	12	53	243	336	465	801	12	75	0.55	0	1	45	222	5.56
2014	MLB	Boston	26	5	8	0	2	308	308	385	692	0	65	0.00	0	0	25	77	4.02

Big, strong OF who missed time with hamstring injury. Reached majors based on plus raw power and bat speed. Ideal platoon player as he crushes LHP. Selectivity is subpar and pitch recognition hinders BA potential. Not much speed and likely limited to LF, but has plus arm strength.

Brett,Ryan | 4 | Tampa Bay

Bats R Age 23 — 2010 (3) HS (WA)

EXP MLB DEBUT: 2015 | H/W: 5-9 180 | FUT: Starting 2B | 7B

Pwr ++ | BAvg ++++ | Spd ++++ | Def +++

Year	Lev	Team	AB	R	H	HR	RBI	Avg	OB	Slg	OPS	bb%	ct%	Eye	SB	CS	x/h%	Iso	RC/G
2012	A	Bowling Green	410	77	117	6	35	285	345	393	737	8	82	0.51	48	8	25	107	4.66
2013	Rk	GCL Devil Rays	4	0	0	0	0	0	0	0	0	0	50	0.00	0	0		0	-7.85
2013	A+	Charlotte	206	38	70	4	22	340	385	490	875	7	87	0.56	22	7	27	150	6.21
2013	AA	Montgomery	105	19	25	3	16	238	292	400	692	7	87	0.57	4	0	40	162	4.10
2014	AA	Montgomery	422	64	128	8	38	303	341	448	789	5	82	0.32	27	7	30	145	5.12

Fundamentally-sound INF with steady approach to game. Makes good contact with compact stroke, and understands strike zone. Reads spin well and has punch in bat to hit doubles to gaps. Posted high in BA and HR. Owns above average wheels. Solid range, quickness, and instincts at 2B.

Briceno,Jose | 2 | Colorado

Bats R Age 22 — 2009 FA (Venezuela)

EXP MLB DEBUT: 2017 | H/W: 6-1 210 | FUT: Starting C | 8D

Pwr +++ | BAvg ++ | Spd ++ | Def +++

Year	Lev	Team	AB	R	H	HR	RBI	Avg	OB	Slg	OPS	bb%	ct%	Eye	SB	CS	x/h%	Iso	RC/G
2012	Rk	Grand Junction	23	5	9	2	5	391	440	652	1092	8	91	1.00	0	0	22	261	8.29
2013	Rk	Grand Junction	153	32	51	9	30	333	354	614	969	3	80	0.17	8	2	49	281	7.07
2013	A	Asheville	91	12	24	1	8	264	302	363	665	5	78	0.25	1	0	29	99	3.58
2014	A	Asheville	315	38	89	12	50	283	317	476	793	5	82	0.28	8	4	40	194	5.06

Raw but athletic backstop continues to make progress. He moves well behind the plate with good hands and a strong arm, but needs to improve his blocking and receiving skills. Has good bat speed and above-average raw power, but can be overly aggressive and pull conscious.

Brinson,Lewis | 789 | Texas

Bats R Age 20 — 2012 (1) HS (FL)

EXP MLB DEBUT: 2017 | H/W: 6-3 170 | FUT: Starting OF | 9D

Pwr +++ | BAvg ++ | Spd ++++ | Def +++

Year	Lev	Team	AB	R	H	HR	RBI	Avg	OB	Slg	OPS	bb%	ct%	Eye	SB	CS	x/h%	Iso	RC/G
2012	Rk	AZL Rangers	237	54	67	7	42	283	341	523	864	8	69	0.28	14	2	54	241	6.76
2013	A	Hickory	447	64	106	21	52	237	311	427	738	10	57	0.25	24	7	39	190	5.36
2014	A	Hickory	164	36	55	10	28	335	401	579	980	10	72	0.39	7	4	35	244	7.96
2014	A+	Myrtle Beach	183	17	45	3	22	246	303	350	653	8	73	0.30	5	5	27	104	3.50

Athletic, strong OF who showed significant improvement in Low-A before promotion. Drastically cut down on Ks, but contact still issue with uppercut stroke. Owns plus bat speed and raw power to all fields, though can get pull happy. Improving CF defender with good speed and arm.

Brito,Gabriel | 2 | Pittsburgh

Bats R Age 17 — 2014 FA (DR)

EXP MLB DEBUT: 2019 | H/W: 5-10 160 | FUT: Starting C | 7D

Pwr ++ | BAvg +++ | Spd ++ | Def +++

Year	Lev	Team	AB	R	H	HR	RBI	Avg	OB	Slg	OPS	bb%	ct%	Eye	SB	CS	x/h%	Iso	RC/G
2014		(did not play in the US in 2014)																	

Signed by the Pirates for $200,000 in July 2014. Has good bat speed and a nice line-drive approach and is willing to use the entire field. Moves well behind the plate with good blocking skills and a strong arm. Will likely make his U.S. debut in '15.

Brito,Socrates | 89 | Arizona

Bats L Age 22 — 2011 FA (DR)

EXP MLB DEBUT: 2016 | H/W: 6-2 200 | FUT: Starting CF | 7C

Pwr +++ | BAvg +++ | Spd +++ | Def +++

Year	Lev	Team	AB	R	H	HR	RBI	Avg	OB	Slg	OPS	bb%	ct%	Eye	SB	CS	x/h%	Iso	RC/G
2011	Rk	AZL Dbacks	236	29	65	1	29	275	313	360	673	5	79	0.26	18	10	17	85	3.73
2012	Rk	Missoula	279	47	87	4	39	312	360	444	804	7	74	0.29	15	9	28	133	5.57
2013	A	South Bend	523	61	138	2	49	264	313	356	668	7	76	0.30	27	9	25	92	3.75
2014	A+	Visalia	518	82	152	10	62	293	339	429	768	6	79	0.33	38	10	30	135	4.94

Speedy, athletic player had a nice breakout, showing improved power and plus speed. Has plus bat speed and hit a career high 10 HR to go along with 38 SB. Plays solid defense, but needs to be more selective at the plate, but has the tools to be an interesting fantasy prospect.

Brown,Aaron | 8 | Philadelphia

Bats L Age 22 — 2013 (3) Pepperdine

EXP MLB DEBUT: 2017 | H/W: 6-2 220 | FUT: Starting RF | 8D

Pwr +++ | BAvg ++ | Spd ++ | Def +++

Year	Lev	Team	AB	R	H	HR	RBI	Avg	OB	Slg	OPS	bb%	ct%	Eye	SB	CS	x/h%	Iso	RC/G
2012	NCAA	Pepperdine	117	9	31	1	24	265	301	350	651	5	74	0.19	3	1	23	85	3.39
2013	NCAA	Pepperdine	46	10	15	2	3	326	340	500	840	2	74	0.08	2	0	27	174	5.55
2014	NCAA	Pepperdine	242	44	76	13	49	314	339	554	892	4	79	0.17	5	3	38	240	6.19
2014	A-	Williamsport	180	23	46	3	16	256	280	356	635	3	77	0.15	8	4	24	100	3.05
2014	A	Lakewood	55	3	17	1	5	309	321	473	794	2	65	0.05	0	1	41	164	5.62

A physical and intense two-way player in college, was drafted as an OF. Though not reflected in his stats, has an advanced hit tool, a fluid and balanced swing, and above-average raw power with exceptional hand/eye coordination. Can be too aggressive at the plate—but with polish, could rise quickly due to broad base of skills.

Brown,Gary

8 | San Francisco | EXP MLB DEBUT: 2014 | H/W: 6-1 190 | FUT: Backup OF | 7D

Bats R Age 26 — 2010 (1) Cal State Fullerton

Pwr ++ | BAvg ++ | Spd ++++ | Def +++

Year	Lev	Team	AB	R	H	HR	RBI	Avg	OB	Slg	OPS	bb%	ct%	Eye	SB	CS	x/h%	Iso	RC/G
2011	A+	San Jose	559	115	188	14	80	336	387	519	906	8	86	0.60	53	19	32	182	6.63
2012	AA	Richmond	538	73	150	7	42	279	329	385	713	7	84	0.46	33	18	27	106	4.32
2013	AAA	Fresno	558	79	129	13	50	231	274	375	649	6	76	0.24	17	11	37	143	3.36
2014	AAA	Fresno	536	89	145	10	53	271	316	394	710	6	78	0.30	36	20	28	123	4.19
2014	MLB	San Francisco	7	1	3	0	1	429	429	429	857	0	100		0	0	0	0	5.47

Brown showed signs of life in 2014, with his ct% and bb% both trending upward after a dismal 2013. Still has an exciting mix of skills: plus speed, good defense with plus range and a strong arm. Runs into one on occasion, but limited to CF since power won't play in the corner. Role to be determined by how much he hits.

Brugman,Jaycob

79 | Oakland | EXP MLB DEBUT: 2016 | H/W: 6-0 195 | FUT: Starting OF | 7C

Bats L Age 23 — 2013 (17) Brigham Young

Pwr +++ | BAvg +++ | Spd +++ | Def ++

Year	Lev	Team	AB	R	H	HR	RBI	Avg	OB	Slg	OPS	bb%	ct%	Eye	SB	CS	x/h%	Iso	RC/G
2012	NCAA	BYU	172	25	48	2	30	279	347	395	743	9	76	0.43	12	6	23	116	4.85
2013	NCAA	BYU	202	39	64	11	52	317	405	609	1014	13	76	0.63	8	2	50	292	8.50
2013	A-	Vermont	165	13	43	1	23	261	291	382	673	4	71	0.15	7	0	33	121	3.78
2014	A	Beloit	248	33	69	8	37	278	367	484	851	12	74	0.54	5	2	45	206	6.45
2014	A+	Stockton	195	34	55	13	35	282	336	533	870	8	74	0.32	3	3	38	251	6.17

Sleeper prospect who put himself on map after standout Aug in High-A. Smooth lefty stroke produces good pop, and he can stand in against LHP with disciplined approach. Holes in swing can be exploited, but power will determine future. Runs well, but not a burner and plus arm is best tool.

Bruno,Stephen

4 | Chicago (N) | EXP MLB DEBUT: 2016 | H/W: 5-9 165 | FUT: Starting 2B | 7D

Bats R Age 24 — 2012 (7) Virginia

Pwr + | BAvg +++ | Spd ++ | Def ++

Year	Lev	Team	AB	R	H	HR	RBI	Avg	OB	Slg	OPS	bb%	ct%	Eye	SB	CS	x/h%	Iso	RC/G
2011	NCAA	Virginia	25	4	6	0	2	240	240	320	560	0	72	0.00	0	1	33	80	2.03
2012	NCAA	Virginia	238	49	88	6	54	370	405	559	964	6	89	0.52	11	3	35	189	7.11
2012	A-	Boise	252	51	91	3	37	361	404	496	900	7	81	0.38	2	7	27	135	6.59
2013	A+	Daytona	69	16	25	0	7	362	405	478	884	7	77	0.31	2	1	32	116	6.61
2014	AA	Tennessee	384	54	106	3	42	276	324	393	717	7	80	0.35	6	2	32	117	4.38

Small-framed 2B prospect was a mild surprise. Has a short, compact stroke and a good understanding of the strike zone. Makes consistent contact with moderate power. Has decent speed with a good glove, but is not going to be a SB threat. Will likely get another year at AA.

Bryan,Vaughn

789 | St. Louis | EXP MLB DEBUT: 2018 | H/W: 6-0 185 | FUT: Starting CF | 7D

Bats B Age 21 — 2013 (35) Broward CC

Pwr ++ | BAvg +++ | Spd +++ | Def +++

Year	Lev	Team	AB	R	H	HR	RBI	Avg	OB	Slg	OPS	bb%	ct%	Eye	SB	CS	x/h%	Iso	RC/G
2012	NCAA	PalmBch Atlntc	90	15	25	0	9	278	316	311	627	5	82	0.31	5	3	12	33	3.15
2013	NCAA	Broward Col	187	26	66	2	33	353	392	444	836	6	83	0.38	16	5	15	91	5.69
2013	Rk	Johnson City	236	45	66	3	24	280	341	394	735	9	77	0.41	13	3	24	114	4.67
2013	A-	State College	8	1	1	0	0	125	125	250	375	0	75	0.00	0	0	100	125	-0.19
2014	A	Peoria	317	47	83	1	15	262	320	382	701	8	77	0.37	11	7	33	120	4.31

Switch-hitting OF is a pure athlete, but remains raw. Played SS in HS but poor mechanics forced a move to the OF. Plus runner with enough speed and range for CF, but he split time at all three positions. Good bat speed, but swing can get long and loopy.

Bryant,Kris

5 | Chicago (N) | EXP MLB DEBUT: 2015 | H/W: 6-5 215 | FUT: Starting 3B | 9A

Bats R Age 23 — 2013 (1) San Diego

Pwr +++++ | BAvg ++++ | Spd ++ | Def +++

Year	Lev	Team	AB	R	H	HR	RBI	Avg	OB	Slg	OPS	bb%	ct%	Eye	SB	CS	x/h%	Iso	RC/G
2013	Rk	AZL Cubs	6	0	1	0	2	167	167	333	500	0	83	0.00	0	0	100	167	1.68
2013	A-	Boise	65	13	23	4	16	354	425	692	1117	11	74	0.47	0	0	57	338	9.93
2013	A+	Daytona	57	9	19	5	14	333	367	719	1086	5	70	0.18	1	0	58	386	9.31
2014	AA	Tennessee	248	61	88	22	58	355	450	702	1152	15	69	0.56	8	2	48	347	10.82
2014	AAA	Iowa	244	57	72	21	52	295	401	619	1020	15	65	0.51	7	2	50	324	9.19

Plus bat speed, good pitch recognition, and ability to make consistent hard contact give him the potential to hit .300 with 30 HR in the majors. Hit a minor league leading 43 HR. There is some swing-and-miss as he hunts for power, but that is mitigated by advanced plate discipline.

Burns,Andy

456 | Toronto | EXP MLB DEBUT: 2015 | H/W: 6-2 205 | FUT: Starting 3B | 7B

Bats R Age 24 — 2011 (11) Arizona

Pwr +++ | BAvg +++ | Spd +++ | Def +++

Year	Lev	Team	AB	R	H	HR	RBI	Avg	OB	Slg	OPS	bb%	ct%	Eye	SB	CS	x/h%	Iso	RC/G
2011	A-	Vancouver	84	10	15	2	7	179	233	298	531	7	83	0.43	2	1	40	119	2.07
2012	A	Lansing	278	57	69	9	37	248	339	464	803	12	73	0.51	15	2	55	216	5.80
2013	A+	Dunedin	248	45	81	8	53	327	388	524	912	9	85	0.66	21	9	35	198	6.79
2013	AA	New Hampshire	265	40	67	7	32	253	313	419	731	8	79	0.42	12	5	42	166	4.56
2014	AA	New Hampshire	495	71	126	15	63	255	312	430	742	8	80	0.41	18	8	41	176	4.65

A fundamentally sound, tall INF who can play any infield spot. Has decent quickness, hands, and arm strength. Runs fairly well and can steal bases with instincts. Owns nice bat speed and matched high in HR while successful against LHP. Should hit enough to be regular with gap power.

Burns,Billy

8 | Oakland | EXP MLB DEBUT: 2014 | H/W: 5-9 180 | FUT: Reserve OF | 6A

Bats B Age 25 — 2011 (32) Mercer

Pwr + | BAvg ++ | Spd ++++ | Def +++

Year	Lev	Team	AB	R	H	HR	RBI	Avg	OB	Slg	OPS	bb%	ct%	Eye	SB	CS	x/h%	Iso	RC/G
2013	A+	Potomac	330	70	103	0	29	312	406	391	797	14	89	1.41	54	5	17	79	5.87
2013	AA	Harrisburg	114	26	37	0	8	325	425	360	785	15	85	1.18	20	2	11	35	5.71
2014	AA	Midland	364	57	91	1	23	250	331	330	661	11	82	0.68	51	5	26	80	3.94
2014	AAA	Sacramento	109	17	21	0	5	193	254	211	465	8	83	0.47	3	1	10	18	1.34
2014	MLB	Oakland	6	4	1	0	0	167	167	167	333	0	100		3	1	0	0	0.50

Short, swift OF who finished 2nd in TL in SB despite promotion to AAA and OAK. Has plus plate discipline and is excellent bunter. Lacks any semblance of power due to slap stroke and can be beaten with two strikes. Possesses nifty range in CF, but owns below average arm.

Buxton,Byron

8 | Minnesota | EXP MLB DEBUT: 2015 | H/W: 6-2 190 | FUT: Starting OF | 9A

Bats R Age 21 — 2012 (1) HS (GA)

Pwr +++ | BAvg ++++ | Spd +++++ | Def ++++

Year	Lev	Team	AB	R	H	HR	RBI	Avg	OB	Slg	OPS	bb%	ct%	Eye	SB	CS	x/h%	Iso	RC/G
2012	Rk	Elizabethton	77	16	22	1	6	286	353	429	782	9	81	0.53	7	0	36	143	5.34
2013	A	Cedar Rapids	270	68	92	8	55	341	433	559	992	14	79	0.79	32	11	36	219	8.28
2013	A+	Fort Myers	218	41	71	4	22	326	412	472	884	13	78	0.65	23	8	23	147	6.85
2014	A+	Fort Myers	121	19	29	4	16	240	298	405	703	8	73	0.30	6	2	34	165	4.14
2014	AA	New Britain	3	0	0	0	0	0	0	0	0	0	0	0.00	0	0		0	

Ultra-athletic OF who missed significant time with variety of injuries. Should be ready by spring training. Possesses elite speed and above average range that makes CF look easy. Swings very fast bat with quick wrists and recognizes pitches to supply high BA. Needs loft to add to average pop.

Cabrera,Gustavo

8 | San Francisco | EXP MLB DEBUT: 2018 | H/W: 6-2 190 | FUT: Starting OF | 8E

Bats R Age 19 — 2012 FA (DR)

Pwr ++ | BAvg ++ | Spd ++++ | Def ++++

Year	Lev	Team	AB	R	H	HR	RBI	Avg	OB	Slg	OPS	bb%	ct%	Eye	SB	CS	x/h%	Iso	RC/G
2014		(did not play in the US in 2014)																	

Former top international player did not play in 2014 due to wrist injury. Oozes with talent, showing plus-plus speed on the bases and in the field. Raw hitting mechanics will take time and may hinder ct% early in develeopment. Plus raw power should become playable with reps. Very raw, but potential five average or better tools.

Calixte,Orlando

6 | Kansas City | EXP MLB DEBUT: 2015 | H/W: 5-11 160 | FUT: Starting SS | 7C

Bats R Age 23 — 2011 FA (DR)

Pwr ++ | BAvg ++ | Spd +++ | Def +++

Year	Lev	Team	AB	R	H	HR	RBI	Avg	OB	Slg	OPS	bb%	ct%	Eye	SB	CS	x/h%	Iso	RC/G
2011	A	Kane County	289	19	60	3	31	208	259	263	522	6	76	0.29	11	4	15	55	1.71
2012	A	Kane County	228	31	55	10	34	241	305	465	770	8	81	0.48	2	5	49	224	5.00
2012	A+	Wilmington	256	38	72	4	28	281	321	426	747	6	75	0.23	8	3	35	145	4.73
2013	AA	NW Arkansas	484	59	121	8	36	250	310	368	678	8	73	0.32	14	11	31	118	3.89
2014	AA	NW Arkansas	374	43	90	11	37	241	292	374	666	7	75	0.29	9	5	30	134	3.56

Athletic INF who repeated AA and had similar results. Produces consistent numbers and offers pop in lithe frame. Has decent BA potential due to quick stroke, though has little patience in aggressive approach. Likes to swing early in count. Has strong arm and can be plus defender.

Camargo,Johan

6 | Atlanta | EXP MLB DEBUT: 2017 | H/W: 6-0 160 | FUT: Starting SS | 7D

Bats B Age 21 — 2010 FA (Panama)

Pwr + | BAvg +++ | Spd ++ | Def +++

Year	Lev	Team	AB	R	H	HR	RBI	Avg	OB	Slg	OPS	bb%	ct%	Eye	SB	CS	x/h%	Iso	RC/G
2013	Rk	Danville	228	28	67	0	14	294	346	360	705	7	86	0.58	3	3	16	66	4.33
2014	A	Rome	420	53	112	0	40	267	322	324	645	7	88	0.68	7	6	18	57	3.70
2014	A+	Lynchburg	58	7	15	1	6	259	271	345	616	2	78	0.08	0	0	20	86	2.69

Switch-hitting SS had a decent full-season debut. Contact approach at the plate gives him the chance to hit for BA, but he has almost no power. Above-average defender with good range, soft hands, and a strong arm. Heady player who should be able to stick at the position.

Candelario,Jeimer

5 | Chicago (N) | EXP MLB DEBUT: 2017 | H/W: 6-1 180 | FUT: Starting 3B | 7D

Bats B Age 21
2010 FA (DR)
Pwr ++
BAvg ++
Spd ++
Def ++

Year	Lev	Team	AB	R	H	HR	RBI	Avg	OB	Slg	OPS	bb%	ct%	Eye	SB	CS	x/h%	Iso	RC/G
2012	A-	Boise	278	34	78	6	47	281	342	396	738	9	80	0.47	2	1	26	115	4.62
2013	A	Kane County	500	71	128	11	57	256	345	396	741	12	82	0.77	1	0	37	140	4.92
2014	A	Kane County	244	32	61	6	37	250	302	426	728	7	82	0.40	0	1	46	176	4.49
2014	A+	Daytona	218	24	42	5	26	193	270	326	595	10	80	0.52	0	3	40	133	2.92

Switch-hitting 3B continues to be moved up aggressively despite not dominating any one level. Has good power, a nice swing, and a adequate understanding of the strike zone. Was more aggressive at the plate as he hunted for power. He's an avg defender at 3B with good hands, but limited speed.

Capellan,Christian

79 | Miami | EXP MLB DEBUT: 2019 | H/W: 6-4 200 | FUT: Starting LF | 7D

Bats R Age 17
2014 FA (DR)
Pwr +++
BAvg ++
Spd +
Def ++

Year	Lev	Team	AB	R	H	HR	RBI	Avg	OB	Slg	OPS	bb%	ct%	Eye	SB	CS	x/h%	Iso	RC/G
2014		(did not play in the US in 2014)																	

Teenage OF has plus raw power. Approach at the plate is awkward, resulting in a good deal of swing-and-miss and struggles with breaking balls. Below-avg runner with a decent arm, should settle in as a corner OF. Ability to hit and make adjustments will be key to development.

Caratini,Victor

2 | Chicago (N) | EXP MLB DEBUT: 2017 | H/W: 6-0 195 | FUT: Starting C | 8D

Bats B Age 21
2013 (2) Miami Dade JC
Pwr ++
BAvg +++
Spd +
Def +++

Year	Lev	Team	AB	R	H	HR	RBI	Avg	OB	Slg	OPS	bb%	ct%	Eye	SB	CS	x/h%	Iso	RC/G
2013	NCAA	Miami-DadeCol	175	44	66	6	66	377	463	549	1012	14	85	1.08	10	1	27	171	8.24
2013	Rk	Danville	200	29	58	1	25	290	406	430	836	16	76	0.80	0	2	43	140	6.57
2014	A	Rome	323	42	90	5	42	279	347	406	753	10	82	0.58	1	1	30	127	4.95
2014	A	Kane County	53	7	14	0	13	264	316	377	693	7	81	0.40	0	0	36	113	4.19

Cubs used him exclusively behind the plate and he becomes the organization's top catching prospect. Uses a line-drive swing to shoot balls into the gaps and has good patience at the plate. Could develop above-average power once he matures, but his swing can get long.

Carey,D.K.

7 | Washington | EXP MLB DEBUT: 2018 | H/W: 6-2 207 | FUT: Backup OF | 7D

Bats R Age 23
2014 (7) Miami
Pwr +++
BAvg ++
Spd +++
Def ++

Year	Lev	Team	AB	R	H	HR	RBI	Avg	OB	Slg	OPS	bb%	ct%	Eye	SB	CS	x/h%	Iso	RC/G
2011	NCAA	Miami	155	30	42	1	24	271	347	342	689	10	72	0.42	5	2	21	71	4.17
2012	NCAA	Miami	214	42	58	2	20	271	363	369	732	13	78	0.65	9	5	26	98	4.87
2013	NCAA	Miami	145	22	28	1	12	193	269	276	545	9	80	0.52	12	5	29	83	2.35
2014	NCAA	Miami	246	53	75	7	29	305	380	463	844	11	83	0.70	16	9	32	159	6.07
2014	A-	Auburn	157	21	39	3	18	248	330	357	686	11	83	0.73	6	2	28	108	4.17

A plus athlete came on with a great college season at Miami to raise his draft stock. No one tool stands out; he has gap power and a below-average hit tool due to a long swing. Can run a little bit, but is just a fringe defender in the OF.

Casali,Curt

2 | Tampa Bay | EXP MLB DEBUT: 2014 | H/W: 6-2 225 | FUT: Backup C | 6B

Bats R Age 26
2011 (10) Vanderbilt
Pwr ++
BAvg ++
Spd +
Def +++

Year	Lev	Team	AB	R	H	HR	RBI	Avg	OB	Slg	OPS	bb%	ct%	Eye	SB	CS	x/h%	Iso	RC/G
2013	AA	Montgomery	120	25	46	5	31	383	475	600	1075	15	85	1.17	0	0	35	217	9.08
2014	A+	Charlotte	7	0	0	0	0	0	0	0	0	0	57	0.00	0	0		0	-7.11
2014	AA	Montgomery	70	7	22	1	13	314	484	429	912	25	77	1.44	0	0	27	114	7.91
2014	AAA	Durham	156	11	37	3	15	237	331	359	690	12	68	0.44	0	0	35	122	4.29
2014	MLB	Tampa Bay	72	10	12	0	3	167	250	208	458	10	68	0.35	0	0	25	42	0.85

Strong backstop who is improving defender with average arm and quick release. Cleaner footwork has led to better accuracy. Brings polished approach to plate, but doesn't profile for BA with fringy bat speed and instincts. Has strength, but mostly gap power at present.

Casteel,Ryan

23 | Colorado | EXP MLB DEBUT: 2016 | H/W: 5-11 205 | FUT: Starting C | 7D

Bats R Age 23
2010 (17) Cleveland St(TN)JC
Pwr +++
BAvg +++
Spd ++
Def ++

Year	Lev	Team	AB	R	H	HR	RBI	Avg	OB	Slg	OPS	bb%	ct%	Eye	SB	CS	x/h%	Iso	RC/G
2010	Rk	Casper	177	21	54	3	22	305	342	412	755	5	80	0.29	2	0	22	107	4.66
2011	A-	Tri-City	198	31	54	1	30	273	351	394	745	11	80	0.60	8	5	37	121	5.01
2012	A	Asheville	251	28	70	2	28	279	330	414	744	7	82	0.43	6	2	40	135	4.78
2013	A+	Modesto	411	67	111	22	76	270	349	523	872	11	71	0.42	1	0	50	253	6.63
2014	AA	Tulsa	436	63	122	16	56	280	339	445	784	8	78	0.41	3	3	32	165	5.13

23-year-old backstop had a solid season, proving his breakout was no fluke. Has a strong arm and has improved his blocking and receiving skills though he only logged 36 games behind the plate, seeing more action at 1B. Makes consistent contact with above-average power.

Castillo,Rusney

8 | Boston | EXP MLB DEBUT: 2014 | H/W: 5-8 185 | FUT: Starting CF | 8B

Bats R Age 27
2014 FA (Cuba)
Pwr +++
BAvg ++++
Spd +++
Def +++

Year	Lev	Team	AB	R	H	HR	RBI	Avg	OB	Slg	OPS	bb%	ct%	Eye	SB	CS	x/h%	Iso	RC/G
2010		Cuba	99	11	30	1	10	303	317	374	691	2	81	0.11	2	4	13	71	3.66
2011		Cuba	441	91	141	22	95	320	351	553	904	5	88	0.40	32	7	38	234	6.26
2012		Cuba	448	101	153	21	84	342	397	574	970	8	89	0.84	27	7	39	232	7.29
2013		Cuba	234	41	64	6	29	274	358	393	752	12	88	1.07	15	9	22	120	5.04
2014	MLB	Boston	36	6	12	2	6	333	385	528	912	8	83	0.50	3	0	25	194	6.49

Short, strong OF who was high-profile international sign. Makes easy contact and exhibits above average power to all fields. Knows strike zone and couples with hand-eye coordination to hit for high BA. Nice speed/power combo and potential 20/20 player. Solid CF with ideal range and arm.

Castro,Anderson

79 | Miami | EXP MLB DEBUT: 2019 | H/W: 6-4 195 | FUT: Starting CF | 8E

Bats R Age 18
2014 FA (DR)
Pwr +++
BAvg ++
Spd +++
Def +++

Year	Lev	Team	AB	R	H	HR	RBI	Avg	OB	Slg	OPS	bb%	ct%	Eye	SB	CS	x/h%	Iso	RC/G
2014		(did not play in the US in 2014)																	

Dominican OF has good athleticism. Raw at the plate but has good bat speed and some feel for squaring up the ball. Should develop above-average power once he matures. Has plus speed and could stick in CF for now, though his frame profiles better as a corner OF.

Castro,Harold

4 | Detroit | EXP MLB DEBUT: 2017 | H/W: 6-0 165 | FUT: Starting 2B | 7E

Bats L Age 21
2011 FA (Venezuela)
Pwr ++
BAvg +++
Spd +++
Def ++

Year	Lev	Team	AB	R	H	HR	RBI	Avg	OB	Slg	OPS	bb%	ct%	Eye	SB	CS	x/h%	Iso	RC/G
2012	Rk	GCL Tigers	193	24	60	1	21	311	345	420	765	5	87	0.40	15	3	28	109	4.88
2013	A	West Michigan	147	17	34	1	11	231	242	313	555	1	73	0.05	5	1	26	82	1.95
2013	A+	Lakeland	73	8	20	0	11	274	321	329	649	6	70	0.23	3	2	15	55	3.50
2014	A	West Michigan	72	8	18	0	3	250	299	319	618	6	90	0.71	3	2	28	69	3.42
2014	A+	Lakeland	211	17	63	0	10	299	327	322	650	4	81	0.23	8	8	8	24	3.30

Free-swinging INF with exciting athleticism and ability to hit. Lacks strength for power and is raw defender, but has room to improve. Average speed enhances value and has enough arm for 2B. Displays quick hands, though needs better footwork. Goes to gaps with line drive stroke.

Cave,Jake

8 | New York (A) | EXP MLB DEBUT: 2016 | H/W: 6-0 180 | FUT: Fourth OF | 6B

Bats L Age 22
2011 (6) HS (VA)
Pwr ++
BAvg +++
Spd +++
Def +++

Year	Lev	Team	AB	R	H	HR	RBI	Avg	OB	Slg	OPS	bb%	ct%	Eye	SB	CS	x/h%	Iso	RC/G
2011	Rk	GCL Yankees	1	0	0	0	0	0	500	0	500	50	100		0	0		0	4.75
2013	A	CharlestonSC	464	69	131	2	31	282	339	401	740	8	76	0.36	18	9	34	119	4.80
2014	A+	Tampa	385	50	117	3	24	304	351	395	746	7	79	0.35	10	3	21	91	4.70
2014	AA	Trenton	176	24	48	4	18	273	340	455	795	9	75	0.41	2	3	40	182	5.55

Rapidly developing OF who maximizes average tools. Swings quick bat and has understanding of strike zone. Patient enough to work counts and aggressive enough to jump on hittable pitch. Has some power to pull side and can shoot liners to opp field. Can play all OF positions.

Cecchini,Garin

57 | Boston | EXP MLB DEBUT: 2014 | H/W: 6-3 220 | FUT: Starting 3B | 8C

Bats L Age 23
2010 (4) HS (LA)
Pwr ++
BAvg ++++
Spd +++
Def +++

Year	Lev	Team	AB	R	H	HR	RBI	Avg	OB	Slg	OPS	bb%	ct%	Eye	SB	CS	x/h%	Iso	RC/G
2012	A	Greenville	455	84	139	4	62	305	388	433	821	12	80	0.68	51	6	33	127	5.99
2013	A+	Salem	214	44	75	5	33	350	459	547	1006	17	84	1.26	15	7	37	196	8.52
2013	AA	Portland	240	36	71	2	28	296	419	404	823	18	78	0.98	8	2	27	108	6.35
2014	AAA	Pawtucket	407	52	107	7	57	263	335	371	706	10	76	0.44	11	1	27	108	4.31
2014	MLB	Boston	31	6	8	1	4	258	324	452	775	9	65	0.27	0	0	50	194	5.59

Tall hitter with great feel for game. Works counts and draws walks to get on base, though lacks plus power and K rate increasing. Level swing path and strength leads to doubles. Intelligent hitter who recognizes spin. Played mostly 3B where he lacks range, but also saw time in LF.

Cecchini,Gavin — 6 — New York (N)

EXP MLB DEBUT: 2017 | H/W: 6-1 180 | FUT: Starting SS | 7D

Bats R Age 21 — 2012 (1) HS (LA)

Pwr ++ / BAvg +++ / Spd +++ / Def +++

Year	Lev	Team	AB	R	H	HR	RBI	Avg	OB	Slg	OPS	bb%	ct%	Eye	SB	CS	x/h%	Iso	RC/G
2012	A-	Brooklyn	5	2	0	0	0	0	0	0	0	0	80	0.00	0	0		0	-4.74
2013	A-	Brooklyn	194	18	53	0	14	273	322	314	637	7	85	0.47	2	3	15	41	3.42
2014	A	Savannah	228	42	59	3	25	259	332	408	740	10	82	0.61	7	1	41	149	4.87
2014	A+	St. Lucie	233	36	55	5	31	236	328	352	680	12	83	0.80	3	3	29	116	4.15
2014	AA	Binghamton	4	1	1	0	0	250	250	250	500	0	75	0.00	0	0	0	0	1.07

Finally healthy, Cecchini showed some pop (8 HR) for the first time. Offensive skills all took a step forward in '14. Lacks a plus tool but all solid-average or a tick better, and his instincts help them play up. Pulling ball more as he adds strength. Strong defender with quick hands and good arm.

Centeno,Juan — 2 — Milwaukee

EXP MLB DEBUT: 2013 | H/W: 5-9 195 | FUT: Backup C | 5B

Bats L Age 25 — 2007 (32) HS (PR)

Pwr + / BAvg ++ / Spd + / Def +++

Year	Lev	Team	AB	R	H	HR	RBI	Avg	OB	Slg	OPS	bb%	ct%	Eye	SB	CS	x/h%	Iso	RC/G
2013	AAA	Las Vegas	213	25	65	0	28	305	342	371	713	5	89	0.50	1	1	18	66	4.33
2013	MLB	NY Mets	10	0	3	0	1	300	300	300	600	0	90	0.00	0	0	0	0	2.63
2014	AA	Binghamton	77	8	22	0	8	286	337	351	688	7	86	0.55	0	1	23	65	4.12
2014	AAA	Las Vegas	179	19	52	1	17	291	345	335	681	8	85	0.58	2	0	12	45	3.97
2014	MLB	NY Mets	30	1	6	0	2	200	273	200	473	9	83	0.60	0	0	0	0	1.51

His defense earned him MLB time in '13 and '14. Has steadily improved OBP skills each year. Offers no power because of long, uppercut swing and poor utilization of lower half. Could be serviceable backup thanks to plus receiving skills and throwing arm; also slowing improving on-base ability.

Chang,Yu-Cheng — 56 — Cleveland

EXP MLB DEBUT: 2018 | H/W: 6-1 175 | FUT: Starting 3B | 7D

Bats R Age 19 — 2013 FA (Taiwan)

Pwr ++ / BAvg +++ / Spd +++ / Def +++

Year	Lev	Team	AB	R	H	HR	RBI	Avg	OB	Slg	OPS	bb%	ct%	Eye	SB	CS	x/h%	Iso	RC/G
2014	Rk	AZL Indians	159	39	55	6	25	346	412	566	978	10	82	0.64	6	1	35	220	7.68

Natural-hitting INF who split time between 3B and SS. Owns quality defensive tools and has strong arm to play either spot. Some talk of moving to CF to take advantage of speed and instincts. Has controlled stroke to make contact and hit for BA and has shown average pull power potential.

Chapman,Matt — 5 — Oakland

EXP MLB DEBUT: 2016 | H/W: 6-2 205 | FUT: Starting 3B | 8D

Bats R Age 21 — 2014 (1) Cal State Fullerton

Pwr +++ / BAvg +++ / Spd ++ / Def +++

Year	Lev	Team	AB	R	H	HR	RBI	Avg	OB	Slg	OPS	bb%	ct%	Eye	SB	CS	x/h%	Iso	RC/G
2013	NCAA	Cal St. Fullerton	186	41	53	5	37	285	395	457	852	15	84	1.17	6	2	36	172	6.50
2014	NCAA	Cal St. Fullerton	205	37	64	6	48	312	392	498	890	12	87	1.04	6	2	38	185	6.70
2014	Rk	AZL Athletics	14	1	6	0	0	429	467	643	1110	7	93	1.00	0	0	33	214	8.97
2014	A	Beloit	190	22	45	5	20	237	264	389	653	4	76	0.15	2	1	36	153	3.31
2014	AA	Midland	3	0	0	0	0	0	0	0	0	0	100		0	0		0	-2.66

Tall, instinctual INF who has potential to move quickly due to quality overall skills. Has tendency to expand strike zone, but projects to good power despite line drive stroke. Recognizes pitches and makes hard contact with textbook swing. Defense is solid with plus arm and clean feet/hands.

Chavis,Michael — 56 — Boston

EXP MLB DEBUT: 2017 | H/W: 5-10 190 | FUT: Starting 3B | 8D

Bats R Age 19 — 2014 (1) HS (GA)

Pwr +++ / BAvg +++ / Spd ++ / Def ++

Year	Lev	Team	AB	R	H	HR	RBI	Avg	OB	Slg	OPS	bb%	ct%	Eye	SB	CS	x/h%	Iso	RC/G
2014	Rk	GCL Red Sox	134	21	36	1	16	269	342	425	768	10	72	0.39	5	3	44	157	5.42

Strong INF who moved to 3B upon signing. Known mostly for bat with short, powerful stroke. Profiles to above average power and plus BA potential. Arm strength is suitable for 3B, though needs to improve footwork and range. Maximizes talent with work ethic and grinder approach.

Chigbogu,Justin — 3 — Los Angeles (N)

EXP MLB DEBUT: 2018 | H/W: 6-1 240 | FUT: Starting 1B | 7E

Bats L Age 20 — 2012 (4) HS (MO)

Pwr ++++ / BAvg + / Spd ++ / Def ++

Year	Lev	Team	AB	R	H	HR	RBI	Avg	OB	Slg	OPS	bb%	ct%	Eye	SB	CS	x/h%	Iso	RC/G
2012	Rk	AZL Dodgers	115	18	23	3	12	200	287	313	600	11	57	0.28	2	3	30	113	3.08
2013	Rk	Ogden	189	34	48	9	31	254	332	455	787	10	62	0.31	2	1	40	201	5.83
2013	Rk	AZL Dodgers	46	12	15	5	19	326	367	761	1128	6	61	0.17	0	0	60	435	11.13
2014	Rk	Ogden	254	45	63	20	56	248	318	520	838	9	60	0.26	3	2	44	272	6.55
2014	A	Great Lakes	90	13	14	3	12	156	200	322	522	5	57	0.13	1	0	57	167	1.73

LH masher has plus raw power hit a career high 23 HR. Has good bat speed but struggles to read pitches and can be beat by breaking balls. Is athletic with the hands to be a good defender at 1B. Whiffed 140 times in 344 AB and struggled mightily when moved up to Low-A.

Choi,Ji-Man — 37 — Seattle

EXP MLB DEBUT: 2015 | H/W: 6-1 225 | FUT: Starting 1B | 7D

Bats L Age 23 — 2009 FA (South Korea)

Pwr ++ / BAvg +++ / Spd + / Def ++

Year	Lev	Team	AB	R	H	HR	RBI	Avg	OB	Slg	OPS	bb%	ct%	Eye	SB	CS	x/h%	Iso	RC/G
2013	A+	High Desert	181	34	61	7	40	337	423	619	1042	13	82	0.82	0	1	56	282	8.76
2013	AA	Jackson	198	21	53	9	39	268	370	485	854	14	86	1.14	2	2	42	217	6.33
2013	AAA	Tacoma	45	9	11	2	6	244	306	422	728	8	84	0.57	0	0	36	178	4.43
2014	AA	Jackson	11	3	3	1	5	273	467	636	1103	27	82	2.00	0	0	67	364	9.95
2014	AAA	Tacoma	237	41	67	5	30	283	377	392	770	13	82	0.86	2	2	21	110	5.30

Natural hitter who missed time for PED suspension and injury. Posts high OBP with discerning eye and puts bat to ball with quick, compact stroke. Doesn't have ideal power for 1B or OF corner and doesn't have much speed. Hits LHP. Has passable range and hands for 1B or LF.

Ciuffo,Nick — 2 — Tampa Bay

EXP MLB DEBUT: 2018 | H/W: 6-1 205 | FUT: Starting C | 8E

Bats L Age 20 — 2013 (1) HS (SC)

Pwr ++ / BAvg ++ / Spd ++ / Def +++

Year	Lev	Team	AB	R	H	HR	RBI	Avg	OB	Slg	OPS	bb%	ct%	Eye	SB	CS	x/h%	Iso	RC/G
2013	Rk	GCL Devil Rays	159	11	41	0	25	258	298	308	606	5	75	0.23	0	0	17	50	2.83
2014	Rk	Princeton	192	25	43	4	20	224	287	333	620	8	77	0.38	2	1	28	109	3.08

Athletic, strong C with high upside. Very rough around edges and showed improvement at end of year. Has plus bat speed that could result in above average power and BA output. Bails on LHH and needs swing adjustment. Has arm strength and quick release while he is good receiver.

Collins,Tyler — 79 — Detroit

EXP MLB DEBUT: 2014 | H/W: 5-11 215 | FUT: Starting OF | 7C

Bats L Age 24 — 2011 (6) Howard JC

Pwr +++ / BAvg ++ / Spd ++ / Def +++

Year	Lev	Team	AB	R	H	HR	RBI	Avg	OB	Slg	OPS	bb%	ct%	Eye	SB	CS	x/h%	Iso	RC/G
2011	A-	Connecticut	163	28	51	8	31	313	353	534	886	6	90	0.59	6	1	37	221	6.14
2012	A+	Lakeland	473	68	137	7	66	290	367	429	796	11	86	0.91	20	3	34	140	5.62
2013	AA	Erie	466	67	112	21	79	240	315	438	753	10	74	0.42	4	5	45	197	4.85
2014	AAA	Toledo	468	63	123	18	62	263	333	423	756	9	75	0.42	12	4	30	160	4.84
2014	MLB	Detroit	24	3	6	1	4	250	280	375	655	4	83	0.25	0	0	17	125	3.23

Short, stocky OF who made DET roster on opening day. Makes acceptable contact with average power profile. Can get pull happy and struggles with LHP and pitch recognition. Fringy speed, but can steal bases and gets good jumps in OF corner. Adds value with instincts and work ethic.

Colon,Christian — 456 — Kansas City

EXP MLB DEBUT: 2014 | H/W: 5-10 190 | FUT: Utility INF | 6A

Bats R Age 25 — 2010 (1) Cal State Fullerton

Pwr ++ / BAvg +++ / Spd +++ / Def +++

Year	Lev	Team	AB	R	H	HR	RBI	Avg	OB	Slg	OPS	bb%	ct%	Eye	SB	CS	x/h%	Iso	RC/G
2012	AAA	Omaha	17	4	7	1	5	412	474	647	1121	11	94	2.00	0	0	29	235	8.96
2013	AAA	Omaha	512	72	140	12	58	273	327	379	706	7	89	0.72	15	4	19	105	4.27
2014	AA	NW Arkansas	8	1	2	0	0	250	333	375	708	11	75	0.50	1	0	50	125	4.62
2014	AAA	Omaha	344	55	107	8	47	311	366	433	799	8	92	1.03	15	4	24	122	5.43
2014	MLB	Kansas City	45	8	15	0	6	333	375	489	864	6	91	0.75	2	0	40	156	6.23

Fundamentally-sound INF who emerged in career year. Extreme contact ability to give BA potential and has plus hand-eye coordination. Power isn't part of game, though can steal occasional base despite average wheels. Versatile defender who can play any spot with plus instincts.

Conforto,Michael — 7 — New York (N)

EXP MLB DEBUT: 2017 | H/W: 6-1 210 | FUT: Starting LF | 8D

Bats L Age 22 — 2014 (1) Oregon State

Pwr ++++ / BAvg ++ / Spd ++ / Def +

Year	Lev	Team	AB	R	H	HR	RBI	Avg	OB	Slg	OPS	bb%	ct%	Eye	SB	CS	x/h%	Iso	RC/G
2012	NCAA	Oregon State	218	45	76	13	76	349	413	601	1014	10	83	0.65	1	1	37	252	7.93
2013	NCAA	Oregon State	247	48	81	11	47	328	424	526	950	14	81	0.87	6	5	32	198	7.53
2014	NCAA	Oregon State	203	52	70	7	56	345	484	547	1031	21	81	1.45	4	4	36	202	9.11
2014	A-	Brooklyn	163	30	54	3	19	331	391	448	839	9	82	0.55	3	0	24	117	5.91

Consistent offensive producer with big-time power upside. Uses quick uppercut swing to drive everything he connects with. Hits to all fields and plenty over the fence. Eye improved each season in college and can work a walk. Swing-and-miss in his game. Average defender without much speed.

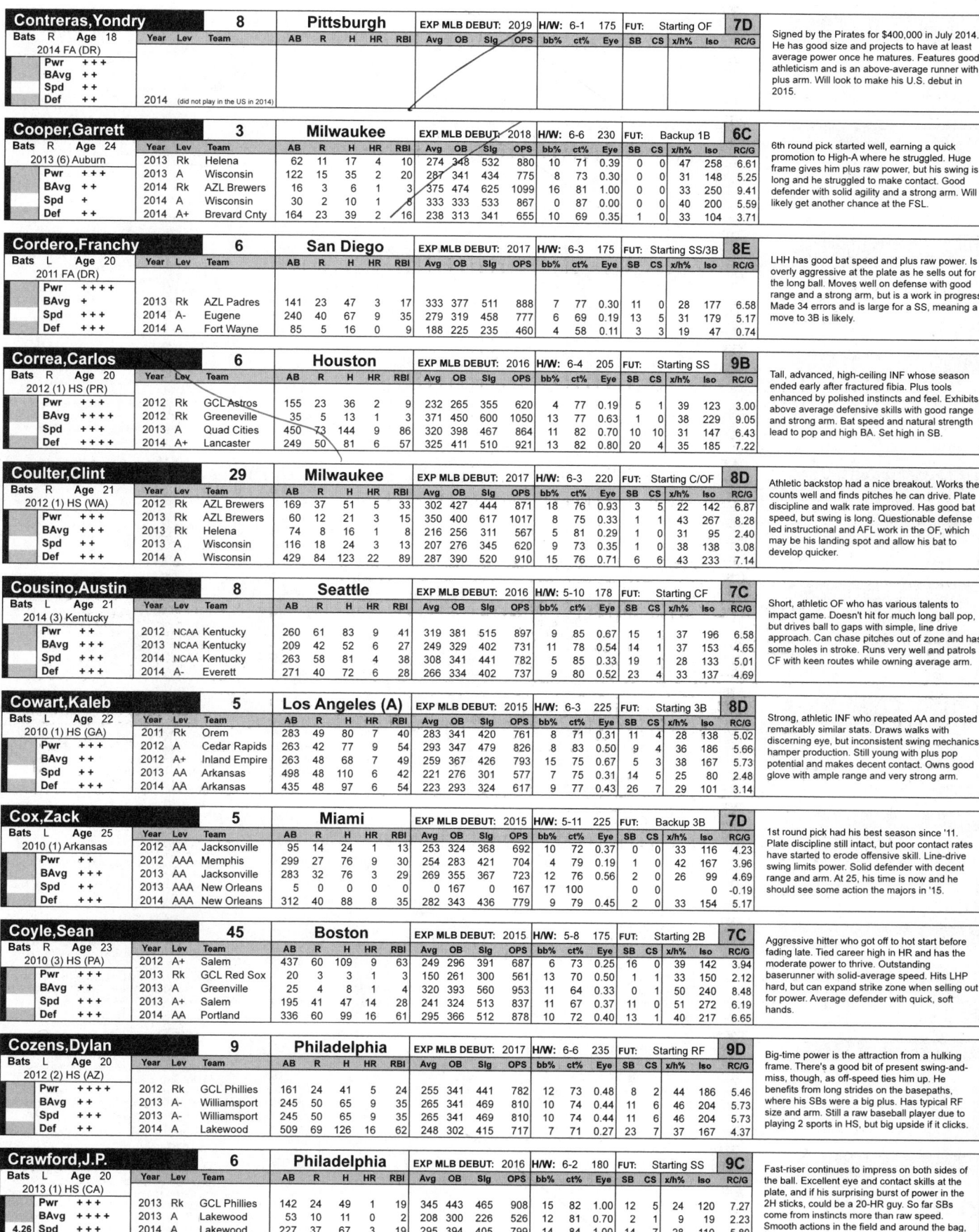

Contreras,Yondry

8 | Pittsburgh | EXP MLB DEBUT: 2019 | H/W: 6-1 175 | FUT: Starting OF | 7D

Bats R Age 18
2014 FA (DR)
Pwr +++
BAvg ++
Spd ++
Def ++

Year	Lev	Team	AB	R	H	HR	RBI	Avg	OB	Slg	OPS	bb%	ct%	Eye	SB	CS	x/h%	Iso	RC/G
2014	(did not play in the US in 2014)																		

Signed by the Pirates for $400,000 in July 2014. He has good size and projects to have at least average power once he matures. Features good athleticism and is an above-average runner with a plus arm. Will look to make his U.S. debut in 2015.

Cooper,Garrett

3 | Milwaukee | EXP MLB DEBUT: 2018 | H/W: 6-6 230 | FUT: Backup 1B | 6C

Bats R Age 24
2013 (6) Auburn
Pwr +++
BAvg ++
Spd +
Def ++

Year	Lev	Team	AB	R	H	HR	RBI	Avg	OB	Slg	OPS	bb%	ct%	Eye	SB	CS	x/h%	Iso	RC/G
2013	Rk	Helena	62	11	17	4	10	274	348	532	880	10	71	0.39	0	0	47	258	6.61
2013	A	Wisconsin	122	15	35	2	20	287	341	434	775	8	73	0.30	0	0	31	148	5.25
2014	Rk	AZL Brewers	16	3	6	1	3	375	474	625	1099	16	81	1.00	0	0	33	250	9.41
2014	A	Wisconsin	30	2	10	1	8	333	333	533	867	0	87	0.00	0	0	40	200	5.59
2014	A+	Brevard Cnty	164	23	39	2	16	238	313	341	655	10	69	0.35	1	0	33	104	3.71

6th round pick started well, earning a quick promotion to High-A where he struggled. Huge frame gives him plus raw power, but his swing is long and he struggled to make contact. Good defender with solid agility and a strong arm. Will likely get another chance at the FSL.

Cordero,Franchy

6 | San Diego | EXP MLB DEBUT: 2017 | H/W: 6-3 175 | FUT: Starting SS/3B | 8E

Bats L Age 20
2011 FA (DR)
Pwr ++++
BAvg +
Spd +++
Def +++

Year	Lev	Team	AB	R	H	HR	RBI	Avg	OB	Slg	OPS	bb%	ct%	Eye	SB	CS	x/h%	Iso	RC/G
2013	Rk	AZL Padres	141	23	47	3	17	333	377	511	888	7	77	0.30	11	0	28	177	6.58
2014	A-	Eugene	240	40	67	9	35	279	319	458	777	6	69	0.19	13	5	31	179	5.17
2014	A	Fort Wayne	85	5	16	0	9	188	225	235	460	4	58	0.11	3	3	19	47	0.74

LHH has good bat speed and plus raw power. Is overly aggressive at the plate as he sells out for the long ball. Moves well on defense with good range and a strong arm, but is a work in progress. Made 34 errors and is large for a SS, meaning a move to 3B is likely.

Correa,Carlos

6 | Houston | EXP MLB DEBUT: 2016 | H/W: 6-4 205 | FUT: Starting SS | 9B

Bats R Age 20
2012 (1) HS (PR)
Pwr +++
BAvg ++++
Spd +++
Def ++++

Year	Lev	Team	AB	R	H	HR	RBI	Avg	OB	Slg	OPS	bb%	ct%	Eye	SB	CS	x/h%	Iso	RC/G
2012	Rk	GCL Astros	155	23	36	2	9	232	265	355	620	4	77	0.19	5	1	39	123	3.00
2012	Rk	Greeneville	35	5	13	1	3	371	450	600	1050	13	77	0.63	1	0	38	229	9.05
2013	A	Quad Cities	450	73	144	9	86	320	398	467	864	11	82	0.70	10	10	31	147	6.43
2014	A+	Lancaster	249	50	81	6	57	325	411	510	921	13	82	0.80	20	4	35	185	7.22

Tall, advanced, high-ceiling INF whose season ended early after fractured fibia. Plus tools enhanced by polished instincts and feel. Exhibits above average defensive skills with good range and strong arm. Bat speed and natural strength lead to pop and high BA. Set high in SB.

Coulter,Clint

29 | Milwaukee | EXP MLB DEBUT: 2017 | H/W: 6-3 220 | FUT: Starting C/OF | 8D

Bats R Age 21
2012 (1) HS (WA)
Pwr +++
BAvg +++
Spd ++
Def +++

Year	Lev	Team	AB	R	H	HR	RBI	Avg	OB	Slg	OPS	bb%	ct%	Eye	SB	CS	x/h%	Iso	RC/G
2012	Rk	AZL Brewers	169	37	51	5	33	302	427	444	871	18	76	0.93	3	5	22	142	6.87
2013	Rk	AZL Brewers	60	12	21	3	15	350	400	617	1017	8	75	0.33	1	1	43	267	8.28
2013	Rk	Helena	74	8	16	1	8	216	256	311	567	5	81	0.29	1	0	31	95	2.40
2013	A	Wisconsin	116	18	24	3	13	207	276	345	620	9	73	0.35	1	0	38	138	3.08
2014	A	Wisconsin	429	84	123	22	89	287	390	520	910	15	76	0.71	6	6	43	233	7.14

Athletic backstop had a nice breakout. Works the counts well and finds pitches he can drive. Plate discipline and walk rate improved. Has good bat speed, but swing is long. Questionable defense led instructional and AFL work in the OF, which may be his landing spot and allow his bat to develop quicker.

Cousino,Austin

8 | Seattle | EXP MLB DEBUT: 2016 | H/W: 5-10 178 | FUT: Starting CF | 7C

Bats L Age 21
2014 (3) Kentucky
Pwr ++
BAvg +++
Spd +++
Def +++

Year	Lev	Team	AB	R	H	HR	RBI	Avg	OB	Slg	OPS	bb%	ct%	Eye	SB	CS	x/h%	Iso	RC/G
2012	NCAA	Kentucky	260	61	83	9	41	319	381	515	897	9	85	0.67	15	1	37	196	6.58
2013	NCAA	Kentucky	209	42	52	6	27	249	329	402	731	11	78	0.54	14	1	37	153	4.65
2014	NCAA	Kentucky	263	58	81	4	38	308	341	441	782	5	85	0.33	19	1	28	133	5.01
2014	A-	Everett	271	40	72	6	28	266	334	402	737	9	80	0.52	23	4	33	137	4.69

Short, athletic OF who has various talents to impact game. Doesn't hit for much long ball pop, but drives ball to gaps with simple, line drive approach. Can chase pitches out of zone and has some holes in stroke. Runs very well and patrols CF with keen routes while owning average arm.

Cowart,Kaleb

5 | Los Angeles (A) | EXP MLB DEBUT: 2015 | H/W: 6-3 225 | FUT: Starting 3B | 8D

Bats L Age 22
2010 (1) HS (GA)
Pwr +++
BAvg ++
Spd ++
Def +++

Year	Lev	Team	AB	R	H	HR	RBI	Avg	OB	Slg	OPS	bb%	ct%	Eye	SB	CS	x/h%	Iso	RC/G
2011	Rk	Orem	283	49	80	7	40	283	341	420	761	8	71	0.31	11	4	28	138	5.02
2012	A	Cedar Rapids	263	42	77	9	54	293	347	479	826	8	83	0.50	9	4	36	186	5.66
2012	A+	Inland Empire	263	48	68	7	49	259	367	426	793	15	75	0.67	5	3	38	167	5.73
2013	AA	Arkansas	498	48	110	6	42	221	276	301	577	7	75	0.31	14	5	25	80	2.48
2014	AA	Arkansas	435	48	97	6	54	223	293	324	617	9	77	0.43	26	7	29	101	3.14

Strong, athletic INF who repeated AA and posted remarkably similar stats. Draws walks with discerning eye, but inconsistent swing mechanics hamper production. Still young with plus pop potential and makes decent contact. Owns good glove with ample range and very strong arm.

Cox,Zack

5 | Miami | EXP MLB DEBUT: 2015 | H/W: 5-11 225 | FUT: Backup 3B | 7D

Bats L Age 25
2010 (1) Arkansas
Pwr ++
BAvg +++
Spd ++
Def +++

Year	Lev	Team	AB	R	H	HR	RBI	Avg	OB	Slg	OPS	bb%	ct%	Eye	SB	CS	x/h%	Iso	RC/G
2012	AA	Jacksonville	95	14	24	1	13	253	324	368	692	10	72	0.37	0	0	33	116	4.23
2012	AAA	Memphis	299	27	76	9	30	254	283	421	704	4	79	0.19	1	0	42	167	3.96
2013	AA	Jacksonville	283	32	76	3	29	269	355	367	723	12	76	0.56	2	0	26	99	4.69
2013	AAA	New Orleans	5	0	0	0	0	0	167	0	167	17	100		0	0		0	-0.19
2014	AAA	New Orleans	312	40	88	8	35	282	343	436	779	9	79	0.45	2	0	33	154	5.17

1st round pick had his best season since '11. Plate discipline still intact, but poor contact rates have started to erode offensive skill. Line-drive swing limits power. Solid defender with decent range and arm. At 25, his time is now and he should see some action the majors in '15.

Coyle,Sean

45 | Boston | EXP MLB DEBUT: 2015 | H/W: 5-8 175 | FUT: Starting 2B | 7C

Bats R Age 23
2010 (3) HS (PA)
Pwr +++
BAvg ++
Spd +++
Def +++

Year	Lev	Team	AB	R	H	HR	RBI	Avg	OB	Slg	OPS	bb%	ct%	Eye	SB	CS	x/h%	Iso	RC/G
2012	A+	Salem	437	60	109	9	63	249	296	391	687	6	73	0.25	16	0	39	142	3.94
2013	Rk	GCL Red Sox	20	3	3	1	3	150	261	300	561	13	70	0.50	1	1	33	150	2.12
2013	A	Greenville	25	4	8	1	4	320	393	560	953	11	64	0.33	0	1	50	240	8.48
2013	A+	Salem	195	41	47	14	28	241	324	513	837	11	67	0.37	11	0	51	272	6.19
2014	AA	Portland	336	60	99	16	61	295	366	512	878	10	72	0.40	13	1	40	217	6.65

Aggressive hitter who got off to hot start before fading late. Tied career high in HR and has the moderate power to thrive. Outstanding baserunner with solid-average speed. Hits LHP hard, but can expand strike zone when selling out for power. Average defender with quick, soft hands.

Cozens,Dylan

9 | Philadelphia | EXP MLB DEBUT: 2017 | H/W: 6-6 235 | FUT: Starting RF | 9D

Bats L Age 20
2012 (2) HS (AZ)
Pwr ++++
BAvg ++
Spd +++
Def ++

Year	Lev	Team	AB	R	H	HR	RBI	Avg	OB	Slg	OPS	bb%	ct%	Eye	SB	CS	x/h%	Iso	RC/G
2012	Rk	GCL Phillies	161	24	41	5	24	255	341	441	782	12	73	0.48	8	2	44	186	5.46
2013	A-	Williamsport	245	50	65	9	35	265	341	469	810	10	74	0.44	11	6	46	204	5.73
2013	A-	Williamsport	245	50	65	9	35	265	341	469	810	10	74	0.44	11	6	46	204	5.73
2014	A	Lakewood	509	69	126	16	62	248	302	415	717	7	71	0.27	23	7	37	167	4.37

Big-time power is the attraction from a hulking frame. There's a good bit of present swing-and-miss, though, as off-speed ties him up. He benefits from long strides on the basepaths, where his SBs were a big plus. Has typical RF size and arm. Still a raw baseball player due to playing 2 sports in HS, but big upside if it clicks.

Crawford,J.P.

6 | Philadelphia | EXP MLB DEBUT: 2016 | H/W: 6-2 180 | FUT: Starting SS | 9C

Bats L Age 20
2013 (1) HS (CA)
Pwr +++
BAvg ++++
4.26 Spd +++
Def ++++

Year	Lev	Team	AB	R	H	HR	RBI	Avg	OB	Slg	OPS	bb%	ct%	Eye	SB	CS	x/h%	Iso	RC/G
2013	Rk	GCL Phillies	142	24	49	1	19	345	443	465	908	15	82	1.00	12	5	24	120	7.27
2013	A	Lakewood	53	10	11	0	2	208	300	226	526	12	81	0.70	2	1	9	19	2.23
2014	A	Lakewood	227	37	67	3	19	295	394	405	799	14	84	1.00	14	7	28	110	5.80
2014	A+	Clearwater	236	32	65	8	29	275	352	407	759	11	84	0.76	10	7	23	131	4.95

Fast-riser continues to impress on both sides of the ball. Excellent eye and contact skills at the plate, and if his surprising burst of power in the 2H sticks, could be a 20-HR guy. So far SBs come from instincts more than raw speed. Smooth actions in the field and around the bag, and has a rifle arm.

Crawford,Rashad

8 | Chicago (N) | EXP MLB DEBUT: 2018 | H/W: 6-3 185 | FUT: Backup OF | 7E

Bats B Age 21
2012 (11) HS (GA)
Pwr ++
BAvg ++
Spd +++
Def ++

Year	Lev	Team	AB	R	H	HR	RBI	Avg	OB	Slg	OPS	bb%	ct%	Eye	SB	CS	x/h%	Iso	RC/G
2012	Rk	AZL Cubs	30	6	5	0	3	167	324	167	491	19	70	0.78	4	0	0	0	1.55
2013	Rk	AZL Cubs	138	20	29	0	8	210	292	275	568	10	72	0.41	10	1	21	65	2.54
2014	A-	Boise	297	45	77	1	34	259	297	360	657	5	72	0.19	14	5	27	101	3.59

Raw, but athletic CF made a nice impact in short-season ball. Plus runner, but stole just 13 bases. Approach at the plate remains raw and too often he swings and misses, striking out 83 times. Covers ground well in CF. Lots of work to do, but tons of potential.

Cuadrado,Romer

8 | Los Angeles (N) | EXP MLB DEBUT: 2018 | H/W: 6-4 195 | FUT: Starting OF | 8E

Bats R Age 18
2014 FA (Venezuela)
Pwr +++
BAvg ++
Spd ++
Def ++

Year	Lev	Team	AB	R	H	HR	RBI	Avg	OB	Slg	OPS	bb%	ct%	Eye	SB	CS	x/h%	Iso	RC/G
2014	(did not play in the US in 2014)																		

Was one of the best July 2 prospects in 2014 and signed with the Dodgers for $750,000. He has a lean, projectable frame and should add power as he matures. Moves well in the OF and profiles as a power-hitting corner OF. Has yet to make his state-side debut.

Cunningham,Todd

8 | Atlanta | EXP MLB DEBUT: 2013 | H/W: 6-0 205 | FUT: Backup OF | 6B

Bats B Age 26
2010 (2) Jacksonville State
Pwr ++
BAvg +++
Spd +++
Def ++

Year	Lev	Team	AB	R	H	HR	RBI	Avg	OB	Slg	OPS	bb%	ct%	Eye	SB	CS	x/h%	Iso	RC/G
2011	A+	Lynchburg	334	59	86	4	20	257	324	353	678	9	86	0.70	14	6	23	96	4.06
2012	AA	Mississippi	466	77	144	3	51	309	361	403	765	8	89	0.75	24	8	22	94	5.06
2013	AAA	Gwinnett	427	60	113	2	38	265	329	333	662	9	85	0.66	20	7	18	68	3.87
2013	MLB	Atlanta	8	2	2	0	0	250	250	250	500	0	63	0.00	0	0	0	0	1.04
2014	AAA	Gwinnett	470	59	135	8	58	287	337	406	743	7	83	0.44	19	8	28	119	4.65

Switch-hitter lacks a standout tool, but has a good approach at the plate. Makes consistent contact with a short stroke and good plate discipline. Strength and bat speed to hit for moderate power, but is more content with putting the ball in play. Runs well, but range is a short for CF.

Cuthbert,Cheslor

35 | Kansas City | EXP MLB DEBUT: 2015 | H/W: 6-1 190 | FUT: Starting 3B | 8D

Bats R Age 22
2009 FA (Nicaragua)
Pwr +++
BAvg ++
Spd ++
Def +++

Year	Lev	Team	AB	R	H	HR	RBI	Avg	OB	Slg	OPS	bb%	ct%	Eye	SB	CS	x/h%	Iso	RC/G
2012	A+	Wilmington	475	47	114	7	59	240	295	322	617	7	83	0.46	6	3	22	82	3.13
2013	A+	Wilmington	225	32	63	2	31	280	357	418	775	11	84	0.73	1	2	40	138	5.38
2013	AA	NW Arkansas	237	25	51	6	28	215	276	359	635	8	78	0.39	5	2	43	143	3.30
2014	AA	NW Arkansas	355	35	98	10	48	276	343	420	762	9	81	0.54	9	3	31	144	4.96
2014	AAA	Omaha	91	12	24	2	16	264	330	385	715	9	87	0.75	1	1	29	121	4.46

Natural hitting INF with emerging long ball pop. Makes splendid contact with short swing and produces above average raw power with quick wrists and bat speed. Set highs in HR and SB, though not a burner. Thick lower half mutes speed and quickness. Good defender with arm strength.

Dahl,David

8 | Colorado | EXP MLB DEBUT: 2016 | H/W: 6-2 195 | FUT: Starting CF | 9C

Bats L Age 21
2012 (1) HS (AL)
Pwr ++++
BAvg ++++
Spd +++
Def +++

Year	Lev	Team	AB	R	H	HR	RBI	Avg	OB	Slg	OPS	bb%	ct%	Eye	SB	CS	x/h%	Iso	RC/G
2012	Rk	Grand Junction	280	62	106	9	57	379	422	625	1047	7	85	0.50	12	7	39	246	8.28
2013	A	Asheville	40	9	11	0	7	275	310	425	735	5	80	0.25	2	0	45	150	4.63
2014	A	Asheville	392	69	121	10	41	309	347	500	847	6	83	0.35	18	5	40	191	5.84
2014	A+	Modesto	120	14	32	4	14	267	296	467	763	4	78	0.19	3	0	44	200	4.74

Natural, athletic hitter has the tools to hit for BA due to plus bat speed and a short stroke. Swing produces plenty of line drives, but has over the fence power as well. He is a solid-average CF with plus speed and a good arm. Has a good approach at the plate, and there is more power in his frame.

Davidson,Braxton

7 | Atlanta | EXP MLB DEBUT: 2017 | H/W: 6-2 210 | FUT: Starting LF | 8D

Bats L Age 18
2014 (1) HS (NC)
Pwr +++
BAvg +++
Spd ++
Def ++

Year	Lev	Team	AB	R	H	HR	RBI	Avg	OB	Slg	OPS	bb%	ct%	Eye	SB	CS	x/h%	Iso	RC/G
2014	Rk	Danville	36	1	6	0	3	167	333	222	556	20	72	0.90	0	0	33	56	2.67
2014	Rk	GCL Braves	111	23	27	0	8	243	368	324	693	17	71	0.69	0	0	30	81	4.58

Good approach at the plate with a balanced swing and the ability to generate bat speed, but needs to use his lower half better. Solid understanding of the strike zone, but does have some swing-and-miss. Smart player and positions himself well with enough arm strength for RF.

Davidson,Matt

5 | Chicago (A) | EXP MLB DEBUT: 2013 | H/W: 6-2 225 | FUT: Starting 3B | 7C

Bats R Age 24
2009 (1-S) HS (CA)
Pwr ++++
BAvg ++
Spd ++
Def +++

Year	Lev	Team	AB	R	H	HR	RBI	Avg	OB	Slg	OPS	bb%	ct%	Eye	SB	CS	x/h%	Iso	RC/G
2011	A+	Visalia	535	93	148	20	106	277	341	465	806	9	73	0.35	0	1	41	189	5.61
2012	AA	Mobile	486	81	127	23	76	261	353	469	822	12	74	0.55	3	4	42	208	5.90
2013	AAA	Reno	443	55	124	17	74	280	348	481	828	9	70	0.34	1	0	42	201	6.07
2013	MLB	Arizona	76	8	18	3	12	237	326	434	760	12	68	0.42	0	1	50	197	5.20
2014	AAA	Charlotte	478	59	95	20	55	199	273	362	635	9	66	0.30	0	0	40	163	3.24

Big, strong 3B who had disappointing year and led IL in K. Provides consistent long ball pop to all fields and has selective approach at plate. Can be asset defender with strong arm and range. Long swing can be exploited and struggles with 2 strikes. Poor speed results in few SB.

Davis,D.J.

8 | Toronto | EXP MLB DEBUT: 2017 | H/W: 6-1 180 | FUT: Starting OF | 8E

Bats L Age 20
2012 (1) HS (MS)
Pwr +++
BAvg ++
Spd ++++
Def +++

Year	Lev	Team	AB	R	H	HR	RBI	Avg	OB	Slg	OPS	bb%	ct%	Eye	SB	CS	x/h%	Iso	RC/G
2012	Rk	Bluefield	47	9	16	1	6	340	392	511	903	8	79	0.40	6	2	31	170	6.76
2012	Rk	GCL Blue Jays	163	30	38	4	12	233	309	374	684	10	67	0.33	18	7	34	141	4.12
2012	A-	Vancouver	18	3	3	0	0	167	348	167	514	22	67	0.83	1	1	0	0	1.84
2013	Rk	Bluefield	225	35	54	6	25	240	319	418	737	10	66	0.34	13	8	39	178	5.00
2014	A	Lansing	494	56	105	8	52	213	266	316	582	7	66	0.22	19	20	27	103	2.52

Athletic, fast OF who had poor year in first full season. Never got on track with tons of Ks and poor BA against LHP (.161). Very raw hitter with aggressive, swing-happy approach. Does project to average power. Has incredible speed with plus CF range. Has impact potential, but needs time.

Davis,Glynn

78 | Baltimore | EXP MLB DEBUT: 2016 | H/W: 6-3 170 | FUT: Reserve OF | 6B

Bats R Age 23
2010 FA (CC -Balt County)
Pwr ++
BAvg ++
Spd ++++
Def +++

Year	Lev	Team	AB	R	H	HR	RBI	Avg	OB	Slg	OPS	bb%	ct%	Eye	SB	CS	x/h%	Iso	RC/G
2012	A	Delmarva	397	53	100	0	25	252	337	302	639	11	77	0.56	29	9	18	50	3.59
2012	A+	Frederick	82	11	21	0	4	256	351	293	644	13	70	0.48	8	1	10	37	3.66
2013	A+	Frederick	364	42	85	2	32	234	314	313	628	11	80	0.58	19	7	26	80	3.44
2014	A+	Frederick	352	65	104	1	31	295	361	386	747	9	80	0.52	20	8	25	91	4.92
2014	AA	Bowie	96	9	30	1	12	313	327	406	733	2	79	0.10	3	1	23	94	4.22

Sleeper prospect who had career year. Repeated High-A until July promotion. Lean frame growing into some power, but still more of a slap style. Chases pitches in poor approach, though has plus-plus speed on base. Solid CF with excellent range and decent arm strength.

Davis,J.D.

5 | Houston | EXP MLB DEBUT: 2017 | H/W: 6-3 215 | FUT: Starting 3B | 7D

Bats R Age 21
2014 (3) Cal State Fullerton
Pwr +++
BAvg +++
Spd +
Def ++

Year	Lev	Team	AB	R	H	HR	RBI	Avg	OB	Slg	OPS	bb%	ct%	Eye	SB	CS	x/h%	Iso	RC/G
2012	NCAA	Cal St. Fullerton	118	12	27	4	20	229	311	381	692	11	79	0.56	2	2	37	153	4.10
2013	NCAA	Cal St. Fullerton	211	40	67	4	50	318	405	436	841	13	82	0.84	1	1	24	118	6.19
2014	NCAA	Cal St. Fullerton	237	34	80	6	43	338	416	523	940	12	78	0.60	7	0	34	186	7.51
2014	A-	Tri City	111	18	31	5	20	279	365	495	861	12	77	0.60	1	0	42	216	6.34
2014	A	Quad Cities	155	20	47	8	32	303	357	516	873	8	74	0.32	4	0	36	213	6.33

Big, strong 3B with tons of raw power. Combines premier bat speed and wrist strength to produce all-fields pop. Should produce sufficient BA despite long swing and poor pitch recognition. Improving defender with some agility and hands while arm is strong. Could move to 1B or LF.

De La Cruz,Michael

8 | Pittsburgh | EXP MLB DEBUT: 2018 | H/W: 6-1 165 | FUT: Starting OF | 8E

Bats L Age 18
2012 FA (DR)
Pwr +++
BAvg +++
Spd +++
Def +++

Year	Lev	Team	AB	R	H	HR	RBI	Avg	OB	Slg	OPS	bb%	ct%	Eye	SB	CS	x/h%	Iso	RC/G
2013	Rk	DSL Pirates	226	51	66	0	20	292	437	367	804	20	78	1.16	14	11	21	75	6.29
2014	Rk	GCL Pirates	91	10	15	1	7	165	283	198	481	14	73	0.60	4	1	7	33	1.30

Athletic OF had a dreadful season. Previously had shown good plate discipline and a nice line-drive approach. Has good speed and should be able to stick in CF where he has good range and a strong arm. Did not turn 18 until mid-year and could use additional time in rookie ball.

Dean,Austin — 7 — Miami

EXP MLB DEBUT: 2017 | H/W: 6-1 190 | FUT: Starting OF | 7D

Bats R Age 21
2012 (4) HS (TX)

- Pwr +++
- BAvg ++
- Spd ++
- Def +++

Year	Lev	Team	AB	R	H	HR	RBI	Avg	OB	Slg	OPS	bb%	ct%	Eye	SB	CS	x/h%	Iso	RC/G
2012	Rk	GCL Marlins	148	15	33	2	15	223	331	338	669	14	76	0.69	2	2	39	115	4.07
2013	A-	Batavia	213	28	57	2	19	268	322	418	740	7	78	0.36	0	2	37	150	4.77
2013	A	Greensboro	20	4	4	1	3	200	333	400	733	17	75	0.80	0	0	50	200	4.81
2014	A	Greensboro	403	67	124	9	58	308	367	444	812	9	82	0.53	4	4	27	136	5.56

Had his best season as a pro. Has a contact-oriented approach with good bat speed and can drive the ball into the gaps. Has avg speed but that isn't going to be part of his game. Covers ground well in the OF with an avg arm. Sum: A ballplayer with no standout tool.

Dean,Matt — 35 — Toronto

EXP MLB DEBUT: 2017 | H/W: 6-3 215 | FUT: Starting 1B | 8D

Bats R Age 22
2011 (13) HS (TX)

- Pwr ++++
- BAvg +++
- Spd ++
- Def ++

Year	Lev	Team	AB	R	H	HR	RBI	Avg	OB	Slg	OPS	bb%	ct%	Eye	SB	CS	x/h%	Iso	RC/G
2012	Rk	Bluefield	167	22	37	2	24	222	274	353	627	7	64	0.20	3	2	38	132	3.37
2013	Rk	Bluefield	210	37	71	6	35	338	379	519	899	6	73	0.25	8	5	32	181	6.79
2014	A	Lansing	448	58	126	9	51	281	322	429	751	6	74	0.23	2	1	34	147	4.76

Aggressive hitter with athletic build who played both 1B and 3B in first full season. Succeeds with BA despite approach and has plus raw power to all fields. Brute strength supplies the pop, though draws few walks and Ks often. Has fringy wheels and suitable arm strength for corner INF.

Decker,Jaff — 7 — Pittsburgh

EXP MLB DEBUT: 2013 | H/W: 5-9 190 | FUT: Backup OF | 6C

Bats L Age 25
2008 (S-1) HS (AZ)

- Pwr +++
- BAvg ++
- Spd +
- Def ++

Year	Lev	Team	AB	R	H	HR	RBI	Avg	OB	Slg	OPS	bb%	ct%	Eye	SB	CS	x/h%	Iso	RC/G
2012	AA	San Antonio	147	30	27	3	9	184	358	293	651	21	75	1.08	6	2	30	109	4.00
2013	AAA	Tucson	350	63	100	10	40	286	383	443	826	14	73	0.59	4	6	34	157	6.13
2013	MLB	San Diego	26	3	4	1	2	154	241	269	511	10	85	0.75	0	1	25	115	1.93
2014	AAA	Indianapolis	350	41	90	6	39	257	352	391	743	13	79	0.70	7	6	38	134	4.99
2014	MLB	Pittsburgh	5	0	0	0	0	0	0	0	0	0	40	0.00	0	0		0	-8.89

Strong outfielder who has extreme strike zone knowledge and discerning eye. Exhibits good power to pull side, though vicious uppercut limits contact and BA ability. Can be too patient. Strikes out too much and lacks foot speed for SB. Can play all OF spots, though best in corner.

Deglan,Kellin — 2 — Texas

EXP MLB DEBUT: 2016 | H/W: 6-2 195 | FUT: Reserve C | 7E

Bats L Age 22
2010 (1) HS (CAN)

- Pwr +++
- BAvg ++
- Spd ++
- Def ++

Year	Lev	Team	AB	R	H	HR	RBI	Avg	OB	Slg	OPS	bb%	ct%	Eye	SB	CS	x/h%	Iso	RC/G
2011	A	Hickory	291	39	66	6	39	227	308	347	655	10	69	0.37	2	0	33	120	3.67
2012	A	Hickory	320	46	75	12	41	234	304	438	741	9	70	0.33	4	4	52	203	4.83
2013	A+	Myrtle Beach	308	37	71	12	49	231	305	393	698	10	69	0.35	0	0	34	162	4.14
2014	A	Hickory	327	46	82	15	60	251	321	465	786	9	73	0.39	2	0	46	214	5.31
2014	A+	Myrtle Beach	46	3	10	1	8	217	234	348	582	2	65	0.06	0	0	40	130	2.40

Atheltic catcher who returned to Low-A for bulk of year. Has been slow to develop, though has nice tools to cultivate. Has burgeoning power from left side, but poor pitch recognition hinders BA growth. Has improved receiving while arm remains plus. Throwing accuracy a little short.

Delgado,Natanael — 79 — Los Angeles (A)

EXP MLB DEBUT: 2018 | H/W: 6-1 170 | FUT: Starting OF | 8D

Bats L Age 19
2012 FA (DR)

- Pwr +++
- BAvg +++
- Spd ++
- Def ++

Year	Lev	Team	AB	R	H	HR	RBI	Avg	OB	Slg	OPS	bb%	ct%	Eye	SB	CS	x/h%	Iso	RC/G
2013	Rk	AZL Angels	192	23	52	3	33	271	310	422	732	5	78	0.26	4	0	40	151	4.51
2014	Rk	Orem	153	23	46	3	21	301	323	464	787	3	78	0.15	4	0	33	163	5.04

Wiry strong prospect who has yet to make full season debut, but possesses nice tools. Should grow into above average power thanks to plus bat speed; can hit for BA with controlled stroke. Can be too overzealous at plate and rarely walks. Needs to improve routes and arm in LF.

Delmonico,Nick — 35 — Milwaukee

EXP MLB DEBUT: 2016 | H/W: 6-2 200 | FUT: Starting 3B | 6C

Bats L Age 22
2011 (6) HS (TN)

- Pwr +++
- BAvg ++
- Spd ++
- Def ++

Year	Lev	Team	AB	R	H	HR	RBI	Avg	OB	Slg	OPS	bb%	ct%	Eye	SB	CS	x/h%	Iso	RC/G
2012	A	Delmarva	338	49	84	11	54	249	340	411	752	12	78	0.64	8	1	39	163	4.97
2013	A+	Brevard Cnty	72	8	14	0	9	194	310	278	587	14	71	0.57	2	1	36	83	2.98
2013	A+	Frederick	226	33	55	13	30	243	347	469	816	14	74	0.61	5	1	45	226	5.80
2014	A+	Brevard Cnty	141	11	37	4	15	262	297	404	702	5	76	0.21	2	2	32	142	3.95

Strong LHH has good raw power, but it has yet to translate to game action. Understands strike zone, but making consistent contact has been an issue. Has strong wrists and good bat speed. Needs to improve pitch recognition. Instinctual baserunner, but below avg speed.

Demeritte,Travis — 45 — Texas

EXP MLB DEBUT: 2017 | H/W: 6-0 178 | FUT: Starting 2B/3B | 8D

Bats R Age 20
2013 (1) HS (GA)

- Pwr ++++
- BAvg ++
- Spd +++
- Def ++

Year	Lev	Team	AB	R	H	HR	RBI	Avg	OB	Slg	OPS	bb%	ct%	Eye	SB	CS	x/h%	Iso	RC/G
2013	Rk	AZL Rangers	144	31	41	4	20	285	405	444	849	17	66	0.59	5	1	29	160	6.92
2014	A	Hickory	398	77	84	25	66	211	299	450	749	11	57	0.29	6	2	51	239	5.49

Strong INF who led SAL in HR, but finished 2nd in Ks. Mostly played 2B in position change and has arm strength for any spot. Works counts to find good pitches to drive and couples bat speed with strength to create plus pop. K rate is significant concern and may struggle to hit for BA.

DeShields,Delino — 478 — Texas

EXP MLB DEBUT: 2015 | H/W: 5-9 210 | FUT: Starting 2B/OF | 7C

Bats R Age 22
2010 (1) HS (GA)

- Pwr ++
- BAvg ++
- Spd ++++
- Def ++

Year	Lev	Team	AB	R	H	HR	RBI	Avg	OB	Slg	OPS	bb%	ct%	Eye	SB	CS	x/h%	Iso	RC/G
2011	A	Lexington	469	73	103	9	48	220	298	322	619	10	75	0.44	30	11	27	102	3.14
2012	A	Lexington	440	96	131	10	52	298	394	439	833	14	75	0.65	83	14	28	141	6.21
2012	A+	Lancaster	97	17	23	2	9	237	327	381	709	12	76	0.57	18	5	30	144	4.48
2013	A+	Lancaster	451	100	143	5	54	317	394	468	862	11	80	0.63	51	18	31	151	6.49
2014	AA	Corpus Christi	411	75	97	11	57	236	335	360	695	13	73	0.54	54	14	28	124	4.25

Rangy, fast OF who led TL in SB despite missing time after HBP in face. Selected in Rule 5 draft. Improving CF defender with plus range, though arm is a bit short. Speed is best tool and uses patient approach to get on base. Swings hard and has inconsistent pop, but has good strength. Can sell out for power.

Devers,Rafael — 5 — Boston

EXP MLB DEBUT: 2018 | H/W: 6-0 200 | FUT: Starting 3B | 9D

Bats L Age 18
2013 FA (DR)

- Pwr ++++
- BAvg +++
- Spd ++
- Def ++

Year	Lev	Team	AB	R	H	HR	RBI	Avg	OB	Slg	OPS	bb%	ct%	Eye	SB	CS	x/h%	Iso	RC/G
2014	Rk	DSL Red Sox	104	26	35	3	21	337	448	538	986	17	81	1.05	4	1	34	202	8.32
2014	Rk	GCL Red Sox	157	21	49	4	36	312	368	484	852	8	81	0.47	1	0	35	172	6.07

Strong, gifted 3B who had success in first year in U.S. Smooth lefty swing hits hard line drives to gaps and has plus-plus raw power. Generates easy bat speed with solid strength. Uses advanced approach and reads pitches well. Can make careless errors, but has right tools to stick at 3B.

Diaz,Elias — 2 — Pittsburgh

EXP MLB DEBUT: 2015 | H/W: 6-1 175 | FUT: Starting C | 7B

Bats R Age 24
2008 FA (Venezuela)

- Pwr ++
- BAvg +++
- Spd ++
- Def ++++

Year	Lev	Team	AB	R	H	HR	RBI	Avg	OB	Slg	OPS	bb%	ct%	Eye	SB	CS	x/h%	Iso	RC/G
2011	A	West Virginia	326	38	72	2	45	221	272	328	600	7	79	0.33	6	1	39	107	2.93
2012	A	West Virginia	313	32	65	3	26	208	260	288	547	7	84	0.43	2	2	28	80	2.33
2013	A+	Bradenton	183	30	51	2	15	279	383	399	782	14	82	0.94	4	4	31	120	5.64
2014	AA	Altoona	326	41	107	6	54	328	385	445	830	8	84	0.59	3	2	24	117	5.76
2014	AAA	Indianapolis	33	4	5	0	0	152	222	182	404	8	82	0.50	0	1	20	30	0.62

Breakout season, hitting .328 with good contact ability and good plate discipline. Continues to improve defensively and threw out 33% of baserunners. Not much power, but should be able to hit for average and has developed into on of the better defensive backstops in the minors.

Diaz,Isan — 6 — Arizona

EXP MLB DEBUT: 2018 | H/W: 5-10 185 | FUT: Starting SS | 7D

Bats L Age 18
2014 (S-2) HS (MA)

- Pwr +++
- BAvg ++
- Spd ++
- Def ++

Year	Lev	Team	AB	R	H	HR	RBI	Avg	OB	Slg	OPS	bb%	ct%	Eye	SB	CS	x/h%	Iso	RC/G
2014	Rk	AZL Dbacks	182	22	34	3	21	187	285	330	615	12	69	0.45	6	5	44	143	3.23

Struggled in his debut, hitting just .187 with 56 K in only 182 AB. Runs well with good range at SS, but his actions might work better at 2B. Should develop moderate power as he matures, but lots of work to do here.

Dickerson,Alex — 39 — San Diego

EXP MLB DEBUT: 2015 | H/W: 6-3 230 | FUT: Starting RF | 8D

Bats L Age 24
2011 (3) Indiana
Pwr ++++
BAvg +++
Spd ++
Def ++

Year	Lev	Team	AB	R	H	HR	RBI	Avg	OB	Slg	OPS	bb%	ct%	Eye	SB	CS	x/h%	Iso	RC/G
2012	A+	Bradenton	488	65	144	13	90	295	347	451	798	7	81	0.42	12	7	33	156	5.32
2013	AA	Altoona	451	61	130	17	68	288	328	494	823	6	80	0.30	10	7	43	206	5.51
2014	Rk	AZL Padres	14	3	4	0	0	286	286	643	929	0	79	0.00	0	0	75	357	7.19
2014	A-	Eugene	10	3	3	0	2	300	462	400	862	23	80	1.50	0	0	33	100	7.22
2014	AA	San Antonio	137	20	44	3	24	321	363	496	859	6	80	0.32	0	1	36	175	6.09

Broken ankle limited him to 161 AB. Has a smooth LH stroke, but can be overly aggressive as he hunts for power. At his best when he uses the whole field; not likely to hit for both power and average. Avg runner, he covers ground in RF with a decent arm.

Dickson,O'Koyea — 3 — Los Angeles (N)

EXP MLB DEBUT: 2015 | H/W: 5-11 215 | FUT: Backup 1B | 6B

Bats R Age 25
2011 (12) Sonoma State
Pwr +++
BAvg ++
Spd ++
Def ++

Year	Lev	Team	AB	R	H	HR	RBI	Avg	OB	Slg	OPS	bb%	ct%	Eye	SB	CS	x/h%	Iso	RC/G
2011	NCAA	Sonoma State	214	61	73	11	52	341	431	565	997	14	88	1.36	9	2	34	224	7.94
2011	Rk	Ogden	189	33	63	13	38	333	394	603	997	9	77	0.43	1	1	38	270	7.85
2012	A	Great Lakes	386	63	105	17	48	272	350	479	829	11	83	0.71	11	6	43	207	5.81
2013	A+	Rancho Cuca	468	68	131	15	88	280	322	457	779	6	85	0.43	4	2	38	177	4.99
2014	AA	Chattanooga	461	71	124	17	73	269	325	471	795	8	85	0.57	5	6	45	202	5.29

Short, stocky 1B prospect has plus raw power and good plate coverage. Solid, balanced approach at the plate allows him to hit for both average and power. Slightly below average runner and defender, limited to 1B and likely a back-up bench player with some power.

Difo,Wilmer — 6 — Washington

EXP MLB DEBUT: 2017 | H/W: 6-0 175 | FUT: Starting SS | 8C

Bats B Age 23
2012 FA (DR)
Pwr +++
BAvg +++
Spd ++++
Def +++

Year	Lev	Team	AB	R	H	HR	RBI	Avg	OB	Slg	OPS	bb%	ct%	Eye	SB	CS	x/h%	Iso	RC/G
2013	Rk	GCL Nationals	19	6	4	1	3	211	348	421	769	17	84	1.33	2	0	50	211	5.39
2013	A-	Auburn	120	15	26	1	6	217	277	333	610	8	86	0.59	3	2	31	117	3.27
2013	A	Hagerstown	50	7	11	2	11	220	291	380	671	9	74	0.38	4	1	36	160	3.68
2013	A+	Potomac	18	2	4	0	1	222	300	278	578	10	83	0.67	0	1	25	56	2.91
2014	A	Hagerstown	559	91	176	14	90	315	357	470	828	6	88	0.57	49	9	30	156	5.60

Pop-up prospect with outstanding season in Low-A. Speed heads the list, but biggest surprise was his power. Controls the strike zone from both sides of the plate; has smooth SS actions and enough arm. Some question whether power will play as he ascends the ladder, but shows hitting acumen and athleticism.

Dosch,Drew — 5 — Baltimore

EXP MLB DEBUT: 2017 | H/W: 6-2 200 | FUT: Starting 3B | 7D

Bats L Age 22
2013 (7) Youngstown State
Pwr ++
BAvg +++
Spd ++
Def +++

Year	Lev	Team	AB	R	H	HR	RBI	Avg	OB	Slg	OPS	bb%	ct%	Eye	SB	CS	x/h%	Iso	RC/G
2011	NCAA	Youngstown St	145	15	38	0	11	262	327	269	596	9	88	0.82	5	2	3	7	3.15
2012	NCAA	Youngstown St	224	36	79	8	42	353	413	527	940	9	91	1.10	5	2	28	174	7.02
2013	NCAA	Youngstown St	201	40	68	3	30	338	439	488	926	15	88	1.44	3	3	31	149	7.44
2014	A	Delmarva	500	76	157	5	50	314	373	404	777	9	81	0.48	5	3	20	90	5.17

Pure-hitting INF with smooth swing and barrel awareness. Not much power projection despite natural bat speed and strength as he owns flat swing path. Puts bat to ball with ease and works counts to get on base. Lacks agility, but makes routine plays with solid-average arm strength.

Dozier,Hunter — 5 — Kansas City

EXP MLB DEBUT: 2015 | H/W: 6-4 220 | FUT: Starting 3B | 8B

Bats R Age 23
2013 (1) Stephen F. Austin
Pwr +++
BAvg +++
Spd +++
Def +++

Year	Lev	Team	AB	R	H	HR	RBI	Avg	OB	Slg	OPS	bb%	ct%	Eye	SB	CS	x/h%	Iso	RC/G
2013	NCAA	StephenF.Austin	212	47	84	17	52	396	480	755	1234	14	83	0.97	12	5	50	358	10.84
2013	Rk	Idaho Falls	218	43	66	7	43	303	399	509	908	14	85	1.09	3	1	47	206	7.07
2013	A	Lexington	55	6	18	0	9	327	362	436	798	5	91	0.60	0	0	33	109	5.36
2014	A+	Wilmington	224	36	66	4	39	295	390	429	819	14	75	0.63	7	3	33	134	6.06
2014	AA	NW Arkansas	234	33	49	4	21	209	302	312	614	12	70	0.44	3	2	33	103	3.12

Tall, advanced INF with terrific approach, bat control, plate coverage, and raw pop. Recognizes pitches with aplomb and can hit for both BA and power. Draws walks with selective eye and is smart baserunner with average speed. Sufficient defender at 3B with ample range and strong arm.

Drury,Brandon — 5 — Arizona

EXP MLB DEBUT: 2015 | H/W: 6-2 190 | FUT: Starting 3B | 8D

Bats R Age 22
2010 (13) HS (OR)
Pwr ++++
BAvg +++
Spd ++
Def ++

Year	Lev	Team	AB	R	H	HR	RBI	Avg	OB	Slg	OPS	bb%	ct%	Eye	SB	CS	x/h%	Iso	RC/G
2011	Rk	Danville	265	40	92	8	54	347	362	525	886	2	87	0.17	3	0	34	177	5.95
2012	A	Rome	445	47	102	6	51	229	262	333	595	4	84	0.27	3	4	30	103	2.76
2013	A	South Bend	526	78	159	15	85	302	360	500	860	8	83	0.51	1	1	44	198	6.16
2014	A+	Visalia	430	73	129	19	81	300	361	519	880	9	82	0.54	4	3	43	219	6.33
2014	AA	Mobile	105	12	31	4	14	295	339	476	815	6	82	0.37	0	0	35	181	5.39

Has a simple, balanced stroke that allows him to drive balls into the gaps and over the fence. Destroys LHP, but also holds his own vs. RHP. Continues to improve defensively and now projects to be at least average with good hands and a strong arm. Speed is not a part of his game.

Duenez,Samir — 3 — Kansas City

EXP MLB DEBUT: 2018 | H/W: 6-1 195 | FUT: Starting 1B/LF | 7C

Bats L Age 18
2012 FA (Venezuela)
Pwr ++
BAvg +++
Spd ++
Def ++

Year	Lev	Team	AB	R	H	HR	RBI	Avg	OB	Slg	OPS	bb%	ct%	Eye	SB	CS	x/h%	Iso	RC/G
2013	Rk	AZL Royals	187	26	55	0	19	294	337	380	716	6	86	0.44	6	4	25	86	4.40
2014	Rk	Idaho Falls	135	16	41	1	27	304	352	393	744	7	85	0.50	4	2	22	89	4.71
2014	A	Lexington	142	12	33	0	9	232	268	324	592	5	87	0.37	2	1	33	92	2.94

Natural hitting 1B who was demoted to rookie ball after struggles in Low-A. Has ability to hit to all fields with plus bat speed and bat control. Offers some power potential, but focuses more on contact. Needs to add strength and could stand to be more selective. Lacks foot speed and agility.

Duffy,Matt — 6 — San Francisco

EXP MLB DEBUT: 2014 | H/W: 6-2 170 | FUT: Utility IF | 7C

Bats R Age 24
2012 (8) Long Beach State
Pwr +
BAvg +++
Spd +++
Def ++

Year	Lev	Team	AB	R	H	HR	RBI	Avg	OB	Slg	OPS	bb%	ct%	Eye	SB	CS	x/h%	Iso	RC/G
2012	A-	Salem-Kaizer	182	31	45	1	16	247	341	286	627	13	88	1.18	10	1	11	38	3.73
2013	A	Augusta	287	48	88	4	43	307	401	418	819	14	86	1.10	22	6	24	111	6.01
2013	A+	San Jose	106	17	31	5	14	292	336	509	846	6	85	0.44	3	1	39	217	5.72
2014	AA	Richmond	367	53	122	3	62	332	401	444	845	10	82	0.64	20	4	25	112	6.16
2014	MLB	SF Giants	60	5	16	0	8	267	279	300	579	2	77	0.07	0	1	13	33	2.26

Duffy put up another impressive season in 2014, getting a quick taste of the bigs the finish the season. He has good bat speed, making consistent contact with gap power and decent plate discipline. He is a smart base runner, capable of 10+ SB in a full time role. He isn't a standout at SS, but will not be a liability, either.

Dugan,Kelly — 9 — Philadelphia

EXP MLB DEBUT: 2015 | H/W: 6-3 215 | FUT: Starting RF | 7B

Bats L Age 24
2009 (2) HS (CA)
Pwr +++
BAvg ++
Spd +
Def +++

Year	Lev	Team	AB	R	H	HR	RBI	Avg	OB	Slg	OPS	bb%	ct%	Eye	SB	CS	x/h%	Iso	RC/G
2011	A-	Williamsport	176	25	50	2	21	284	337	386	723	7	81	0.41	6	0	20	102	4.45
2012	A	Lakewood	430	83	129	12	60	300	370	470	840	10	72	0.39	5	1	36	170	6.23
2013	A+	Clearwater	217	37	69	10	36	318	386	539	925	10	72	0.40	1	3	36	221	7.28
2013	AA	Reading	212	25	56	10	23	264	281	472	753	2	75	0.09	0	1	41	208	4.46
2014	AA	Reading	253	43	75	5	34	296	367	435	801	10	78	0.50	1	0	32	138	5.57

Often overlooked due to lack of loud tools and recurring injury troubles, he has been a quiet producer when on the field. Knows the strike zone, hits for average and a bit of power, a solid defender with above-average arm. A high-floor, low-ceiling type.

Duvall,Adam — 5 — San Francisco

EXP MLB DEBUT: 2014 | H/W: 6-1 205 | FUT: Backup 3B | 6C

Bats R Age 26
2010 (11) Louisville
Pwr ++++
BAvg ++
Spd +
Def ++

Year	Lev	Team	AB	R	H	HR	RBI	Avg	OB	Slg	OPS	bb%	ct%	Eye	SB	CS	x/h%	Iso	RC/G
2011	A	Augusta	431	69	123	22	87	285	371	527	898	12	77	0.60	4	4	46	241	6.83
2012	A+	San Jose	534	101	138	30	100	258	318	487	805	8	78	0.41	8	2	42	228	5.33
2013	AA	Richmond	385	61	97	17	58	252	314	465	779	8	81	0.49	2	1	45	213	5.09
2014	AAA	Fresno	359	67	107	27	90	298	352	599	951	8	77	0.37	2	0	48	301	7.14
2014	MLB	SF Giants	73	8	14	3	5	192	224	342	566	4	73	0.15	0	0	36	151	2.03

Big, strong 3B continued his minor league power surge in AAA hitting 27 HR, getting a cup of coffee in '14. Aside from plus power, he is slightly below average across the board. Respectable ct%, but strikes out a lot and won't hit for BA. Limited to a corner position and runs below average. Power off the bench is an asset.

Eaves,Kody — 4 — Los Angeles (A)

EXP MLB DEBUT: 2017 | H/W: 6-0 175 | FUT: Utility player | 6B

Bats L Age 21
2012 (16) HS (TX)
Pwr ++
BAvg ++
Spd +++
Def +++

Year	Lev	Team	AB	R	H	HR	RBI	Avg	OB	Slg	OPS	bb%	ct%	Eye	SB	CS	x/h%	Iso	RC/G
2012	Rk	AZL Angels	165	25	43	2	19	261	326	400	726	9	79	0.47	6	0	33	139	4.62
2013	Rk	Orem	264	45	73	1	24	277	327	386	714	7	85	0.50	22	6	29	110	4.44
2014	A	Burlington	549	74	147	10	45	268	304	415	720	5	74	0.20	25	10	37	148	4.33

Instinctual, smart INF who has been steady performer. Maximizes average tools with grinder approach. Tweaked swing to leverage natural strength, though power doesn't project well. Swings and misses a lot and can bail against LHP. Runs bases well and ranges to both sides at 2B.

Eibner,Brett — 89 — Kansas City
EXP MLB DEBUT: 2015 | H/W: 6-3 195 | FUT: Starting OF | 7D

Bats R Age 26 — 2010 (2) Arkansas

Skill	Rating	Year	Lev	Team	AB	R	H	HR	RBI	Avg	OB	Slg	OPS	bb%	ct%	Eye	SB	CS	x/h%	Iso	RC/G
		2011	A	Kane County	272	46	58	12	31	213	331	408	739	15	67	0.53	2	3	47	195	4.99
Pwr	++++	2012	A+	Wilmington	423	60	83	15	53	196	292	388	679	12	61	0.35	5	2	55	191	4.29
BAvg	++	2013	AA	NW Arkansas	441	74	107	19	41	243	324	451	775	11	66	0.36	7	3	42	209	5.47
Spd	++	2014	A+	Wilmington	41	5	9	1	3	220	373	366	738	20	61	0.63	3	2	44	146	5.46
Def	+++	2014	AAA	Omaha	274	42	66	7	27	241	316	380	695	10	72	0.38	5	2	33	139	4.17

Powerful OF who missed significant time during season. Vicious swing results in Ks, though the trade-off is plus power to all fields. Runs well for size and gets on base consistently. Can play CF, but projects better in RF where arm stands out. Very low BA due to poor plate coverage.

Elander,Josh — 7 — Atlanta
EXP MLB DEBUT: 2016 | H/W: 6-1 220 | FUT: Starting LF | 7D

Bats R Age 24 — 2012 (6) TCU

Skill	Rating	Year	Lev	Team	AB	R	H	HR	RBI	Avg	OB	Slg	OPS	bb%	ct%	Eye	SB	CS	x/h%	Iso	RC/G
		2012	NCAA	Texas Christian	223	56	70	11	43	314	423	525	947	16	80	0.95	14	7	34	211	7.59
Pwr	+++	2012	Rk	Danville	123	19	32	4	19	260	345	439	784	12	85	0.84	3	1	38	179	5.40
BAvg	+++	2013	A	Rome	280	47	89	11	61	318	382	536	918	9	78	0.48	6	2	40	218	6.97
Spd	++	2013	A+	Lynchburg	221	28	58	4	32	262	340	371	711	11	78	0.54	3	1	28	109	4.41
Def	++	2014	A+	Lynchburg	137	19	30	2	21	219	318	328	647	13	77	0.63	6	0	37	109	3.71

Was limited by a nagging shoulder injury. Continues to make the transition from behind the plate. Prior to the injury, showed impressive power and he squares the ball up well, but remains a below average runner and defender. Has above-average power, but owns no other plus tool.

Elizalde,Sebastian — 79 — Cincinnati
EXP MLB DEBUT: 2017 | H/W: 6-0 175 | FUT: Starting OF | 7C

Bats L Age 23 — 2013 FA (Mexico)

Skill	Rating	Year	Lev	Team	AB	R	H	HR	RBI	Avg	OB	Slg	OPS	bb%	ct%	Eye	SB	CS	x/h%	Iso	RC/G
		2011	MEX	Monterrey	36	8	11	1	5	306	342	472	814	5	83	0.33	0	0	36	167	5.37
Pwr	+++	2012	MEX	Monterrey	134	25	37	2	14	276	349	448	797	10	72	0.41	7	3	41	172	5.75
BAvg	+++	2013	MEX	Monterrey	116	24	38	3	10	328	355	448	804	4	81	0.23	5	3	21	121	5.11
Spd	++++	2014	A	Dayton	183	29	57	7	34	311	438	503	940	18	74	0.85	9	10	35	191	7.90
Def	+++	2014	A+	Bakersfield	243	35	66	9	37	272	324	461	785	7	82	0.43	10	7	41	189	5.12

Signed as older international prospect and held his own during U.S. debut. Shows solid plate approach and advanced knowledge of hitting. Still learning to read breaking balls. Has plus speed but hasn't yet mastered stealing bases. Can play all three outfield positions well. Solid all-around player.

Engel,Adam — 8 — Chicago (A)
EXP MLB DEBUT: 2016 | H/W: 6-1 215 | FUT: Starting CF | 7C

Bats R Age 23 — 2013 (19) Louisville

Skill	Rating	Year	Lev	Team	AB	R	H	HR	RBI	Avg	OB	Slg	OPS	bb%	ct%	Eye	SB	CS	x/h%	Iso	RC/G
		2013	NCAA	Louisville	246	51	58	1	28	236	324	301	625	12	86	0.91	41	13	21	65	3.61
Pwr	++	2013	Rk	Great Falls	239	44	72	3	30	301	358	414	772	8	86	0.62	31	8	25	113	5.11
BAvg	+++	2014	Rk	AZL White Sox	33	6	12	1	3	364	417	727	1144	8	82	0.50	2	0	58	364	9.90
Spd	++++	2014	A	Kannapolis	307	54	80	6	30	261	324	410	735	9	72	0.34	28	11	34	150	4.75
Def	+++	2014	A+	Winston-Salem	88	11	21	0	5	239	287	239	526	6	76	0.29	9	1	0	0	1.76

Plus athlete who relies on speed and defense to add value. Offers strength, but instead focuses on bat-to-ball and using legs to get on base. Can flail at breaking balls and may not have enough bat speed to hit for BA. Owns instincts and range in CF while arm strength is fringy at best.

Ervin,Phillip — 89 — Cincinnati
EXP MLB DEBUT: 2017 | H/W: 5-10 205 | FUT: Starting OF | 9E

Bats R Age 22 — 2013 (1) Samford

Skill	Rating	Year	Lev	Team	AB	R	H	HR	RBI	Avg	OB	Slg	OPS	bb%	ct%	Eye	SB	CS	x/h%	Iso	RC/G
		2012	NCAA	Samford	260	55	85	10	52	327	382	519	901	8	85	0.59	16	5	34	192	6.52
Pwr	+++	2013	NCAA	Samford	196	58	66	11	40	337	447	597	1044	17	87	1.56	21	2	41	260	8.71
BAvg	+++	2013	Rk	Billings	129	27	42	8	29	326	404	597	1001	12	81	0.71	12	0	43	271	7.94
Spd	++++	2013	A	Dayton	43	7	15	1	6	349	451	465	916	16	77	0.80	2	1	20	116	7.37
Def	++++	2014	A	Dayton	498	68	118	7	68	237	301	376	677	8	78	0.42	30	5	41	139	3.96

2014 was a significant setback. Regression in OBP and approach concerning, but could be result of offseason wrist surgery. Showed glimpses of pre-surgery tools, but no consistency. Given age and experience, needs a rebound 2015. Improved outfield defense and did nice job on basepaths.

Escobar,Elvis — 79 — Pittsburgh
EXP MLB DEBUT: 2017 | H/W: 5-10 180 | FUT: Starting CF | 7D

Bats L Age 20 — 2011 FA (Venezuela)

Skill	Rating	Year	Lev	Team	AB	R	H	HR	RBI	Avg	OB	Slg	OPS	bb%	ct%	Eye	SB	CS	x/h%	Iso	RC/G
Pwr	+	2012	Rk	GCL Pirates	190	29	52	2	18	274	337	374	710	9	76	0.39	6	5	21	100	4.36
BAvg	+++	2013	A-	Jamestown	183	25	49	1	23	268	302	350	652	5	74	0.19	9	4	22	82	3.41
Spd	+++	2014	A-	Jamestown	146	18	40	1	9	274	321	349	670	6	81	0.36	6	3	20	75	3.73
Def	+++	2014	A	West Virginia	200	18	42	2	29	210	237	315	552	3	73	0.13	3	2	36	105	2.03

Showed some signs of progress in 2014. Started the year at Low-A, but hit just .210 and was sent to short-season ball, where he fared better. Made more consistent contact and played CF all season. Struggles mightily vs. LHP, hitting just .157 with 28 K in 84 AB.

Estrada,Thairo — 6 — New York (A)
EXP MLB DEBUT: 2018 | H/W: 5-10 155 | FUT: Starting 2B/SS | 7D

Bats R Age 19 — 2012 FA (Venezuela)

Skill	Rating	Year	Lev	Team	AB	R	H	HR	RBI	Avg	OB	Slg	OPS	bb%	ct%	Eye	SB	CS	x/h%	Iso	RC/G
Pwr	++																				
BAvg	+++	2013	Rk	GCL Yankees 2	176	28	49	2	17	278	324	432	756	6	83	0.40	7	5	37	153	4.89
Spd	+++	2014	Rk	GCL Yankees	22	2	6	0	4	273	304	364	668	4	82	0.25	0	0	33	91	3.69
Def	+++	2014	A-	Staten Island	59	11	16	0	2	271	338	288	627	9	88	0.86	8	1	6	17	3.53

Quick, advanced INF with requisite hands, feet, and arm for middle infield. Positions himself well and makes all routine plays. Has short stroke to put ball in play and rarely fans. Very limited power outlook as he has small frame with poor strength. Runs extremely well and steals bases.

Evans,Zane — 2 — Kansas City
EXP MLB DEBUT: 2016 | H/W: 6-2 205 | FUT: Starting C | 7D

Bats R Age 23 — 2013 (4) Georgia Tech

Skill	Rating	Year	Lev	Team	AB	R	H	HR	RBI	Avg	OB	Slg	OPS	bb%	ct%	Eye	SB	CS	x/h%	Iso	RC/G
		2011	NCAA	Georgia Tech	226	34	61	5	46	270	329	398	727	8	77	0.38	2	0	31	128	4.49
Pwr	+++	2012	NCAA	Georgia Tech	224	34	66	4	51	295	363	433	796	10	80	0.53	1	0	33	138	5.49
BAvg	+++	2013	NCAA	Georgia Tech	244	47	88	14	66	361	437	590	1027	12	84	0.83	0	1	31	230	8.20
Spd	+	2013	Rk	Idaho Falls	162	26	57	4	31	352	393	537	930	6	85	0.44	1	0	39	185	6.85
Def	++	2014	A+	Wilmington	371	34	84	5	36	226	279	332	610	7	75	0.29	2	1	35	105	2.94

Large-framed C who was aggressively placed at High-A. Has potential to be average behind plate, but needs better footwork and release. Can be free-swinger at plate and doesn't recognize spin well. Offers average pop and can hit for BA due to compact stroke and use of entire field.

Fargas,Johneshwy — 8 — San Francisco
EXP MLB DEBUT: 2017 | H/W: 6-1 165 | FUT: Starting OF | 8E

Bats R Age 20 — 2013 (11) HS (PR)

Skill	Rating	Year	Lev	Team	AB	R	H	HR	RBI	Avg	OB	Slg	OPS	bb%	ct%	Eye	SB	CS	x/h%	Iso	RC/G
Pwr	++																				
BAvg	+++																				
Spd	++++	2013	Rk	AZL Giants	77	21	23	0	2	299	372	351	723	10	86	0.82	8	3	17	52	4.71
Def	+++	2014	A-	Salem-Kaizer	167	33	40	3	13	240	335	329	664	13	84	0.89	15	6	23	90	4.00

Lanky speedster controls zone extremely well, drawing BBs and barreling the ball at an above average rate. Plus bat speed makes up for his long swing now, but he will have to tone it down or Ks will follow. His wiry frame contributes to his plus SB potential and good range in the OF where his arm plays average.

Farmer,Kyle — 2 — Los Angeles (N)
EXP MLB DEBUT: 2017 | H/W: 6-0 200 | FUT: Starting C | 7D

Bats R Age 24 — 2013 (8) Georgia

Skill	Rating	Year	Lev	Team	AB	R	H	HR	RBI	Avg	OB	Slg	OPS	bb%	ct%	Eye	SB	CS	x/h%	Iso	RC/G
		2012	NCAA	Georgia	245	35	74	4	41	302	324	453	777	3	89	0.31	3	0	35	151	4.91
Pwr	++	2013	NCAA	Georgia	210	26	61	3	44	290	329	410	738	5	94	1.00	0	2	28	119	4.72
BAvg	+++	2013	Rk	Ogden	167	37	58	4	36	347	374	533	906	4	87	0.33	1	1	40	186	6.38
Spd	++	2014	A	Great Lakes	229	25	71	2	35	310	352	441	794	6	90	0.63	9	3	31	131	5.33
Def	+++	2014	A+	Rancho Cuca	130	8	31	0	15	238	293	292	585	7	78	0.36	2	0	19	54	2.71

Collegiate SS was converted to C and made steady progress behind the plate, hitting well and proving he can handle the position. Nailed 32% of baserunners, but still has work to do. Barrels the ball well and makes decent contact. A work in progress, but one that is worth watching.

Featherston,Taylor — 46 — Los Angeles (A)
EXP MLB DEBUT: 2017 | H/W: 6-1 185 | FUT: Utility INF | 6C

Bats R Age 25 — 2011 (5) TCU

Skill	Rating	Year	Lev	Team	AB	R	H	HR	RBI	Avg	OB	Slg	OPS	bb%	ct%	Eye	SB	CS	x/h%	Iso	RC/G
		2011	NCAA	Texas Christian	245	53	82	3	42	335	380	457	837	7	87	0.56	6	5	24	122	5.80
Pwr	+++	2011	A-	Tri-City	169	19	39	2	20	231	301	349	650	9	78	0.45	3	1	33	118	3.63
BAvg	++	2012	A	Asheville	378	75	113	12	53	299	385	495	880	12	77	0.61	15	4	41	196	6.73
Spd	+++	2013	A+	Modesto	469	87	137	13	81	292	335	484	819	6	77	0.27	17	4	39	192	5.62
Def	++	2014	AA	Tulsa	497	69	129	16	57	260	312	439	751	7	77	0.33	14	6	41	179	4.73

Strong, offensive-minded SS was taken by the Angels in the Rule 5 draft. He has offensive potential and above-average speed. Makes consistent contact, but sells out plate discipline for power. Strong arm with good range and should be able to stick at 2B with 15-20 HR potential.

Fields,Daniel — 78 — Detroit

EXP MLB DEBUT: 2015 | H/W: 6-2 215 | FUT: Starting OF | 7D

Bats R Age 24
2009 (6) HS (MI)
Pwr +++
BAvg ++
Spd +++
Def +++

Year	Lev	Team	AB	R	H	HR	RBI	Avg	OB	Slg	OPS	bb%	ct%	Eye	SB	CS	x/h%	Iso	RC/G
2012	AA	Erie	106	13	28	2	7	264	345	358	703	11	80	0.62	9	1	21	94	4.31
2013	AA	Erie	457	71	130	10	58	284	349	435	784	9	72	0.35	24	7	33	151	5.43
2014	Rk	GCL Tigers	6	2	1	0	0	167	167	333	500	0	67	0.00	0	0	100	167	1.47
2014	AA	Erie	28	4	8	0	9	286	412	464	876	18	75	0.86	2	0	50	179	7.30
2014	AAA	Toledo	274	29	60	6	26	219	260	343	603	5	72	0.20	8	2	32	124	2.71

Athletic, strong OF whose tools exceed performance. Uppercut stroke leads to Ks and aggressive approach results in low OBP. BA in question, though has plus bat speed and uses entire field. Has become stellar defender who takes direct routes and has strong arm, but better in corner.

Fields,Roemon — 8 — Toronto

EXP MLB DEBUT: 2017 | H/W: 5-11 185 | FUT: Reserve OF | 7D

Bats L Age 24
2013 FA (Bethany Col)
Pwr +
BAvg ++
Spd +++++
Def ++++

Year	Lev	Team	AB	R	H	HR	RBI	Avg	OB	Slg	OPS	bb%	ct%	Eye	SB	CS	x/h%	Iso	RC/G
2014	A-	Vancouver	294	64	79	1	26	269	330	350	681	8	79	0.44	48	9	23	82	4.01

Short, lean OF who has as much speed as any in minors. Steals bases easily and has decent instincts and jumps. Can hit LHP with simple stroke and likes to use entire field. Not a strong bunter and will not hit for much pop. Has strength to drive balls to gaps. Gifted CF with great range.

Fish,Mike — 789 — Los Angeles (A)

EXP MLB DEBUT: 2017 | H/W: 6-1 190 | FUT: Reserve OF | 7E

Bats R Age 24
2013 (32) Siena
Pwr +++
BAvg ++
Spd +++
Def ++

Year	Lev	Team	AB	R	H	HR	RBI	Avg	OB	Slg	OPS	bb%	ct%	Eye	SB	CS	x/h%	Iso	RC/G
2012	NCAA	Siena Col	105	18	32	3	11	305	348	448	796	6	90	0.64	3	0	28	143	5.21
2013	NCAA	Siena Col	231	55	84	12	51	364	414	602	1016	8	90	0.87	14	2	36	238	7.72
2013	Rk	AZL Angels	66	19	27	2	9	409	451	712	1163	7	79	0.36	6	0	52	303	10.12
2013	Rk	Orem	98	27	33	7	33	337	381	673	1054	7	84	0.44	1	2	52	337	8.21
2014	A	Burlington	428	51	108	9	57	252	301	402	703	7	82	0.38	8	3	37	150	4.16

Aggressive OF who faded down stretch. Makes easy contact with simple swing and possesses good speed. Pitch selection needs attention and can be pull-conscious. Quick wrists produce bat speed and average pop. Can play all OF positions, though best in LF with solid average arm.

Fisher,Derek — 7 — Houston

EXP MLB DEBUT: 2017 | H/W: 6-1 205 | FUT: Starting OF | 7B

Bats L Age 21
2014 (1-S) Virginia
Pwr +++
BAvg +++
Spd ++++
Def ++

Year	Lev	Team	AB	R	H	HR	RBI	Avg	OB	Slg	OPS	bb%	ct%	Eye	SB	CS	x/h%	Iso	RC/G
2012	NCAA	Virginia	219	44	63	7	50	288	353	507	860	9	72	0.36	4	5	41	219	6.49
2013	NCAA	Virginia	205	43	60	7	48	293	378	483	861	12	80	0.70	8	3	37	190	6.37
2014	NCAA	Virginia	177	24	46	3	29	260	307	362	668	6	84	0.43	5	3	24	102	3.72
2014	Rk	GCL Astros	3	0	2	0	0	667	750	1000	1750	25	100		0	0	50	333	17.49
2014	A-	Tri City	152	31	46	2	18	303	369	408	777	10	77	0.46	17	4	20	105	5.25

Athletic, strong OF with solid set of tools. Possesses clean, fluid swing and combines disciplined approach with natural strength to project to above average pop. Excellent baserunner with plus speed and ranges well in OF. Relegated to LF with poor arm and unpolished routes to ball.

Flores,Ramon — 789 — New York (A)

EXP MLB DEBUT: 2015 | H/W: 5-10 150 | FUT: Reserve OF | 6A

Bats L Age 23
2008 FA (Venezuela)
Pwr ++
BAvg +++
Spd ++
Def ++

Year	Lev	Team	AB	R	H	HR	RBI	Avg	OB	Slg	OPS	bb%	ct%	Eye	SB	CS	x/h%	Iso	RC/G
2012	AA	Trenton	5	2	2	1	2	400	400	1000	1400	0	100		0	0	50	600	10.25
2013	AA	Trenton	534	79	139	6	55	260	354	363	717	13	82	0.79	7	6	27	103	4.68
2014	Rk	GCL Yankees 2	9	2	3	1	1	333	400	778	1178	10	67	0.33	0	0	67	444	11.18
2014	Rk	GCL Yankees	8	2	3	1	2	375	375	1000	1375	0	75	0.00	0	0	100	625	12.46
2014	AAA	Scranton/WB	235	30	58	7	23	247	340	443	782	12	81	0.73	3	2	48	196	5.45

Short, versatile OF who may not have power to be everyday corner OF, but has plus on base skills and ability to supply line-drive pop. Can play CF, but lacks the speed for effective range. Advancing one level per year and adding strength along way. Can hit LHP and has useful bat.

Fontana,Nolan — 46 — Houston

EXP MLB DEBUT: 2015 | H/W: 5-11 190 | FUT: Utility player | 6B

Bats L Age 23
2012 (2) Florida
Pwr ++
BAvg ++
Spd +++
Def +++

Year	Lev	Team	AB	R	H	HR	RBI	Avg	OB	Slg	OPS	bb%	ct%	Eye	SB	CS	x/h%	Iso	RC/G
2011	NCAA	Florida	256	57	74	5	49	289	409	434	843	17	88	1.73	6	4	30	145	6.54
2012	NCAA	Florida	243	59	69	9	30	284	402	444	847	16	89	1.78	13	1	29	160	6.43
2012	A	Lexington	151	37	34	2	25	225	458	338	796	30	71	1.48	12	2	35	113	6.47
2013	A+	Lancaster	386	88	100	8	60	259	414	399	813	21	74	1.02	16	5	32	140	6.32
2014	AA	Corpus Christi	229	33	60	1	26	262	417	376	793	21	67	0.80	5	8	38	114	6.34

Fundamentally-sound INF who ended season in June after breaking finger. Split time bewteen 2B and SS and makes routine plays despite limited range and average arm. Posts very high OBP due to ultra-patient approach. Not much thunder in bat and struggles to make contact.

Forbes,Tiquan — 56 — Texas

EXP MLB DEBUT: 2019 | H/W: 6-3 180 | FUT: Starting 3B | 9E

Bats R Age 18
2014 (2) HS (MS)
Pwr ++
BAvg ++
Spd ++++
Def +++

Year	Lev	Team	AB	R	H	HR	RBI	Avg	OB	Slg	OPS	bb%	ct%	Eye	SB	CS	x/h%	Iso	RC/G
2014	Rk	AZL Rangers	174	27	42	0	16	241	330	282	612	12	73	0.49	10	1	12	40	3.17

Exciting, lean INF with plus projection. Could evolve into offensive producer once he adds strength. Swings and misses too often and swing path more conducive to gap pop now. Has above average speed which could mean move to CF where arm plays. Split time between 3B and SS.

Franco,Maikel — 5 — Philadelphia

EXP MLB DEBUT: 2014 | H/W: 6-1 180 | FUT: Starting 3B | 9C

Bats R Age 22
2008 FA (DR)
Pwr ++++
BAvg +++
Spd +
Def ++

Year	Lev	Team	AB	R	H	HR	RBI	Avg	OB	Slg	OPS	bb%	ct%	Eye	SB	CS	x/h%	Iso	RC/G
2012	A	Lakewood	503	70	141	14	84	280	331	439	770	7	84	0.48	3	1	35	159	4.96
2013	A+	Clearwater	264	42	79	16	52	299	349	576	924	7	85	0.51	0	0	51	277	6.67
2013	AA	Reading	277	47	94	15	51	339	362	563	926	3	89	0.32	1	2	32	224	6.35
2014	AAA	Lehigh Valley	521	64	134	16	78	257	298	428	726	5	84	0.37	3	1	40	171	4.34
2014	MLB	Philadelphia	56	5	10	0	5	179	193	214	407	2	77	0.08	0	0	20	36	0.13

Triple-A pitchers had their way with him early on, exposing his long swing and impatient approach. A second-half rebound helped his final line, but still gets fooled by offspeed stuff and can be beaten inside. Shows enough in the field to stay at 3B for now. Likely needs more seasoning.

Franklin,Kevin — 3 — Cincinnati

EXP MLB DEBUT: 2017 | H/W: 6-1 220 | FUT: Starting 1B | 7E

Bats R Age 20
2013 (2) HS (CA)
Pwr ++++
BAvg ++
Spd ++
Def ++

Year	Lev	Team	AB	R	H	HR	RBI	Avg	OB	Slg	OPS	bb%	ct%	Eye	SB	CS	x/h%	Iso	RC/G
2013	Rk	AZL Reds	173	17	45	1	25	260	312	364	676	7	69	0.25	1	1	36	104	3.96
2014	Rk	Billings	237	28	50	4	30	211	234	325	559	3	73	0.11	4	1	34	114	2.05

Move from 3B to 1B is off to a successful start. Still very raw with lots of tools, but continues to struggle at the plate. Possesses good bat speed and power potential but easily fooled by off-speed pitches. 65/7 K/BB in 237 AB.

Frazier,Clint — 8 — Cleveland

EXP MLB DEBUT: 2017 | H/W: 6-1 190 | FUT: Starting CF | 9D

Bats R Age 20
2013 (1) HS (GA)
Pwr ++++
BAvg +++
Spd +++
Def ++

Year	Lev	Team	AB	R	H	HR	RBI	Avg	OB	Slg	OPS	bb%	ct%	Eye	SB	CS	x/h%	Iso	RC/G
2013	Rk	AZL Indians	172	32	51	5	28	297	360	506	866	9	65	0.28	3	2	41	209	7.06
2014	A	Lake County	474	70	126	13	50	266	343	411	755	11	66	0.35	12	6	29	146	5.21

Strong OF who got better as season progressed. Finished 3rd in MWL in K, but has plus raw power and BA potential despite swing and miss in game. Exhibits quick, leveraged stroke and draws walks with good eye. Average speed enhances defense and could become average CF.

Fuentes,Reymond — 78 — Kansas City

EXP MLB DEBUT: 2013 | H/W: 6-0 160 | FUT: Starting CF | 7B

Bats L Age 24
2009 (1) HS (PR)
Pwr ++
BAvg +++
Spd ++++
Def ++

Year	Lev	Team	AB	R	H	HR	RBI	Avg	OB	Slg	OPS	bb%	ct%	Eye	SB	CS	x/h%	Iso	RC/G
2013	AA	San Antonio	345	56	109	6	35	316	389	441	829	11	79	0.58	29	10	27	125	5.95
2013	AAA	Tucson	55	17	23	0	8	418	508	491	999	15	82	1.00	6	1	17	73	8.44
2013	MLB	San Diego	33	4	5	0	1	152	222	152	374	8	52	0.19	3	0	0	0	-0.88
2014	AA	San Antonio	170	25	55	4	17	324	382	453	835	9	78	0.43	12	1	22	129	5.86
2014	AAA	El Paso	157	29	41	1	16	261	333	376	709	10	83	0.63	13	2	32	115	4.51

Slender speedster whose power has never really developed. Has shown the ability to hit for average with decent plate discipline, but he doesn't draw enough walks to take advantage of his speed. A below-avg arm makes CF unlikely in the majors and he split time between CF and LF in '15.

Gallagher,Cameron — 2 — Kansas City

EXP MLB DEBUT: 2017 | H/W: 6-3 210 | FUT: Starting C | 7D

Bats R Age 22	Year	Lev	Team	AB	R	H	HR	RBI	Avg	OB	Slg	OPS	bb%	ct%	Eye	SB	CS	x/h%	Iso	RC/G
2011 (2) HS (PA)	2011	Rk	Idaho Falls	30	2	6	1	2	200	273	300	573	9	87	0.75	0	0	17	100	2.70
Pwr ++	2011	Rk	AZL Royals	78	6	11	1	7	141	212	179	391	8	81	0.47	0	0	9	38	0.30
BAvg ++	2012	Rk	Burlington	127	13	35	3	15	276	328	425	754	7	87	0.63	1	3	37	150	4.84
Spd +	2013	A	Lexington	222	19	47	2	18	212	289	306	595	10	87	0.86	0	0	36	95	3.23
Def +++	2014	A+	Wilmington	312	24	71	5	34	228	309	333	643	11	88	0.97	1	0	32	106	3.80

Injury-prone backstop who is solid defender and leader behind plate. Quick release accentuates solid arm. Willing to work counts and get on base while short swing makes easy contact. Set career high in HR, though doesn't project well in BA or power as he lacks load in level path.

Gallo,Joey — 35 — Texas

EXP MLB DEBUT: 2015 | H/W: 6-5 205 | FUT: Starting 3B | 8B

Bats L Age 21	Year	Lev	Team	AB	R	H	HR	RBI	Avg	OB	Slg	OPS	bb%	ct%	Eye	SB	CS	x/h%	Iso	RC/G
2012 (1-S) HS (NV)	2012	A-	Spokane	56	9	12	4	9	214	343	464	808	16	54	0.42	0	0	50	250	6.85
Pwr +++++	2013	Rk	AZL Rangers	19	4	7	2	10	368	429	895	1323	10	63	0.29	1	0	86	526	14.22
BAvg ++	2013	A	Hickory	392	82	96	38	78	245	327	610	937	11	58	0.29	14	1	65	365	8.52
Spd ++	2014	A+	Myrtle Beach	189	53	61	21	50	323	467	735	1202	21	66	0.80	5	3	54	413	12.07
Def ++	2014	AA	Frisco	250	44	58	21	56	232	329	524	853	13	54	0.31	2	0	53	292	7.56

Big, strong hitter who set career high in HR and has best raw power in minors. Plenty of bat speed generates plus-plus pop and willing to draw walks to get on base. Ks will always be issue, but OK trade-off. Trying OF in offseason and has arm for it, but secondary skills are a bit behind.

Garcia,Anthony — 7 — St. Louis

EXP MLB DEBUT: 2016 | H/W: 6-0 180 | FUT: Backup OF | 6C

Bats R Age 23	Year	Lev	Team	AB	R	H	HR	RBI	Avg	OB	Slg	OPS	bb%	ct%	Eye	SB	CS	x/h%	Iso	RC/G
2009 (18) HS (PR)	2011	Rk	Johnson City	182	38	56	6	31	308	379	527	907	10	80	0.58	4	1	43	220	6.91
Pwr +++	2012	A	Quad Cities	396	63	111	19	74	280	337	525	862	8	73	0.32	3	6	50	245	6.32
BAvg ++	2013	Rk	GCL Cardinals	4	0	0	0	0	0	0	0	0	0	75	0.00	0	0		0	-5.26
Spd ++	2013	A+	Palm Beach	345	37	75	13	45	217	272	383	655	7	72	0.27	6	2	40	165	3.42
Def ++	2014	A+	Palm Beach	343	56	78	10	44	227	304	385	689	10	81	0.59	3	4	41	157	4.12

Strong, power-hitting OF continued to scuffle in repeat of High-A. Garcia has plus raw power, but can be overly aggressive. Ball jumps off of his bat when he does make contact. Is a below-average runner and is questionable on defense.

Garcia,Aramis — 2 — San Francisco

EXP MLB DEBUT: 2017 | H/W: 6-2 195 | FUT: Starting C | 8D

Bats R Age 22	Year	Lev	Team	AB	R	H	HR	RBI	Avg	OB	Slg	OPS	bb%	ct%	Eye	SB	CS	x/h%	Iso	RC/G
2014 (2) Florida Intl	2012	NCAA	Florida Intl	192	24	52	6	29	271	336	417	753	9	78	0.44	1	3	29	146	4.81
Pwr +++	2013	NCAA	Florida Intl	224	37	72	11	51	321	369	522	892	7	83	0.44	0	1	32	201	6.28
BAvg +++	2014	NCAA	Florida Intl	163	34	60	8	37	368	452	626	1078	13	86	1.09	4	1	40	258	8.96
Spd ++	2014	Rk	AZL Giants	32	6	7	0	3	219	324	313	637	14	81	0.83	0	0	43	94	3.82
Def ++	2014	A-	Salem-Kaizer	70	5	16	2	12	229	280	357	637	7	73	0.26	0	0	31	129	3.18

Lean, athletic C joins an org swimming in C depth, but Garcia's mature approach and LD oriented swing will look to make an immediate impact. Uses whole field now, but raw power make 15-20 HR seem realistic as he matures. Needs to improve receiving skills but has the work ethic to remain behind the plate.

Garcia,Greg — 456 — St. Louis

EXP MLB DEBUT: 2014 | H/W: 6-0 190 | FUT: Utility INF | 6C

Bats L Age 25	Year	Lev	Team	AB	R	H	HR	RBI	Avg	OB	Slg	OPS	bb%	ct%	Eye	SB	CS	x/h%	Iso	RC/G
2010 (7) Hawaii	2012	AA	Springfield	412	81	117	10	51	284	400	420	820	16	80	0.96	10	5	28	136	6.11
Pwr +	2013	AAA	Memphis	354	50	96	3	35	271	360	384	744	12	80	0.70	14	2	31	113	5.03
BAvg ++	2014	AA	Springfield	15	2	5	0	1	333	375	467	842	6	73	0.25	1	0	40	133	6.20
Spd ++	2014	AAA	Memphis	382	60	104	8	40	272	343	382	725	10	75	0.43	7	5	22	110	4.53
Def ++	2014	MLB	St. Louis	14	2	2	0	1	143	200	214	414	7	57	0.17	0	0	50	71	0.05

LH hitting shortstop from Hawaii has shown the ability to hit for average. Has a short, compact line-drive stroke, but only moderate power. Is an average defender, but his arm and range are light for SS and he profiles best as a utility player.

Garcia,Willy — 9 — Pittsburgh

EXP MLB DEBUT: 2016 | H/W: 6-3 180 | FUT: Starting OF | 7D

Bats R Age 22	Year	Lev	Team	AB	R	H	HR	RBI	Avg	OB	Slg	OPS	bb%	ct%	Eye	SB	CS	x/h%	Iso	RC/G
2010 FA (DR)	2011	Rk	GCL Pirates	177	26	47	5	35	266	309	446	755	6	72	0.22	7	5	38	181	4.85
Pwr +++	2011	A-	State College	7	1	2	0	0	286	286	286	571	0	100		0	0	0	0	2.76
BAvg ++	2012	A	West Virginia	459	57	110	18	77	240	289	403	692	7	71	0.24	10	8	34	163	3.90
Spd +++	2013	A+	Bradenton	449	51	115	16	60	256	292	437	729	5	66	0.15	13	6	37	180	4.62
Def +++	2014	AA	Altoona	439	59	119	18	63	271	309	478	787	5	67	0.17	8	4	42	207	5.42

Athletic OF has plus raw tools, but is too aggressive at the plate. Has good range and arm strength. Went on a tear in the middle of the season and was equally effective against both RHP and LHP, but struck out 145 times. The power is legit and hit 52 HR in the past 3 yrs.

Gardner,Jeff — 7 — Washington

EXP MLB DEBUT: 2018 | H/W: 6-2 210 | FUT: Starting OF | 7C

Bats L Age 23	Year	Lev	Team	AB	R	H	HR	RBI	Avg	OB	Slg	OPS	bb%	ct%	Eye	SB	CS	x/h%	Iso	RC/G
2014 (8) Louisville	2011	NCAA	Louisville	91	20	30	3	13	330	351	527	879	3	85	0.21	3	0	40	198	5.98
Pwr +++	2012	NCAA	Louisville	167	35	50	2	34	299	357	413	770	8	80	0.45	2	3	26	114	5.09
BAvg +++	2013	NCAA	Louisville	163	28	55	9	43	337	403	632	1035	10	87	0.86	1	2	49	294	8.20
Spd ++	2014	NCAA	Louisville	240	37	75	9	68	313	370	525	895	8	82	0.50	2	1	41	213	6.56
Def +++	2014	A-	Auburn	165	20	34	4	11	206	276	327	604	9	67	0.30	2	5	32	121	2.84

Has a fluid LH swing and an advanced sense for the craft. Quick to the ball, he also has strength for extra-base power. Only an average defender in the outfield, so he'll need to hit to succeed. Could move quickly given his advanced college program.

Gasparini,Marten — 6 — Kansas City

EXP MLB DEBUT: 2019 | H/W: 6-0 165 | FUT: Starting SS | 8E

Bats B Age 17	Year	Lev	Team	AB	R	H	HR	RBI	Avg	OB	Slg	OPS	bb%	ct%	Eye	SB	CS	x/h%	Iso	RC/G
2013 FA (Italy)																				
Pwr +																				
BAvg ++																				
Spd ++++	2014	Rk	Idaho Falls	11	4	5	1	3	455	500	727	1227	8	82	0.50	2	0	20	273	10.18
Def +++	2014	Rk	Burlington	68	11	13	0	1	191	225	250	475	4	53	0.09	4	1	23	59	1.20

Raw, thin INF who is very athletic. Missed lots of action due to injuries in first year in U.S. Defense and speed well ahead of bat at present. Has quick actions to stand out with glove and only needs stronger arm to be plus at SS. Has bat speed with fluidity, but doesn't profile for power.

Gatewood,Jacob — 6 — Milwaukee

EXP MLB DEBUT: 2018 | H/W: 6-5 190 | FUT: Starting 3B | 8D

Bats R Age 19	Year	Lev	Team	AB	R	H	HR	RBI	Avg	OB	Slg	OPS	bb%	ct%	Eye	SB	CS	x/h%	Iso	RC/G
2014 (S-1) HS (CA)																				
Pwr +++																				
BAvg ++																				
Spd ++																				
Def +++	2014	Rk	AZL Brewers	204	19	42	3	32	206	253	279	533	6	65	0.18	7	8	21	74	1.72

Has good bat speed and plus raw power, but swing can get long and he struck out 71 times in debut. Moves well defensively with smooth actions, good range, and a strong arm. Should be able to stick at SS for now, but not a lot of 6'5" SS in the majors, so a move to 3B seems likely.

Gelalich,Jeff — 97 — Cincinnati

EXP MLB DEBUT: 2017 | H/W: 6-0 210 | FUT: Starting OF | 7D

Bats L Age 24	Year	Lev	Team	AB	R	H	HR	RBI	Avg	OB	Slg	OPS	bb%	ct%	Eye	SB	CS	x/h%	Iso	RC/G
2012 (1) UCLA	2012	NCAA	UCLA	245	56	86	11	48	351	430	535	965	12	82	0.76	16	5	26	184	7.54
Pwr ++	2012	Rk	Billings	127	27	31	2	9	244	319	378	697	10	67	0.33	4	1	35	134	4.40
BAvg +++	2013	A	Dayton	444	61	109	1	37	245	331	300	631	11	76	0.53	20	6	18	54	3.45
Spd +++	2014	A	Dayton	212	30	47	2	21	222	301	311	612	10	72	0.41	12	4	26	90	3.10
Def ++	2014	A+	Bakersfield	234	42	59	9	28	252	324	415	739	10	69	0.35	9	1	34	162	4.74

Finally showed pop amidst second consecutive season with 20+ steals. Promising toolset, but hasn't put everything together as quickly as hoped. Shows good speed and compact stroke, but persistent contact issues. Has played mostly RF, but lacks arm to stick long-term.

George,Max — 46 — Colorado

EXP MLB DEBUT: 2018 | H/W: 5-9 180 | FUT: Starting 2B | 7C

Bats R Age 18	Year	Lev	Team	AB	R	H	HR	RBI	Avg	OB	Slg	OPS	bb%	ct%	Eye	SB	CS	x/h%	Iso	RC/G
2014 (6) HS (CO)																				
Pwr ++																				
BAvg +++																				
Spd +++																				
Def +++	2014	Rk	Grand Junction	136	30	41	4	19	301	410	463	873	16	68	0.57	10	3	32	162	7.13

Impressive pro debut. Has plus bat speed and makes consistent contact and has good plate discipline. Saw most of his action at SS, but profiles better at 2B. Avg runner with good hands and a strong arm. Scrappy, instinctual player who gets the most of his abilities.

Gettys,Michael — 89 — San Diego

EXP MLB DEBUT: 2018 | H/W: 6-1 205 | FUT: Starting RF | **9D**

Bats R Age 19
2014 (2) HS (GA)
Pwr +++
BAvg +++
4.00 Spd ++++
Def +++

Year	Lev	Team	AB	R	H	HR	RBI	Avg	OB	Slg	OPS	bb%	ct%	Eye	SB	CS	x/h%	Iso	RC/G
2014	Rk	AZL Padres	213	29	66	3	38	310	355	437	792	7	69	0.23	14	2	24	127	5.56

Toolsy, athletic OF had a good debut. Has some swing-and-miss, but shows good speed and power. Plays hard at all times and covers ground well in the OF. Has easy bat speed and quick hands, but scouts are mixed on his power upside due to aggressive approach. Good tools.

Gillaspie,Casey — 3 — Tampa Bay

EXP MLB DEBUT: 2016 | H/W: 6-4 240 | FUT: Starting 1B | **8D**

Bats B Age 22
2014 (1) Wichita State
Pwr ++++
BAvg +++
Spd +
Def ++

Year	Lev	Team	AB	R	H	HR	RBI	Avg	OB	Slg	OPS	bb%	ct%	Eye	SB	CS	x/h%	Iso	RC/G
2012	NCAA	Wichita State	215	29	59	8	32	274	373	442	815	14	80	0.79	1	0	32	167	5.83
2013	NCAA	Wichita State	234	49	70	11	46	299	446	517	963	21	85	1.77	5	3	40	218	8.06
2014	NCAA	Wichita State	211	50	82	15	50	389	520	682	1203	22	87	2.07	8	0	38	294	10.90
2014	A-	Hudson Valley	263	27	69	7	42	262	364	411	775	14	75	0.65	2	3	35	148	5.40

Big, strong 1B with significant power from both sides, plus owns mature approach at plate. Could move quickly, as bat ready for upper levels. A lot of swing and miss to his game, but has discerning eye and works counts. Limited to 1B with poor hands and agility, but can make routine plays.

Goeddel,Tyler — 5 — Tampa Bay

EXP MLB DEBUT: 2016 | H/W: 6-4 185 | FUT: Starting 3B | **7C**

Bats R Age 22
2011 (1-S) HS (CA)
Pwr ++
BAvg +++
Spd +++
Def ++

Year	Lev	Team	AB	R	H	HR	RBI	Avg	OB	Slg	OPS	bb%	ct%	Eye	SB	CS	x/h%	Iso	RC/G
2012	A	Bowling Green	329	52	81	6	46	246	324	371	695	10	71	0.40	30	5	33	125	4.24
2013	A	Bowling Green	450	63	112	7	65	249	310	389	699	8	78	0.41	30	5	33	140	4.21
2014	A+	Charlotte	424	41	114	6	61	269	340	408	748	10	77	0.47	20	9	34	139	4.95

Tall, lean INF who is terrific athlete for size. Hasn't tapped into power potential and needs to add strength and loft to stroke. Drives balls to all fields and has speed to leg out doubles and steal bases. Displays good instincts to help defense, but is error-prone with shoddy footwork.

Gonzalez,Erik — 6 — Cleveland

EXP MLB DEBUT: 2015 | H/W: 6-0 175 | FUT: Utility player | **6A**

Bats R Age 23
2008 FA (DR)
Pwr ++
BAvg +++
Spd +++
Def ++++

Year	Lev	Team	AB	R	H	HR	RBI	Avg	OB	Slg	OPS	bb%	ct%	Eye	SB	CS	x/h%	Iso	RC/G
2012	A-	Mahoning Val	214	30	47	2	18	220	258	299	557	5	77	0.22	9	1	26	79	2.17
2013	A	Lake County	355	59	92	9	49	259	306	439	746	6	80	0.34	10	4	42	180	4.68
2013	A+	Carolina	153	16	37	0	27	242	266	366	632	3	75	0.13	1	2	38	124	3.22
2014	A+	Carolina	308	44	89	3	46	289	338	409	747	7	79	0.35	15	6	27	120	4.77
2014	AA	Akron	129	21	46	1	16	357	390	473	863	5	82	0.30	6	1	22	116	6.03

Very athletic, quick INF who posted career highs in BA and SB. Tools may be short for everyday role, but can contribute with glove and contact approach. Uses quick, soft hands, plus range, and strong arm to make plays. Hits line drives to gaps, but struggles with good FB and spin.

Gonzalez,Pedro — 6 — Colorado

EXP MLB DEBUT: 2019 | H/W: 6-4 160 | FUT: Starting OF | **8E**

Bats R Age 17
2014 FA (DR)
Pwr +++
BAvg +++
Spd ++
Def +++

Year	Lev	Team	AB	R	H	HR	RBI	Avg	OB	Slg	OPS	bb%	ct%	Eye	SB	CS	x/h%	Iso	RC/G
2014		(did not play in the US in 2014)																	

Signed with the Rockies for $1.3 million. Switch-hitter has fluid motions at the plate, but because of his long arms there is length to his swing, That should be off-set by the bat speed and ability to square up the ball. Because of his size, he will likely move to 3B or OF.

Goodrum,Niko — 56 — Minnesota

EXP MLB DEBUT: 2016 | H/W: 6-3 200 | FUT: Starting 3B/SS | **7C**

Bats B Age 23
2010 (2) HS (GA)
Pwr ++
BAvg +++
Spd +++
Def +++

Year	Lev	Team	AB	R	H	HR	RBI	Avg	OB	Slg	OPS	bb%	ct%	Eye	SB	CS	x/h%	Iso	RC/G
2010	Rk	GCL Twins	118	10	19	0	5	161	220	195	415	7	71	0.26	4	2	21	34	0.23
2011	Rk	Elizabethton	204	39	56	2	20	275	342	382	725	9	73	0.38	8	1	27	108	4.64
2012	Rk	Elizabethton	227	38	55	4	38	242	351	419	769	14	75	0.68	6	3	44	176	5.49
2013	A	Cedar Rapids	385	62	100	4	45	260	360	369	728	13	73	0.57	20	4	30	109	4.88
2014	A+	Fort Myers	438	63	109	3	49	249	337	336	672	12	77	0.59	35	4	25	87	4.04

Tall, lanky INF who led FSL in SB. Played mostly 3B and some SS and exhibits very strong arm and good range. Quick, fast hands fine for either spot. Makes decent contact with quiet swing, particularly from right side. Has frame to add strength for power and has become more selective.

Goodwin,Brian — 8 — Washington

EXP MLB DEBUT: 2015 | H/W: 6-0 200 | FUT: Starting OF | **7C**

Bats L Age 24
2011 (1) Miami Dade CC
Pwr +++
BAvg ++
Spd ++++
Def ++++

Year	Lev	Team	AB	R	H	HR	RBI	Avg	OB	Slg	OPS	bb%	ct%	Eye	SB	CS	x/h%	Iso	RC/G
2011	NCAA	Miami-DadeCol	157	42	60	8	37	382	500	631	1131	19	100		16	2	35	248	9.86
2012	A	Hagerstown	216	47	70	9	38	324	436	542	978	17	82	1.10	15	4	40	218	8.07
2012	AA	Harrisburg	166	17	37	5	14	223	299	373	672	10	70	0.36	3	3	38	151	3.84
2013	AA	Harrisburg	457	82	115	10	40	252	346	407	753	13	74	0.55	19	11	35	155	5.14
2014	AAA	Syracuse	274	31	60	4	32	219	340	328	668	15	65	0.53	6	4	30	109	4.13

Toolsy player that has stalled in the high minors. Knows balls and strikes, but contact rate has worsened, and breaking stuff—especially from LHP—still gives him fits. Has speed and solid defender in CF, but not an effective base-stealer. Shoulder injury wiped out half his 2014, but organizational patience may be wearing thin.

Gordon,Nick — 6 — Minnesota

EXP MLB DEBUT: 2018 | H/W: 6-0 160 | FUT: Starting SS | **9D**

Bats L Age 19
2014 (1) HS (FL)
Pwr ++
BAvg ++++
Spd ++++
Def +++

Year	Lev	Team	AB	R	H	HR	RBI	Avg	OB	Slg	OPS	bb%	ct%	Eye	SB	CS	x/h%	Iso	RC/G
2014	Rk	Elizabethton	235	46	69	1	28	294	325	366	691	4	81	0.24	11	7	16	72	3.89

Lean, instinctual INF with solid tools across board. Power short at present, but can hit for high BA with quick stroke and hand-eye coordination. Controlled swing puts ball in play and uses above average speed effectively. Nimble defender with strong arm, soft hands, and sufficient range.

Gosselin,Phil — 456 — Atlanta

EXP MLB DEBUT: 2013 | H/W: 6-1 200 | FUT: Backup 2B | **6C**

Bats R Age 26
2010 (5) Virginia
Pwr +
BAvg +++
Spd ++
Def +++

Year	Lev	Team	AB	R	H	HR	RBI	Avg	OB	Slg	OPS	bb%	ct%	Eye	SB	CS	x/h%	Iso	RC/G
2013	AA	Mississippi	218	27	53	1	23	243	283	312	595	5	86	0.39	5	1	23	69	2.89
2013	AAA	Gwinnett	207	17	55	2	15	266	306	324	630	5	82	0.32	1	0	13	58	3.14
2013	MLB	Atlanta	6	2	2	0	0	333	429	333	762	14	67	0.50	0	0	0	0	5.49
2014	AAA	Gwinnett	378	58	130	5	31	344	375	487	862	5	84	0.31	6	1	30	143	5.98
2014	MLB	Atlanta	128	17	34	1	3	266	293	320	614	4	79	0.19	2	2	15	55	2.81

Infielder put up impressive numbers at AAA and then saw important AB in the majors down the stretch. Has no standout tools other than the ability to hit, but plays the game hard and gets the most of his ability. Not likely to be more than a utility player in the majors.

Green,Zach — 5 — Philadelphia

EXP MLB DEBUT: 2017 | H/W: 6-3 210 | FUT: Starting 3B | **8D**

Bats R Age 21
2012 (3) HS (CA)
Pwr ++++
BAvg ++
Spd ++
Def +++

Year	Lev	Team	AB	R	H	HR	RBI	Avg	OB	Slg	OPS	bb%	ct%	Eye	SB	CS	x/h%	Iso	RC/G
2012	Rk	GCL Phillies	169	20	48	3	21	284	316	426	742	5	75	0.19	2	2	35	142	4.59
2013	A-	Williamsport	270	52	68	13	41	252	329	478	807	10	66	0.34	8	5	50	226	5.91
2014	A	Lakewood	328	41	88	6	43	268	318	402	721	7	80	0.37	7	1	34	134	4.38

Took some big steps forward in making better contact, but season cut short by back/leg issues. Given his power potential and good size, could be ready for some additional power growth in 2015. Still some question as to whether long-term he'll stick at 3B due to a slow first step. One to watch at High-A.

Gregor,Conrad — 3 — Houston

EXP MLB DEBUT: 2016 | H/W: 6-3 225 | FUT: Starting 1B | **7C**

Bats L Age 23
2013 (4) Vanderbilt
Pwr +++
BAvg +++
Spd +
Def ++

Year	Lev	Team	AB	R	H	HR	RBI	Avg	OB	Slg	OPS	bb%	ct%	Eye	SB	CS	x/h%	Iso	RC/G
2013	NCAA	Vanderbilt	227	47	70	3	48	308	441	410	851	19	87	1.86	21	3	24	101	6.78
2013	A-	Tri City	270	36	78	4	35	289	375	385	760	12	84	0.86	2	2	22	96	5.16
2014	A	Quad Cities	161	26	48	1	28	298	402	410	812	15	79	0.82	0	0	31	112	6.07
2014	A+	Lancaster	180	43	66	12	45	367	449	678	1127	13	86	1.08	1	1	44	311	9.44
2014	AA	Corpus Christi	109	14	26	3	13	239	320	376	696	11	81	0.62	0	1	31	138	4.21

Large-framed 1B who produces with raw power and balanced approach. Offers strength in wrists to produce pop. Long swing can be exploited, particularly with breaking balls. BA doesn't project at higher levels due to stroke, though can hit LHP. Lacks speed and not a good defender.

Greiner,Grayson

2 | Detroit | EXP MLB DEBUT: 2017 | H/W: 6-6 215 | FUT: Starting C | 8E

Bats R Age 22
2014 (3) South Carolina

- Pwr +++
- BAvg ++
- Spd +
- Def +++

Year	Lev	Team	AB	R	H	HR	RBI	Avg	OB	Slg	OPS	bb%	ct%	Eye	SB	CS	x/h%	Iso	RC/G
2012	NCAA	South Carolina	194	26	43	6	32	222	326	392	718	13	75	0.63	0	1	47	170	4.61
2013	NCAA	South Carolina	205	32	61	4	38	298	371	424	796	10	86	0.86	5	4	26	127	5.52
2014	NCAA	South Carolina	212	39	66	8	50	311	394	486	880	12	82	0.74	0	0	32	175	6.54
2014	A	West Michigan	90	11	29	2	16	322	396	444	840	11	80	0.61	0	0	24	122	6.05

Very tall catcher who ended season early after breaking wrist. Long swing tames BA potential, but can give ball ride when arms extended. Only has average bat speed, but brute strength is weapon. Release can be slow, but has strong arm and steady receiving. Needs to hit to have value.

Grichuk,Randal

89 | St. Louis | EXP MLB DEBUT: 2014 | H/W: 6-1 195 | FUT: Starting OF | 8C

Bats R Age 23
2009 (1) HS (TX)

- Pwr ++++
- BAvg ++
- Spd +++
- Def +++

Year	Lev	Team	AB	R	H	HR	RBI	Avg	OB	Slg	OPS	bb%	ct%	Eye	SB	CS	x/h%	Iso	RC/G
2011	A+	Inland Empire	53	13	15	1	6	283	283	491	774	0	75	0.00	0	0	47	208	4.85
2012	A+	Inland Empire	537	79	160	18	71	298	327	488	815	4	83	0.25	16	6	36	190	5.30
2013	AA	Arkansas	500	85	128	22	64	256	295	474	769	5	82	0.30	9	5	45	218	4.80
2014	AAA	Memphis	436	73	113	25	71	259	304	493	797	6	75	0.26	8	5	44	234	5.16
2014	MLB	St. Louis	110	11	27	3	8	245	278	400	678	4	72	0.16	0	2	37	155	3.71

Athletic OF saw playing time in the majors as the Cards made a push for the post-season. Has plus raw power and swatted a career-high 28 HR, but continues to be overly aggressive, striking out 141 times. Does have plus bat speed and the power to hit 20+ HR in the majors.

Grullon,Deivi

2 | Philadelphia | EXP MLB DEBUT: 2018 | H/W: 6-1 180 | FUT: Starting C | 8C

Bats R Age 19
2012 FA (DR)

- Pwr ++
- BAvg ++
- Spd ++
- Def ++++

Year	Lev	Team	AB	R	H	HR	RBI	Avg	OB	Slg	OPS	bb%	ct%	Eye	SB	CS	x/h%	Iso	RC/G
2013	Rk	GCL Phillies	121	13	33	1	14	273	328	364	692	8	85	0.56	0	0	27	91	4.15
2014	A-	Williamsport	187	14	42	0	18	225	260	283	544	5	79	0.23	3	0	24	59	2.09
2014	A	Lakewood	76	9	18	1	7	237	266	342	608	4	83	0.23	0	0	33	105	2.88
2014	A+	Clearwater	10	0	2	0	1	200	200	200	400	0	90	0.00	0	0	0	0	0.52

Defense-first catcher, but is still young enough and strong enough to consider the possiblity that he grows into a bit of power. Has a rifle arm and good base of other defensive skills behind the plate, and that will be what carries him to the majors.

Guerra,Javier

6 | Boston | EXP MLB DEBUT: 2018 | H/W: 5-11 155 | FUT: Starting SS | 7D

Bats L Age 19
2012 FA (Panama)

- Pwr +
- BAvg +++
- Spd ++
- Def ++++

Year	Lev	Team	AB	R	H	HR	RBI	Avg	OB	Slg	OPS	bb%	ct%	Eye	SB	CS	x/h%	Iso	RC/G
2013	Rk	DSL Red Sox	210	27	52	0	23	248	350	290	640	14	81	0.83	7	4	17	43	3.78
2014	Rk	GCL Red Sox	201	21	54	2	26	269	286	408	694	2	79	0.12	1	5	37	139	3.89

Diminutive INF with contact-oriented approach, though swings early in count and rarely walks. Has room to grow into lean frame, though power will never be part of game. Displays athletic actions in middle infield and has exceptional arm strength. Despite quickness, does not steal bases.

Guerrero,Alexander

4 | Los Angeles (N) | EXP MLB DEBUT: 2014 | H/W: 5-10 205 | FUT: Starting 2B | 8C

Bats R Age 28
2013 FA (Cuba)

- Pwr +++
- BAvg +++
- Spd +++
- Def +++

Year	Lev	Team	AB	R	H	HR	RBI	Avg	OB	Slg	OPS	bb%	ct%	Eye	SB	CS	x/h%	Iso	RC/G
2014	Rk	AZL Dodgers	23	6	8	2	6	348	423	652	1075	12	78	0.60	0	0	38	304	8.81
2014	A+	Rancho Cuca	19	3	7	0	2	368	429	684	1113	10	89	1.00	0	0	71	316	9.49
2014	AAA	Albuquerque	243	38	80	15	49	329	356	613	969	4	82	0.23	4	0	43	284	7.05
2014	MLB	LA Dodgers	13	0	1	0	0	77	77	77	154	0	54	0.00	0	0	0	0	-4.74

Event-filled pro debut. Hit .333 and had part of his ear bitten off by a teammate. A compact but surprisingly strong player, he proved he can hit. Squares the ball up well and makes consistent hard contact. Can be overly aggressive, but doesn't strikeout much. Also has decent speed.

Guerrero,Gabriel

9 | Seattle | EXP MLB DEBUT: 2016 | H/W: 6-3 190 | FUT: Starting OF | 8C

Bats R Age 21
2011 FA (DR)

- Pwr ++++
- BAvg +++
- Spd ++
- Def +++

Year	Lev	Team	AB	R	H	HR	RBI	Avg	OB	Slg	OPS	bb%	ct%	Eye	SB	CS	x/h%	Iso	RC/G
2012	Rk	AZL Mariners	75	17	25	4	18	333	359	560	919	4	83	0.23	0	0	36	227	6.40
2013	A	Clinton	469	60	127	4	50	271	302	358	660	4	76	0.19	12	3	24	87	3.47
2014	A+	High Desert	538	97	165	18	96	307	348	467	814	6	76	0.26	18	6	29	160	5.46

Lean, strong OF who set highs in HR and SB. Very aggressive free-swinger, but makes contact and covers plate well with hand-eye coordination. Emerging power is best tool, but also has ideal gun for RF. Owns high ceiling and should be middle-of-order run producer at maturity.

Gushue,Taylor

2 | Pittsburgh | EXP MLB DEBUT: 2017 | H/W: 6-1 215 | FUT: Starting C | 7D

Bats B Age 21
2014 (4) Florida

- Pwr +++
- BAvg ++
- Spd ++
- Def ++

Year	Lev	Team	AB	R	H	HR	RBI	Avg	OB	Slg	OPS	bb%	ct%	Eye	SB	CS	x/h%	Iso	RC/G
2012	NCAA	Florida	141	21	29	5	21	206	317	383	700	14	77	0.70	1	2	48	177	4.37
2013	NCAA	Florida	216	27	58	5	33	269	336	417	753	9	81	0.54	3	3	34	148	4.89
2014	NCAA	Florida	222	30	71	6	49	320	389	473	862	10	83	0.68	1	0	31	153	6.24
2014	A-	Jamestown	199	25	48	5	29	241	332	402	734	12	81	0.73	0	1	42	161	4.82

4th round pick is new to catching. Strong, compact swing with above-average power. Made decent contact, but scouts are not convinced he will hit for average. Got off to a good start, but faded down the stretch. Only an average defender who threw out 23% of baserunners in his debut.

Guzman,Ronald

3 | Texas | EXP MLB DEBUT: 2017 | H/W: 6-5 205 | FUT: Starting 1B | 7C

Bats L Age 20
2011 FA (DR)

- Pwr +++
- BAvg +++
- Spd ++
- Def ++

Year	Lev	Team	AB	R	H	HR	RBI	Avg	OB	Slg	OPS	bb%	ct%	Eye	SB	CS	x/h%	Iso	RC/G
2012	Rk	AZL Rangers	212	29	68	1	33	321	377	434	811	8	80	0.45	7	1	28	113	5.66
2013	A	Hickory	173	17	47	4	26	272	315	387	703	6	84	0.41	0	0	26	116	4.07
2014	A	Hickory	445	46	97	6	63	218	278	330	608	8	76	0.35	6	3	39	112	2.98

Long, lean INF who repeated Low-A, but fell apart after April. Hand-eye coordination is ideal for potential BA and can use entire field. Has long arms to generate power, though bat speed doesn't project to plus pop. Is a slow runner and not a polished defender. Has clean swing mechanics.

Hager,Jake

6 | Tampa Bay | EXP MLB DEBUT: 2016 | H/W: 6-1 170 | FUT: Starting SS | 7D

Bats R Age 22
2011 (1) HS (NV)

- Pwr ++
- BAvg +++
- Spd +++
- Def +++

Year	Lev	Team	AB	R	H	HR	RBI	Avg	OB	Slg	OPS	bb%	ct%	Eye	SB	CS	x/h%	Iso	RC/G
2011	Rk	Princeton	193	29	52	4	17	269	302	399	701	4	87	0.35	5	7	31	130	4.03
2012	A	Bowling Green	442	63	124	10	72	281	340	412	752	8	86	0.67	17	11	28	131	4.85
2013	Rk	GCL Devil Rays	4	1	2	0	1	500	500	750	1250	0	100		0	0	50	250	9.68
2013	A+	Charlotte	449	56	116	0	33	258	316	305	621	8	82	0.47	12	8	16	47	3.26
2014	AA	Montgomery	447	42	121	4	47	271	317	376	692	6	80	0.33	4	4	29	105	4.03

Reliable INF who is steadily progressing one level per year and has glove to contribute. Has average, accurate arm and the textbook actions necessary to stick at SS. Aggressive hitter with moderate doubles power and can move runners along with contact approach. Profiles as #2 hitter.

Haniger,Mitch

89 | Arizona | EXP MLB DEBUT: 2015 | H/W: 6-2 215 | FUT: Starting OF | 7C

Bats R Age 24
2012 (1-S) Cal Poly

- Pwr +++
- BAvg +++
- Spd ++
- Def +++

Year	Lev	Team	AB	R	H	HR	RBI	Avg	OB	Slg	OPS	bb%	ct%	Eye	SB	CS	x/h%	Iso	RC/G
2013	A	Wisconsin	145	24	43	5	25	297	400	510	910	15	83	1.04	7	0	44	214	7.15
2013	A+	Brevard Cnty	328	52	82	6	43	250	317	396	713	9	79	0.47	2	2	40	146	4.42
2014	Rk	AZL Dbacks	15	4	3	1	4	200	250	467	717	6	60	0.17	0	0	67	267	4.66
2014	AA	Huntsville	243	41	62	10	34	255	309	416	725	7	83	0.46	4	0	29	160	4.31
2014	AA	Mobile	24	5	8	0	5	333	407	458	866	11	83	0.75	0	0	38	125	6.56

Toolsy OF took a step back and was traded. A quick bat and good approach give him the tools to hit for avg with above-avg power. Has decent speed, but not enough to stick in CF. Has good speed under way, but not a base-stealing threat. Works hard and gets the most of his tools.

Hannemann,Jacob

8 | Chicago (N) | EXP MLB DEBUT: 2017 | H/W: 6-1 195 | FUT: Starting OF | 7D

Bats L Age 23
2013 (3) Brigham Young

- Pwr ++
- BAvg +++
- Spd ++++
- Def ++

Year	Lev	Team	AB	R	H	HR	RBI	Avg	OB	Slg	OPS	bb%	ct%	Eye	SB	CS	x/h%	Iso	RC/G
2013	NCAA	BYU	215	53	74	5	29	344	410	553	964	10	83	0.65	14	1	38	209	7.60
2013	Rk	AZL Cubs	9	1	1	0	2	111	111	222	333	0	89	0.00	1	0	100	111	-0.02
2013	A-	Boise	62	8	18	1	5	290	313	468	780	3	82	0.18	3	1	39	177	4.97
2014	A	Kane County	342	57	87	6	39	254	316	377	694	8	77	0.40	32	4	29	123	4.10
2014	A+	Daytona	145	17	35	2	12	241	295	345	640	7	77	0.32	5	3	31	103	3.34

3rd round pick scuffled in his full-season debut. Remains raw on the diamond, but has good athleticism. Smooth LH stroke generates moderate power and consistent contact with good balance and bat speed. Runs well and stole 37 bases and should be able to stick in CF.

Hanson,Alen — 46 — Pittsburgh

EXP MLB DEBUT: 2015 | H/W: 5-11 170 | FUT: Starting SS/2B | 8C

Bats B Age 22 | 2009 FA (DR) | Pwr +++ | BAvg +++ | Spd ++++ | Def ++

Year	Lev	Team	AB	R	H	HR	RBI	Avg	OB	Sig	OPS	bb%	ct%	Eye	SB	CS	x/h%	Iso	RC/G
2011	A-	State College	10	1	2	0	0	200	273	200	473	9	80	0.50	0	0	0	0	1.36
2012	A	West Virginia	489	99	151	16	62	309	379	528	906	10	79	0.52	35	19	41	219	6.93
2013	A+	Bradenton	367	51	103	7	48	281	340	444	784	8	81	0.47	24	14	37	163	5.29
2013	AA	Altoona	137	13	35	1	10	255	297	380	676	6	81	0.31	6	2	29	124	3.85
2014	AA	Altoona	482	64	135	11	58	280	324	442	765	6	82	0.35	25	11	33	162	4.89

Switch-hitter has tools to be a 20/20 player in the majors. Has plus speed and a line-drive approach. Is aggressive at the plate, but makes enough contact that he should be able to hit for average. Remains below-average defensively, but his bat is good enough that it won't matter.

Harrison,Monte — 89 — Milwaukee

EXP MLB DEBUT: 2018 | H/W: 6-3 200 | FUT: Starting RF | 8D

Bats R Age 19 | 2014 (2) HS (MO) | Pwr ++ | BAvg +++ | Spd ++++ | Def ++++

Year	Lev	Team	AB	R	H	HR	RBI	Avg	OB	Sig	OPS	bb%	ct%	Eye	SB	CS	x/h%	Iso	RC/G
2014	Rk	AZL Brewers	180	37	47	1	20	261	370	339	709	15	73	0.65	32	2	21	78	4.66

High-energy OF was a three-sport star in high school. Is raw on the field, but had a solid debut. Has good hand-eye coordination and barrels the ball consistently. Needs to improve his timing to drive balls over the fence. Has good speed and one of the best arms in the draft class.

Harrison,Travis — 57 — Minnesota

EXP MLB DEBUT: 2016 | H/W: 6-1 215 | FUT: Starting 3B/LF | 7C

Bats R Age 22 | 2011 (1-S) HS (CA) | Pwr +++ | BAvg ++ | Spd + | Def ++

Year	Lev	Team	AB	R	H	HR	RBI	Avg	OB	Sig	OPS	bb%	ct%	Eye	SB	CS	x/h%	Iso	RC/G
2012	Rk	Elizabethton	219	39	66	5	27	301	370	461	832	10	77	0.47	3	0	32	160	5.99
2013	A	Cedar Rapids	450	66	114	15	59	253	351	416	767	13	72	0.54	2	4	38	162	5.27
2014	A+	Fort Myers	458	80	123	3	59	269	358	365	723	12	81	0.74	7	5	30	96	4.77

Strong hitter who moved to LF from 3B in '14. Saw large drop off in power, but also in K rate. Makes good contact with bat speed and sound hitting instincts. Has power to all fields, but can get pull-conscious. Has disciplined eye to draw walks. Very poor runner and is raw in OF with routes.

Hart,Josh — 8 — Baltimore

EXP MLB DEBUT: 2017 | H/W: 6-1 180 | FUT: Starting CF | 8E

Bats L Age 20 | 2013 (1-S) HS (GA) | Pwr + | BAvg ++ | Spd ++++ | Def ++++

Year	Lev	Team	AB	R	H	HR	RBI	Avg	OB	Sig	OPS	bb%	ct%	Eye	SB	CS	x/h%	Iso	RC/G
2013	Rk	GCL Orioles	123	14	28	0	9	228	301	301	602	10	81	0.57	11	3	25	73	3.15
2013	A-	Aberdeen	10	0	1	0	0	100	182	100	282	9	60	0.25	0	0	0	0	-2.30
2014	Rk	GCL Orioles	24	2	4	0	0	167	200	250	450	4	92	0.50	2	0	25	83	1.55
2014	A	Delmarva	326	22	83	1	28	255	300	285	585	6	74	0.24	11	5	8	31	2.50

Small, wiry OF with high upside, but little present production. Plus speed is best attribute and is solid defensive CF with plus range and instincts. Potential to be top-of-order hitter, but needs more patience and contact. Sprays ball to all fields, but inconsistent stroke limits BA and pop.

Hassan,Alex — 79 — Baltimore

EXP MLB DEBUT: 2014 | H/W: 6-3 220 | FUT: Reserve OF | 6B

Bats R Age 27 | 2009 (20) Duke | Pwr ++ | BAvg +++ | Spd ++ | Def +++

Year	Lev	Team	AB	R	H	HR	RBI	Avg	OB	Sig	OPS	bb%	ct%	Eye	SB	CS	x/h%	Iso	RC/G
2012	AAA	Pawtucket	312	39	80	7	46	256	368	365	733	15	78	0.79	1	1	25	109	4.89
2013	A	Greenville	23	4	11	0	7	478	636	565	1202	30	91	5.00	0	0	18	87	11.95
2013	AAA	Pawtucket	187	26	60	4	28	321	430	460	890	16	73	0.72	0	1	30	139	7.21
2014	AAA	Pawtucket	408	66	117	8	55	287	378	426	805	13	73	0.55	2	2	34	140	5.86
2014	MLB	Boston	8	1	1	0	0	125	222	125	347	11	38	0.20	0	0	0	0	-1.18

Patient hitter who has spent last 3 years in Triple-A. Focuses on OBP with mature strike zone judgment and drives ball to all fields. Too much swing and miss in game, especially with lack of punch. Not much foot speed, though has instincts on base and in OF. Average arm with OK range.

Hawkins,Courtney — 7 — Chicago (A)

EXP MLB DEBUT: 2016 | H/W: 6-3 220 | FUT: Starting OF | 8D

Bats R Age 21 | 2012 (1) HS (TX) | Pwr ++++ | BAvg ++ | Spd +++ | Def +++

Year	Lev	Team	AB	R	H	HR	RBI	Avg	OB	Sig	OPS	bb%	ct%	Eye	SB	CS	x/h%	Iso	RC/G
2012	Rk	Bristol	147	25	40	3	16	272	305	401	707	5	75	0.19	8	2	30	129	4.06
2012	A	Kannapolis	65	11	20	4	15	308	348	631	979	6	74	0.24	3	2	55	323	7.74
2012	A+	Winston-Salem	17	3	5	1	2	294	294	588	882	0	88	0.00	0	1	60	294	5.74
2013	A+	Winston-Salem	383	48	68	19	62	178	235	384	619	7	58	0.18	10	5	56	206	3.22
2014	A+	Winston-Salem	449	65	112	19	84	249	329	450	779	11	68	0.37	11	3	43	200	5.42

Thick, strong OF who repeated High-A and was better. Finished 2nd in CAR in HR and 3rd in K. Draws walks, but too much swing and miss hinders BA potential. Owns significant power to pull side and runs well for size. Struggles with breaking balls, pitch recognition, and LHP.

Healy,Ryon — 35 — Oakland

EXP MLB DEBUT: 2016 | H/W: 6-5 205 | FUT: Starting 1B | 7C

Bats R Age 23 | 2013 (3) Oregon | Pwr +++ | BAvg +++ | Spd + | Def ++

Year	Lev	Team	AB	R	H	HR	RBI	Avg	OB	Sig	OPS	bb%	ct%	Eye	SB	CS	x/h%	Iso	RC/G
2012	NCAA	Oregon	253	35	79	4	42	312	370	419	789	8	82	0.51	3	2	23	107	5.27
2013	NCAA	Oregon	228	44	76	11	56	333	406	566	972	11	89	1.17	5	3	41	232	7.49
2013	Rk	AZL Athletics	28	4	6	2	8	214	290	500	790	10	86	0.75	0	0	50	286	5.20
2013	A-	Vermont	146	12	34	4	21	233	243	384	627	1	84	0.08	2	1	41	151	2.93
2014	A+	Stockton	561	73	160	16	83	285	319	428	747	5	86	0.35	0	0	29	143	4.52

Large-framed corner INF who is bat-only prospect. Offers plenty of strength and leverage to generate power to all fields. Knows how to hit and has great plate coverage. Doesn't walk much, but makes easy contact. Speed is well below average and is poor with glove at 1B or 3B. Likely DH.

Heathcott,Slade — 89 — New York (A)

EXP MLB DEBUT: 2015 | H/W: 6-1 190 | FUT: Starting OF | 7E

Bats L Age 24 | 2009 (1) HS (TX) | Pwr ++ | BAvg ++ | Spd +++ | Def ++++

Year	Lev	Team	AB	R	H	HR	RBI	Avg	OB	Sig	OPS	bb%	ct%	Eye	SB	CS	x/h%	Iso	RC/G
2011	A+	Tampa	5	2	3	1	1	600	600	1200	1800	0	80	0.00	0	0	33	600	16.14
2012	Rk	GCL Yankees	17	3	4	0	2	235	409	353	762	23	76	1.25	2	0	50	118	5.86
2012	A+	Tampa	215	38	66	5	27	307	366	470	836	9	69	0.30	17	4	35	163	6.24
2013	AA	Trenton	399	59	104	8	49	261	322	411	733	8	73	0.34	15	8	36	150	4.67
2014	AA	Trenton	33	4	6	0	1	182	250	242	492	8	61	0.23	0	1	33	61	1.32

Injury-prone OF who missed most of season—again—after knee surgery. Cannot stay on field and status dwindling. Had plus speed at one time, but not nearly as quick now. Still remains strong CF defender with above average arm. Has bat speed for some pop, but long swing hurts BA.

Hedges,Austin — 2 — San Diego

EXP MLB DEBUT: 2015 | H/W: 6-1 190 | FUT: Starting C | 7B

Bats R Age 22 | 2011 (2) HS (CA) | Pwr ++ | BAvg ++ | Spd ++ | Def ++++

Year	Lev	Team	AB	R	H	HR	RBI	Avg	OB	Sig	OPS	bb%	ct%	Eye	SB	CS	x/h%	Iso	RC/G
2011	A-	Eugene	10	0	1	0	0	100	250	200	450	17	70	0.67	0	0	100	100	1.03
2012	A	Fort Wayne	337	44	94	10	56	279	325	451	776	6	82	0.37	14	9	40	172	4.99
2013	A+	Lake Elsinore	233	34	63	4	30	270	333	425	758	9	81	0.49	5	4	43	155	4.99
2013	AA	San Antonio	67	4	15	0	8	224	288	269	556	8	87	0.67	3	1	20	45	2.66
2014	AA	San Antonio	427	31	96	6	44	225	264	321	585	5	79	0.26	1	3	28	96	2.57

Remains an elite defensive C and has the tools to handle a major league staff right now. Moves well behind the plate with good hands and strong blocking skills. Nailed almost 40% of baserunners. Has some offensive potential, but overall his production continues to stagnate.

Henry,Jabari — 79 — Seattle

EXP MLB DEBUT: 2016 | H/W: 6-1 200 | FUT: Reserve OF | 7D

Bats R Age 24 | 2012 (18) Florida Intl | Pwr ++++ | BAvg +++ | Spd ++ | Def ++

Year	Lev	Team	AB	R	H	HR	RBI	Avg	OB	Sig	OPS	bb%	ct%	Eye	SB	CS	x/h%	Iso	RC/G
2012	Rk	Pulaski	207	35	56	8	42	271	355	488	843	12	78	0.59	5	2	46	217	6.15
2012	A-	Everett	6	0	2	0	0	333	500	333	833	25	83	2.00	0	0	0	0	6.90
2013	A	Clinton	257	41	69	7	40	268	382	436	817	15	81	0.96	9	6	39	167	6.05
2013	A+	High Desert	105	19	25	4	17	238	339	438	777	13	77	0.67	0	1	44	200	5.36
2014	A+	High Desert	430	79	125	30	95	291	389	584	972	14	75	0.63	6	9	49	293	7.91

Breakout prospect with significant increase in HR output while maintaining very selective eye. Exhibits athleticism and decent speed, though is inefficient baserunner. Has exploitable swing and will flail at breaking balls. Strong arm highlights OF play, but needs work on routes and reads.

Hernandez,Elier — 89 — Kansas City

EXP MLB DEBUT: 2017 | H/W: 6-3 200 | FUT: Starting OF | 8D

Bats R Age 20 | 2011 FA (DR) | Pwr +++ | BAvg +++ | Spd +++ | Def ++

Year	Lev	Team	AB	R	H	HR	RBI	Avg	OB	Sig	OPS	bb%	ct%	Eye	SB	CS	x/h%	Iso	RC/G
2012	Rk	Idaho Falls	250	30	52	0	34	208	250	280	530	5	74	0.21	2	0	27	72	1.86
2013	Rk	Idaho Falls	289	44	87	3	44	301	342	439	781	6	79	0.29	9	2	30	138	5.16
2014	A	Lexington	420	54	111	9	34	264	291	393	684	4	76	0.16	5	5	29	129	3.70

High-ceiling OF who was very good last 2 months. Started to break out by driving ball consistently and tapping into average pop. Plus bat speed gives him BA potential, though needs to be more selective in undisciplined approach. Subpar defender now with poor routes and reads.

Hernandez,Oscar — 2 — Arizona

EXP MLB DEBUT: 2017 | H/W: 6-0 195 | FUT: Starting C | **8D**

Bats R Age 21 — 2009 FA (Venezuela)
Pwr +++ / BAvg ++ / Spd ++ / Def ++++

Year	Lev	Team	AB	R	H	HR	RBI	Avg	OB	Slg	OPS	bb%	ct%	Eye	SB	CS	x/h%	Iso	RC/G
2012	Rk	Princeton	160	25	37	5	24	231	328	394	722	13	81	0.74	0	1	41	163	4.64
2013	A-	Hudson Valley	167	22	38	6	33	228	275	371	647	6	86	0.46	9	1	32	144	3.40
2013	A	Bowling Green	9	1	2	0	1	222	364	222	586	18	89	2.00	0	0	0	0	3.62
2014	A	Bowling Green	362	43	90	9	63	249	297	401	698	6	78	0.32	3	6	36	152	4.04

Sleeper prospect who is athletic, excellent defender. Selected in Rule 5 draft.Blessed with catch-and-throw skills and easy receiving ability. Can get pull happy with uppercut stroke, but bat speed and strength should lead to both BA and power with proper adjustments. Handles pitching staff and is strong leader.

Hernandez,Teoscar — 89 — Houston

EXP MLB DEBUT: 2017 | H/W: 6-2 180 | FUT: Starting OF | **8D**

Bats R Age 22 — 2011 FA (DR)
Pwr +++ / BAvg +++ / Spd ++++ / Def +++

Year	Lev	Team	AB	R	H	HR	RBI	Avg	OB	Slg	OPS	bb%	ct%	Eye	SB	CS	x/h%	Iso	RC/G
2012	Rk	GCL Astros	177	25	43	4	18	243	316	395	712	10	69	0.35	10	1	40	153	4.50
2012	A	Lexington	25	2	6	1	5	240	321	440	761	11	52	0.25	1	0	50	200	6.50
2013	A	Quad Cities	499	97	135	13	55	271	326	435	761	8	73	0.30	24	11	35	164	4.99
2014	A+	Lancaster	391	72	115	17	75	294	373	550	923	11	70	0.42	31	6	50	256	7.53
2014	AA	Corpus Christi	95	12	27	4	10	284	299	474	773	2	62	0.06	2	3	33	189	5.36

Tall, lean OF who had career year with highs in HR, 2B, SB, BA, and BB. Owns nice tools with speed being best attribute. Swings hard and prone to Ks with some swing and miss, but puts charge into ball with bat speed and strength. Uses whole field. Potential 20 HR / 20 SB player.

Herrera,Carlos — 6 — Colorado

EXP MLB DEBUT: 2018 | H/W: 6-0 150 | FUT: Starting SS | **7D**

Bats L Age 18 — 2013 FA (Venezuela)
Pwr + / BAvg +++ / Spd ++++ / Def +++

Year	Lev	Team	AB	R	H	HR	RBI	Avg	OB	Slg	OPS	bb%	ct%	Eye	SB	CS	x/h%	Iso	RC/G
2014	Rk	DSL Rockies	139	18	32	0	11	230	287	281	567	7	82	0.44	6	4	22	50	2.59

Venezuelan SS has plus speed and good athleticism. Has yet to make his U.S. debut, but struggled in the DSL. Should develop average power once he matures and has the range and arm to stick at SS, but needs to work on mechanics and footwork. Lots of raw talent, but years away.

Herrera,Dilson — 4 — New York (N)

EXP MLB DEBUT: 2014 | H/W: 5-10 150 | FUT: Starting 2B | **8C**

Bats R Age 21 — 2010 FA (Colombia)
Pwr ++++ / BAvg +++ / Spd ++++ / Def ++

Year	Lev	Team	AB	R	H	HR	RBI	Avg	OB	Slg	OPS	bb%	ct%	Eye	SB	CS	x/h%	Iso	RC/G
2013	A	Savannah	19	6	6	0	4	316	409	316	725	14	68	0.50	3	0	0	0	4.84
2013	A	West Virginia	423	69	112	11	56	265	324	421	745	8	74	0.34	11	6	37	156	4.76
2014	A+	St. Lucie	283	48	87	3	23	307	349	410	759	6	84	0.41	14	3	24	102	4.81
2014	AA	Binghamton	241	50	82	10	48	340	411	560	971	11	78	0.56	9	4	37	220	7.72
2014	MLB	NY Mets	59	6	13	3	11	220	303	407	710	11	71	0.41	0	0	31	186	4.23

Rose from A ball to the majors. Exciting amount of power for a MI due to natural strength and above-average bat speed. Quick hands and hand-eye coordination should produce nice BA despite being a free swinger. Average defender showing improvements. Double-digit HR/SB potential.

Herrera,Jose — 2 — Arizona

EXP MLB DEBUT: 2018 | H/W: 5-10 185 | FUT: Starting C | **7D**

Bats B Age 18 — 2013 FA (Venezuela)
Pwr ++ / BAvg ++ / Spd ++ / Def +++

Year	Lev	Team	AB	R	H	HR	RBI	Avg	OB	Slg	OPS	bb%	ct%	Eye	SB	CS	x/h%	Iso	RC/G
2014	Rk	Missoula	7	2	2	0	1	286	444	429	873	22	71	1.00	0	0	50	143	7.53
2014	Rk	AZL Dbacks	154	24	35	0	14	227	328	266	594	13	76	0.62	1	0	14	39	3.03

Squat, strong-bodied backstop from Venezuela. Moves well behind the plate with a strong arm and good receiving skills. Switch-hitter projects to have above-average power from both sides, but failed to hit in his U.S. debut, hitting just .230/.342/.273.

Herrera,Juan — 6 — St. Louis

EXP MLB DEBUT: 2017 | H/W: 5-11 165 | FUT: Starting 2B/SS | **7D**

Bats R Age 21 — 2010 FA (DR)
Pwr ++ / BAvg +++ / Spd +++ / Def ++++

Year	Lev	Team	AB	R	H	HR	RBI	Avg	OB	Slg	OPS	bb%	ct%	Eye	SB	CS	x/h%	Iso	RC/G
2013	A-	Mahoning Val	149	20	41	1	11	275	345	369	715	10	80	0.53	2	1	27	94	4.50
2013	A-	State College	15	1	1	0	0	67	176	67	243	12	93	2.00	0	0	0	0	-0.25
2013	A	Peoria	85	5	23	0	3	271	326	318	644	8	74	0.32	2	0	17	47	3.43
2014	A	Peoria	379	50	104	2	56	274	318	364	682	6	85	0.42	27	13	26	90	3.95
2014	A+	Palm Beach	31	3	6	0	0	194	219	194	412	3	84	0.20	1	0	0	0	0.51

Defensively Herrera has the tools to make all of the plays. He has good range, quick feet, soft hands, and a strong arm. He has a good approach at the plate and makes consistent contact, but is not likely to ever hit for much power. He does have good speed and stole 28 bases.

Herrera,Rosell — 56 — Colorado

EXP MLB DEBUT: 2016 | H/W: 6-3 190 | FUT: Starting SS | **9D**

Bats B Age 22 — 2009 FA (DR)
Pwr +++ / BAvg ++++ / Spd ++ / Def +++

Year	Lev	Team	AB	R	H	HR	RBI	Avg	OB	Slg	OPS	bb%	ct%	Eye	SB	CS	x/h%	Iso	RC/G
2011	Rk	Casper	243	38	69	6	34	284	356	449	804	10	74	0.44	5	4	29	165	5.67
2012	A-	Tri-City	194	30	55	1	30	284	332	351	682	7	82	0.41	7	3	16	67	3.92
2012	A	Asheville	213	22	43	1	26	202	274	272	546	9	77	0.43	6	3	26	70	2.25
2013	A	Asheville	472	83	162	16	76	343	418	515	933	11	80	0.64	21	8	30	172	7.23
2014	A+	Modesto	275	31	67	4	23	244	304	335	639	8	81	0.46	9	7	24	91	3.41

Switch-hitting SS came back to earth. A wrist injury cost him five weeks and hampered his production all season. Has good size and above-avg power. Can be overly aggressive and struggles to hit LHP. Speed is not a big part of his game, but does have good instincts on the bases.

Hicks,John — 2 — Seattle

EXP MLB DEBUT: 2015 | H/W: 6-2 210 | FUT: Starting C | **7E**

Bats R Age 25 — 2011 (4) Virginia
Pwr ++ / BAvg +++ / Spd ++ / Def +++

Year	Lev	Team	AB	R	H	HR	RBI	Avg	OB	Slg	OPS	bb%	ct%	Eye	SB	CS	x/h%	Iso	RC/G
2011	A	Clinton	139	21	43	2	26	309	333	446	779	3	88	0.29	2	3	30	137	4.92
2012	A+	High Desert	506	87	158	15	79	312	348	472	821	5	80	0.38	22	8	31	160	5.41
2013	AA	Jackson	296	40	70	4	29	236	289	331	620	7	79	0.35	13	4	27	95	3.10
2014	AA	Jackson	189	29	56	3	27	296	364	418	782	10	78	0.48	6	3	27	122	5.31
2014	AAA	Tacoma	101	13	28	2	20	277	324	376	700	6	76	0.29	1	0	18	99	4.02

Strong catcher with decent all-around game. Has improved receiving while catch-and-throw skills are solid. Expands strike zone at times with long swing, but can make hard contact and give ball a ride. Swing path more conducive for doubles, but can catch up to good FB. Runs OK for C.

Hill,Derek — 8 — Detroit

EXP MLB DEBUT: 2018 | H/W: 6-2 195 | FUT: Starting CF | **8C**

Bats R Age 19 — 2014 (1) HS (CA)
Pwr ++ / BAvg ++++ / Spd ++++ / Def +++

Year	Lev	Team	AB	R	H	HR	RBI	Avg	OB	Slg	OPS	bb%	ct%	Eye	SB	CS	x/h%	Iso	RC/G
2014	Rk	GCL Tigers	99	12	21	2	11	212	322	333	655	14	81	0.84	9	1	29	121	3.91
2014	A-	Connecticut	74	8	15	0	3	203	224	243	467	3	65	0.08	2	1	13	41	0.73

Rangy, fast CF with polished feel for game. Frame could add strength and more loft in stroke could lead to above average power. Makes OK contact with quick, short swing and focuses on line drives to gaps. Knows strike zone and uses plus speed well on base. Accurate arm asset in CF.

Hoying,Jared — 89 — Texas

EXP MLB DEBUT: 2015 | H/W: 6-3 190 | FUT: Reserve OF | **6B**

Bats L Age 25 — 2010 (10) Toledo
Pwr +++ / BAvg ++ / Spd +++ / Def ++

Year	Lev	Team	AB	R	H	HR	RBI	Avg	OB	Slg	OPS	bb%	ct%	Eye	SB	CS	x/h%	Iso	RC/G
2012	A+	Myrtle Beach	218	37	60	4	17	275	339	404	743	9	76	0.40	8	4	30	128	4.76
2012	AA	Frisco	246	39	68	4	25	276	326	378	704	7	80	0.36	9	5	21	102	4.12
2013	AA	Frisco	153	17	37	5	24	242	301	438	739	8	71	0.29	3	1	46	196	4.76
2013	AAA	Round Rock	188	31	50	8	24	266	289	473	762	3	68	0.10	4	2	36	207	4.89
2014	AAA	Round Rock	509	86	138	26	78	271	324	517	841	7	72	0.29	20	7	48	246	5.99

Athletic OF who doubled career high in HR and matched high in SB. Has bat speed and barrel control to contribute in power department. Consistently drives balls and can hit LHP. Runs well for size and can play CF with sufficient range. Profiles as reserve who can help with HR and SB.

Jackson,Alex — 79 — Seattle

EXP MLB DEBUT: 2017 | H/W: 6-2 215 | FUT: Starting OF | **9D**

Bats R Age 19 — 2014 (1) HS (CA)
Pwr ++++ / BAvg +++ / Spd ++ / Def ++

Year	Lev	Team	AB	R	H	HR	RBI	Avg	OB	Slg	OPS	bb%	ct%	Eye	SB	CS	x/h%	Iso	RC/G
2014	Rk	AZL Mariners	82	11	23	2	16	280	352	476	827	10	71	0.38	0	1	43	195	6.17

Strong, powerful prospect who moved from C to OF as pro. Missed time with fractured cheek, but has significant upside with bat. Drives ball to all fields with plus power and bat speed. Long swing can be exploited, but should hit for power and BA. Lacks foot speed and needs reps in OF.

Jagielo, Eric — 5 — New York (A)

EXP MLB DEBUT: 2016 | H/W: 6-2 195 | FUT: Starting 3B | 8D

Bats L | Age 22
2013 (1) Notre Dame
Pwr +++
BAvg +++
Spd +
Def ++

Year	Lev	Team	AB	R	H	HR	RBI	Avg	OB	Slg	OPS	bb%	ct%	Eye	SB	CS	x/h%	Iso	RC/G
2013	Rk	GCL Yankees	2	1	0	0	0	0	0	0	0	0	100		0	0		0	-2.66
2013	Rk	GCL Yankees 2	7	2	2	0	0	286	375	571	946	13	71	0.50	0	0	100	286	8.37
2013	A-	Staten Island	184	19	49	6	27	266	357	451	808	12	71	0.48	0	0	43	185	5.91
2014	Rk	GCL Yankees	23	3	5	2	4	217	308	478	786	12	96	3.00	0	0	40	261	5.33
2014	A+	Tampa	309	43	80	16	54	259	340	460	800	11	70	0.41	0	0	38	201	5.57

Tall INF who missed time with oblique injury. Has a polished approach, though can struggle with LHP. Knows strike zone and has above average power potential with loft. Swings hard and has hand-eye coordination for moderate BA. Not much agility or range at 3B and could move to 1B.

Jankowski, Travis — 8 — San Diego

EXP MLB DEBUT: 2016 | H/W: 6-2 190 | FUT: Backup OF | 6B

Bats L | Age 23
2012 (S-1) Stony Brook
Pwr ++
BAvg +++
Spd ++++
Def ++++

Year	Lev	Team	AB	R	H	HR	RBI	Avg	OB	Slg	OPS	bb%	ct%	Eye	SB	CS	x/h%	Iso	RC/G
2013	A+	Lake Elsinore	493	89	141	1	38	286	356	355	711	10	81	0.56	71	14	18	69	4.48
2014	Rk	AZL Padres	14	5	6	0	3	429	467	500	967	7	93	1.00	2	1	17	71	7.22
2014	A-	Eugene	33	6	6	0	1	182	250	182	432	8	85	0.60	4	0	0	0	1.07
2014	A+	Lake Elsinore	18	2	3	0	1	167	375	222	597	25	83	2.00	1	0	33	56	3.87
2014	AA	San Antonio	100	14	24	0	10	240	296	300	596	7	86	0.57	10	2	21	60	3.08

Limited to just 165 AB due to a fractured wrist. Plus speed and good instincts on the bases gives him a chance, but lack of power works against him. Struggles with breaking stuff, though makes decent contact with line drive approach. Plays solid CF with plus range.

Jansen, Danny — 2 — Toronto

EXP MLB DEBUT: 2018 | H/W: 6-2 210 | FUT: Starting C | 7D

Bats R | Age 19
2013 (16) HS (WI)
Pwr +++
BAvg +++
Spd +
Def ++

Year	Lev	Team	AB	R	H	HR	RBI	Avg	OB	Slg	OPS	bb%	ct%	Eye	SB	CS	x/h%	Iso	RC/G
2013	Rk	GCL Blue Jays	114	19	28	0	18	246	363	281	644	16	91	2.10	0	0	14	35	4.28
2014	Rk	Bluefield	124	22	35	5	17	282	364	484	848	11	86	0.94	2	1	43	202	6.12

Strong catcher who makes easy contact with compact, quick stroke. Understands balls and strikes and has enough bat speed to own average pop to pull side. Has improved behind plate, but lacks ideal footwork and agility. Arm strength is a bit light, but plays up due to quick transfer.

Jean, Luis — 6 — Colorado

EXP MLB DEBUT: 2018 | H/W: 6-1 150 | FUT: Starting SS | 7D

Bats R | Age 20
2011 FA (DR)
Pwr ++
BAvg +++
Spd +++
Def +++

Year	Lev	Team	AB	R	H	HR	RBI	Avg	OB	Slg	OPS	bb%	ct%	Eye	SB	CS	x/h%	Iso	RC/G
2013	Rk	DSL Rockies	164	26	48	1	17	293	348	360	708	8	93	1.17	19	4	19	67	4.51
2014	Rk	Grand Junction	158	22	45	1	25	285	327	386	713	6	88	0.53	13	8	22	101	4.37

Versatile infielder from the Dominican had a solid U.S. debut. For now Jean is a contact-oriented hitter who puts the ball into play and uses his above-average speed well on the bases. Moves well defensively with a plus arm and proved he can handle SS/2B/3B.

Jensen, Kyle — 79 — Los Angeles (N)

EXP MLB DEBUT: 2015 | H/W: 6-3 250 | FUT: Backup OF | 6C

Bats R | Age 26
2009 (12) St. Mary's
Pwr ++++
BAvg +
Spd +
Def +

Year	Lev	Team	AB	R	H	HR	RBI	Avg	OB	Slg	OPS	bb%	ct%	Eye	SB	CS	x/h%	Iso	RC/G
2011	AA	Jacksonville	80	14	20	5	10	250	310	475	785	8	71	0.30	1	0	35	225	5.14
2012	AA	Jacksonville	445	70	104	24	84	234	337	452	788	13	64	0.43	1	1	45	218	5.78
2013	AA	Jacksonville	245	43	58	16	42	237	327	498	825	12	70	0.45	5	3	55	261	5.94
2013	AAA	New Orleans	202	31	47	12	36	233	292	485	777	8	65	0.24	1	0	57	252	5.39
2014	AAA	New Orleans	497	70	129	27	92	260	325	481	806	9	70	0.33	1	0	43	221	5.56

Tall, thick-bodied OF has plus raw power, that is about the extent of his tool box. Launched 27 HR at AAA, but also struck out 147 times. Struggles to hit breaking balls and is essentially a mistake hitter. Below avg at every other facet of the game though he can play both LF and 1B.

Jhang, Jin-De — 2 — Pittsburgh

EXP MLB DEBUT: 2016 | H/W: 5-11 220 | FUT: Starting C | 7C

Bats L | Age 21
2011 FA (Taiwan)
Pwr ++
BAvg ++
4.30 Spd +++
Def +++

Year	Lev	Team	AB	R	H	HR	RBI	Avg	OB	Slg	OPS	bb%	ct%	Eye	SB	CS	x/h%	Iso	RC/G
2012	Rk	GCL Pirates	128	12	39	1	23	305	373	398	772	10	88	0.88	1	1	21	94	5.26
2013	A-	Jamestown	184	22	51	5	34	277	338	413	751	8	87	0.71	0	1	27	136	4.83
2014	A+	Bradenton	269	29	59	2	35	219	261	301	562	5	87	0.42	3	0	27	82	2.55

Power has yet to develop, but it should as he moves up. Continues to improve defensively. Despite stocky frame, he moves well behind the plate and nailed 32% of baserunners. Struggles vs. LHP and will need to work hard to remain behind the dish as the Pirates have depth at C.

Jimenez, A.J. — 2 — Toronto

EXP MLB DEBUT: 2015 | H/W: 6-0 225 | FUT: Starting C | 7C

Bats R | Age 24
2008 (9) HS (PR)
Pwr +++
BAvg ++
Spd ++
Def ++++

Year	Lev	Team	AB	R	H	HR	RBI	Avg	OB	Slg	OPS	bb%	ct%	Eye	SB	CS	x/h%	Iso	RC/G
2013	A+	Dunedin	28	5	12	1	9	429	448	643	1091	3	89	0.33	0	0	33	214	8.28
2013	AA	New Hampshire	203	28	56	3	29	276	329	394	723	7	82	0.43	1	2	32	118	4.44
2013	AAA	Buffalo	30	0	7	0	0	233	258	267	525	3	93	0.50	0	1	14	33	2.28
2014	AA	New Hampshire	94	11	21	1	13	223	270	340	610	6	80	0.32	1	0	43	117	3.01
2014	AAA	Buffalo	219	21	57	2	24	260	302	356	658	6	85	0.39	1	1	28	96	3.63

Injury-riddled C who had over 300 AB for first time since '11. May not project to high BA, but has plus bat speed with some HR potential. Mostly lines ball to gaps. Mostly known for athleticism and excellent defense. Receives and frames well while possessing strong, accurate arm.

Jimenez, Eloy — 79 — Chicago (N)

EXP MLB DEBUT: 2018 | H/W: 6-4 205 | FUT: Starting RF | 9E

Bats R | Age 18
2013 FA (DR)
Pwr ++++
BAvg ++
Spd +++
Def +++

Year	Lev	Team	AB	R	H	HR	RBI	Avg	OB	Slg	OPS	bb%	ct%	Eye	SB	CS	x/h%	Iso	RC/G
2014	Rk	AZL Cubs	150	13	34	3	27	227	275	367	642	6	79	0.31	3	1	38	140	3.35

Lean, projectable OF has plus raw power. Swing can get long and scouts are mixed on whether he will hit for avg. Makes consistent contact and has plus bat speed, but makes weak contact at present. Can be a beast in batting practice and already has impressive physicality.

Jimenez, Emerson — 6 — Colorado

EXP MLB DEBUT: 2017 | H/W: 6-1 160 | FUT: Starting SS | 8D

Bats L | Age 20
2011 FA (DR)
Pwr ++
BAvg +++
Spd ++++
Def ++++

Year	Lev	Team	AB	R	H	HR	RBI	Avg	OB	Slg	OPS	bb%	ct%	Eye	SB	CS	x/h%	Iso	RC/G
2013	Rk	DSL Rockies	36	3	8	0	4	222	243	250	493	3	89	0.25	1	2	13	28	1.69
2013	Rk	Grand Junction	181	32	56	3	20	309	342	414	756	5	77	0.21	6	3	21	105	4.67
2014	A	Asheville	266	36	69	1	28	259	273	342	615	2	78	0.09	16	7	23	83	2.81

Slick fielding SS put up respectable numbers in the SAL. Has good bat speed and the potential to develop avg power, but needs a better understanding of the strike zone. Plus speed gives him SB potential and range at SS. Makes all the plays defensive and his glove is plus.

Joe, Connor — 9 — Pittsburgh

EXP MLB DEBUT: 2017 | H/W: 6-0 205 | FUT: Starting RF | 7D

Bats R | Age 22
2014 (1-S) San Diego
Pwr +++
BAvg +++
Spd +++
Def ++

Year	Lev	Team	AB	R	H	HR	RBI	Avg	OB	Slg	OPS	bb%	ct%	Eye	SB	CS	x/h%	Iso	RC/G
2014	(did not play in 2014)																		

39th pick in the 2014 draft. Has average speed and defense in the OF with a good arm. Quick bat with solid plate discipline and gap power. Given org depth at C he will likely play the OF. Back injury prevented him from making his pro debut.

Johnson, Micah — 4 — Chicago (A)

EXP MLB DEBUT: 2015 | H/W: 6-0 190 | FUT: Starting 2B | 7C

Bats B | Age 24
2012 (9) Indiana
Pwr ++
BAvg +++
Spd ++++
Def ++

Year	Lev	Team	AB	R	H	HR	RBI	Avg	OB	Slg	OPS	bb%	ct%	Eye	SB	CS	x/h%	Iso	RC/G
2013	A	Kannapolis	304	76	104	6	42	342	419	530	948	12	78	0.60	61	19	33	188	7.65
2013	A+	Winston-Salem	211	28	58	1	15	275	308	360	668	5	87	0.37	22	7	21	85	3.74
2013	AA	Birmingham	21	2	5	0	1	238	238	238	476	0	81	0.00	1	0	0	0	0.95
2014	AA	Birmingham	146	18	48	3	16	329	413	466	879	13	82	0.78	10	7	27	137	6.66
2014	AAA	Charlotte	273	30	75	2	28	275	315	370	685	6	85	0.38	12	6	23	95	3.94

Patient, fast INF who saw SB plummet due to hamstring ailments. Leadoff hitter who sees pitches and controls bat while using entire field. Is a menace while on base and has plus speed for XBH and SB. Exhibits some strength, but HR not in game. Defense isn't strong suit, nor is his arm.

Jones,JaCoby

6 | **Pittsburgh** | EXP MLB DEBUT: 2016 | H/W: 6-3 200 | FUT: Starting SS | **8D**

Bats R Age 22 — 2013 (3) LSU

Pwr ++ | BAvg ++ | Spd +++ | Def ++

Year	Lev	Team	AB	R	H	HR	RBI	Avg	OB	Slg	OPS	bb%	ct%	Eye	SB	CS	x/h%	Iso	RC/G
2011	NCAA	LSU	195	36	66	4	32	338	377	467	843	6	81	0.32	13	8	24	128	5.77
2012	NCAA	LSU	245	42	62	4	29	253	296	363	659	6	81	0.32	11	5	29	110	3.55
2013	NCAA	LSU	201	42	59	6	31	294	385	448	833	13	78	0.68	12	3	31	154	6.08
2013	A-	Jamestown	61	14	19	1	10	311	344	459	803	5	77	0.21	3	2	26	148	5.34
2014	A	West Virginia	445	72	128	23	70	288	337	503	840	7	70	0.25	17	9	37	216	5.98

Was moved from CF to SS and had an impressive breakout. At the plate has plus bat speed and a swing-for-the-fences approach. Can be overly aggressive and raises questions about ability to hit. Defensively is below avg with a strong arm, but inconsistent footwork. Made 24 errors.

Jones,Ryder

56 | **San Francisco** | EXP MLB DEBUT: 2017 | H/W: 6-2 200 | FUT: Starting 3B | **8E**

Bats L Age 20 — 2013 (2) HS (NC)

Pwr +++ | BAvg ++ | Spd ++ | Def +++

Year	Lev	Team	AB	R	H	HR	RBI	Avg	OB	Slg	OPS	bb%	ct%	Eye	SB	CS	x/h%	Iso	RC/G
2013	Rk	AZL Giants	145	29	46	1	18	317	377	400	777	9	74	0.37	0	0	22	83	5.29
2014	A-	Salem-Kaizer	107	17	26	3	18	243	289	393	682	6	80	0.33	1	0	35	150	3.80
2014	A	Augusta	369	43	81	7	49	220	256	339	595	5	75	0.19	6	1	36	119	2.61

Strong, athletic IF struggled across two levels in '14, splitting time at 3B and SS, though his future will be at the hot corner where he'll be average with a strong arm. He has plus raw power and a good, smooth stroke, but as many scouts thought, he struggled making consistent contact against better pitching and needs to adjust approach.

Judge,Aaron

9 | **New York (A)** | EXP MLB DEBUT: 2016 | H/W: 6-7 230 | FUT: Starting RF | **9D**

Bats R Age 22 — 2013 (1) Fresno State

Pwr ++++ | BAvg +++ | Spd +++ | Def +++

Year	Lev	Team	AB	R	H	HR	RBI	Avg	OB	Slg	OPS	bb%	ct%	Eye	SB	CS	x/h%	Iso	RC/G
2011	NCAA	Fresno State	187	38	67	2	30	358	434	465	899	12	78	0.60	11	1	22	107	6.99
2012	NCAA	Fresno State	201	47	62	4	27	308	442	458	899	19	79	1.14	13	2	32	149	7.38
2013	NCAA	Fresno State	206	45	76	12	36	369	461	655	1116	15	74	0.66	12	2	41	286	10.04
2014	A	CharlestonSC	234	36	78	9	45	333	429	530	958	14	75	0.66	1	0	33	197	7.90
2014	A+	Tampa	233	44	66	8	33	283	410	442	852	18	69	0.69	0	0	29	159	6.77

Physical OF who stood out in pro debut. Brings patience and plus power to plate and destroys LHP. Has leverage and fluidity in swing to hit for more than just power, but will strike out. Owns nice athleticism and speed for size and profiles as big league RF with plus-plus arm strength.

Katoh,Gosuke

4 | **New York (A)** | EXP MLB DEBUT: 2018 | H/W: 6-2 180 | FUT: Starting 2B | **7E**

Bats L Age 20 — 2013 (2) HS (CA)

Pwr ++ | BAvg ++ | Spd ++++ | Def ++

Year	Lev	Team	AB	R	H	HR	RBI	Avg	OB	Slg	OPS	bb%	ct%	Eye	SB	CS	x/h%	Iso	RC/G
2013	Rk	GCL Yankees	184	28	57	6	25	310	398	522	920	13	76	0.61	4	2	39	212	7.33
2014	A	CharlestonSC	383	58	85	3	37	222	344	326	670	16	63	0.50	20	10	33	104	4.30

Lean 2B who suffered thru inconsistent season. Has plate patience, but doesn't have good 2-strike approach. Swings and misses too much and has significant holes in swing. Some hope that power will emerge, but needs more contact. Owns plus speed and range, but sloppy defender.

Kelly,Carson

2 | **St. Louis** | EXP MLB DEBUT: 2017 | H/W: 6-2 200 | FUT: Starting C | **7D**

Bats R Age 20 — 2012 (2) HS (OR)

Pwr +++ | BAvg ++ | Spd ++ | Def ++

Year	Lev	Team	AB	R	H	HR	RBI	Avg	OB	Slg	OPS	bb%	ct%	Eye	SB	CS	x/h%	Iso	RC/G
2012	Rk	Johnson City	213	24	48	9	25	225	260	399	659	4	85	0.30	0	0	40	174	3.42
2013	A-	State College	271	35	75	4	32	277	326	387	714	7	89	0.65	1	0	28	111	4.40
2013	A	Peoria	146	18	32	2	13	219	283	301	584	8	83	0.52	0	0	25	82	2.80
2014	A	Peoria	363	41	90	6	49	248	318	366	684	9	85	0.69	1	0	30	118	4.13

Has yet to hit his stride, but does have good power. Makes consistent contact, but lacks a feel for hitting. Could be more selective in his approach. Defensively has good hands a plus arm and made great strides. Moves well behind the plate.

Kemp,Tony

478 | **Houston** | EXP MLB DEBUT: 2015 | H/W: 5-6 165 | FUT: Utility player | **6A**

Bats L Age 23 — 2013 (5) Vanderbilt

Pwr ++ | BAvg +++ | Spd ++++ | Def ++

Year	Lev	Team	AB	R	H	HR	RBI	Avg	OB	Slg	OPS	bb%	ct%	Eye	SB	CS	x/h%	Iso	RC/G
2013	NCAA	Vanderbilt	266	64	104	0	33	391	462	485	947	12	88	1.09	34	14	18	94	7.47
2013	A-	Vermont	177	25	50	1	13	282	359	362	720	11	84	0.72	17	9	20	79	4.65
2013	A	Quad Cities	98	21	25	1	9	255	376	316	692	16	82	1.06	4	2	12	61	4.53
2014	A+	Lancaster	295	79	99	4	37	336	424	468	891	13	88	1.29	28	7	27	132	6.89
2014	AA	Corpus Christi	233	42	68	4	21	292	368	425	793	11	86	0.88	13	6	28	133	5.53

Diminutive, consistent INF who knows role. Ideal leadoff hitter with high OBP and line drive approach. Can play small ball with plus bat control and easy contact. Offers some pop, though not effective against LHP. Will be given shot in CF and has the speed and instincts to succeed there.

Kepler-Rozycki,Max

3789 | **Minnesota** | EXP MLB DEBUT: 2016 | H/W: 6-4 205 | FUT: Starting OF | **7C**

Bats L Age 22 — 2009 FA (Germany)

Pwr +++ | BAvg ++ | Spd +++ | Def ++

Year	Lev	Team	AB	R	H	HR	RBI	Avg	OB	Slg	OPS	bb%	ct%	Eye	SB	CS	x/h%	Iso	RC/G
2010	Rk	GCL Twins	140	15	40	0	11	286	346	343	689	8	81	0.48	6	1	18	57	4.12
2011	Rk	Elizabethton	191	29	50	1	24	262	341	366	708	11	72	0.43	1	1	30	105	4.53
2012	Rk	Elizabethton	232	40	69	10	49	297	371	539	909	10	86	0.82	7	0	45	241	6.81
2013	A	Cedar Rapids	236	35	56	9	40	237	308	424	731	9	82	0.56	2	0	41	186	4.57
2014	A+	Fort Myers	364	53	96	5	59	264	327	393	719	9	83	0.55	6	2	32	129	4.52

Athletic prospect who is making progress and ended year strong. Has size and strength to add more power to arsenal and owns balanced swing and ability to hit LHP. Drives ball to all fields with easy contact. Played mostly CF after 1B in '13. Has good speed, but owns below average arm.

Kivlehan,Patrick

35 | **Seattle** | EXP MLB DEBUT: 2015 | H/W: 6-2 210 | FUT: Starting 3B | **7B**

Bats R Age 25 — 2012 (4) Rutgers

Pwr +++ | BAvg +++ | Spd ++ | Def +++

Year	Lev	Team	AB	R	H	HR	RBI	Avg	OB	Slg	OPS	bb%	ct%	Eye	SB	CS	x/h%	Iso	RC/G
2012	A-	Everett	282	46	85	12	52	301	346	511	856	6	67	0.20	14	1	38	209	6.46
2013	A	Clinton	223	26	63	3	31	283	333	386	719	7	81	0.40	5	3	25	103	4.36
2013	A+	High Desert	266	48	85	13	59	320	380	530	910	9	76	0.40	10	3	33	211	6.83
2014	A+	High Desert	142	24	40	9	35	282	338	563	901	8	77	0.38	2	0	50	282	6.58
2014	AA	Jackson	377	60	113	11	68	300	373	485	858	10	79	0.56	9	4	36	186	6.30

Versatile, athletic player who set highs in HR and BB. Becoming complete player with improving power and ability to hit for BA. Draws walks with advanced approach and can steal occasional bag. Played mostly 3B, but also saw action at 1B and OF. Not the quickest guy, but makes plays.

Knapp,Andrew

2 | **Philadelphia** | EXP MLB DEBUT: 2017 | H/W: 6-1 190 | FUT: Starting C | **7D**

Bats B Age 23 — 2013 (2) California

Pwr ++ | BAvg +++ | Spd + | Def ++

Year	Lev	Team	AB	R	H	HR	RBI	Avg	OB	Slg	OPS	bb%	ct%	Eye	SB	CS	x/h%	Iso	RC/G
2012	NCAA	California	211	36	56	5	26	265	338	412	750	10	84	0.68	4	3	38	147	4.91
2013	NCAA	California	206	34	72	8	41	350	425	544	969	12	83	0.77	4	2	33	194	7.59
2013	A-	Williamsport	217	30	55	4	23	253	322	401	723	9	74	0.39	7	5	44	147	4.59
2014	A	Lakewood	283	39	82	5	25	290	352	438	790	9	75	0.38	3	3	34	148	5.44
2014	A+	Clearwater	83	7	13	1	7	157	205	205	409	6	69	0.19	1	0	15	48	-0.08

Only played about a half-season due to Tommy John surgery in 2013, but showed the hitting chops with an up-the-middle approach. Can barrel balls into the gaps, especially from the left side. Defense is improving to the point that he should be able to stick, though has athleticism to move to back to OF (his college position) if needed.

Kobernus,Jeff

8 | **Washington** | EXP MLB DEBUT: 2014 | H/W: 6-2 195 | FUT: Backup OF | **6B**

Bats R Age 26 — 2009 (2) California

Pwr + | BAvg +++ | Spd ++++ | Def +++

Year	Lev	Team	AB	R	H	HR	RBI	Avg	OB	Slg	OPS	bb%	ct%	Eye	SB	CS	x/h%	Iso	RC/G
2014	A	Hagerstown	13	6	3	1	2	231	375	462	837	19	77	1.00	2	1	33	231	6.07
2014	A+	Potomac	15	5	5	0	3	333	444	333	778	17	87	1.50	5	0	0	0	5.72
2014	AA	Harrisburg	24	2	7	0	3	292	346	333	679	8	83	0.50	2	0	14	42	3.96
2014	AAA	Syracuse	206	28	53	2	23	257	332	359	691	10	79	0.52	15	3	30	102	4.20
2014	MLB	Washington	6	2	0	0	0	0	143	0	143	14	83	1.00	0	0		0	-2.27

Becoming a usable utliity player who can help out at all OF positions and at 2B in a pinch. No power to speak of, but hits line drives, can draw walks, and still has base-stealing ability. Uses speed to close gaps in the OF.

Kubitza,Kyle

5 | **Los Angeles (A)** | EXP MLB DEBUT: 2015 | H/W: 6-3 215 | FUT: Backup 3B | **7B**

Bats L Age 24 — 2011 (3) Texas State

Pwr +++ | BAvg +++ | Spd +++ | Def ++

Year	Lev	Team	AB	R	H	HR	RBI	Avg	OB	Slg	OPS	bb%	ct%	Eye	SB	CS	x/h%	Iso	RC/G
2011	NCAA	Texas State	226	59	70	10	66	310	443	558	1000	19	79	1.13	16	3	41	248	8.61
2011	Rk	Danville	162	36	52	1	34	321	409	475	884	13	77	0.63	9	3	38	154	7.01
2012	A	Rome	448	68	107	9	59	239	345	393	738	14	72	0.57	18	11	39	154	5.03
2013	A+	Lynchburg	435	75	113	12	57	260	375	434	809	16	70	0.61	8	16	41	175	6.12
2014	AA	Mississippi	440	76	130	8	55	295	400	470	871	15	70	0.58	21	6	38	175	7.10

3B had an impressive breakout hitting .295 with 50 extra-base hits. Does a good job of not chasing balls out of the zone and swinging at pitches he can drive. Solid defender at 3B with a strong arm, good feet, and soft hands. Shows surprising speed and agility for his size.

Lamb,Jake — 5 — Arizona

EXP MLB DEBUT: 2014 | H/W: 6-3 220 | FUT: Starting 3B | 8D

Bats L Age 24 — 2012 (6) Washington
Pwr +++ | BAvg +++ | Spd ++ | Def ++++

Year	Lev	Team	AB	R	H	HR	RBI	Avg	OB	Slg	OPS	bb%	ct%	Eye	SB	CS	x/h%	Iso	RC/G
2013	Rk	AZL Dbacks	17	4	5	0	5	294	368	412	780	11	71	0.40	0	0	40	118	5.65
2013	A+	Visalia	231	44	70	13	47	303	423	558	981	17	70	0.69	0	0	47	255	8.55
2014	AA	Mobile	374	60	119	14	79	318	399	551	949	12	74	0.51	0	0	45	233	7.77
2014	AAA	Reno	18	3	9	1	5	500	571	889	1460	14	78	0.75	2	0	56	389	14.50
2014	MLB	Arizona	126	15	29	4	11	230	265	373	638	5	71	0.16	1	1	31	143	3.11

Proved that '13 was no fluke, hitting .318 at AA, but struggled in the majors. Has a good approach at the plate with solid power. Doesn't have premium bat speed, and his stroke can get long, which was exploited. He moves well for his size and is a good defender with a strong arm.

Lambo,Andrew — 379 — Pittsburgh

EXP MLB DEBUT: 2013 | H/W: 6-3 225 | FUT: Backup OF | 6C

Bats L Age 26 — 2007 (4) HS (CA)
Pwr +++ | BAvg ++ | Spd + | Def ++

Year	Lev	Team	AB	R	H	HR	RBI	Avg	OB	Slg	OPS	bb%	ct%	Eye	SB	CS	x/h%	Iso	RC/G
2013	MLB	Pittsburgh	30	4	7	1	2	233	303	400	703	9	63	0.27	0	1	43	167	4.47
2014	Rk	GCL Pirates	13	3	2	1	1	154	353	385	738	24	77	1.33	0	0	50	231	4.88
2014	A-	Jamestown	12	2	2	0	1	167	375	167	542	25	83	2.00	0	0	0	0	3.11
2014	AAA	Indianapolis	238	44	78	11	42	328	385	563	948	8	80	0.47	3	2	41	235	7.20
2014	MLB	Pittsburgh	39	3	10	0	1	256	256	359	615	0	79	0.00	0	0	40	103	2.80

Another impressive season at AAA, hitting .328/.389/.565. Still has plus raw power and could hit 25+ HR if he played everyday. Worked to make more consistent contact, but it resulted in a dip in production, and he may have to decide whether to hit for power or BA.

Lara,Gilbert — 6 — Milwaukee

EXP MLB DEBUT: 2019 | H/W: 6-3 185 | FUT: Starting 3B | 8E

Bats R Age 17 — 2014 FA (DR)
Pwr +++ | BAvg ++ | Spd +++ | Def +++

Year	Lev	Team	AB	R	H	HR	RBI	Avg	OB	Slg	OPS	bb%	ct%	Eye	SB	CS	x/h%	Iso	RC/G
2014		(did not play in the US in 2014)																	

Dominican SS has good bat speed, but scouts are mixed on whether he will hit for average. Did show the ability to make good hard contact, but might struggle against more advanced pitching. Lara was drafted as a shortstop, but most evaluators see him moving to 3B in the future.

Lee,Hak-Ju — 6 — Tampa Bay

EXP MLB DEBUT: 2015 | H/W: 6-2 170 | FUT: Starting SS | 7B

Bats L Age 24 — 2008 FA (South Korea)
Pwr ++ | BAvg +++ | Spd ++++ | Def ++++

Year	Lev	Team	AB	R	H	HR	RBI	Avg	OB	Slg	OPS	bb%	ct%	Eye	SB	CS	x/h%	Iso	RC/G
2011	A+	Charlotte	400	82	127	4	23	318	382	443	825	10	82	0.58	28	14	24	125	5.87
2011	AA	Montgomery	100	16	19	1	7	190	270	310	580	10	78	0.50	5	2	32	120	2.80
2012	AA	Montgomery	475	68	124	4	37	261	333	360	693	10	79	0.50	37	9	23	99	4.21
2013	AAA	Durham	45	13	19	1	7	422	536	600	1136	20	80	1.22	6	2	26	178	10.51
2014	AAA	Durham	315	36	64	4	23	203	287	276	563	11	73	0.43	12	5	22	73	2.38

Long, lean INF who has missed lots of time past 2 seasons. Possesses instincts and the requisite hands, range, and arm for SS. More of a slap approach which limits power and batting eye fell apart in '14. Can go to opposite field and at best when drawing walks and using speed.

Leon,Julian — 2 — Los Angeles (N)

EXP MLB DEBUT: 2017 | H/W: 5-11 215 | FUT: Starting C | 8D

Bats R Age 19 — 2012 FA (Mexico)
Pwr +++ | BAvg +++ | Spd + | Def ++

Year	Lev	Team	AB	R	H	HR	RBI	Avg	OB	Slg	OPS	bb%	ct%	Eye	SB	CS	x/h%	Iso	RC/G
2013	Rk	AZL Dodgers	81	12	20	3	19	247	307	420	727	8	74	0.33	0	1	35	173	4.43
2014	Rk	Ogden	223	39	74	12	57	332	413	565	978	12	76	0.58	1	1	36	233	7.89

Top C prospect in the system. Is already physically mature. Has plus power and drives the ball to all fields. Moves well behind the dish with a strong arm, but needs to improve his footwork and blocking skills. Showed enough to stick behind the plate and his bat will be carrying tool.

Leonard,Patrick — 35 — Tampa Bay

EXP MLB DEBUT: 2016 | H/W: 6-4 225 | FUT: Starting 1B | 7C

Bats R Age 22 — 2011 (5) HS (TX)
Pwr +++ | BAvg +++ | Spd ++ | Def +++

Year	Lev	Team	AB	R	H	HR	RBI	Avg	OB	Slg	OPS	bb%	ct%	Eye	SB	CS	x/h%	Iso	RC/G
2012	Rk	Burlington	235	37	59	14	46	251	336	494	829	11	77	0.55	6	2	44	243	5.82
2013	A	Bowling Green	440	52	99	9	57	225	293	345	638	9	73	0.36	4	1	35	120	3.34
2014	A+	Charlotte	455	79	129	13	58	284	353	448	802	10	76	0.46	14	0	34	165	5.55

Tall INF who showed improvement with emerging power. Tweaked swing to tap into natural power and continues to show polished pitch recognition. Bat speed is only average, but he uses entire field. Excellent defender with OK quickness and range. Lacks foot speed, but can steal bases.

Leyba,Domingo — 46 — Arizona

EXP MLB DEBUT: 2018 | H/W: 5-11 160 | FUT: Starting 2B/SS | 7C

Bats B Age 19 — 2012 FA (DR)
Pwr ++ | BAvg +++ | Spd +++ | Def +++

Year	Lev	Team	AB	R	H	HR	RBI	Avg	OB	Slg	OPS	bb%	ct%	Eye	SB	CS	x/h%	Iso	RC/G
2013	Rk	DSL Tigers	201	51	70	5	36	348	443	577	1020	14	87	1.31	16	8	40	229	8.51
2014	A-	Connecticut	144	20	38	1	17	264	303	375	678	5	88	0.47	1	2	34	111	3.95
2014	A	West Michigan	116	20	46	1	7	397	426	483	909	5	89	0.46	1	2	17	86	6.41

Young, advanced INF who has knowledge of strike zone, and a contact approach to get on base. Controls bat from both sides and has strength for doubles. Should add some pop in due time for double-digit HR. Moves well in middle infield with quick hands and feet. Speed, range, and arm are average.

Lin,Tzu-Wei — 6 — Boston

EXP MLB DEBUT: 2017 | H/W: 5-9 155 | FUT: Starting SS | 7D

Bats L Age 21 — 2012 FA (Taiwan)
Pwr + | BAvg +++ | Spd ++++ | Def +++

Year	Lev	Team	AB	R	H	HR	RBI	Avg	OB	Slg	OPS	bb%	ct%	Eye	SB	CS	x/h%	Iso	RC/G
2012	Rk	GCL Red Sox	110	21	28	0	16	255	349	318	667	13	75	0.57	4	2	21	64	4.03
2013	A-	Lowell	230	34	52	1	20	226	310	296	606	11	74	0.47	12	4	23	70	3.08
2014	A	Greenville	402	55	92	1	42	229	320	296	616	12	82	0.73	10	7	26	67	3.42

Short, quick INF who benefits by working counts and getting on base. Has bat speed to smash line drives to gaps and likes to use opposite field. Lacks physical frame and power projection, but has plus speed. Natural SS with smooth actions and strong arm. Gets to balls deep in hole.

Lindor,Francisco — 6 — Cleveland

EXP MLB DEBUT: 2015 | H/W: 5-11 175 | FUT: Starting SS | 9B

Bats B Age 21 — 2011 (1) HS (PR)
Pwr +++ | BAvg ++++ | Spd +++ | Def +++++

Year	Lev	Team	AB	R	H	HR	RBI	Avg	OB	Slg	OPS	bb%	ct%	Eye	SB	CS	x/h%	Iso	RC/G
2012	A	Lake County	490	83	126	6	42	257	339	355	694	11	84	0.78	27	12	26	98	4.35
2013	A+	Carolina	327	51	100	1	27	306	373	410	783	10	88	0.90	20	5	26	104	5.44
2013	AA	Akron	76	14	22	1	7	289	400	395	795	16	91	2.00	5	2	23	105	5.95
2014	AA	Akron	342	51	95	6	48	278	353	389	742	10	82	0.66	25	9	23	111	4.83
2014	AAA	Columbus	165	24	45	5	14	273	310	388	698	5	78	0.25	3	7	20	115	3.85

Instinctual INF with emerging power to add to elite defense. Understands strike zone and covers plate well with compact stroke from both sides. Hard line drives evolving into HR; set highs in HR and SB. Can impact game in variety of ways. Can hit leadoff with contact, eye, and speed.

Lindsey,Taylor — 4 — San Diego

EXP MLB DEBUT: 2015 | H/W: 6-0 195 | FUT: Starting 2B | 7B

Bats L Age 23 — 2010 (S-1) HS (AZ)
Pwr +++ | BAvg +++ | Spd +++ | Def +++

Year	Lev	Team	AB	R	H	HR	RBI	Avg	OB	Slg	OPS	bb%	ct%	Eye	SB	CS	x/h%	Iso	RC/G
2013	AA	Arkansas	508	68	139	17	56	274	336	441	777	9	82	0.53	4	4	32	167	5.10
2014	Rk	AZL Angels	3	1	1	0	0	333	500	333	833	25	100		0	0	0	0	7.37
2014	Rk	Orem	5	0	1	0	1	200	200	400	600	0	100		0	0	100	200	3.41
2014	AAA	Salt Lake	295	50	73	8	30	247	319	400	719	10	85	0.70	7	2	34	153	4.52
2014	AAA	El Paso	146	18	32	2	17	219	265	315	580	6	90	0.60	0	2	28	96	2.87

Took a step back after power surge in '13 and was dealt to the Padres. Sprays line drives and has a nice gap-to-gap approach. Good eye-hand coordination and nice bat speed allow him to make contact. Speed is below avg and lack of range and quickness keeps him at 2B.

Liriano,Rymer — 789 — San Diego

EXP MLB DEBUT: 2014 | H/W: 6-0 230 | FUT: Starting CF | 8C

Bats R Age 23 — 2007 FA (DR)
Pwr ++++ | BAvg ++ | Spd ++++ | Def +++

Year	Lev	Team	AB	R	H	HR	RBI	Avg	OB	Slg	OPS	bb%	ct%	Eye	SB	CS	x/h%	Iso	RC/G
2012	A+	Lake Elsinore	282	41	84	5	41	298	347	443	790	7	76	0.30	22	7	35	145	5.33
2012	AA	San Antonio	183	24	46	3	20	251	325	377	702	10	73	0.40	10	1	33	126	4.33
2014	AA	San Antonio	371	55	98	14	53	264	328	442	770	9	73	0.34	17	7	37	178	5.08
2014	AAA	El Paso	62	14	28	0	13	452	514	661	1176	11	77	0.57	3	1	43	210	10.84
2014	MLB	San Diego	109	13	24	1	6	220	280	266	546	8	64	0.23	4	1	13	46	1.97

He has plus raw power that is still developing and hit a career-high 15 HR. Has plus speed, though plate discipline and pitch recognition are an issue. That shortcoming is the only thing holding him back from being an elite prospect, as he does everything else well and with ease.

Loehr,Trace — 46 — Oakland

EXP MLB DEBUT: 2018 | H/W: 5-10 175 | FUT: Starting 2B/SS | 7D

Bats L Age 19
2014 (6) HS (OR)

Pwr +
BAvg + + +
Spd + + +
Def + + +

Year	Lev	Team	AB	R	H	HR	RBI	Avg	OB	Slg	OPS	bb%	ct%	Eye	SB	CS	x/h%	Iso	RC/G
2014	Rk	AZL Athletics	160	22	39	0	14	244	309	288	596	9	81	0.48	6	2	13	44	2.95

Short, agile INF who maximizes ability. Ranges well to both sides and has first step quickness and speed. Possesses soft hands and ideal footwork. Swings quick bat and makes good contact, but not much pop. Can hit LHP and should grow to hit for BA. Tools play up due to instincts.

Longhi,Nick — 79 — Boston

EXP MLB DEBUT: 2018 | H/W: 6-2 205 | FUT: Starting OF | 8E

Bats R Age 19
2013 (30) HS (FL)

Pwr + + +
BAvg + + +
Spd +
Def + +

Year	Lev	Team	AB	R	H	HR	RBI	Avg	OB	Slg	OPS	bb%	ct%	Eye	SB	CS	x/h%	Iso	RC/G
2013	Rk	GCL Red Sox	45	4	8	1	4	178	229	356	585	6	73	0.25	1	0	75	178	2.63
2014	A-	Lowell	109	19	36	0	10	330	392	440	832	9	80	0.50	0	3	31	110	6.03

Projectable sleeper prospect with intriging tools and raw ability. Fluid, repeatable swing could lead to offensive upside. Possesses natural strength and brute raw power, but may not have bat speed for quality fastballs. Doesn't run well and has limited range, though has plus arm.

Lopez,Carlos — 789 — Miami

EXP MLB DEBUT: 2018 | H/W: 6-2 210 | FUT: Starting LF | 7D

Bats L Age 25
2013 (10) Cal St Fullerton

Pwr +
BAvg + + +
Spd + +
Def + +

Year	Lev	Team	AB	R	H	HR	RBI	Avg	OB	Slg	OPS	bb%	ct%	Eye	SB	CS	x/h%	Iso	RC/G
2011	NCAA	Cal St. Fullerton	148	15	50	2	33	338	399	480	879	9	93	1.50	7	0	26	142	6.50
2012	NCAA	Cal St. Fullerton	218	32	69	1	35	317	402	413	814	12	90	1.41	7	1	28	96	6.00
2013	NCAA	Cal St. Fullerton	236	52	80	4	34	339	405	462	866	10	91	1.24	15	4	23	123	6.34
2013	A-	Batavia	223	28	71	0	24	318	390	417	807	10	86	0.81	1	3	23	99	5.76
2014	A	Greensboro	507	85	164	7	74	323	394	438	832	10	87	0.92	5	2	24	114	5.97

Has a good approach at the plate and a pretty LH swing. Has some power, but prefers to work counts, get on base, and shoot balls in the gap. Worked hard to become an avg defender. Was old for this level and will need to prove he can do this against more advanced competition.

Lugo,Dawel — 6 — Toronto

EXP MLB DEBUT: 2017 | H/W: 6-0 190 | FUT: Starting SS | 7C

Bats R Age 20
2011 FA (DR)

Pwr + +
BAvg + + +
Spd + +
Def + + +

Year	Lev	Team	AB	R	H	HR	RBI	Avg	OB	Slg	OPS	bb%	ct%	Eye	SB	CS	x/h%	Iso	RC/G
2012	Rk	GCL Blue Jays	170	20	38	2	20	224	254	329	584	4	85	0.28	5	1	24	106	2.68
2013	Rk	Bluefield	192	28	57	6	36	297	315	469	783	3	85	0.18	1	0	33	172	4.81
2013	A-	Vancouver	69	6	17	1	8	246	257	348	605	1	81	0.08	0	0	29	101	2.65
2014	A	Lansing	474	40	123	4	53	259	287	329	616	4	85	0.25	3	3	19	70	2.97

Pure-hitting SS who was inconsistent from month to month in first full season. Has hand-eye coordination to make contact, though hesitant to work counts. Can catch up to good FB with quick stroke and has surprising pop in lean frame. Smooth actions at SS with strong arm, but limited range.

Machado,Dixon — 6 — Detroit

EXP MLB DEBUT: 2015 | H/W: 6-1 170 | FUT: Utility player | 6A

Bats R Age 23
2008 FA (Venezuela)

Pwr +
BAvg + +
Spd + + +
Def + + + +

Year	Lev	Team	AB	R	H	HR	RBI	Avg	OB	Slg	OPS	bb%	ct%	Eye	SB	CS	x/h%	Iso	RC/G
2012	A+	Lakeland	421	59	82	2	37	195	282	252	534	11	86	0.84	23	5	23	57	2.48
2013	Rk	GCL Tigers	28	3	9	0	2	321	345	393	738	3	82	0.20	0	0	22	71	4.41
2013	A+	Lakeland	149	19	32	1	12	215	264	295	559	6	87	0.53	1	0	25	81	2.61
2014	A+	Lakeland	159	30	40	1	8	252	346	333	679	13	79	0.68	2	1	25	82	4.19
2014	AA	Erie	292	45	89	5	32	305	389	442	830	12	88	1.11	8	5	33	137	6.07

Agile, lean INF who returned to prospect map with career high in HR and more mature approach. Has always been standout with glove with plus range to both sides and clean, quick hands. Brings average speed to game and can beat out grounders. Can add strength to lithe frame.

Mahtook,Mikie — 789 — Tampa Bay

EXP MLB DEBUT: 2015 | H/W: 6-1 200 | FUT: Starting OF | 7B

Bats R Age 25
2011 (1) LSU

Pwr + + +
BAvg + + +
Spd + + +
Def + + +

Year	Lev	Team	AB	R	H	HR	RBI	Avg	OB	Slg	OPS	bb%	ct%	Eye	SB	CS	x/h%	Iso	RC/G
2011	NCAA	LSU	196	61	75	14	56	383	489	709	1199	17	84	1.28	29	9	41	327	10.68
2012	A+	Charlotte	341	44	99	5	37	290	346	419	765	8	79	0.41	19	6	27	129	5.01
2012	AA	Montgomery	153	17	38	4	25	248	299	405	704	7	80	0.35	4	3	39	157	4.13
2013	AA	Montgomery	511	71	130	7	68	254	312	386	698	8	80	0.42	25	8	35	131	4.19
2014	AAA	Durham	489	56	143	12	68	292	353	458	811	9	72	0.34	18	5	36	166	5.78

Instinctual OF who had career year with highs in HR and BB. Destroys LHP and uses speed effectively on base and in OF. Holes in swing lead to Ks, but works counts and gets on base. Should get to average pop in time, but needs to recognize pitches better. Solid OF with strong arm.

Mancini,Trey — 3 — Baltimore

EXP MLB DEBUT: 2016 | H/W: 6-4 215 | FUT: Starting 1B | 7D

Bats R Age 23
2013 (8) Notre Dame

Pwr + + +
BAvg + + +
Spd +
Def + +

Year	Lev	Team	AB	R	H	HR	RBI	Avg	OB	Slg	OPS	bb%	ct%	Eye	SB	CS	x/h%	Iso	RC/G
2012	NCAA	Notre Dame	202	47	64	12	45	317	384	545	928	10	82	0.59	3	4	34	228	6.88
2013	NCAA	Notre Dame	229	29	89	7	54	389	440	603	1043	8	90	0.91	3	0	31	214	8.19
2013	A-	Aberdeen	256	43	84	3	35	328	377	449	826	7	83	0.47	3	1	27	121	5.71
2014	A	Delmarva	268	30	85	3	42	317	351	422	773	5	81	0.27	1	1	22	104	4.90
2014	A+	Frederick	275	37	69	7	41	251	287	396	684	5	84	0.33	0	1	38	145	3.81

Big, strong 1B with natural hitting ability. Got ott to hot start before promotion to High-A in June. Hits to all fields with line drive stroke and has enough strength for long ball pop. Needs to pull more to realize power and needs to shorten swing at times. Lacks speed and rarely steals bases.

Margot,Manuel — 8 — Boston

EXP MLB DEBUT: 2017 | H/W: 5-11 170 | FUT: Starting CF | 8C

Bats R Age 20
2011 FA (DR)

Pwr + + +
BAvg + + +
Spd + + + +
Def + + +

Year	Lev	Team	AB	R	H	HR	RBI	Avg	OB	Slg	OPS	bb%	ct%	Eye	SB	CS	x/h%	Iso	RC/G
2013	A-	Lowell	185	29	50	1	21	270	348	351	699	11	78	0.55	18	8	22	81	4.34
2014	A	Greenville	370	61	106	10	45	286	351	449	800	9	87	0.76	39	13	33	162	5.47
2014	A+	Salem	50	4	17	2	14	340	365	560	925	4	90	0.40	3	2	41	220	6.49

Lean, strong OF who is evolving into top prospect. True 5-tool talent who has instincts and high upside. Brings disciplined eye to plate and makes easy contact; is a tough out. Plus bat speed has led to emerging power and can hit for BA. Solid CF with plus speed and ample range.

Marin,Adrian — 6 — Baltimore

EXP MLB DEBUT: 2016 | H/W: 6-0 180 | FUT: Starting SS | 7D

Bats R Age 21
2012 (3) HS (FL)

Pwr + +
BAvg + +
Spd + + +
Def + + +

Year	Lev	Team	AB	R	H	HR	RBI	Avg	OB	Slg	OPS	bb%	ct%	Eye	SB	CS	x/h%	Iso	RC/G
2012	Rk	GCL Orioles	178	24	51	0	13	287	328	360	688	6	81	0.32	6	1	20	73	3.97
2012	A	Delmarva	21	5	6	0	2	286	318	286	604	5	90	0.50	2	0	0	0	3.02
2013	A	Delmarva	388	30	103	4	48	265	307	356	662	6	77	0.26	11	4	24	90	3.56
2014	A+	Frederick	431	40	100	5	42	232	268	341	609	5	76	0.20	12	4	36	109	2.85

Agile, quick INF with natural defensive skills and offensive potential. Possesses innate instincts and feel for glove. Owns textbook footwork, ample range, and average arm. Inconsistent approach hinders BA and small frame lacks strength for power. Swings fast bat and hits lots of doubles.

Marlette,Tyler — 2 — Seattle

EXP MLB DEBUT: 2016 | H/W: 5-11 195 | FUT: Starting C | 7C

Bats R Age 22
2011 (5) HS (FL)

Pwr + + +
BAvg + + +
Spd + +
Def + +

Year	Lev	Team	AB	R	H	HR	RBI	Avg	OB	Slg	OPS	bb%	ct%	Eye	SB	CS	x/h%	Iso	RC/G
2012	Rk	Pulaski	208	23	59	5	23	284	304	423	727	3	78	0.13	3	1	32	139	4.18
2012	A-	Everett	5	0	2	0	0	400	400	600	1000	0	80	0.00	0	1	50	200	7.60
2013	A	Clinton	270	36	82	6	37	304	361	448	809	8	80	0.45	10	4	30	144	5.52
2014	A+	High Desert	312	51	94	15	49	301	351	519	870	7	80	0.39	9	2	40	218	6.11
2014	AA	Jackson	32	3	8	2	2	250	333	500	833	11	69	0.40	0	1	50	250	6.09

Strong backstop who built upon breakout in '13 to set high in HR. Can hit for BA due to disciplined eye and ability to use whole field. Improving as receiver, but lacks ideal footwork and agility. Possesses strong arm, though accuracy needs help. Mostly bat first catcher at present.

Marrero,Deven — 6 — Boston

EXP MLB DEBUT: 2015 | H/W: 6-1 195 | FUT: Starting SS | 7B

Bats R Age 24
2012 (1) Arizona State

Pwr + +
BAvg + +
Spd + + + +
Def + + + +

Year	Lev	Team	AB	R	H	HR	RBI	Avg	OB	Slg	OPS	bb%	ct%	Eye	SB	CS	x/h%	Iso	RC/G
2012	A-	Lowell	246	45	66	2	24	268	357	374	731	12	80	0.71	24	6	29	106	4.86
2013	A+	Salem	332	50	85	2	21	256	340	334	674	11	82	0.70	21	2	26	78	4.09
2013	AA	Portland	72	7	17	0	5	236	329	236	565	12	78	0.63	6	0	0	0	2.60
2014	AA	Portland	268	42	78	5	39	291	371	433	804	11	79	0.60	12	7	33	142	5.69
2014	AAA	Pawtucket	186	23	39	1	20	210	258	285	543	6	80	0.32	4	1	31	75	2.16

Instinctual INF who is on verge of majors. Not a top hitter, but is terrific defender who makes routine and tough plays. Possesses plus range and soft, quick hands along with strong arm. Knows strike zone and set highs in 2B and HR. Hits LHP with short stroke and runs quite well for SB.

Marte,Ketel — 46 — Seattle

EXP MLB DEBUT: 2016 | H/W: 6-1 180 | FUT: Starting 2B/SS | **7C**

Bats B Age 21 — 2010 FA (DR)
- Pwr +
- BAvg + + +
- Spd + + + +
- Def + + + +

Year	Lev	Team	AB	R	H	HR	RBI	Avg	OB	Slg	OPS	bb%	ct%	Eye	SB	CS	x/h%	Iso	RC/G
2012	A	Clinton	14	3	4	0	2	286	375	286	661	13	79	0.67	1	0	0	0	3.87
2013	A	Clinton	378	61	115	0	29	304	331	370	701	4	90	0.38	16	8	17	66	4.11
2013	A+	High Desert	86	18	22	1	8	256	289	337	626	4	87	0.36	4	3	14	81	3.20
2014	AA	Jackson	443	63	134	2	46	302	331	404	735	4	85	0.29	23	10	26	102	4.47
2014	AAA	Tacoma	80	16	25	2	9	313	375	450	825	9	84	0.62	6	0	28	138	5.72

Young, advanced INF who can play both middle infield spots with precision. Owns quick, soft hands and exemplary range and arm. Profiles as #2 hitter with ability to make contact from both sides of plate. Lacks power projection, but drives ball to gaps. Can be too much of free swinger.

Mateo,Jorge — 6 — New York (A)

EXP MLB DEBUT: 2018 | H/W: 6-0 188 | FUT: Starting SS | **9E**

Bats R Age 19 — 2012 FA (DR)
- Pwr + +
- BAvg + + +
- Spd + + + +
- Def + + +

Year	Lev	Team	AB	R	H	HR	RBI	Avg	OB	Slg	OPS	bb%	ct%	Eye	SB	CS	x/h%	Iso	RC/G
2013	Rk	DSL Yankees	258	50	74	7	26	287	370	450	819	12	80	0.65	49	10	30	163	5.85
2014	Rk	GCL Yankees	58	14	16	0	1	276	354	397	750	11	71	0.41	11	1	38	121	5.24

High-upside INF who broke wrist and missed time in 1st year in U.S. Possesses athleticism and strength to project to BA and pop. Plus speed is best current tool and has the range and arm for SS. Makes hard contact with plus bat speed and gets on base with mature, disciplined approach.

Mathisen,Wyatt — 5 — Pittsburgh

EXP MLB DEBUT: 2016 | H/W: 6-1 210 | FUT: Starting 3B | **7D**

Bats R Age 21 — 2012 (2) HS (TX)
- Pwr + +
- BAvg + + +
- Spd + + +
- Def + +

Year	Lev	Team	AB	R	H	HR	RBI	Avg	OB	Slg	OPS	bb%	ct%	Eye	SB	CS	x/h%	Iso	RC/G
2012	Rk	GCL Pirates	139	24	41	1	15	295	368	374	742	10	86	0.84	10	8	22	79	4.92
2013	Rk	GCL Pirates	22	5	9	0	3	409	552	455	1006	24	91	3.50	0	0	11	45	9.08
2013	A-	Jamestown	26	4	7	0	3	269	387	269	656	16	73	0.71	1	0	0	0	3.93
2013	A	West Virginia	119	13	22	0	9	185	242	210	452	7	82	0.41	1	0	14	25	1.12
2014	A	West Virginia	375	48	105	3	42	280	338	360	698	8	86	0.61	6	2	21	80	4.24

Good approach at the plate and makes consistent contact. Struggles to hit RHP, but has a good understanding of the strike zone. Power has yet to show up in game action. Move to 3B is a work in progress where his footwork and range are below-avg. Hit .308 after the break.

Maxwell,Bruce — 2 — Oakland

EXP MLB DEBUT: 2016 | H/W: 6-2 235 | FUT: Starting C | **7D**

Bats L Age 24 — 2012 (2) Birmingham So.
- Pwr + + +
- BAvg + +
- Spd +
- Def + +

Year	Lev	Team	AB	R	H	HR	RBI	Avg	OB	Slg	OPS	bb%	ct%	Eye	SB	CS	x/h%	Iso	RC/G
2012	A-	Vermont	228	22	58	0	22	254	331	316	646	10	85	0.74	1	0	24	61	3.79
2013	A	Beloit	199	25	57	2	28	286	363	387	750	11	85	0.83	0	0	28	101	5.04
2013	A+	Stockton	175	19	46	5	21	263	335	394	729	10	81	0.56	0	0	28	131	4.55
2014	A+	Stockton	289	33	79	6	35	273	364	381	744	12	80	0.71	0	1	23	107	4.92
2014	AA	Midland	85	8	12	0	2	141	223	176	400	10	62	0.28	0	1	25	35	-0.21

Powerful C who was horrific upon promotion to AA. Showing improved agility behind plate with decent hands and quick transfer. Has bat speed to hit for power, especially against LHP, and gets on base due to knowledge of strike zone. Can have contact issues in long swing.

May,Jacob — 8 — Chicago (A)

EXP MLB DEBUT: 2016 | H/W: 5-10 180 | FUT: Starting OF | **7D**

Bats B Age 23 — 2013 (3) Coastal Carolina
- Pwr + +
- BAvg + + +
- Spd + + + +
- Def + + +

Year	Lev	Team	AB	R	H	HR	RBI	Avg	OB	Slg	OPS	bb%	ct%	Eye	SB	CS	x/h%	Iso	RC/G
2012	NCAA	Coastal Carolina	209	43	64	2	18	306	383	407	790	11	88	1.00	27	5	20	100	5.55
2013	NCAA	Coastal Carolina	216	42	70	7	31	324	387	495	882	9	88	0.85	16	10	30	171	6.39
2013	Rk	Great Falls	45	5	17	0	7	378	462	444	906	13	87	1.17	5	1	12	67	7.10
2013	A	Kannapolis	206	36	59	8	28	286	338	461	799	7	79	0.37	19	5	29	175	5.25
2014	A+	Winston-Salem	415	66	107	2	27	258	326	395	721	9	83	0.59	37	8	40	137	4.67

Contact hitter with plus speed who finished 3rd in CAR in SB. Tracks balls well in CF and has enough arm and instincts to stay there. Hits for decent BA from both sides of plate and is difficult to fan. Knows strike zone and draws walks. Won't hit many HR, but makes loud contact to gaps.

Mazara,Nomar — 9 — Texas

EXP MLB DEBUT: 2017 | H/W: 6-4 195 | FUT: Starting OF | **8D**

Bats L Age 19 — 2011 FA (DR)
- Pwr + + + +
- BAvg + + +
- Spd + +
- Def + +

Year	Lev	Team	AB	R	H	HR	RBI	Avg	OB	Slg	OPS	bb%	ct%	Eye	SB	CS	x/h%	Iso	RC/G
2012	Rk	AZL Rangers	201	40	53	6	39	264	378	448	826	16	65	0.53	5	2	42	184	6.58
2013	A	Hickory	453	48	107	13	62	236	304	382	686	9	71	0.34	1	2	36	146	3.98
2014	A	Hickory	398	68	105	19	73	264	356	470	826	13	75	0.58	4	3	40	206	5.92
2014	AA	Frisco	85	10	26	3	16	306	372	518	890	10	74	0.41	0	0	42	212	6.80

Tall, strong OF who repeated Low-A to begin year but caught fire and bypassed High-A upon promotion. Showed improved power, eye and contact while killing RHP. Cleaner swing led to improved profile, but holes still exist and struggles with LHP. Not much speed and is fringy defender.

Mazzilli,L.J. — 4 — New York (N)

EXP MLB DEBUT: 2017 | H/W: 6-1 190 | FUT: Platoon 2B | **6D**

Bats R Age 24 — 2013 (4) Connecticut
- Pwr + + +
- BAvg + +
- Spd + +
- Def + + +

Year	Lev	Team	AB	R	H	HR	RBI	Avg	OB	Slg	OPS	bb%	ct%	Eye	SB	CS	x/h%	Iso	RC/G
2013	NCAA	Connecticut	260	50	92	6	51	354	417	515	932	10	90	1.08	29	4	28	162	7.05
2013	A-	Brooklyn	273	24	76	4	34	278	332	381	713	7	81	0.42	3	0	24	103	4.30
2014	A	Savannah	250	39	73	7	45	292	366	428	794	10	81	0.60	11	1	25	136	5.40
2014	A+	St. Lucie	250	40	78	4	34	312	353	456	809	6	87	0.48	3	3	33	144	5.43
2014	AAA	Las Vegas	5	0	1	0	0	200	200	200	400	0	80	0.00	0	0	0	0	0.01

Will miss first 50 games of '15 due to drug suspension. Suspension clouds legitimacy of gains at plate and SB in '14. Demonstrates good approach and high ct%. Sprays lots of line drives to both gaps. Average speed but can steal a base. Steady defender but arm locks him in at 2B.

McCann,James — 2 — Detroit

EXP MLB DEBUT: 2014 | H/W: 6-2 210 | FUT: Starting C | **7B**

Bats R Age 24 — 2011 (2) Arkansas
- Pwr + +
- BAvg + + +
- Spd + +
- Def + + + +

Year	Lev	Team	AB	R	H	HR	RBI	Avg	OB	Slg	OPS	bb%	ct%	Eye	SB	CS	x/h%	Iso	RC/G
2012	A+	Lakeland	160	24	46	0	20	288	329	350	679	6	82	0.34	3	0	22	63	3.86
2012	AA	Erie	220	15	44	2	19	200	228	282	510	4	80	0.18	2	2	32	82	1.61
2013	AA	Erie	441	50	122	8	54	277	323	404	726	6	81	0.35	3	3	32	127	4.41
2014	AAA	Toledo	417	49	123	7	54	295	335	427	762	6	78	0.28	9	2	33	132	4.83
2014	MLB	Detroit	12	2	3	0	0	250	250	333	583	0	83	0.00	1	0	33	83	2.44

Intelligent backstop who tweaked swing to add more lift and power. More known for receiving and framing with solid catch-and-throw skills. Hits for BA with bat to ball ability and reading spin. Not much speed, but has sound baserunning acumen. Power output will dictate whether he starts.

McElroy,C.J. — 78 — St. Louis

EXP MLB DEBUT: 2017 | H/W: 5-10 180 | FUT: Starting CF | **7D**

Bats R Age 21 — 2011 (3) HS (TX)
- Pwr +
- BAvg + +
- Spd + + + +
- Def + + +

Year	Lev	Team	AB	R	H	HR	RBI	Avg	OB	Slg	OPS	bb%	ct%	Eye	SB	CS	x/h%	Iso	RC/G
2011	Rk	GCL Cardinals	79	10	18	0	7	228	291	278	569	8	81	0.47	8	2	17	51	2.62
2012	Rk	Johnson City	247	40	67	0	22	271	313	332	645	6	83	0.36	24	5	19	61	3.46
2013	Rk	GCL Cardinals	10	0	3	0	0	300	300	400	700	0	80	0.00	1	1	33	100	3.81
2013	A	Peoria	242	24	58	0	23	240	290	302	591	7	83	0.43	8	8	21	62	2.89
2014	A	Peoria	490	74	131	0	29	267	323	298	621	8	83	0.48	41	18	10	31	3.22

Fleet-footed CF has nice athleticism and a good line-drive stroke. Can occasionally drive the ball, but is not going to hit for power and has yet to hit a HR as a pro. Uses his plus speed well on the bases and in the field and he swiped a career-high 41 bases.

McFarland,Christopher — 4 — Milwaukee

EXP MLB DEBUT: 2018 | H/W: 6-0 190 | FUT: Backup 2B | **6C**

Bats R Age 22 — 2011 (18) HS (TX)
- Pwr + +
- BAvg + +
- Spd + + +
- Def + +

Year	Lev	Team	AB	R	H	HR	RBI	Avg	OB	Slg	OPS	bb%	ct%	Eye	SB	CS	x/h%	Iso	RC/G
2012	Rk	Helena	282	48	85	6	42	301	354	433	787	8	72	0.29	15	6	28	131	5.35
2013	A	Wisconsin	307	35	73	3	42	238	289	358	647	7	71	0.24	7	3	32	121	3.51
2014	A	Wisconsin	394	55	112	6	39	284	325	388	714	6	78	0.27	30	9	23	104	4.20

Brewers 2B prospect was an 18th round pick. Solid, line-drive hitter put up good numbers in a return trip to the MWL, hitting .284. Doesn't project to have much power, but he runs well and swiped 30 bases. Fringy defender should have enough range and arm strength to stick at 2B.

McGuire,Reese — 2 — Pittsburgh

EXP MLB DEBUT: 2017 | H/W: 6-0 180 | FUT: Starting C | **8D**

Bats L Age 20 — 2013 (1) HS (WA)
- Pwr + + +
- BAvg + + +
- Spd + +
- Def + + + +

Year	Lev	Team	AB	R	H	HR	RBI	Avg	OB	Slg	OPS	bb%	ct%	Eye	SB	CS	x/h%	Iso	RC/G
2013	Rk	GCL Pirates	176	30	58	0	21	330	382	392	774	8	90	0.83	5	1	19	63	5.20
2013	A-	Jamestown	16	3	4	0	0	250	294	250	544	6	94	1.00	1	0	0	0	2.62
2014	A	West Virginia	389	46	102	3	45	262	305	334	639	6	89	0.55	7	2	18	72	3.50

Has yet to develop as many anticipated. Behind the plate, blocks and receives the ball well and nailed 39% of baserunners. At the plate, has a good approach, good bat speed, and plate discipline. Shows a willingness to go the other way and should develop moderate power.

McKinney,Billy — 89 — Chicago (N)

EXP MLB DEBUT: 2016 | H/W: 6-1 195 | FUT: Starting CF | 8C

Bats L Age 20
2013 (1) HS (TX)

Pwr	+++	
BAvg	++++	
Spd	+++	
Def	++	

Year	Lev	Team	AB	R	H	HR	RBI	Avg	OB	Slg	OPS	bb%	ct%	Eye	SB	CS	x/h%	Iso	RC/G
2013	Rk	AZL Athletics	181	31	58	2	20	320	379	414	793	9	84	0.59	7	0	19	94	5.36
2013	A-	Vermont	34	5	12	1	6	353	405	559	964	8	88	0.75	1	1	33	206	7.32
2014	A+	Daytona	176	30	53	1	36	301	388	432	820	12	76	0.60	1	0	32	131	6.11
2014	A+	Stockton	290	42	70	10	33	241	325	400	725	11	80	0.62	5	3	34	159	4.56

Has plus bat speed and makes consistent contact with good plate discipline. Has avg power potential, but is willing to use the entire field. Sweet LH stroke is textbook and could develop power as he matures. Avg speed helps range, but mostly relegated to LF due to subpar arm.

McMahon,Ryan — 5 — Colorado

EXP MLB DEBUT: 2017 | H/W: 6-2 185 | FUT: Starting 3B | 9D

Bats L Age 20
2013 (2) HS (CA)

Pwr	++++	
BAvg	+++	
Spd	++	
Def	+++	

Year	Lev	Team	AB	R	H	HR	RBI	Avg	OB	Slg	OPS	bb%	ct%	Eye	SB	CS	x/h%	Iso	RC/G
2013	Rk	Grand Junction	218	42	70	11	52	321	398	583	981	11	73	0.47	4	6	46	261	8.13
2014	A	Asheville	482	93	136	18	102	282	354	502	857	10	70	0.38	8	5	49	220	6.52

Impressive full-season debut, with 46 2B and 18 HR. Quick LH stroke and has plus power. Makes good contact and has a solid approach at the plate. An avg runner, but has soft hands, good lateral movement, and a strong arm. Will need to become more consistent as he moves up.

McPhearson,Matt — 78 — Arizona

EXP MLB DEBUT: 2017 | H/W: 5-8 165 | FUT: Starting LF | 7D

Bats L Age 19
2013 (4) HS, MD

Pwr	+	
BAvg	+++	
Spd	++++	
Def	++++	

Year	Lev	Team	AB	R	H	HR	RBI	Avg	OB	Slg	OPS	bb%	ct%	Eye	SB	CS	x/h%	Iso	RC/G
2013	Rk	AZL Dbacks	130	20	26	0	7	200	311	238	550	14	65	0.47	15	3	15	38	2.28
2014	Rk	AZL Dbacks	160	32	45	0	16	281	372	294	665	13	73	0.53	23	3	4	13	3.91

Short, fleet-footed LHH OF was impressive, hitting .281 with 23 SB in 43 games. There is some length to his swing and his contact rate is not ideal, but he is willing to take walk. Has some loft to his swing and he could add power. Plus speed is his main tool and he is a 70 runner.

Meadows,Austin — 8 — Pittsburgh

EXP MLB DEBUT: 2017 | H/W: 6-3 200 | FUT: Starting LF | 9D

Bats L Age 19
2013 (1) HS (GA)

Pwr	++++	
BAvg	++++	
Spd	+++	
Def	++	

Year	Lev	Team	AB	R	H	HR	RBI	Avg	OB	Slg	OPS	bb%	ct%	Eye	SB	CS	x/h%	Iso	RC/G
2013	Rk	GCL Pirates	160	29	47	5	20	294	386	519	905	13	74	0.57	3	2	45	225	7.26
2013	A-	Jamestown	17	8	9	2	2	529	636	882	1519	23	76	1.25	0	0	22	353	15.49
2014	Rk	Bristol	14	2	1	0	0	71	235	71	307	18	79	1.00	0	0	0	0	-0.55
2014	Rk	GCL Pirates	4	1	4	0	1	1000	2000	3000	3000	33	100		0	0	75	1000	32.64
2014	A	West Virginia	146	18	47	3	15	322	381	486	868	9	79	0.47	2	3	36	164	6.35

Missed games until June with a hamstring injury. Has a simple, compact LH stroke and the ball jumps off his bat. He's an above-avg runner, but speed is not part of his game. Average arm could result in a shift to LF where his power profiles well. Shows good patience at the plate.

Mejia,Francisco — 2 — Cleveland

EXP MLB DEBUT: 2018 | H/W: 5-10 175 | FUT: Starting C | 7C

Bats B Age 19
2012 FA (DR)

Pwr	++	
BAvg	+++	
Spd	++	
Def	+++	

Year	Lev	Team	AB	R	H	HR	RBI	Avg	OB	Slg	OPS	bb%	ct%	Eye	SB	CS	x/h%	Iso	RC/G
2013	Rk	AZL Indians	105	16	32	4	24	305	336	524	860	5	83	0.28	3	1	44	219	5.88
2014	A-	Mahoning Val	248	32	70	2	36	282	331	407	738	7	81	0.38	2	4	33	125	4.67

Wiry backstop who is natural hitter with line drive approach. Fast bat and feel for zone give him BA potential and should add strength as he ages for more pop. Makes good contact, but can chase balls at times. Receiving needs attention and is raw defender, but owns strong, accurate arm.

Mejias-Brean,Seth — 5 — Cincinnati

EXP MLB DEBUT: 2016 | H/W: 6-2 215 | FUT: Starting 3B | 7C

Bats R Age 24
2012 (8) Arizona

Pwr	+++	
BAvg	+++	
Spd	+++	
Def	++++	

Year	Lev	Team	AB	R	H	HR	RBI	Avg	OB	Slg	OPS	bb%	ct%	Eye	SB	CS	x/h%	Iso	RC/G
2012	Rk	Billings	179	35	56	8	40	313	385	536	921	11	84	0.72	6	0	39	223	6.93
2013	A	Dayton	479	70	146	10	79	305	376	453	829	10	83	0.66	3	2	33	148	5.93
2013	A+	Bakersfield	13	3	4	1	3	308	308	615	923	0	100		1	0	50	308	6.10
2014	A+	Bakersfield	267	56	80	11	45	300	399	476	874	14	82	0.90	7	1	28	176	6.57
2014	AA	Pensacola	226	23	53	3	22	235	329	323	652	12	78	0.64	1	4	23	88	3.76

Balanced, disciplined offensive approach. Hits for decent power, makes excellent contact, and can draw a walk. GB% spiked upon promotion to Double-A and needs to modify swing path based on his power potential. Excellent defender at 3B with plus arm.

Mercado,Oscar — 6 — St. Louis

EXP MLB DEBUT: 2018 | H/W: 6-2 175 | FUT: Starting SS | 7E

Bats R Age 20
2013 (2) HS (FL)

Pwr	++	
BAvg	++	
Spd	++++	
Def	++++	

Year	Lev	Team	AB	R	H	HR	RBI	Avg	OB	Slg	OPS	bb%	ct%	Eye	SB	CS	x/h%	Iso	RC/G
2013	Rk	GCL Cardinals	163	18	34	1	14	209	283	307	590	9	76	0.44	12	4	29	98	2.87
2014	Rk	Johnson City	245	41	55	3	25	224	283	306	589	8	85	0.54	26	7	24	82	2.89

Slick-fielding SS with plus speed has yet to prove he can hit. Does have a good line-drive approach that is geared more towards gap power and makes decent contact, but doesn't yet hit the ball with authority. Pitch recognition needs to improve. Solid defender with good range.

Merrifield,Whit — 479 — Kansas City

EXP MLB DEBUT: 2015 | H/W: 6-1 175 | FUT: Utility player | 6B

Bats R Age 26
2010 (9) South Carolina

Pwr	++	
BAvg	+++	
Spd	+++	
Def	++	

Year	Lev	Team	AB	R	H	HR	RBI	Avg	OB	Slg	OPS	bb%	ct%	Eye	SB	CS	x/h%	Iso	RC/G
2012	A+	Wilmington	380	59	98	8	36	258	330	389	720	10	82	0.59	25	5	32	132	4.51
2012	AA	NW Arkansas	96	12	25	1	8	260	317	333	651	8	80	0.42	3	2	16	73	3.52
2013	AA	NW Arkansas	322	31	87	3	43	270	317	391	708	6	82	0.39	17	7	32	121	4.27
2014	AA	NW Arkansas	162	22	45	5	20	278	364	463	827	12	83	0.81	5	4	42	185	5.96
2014	AAA	Omaha	321	57	109	3	29	340	373	474	846	5	84	0.33	11	7	31	134	5.83

Athletic grinder who hit over .300 each month but April. Has simple approach and level swing to hit for BA. Likes to hack early in count, but makes easy contact. Power is short for everyday run. Has versatility to play any position on diamond, though best at 2B with good hands and arm.

Michalczewski,Trey — 5 — Chicago (A)

EXP MLB DEBUT: 2017 | H/W: 6-3 210 | FUT: Starting 1B/3B | 8D

Bats B Age 20
2013 (7) HS (OK)

Pwr	+++	
BAvg	+++	
Spd	++	
Def	++	

Year	Lev	Team	AB	R	H	HR	RBI	Avg	OB	Slg	OPS	bb%	ct%	Eye	SB	CS	x/h%	Iso	RC/G
2013	Rk	Bristol	195	25	46	3	21	236	317	328	645	11	71	0.41	2	0	22	92	3.51
2014	A	Kannapolis	432	57	118	10	70	273	342	433	775	9	68	0.32	6	3	36	160	5.47
2014	A+	Winston-Salem	72	15	14	0	5	194	284	222	506	11	71	0.43	1	0	14	28	1.61

Tall, athletic INF who has interesting tools and high upside. Projects to plus power once he adds loft to stroke. Fluid swing from both sides produces BA thanks to discerning eye at plate. Runs well underway and can steal occasional base. Owns strong arm, but may move to 1B long-term.

Milone,Thomas — 8 — Tampa Bay

EXP MLB DEBUT: 2018 | H/W: 5-11 190 | FUT: Starting CF | 8E

Bats B Age 20
2013 (3) HS (CT)

Pwr	++	
BAvg	++	
Spd	++++	
Def	+++	

Year	Lev	Team	AB	R	H	HR	RBI	Avg	OB	Slg	OPS	bb%	ct%	Eye	SB	CS	x/h%	Iso	RC/G
2013	Rk	GCL Devil Rays	142	18	27	0	4	190	228	261	489	5	73	0.18	5	1	22	70	1.28
2013	A-	Hudson Valley	6	3	4	1	2	667	667	1167	1833	0	83	0.00	1	0	25	500	16.11
2014	Rk	Princeton	233	30	62	2	23	266	345	378	723	11	74	0.46	12	5	29	112	4.69

Athletic, fast OF with impressive natural tools. Has good strength, but swing not conducive to power. Takes slap approach and doesn't drive ball enough. Has plus speed and instincts on base, but has raw routes in CF. Yet to see full season and may take time to develop.

Minier,Amaurys — 37 — Minnesota

EXP MLB DEBUT: 2018 | H/W: 6-2 190 | FUT: Starting 1B/LF | 8D

Bats B Age 19
2012 FA (DR)

Pwr	++++	
BAvg	+++	
Spd	+	
Def	+	

Year	Lev	Team	AB	R	H	HR	RBI	Avg	OB	Slg	OPS	bb%	ct%	Eye	SB	CS	x/h%	Iso	RC/G
2013	Rk	GCL Twins	112	10	24	6	17	214	254	455	710	5	74	0.21	1	1	54	241	4.05
2014	Rk	GCL Twins	171	25	50	8	23	292	395	520	915	15	70	0.56	2	2	42	228	7.53

Strong, thick prospect who repeated rookie ball and led GCL in HR. Projects very well with bat and has hitting acumen to hit for BA from both sides. Can expand strike zone and sell out for power. Very raw defender with strong arm, but limited speed. Split time between LF and 1B.

Mitchell,Jared — 78 — Chicago (A)

EXP MLB DEBUT: 2015 | H/W: 6-0 205 | FUT: Starting OF | 7E

Bats L Age 26
2009 (1) LSU
Pwr +++
BAvg +
Spd +++
Def +++

Year	Lev	Team	AB	R	H	HR	RBI	Avg	OB	Slg	OPS	bb%	ct%	Eye	SB	CS	x/h%	Iso	RC/G
2012	AAA	Charlotte	121	18	28	1	13	231	321	364	685	12	56	0.30	1	1	46	132	4.91
2013	AA	Birmingham	247	23	43	5	20	174	292	275	567	14	61	0.43	13	5	30	101	2.45
2013	AAA	Charlotte	53	7	7	0	3	132	270	170	440	16	49	0.37	4	1	29	38	0.39
2014	AA	Birmingham	157	32	47	10	20	299	364	561	925	9	75	0.40	4	5	38	261	7.03
2014	AAA	Charlotte	269	41	62	9	30	230	349	375	725	15	59	0.44	11	7	31	145	5.17

Premium athlete who has bounced between AA and AAA for 3 years. Got on track upon demotion to AA and posted career high in HR. Has very patient, yet passive approach to get on base. Lacks feel for bat and has trouble hitting breaking balls. Poor reads in OF but has speed and arm.

Moncrief,Carlos — 9 — Cleveland

EXP MLB DEBUT: 2015 | H/W: 6-0 220 | FUT: Starting OF | 7D

Bats L Age 26
2008 (14) Chipola JC
Pwr +++
BAvg ++
Spd +++
Def +++

Year	Lev	Team	AB	R	H	HR	RBI	Avg	OB	Slg	OPS	bb%	ct%	Eye	SB	CS	x/h%	Iso	RC/G
2010	A+	Kinston	9	1	1	0	0	111	200	222	422	10	56	0.25	0	0	100	111	0.28
2011	A	Lake County	464	73	108	16	53	233	341	422	763	14	66	0.48	20	7	45	190	5.47
2012	A+	Carolina	353	57	88	15	53	249	336	465	800	12	64	0.37	17	2	48	215	6.01
2013	AA	Akron	489	77	139	17	75	284	357	470	827	10	80	0.56	15	7	36	186	5.82
2014	AAA	Columbus	480	64	130	12	63	271	324	431	756	7	73	0.29	8	3	38	160	4.91

Strong, toolsy OF who took step back after career year. Has nice power/speed combo to go with plus arm strength. Erratic approach and poor pitch recognition mute BA and lead to Ks, but has pull power and speed to be threat on base. Could be platoon guy due to struggles with LHP.

Mondesi,Raul — 6 — Kansas City

EXP MLB DEBUT: 2017 | H/W: 6-1 165 | FUT: Starting SS | 9D

Bats B Age 19
2011 FA (DR)
Pwr +++
BAvg +++
Spd ++++
Def ++++

Year	Lev	Team	AB	R	H	HR	RBI	Avg	OB	Slg	OPS	bb%	ct%	Eye	SB	CS	x/h%	Iso	RC/G
2012	Rk	Helena	273	43	63	5	32	231	268	374	642	5	68	0.16	8	4	37	143	3.37
2012	Rk	Idaho Falls	207	35	60	3	30	290	350	386	736	8	69	0.29	11	2	20	97	4.79
2013	A	Lexington	482	61	126	7	47	261	310	361	671	7	76	0.29	24	10	21	100	3.70
2014	A+	Wilmington	435	54	92	8	33	211	253	354	607	5	72	0.20	17	4	37	143	2.84

Young, projectable INF who had tough year at plate. Stands out with glove with first step quickness, plus range, and strong arm. Uses simple swing from both sides, but expands zone in erratic approach. Has plus upside due to extreme bat speed and ability to make hard contact to gaps.

Moran,Colin — 5 — Houston

EXP MLB DEBUT: 2015 | H/W: 6-4 215 | FUT: Starting 3B | 7B

Bats L Age 22
2013 (1) North Carolina
Pwr ++
BAvg ++++
Spd ++
Def +++

Year	Lev	Team	AB	R	H	HR	RBI	Avg	OB	Slg	OPS	bb%	ct%	Eye	SB	CS	x/h%	Iso	RC/G
2012	NCAA	North Carolina	170	30	62	3	35	365	435	494	929	11	86	0.88	1	2	24	129	7.12
2013	NCAA	North Carolina	281	76	97	13	91	345	465	544	1010	18	91	2.52	1	0	28	199	8.43
2013	A	Greensboro	154	19	46	4	23	299	361	442	803	9	84	0.60	1	0	28	143	5.44
2014	A+	Jupiter	361	34	106	5	33	294	344	393	738	7	85	0.53	1	2	25	100	4.62
2014	AA	Corpus Christi	112	12	34	2	22	304	355	411	766	7	79	0.39	0	1	24	107	4.93

Pure-hitting prospect who projects to high BA due to easy, clean swing and strike zone knowledge. Makes easy contact with short stroke, but lacks punch. Doesn't drive ball despite size and lacks foot speed. Not the most nimble defender, but has soft hands and strong, accurate arm.

Morban,Julio — 79 — Seattle

EXP MLB DEBUT: 2015 | H/W: 6-1 210 | FUT: Starting OF | 7E

Bats L Age 23
2008 FA (DR)
Pwr +++
BAvg ++
Spd ++
Def ++

Year	Lev	Team	AB	R	H	HR	RBI	Avg	OB	Slg	OPS	bb%	ct%	Eye	SB	CS	x/h%	Iso	RC/G
2012	Rk	AZL Mariners	21	2	5	0	3	238	238	238	476	0	86	0.00	0	0	0	0	1.13
2012	A+	High Desert	300	56	94	17	52	313	358	550	908	7	78	0.31	5	1	37	237	6.56
2013	AA	Jackson	295	46	87	7	44	295	356	468	824	9	68	0.29	7	2	37	173	6.18
2014	AA	Jackson	115	14	29	1	11	252	306	339	646	7	70	0.26	0	0	24	87	3.46
2014	AAA	Tacoma	99	10	24	0	7	242	312	303	615	9	68	0.31	0	0	21	61	3.16

Free-swinging OF who missed time recovering from broken leg in '13. Has good power potential, but only has reached double-digit HR once. Strikes out a lot and has shown ability to hit LHP and owns impressive, natural tools. Not much speed and range in OF, but has strong arm.

Moreno,Angel — 89 — Tampa Bay

EXP MLB DEBUT: 2019 | H/W: 6-2 180 | FUT: Starting OF | 9E

Bats R Age 18
2012 FA (DR)
Pwr +++
BAvg ++
Spd ++++
Def +++

Year	Lev	Team	AB	R	H	HR	RBI	Avg	OB	Slg	OPS	bb%	ct%	Eye	SB	CS	x/h%	Iso	RC/G
2013	Rk	DSL Devil Rays	141	26	43	4	22	305	351	496	847	7	83	0.42	5	4	37	191	5.90
2014	Rk	Princeton	196	15	46	4	22	235	246	367	614	2	73	0.06	10	1	33	133	2.72

Young, raw OF with enticing speed/power combo. Has extremely poor eye at plate and swings hard early in count. Gets himself out with long swing and subpar pitch recognition. Has impact potential with plus speed and raw power. Also displays quality glovework in RF with good arm.

Morgan,Gareth — 789 — Seattle

EXP MLB DEBUT: 2018 | H/W: 6-4 220 | FUT: Starting OF | 8E

Bats R Age 18
2014 (2-S) HS (Canada)
Pwr ++++
BAvg +
Spd ++
Def ++

Year	Lev	Team	AB	R	H	HR	RBI	Avg	OB	Slg	OPS	bb%	ct%	Eye	SB	CS	x/h%	Iso	RC/G
2014	Rk	AZL Mariners	155	15	23	2	12	148	228	252	480	9	53	0.22	4	1	48	103	1.20

Athletic OF with as much bat speed and raw power as any in org. Has tall frame and existing strength for plus pop, but is very raw with stick. Can be easy out with poor swing fundamentals and pitch recognition. Possesses strong arm, but has limited speed which impacts range in OF.

Morgan,Joshua — 46 — Texas

EXP MLB DEBUT: 2018 | H/W: 5-11 185 | FUT: Starting 2B/SS | 7C

Bats R Age 19
2014 (3) HS (CA)
Pwr +
BAvg +++
Spd +++
Def +++

Year	Lev	Team	AB	R	H	HR	RBI	Avg	OB	Slg	OPS	bb%	ct%	Eye	SB	CS	x/h%	Iso	RC/G
2014	Rk	AZL Rangers	113	26	38	0	10	336	432	372	803	14	88	1.46	2	2	8	35	5.95
2014	A-	Spokane	89	11	27	0	9	303	374	315	688	10	89	1.00	1	1	4	11	4.30

Advanced INF who led AZL in OBP. Split time between SS and 2B and has good arm and quick hands. May not have range for SS in upper levels. Swings a quick bat and contact comes naturally. Has high BA capability with use of whole field and good speed to beat out groundballs.

Morris,Hunter — 3 — Milwaukee

EXP MLB DEBUT: 2015 | H/W: 6-2 225 | FUT: Backup 1B | 6B

Bats L Age 26
2010 (4) Auburn
Pwr +++
BAvg ++
Spd ++
Def ++

Year	Lev	Team	AB	R	H	HR	RBI	Avg	OB	Slg	OPS	bb%	ct%	Eye	SB	CS	x/h%	Iso	RC/G
2012	AA	Huntsville	522	77	158	28	113	303	352	563	916	7	78	0.34	2	1	47	261	6.77
2013	AAA	Nashville	497	61	123	24	73	247	307	457	764	8	75	0.35	3	1	43	209	4.87
2014	Rk	AZL Brewers	15	2	3	0	1	200	333	400	733	17	80	1.00	0	0	67	200	5.32
2014	AA	Huntsville	26	3	7	0	2	269	296	269	566	4	85	0.25	0	0	0	0	2.33
2014	AAA	Nashville	330	46	92	11	42	279	320	448	768	6	78	0.27	0	0	36	170	4.84

Was limited by an arm injury. Power is a strength, but he makes below avg contact, struggles against LHP, and Ks too often, limiting his BA ceiling. Still, has the potential to hit 20+ HR. Below average runner with limited range, making 1B his only option.

Moya,Steven — 9 — Detroit

EXP MLB DEBUT: 2014 | H/W: 6-6 230 | FUT: Starting OF | 8D

Bats L Age 23
2008 FA (PR)
Pwr ++++
BAvg ++
Spd +++
Def +++

Year	Lev	Team	AB	R	H	HR	RBI	Avg	OB	Slg	OPS	bb%	ct%	Eye	SB	CS	x/h%	Iso	RC/G
2011	A	West Michigan	323	38	66	13	39	204	233	362	595	4	61	0.09	1	1	36	158	2.64
2012	A	West Michigan	243	28	70	9	47	288	319	481	800	4	76	0.19	5	3	37	193	5.22
2013	A+	Lakeland	365	52	93	12	55	255	290	433	723	5	71	0.17	6	0	39	178	4.34
2014	AA	Erie	515	81	142	35	105	276	307	555	862	4	69	0.14	16	4	50	280	6.22
2014	MLB	Detroit	8	2	3	0	0	375	375	375	750	0	75	0.00	0	0	0	0	4.24

Long OF with huge frame and won EL MVP after leading league in HR by 12. Also led league in K due to holes in long swing. Owns plus-plus pop to all fields and takes aggressive cuts. Posted easy highs in HR and SB. Can hit LHP, but rarely walks. Has good speed and is solid defender.

Muncy,Max — 35 — Oakland

EXP MLB DEBUT: 2015 | H/W: 6-0 205 | FUT: Platoon 1B/3B | 6A

Bats L Age 24
2012 (5) Baylor
Pwr ++
BAvg +++
Spd +
Def ++

Year	Lev	Team	AB	R	H	HR	RBI	Avg	OB	Slg	OPS	bb%	ct%	Eye	SB	CS	x/h%	Iso	RC/G
2012	NCAA	Baylor	255	55	82	7	56	322	416	494	910	14	87	1.28	7	5	33	173	7.08
2012	A	Burlington	229	34	63	4	23	275	385	432	817	15	84	1.11	3	1	41	157	6.12
2013	A+	Stockton	351	67	100	21	76	285	395	507	902	15	81	0.94	1	1	35	222	6.90
2013	AA	Midland	172	22	43	4	24	250	342	413	755	12	80	0.71	0	1	42	163	5.11
2014	AA	Midland	435	59	115	7	63	264	387	379	766	17	79	0.95	7	2	29	115	5.48

Instinctual hitter who led TL in OBP. Saw huge decline in power output as he focused on shortening stroke and using entire field. Power predicated more on strength than bat speed and doesn't profile well. Has well below aveage speed. Owns average arm and can play 1B or 3B.

Munoz,Joe — 56 — Arizona

EXP MLB DEBUT: 2017 | H/W: 6-3 195 | FUT: Starting 3B | 7D

Bats R Age 21
2012 (2) HS (CA)
Pwr ++
BAvg +++
Spd +
Def ++

Year	Lev	Team	AB	R	H	HR	RBI	Avg	OB	Slg	OPS	bb%	ct%	Eye	SB	CS	x/h%	Iso	RC/G
2012	Rk	AZL Dbacks	173	25	45	2	20	260	323	341	664	8	69	0.30	4	4	18	81	3.73
2013	Rk	Missoula	194	32	51	6	30	263	332	448	780	9	69	0.33	5	0	41	186	5.48
2014	Rk	AZL Dbacks	17	1	5	0	2	294	368	294	663	11	82	0.67	0	0	0	0	3.85
2014	A	South Bend	301	48	74	9	44	246	316	402	718	9	71	0.35	1	1	38	156	4.47

Former 2nd round pick is tall and athletic and starting to fill out. Moved from SS to 3B and he put in a full season in the MWL. Struggles to make consistent contact and has struck out 205 times in 685 pro AB. Fits better at 3B than SS with good hands and a strong arm.

Munoz,Yairo — 6 — Oakland

EXP MLB DEBUT: 2018 | H/W: 6-1 165 | FUT: Starting SS | 8D

Bats R Age 20
2012 FA (DR)
Pwr ++
BAvg +++
Spd ++++
Def ++++

Year	Lev	Team	AB	R	H	HR	RBI	Avg	OB	Slg	OPS	bb%	ct%	Eye	SB	CS	x/h%	Iso	RC/G
2013	Rk	AZL Athletics	67	8	13	1	5	194	270	284	554	9	84	0.64	1	0	31	90	2.53
2014	A-	Vermont	252	29	75	5	20	298	317	448	765	3	83	0.17	14	6	33	151	4.67

Thin, quick INF with plus athleticism. Plays excellent SS defense with great range and strong arm. Needs to focus on contact and approach as he chases pitches and doesn't get on base enough. Quick swing can produce some power and can use entire field with solid plate coverage.

Murphy,J.R. — 2 — New York (A)

EXP MLB DEBUT: 2013 | H/W: 5-11 195 | FUT: Starting C | 7D

Bats R Age 23
2009 (2) HS (FL)
Pwr ++
BAvg +++
Spd ++
Def +++

Year	Lev	Team	AB	R	H	HR	RBI	Avg	OB	Slg	OPS	bb%	ct%	Eye	SB	CS	x/h%	Iso	RC/G
2013	AA	Trenton	183	34	49	6	25	268	353	421	773	12	83	0.75	1	0	33	153	5.21
2013	AAA	Scranton/WB	230	26	62	6	21	270	336	430	766	9	82	0.56	0	1	40	161	5.05
2013	MLB	NY Yankees	26	3	4	0	1	154	185	192	377	4	65	0.11	0	0	25	38	-0.57
2014	AAA	Scranton/WB	179	17	44	6	28	246	297	397	694	7	77	0.31	0	0	34	151	3.91
2014	MLB	NY Yankees	81	7	23	1	9	284	318	370	688	5	73	0.18	0	0	22	86	3.84

Durable backstop who has evolved into solid defender. Receives ball with soft hands and blocks well. Quick release accentuates strong arm. Makes easy contact with level swing, though expands strike zone and rarely walks. Can muscle balls out on occasion, but power isn't his game.

Murphy,Max — 789 — Minnesota

EXP MLB DEBUT: 2017 | H/W: 5-11 195 | FUT: Fourth OF | 7D

Bats R Age 22
2014 (9) Bradley
Pwr +++
BAvg +++
Spd ++
Def ++

Year	Lev	Team	AB	R	H	HR	RBI	Avg	OB	Slg	OPS	bb%	ct%	Eye	SB	CS	x/h%	Iso	RC/G
2012	NCAA	Bradley	200	32	57	9	38	285	353	495	848	10	75	0.41	9	4	39	210	6.11
2013	NCAA	Bradley	183	34	51	6	34	279	323	459	782	6	85	0.44	2	3	37	180	5.04
2014	NCAA	Bradley	194	47	61	12	42	314	387	598	985	11	79	0.56	10	2	48	284	7.78
2014	Rk	Elizabethton	119	34	45	10	26	378	475	723	1198	16	71	0.65	4	0	42	345	11.33
2014	A	Cedar Rapids	124	15	30	4	15	242	288	395	683	6	68	0.20	1	1	37	153	3.88

Short, strong OF who plays above limited tools. Swings fast bat and has average power to all fields. Muscles balls out with natural strength. Struggles with breaking balls and two-strike approach. Runs OK underway and has enough range and arm strength to be passable in OF corner.

Murphy,Tanner — 2 — Atlanta

EXP MLB DEBUT: 2018 | H/W: 6-1 215 | FUT: Starting C | 7D

Bats R Age 20
2013 (4) HS (MO)
Pwr ++
BAvg ++
Spd +
Def +++

Year	Lev	Team	AB	R	H	HR	RBI	Avg	OB	Slg	OPS	bb%	ct%	Eye	SB	CS	x/h%	Iso	RC/G
2013	Rk	GCL Braves	97	7	22	0	8	227	312	258	570	11	65	0.35	5	0	14	31	2.50
2014	Rk	Danville	157	21	38	5	19	242	364	389	752	16	76	0.79	2	1	34	146	5.15

Strong backstop who moves well behind the plate and has a plus arm. Draws rave reviews for his signal calling, but needs to refine his game and threw out just 24% of runners. Swing can get long, but has made solid adjustments and has shown ability to take a walk. Power ceiling still in question.

Murphy,Tom — 2 — Colorado

EXP MLB DEBUT: 2016 | H/W: 6-1 220 | FUT: Starting C | 8D

Bats R Age 24
2012 (3) Buffalo
Pwr +++
BAvg +++
Spd ++
Def ++

Year	Lev	Team	AB	R	H	HR	RBI	Avg	OB	Slg	OPS	bb%	ct%	Eye	SB	CS	x/h%	Iso	RC/G
2012	NCAA	Univ at Buffalo	219	46	68	13	51	311	398	616	1015	13	79	0.70	6	3	54	306	8.35
2012	A-	Tri-City	212	26	61	6	38	288	332	462	794	6	75	0.27	1	1	36	175	5.30
2013	A	Asheville	288	55	83	19	74	288	369	590	960	11	70	0.43	4	5	57	302	7.94
2013	AA	Tulsa	69	9	20	3	9	290	329	493	822	5	77	0.25	0	0	40	203	5.49
2014	AA	Tulsa	94	16	20	5	15	213	315	415	730	13	71	0.52	0	0	45	202	4.61

Injury limited him to 94 AB. When healthy, has a good approach that generates above-avg power. Has good bat speed, but struggles to make contact, though he does draw walks. Moves well behind the plate with a strong throwing arm but needs to improve as he progresses.

Naquin,Tyler — 8 — Cleveland

EXP MLB DEBUT: 2015 | H/W: 6-3 190 | FUT: Starting CF | 7B

Bats L Age 23
2012 (1) Texas A&M
Pwr ++
BAvg +++
Spd +++
Def +++

Year	Lev	Team	AB	R	H	HR	RBI	Avg	OB	Slg	OPS	bb%	ct%	Eye	SB	CS	x/h%	Iso	RC/G
2012	NCAA	Texas A&M	242	56	92	3	49	380	438	541	980	9	85	0.68	21	5	29	161	7.71
2012	A-	Mahoning Val	137	22	37	0	13	270	351	380	730	11	81	0.65	4	3	35	109	4.87
2013	A+	Carolina	448	69	124	9	42	277	337	424	762	8	75	0.37	14	7	34	147	5.02
2013	AA	Akron	80	9	18	1	6	225	271	300	571	6	73	0.23	1	3	22	75	2.29
2014	AA	Akron	304	54	95	4	30	313	372	424	797	9	77	0.41	14	3	22	112	5.48

Tall, quick OF whose season ended early due to fractured hand. Controls bat well, but needs to pull ball more to realize power. Speed is best current tool which helps plus CF range. Owns strong, accurate arm. Could be catalyst at top of lineup with on base skills and baserunning instincts.

Nay,Mitch — 5 — Toronto

EXP MLB DEBUT: 2017 | H/W: 6-3 195 | FUT: Starting 3B | 8D

Bats R Age 21
2012 (1-S) HS (AZ)
Pwr +++
BAvg +++
Spd ++
Def +++

Year	Lev	Team	AB	R	H	HR	RBI	Avg	OB	Slg	OPS	bb%	ct%	Eye	SB	CS	x/h%	Iso	RC/G
2013	Rk	Bluefield	230	41	69	6	42	300	369	426	795	10	85	0.71	0	1	25	126	5.39
2014	A	Lansing	473	57	135	3	59	285	340	389	729	8	83	0.49	6	2	30	104	4.60
2014	A+	Dunedin	37	2	7	0	1	189	250	216	466	8	76	0.33	0	0	14	27	1.08

Large, strong 3B with plus, raw power. Hasn't yet tapped into natural pop as he focuses on going to opposite field with short, quick stroke. Puts bat to ball with ease and will need to pull more to realize power. Improved defender with acceptable range and strong arm. Lacks foot speed.

Nessy,Santiago — 2 — Kansas City

EXP MLB DEBUT: 2016 | H/W: 6-2 230 | FUT: Starting C | 7E

Bats R Age 22
2009 FA (Venezuela)
Pwr +++
BAvg ++
Spd +
Def +++

Year	Lev	Team	AB	R	H	HR	RBI	Avg	OB	Slg	OPS	bb%	ct%	Eye	SB	CS	x/h%	Iso	RC/G
2012	Rk	Bluefield	160	26	41	8	23	256	312	456	768	8	71	0.28	0	0	39	200	4.98
2012	A-	Vancouver	22	4	2	1	3	91	200	273	473	12	68	0.43	0	0	100	182	0.88
2013	A	Lansing	224	23	54	5	23	241	283	375	658	5	74	0.22	0	0	37	134	3.47
2014	A	Lansing	148	20	36	1	16	243	325	351	677	11	76	0.51	0	0	33	108	4.08
2014	A+	Dunedin	90	9	19	0	12	211	268	300	568	7	76	0.32	0	0	42	89	2.51

Big, durable backstop who has decent tools, but hasn't lived up to expectations. Possesses above average bat speed and projects to at least average power, but has long swing and poor instincts that mute BA. Solid defender with strong arm and average agility. Good catch-and-throw skills.

Neuhaus,Tucker — 56 — Milwaukee

EXP MLB DEBUT: 2017 | H/W: 6-3 190 | FUT: Backup INF | 6C

Bats L Age 19
2013 (S-2) HS (FL)
Pwr ++
BAvg +++
Spd +++
Def +++

Year	Lev	Team	AB	R	H	HR	RBI	Avg	OB	Slg	OPS	bb%	ct%	Eye	SB	CS	x/h%	Iso	RC/G
2013	Rk	AZL Brewers	195	29	45	0	24	231	312	303	614	11	71	0.41	6	3	29	72	3.21
2014	Rk	Helena	232	31	54	3	21	233	294	328	621	8	67	0.26	9	2	30	95	3.15

Batting average has yet to click, but does have a good approach at the plate with a smooth stroke. Has shwon little ability to make contact or recognize pitches. Sound fundamentals in the field with good hands and above-avg speed. Could move to 3B down the road.

Ngoepe,Gift — 46 — Pittsburgh

EXP MLB DEBUT: 2016 | H/W: 5-10 165 | FUT: Utility INF | 6C

Bats B Age 25
2008 FA (South Africa)
Pwr ++
BAvg ++
Spd +++
Def ++++

Year	Lev	Team	AB	R	H	HR	RBI	Avg	OB	Slg	OPS	bb%	ct%	Eye	SB	CS	x/h%	Iso	RC/G
2011	A	West Virginia	85	14	26	2	5	306	359	459	818	8	84	0.50	3	3	31	153	5.58
2012	A+	Bradenton	456	66	106	9	36	232	326	338	663	12	71	0.48	22	14	24	105	3.82
2013	A+	Bradenton	96	17	28	0	6	292	419	427	846	18	64	0.60	7	1	36	135	7.35
2013	AA	Altoona	220	29	39	3	16	177	270	282	552	11	63	0.34	10	3	38	105	2.24
2014	AA	Altoona	437	58	104	9	52	238	318	380	697	10	69	0.38	13	8	34	142	4.33

Athletic infielder split time between 2B and SS. Struggled to make contact and struck out 135 times and has yet to prove he can hit a breaking ball. Did show a slight spike in power, hitting a career-high 9 HR. Runs well, but swiped just 13 bases in 21 attempts. Plus defender.

Nicholas,Brett — 23 — Texas

EXP MLB DEBUT: 2015 | H/W: 6-2 215 | FUT: Reserve C/1B | **6C**

Bats L Age 26
2010 (6) Missouri
Pwr +++
BAvg ++
Spd +
Def ++

Year	Lev	Team	AB	R	H	HR	RBI	Avg	OB	Slg	OPS	bb%	ct%	Eye	SB	CS	x/h%	Iso	RC/G
2011	A-	Spokane	224	35	62	6	45	277	382	451	833	15	80	0.84	1	0	44	174	6.20
2011	A+	Myrtle Beach	9	0	1	0	0	111	273	222	495	18	67	0.67	0	0	100	111	1.63
2012	A+	Myrtle Beach	446	49	127	8	63	285	349	413	762	9	81	0.52	5	1	32	128	5.00
2013	AA	Frisco	506	71	146	21	91	289	348	474	822	8	76	0.37	2	1	34	186	5.66
2014	AAA	Round Rock	452	40	124	10	58	274	315	389	705	6	75	0.24	4	1	25	115	4.04

Low-upside hitter who can play both C and 1B. Doesn't project as a starter as he hasn't mastered either spot. Lacks agility and footwork to be regular receiver, but has moderate power to pull side while showing barrel control. Needs to be more selective at plate to realize potential.

Nimmo,Brandon — 8 — New York (N)

EXP MLB DEBUT: 2017 | H/W: 6-3 205 | FUT: Starting LF/RF | **8D**

Bats L Age 22
2011 (1) HS (WY)
Pwr ++++
BAvg +++
Spd +++
Def +++

Year	Lev	Team	AB	R	H	HR	RBI	Avg	OB	Slg	OPS	bb%	ct%	Eye	SB	CS	x/h%	Iso	RC/G
2011	Rk	Kingsport	9	0	1	0	0	111	333	111	444	25	44	0.60	0	0	0	0	0.02
2012	A-	Brooklyn	266	41	66	6	40	248	359	406	765	15	71	0.59	1	5	42	158	5.44
2013	A	Savannah	395	62	108	2	40	273	384	359	744	15	67	0.54	10	7	22	86	5.33
2014	A+	St. Lucie	227	59	73	4	25	322	444	458	902	18	78	0.98	9	3	25	137	7.39
2014	AA	Binghamton	240	38	57	6	26	238	337	396	733	13	78	0.67	5	1	39	158	4.83

Starting to tap into plus power potential. Owns diverse skill set with a mature approach and solid instincts. Has ability to get on-base at a high clip thanks to knowledge of zone and knack for hard contact. Swing gets long but has quick hands. Solid OF range and base-stealing ability.

Nunez,Dom — 2 — Colorado

EXP MLB DEBUT: 2018 | H/W: 6-0 175 | FUT: Starting C | **8D**

Bats L Age 20
2013 (6) HS (CA)
Pwr ++
BAvg +++
Spd ++
Def +++

Year	Lev	Team	AB	R	H	HR	RBI	Avg	OB	Slg	OPS	bb%	ct%	Eye	SB	CS	x/h%	Iso	RC/G
2013	Rk	Grand Junction	195	24	39	3	23	200	268	323	591	8	83	0.53	11	8	44	123	2.94
2014	Rk	Grand Junction	176	30	55	8	40	313	386	517	903	11	84	0.75	5	7	36	205	6.68

Strong, athletic player made impressive strides behind the plate, showing good receiving and blocking skills. Has a strong, accurate arm with a quick release and nailed 36% of runners. Good approach at the plate with a compact LH stroke that is geared towards making contact.

Nunez,Renato — 5 — Oakland

EXP MLB DEBUT: 2016 | H/W: 6-1 185 | FUT: Starting 3B | **8D**

Bats R Age 21
2010 FA (Venezuela)
Pwr ++++
BAvg ++
Spd ++
Def ++

Year	Lev	Team	AB	R	H	HR	RBI	Avg	OB	Slg	OPS	bb%	ct%	Eye	SB	CS	x/h%	Iso	RC/G
2012	Rk	AZL Athletics	160	31	52	4	42	325	390	550	940	10	80	0.53	4	0	48	225	7.36
2013	A	Beloit	508	69	131	19	85	258	297	423	720	5	73	0.21	2	2	35	165	4.20
2014	A+	Stockton	509	75	142	29	96	279	324	517	841	6	78	0.30	2	0	42	238	5.69

Offensive INF who saw immense power spike along with improved contact rate. Destroys LHP with hard contact and has BA potential due to feel for bat and swing. Uses entire field and only needs to rein in swing-happy approach. Doesn't run well and lacks ideal defensive skills at 3B.

O'Brien,Peter — 23 — Arizona

EXP MLB DEBUT: 2015 | H/W: 6-3 215 | FUT: Starting 1B | **7D**

Bats R Age 24
2012 (2) Miami
Pwr ++++
BAvg ++
Spd +
Def ++

Year	Lev	Team	AB	R	H	HR	RBI	Avg	OB	Slg	OPS	bb%	ct%	Eye	SB	CS	x/h%	Iso	RC/G
2013	A	CharlestonSC	194	47	63	11	41	325	394	619	1012	10	70	0.38	0	0	54	294	8.70
2013	A+	Tampa	253	31	67	11	55	265	316	486	802	7	70	0.25	0	1	46	221	5.57
2014	A+	Tampa	112	19	36	10	19	321	345	688	1032	3	74	0.14	0	0	56	366	8.11
2014	AA	Trenton	274	47	67	23	51	245	286	555	841	6	72	0.21	0	0	57	310	5.72
2014	AA	Mobile	13	1	5	1	4	385	429	615	1044	7	62	0.20	0	0	20	231	9.59

Slugging C/1B was traded and the Snakes had him play 1B as he was a below average defender behind the dish. Atrocious strike zone judgment makes it unlikely that he will hit for BA. Does have plus raw power and hit 34 HR in just 399 AB. Swing-and-miss will be part of his game.

O'Conner,Justin — 2 — Tampa Bay

EXP MLB DEBUT: 2016 | H/W: 6-0 190 | FUT: Starting C | **8D**

Bats R Age 23
2010 (1) HS (IN)
Pwr +++
BAvg ++
Spd ++
Def ++++

Year	Lev	Team	AB	R	H	HR	RBI	Avg	OB	Slg	OPS	bb%	ct%	Eye	SB	CS	x/h%	Iso	RC/G
2011	Rk	Princeton	178	18	28	9	29	157	231	354	585	9	56	0.22	4	1	61	197	2.70
2012	A-	Hudson Valley	238	39	53	5	29	223	277	370	647	7	69	0.25	2	0	45	147	3.48
2013	A	Bowling Green	399	49	93	14	56	233	288	381	669	7	72	0.28	5	0	33	148	3.61
2014	A+	Charlotte	319	40	90	10	44	282	314	486	800	4	76	0.19	0	0	48	204	5.31
2014	AA	Montgomery	80	9	21	2	3	263	272	388	659	1	75	0.05	0	0	29	125	3.22

Athletic receiver who is starting to emerge. Already an established backstop with agility, framing ability, and plus arm. Ready for majors now with glove. Bat still needs work. Exhibits plus raw power, but is too aggressive and flails against breakers. Has good bat speed and uses whole field.

Ogle,Tyler — 2 — Los Angeles (N)

EXP MLB DEBUT: 2017 | H/W: 5-10 210 | FUT: Backup C | **6C**

Bats R Age 24
2011 (9) Oklahoma
Pwr ++
BAvg ++
Spd ++
Def ++

Year	Lev	Team	AB	R	H	HR	RBI	Avg	OB	Slg	OPS	bb%	ct%	Eye	SB	CS	x/h%	Iso	RC/G
2012	Rk	AZL Dodgers	60	22	29	5	24	483	563	883	1447	15	80	0.92	1	1	48	400	13.93
2012	A	Great Lakes	62	10	13	3	7	210	279	371	650	9	74	0.38	0	0	31	161	3.31
2012	AAA	Albuquerque	3	0	3	0	4	1000		1000	2000	25	100		0	0	0	0	20.02
2013	A	Great Lakes	437	60	110	12	57	252	386	389	776	18	83	1.26	6	7	33	137	5.63
2014	A+	Rancho Cuca	267	40	73	7	26	273	376	423	799	14	78	0.75	0	1	33	150	5.74

Short, compact C fared well in High-A. Has a good understanding of the strike zone, and a nice line-drive approach with gap power. Below-average defender and split time between C/1B/DH and isn't likely to stick behind the plate long-term.

O'Hearn,Ryan — 39 — Kansas City

EXP MLB DEBUT: 2017 | H/W: 6-3 200 | FUT: Starting 1B | **7C**

Bats L Age 21
2014 (8) Sam Houston St
Pwr ++++
BAvg ++
Spd +
Def ++

Year	Lev	Team	AB	R	H	HR	RBI	Avg	OB	Slg	OPS	bb%	ct%	Eye	SB	CS	x/h%	Iso	RC/G
2012	NCAA	Sam Houston St	227	34	69	2	30	304	373	388	761	10	74	0.42	5	1	19	84	5.10
2013	NCAA	Sam Houston St	183	19	48	1	25	262	345	361	705	11	77	0.55	0	1	25	98	4.47
2014	NCAA	Sam Houston St	257	37	75	8	44	292	348	451	799	8	79	0.42	1	1	29	160	5.34
2014	Rk	Idaho Falls	249	61	90	13	54	361	448	590	1038	14	76	0.66	3	2	33	229	8.77

Bat-only prospect who was MVP of Pioneer League. Has big, strong frame and clean swing to produce plus power to pull side. Free swinging approach brings BA into question and can get pull happy. Can also sell out for power. Played both 1B and RF with nice arm, though lacks range and agility for both.

Ohlman,Michael — 2 — Baltimore

EXP MLB DEBUT: 2015 | H/W: 6-5 215 | FUT: Backup C | **7C**

Bats R Age 24
2009 (11) HS (FL)
Pwr +++
BAvg +++
Spd ++
Def +

Year	Lev	Team	AB	R	H	HR	RBI	Avg	OB	Slg	OPS	bb%	ct%	Eye	SB	CS	x/h%	Iso	RC/G
2011	A	Delmarva	375	38	84	4	51	224	312	307	619	11	74	0.50	1	2	25	83	3.23
2012	Rk	GCL Orioles	29	5	8	1	3	276	323	483	805	6	66	0.20	1	0	50	207	5.90
2012	A	Delmarva	171	27	52	2	28	304	417	456	873	16	84	1.22	0	1	38	152	6.90
2013	A+	Frederick	361	61	113	13	53	313	405	524	929	13	74	0.60	5	0	41	211	7.52
2014	AA	Bowie	403	40	95	2	33	236	309	318	627	10	79	0.50	0	0	29	82	3.38

Large-framed backstop who saw big drop-off from hot 2013. Power output declined, but still has plus power potential. Fluid swing brings hope, but tends to get long. Draws walks due to selectivity, though can sell out for power. Lacks speed and poor footwork hinders solid average arm.

Olson,Matt — 3 — Oakland

EXP MLB DEBUT: 2016 | H/W: 6-4 235 | FUT: Starting 1B | **8B**

Bats L Age 21
2012 (1-S) HS (GA)
Pwr ++++
BAvg ++
Spd +
Def +++

Year	Lev	Team	AB	R	H	HR	RBI	Avg	OB	Slg	OPS	bb%	ct%	Eye	SB	CS	x/h%	Iso	RC/G
2012	Rk	AZL Athletics	177	29	50	8	41	282	342	520	862	8	74	0.35	0	0	50	237	6.30
2012	A-	Vermont	11	3	3	1	4	273	429	545	974	21	64	0.75	0	0	33	273	8.67
2013	A	Beloit	481	69	108	23	93	225	325	435	760	13	69	0.49	4	3	51	210	5.16
2014	A+	Stockton	512	111	134	37	97	262	399	543	942	19	73	0.85	2	0	51	281	7.72

Monstrous hitter who led CAL in HR and BB en route to breakout season. Recognizes pitches and has bat speed and plate coverage for plus-plus pop. Drew 117 BB, but can be too patient. Will also rack up Ks as he struggles with breaking balls. Plays strong defense with good hands.

O'Neill,Michael — 79 — New York (A)

EXP MLB DEBUT: 2016 | H/W: 6-1 195 | FUT: Reserve OF | **6B**

Bats R Age 22
2013 (3) Michigan
Pwr ++
BAvg ++
Spd ++++
Def +++

Year	Lev	Team	AB	R	H	HR	RBI	Avg	OB	Slg	OPS	bb%	ct%	Eye	SB	CS	x/h%	Iso	RC/G
2011	NCAA	Michigan	218	30	67	2	29	307	346	390	736	6	79	0.28	29	8	18	83	4.48
2012	NCAA	Michigan	158	31	52	6	30	329	365	525	891	5	87	0.43	19	5	35	196	6.21
2013	NCAA	Michigan	239	46	85	5	37	356	384	498	882	4	83	0.28	23	4	27	142	6.12
2013	A-	Staten Island	256	26	56	0	14	219	259	293	552	5	64	0.15	9	7	32	74	2.19
2014	A	CharlestonSC	489	80	125	10	57	256	315	384	699	8	73	0.32	42	9	30	129	4.15

Athletic OF who offers versatility in ability to play all OF positions. Speed playable in field and on base where he runs aggressively. Has the strength for some long ball pop. Bat control not ideal for contact or BA potential. Should hit ball on ground more to take advantage of wheels.

O'Neill,Mike — 7 — St. Louis

EXP MLB DEBUT: 2015 | H/W: 5-9 170 | FUT: Backup OF | 6A

Bats L Age 27
2010 (31) USC
Pwr +
BAvg + + + +
Spd + +
Def + +

Year	Lev	Team	AB	R	H	HR	RBI	Avg	OB	Slg	OPS	bb%	ct%	Eye	SB	CS	x/h%	Iso	RC/G
2012	AA	Springfield	32	8	18	0	5	563	650	719	1369	20	94	4.00	3	0	28	156	12.94
2013	AA	Springfield	359	66	115	2	35	320	433	384	817	17	93	2.73	18	4	15	64	6.33
2013	AAA	Memphis	112	16	33	0	3	295	402	321	723	15	90	1.82	1	0	9	27	5.10
2014	AA	Springfield	360	57	97	1	26	269	344	347	691	10	90	1.11	5	7	23	78	4.45
2014	AAA	Memphis	57	3	19	0	8	333	406	386	792	11	93	1.75	0	1	11	53	5.68

Sparkplug of a player is a pure hitter. Short, compact stroke and plus-plus strike zone judgment allow him to hit and get on base. Now has a career .414 OB%. Almost no power, but does have good speed and is a solid defender. Hit .278/.351/.353 between Double and Triple-A.

O'Neill,Tyler — 79 — Seattle

EXP MLB DEBUT: 2018 | H/W: 5-11 210 | FUT: Starting OF | 7C

Bats R Age 19
2013 (3) HS (Canada)
Pwr + + +
BAvg + +
Spd + + +
Def + +

Year	Lev	Team	AB	R	H	HR	RBI	Avg	OB	Slg	OPS	bb%	ct%	Eye	SB	CS	x/h%	Iso	RC/G
2013	Rk	AZL Mariners	100	12	31	1	15	310	384	450	834	11	73	0.44	2	4	29	140	6.26
2014	Rk	AZL Mariners	2	0	0	0	0	0	0	0	0	0	50	0.00	0	0		0	-7.85
2014	A-	Everett	10	2	4	0	2	400	455	600	1055	9	50	0.20	0	0	50	200	13.24
2014	A	Clinton	219	31	54	13	38	247	310	466	775	8	64	0.25	5	0	41	219	5.36

Strong, stocky OF who missed time with broken hand after punching wall. Combines level swing with bat speed and pitch recognition to project to average pop. Likes to swing early in count and could be more patient. Runs well underway, but lacks range in OF and only has average arm.

Ortiz,Jose — 2 — Cincinnati

EXP MLB DEBUT: 2017 | H/W: 5-11 205 | FUT: Starting C | 7D

Bats R Age 20
2012 (17) HS (PR)
Pwr + + +
BAvg + +
Spd + +
Def + + +

Year	Lev	Team	AB	R	H	HR	RBI	Avg	OB	Slg	OPS	bb%	ct%	Eye	SB	CS	x/h%	Iso	RC/G
2012	Rk	AZL Reds	39	10	14	0	6	359	468	538	1007	17	74	0.80	3	0	43	179	9.11
2013	Rk	Billings	164	21	43	8	32	262	320	494	814	8	74	0.33	1	0	51	232	5.59
2014	A	Dayton	131	12	26	3	14	198	245	336	580	6	70	0.21	0	0	42	137	2.45

Began year in extended spring training then split time at Dayton. Struggled to find consistency at plate, but still flashes plus power potential. Only allowed three passed balls and threw out 25% of would-be base stealers. Solid defender but not as advanced as others in system; must hit to play.

Osuna,Jose — 3 — Pittsburgh

EXP MLB DEBUT: 2016 | H/W: 6-2 215 | FUT: Starting 1B | 7D

Bats R Age 22
2009 FA (Venezuela)
Pwr + + +
BAvg + +
Spd +
Def +

Year	Lev	Team	AB	R	H	HR	RBI	Avg	OB	Slg	OPS	bb%	ct%	Eye	SB	CS	x/h%	Iso	RC/G
2011	Rk	GCL Pirates	178	28	59	4	32	331	393	511	904	9	88	0.86	3	2	36	180	6.74
2011	A-	State College	8	2	2	0	1	250	333	375	708	11	100		0	0	50	125	5.15
2012	A	West Virginia	482	68	135	16	72	280	324	454	778	6	83	0.38	4	4	39	174	4.96
2013	A+	Bradenton	454	47	111	8	48	244	299	357	655	7	83	0.46	18	6	31	112	3.61
2014	A+	Bradenton	365	47	108	10	57	296	346	458	804	7	80	0.39	4	2	33	162	5.38

Strong-bodied 1B prospect continues to prove he can hit for avg with power, despite sub-par plate discipline. Moderate bat speed raises questions about his ability to do both in the majors. Below-avg speed limits him to 1B, but continues to make progress and will move up to AA.

Padlo,Kevin — 5 — Colorado

EXP MLB DEBUT: 2018 | H/W: 6-2 200 | FUT: Starting 3B | 8D

Bats R Age 18
2014 (5) HS (CA)
Pwr + + +
BAvg + + +
Spd + + +
Def + + +

Year	Lev	Team	AB	R	H	HR	RBI	Avg	OB	Slg	OPS	bb%	ct%	Eye	SB	CS	x/h%	Iso	RC/G
2014	Rk	Grand Junction	160	32	48	8	44	300	414	594	1007	16	76	0.82	6	1	56	294	8.64

Rockies have to thrilled with the returns so far and he was one of the more dynamic players in the Pioneer League. Flashes a quick bat and above-average power to go along with good strike zone judgment. Moves well defensively with good hands and a strong arm.

Palka,Daniel — 3 — Arizona

EXP MLB DEBUT: 2016 | H/W: 6-2 220 | FUT: Starting 1B | 7C

Bats L Age 23
2013 (3) Georgia Tech
Pwr + + + +
BAvg + +
Spd +
Def +

Year	Lev	Team	AB	R	H	HR	RBI	Avg	OB	Slg	OPS	bb%	ct%	Eye	SB	CS	x/h%	Iso	RC/G
2012	NCAA	Georgia Tech	238	44	72	12	47	303	349	550	899	7	79	0.34	6	1	46	248	6.50
2013	NCAA	Georgia Tech	237	55	81	17	66	342	418	637	1055	12	75	0.52	6	0	41	295	8.89
2013	Rk	Missoula	205	36	62	7	38	302	389	502	891	12	78	0.64	2	2	44	200	6.84
2013	A-	Hillsboro	47	10	16	2	10	340	426	574	1000	13	66	0.44	1	0	31	234	9.07
2014	A	South Bend	455	63	113	22	82	248	331	466	797	11	72	0.43	9	3	44	218	5.55

Strong 1B prospect has some of the best raw power in the D-backs system, but has a hitch at the start of swing and there is plenty of swing-and-miss right now. Is a below average runner, which limits him to 1B, so he needs to hit to have value. Power is only plus tool but is worth watching.

Papi,Mike — 79 — Cleveland

EXP MLB DEBUT: 2017 | H/W: 6-2 190 | FUT: Starting OF | 7C

Bats L Age 22
2014 (1-S) Virginia
Pwr + + +
BAvg + + +
Spd + +
Def + + +

Year	Lev	Team	AB	R	H	HR	RBI	Avg	OB	Slg	OPS	bb%	ct%	Eye	SB	CS	x/h%	Iso	RC/G
2012	NCAA	Virginia	106	24	30	1	17	283	372	387	759	12	84	0.88	5	2	30	104	5.23
2013	NCAA	Virginia	176	57	67	7	57	381	507	619	1126	20	86	1.80	6	2	37	239	10.12
2014	NCAA	Virginia	244	55	75	11	56	307	446	488	934	20	81	1.33	8	3	29	180	7.64
2014	A-	Mahoning Val	9	2	2	0	3	222	222	222	444	0	100		0	0	0	0	1.56
2014	A	Lake County	135	21	24	3	15	178	311	274	585	16	76	0.81	2	0	29	96	2.91

Athletic OF who brings patient eye to plate and posts high OBP. Gets behind in counts and could stand to swing aggressively early. Owns plus power potential and uses entire field in approach, though has trouble with LHP. Lacks speed for plus range, but can play corner OF.

Parker,Kyle — 379 — Colorado

EXP MLB DEBUT: 2014 | H/W: 6-0 205 | FUT: Starting OF/1B | 7C

Bats R Age 25
2010 (1) Clemson
Pwr + + +
BAvg + +
Spd + +
Def + +

Year	Lev	Team	AB	R	H	HR	RBI	Avg	OB	Slg	OPS	bb%	ct%	Eye	SB	CS	x/h%	Iso	RC/G
2011	A	Asheville	445	75	127	21	95	285	355	483	838	10	70	0.36	2	0	35	198	6.11
2012	A+	Modesto	390	86	120	23	73	308	408	562	969	14	77	0.75	1	2	39	254	7.84
2013	AA	Tulsa	480	70	138	23	74	288	342	492	834	8	79	0.40	6	6	36	204	5.68
2014	AAA	ColoradoSprgs	502	73	145	15	72	289	333	450	783	6	80	0.32	4	3	33	161	5.05
2014	MLB	Colorado	26	1	5	0	1	192	192	231	423	0	46	0.00	0	0	20	38	0.61

Strong, athletic player put up respectable numbers and makes consistent contact with above-avg power. Good bat speed, short, compact stroke, and raw strength should allow power to continue to develop. Remains below avg defensively with avg speed, but has a strong arm.

Paroubeck,Jordan — 79 — San Diego

EXP MLB DEBUT: 2018 | H/W: 6-2 185 | FUT: Starting OF | 7D

Bats B Age 20
2013 (S-2) HS (CA)
Pwr + + +
BAvg + + +
Spd + + +
Def + + +

Year	Lev	Team	AB	R	H	HR	RBI	Avg	OB	Slg	OPS	bb%	ct%	Eye	SB	CS	x/h%	Iso	RC/G
2014	Rk	AZL Padres	140	26	40	4	24	286	346	457	804	8	70	0.31	4	2	35	171	5.71

Plus bat speed and size gives him the tools for hit for above-average power, but struggled with making contact in his debut. Plus speed and an above-average throwing arm means he could play either corner slot. Frame still has room to fill out.

Patterson,Jordan — 39 — Colorado

EXP MLB DEBUT: 2017 | H/W: 6-4 215 | FUT: Starting RF | 7D

Bats L Age 23
2013 (4) South Alabama
Pwr + + +
BAvg + +
Spd + + + +
Def + + +

Year	Lev	Team	AB	R	H	HR	RBI	Avg	OB	Slg	OPS	bb%	ct%	Eye	SB	CS	x/h%	Iso	RC/G
2011	NCAA	South Alabama	211	38	60	4	32	284	355	403	758	10	80	0.55	4	2	27	118	4.97
2012	NCAA	South Alabama	217	41	70	8	44	323	388	512	899	10	79	0.51	2	1	34	189	6.69
2013	NCAA	South Alabama	233	69	82	4	49	352	449	519	968	15	85	1.17	4	2	37	167	7.95
2013	Rk	Grand Junction	206	44	60	10	37	291	351	495	846	8	82	0.51	10	6	37	204	5.85
2014	A	Asheville	453	69	126	14	66	278	345	430	775	9	74	0.39	25	8	33	152	5.17

Has good raw power and profiles well as a corner OF, but needs to prove that he can make enough contact. Currently has a line-drive approach, but did manage 27 2B and 14 HR. Also have above-avg speed and swiped 25 bases. Has the tools to be a 20/20 player in the majors.

Paulino,Dorssys — 678 — Cleveland

EXP MLB DEBUT: 2017 | H/W: 6-0 175 | FUT: Starting LF | 7E

Bats R Age 20
2011 FA (DR)
Pwr + +
BAvg + + +
Spd + +
Def + +

Year	Lev	Team	AB	R	H	HR	RBI	Avg	OB	Slg	OPS	bb%	ct%	Eye	SB	CS	x/h%	Iso	RC/G
2012	Rk	AZL Indians	172	42	61	6	30	355	406	610	1017	8	82	0.48	9	1	43	256	8.10
2012	A-	Mahoning Val	59	5	16	1	8	271	306	407	713	5	76	0.21	2	1	38	136	4.20
2013	A	Lake County	476	56	117	5	46	246	291	349	639	6	81	0.33	12	7	31	103	3.35
2014	A	Lake County	427	51	107	3	35	251	304	354	658	7	76	0.33	5	6	31	103	3.64

Young prospect who repeated Low-A, but didn't fare much better. Moved to OF in June to disappointing results. Lacks instincts and jumps, though has speed to cover ground. Ultra aggressive approach hurts BA, though still has bat speed and gap power. Potential still remains.

Pederson,Joc — 8 — Los Angeles (N)

EXP MLB DEBUT: 2014 | H/W: 6-1 185 | FUT: Starting CF | 9D

Bats L Age 22
2010 (11) HS (CA)

- Pwr +++
- BAvg ++++
- Spd +++
- Def +++

Year	Lev	Team	AB	R	H	HR	RBI	Avg	OB	Slg	OPS	bb%	ct%	Eye	SB	CS	x/h%	Iso	RC/G
2011	A	Great Lakes	50	4	8	0	1	160	263	160	423	12	82	0.78	2	0	0	0	0.99
2012	A+	Rancho Cuca	434	96	136	18	70	313	386	516	902	11	81	0.63	26	14	35	203	6.72
2013	AA	Chattanooga	439	81	122	22	58	278	377	497	874	14	74	0.61	31	8	40	219	6.66
2014	AAA	Albuquerque	445	106	135	33	78	303	431	582	1013	18	67	0.67	30	13	40	279	9.16
2014	MLB	LA Dodgers	28	1	4	0	0	143	351	143	494	24	61	0.82	0	0	0	0	1.33

OF had a breakout season, becoming the first player in the PCL to go 30/30 since 1934. Has a balanced approach at the plate, with a smooth stroke and good bat speed, though he needs to take pitches the other way. Average defender with a plus arm and good reads. His speed works.

Peguero,Yelier — 6 — Chicago (N)

EXP MLB DEBUT: 2019 | H/W: 5-10 155 | FUT: Starting SS | 7D

Bats Age 18
2014 FA (DR)

- Pwr ++
- BAvg +++
- Spd +++
- Def +++

Year	Lev	Team	AB	R	H	HR	RBI	Avg	OB	Slg	OPS	bb%	ct%	Eye	SB	CS	x/h%	Iso	RC/G
2014	(did not play in the US in 2014)																		

Short, thin switch-hitting SS prospect was signed by the Cubs for $250,000 in July 2014. Good line-drive approach, but projects to have below-average power. Runs well and has a good glove so should be able to stick at SS.

Pentecost,Max — 2 — Toronto

EXP MLB DEBUT: 2016 | H/W: 6-2 195 | FUT: Starting C | 8C

Bats R Age 22
2014 (1) Kennesaw State

- Pwr ++
- BAvg +++
- Spd +++
- Def +++

Year	Lev	Team	AB	R	H	HR	RBI	Avg	OB	Slg	OPS	bb%	ct%	Eye	SB	CS	x/h%	Iso	RC/G
2012	NCAA	Kennesaw St	191	23	53	0	23	277	349	393	742	10	83	0.66	4	0	36	115	4.97
2013	NCAA	Kennesaw St	212	36	64	3	30	302	368	410	778	9	87	0.81	4	0	27	108	5.27
2014	NCAA	Kennesaw St	268	59	113	9	61	422	480	627	1107	10	90	1.15	17	0	31	205	8.99
2014	Rk	GCL Blue Jays	22	2	8	0	3	364	364	455	818	0	86	0.00	0	1	25	91	5.11
2014	A-	Vancouver	83	15	26	0	9	313	329	410	739	2	78	0.11	2	1	19	96	4.43

Tall, athletic backstop who profiles as offensive catcher as pro. Exhibits excellent barrel control and should hit for high BA with better pitch recognition. Level swing path conducive to doubles, but should add strength in time. Receives balls well and has average arm with quick release.

Peoples-Walls,Kenny — 7 — St. Louis

EXP MLB DEBUT: 2018 | H/W: 6-1 180 | FUT: Starting LF | 7D

Bats R Age 21
2011 (4) HS (CA)

- Pwr ++
- BAvg +++
- Spd +++
- Def ++

Year	Lev	Team	AB	R	H	HR	RBI	Avg	OB	Slg	OPS	bb%	ct%	Eye	SB	CS	x/h%	Iso	RC/G
2011	Rk	GCL Cardinals	88	8	21	0	7	239	309	250	559	9	73	0.38	4	4	5	11	2.29
2012	Rk	GCL Cardinals	150	19	39	2	21	260	293	367	660	4	77	0.20	4	5	23	107	3.47
2013	Rk	Johnson City	237	41	71	7	35	300	341	468	810	6	69	0.21	9	3	31	169	5.69
2014	A-	State College	58	9	13	0	0	224	237	310	548	2	71	0.06	1	0	38	86	1.96
2014	A	Peoria	291	27	68	3	28	234	247	299	546	2	75	0.07	7	6	19	65	1.79

Toolsy, athletic prospect moved to OF, but failed to duplicate his breakout of '13. Overly aggressive approach caught up to him as move advanced hurlers got him to chase. Moves well in the OF with average speed and solid gap power. Still young, but will need to regroup in 2015.

Peraza,Jose — 46 — Atlanta

EXP MLB DEBUT: 2015 | H/W: 6-0 165 | FUT: Starting 2B | 8B

Bats R Age 20
2010 FA (Venezuela)

- Pwr +
- BAvg +++
- Spd +++++
- Def +++

Year	Lev	Team	AB	R	H	HR	RBI	Avg	OB	Slg	OPS	bb%	ct%	Eye	SB	CS	x/h%	Iso	RC/G
2012	Rk	GCL Braves	85	17	27	0	10	318	348	424	772	4	93	0.67	10	3	22	106	5.06
2012	Rk	Danville	121	21	34	1	18	281	331	339	670	7	85	0.50	15	2	15	58	3.79
2013	A	Rome	448	72	129	1	47	288	338	371	709	7	86	0.53	64	15	21	83	4.36
2014	A+	Lynchburg	284	44	97	1	27	342	364	454	818	3	89	0.31	35	7	23	113	5.40
2014	AA	Mississippi	185	35	62	1	17	335	359	422	781	4	92	0.47	25	8	18	86	4.99

Hit .339 between A/AA. Top-of-the-order hitter has plus speed and swiped 60 bases. Handles the bat well with a compact stroke and makes good contact, though he doesn't draw many walks. Good eye-hand coordination and good bat speed, but doesn't project to have much power.

Perez,Hernan — 46 — Detroit

EXP MLB DEBUT: 2012 | H/W: 6-1 185 | FUT: Starting 2B | 7C

Bats R Age 24
2007 FA (Venezuela)

- Pwr ++
- BAvg +++
- Spd +++
- Def +++

Year	Lev	Team	AB	R	H	HR	RBI	Avg	OB	Slg	OPS	bb%	ct%	Eye	SB	CS	x/h%	Iso	RC/G
2013	AA	Erie	362	45	109	4	35	301	324	423	746	3	87	0.25	24	7	31	122	4.53
2013	AAA	Toledo	67	3	20	0	4	299	347	343	691	7	90	0.71	4	0	15	45	4.18
2013	MLB	Detroit	66	13	13	0	5	197	221	227	448	3	77	0.13	1	0	8	30	0.70
2014	AAA	Toledo	547	69	157	6	53	287	331	404	735	6	88	0.55	21	6	29	117	4.62
2014	MLB	Detroit	5	1	1	0	0	200	333	200	533	17	80	1.00	0	0	0	0	2.48

Consistent, steady INF with ideal plate coverage and solid glovework. Reads pitches well and makes easy contact with repeatable stroke. Steals bases with good speed and exhibits quickness and instincts in middle infield. Won't hit for much power, but isn't a liability with bat in hands.

Perez,Michael — 2 — Arizona

EXP MLB DEBUT: 2016 | H/W: 5-11 180 | FUT: Backup C | 7D

Bats L Age 22
2011 (5) HS (PR)

- Pwr +++
- BAvg ++
- Spd +
- Def ++++

Year	Lev	Team	AB	R	H	HR	RBI	Avg	OB	Slg	OPS	bb%	ct%	Eye	SB	CS	x/h%	Iso	RC/G
2011	Rk	AZL D'backs	23	5	5	2	3	217	280	565	845	8	57	0.20	1	0	80	348	7.15
2012	Rk	Missoula	225	43	66	10	60	293	351	542	893	8	68	0.28	0	1	47	249	7.09
2013	A	South Bend	162	20	40	2	14	247	307	383	690	8	66	0.25	0	0	40	136	4.29
2013	A+	Visalia	179	21	31	5	24	173	221	307	528	6	56	0.14	1	1	45	134	1.83
2014	A	South Bend	319	53	76	9	35	238	362	414	776	16	71	0.67	1	1	45	176	5.62

Offensive-minded C struggled through a second stint in the MWL. Improved his selectivity and contact rate, but still whiffed 92 in 319 AB. Remains raw behind the plate, but has a very strong arm and most observers now believe in him as major league catcher.

Perez,Roberto — 2 — Cleveland

EXP MLB DEBUT: 2014 | H/W: 5-11 225 | FUT: Reserve C | 6B

Bats R Age 26
2008 (33) Lake City CC

- Pwr ++
- BAvg ++
- Spd +
- Def ++++

Year	Lev	Team	AB	R	H	HR	RBI	Avg	OB	Slg	OPS	bb%	ct%	Eye	SB	CS	x/h%	Iso	RC/G
2012	AA	Akron	283	31	60	1	31	212	328	293	622	15	76	0.73	0	1	32	81	3.52
2013	AA	Akron	93	10	23	2	10	247	440	376	816	26	73	1.28	1	1	35	129	6.55
2013	AAA	Columbus	187	16	33	0	24	176	263	241	504	11	68	0.37	0	1	36	64	1.58
2014	AAA	Columbus	174	29	53	8	43	305	404	517	921	14	71	0.57	1	0	38	213	7.52
2014	MLB	Cleveland	85	10	23	1	4	271	311	365	676	6	69	0.19	0	0	26	94	3.80

Defense-first backstop who had career year with highs in BA and HR. Gets on base consistently, but long swing can be exploited. Hits lots of groundballs and doesn't run well. Short and stocky frame is good for blocking and has fine agility and footwork. Strong arm with quick release.

Perkins,Cameron — 7 — Philadelphia

EXP MLB DEBUT: 2015 | H/W: 6-5 195 | FUT: Backup OF | 6A

Bats R Age 24
2012 (6) Purdue

- Pwr ++
- BAvg +++
- Spd ++
- Def ++

Year	Lev	Team	AB	R	H	HR	RBI	Avg	OB	Slg	OPS	bb%	ct%	Eye	SB	CS	x/h%	Iso	RC/G
2012	A-	Williamsport	270	31	82	1	38	304	338	407	745	5	85	0.34	5	2	30	104	4.65
2013	Rk	GCL Phillies	7	1	4	1	1	571	625	1143	1768	13	100		0	0	50	571	15.46
2013	A+	Clearwater	387	54	114	6	53	295	337	444	782	6	85	0.44	4	5	36	150	5.13
2014	AA	Reading	196	25	67	3	34	342	403	495	898	9	85	0.67	5	3	34	153	6.70
2014	AAA	Lehigh Valley	255	17	55	2	17	216	254	298	552	5	81	0.27	3	3	25	82	2.22

After a history of strong BAs, ran into first extended trouble in Triple-A in the second half. Tall and lanky, he's more of a gap-to-gap hitter without a lot of power or speed, and advanced age means he has little projection left. Makes good contact, but likely not enough other things to hold down a starting corner OF spot.

Peterson,D.J. — 35 — Seattle

EXP MLB DEBUT: 2015 | H/W: 6-1 190 | FUT: Starting 3B/1B | 8B

Bats R Age 23
2013 (1) New Mexico

- Pwr ++++
- BAvg ++++
- Spd ++
- Def ++

Year	Lev	Team	AB	R	H	HR	RBI	Avg	OB	Slg	OPS	bb%	ct%	Eye	SB	CS	x/h%	Iso	RC/G
2013	NCAA	New Mexico	218	68	89	18	72	408	511	807	1319	17	84	1.31	5	1	53	399	12.15
2013	A-	Everett	109	20	34	6	27	312	385	532	917	11	83	0.72	0	1	35	220	6.80
2013	A	Clinton	99	16	29	7	20	293	340	576	915	7	76	0.29	1	0	45	283	6.68
2014	A+	High Desert	273	51	89	18	73	326	378	615	994	8	76	0.35	6	0	47	289	7.81
2014	AA	Jackson	222	32	58	13	38	261	328	473	801	9	77	0.43	1	1	36	212	5.28

Power-producing INF who was promoted to AA in June. Possesses big-time power from right side, but has controlled swing to make contact. Easy power to all fields and understands strike zone. Can also hit breaking balls. Not much speed and could move to 1B as he has subpar range.

Peterson,Dustin — 5 — Atlanta

EXP MLB DEBUT: 2018 | H/W: 6-2 180 | FUT: Starting 3B | 7D

Bats R Age 20
2013 (2) HS (AZ)

- Pwr +++
- BAvg ++
- Spd ++
- Def ++

Year	Lev	Team	AB	R	H	HR	RBI	Avg	OB	Slg	OPS	bb%	ct%	Eye	SB	CS	x/h%	Iso	RC/G
2013	Rk	AZL Padres	157	20	46	0	18	293	331	344	675	5	79	0.27	3	0	17	51	3.74
2014	A	Fort Wayne	527	64	123	10	79	233	268	361	629	5	74	0.18	1	3	36	127	3.06

Younger brother of D.J. Peterson struggled in full-season debut. Despite being over-matched, has good bat speed and raw athleticism. Projects to develop above-average power and hit 10 HR. Needs to be less aggressive and make more contact. Moves well at 3B with good hands. Traded to ATL in Justin Upton deal.

Peterson,Shane — 789 — Milwaukee

EXP MLB DEBUT: 2013 | H/W: 6-0 210 | FUT: Reserve OF | **6C**

Bats L Age 27 — 2008 (2) Long Beach State
Pwr ++ | BAvg +++ | Spd ++ | Def +++

Year	Lev	Team	AB	R	H	HR	RBI	Avg	OB	Slg	OPS	bb%	ct%	Eye	SB	CS	x/h%	Iso	RC/G
2012	AA	Midland	157	27	43	2	23	274	433	420	853	22	70	0.94	9	3	37	146	7.14
2012	AAA	Sacramento	131	36	51	7	23	389	481	618	1099	15	76	0.74	4	3	29	229	9.66
2013	AAA	Sacramento	463	70	116	12	79	251	357	387	744	14	73	0.61	17	2	33	136	5.02
2013	MLB	Oakland	7	1	1	0	1	143	250	143	393	13	57	0.33	0	0	0	0	-0.51
2014	AAA	Sacramento	543	101	167	11	90	308	383	460	843	11	74	0.47	11	2	34	153	6.27

Consistent, steady OF with gap power and disciplined eye. Hangs in against LHP and smokes hard line drives to pull side. Hits ton of doubles, though power short for everyday corner OF. Can steal occasional base with fringy speed and is smart defender with limited range.

Pham,Tommy — 78 — St. Louis

EXP MLB DEBUT: 2014 | H/W: 6-1 175 | FUT: Backup OF | **6C**

Bats R Age 27 — 2006 (16) HS (NV)
Pwr ++ | BAvg ++ | Spd +++ | Def +++

Year	Lev	Team	AB	R	H	HR	RBI	Avg	OB	Slg	OPS	bb%	ct%	Eye	SB	CS	x/h%	Iso	RC/G
2012	AA	Springfield	39	3	6	1	3	154	233	282	515	9	51	0.21	0	0	50	128	1.82
2013	AA	Springfield	163	27	49	6	28	301	377	521	899	11	74	0.48	6	3	37	221	6.98
2013	AAA	Memphis	106	6	28	1	13	264	310	368	678	6	76	0.28	2	1	29	104	3.82
2014	AAA	Memphis	346	63	112	10	44	324	391	491	882	10	77	0.47	20	2	29	168	6.60
2014	MLB	St. Louis	2	0	0	0	0	0	0	0	0	0	0	0.00	0	0		0	

Athletic OF had his best season as a pro, hitting .324/.395/.491, earning him a cup of coffee in the majors. Has a good approach at the plate with good speed, but avg power. Avg plate discipline and good bat speed allow him to hit for avg and utilize his speed. Has been injury prone.

Phillips,Brett — 89 — Houston

EXP MLB DEBUT: 2017 | H/W: 6-0 175 | FUT: Starting OF | **8D**

Bats L Age 20 — 2012 (6) HS (FL)
Pwr +++ | BAvg +++ | Spd +++ | Def +++

Year	Lev	Team	AB	R	H	HR	RBI	Avg	OB	Slg	OPS	bb%	ct%	Eye	SB	CS	x/h%	Iso	RC/G
2012	Rk	GCL Astros	175	26	44	0	13	251	355	360	715	14	73	0.58	7	5	30	109	4.82
2013	Rk	Greeneville	85	9	21	0	9	247	373	353	725	17	75	0.81	4	3	38	106	5.07
2013	A	Quad Cities	39	4	9	0	3	231	286	282	568	7	74	0.30	1	1	22	51	2.41
2014	A	Quad Cities	384	68	116	13	58	302	362	521	883	9	80	0.47	18	10	40	219	6.49
2014	A+	Lancaster	109	19	37	4	10	339	415	560	974	11	82	0.70	5	4	38	220	7.74

Breakout prospect who led MWL in SLG. Consistent, steady hitter who has added loft to swing to generate good power to all fields. Draws walks, but can be too passive early in count. Swing can get long, but makes loud contact. Can play CF with good speed, strong arm, and range.

Pierre,Nicolas — 789 — Milwaukee

EXP MLB DEBUT: 2017 | H/W: 6-3 170 | FUT: Starting OF | **7C**

Bats R Age 19 — 2013 FA (DR)
Pwr +++ | BAvg +++ | Spd +++ | Def +++

Year	Lev	Team	AB	R	H	HR	RBI	Avg	OB	Slg	OPS	bb%	ct%	Eye	SB	CS	x/h%	Iso	RC/G
2014	Rk	DSL Brewers	252	36	65	6	27	258	294	401	695	5	77	0.22	9	5	34	143	3.92

Tall, slender Dominican OF was signed by the Brewers for $800,000. Scouts like his athleticism and raw power. Features a good line-drive approach, but struggles to make contact. He has good speed and should be able to stick in CF, at least for now. Has yet to make his U.S. debut.

Pimentel,Guillermo — 7 — Seattle

EXP MLB DEBUT: 2016 | H/W: 6-1 205 | FUT: Starting OF | **8E**

Bats L Age 22 — 2009 FA (DR)
Pwr ++++ | BAvg ++ | Spd ++ | Def ++

Year	Lev	Team	AB	R	H	HR	RBI	Avg	OB	Slg	OPS	bb%	ct%	Eye	SB	CS	x/h%	Iso	RC/G
2013	Rk	AZL Mariners	20	1	6	0	2	300	300	400	700	0	70	0.00	0	0	33	100	3.99
2013	A	Clinton	202	24	52	6	30	257	324	416	740	9	66	0.29	4	3	35	158	4.92
2013	A+	High Desert	63	10	21	4	14	333	354	603	957	3	71	0.11	0	0	38	270	7.31
2014	Rk	AZL Mariners	6	1	2	0	2	333	333	333	667	0	50	0.00	0	0	0	0	4.80
2014	A+	High Desert	15	4	5	2	6	333	474	800	1274	21	67	0.80	0	0	60	467	12.94

Powerful OF who missed most of year with stress fracture in tibia. Has exciting power potential with good feel for bat. Secondary skills need polish, but hope is that bat will carry him. Pitch selection needs work and can get himself out with uppercut stroke. Lacks speed and relegated to LF.

Pinder,Chad — 46 — Oakland

EXP MLB DEBUT: 2016 | H/W: 6-2 195 | FUT: Starting 2B/SS | **7C**

Bats R Age 23 — 2013 (2-S) Virginia Tech
Pwr ++ | BAvg +++ | Spd +++ | Def ++

Year	Lev	Team	AB	R	H	HR	RBI	Avg	OB	Slg	OPS	bb%	ct%	Eye	SB	CS	x/h%	Iso	RC/G
2011	NCAA	Virginia Tech	104	21	33	3	14	317	360	510	870	6	82	0.37	4	1	30	192	6.16
2012	NCAA	Virginia Tech	212	36	69	7	37	325	367	538	905	6	80	0.33	6	5	43	212	6.61
2013	NCAA	Virginia Tech	240	49	77	8	50	321	375	483	859	8	84	0.55	5	4	29	163	6.02
2013	A-	Vermont	140	14	28	3	8	200	263	293	556	8	71	0.29	1	0	25	93	2.10
2014	A+	Stockton	403	61	116	13	55	288	325	489	814	5	75	0.22	12	9	43	201	5.51

Savvy INF who bypassed Low-A and had stellar season. Has plus feel for hitting with plus hand-eye coordination and barrel control. Drives ball to gaps, though projects to average pop at best. Exhibits clean hands, but may not have enough range for SS. Arm is playable at any spot.

Pirela,Jose — 479 — New York (A)

EXP MLB DEBUT: 2014 | H/W: 5-11 210 | FUT: Utility player | **6B**

Bats B Age 25 — 2006 FA (Venezuela)
Pwr ++ | BAvg +++ | Spd +++ | Def ++

Year	Lev	Team	AB	R	H	HR	RBI	Avg	OB	Slg	OPS	bb%	ct%	Eye	SB	CS	x/h%	Iso	RC/G
2012	AA	Trenton	317	55	93	8	33	293	347	448	795	8	85	0.54	9	3	32	155	5.30
2013	AA	Trenton	459	73	125	10	62	272	351	418	770	11	87	0.92	18	3	34	146	5.26
2013	AAA	Scranton/WB	23	3	7	0	1	304	333	304	638	4	91	0.50	1	0	0	0	3.38
2014	AAA	Scranton/WB	535	87	163	10	60	305	350	441	791	6	86	0.50	15	7	26	136	5.21
2014	MLB	NY Yankees	24	6	8	0	3	333	360	542	902	4	83	0.25	0	0	38	208	6.64

Short, strong prospect who tied career high in HR while showing solid BA from both sides of plate. Graduated to AAA after 3 yrs in AA and uses limited tools well. Not a gifted glovesman, though has instincts to play any position. Runs well and possesses average arm and range at 2B.

Piscotty,Stephen — 9 — St. Louis

EXP MLB DEBUT: 2015 | H/W: 6-3 210 | FUT: Starting RF | **8C**

Bats R Age 24 — 2012 (S-1) Stanford
Pwr +++ | BAvg +++ | Spd +++ | Def +++

Year	Lev	Team	AB	R	H	HR	RBI	Avg	OB	Slg	OPS	bb%	ct%	Eye	SB	CS	x/h%	Iso	RC/G
2012	NCAA	Stanford	246	44	81	5	56	329	402	467	870	11	91	1.30	4	0	26	138	6.44
2012	A	Quad Cities	210	29	62	4	27	295	351	448	798	8	88	0.72	3	0	37	152	5.44
2013	A+	Palm Beach	243	30	71	9	35	292	341	477	818	7	89	0.67	4	5	35	185	5.50
2013	AA	Springfield	184	17	55	6	24	299	365	446	810	9	90	1.00	7	3	27	147	5.57
2014	AAA	Memphis	500	70	144	9	69	288	344	406	750	8	88	0.70	11	5	28	118	4.85

Does everything above average, but doesn't have a plus tool besides the ability to hit. Makes consistent contact and uses the whole field. Runs well and has a plus arm and range. Does have good bat speed and a discerning eye, so he could develop a bit more power as he matures.

Plawecki,Kevin — 2 — New York (N)

EXP MLB DEBUT: 2015 | H/W: 6-2 225 | FUT: Starting C | **7B**

Bats R Age 24 — 2012 (1) Purdue
Pwr +++ | BAvg +++ | Spd + | Def +++

Year	Lev	Team	AB	R	H	HR	RBI	Avg	OB	Slg	OPS	bb%	ct%	Eye	SB	CS	x/h%	Iso	RC/G
2012	A-	Brooklyn	216	26	54	7	27	250	328	384	712	10	89	1.04	0	0	28	134	4.50
2013	A	Savannah	245	35	77	6	43	314	373	494	867	9	87	0.72	1	0	40	180	6.26
2013	A+	St. Lucie	204	25	60	2	37	294	354	392	746	9	90	0.90	0	0	27	98	4.92
2014	AA	Binghamton	224	33	73	6	43	326	371	487	857	7	88	0.59	0	0	33	161	5.96
2014	AAA	Las Vegas	152	25	43	5	21	283	343	421	764	8	86	0.67	0	0	26	138	4.92

Consistent offensive producer thanks to excellent ability to make contact and use all fields. Has enough strength for double digit HRs and advanced knowledge of strike zone will bodes well for OBP. Continues to improve behind plate. Agile receiver with average arm but improving release.

Polanco,Jorge — 46 — Minnesota

EXP MLB DEBUT: 2014 | H/W: 5-11 165 | FUT: Starting 2B/SS | **7B**

Bats B Age 21 — 2009 FA (DR)
Pwr ++ | BAvg +++ | Spd ++++ | Def +++

Year	Lev	Team	AB	R	H	HR	RBI	Avg	OB	Slg	OPS	bb%	ct%	Eye	SB	CS	x/h%	Iso	RC/G
2012	Rk	Elizabethton	173	35	55	5	27	318	389	514	903	10	85	0.77	6	3	40	197	6.79
2013	A	Cedar Rapids	465	76	143	5	78	308	365	452	817	8	87	0.71	4	4	33	144	5.72
2014	A+	Fort Myers	378	61	110	6	45	291	368	415	783	11	84	0.77	10	8	26	124	5.40
2014	AA	New Britain	146	13	41	1	16	281	323	342	665	6	81	0.32	7	3	17	62	3.61
2014	MLB	Minnesota	6	2	2	0	3	333	500	833	1333	25	67	1.00	0	0	100	500	15.61

Improving INF who reached majors after quick rise. Posted career highs in HR and SB while continuing to show bat control and polished approach. Focuses on line drives with quick, compact stroke. Runs well and possesses positive defensive attributes. Can play either middle infield spot.

Pompey,Dalton — 78 — Toronto

EXP MLB DEBUT: 2014 | H/W: 6-2 195 | FUT: Starting OF | **8B**

Bats B Age 22 — 2010 (16) HS (CAN)
Pwr +++ | BAvg ++++ | Spd ++++ | Def +++

Year	Lev	Team	AB	R	H	HR	RBI	Avg	OB	Slg	OPS	bb%	ct%	Eye	SB	CS	x/h%	Iso	RC/G
2013	A	Lansing	437	68	114	6	40	261	354	394	748	13	76	0.59	38	10	32	133	5.08
2014	A+	Dunedin	276	49	88	6	34	319	395	471	867	11	80	0.63	29	2	27	152	6.46
2014	AA	New Hampshire	112	20	33	3	12	295	373	473	846	11	84	0.78	8	5	33	179	6.16
2014	AAA	Buffalo	53	15	19	0	5	358	393	453	846	5	81	0.30	6	0	26	94	5.89
2014	MLB	Toronto	39	5	9	1	4	231	302	436	738	9	69	0.33	1	0	44	205	4.94

Breakout prospect who set highs in HR and SB. Elite athlete with plus speed and above average CF defense. Tracks balls down with keen instincts and has strong arm. Knows strike zone and sees pitches well. Ability to hit for high BA due to fluid swing and plate patience. High floor player.

Powell,Boog — 8 — Oakland

EXP MLB DEBUT: 2017 | H/W: 5-10 185 | FUT: Fourth OF | **6B**

Bats L Age 22
2012 (20) Orange Coast CC

- Pwr +
- BAvg + + +
- Spd + + +
- Def + +

Year	Lev	Team	AB	R	H	HR	RBI	Avg	OB	Slg	OPS	bb%	ct%	Eye	SB	CS	x/h%	Iso	RC/G
2012	NCAA	Orange Coast CC	191	49	76	0	25	398	431	435	865	5	95	1.10	8	6	7	37	6.01
2012	Rk	AZL Athletics	111	20	34	0	13	306	389	315	704	12	92	1.67	5	2	3	9	4.70
2013	A-	Vermont	212	30	60	0	14	283	361	344	706	11	84	0.76	14	6	17	61	4.52
2014	A	Beloit	254	43	85	3	17	335	450	429	879	17	81	1.08	16	13	16	94	6.99
2014	A+	Stockton	61	11	23	0	11	377	449	459	908	12	93	2.00	0	2	17	82	7.03

Breakout OF who served 50 game suspension for PED. Has extensive knowledge of strike zone and gets on base with consistent approach. Owns balanced swing and puts ball in play. Not much power in stroke and is poor basestealer despite good speed. Defense hurt by poor arm.

Prime,Correlle — 3 — Colorado

EXP MLB DEBUT: 2017 | H/W: 6-5 220 | FUT: Starting 1B | **7D**

Bats R Age 21
2012 (12) HS (FL)

- Pwr + + + +
- BAvg + +
- Spd + +
- Def + +

Year	Lev	Team	AB	R	H	HR	RBI	Avg	OB	Slg	OPS	bb%	ct%	Eye	SB	CS	x/h%	Iso	RC/G
2012	Rk	Grand Junction	127	17	36	1	11	283	372	362	735	12	73	0.53	0	0	22	79	4.89
2013	Rk	Grand Junction	224	30	63	7	39	281	315	446	761	5	75	0.20	11	2	33	165	4.74
2014	A	Asheville	508	84	148	21	102	291	338	520	858	7	74	0.27	8	2	48	228	6.18

Big-bodied prospect had a nice breakout season. Can be overly aggressive searching for power and walked just 36 times, striking out 131. Below average in every other aspect of the game, which means he has to hit to move up and have value.

Puello,Cesar — 9 — New York (N)

EXP MLB DEBUT: 2015 | H/W: 6-2 220 | FUT: Starting RF | **8D**

Bats R Age 24
2007 FA (DR)

- Pwr + + + +
- BAvg + +
- Spd + + + +
- Def + + +

Year	Lev	Team	AB	R	H	HR	RBI	Avg	OB	Slg	OPS	bb%	ct%	Eye	SB	CS	x/h%	Iso	RC/G
2010	A	Savannah	404	80	118	1	34	292	344	359	703	7	80	0.39	45	10	20	67	4.21
2011	A+	St. Lucie	441	67	114	10	50	259	288	397	684	4	77	0.17	19	9	32	138	3.73
2012	A+	St. Lucie	227	36	59	4	21	260	282	423	705	3	74	0.12	19	2	42	163	4.07
2013	AA	Binghamton	331	63	108	16	73	326	379	547	926	8	75	0.34	24	7	36	221	7.01
2014	AAA	Las Vegas	318	59	80	7	37	252	316	393	709	9	77	0.42	13	1	36	142	4.31

Power numbers took a hit which is concerning considering home park and suspension previous season. Struggled against RHP (.101 Iso, .220 BA) but still possesses tantalizing tools. Can hit with power to all fields and good base stealer. Logged time at all OF spots, but RF likely.

Pujols,Jose — 9 — Philadelphia

EXP MLB DEBUT: 2019 | H/W: 6-3 175 | FUT: Starting RF | **9E**

Bats R Age 19
2012 FA (DR)

- Pwr + + + +
- BAvg + +
- Spd + +
- Def + +

Year	Lev	Team	AB	R	H	HR	RBI	Avg	OB	Slg	OPS	bb%	ct%	Eye	SB	CS	x/h%	Iso	RC/G
2013	Rk	GCL Phillies	160	27	30	6	18	188	274	369	642	11	65	0.34	1	3	50	181	3.49
2014	Rk	GCL Phillies	151	21	35	5	28	232	288	411	699	7	64	0.22	1	2	43	179	4.35
2014	A-	Williamsport	61	3	13	0	5	213	213	295	508	0	66	0.00	0	0	38	82	1.36

A high-profile international sign from 2012, his biggest asset is his age. Still far away, but his broad-shouldered frame still can fill out, and he has the plus raw power and elite arm of a classic RFer. Poor plate patience, contact rate, route running are all things that will need to be smoothed out. But he has time.

Pullin,Andrew — 4 — Philadelphia

EXP MLB DEBUT: 2017 | H/W: 6-0 190 | FUT: Starting 2B | **7C**

Bats L Age 21
2012 (5) HS (WA)

- Pwr + + +
- BAvg + + + +
- Spd + +
- Def + +

Year	Lev	Team	AB	R	H	HR	RBI	Avg	OB	Slg	OPS	bb%	ct%	Eye	SB	CS	x/h%	Iso	RC/G
2012	Rk	GCL Phillies	140	16	45	2	13	321	375	436	811	8	77	0.38	3	5	27	114	5.59
2013	A-	Williamsport	211	20	55	3	23	261	284	412	697	3	82	0.19	1	3	38	152	3.96
2014	A	Lakewood	492	67	133	9	61	270	326	374	700	8	81	0.43	6	7	23	104	4.12

Made strides in his plate approach, and when he's on, has sweet, short stroke. Capable of peppering balls up the middle and occasionally lifting one out, but often looks lost and unbalanced against breaking stuff. Took a step back with the glove; didn't look comfortable around the keystone. Good BA, but lots of questions.

Quinn,Roman — 6 — Philadelphia

EXP MLB DEBUT: 2016 | H/W: 5-10 175 | FUT: Starting CF | **8D**

Bats B Age 21
2011 (2) HS (FL)

- Pwr + +
- BAvg + + +
- Spd + + + +
- Def + + +

Year	Lev	Team	AB	R	H	HR	RBI	Avg	OB	Slg	OPS	bb%	ct%	Eye	SB	CS	x/h%	Iso	RC/G
2012	A-	Williamsport	267	56	75	1	23	281	349	408	757	9	77	0.46	30	6	28	127	5.13
2013	A	Lakewood	260	37	62	5	21	238	310	346	656	9	75	0.42	32	9	24	108	3.62
2014	A+	Clearwater	327	51	84	7	36	257	331	370	701	10	76	0.45	32	12	24	113	4.21

Achilles injury kept him out the first half, but grabbed SB in bunches upon return. Still learning routes in the OF (signed as a SS), but has speed to compensate. Has surprising gap power from both sides of the plate; opened some eyes with solid AFL season. Discerning eye, but contact still a question mark.

Quintana,Gabriel — 5 — San Diego

EXP MLB DEBUT: 2016 | H/W: 6-2 190 | FUT: Starting 3B | **8E**

Bats R Age 22
2009 FA (DR)

- Pwr + + + +
- BAvg + +
- Spd + +
- Def + +

Year	Lev	Team	AB	R	H	HR	RBI	Avg	OB	Slg	OPS	bb%	ct%	Eye	SB	CS	x/h%	Iso	RC/G
2012	Rk	AZL Padres	151	25	44	5	36	291	318	483	802	4	75	0.16	2	1	39	192	5.25
2012	A-	Eugene	61	2	14	1	8	230	242	311	553	2	70	0.06	0	0	21	82	1.84
2013	Rk	AZL Padres	21	4	7	0	3	333	364	429	792	5	81	0.25	0	0	29	95	5.19
2013	A	Fort Wayne	347	50	106	9	44	305	327	447	774	3	74	0.12	6	2	28	141	4.84
2014	A+	Lake Elsinore	529	77	139	18	84	263	291	431	722	4	72	0.14	4	1	38	168	4.24

Tall and athletic INF had mixed results, hitting .263 but blasting 35 dbls and 18 HR. Possesses natural hitting skills with average power potential. Free swinging approach may not play well at higher levels and he did strike out 150 times. OK defender with quick hands and feet.

Ragira,Brian — 39 — San Francisco

EXP MLB DEBUT: 2016 | H/W: 6-2 185 | FUT: Backup 1B/OF | **7D**

Bats R Age 23
2013 (4) Stanford

- Pwr + + +
- BAvg + +
- Spd +
- Def + + +

Year	Lev	Team	AB	R	H	HR	RBI	Avg	OB	Slg	OPS	bb%	ct%	Eye	SB	CS	x/h%	Iso	RC/G
2012	NCAA	Stanford	252	41	83	5	50	329	374	448	822	7	81	0.38	3	2	24	119	5.56
2013	NCAA	Stanford	222	34	71	8	42	320	360	482	842	6	89	0.58	4	1	27	162	5.67
2013	Rk	AZL Giants	28	4	10	0	6	357	379	464	844	3	79	0.17	0	0	20	107	5.81
2013	A-	Salem-Kaizer	179	29	47	3	36	263	356	391	747	13	70	0.48	1	1	34	128	5.14
2014	A+	San Jose	457	58	119	20	82	260	316	444	760	7	72	0.29	2	2	37	184	4.85

Strong, athletic 1B tapped into the raw power many scouts saw when he was at Stanford. Decent bat speed allows for average contact rates, but trouble with off speed will affect BA ceiling. Lacks plate discipline, but average power and good defense at 1B will likely carve out a role for him in the future.

Rahier,Tanner — 5 — Cincinnati

EXP MLB DEBUT: 2017 | H/W: 5-11 200 | FUT: Starting 3B | **7E**

Bats R Age 21
2012 (2) HS (CA)

- Pwr + + +
- BAvg + +
- Spd + +
- Def + + +

Year	Lev	Team	AB	R	H	HR	RBI	Avg	OB	Slg	OPS	bb%	ct%	Eye	SB	CS	x/h%	Iso	RC/G
2012	Rk	AZL Reds	193	21	37	4	30	192	271	311	582	10	78	0.49	5	2	38	119	2.71
2013	A	Dayton	410	31	91	7	61	222	244	320	564	3	80	0.15	0	5	26	98	2.18
2014	A	Dayton	421	51	100	9	54	238	293	356	649	7	77	0.34	2	2	30	119	3.43

Got off to decent start, but yet another season of prolonged struggles. Plus power and excellent D will earn him AB while he tries to figure out the systemic cold spells. Can provide nice pop for his size thanks to leveraged stroke. Quick hands and strong arm at the hot corner. Still 15-20 HR upside.

Railey,Matt — 8 — Arizona

EXP MLB DEBUT: 2017 | H/W: 5-11 190 | FUT: Starting LF | **8D**

Bats L Age 20
2014 (3) HS (FL)

- Pwr + + +
- BAvg + + +
- Spd + +
- Def + +

Year	Lev	Team	AB	R	H	HR	RBI	Avg	OB	Slg	OPS	bb%	ct%	Eye	SB	CS	x/h%	Iso	RC/G
2014	Rk	Missoula	45	7	12	2	7	267	327	556	882	8	84	0.57	1	1	67	289	6.42

3rd round pick and looks to be a good one. Has a quick bat with a balanced swing. The ball jumps off his bat and he projects to have above-average power. Can be overly aggressive, and there is swing-and-miss to his game, but showed contact ability in his debut. Above-average speed.

Ramirez,Harold — 789 — Pittsburgh

EXP MLB DEBUT: 2016 | H/W: 5-10 210 | FUT: Starting CF | **8D**

Bats R Age 20
2011 FA (Columbia)

- Pwr + + +
- BAvg + + +
- Spd + + +
- Def + + +

Year	Lev	Team	AB	R	H	HR	RBI	Avg	OB	Slg	OPS	bb%	ct%	Eye	SB	CS	x/h%	Iso	RC/G
2012	Rk	GCL Pirates	135	18	35	1	12	259	291	333	624	4	85	0.30	9	5	20	74	3.13
2013	A-	Jamestown	274	42	78	5	40	285	340	409	749	8	81	0.44	23	11	26	124	4.76
2014	A	West Virginia	204	30	63	1	24	309	344	402	746	5	83	0.31	12	3	25	93	4.63

Leg injuries limited him to 204 AB, but when he was on the field he impressed. Has an aggressive approach with good pop and plus speed. Can be overly aggressive, but makes consistent contact. Good raw power that has yet to translate into game action, but could take off.

Ramirez,Nick
3 | **Milwaukee** | EXP MLB DEBUT: 2016 | H/W: 6-3 225 | FUT: Backup 1B | **6C**

Bats L Age 25 — 2011 (4) Cal St Fullerton — Pwr +++ / BAvg ++ / Spd + / Def ++++

Year	Lev	Team	AB	R	H	HR	RBI	Avg	OB	Slg	OPS	bb%	ct%	Eye	SB	CS	x/h%	Iso	RC/G
2011	Rk	Helena	103	23	38	8	30	369	381	689	1070	2	79	0.09	0	1	45	320	8.20
2011	A	Wisconsin	137	11	27	3	23	197	247	350	597	6	74	0.25	0	0	56	153	2.74
2012	A	Wisconsin	383	46	95	16	70	248	296	446	742	6	62	0.18	0	0	46	198	5.04
2013	A+	Brevard Cnty	500	70	129	19	81	258	330	438	768	10	66	0.32	5	0	38	180	5.35
2014	AA	Huntsville	490	71	113	19	82	231	308	410	718	10	69	0.36	1	4	40	180	4.50

Tall LHH 1B prospect. Most advanced tools is his power and he launched 19 HR in each of the past two season. Making consistent contact is not his forte and it is hard to see how he will hit for avg. Is a career .249 hitter. Below avg speed and defense give him limited value.

Ramos,Henry
789 | **Boston** | EXP MLB DEBUT: 2016 | H/W: 6-2 190 | FUT: Starting OF | **7D**

Bats B Age 22 — 2010 (5) HS (PR) — Pwr +++ / BAvg +++ / Spd + / Def ++

Year	Lev	Team	AB	R	H	HR	RBI	Avg	OB	Slg	OPS	bb%	ct%	Eye	SB	CS	x/h%	Iso	RC/G
2010	A-	Lowell	24	1	3	0	2	125	160	125	285	4	67	0.13	0	0	0	0	-1.97
2011	A	Greenville	332	40	87	5	43	262	298	383	681	5	77	0.22	15	6	30	120	3.77
2012	A	Greenville	441	61	112	8	63	254	322	381	703	9	77	0.44	12	10	32	127	4.26
2013	A+	Salem	469	69	118	12	55	252	330	416	746	10	79	0.55	11	12	39	164	4.88
2014	AA	Portland	181	26	59	2	23	326	365	431	796	6	79	0.29	2	4	22	105	5.25

Steadily improving OF ended season in May after fractured leg. Exhibits good all-around tools, highlighted by raw power and athleticism. Can hit for BA from both sides of plate and makes loud contact with simple stroke. Added strength since signing, but has slowed down considerably.

Ramos,Milton
6 | **New York (N)** | EXP MLB DEBUT: 2019 | H/W: 5-11 160 | FUT: Starting SS | **8E**

Bats R Age 19 — 2014 (3) HS (FL) — Pwr + / BAvg ++ / Spd ++++ / Def ++++

Year	Lev	Team	AB	R	H	HR	RBI	Avg	OB	Slg	OPS	bb%	ct%	Eye	SB	CS	x/h%	Iso	RC/G
2014	Rk	GCL Mets	166	20	40	0	29	241	300	355	655	8	80	0.41	6	6	35	114	3.76

Considered best defender of '14 draft. Offense needs work but early positive returns (14 XBH in 166 AB). Smart player with plus speed, good instincts, and plus arm. Great range at SS. Aggressive swinger with compact line-drive stroke. Plenty of projection but needs to simplify approach.

Ramsey,James
789 | **Cleveland** | EXP MLB DEBUT: 2015 | H/W: 6-0 190 | FUT: Starting OF | **7B**

Bats L Age 25 — 2012 (1) Florida State — Pwr ++ / BAvg +++ / Spd +++ / Def +++

Year	Lev	Team	AB	R	H	HR	RBI	Avg	OB	Slg	OPS	bb%	ct%	Eye	SB	CS	x/h%	Iso	RC/G
2013	A+	Palm Beach	61	17	22	1	7	361	466	557	1023	16	80	1.00	1	0	36	197	8.89
2013	AA	Springfield	347	61	87	15	44	251	350	424	774	13	69	0.49	8	4	32	173	5.36
2013	AAA	Memphis	3	0	0	0	0	0	0	0	0	0	67	0.00	0	0		0	-6.12
2014	AA	Springfield	243	47	73	13	36	300	380	527	906	11	73	0.47	4	2	38	226	7.01
2014	AAA	Columbus	109	17	31	3	16	284	361	468	829	11	69	0.38	1	0	42	183	6.26

Athletic OF who maximizes ability and has no glaring weakness. Set career high in HR, though thrives more with gap power and speed. Doesn't steal many bases despite wheels, but patrols CF well with honed routes and range. Struggles with LHH and could stand to make better contact.

Ratterree,Michael
9 | **Milwaukee** | EXP MLB DEBUT: 2017 | H/W: 6-1 190 | FUT: Backup OF | **6C**

Bats R Age 24 — 2013 (10) Rice — Pwr +++ / BAvg ++ / Spd + / Def ++

Year	Lev	Team	AB	R	H	HR	RBI	Avg	OB	Slg	OPS	bb%	ct%	Eye	SB	CS	x/h%	Iso	RC/G
2012	NCAA	Rice	189	39	44	6	32	233	372	407	780	18	79	1.08	6	2	45	175	5.66
2013	NCAA	Rice	226	48	59	9	41	261	381	425	806	16	81	1.00	13	3	32	164	5.83
2013	Rk	Helena	258	63	81	12	58	314	377	585	962	9	72	0.36	7	3	49	271	7.86
2014	A	Wisconsin	447	91	105	18	71	235	345	452	797	14	66	0.49	4	6	53	217	6.00
2014	AA	Huntsville	26	2	3	1	5	115	233	269	503	13	54	0.33	1	0	67	154	1.30

10th rounder had an impressive debut in 2013, but failed to duplicate it, with 154 K in full-season ball.. Frequently looked over-matched, though he is willing to take a walk and has plus raw power. Runs fairly well underway, but takes bad routes, so he needs to hit to have value.

Ravelo,Rangel
3 | **Oakland** | EXP MLB DEBUT: 2015 | H/W: 6-2 210 | FUT: Starting 1B | **7D**

Bats R Age 22 — 2010 (6) HS (FL) — Pwr ++ / BAvg +++ / Spd ++ / Def ++

Year	Lev	Team	AB	R	H	HR	RBI	Avg	OB	Slg	OPS	bb%	ct%	Eye	SB	CS	x/h%	Iso	RC/G
2011	A	Kannapolis	161	11	51	0	21	317	364	373	737	7	88	0.63	0	1	18	56	4.68
2012	A	Kannapolis	290	32	84	2	39	290	335	397	732	6	87	0.53	6	1	29	107	4.60
2013	A	Kannapolis	53	9	12	0	9	226	359	302	661	17	79	1.00	1	1	33	75	4.24
2013	A+	Winston-Salem	301	43	94	4	53	312	393	455	848	12	85	0.87	4	1	35	143	6.29
2014	AA	Birmingham	476	72	147	11	66	309	382	473	854	11	84	0.73	10	6	35	164	6.23

Consistent, steady 1B who makes very good contact with gap power. Has strength for power, but likes to use opposite field and focus on putting ball in play. Set high in HR while continuing to have discerning eye. Finished 2nd in SL in BA, but doesn't have secondary skills to have value.

Realmuto,J.T.
2 | **Miami** | EXP MLB DEBUT: 2014 | H/W: 6-1 215 | FUT: Starting C | **8C**

Bats R Age 24 — 2010 (3) HS (OK) — Pwr ++ / BAvg +++ / Spd +++ / Def ++++

Year	Lev	Team	AB	R	H	HR	RBI	Avg	OB	Slg	OPS	bb%	ct%	Eye	SB	CS	x/h%	Iso	RC/G
2011	A	Greensboro	348	46	100	12	49	287	337	454	791	7	78	0.33	13	6	31	167	5.18
2012	A+	Jupiter	446	63	114	8	46	256	313	345	658	8	86	0.58	13	5	21	90	3.68
2013	AA	Jacksonville	368	41	88	5	39	239	307	353	660	9	82	0.53	9	1	33	114	3.78
2014	AA	Jacksonville	375	66	112	8	62	299	368	461	829	10	84	0.69	18	5	35	163	5.90
2014	MLB	Miami	29	4	7	0	9	241	267	345	611	3	72	0.13	0	0	29	103	2.92

At the plate he has good bat speed, makes consistent contact, and plate discipline. Power has yet to develop. Shines behind the plate. Uses athleticism to block balls and has a good pop time and quick release. Plus throwing arm allowed him to nail 39% of baserunners in 2014.

Reed,A.J.
3 | **Houston** | EXP MLB DEBUT: 2017 | H/W: 6-4 240 | FUT: Starting 1B | **7C**

Bats L Age 21 — 2014 (2) Kentucky — Pwr ++++ / BAvg ++ / Spd ++ / Def ++

Year	Lev	Team	AB	R	H	HR	RBI	Avg	OB	Slg	OPS	bb%	ct%	Eye	SB	CS	x/h%	Iso	RC/G
2012	NCAA	Kentucky	200	29	60	4	43	300	375	405	780	11	75	0.47	0	1	22	105	5.32
2013	NCAA	Kentucky	214	30	60	13	52	280	358	519	877	11	81	0.63	1	1	38	238	6.33
2014	A-	Tri City	124	22	38	5	30	306	411	516	927	15	82	1.00	2	0	42	210	7.33
2014	A	Quad Cities	125	21	34	7	24	272	316	528	844	6	74	0.25	0	0	50	256	5.86

Astute, professional hitter who combines patient approach with loft in stroke to hit for power. Understands strike zone, but can get himself out when behind in count. Struggles with LHP while fringy bat speed and long swing project to low BA. Owns strong arm, but not as useful at 1B.

Reed,Michael
79 | **Milwaukee** | EXP MLB DEBUT: 2016 | H/W: 6-0 190 | FUT: Starting RF | **7D**

Bats R Age 22 — 2011 (5) HS (TX) — Pwr + / BAvg +++ / Spd ++++ / Def +++

Year	Lev	Team	AB	R	H	HR	RBI	Avg	OB	Slg	OPS	bb%	ct%	Eye	SB	CS	x/h%	Iso	RC/G
2012	Rk	Helena	179	29	44	1	20	246	335	302	637	12	68	0.41	11	1	16	56	3.51
2012	A+	Brevard Cnty	32	5	9	0	5	281	425	281	706	20	75	1.00	3	0	0	0	4.82
2012	AA	Huntsville	7	0	0	0	0	0	0	0	0	0	57	0.00	0	0		0	-7.11
2013	A	Wisconsin	455	68	130	1	40	286	382	400	782	13	76	0.66	26	10	28	114	5.67
2014	A+	Brevard Cnty	365	50	93	5	47	255	386	378	764	18	78	0.99	33	13	32	123	5.53

Well-rounded OF with plus speed. Makes consistent contact and is very patient at the plate. Has yet to have a breakout season, but has the tools to hit for average and get on base with regularity. Possesses decent raw power, but has a contact, line-drive approach.

Reetz,Jakson
2 | **Washington** | EXP MLB DEBUT: 2019 | H/W: 6-1 195 | FUT: Starting C | **8E**

Bats R Age 19 — 2014 (3) HS (NE) — Pwr +++ / BAvg +++ / Spd + / Def +++

Year	Lev	Team	AB	R	H	HR	RBI	Avg	OB	Slg	OPS	bb%	ct%	Eye	SB	CS	x/h%	Iso	RC/G
2014	Rk	GCL Nationals	117	20	32	1	15	274	406	368	773	18	74	0.87	6	3	25	94	5.70

A catching skill set to dream on: Short stroke to all fields, sufficient bat speed, and the strength that portends at least league-average power. Solid frame with room to grow. A bit raw defensively, but plus arm strength, athleticism argue for patience while he develops. A long way off, but raw tools are there.

Refsnyder,Rob
49 | **New York (A)** | EXP MLB DEBUT: 2015 | H/W: 6-1 205 | FUT: Starting 2B | **7B**

Bats R Age 24 — 2012 (5) Arizona — Pwr ++ / BAvg ++++ / Spd +++ / Def ++

Year	Lev	Team	AB	R	H	HR	RBI	Avg	OB	Slg	OPS	bb%	ct%	Eye	SB	CS	x/h%	Iso	RC/G
2012	A	CharlestonSC	162	22	39	4	22	241	309	364	673	9	85	0.64	11	1	31	123	3.91
2013	A	CharlestonSC	54	9	20	0	6	370	433	481	915	10	78	0.50	7	0	25	111	7.18
2013	A+	Tampa	413	66	117	6	51	283	397	404	802	16	83	1.11	16	6	31	121	5.93
2014	AA	Trenton	228	35	78	6	30	342	380	548	928	6	83	0.37	5	5	38	206	6.84
2014	AAA	Scranton/WB	287	47	86	8	33	300	387	456	844	13	77	0.61	4	4	33	157	6.24

Natural hitting player who does many things well with bat. Good situational hitter who makes easy contact and draws walks while exhibiting enough power to keep defenses honest. Not a great athlete, but has average speed. Saw time in OF, but 2B is best spot. Needs to improve hands.

Reinheimer,Jack — 46 — Seattle

EXP MLB DEBUT: 2016 | H/W: 6-1 185 | FUT: Starting 2B/SS | 6B

Bats R Age 22 — 2013 (5) East Carolina
- Pwr ++
- BAvg +++
- Spd +++
- Def +++

Year	Lev	Team	AB	R	H	HR	RBI	Avg	OB	Slg	OPS	bb%	ct%	Eye	SB	CS	x/h%	Iso	RC/G
2012	NCAA	East Carolina	238	36	70	2	22	294	333	374	707	6	88	0.48	9	1	20	80	4.22
2013	NCAA	East Carolina	221	32	60	2	21	271	356	339	695	12	81	0.67	10	3	18	68	4.31
2013	A-	Everett	249	39	67	2	30	269	352	325	678	11	80	0.63	18	5	13	56	4.05
2014	A	Clinton	436	69	115	2	46	264	324	335	659	8	83	0.51	34	9	20	71	3.75
2014	A+	High Desert	85	15	29	1	12	341	371	459	830	4	86	0.33	5	2	24	118	5.54

Smart, savvy INF who has grinder approach. Lacks a standout tool and will rarely hit HR, but knows how to play game, particularly defensively. Range is average, but makes plays with quick, soft hands. Will draw walks and use average speed well. Keeps bat head in zone a long time.

Renda,Tony — 4 — Washington

EXP MLB DEBUT: 2016 | H/W: 5-8 180 | FUT: Backup 2B | 7D

Bats R Age 24 — 2012 (2) California
- Pwr +
- BAvg +++
- Spd +++
- Def ++

Year	Lev	Team	AB	R	H	HR	RBI	Avg	OB	Slg	OPS	bb%	ct%	Eye	SB	CS	x/h%	Iso	RC/G
2011	NCAA	California	265	38	88	3	44	332	363	434	797	5	89	0.46	9	2	22	102	5.18
2012	NCAA	California	219	41	75	5	27	342	419	484	903	12	92	1.61	16	3	28	142	6.87
2012	A-	Auburn	295	47	78	0	32	264	334	295	629	10	89	0.94	15	3	12	31	3.63
2013	A	Hagerstown	521	99	153	3	51	294	375	405	780	12	88	1.05	30	6	32	111	5.52
2014	A+	Potomac	414	75	127	0	47	307	372	377	749	9	86	0.73	19	5	20	70	4.97

Lacks physicality and one standout tool, but a baseball rat who knows how to play the game. Hits for average with a good eye at the plate and an impressive contact rate history, and uses good speed to steal bases. Has a strong arm, but defensive profile limited to 2B. Opened some eyes in the AFL, but it's an uphill battle.

Renfroe,Hunter — 9 — San Diego

EXP MLB DEBUT: 2015 | H/W: 6-1 210 | FUT: Starting RF | 9D

Bats R Age 23 — 2013 (1) Mississippi St
- Pwr ++++
- BAvg +++
- Spd +++
- Def +++

Year	Lev	Team	AB	R	H	HR	RBI	Avg	OB	Slg	OPS	bb%	ct%	Eye	SB	CS	x/h%	Iso	RC/G
2013	NCAA	Mississippi St	255	56	88	16	65	345	424	620	1044	12	83	0.81	9	4	40	275	8.44
2013	A-	Eugene	104	20	32	4	18	308	339	510	849	5	75	0.19	2	0	41	202	5.89
2013	A	Fort Wayne	66	6	14	2	7	212	257	379	636	6	65	0.17	0	0	50	167	3.31
2014	A+	Lake Elsinore	278	46	82	16	52	295	359	565	924	9	71	0.35	9	3	49	270	7.29
2014	AA	San Antonio	224	17	52	5	23	232	309	353	662	10	76	0.47	2	1	33	121	3.72

Classic RF profile with plus power and arm strength. Has tendency to expand strike zone with an unrefined approach, but has decent hitting instincts with quick hands. Generates plus bat speed, but can be fooled by breaking balls. Runs well for size and has enough range in OF.

Reyes,Elmer — 6 — Atlanta

EXP MLB DEBUT: 2015 | H/W: 5-11 175 | FUT: Backup INF | 6C

Bats R Age 24 — 2009 FA (Nicaragua)
- Pwr +
- BAvg +++
- Spd ++
- Def ++

Year	Lev	Team	AB	R	H	HR	RBI	Avg	OB	Slg	OPS	bb%	ct%	Eye	SB	CS	x/h%	Iso	RC/G
2011	A	Rome	237	24	42	1	16	177	207	245	452	4	85	0.26	5	1	33	68	1.16
2012	A	Rome	379	49	95	5	36	251	279	391	670	4	83	0.23	5	5	39	140	3.67
2013	A+	Lynchburg	438	57	125	5	60	285	317	406	723	4	83	0.27	7	1	31	121	4.31
2014	AA	Mississippi	211	25	64	2	28	303	326	417	743	3	77	0.15	3	2	30	114	4.49
2014	AAA	Gwinnett	206	27	59	3	24	286	303	427	731	2	78	0.11	2	0	36	141	4.29

Had his best season as a pro, hitting .295 with 32 doubles between AA/AAA. Short simple stroke results in line drives, but poor pitch recognition leads to poor contact and he was lucky in '14 with a .378 BABIP at AA. Below average arm makes a shift to 2B or a UT role likely.

Reyes,Jomar — 5 — Baltimore

EXP MLB DEBUT: 2018 | H/W: 6-3 220 | FUT: Starting 3B/1B | 8D

Bats R Age 18 — 2014 FA (DR)
- Pwr ++++
- BAvg +++
- Spd +
- Def ++

Year	Lev	Team	AB	R	H	HR	RBI	Avg	OB	Slg	OPS	bb%	ct%	Eye	SB	CS	x/h%	Iso	RC/G
2014	Rk	GCL Orioles	186	23	53	4	29	285	338	425	763	7	80	0.39	1	0	30	140	4.92

Big, strong INF who has ideal power and arm to be standout 3B. Possesses plus bat speed and can drive ball to all fields. Hand-eye coordination a tad short at present, but makes hard contact with lofty stroke. Doesn't run well and subpar footwork and range could lead him to 1B full-time.

Reyes,Victor — 79 — Atlanta

EXP MLB DEBUT: 2018 | H/W: 6-3 170 | FUT: Starting OF | 7D

Bats L Age 20 — 2011 FA (Venezuela)
- Pwr ++
- BAvg +++
- Spd ++
- Def +++

Year	Lev	Team	AB	R	H	HR	RBI	Avg	OB	Slg	OPS	bb%	ct%	Eye	SB	CS	x/h%	Iso	RC/G
2013	Rk	Danville	81	12	26	0	4	321	345	358	703	4	89	0.33	0	0	12	37	4.04
2013	Rk	GCL Braves	112	22	40	0	21	357	419	446	866	10	82	0.60	5	1	23	89	6.41
2014	A	Rome	332	32	86	0	34	259	309	298	607	7	83	0.41	12	7	15	39	3.02

OF regressed in his full-season debut. Remains raw, but does have a good approach and makes consistent contact. Prefers to shoot balls the other way, raising questions long-term power and he has yet to hit a HR. Shows good range in the OF with above-average speed.

Reynolds,Matt — 6 — New York (N)

EXP MLB DEBUT: 2016 | H/W: 6-1 200 | FUT: Platoon SS/2B | 6D

Bats R Age 24 — 2012 (2) Arkansas
- Pwr ++
- BAvg +++
- Spd ++
- Def ++

Year	Lev	Team	AB	R	H	HR	RBI	Avg	OB	Slg	OPS	bb%	ct%	Eye	SB	CS	x/h%	Iso	RC/G
2012	A	Savannah	158	18	41	3	13	259	312	367	679	7	84	0.46	5	1	27	108	3.87
2013	A+	St. Lucie	433	59	98	5	49	226	286	337	623	8	82	0.45	9	2	33	111	3.27
2013	AA	Binghamton	3	0	0	0	0	0	0	0	0	0	100		0	0		0	-2.66
2014	AA	Binghamton	211	33	75	1	21	355	433	422	855	12	81	0.71	6	3	12	66	6.38
2014	AAA	Las Vegas	267	54	89	5	40	333	382	479	861	7	78	0.35	14	4	28	146	6.21

Put together impressive numbers at the plate during first taste of high minors. Shows gap power and willingness to go the other way with a compact, line-drive swing that gets to most anything in the strike zone. Average-at-best power and speed. Good hands but range could force move to 2B.

Reynoso,Jonathan — 89 — Cincinnati

EXP MLB DEBUT: 2017 | H/W: 6-3 175 | FUT: Starting OF | 8E

Bats R Age 22 — 2010 FA (DR)
- Pwr +++
- BAvg ++
- Spd ++++
- Def +++

Year	Lev	Team	AB	R	H	HR	RBI	Avg	OB	Slg	OPS	bb%	ct%	Eye	SB	CS	x/h%	Iso	RC/G
2012	Rk	AZL Reds	190	37	59	2	16	311	332	411	742	3	88	0.26	30	9	20	100	4.45
2013	Rk	Billings	160	16	38	2	12	238	261	306	567	3	82	0.17	9	5	18	69	2.25
2014	A	Dayton	175	20	40	0	13	229	286	263	549	7	77	0.34	8	1	13	34	2.18

Disappointing season across the board offensively considering his tools upside. Didn't get on base enough to utilize plus speed and power was non-existent. He's working to shorten swing path for more consistent contact. Has the arm and range for RF, needs the bat to come around soon.

Rijo,Wendell — 4 — Boston

EXP MLB DEBUT: 2017 | H/W: 5-11 170 | FUT: Starting 2B | 7C

Bats R Age 19 — 2012 FA (DR)
- Pwr ++
- BAvg +++
- Spd +++
- Def ++

Year	Lev	Team	AB	R	H	HR	RBI	Avg	OB	Slg	OPS	bb%	ct%	Eye	SB	CS	x/h%	Iso	RC/G
2013	Rk	GCL Red Sox	170	28	46	0	20	271	354	359	713	11	83	0.76	15	5	33	88	4.67
2013	A-	Lowell	14	1	5	0	0	357	357	571	929	0	79	0.00	0	1	40	214	6.85
2014	A	Greenville	409	56	104	9	46	254	344	416	760	12	75	0.54	16	6	40	161	5.19

Smart, situational hitter who picked up power production late in first full season. Understands strike zone and waits for pitches to drive. Can be too passive at plate and get himself behind in count. Runs well and can steal bases. Arm strength is limited, but is solid defender with quick feet.

Rivera,Yadiel — 6 — Milwaukee

EXP MLB DEBUT: 2015 | H/W: 6-2 175 | FUT: Backup SS | 6C

Bats R Age 22 — 2010 (9) HS (PR)
- Pwr ++
- BAvg +++
- Spd +++
- Def ++++

Year	Lev	Team	AB	R	H	HR	RBI	Avg	OB	Slg	OPS	bb%	ct%	Eye	SB	CS	x/h%	Iso	RC/G
2011	A	Wisconsin	103	6	20	1	5	194	224	262	486	4	67	0.12	0	0	20	68	1.01
2012	A	Wisconsin	465	60	115	12	49	247	287	402	689	5	74	0.22	7	3	37	155	3.88
2013	A+	Brevard Cnty	478	51	115	5	37	241	288	314	602	6	83	0.40	13	8	20	73	2.92
2014	A+	Brevard Cnty	231	35	59	3	17	255	304	346	650	6	78	0.32	5	3	22	91	3.43
2014	AA	Huntsville	183	31	48	2	13	262	301	410	710	5	80	0.28	5	2	35	148	4.25

Lean and athletic SS might be the best defender in the system. He has good range, soft hands, and gets excellent jumps. At the plate he has gap power, but is a free swinger who rarely walks, though he did make more consistent contact '14.

Roache,Victor — 7 — Milwaukee

EXP MLB DEBUT: 2016 | H/W: 6-1 225 | FUT: Starting OF | 8D

Bats R Age 23 — 2012 (1) GA Southern
- Pwr ++++
- BAvg ++
- Spd ++
- Def ++

Year	Lev	Team	AB	R	H	HR	RBI	Avg	OB	Slg	OPS	bb%	ct%	Eye	SB	CS	x/h%	Iso	RC/G
2010	NCAA	GA Southern	151	38	38	8	38	252	379	464	843	17	72	0.74	7	2	39	212	6.38
2011	NCAA	GA Southern	230	58	75	30	84	326	419	778	1198	14	82	0.88	3	4	56	452	10.16
2012	NCAA	GA Southern	17	6	7	2	5	412	583	765	1348	29	94	7.00	0	0	29	353	12.67
2013	A	Wisconsin	459	62	114	22	74	248	317	440	757	9	70	0.34	6	2	35	192	4.90
2014	A+	Brevard Cnty	433	46	98	18	54	226	287	400	687	8	68	0.27	11	4	38	173	3.93

Continues to struggle with the breaking balls and a poor contact rate make it unlikely he will hit for average. Physically mature and has the potential to hit 30 HR in the majors. Limited to LF with an average arm and decent reads, given that he has slightly below average speed.

Robertson,Daniel — 6 — Oakland

EXP MLB DEBUT: 2016 | H/W: 6-0 190 | FUT: Starting SS | 8B

Bats R Age 21 — 2012 (1-S) HS (CA)

Pwr +++ | BAvg ++++ | Spd ++ | Def +++

Year	Lev	Team	AB	R	H	HR	RBI	Avg	OB	Slg	OPS	bb%	ct%	Eye	SB	CS	x/h%	Iso	RC/G
2012	Rk	AZL Athletics	101	25	30	4	22	297	393	554	948	14	85	1.07	2	0	53	257	7.53
2012	A-	Vermont	94	9	17	1	8	181	238	234	472	7	67	0.23	1	1	18	53	0.85
2013	A	Beloit	401	59	111	9	46	277	344	401	745	9	80	0.52	1	7	28	125	4.77
2014	A+	Stockton	548	110	170	15	60	310	390	471	861	12	83	0.77	4	4	32	161	6.34

Disciplined INF who set highs in HR, BA, and BB. Was consistent with approach and leveraged bat speed and compact stroke to make easy, hard contact. Projects to above average bat contributor. Jury is out on defensive home. Can play SS with decent hands, but range better at 2B.

Rodriguez,Luigi — 789 — Cleveland

EXP MLB DEBUT: 2016 | H/W: 5-11 160 | FUT: Starting OF | 7D

Bats B Age 22 — 2009 FA (DR)

Pwr ++ | BAvg +++ | Spd ++++ | Def +++

Year	Lev	Team	AB	R	H	HR	RBI	Avg	OB	Slg	OPS	bb%	ct%	Eye	SB	CS	x/h%	Iso	RC/G
2011	A	Lake County	132	10	33	0	5	250	322	311	633	10	73	0.39	6	5	18	61	3.40
2012	A	Lake County	463	75	124	11	48	268	339	406	745	10	71	0.38	24	9	30	138	4.89
2013	A	Lake County	76	14	20	1	9	263	349	329	678	12	67	0.40	5	3	15	66	4.06
2013	A+	Carolina	113	16	32	0	11	283	382	398	780	14	68	0.50	3	4	38	115	5.88
2014	A+	Carolina	336	50	84	6	30	250	347	366	713	13	74	0.57	15	8	27	116	4.58

Short, lean OF with smooth, compact swing that results in decent pop despite size. Goes gap to gap and draws walks with improving eye. Exhibits plus speed on base and is asset at any OF position. Played mostly RF in '14 where arm is sufficient. Needs to get better jumps to improve.

Rodriguez,Nelson — 3 — Cleveland

EXP MLB DEBUT: 2017 | H/W: 6-2 225 | FUT: Starting 1B | 7D

Bats R Age 20 — 2012 (15) HS (NY)

Pwr ++++ | BAvg ++ | Spd + | Def ++

Year	Lev	Team	AB	R	H	HR	RBI	Avg	OB	Slg	OPS	bb%	ct%	Eye	SB	CS	x/h%	Iso	RC/G
2012	Rk	AZL Indians	109	19	25	4	17	229	368	459	827	18	62	0.59	0	0	56	229	6.83
2013	A-	Mahoning Val	261	32	75	9	37	287	359	452	811	10	77	0.48	0	2	33	165	5.62
2013	A	Lake County	160	18	31	1	13	194	306	256	563	14	67	0.49	0	0	26	63	2.46
2014	A	Lake County	485	67	130	22	88	268	349	482	831	11	71	0.42	0	0	44	214	6.09

Breakout prospect who led MWL in HR. Was spectacular late in season as he gained confidence in big stroke. Learning to use entire field and let bat speed take its course. Will always fan a lot with long swing, but willing to take walks when pitched around. No other average tool in arsenal.

Rodriguez,Ricardo — 2 — San Diego

EXP MLB DEBUT: 2019 | H/W: 5-10 180 | FUT: Starting C | 7C

Bats R Age 17 — 2014 FA (Venezuela)

Pwr +++ | BAvg ++ | Spd ++ | Def +++

Year	Lev	Team	AB	R	H	HR	RBI	Avg	OB	Slg	OPS	bb%	ct%	Eye	SB	CS	x/h%	Iso	RC/G
2014		(did not play in the US in 2014)																	

Doesn't have great bat speed but has good loft to his swing and should be able to develop power. Scouts have questions about his ability to hit for average, but he does have good plate discipline. Is a steady defender who blocks and receives well. Has good arm with quick throws.

Rodriguez,Ronny — 3456 — Cleveland

EXP MLB DEBUT: 2015 | H/W: 6-0 170 | FUT: Starting 2B/SS | 7C

Bats R Age 22 — 2010 FA (DR)

Pwr +++ | BAvg ++ | Spd ++ | Def +++

Year	Lev	Team	AB	R	H	HR	RBI	Avg	OB	Slg	OPS	bb%	ct%	Eye	SB	CS	x/h%	Iso	RC/G
2011	A	Lake County	370	41	91	11	42	246	272	449	720	3	78	0.16	10	7	51	203	4.22
2012	A+	Carolina	454	67	120	19	66	264	294	452	745	4	81	0.22	7	7	36	187	4.40
2013	AA	Akron	468	62	124	5	52	265	289	376	665	3	84	0.21	12	3	29	111	3.56
2014	AA	Akron	413	52	94	5	34	228	272	324	596	6	78	0.27	4	5	32	97	2.73

Versatile INF who regressed in repeat of AA. Has seen power output decline while bat speed and approach eroding. Still hope for improvement as he has athleticism and wiry strength. Makes loud contact and likes to use entire field. Exhibits plus range and has quick hands for any spot.

Rodriguez,Wilfredo — 2 — Colorado

EXP MLB DEBUT: 2018 | H/W: 5-10 200 | FUT: Backup C | 7D

Bats R Age 21 — 2012 (7) HS (PR)

Pwr ++ | BAvg ++++ | Spd ++ | Def ++

Year	Lev	Team	AB	R	H	HR	RBI	Avg	OB	Slg	OPS	bb%	ct%	Eye	SB	CS	x/h%	Iso	RC/G
2012	Rk	Grand Junction	166	26	53	2	27	319	369	452	821	7	86	0.57	1	1	32	133	5.66
2013	A-	Tri-City	141	15	38	1	19	270	352	326	678	11	82	0.72	2	4	16	57	4.11
2014	A	Asheville	281	36	87	3	37	310	358	399	756	7	88	0.64	2	3	22	89	4.87

Athletic C moves well behind the plate with an avg arm. Improved defensively, but still has work to do. Does have a good approach at the plate with a short, balanced stroke. He shoots balls into the gap and could develop power with decent plate discipline. Bat gives him value..

Rodriguez,Yorman — 8 — Cincinnati

EXP MLB DEBUT: 2014 | H/W: 6-3 195 | FUT: Starting OF | 8E

Bats R Age 22 — 2009 FA (Venezuela)

Pwr +++ | BAvg ++ | Spd ++++ | Def ++++

Year	Lev	Team	AB	R	H	HR	RBI	Avg	OB	Slg	OPS	bb%	ct%	Eye	SB	CS	x/h%	Iso	RC/G
2012	A+	Bakersfield	90	7	14	0	7	156	183	200	383	3	57	0.08	4	0	29	44	-0.58
2013	A+	Bakersfield	251	41	63	9	35	251	311	470	781	8	69	0.29	6	3	52	219	5.43
2013	AA	Pensacola	262	30	70	4	31	267	331	385	717	9	71	0.33	4	0	30	118	4.50
2014	AA	Pensacola	450	69	118	9	40	262	332	389	721	9	74	0.40	12	5	29	127	4.51
2014	MLB	Cincinnati	27	3	6	0	2	222	250	222	472	4	56	0.08	0	1	0	0	0.85

Earned September call-up despite sluggish first half. Very exciting tool set though still very raw. Made strides in bb% and ct%. Hits with authority to all fields and hits RHP well. Will become exposed at higher levels if he doesn't improve pitch recognition. 20/20 ceiling. Plus defender in CF or RF.

Rogers,Jason — 35 — Milwaukee

EXP MLB DEBUT: 2014 | H/W: 6-2 245 | FUT: Starting 1B | 7D

Bats R Age 27 — 2010 (32) Columbus State

Pwr ++++ | BAvg +++ | Spd ++ | Def ++

Year	Lev	Team	AB	R	H	HR	RBI	Avg	OB	Slg	OPS	bb%	ct%	Eye	SB	CS	x/h%	Iso	RC/G
2012	A+	Brevard Cnty	233	33	70	5	23	300	407	412	819	15	82	1.00	7	1	23	112	6.04
2013	AA	Huntsville	481	69	130	22	87	270	350	468	818	11	82	0.69	7	2	38	198	5.66
2014	AA	Huntsville	287	42	81	7	43	282	352	432	784	10	80	0.55	5	1	33	150	5.30
2014	AAA	Nashville	206	36	65	11	39	316	382	568	950	10	82	0.58	0	0	40	252	7.23
2014	MLB	Milwaukee	9	0	1	0	0	111	200	222	422	10	89	1.00	0	0	100	111	1.46

32nd round pick has exceeded expectations. Has plus raw power, plus makes decent contact and takes his share of BB. Soft body doesn't play well at 3B and limits his range. His bat will have to carry him and sticking at 3B will be difficult.

Rogers,Wes — 8 — Colorado

EXP MLB DEBUT: 2018 | H/W: 6-3 180 | FUT: Starting CF | 8E

Bats R Age 21 — 2014 (4) SpartanburgMethJC

Pwr ++ | BAvg +++ | Spd +++ | Def +++

Year	Lev	Team	AB	R	H	HR	RBI	Avg	OB	Slg	OPS	bb%	ct%	Eye	SB	CS	x/h%	Iso	RC/G
2013	NCAA	SpartanbrgMth	180	64	60	0	30	333	442	400	842	16	88	1.67	30	2	18	67	6.56
2014	Rk	Grand Junction	113	25	32	3	16	283	357	425	782	10	78	0.52	15	1	25	142	5.29

Raw on the ball field, but has all the tools to be a stud. At 6'3", 180 he has long limbs and quick hands. Has good bat speed and raw power. Covers ground well in CF with long, easy strides. Has a good approach at the plate and good strike zone judgment. Solid debut in the Pioneer League.

Roller,Kyle — 3 — New York (A)

EXP MLB DEBUT: 2015 | H/W: 6-1 250 | FUT: Reserve 1B | 7E

Bats L Age 27 — 2010 (8) East Carolina

Pwr ++++ | BAvg ++ | Spd + | Def ++

Year	Lev	Team	AB	R	H	HR	RBI	Avg	OB	Slg	OPS	bb%	ct%	Eye	SB	CS	x/h%	Iso	RC/G
2011	A+	Tampa	211	27	56	7	28	265	335	427	761	9	69	0.34	1	0	36	161	5.11
2012	A+	Tampa	418	59	111	18	85	266	337	471	808	10	72	0.39	4	2	41	206	5.66
2013	AA	Trenton	443	59	112	17	69	253	333	427	759	11	68	0.37	0	0	38	174	5.15
2014	AA	Trenton	78	18	30	9	23	385	448	808	1256	10	73	0.43	1	0	50	423	11.46
2014	AAA	Scranton/WB	378	59	107	17	51	283	365	497	863	11	67	0.39	0	0	41	214	6.77

Mammoth hitter who possesses selective eye at plate and uses to his advantage. Posted career high in HR and BB while ably hitting LHP. Fastball-only hitter who can be fooled with breaking balls and has swing with holes. Lacks athleticism in large frame, but is passable defender at 1B.

Romero,Avery — 4 — Miami

EXP MLB DEBUT: 2016 | H/W: 5-8 190 | FUT: Starting 2B | 8C

Bats R Age 21 — 2012 (3) HS (FL)

Pwr +++ | BAvg ++++ | Spd ++ | Def ++

Year	Lev	Team	AB	R	H	HR	RBI	Avg	OB	Slg	OPS	bb%	ct%	Eye	SB	CS	x/h%	Iso	RC/G
2012	A-	Jamestown	21	3	8	0	4	381	458	381	839	13	100	####	1	0	0	0	6.42
2013	A-	Batavia	209	27	62	2	30	297	344	411	755	7	84	0.44	3	4	32	115	4.84
2013	A	Greensboro	34	5	5	1	5	147	237	265	502	11	85	0.80	0	0	40	118	1.95
2014	A	Greensboro	366	51	117	5	46	320	363	429	792	6	87	0.53	6	4	25	109	5.22
2014	A+	Jupiter	100	12	32	0	10	320	364	400	764	7	87	0.54	4	1	25	80	4.99

Strong hands and quick wrists generate good bat speed that allows him to go gap-to-gap. Barrels the ball well and relies on contact approach, but does get some leverage and backspin. In the field, his good actions and strong arm work well. The move from SS to 2B was a success.

Rondon,Cleuluis | 46 | Chicago (A)

EXP MLB DEBUT: 2017 | H/W: 6-0 155 | FUT: Utility player | 6B

Bats R Age 20
2010 FA (Venezuela)
Pwr +
BAvg + +
Spd + + + +
Def + + + +

Year	Lev	Team	AB	R	H	HR	RBI	Avg	OB	Slg	OPS	bb%	ct%	Eye	SB	CS	x/h%	Iso	RC/G
2012	A-	Lowell	4	0	0	0	0	0	0	0	0	0	75	0.00	0	0		0	-5.26
2013	A-	Lowell	123	13	34	1	10	276	315	350	665	5	79	0.27	6	1	18	73	3.57
2013	A	Kannapolis	94	11	19	1	6	202	257	234	491	7	74	0.29	1	0	5	32	1.25
2014	A	Kannapolis	301	35	70	0	16	233	294	262	556	8	78	0.40	13	8	13	30	2.34
2014	A+	Winston-Salem	198	24	49	1	24	247	313	354	667	9	83	0.58	3	4	31	106	3.95

Lean, quick INF who won't have much value with bat, but is excellent defender with solid speed. Possesses smooth ability with hands and feet, and moves well to both sides. Exhibits strong, accurate arm. Has simple, compact stroke to make contact, but lacks strength for even gap power.

Rondon,Jose | 6 | San Diego

EXP MLB DEBUT: 2017 | H/W: 6-1 160 | FUT: Starting SS | 7B

Bats R Age 21
2011 FA (Venezuela)
Pwr + +
BAvg + + +
Spd + + +
Def + + +

Year	Lev	Team	AB	R	H	HR	RBI	Avg	OB	Slg	OPS	bb%	ct%	Eye	SB	CS	x/h%	Iso	RC/G
2012	Rk	Orem	20	4	6	0	1	300	364	450	814	9	85	0.67	1	0	33	150	5.84
2013	Rk	Orem	276	45	81	1	50	293	363	399	761	10	89	0.97	13	8	31	105	5.22
2014	Rk	AZL Angels	8	3	1	0	0	125	222	125	347	11	100	####	2	1	0	0	1.36
2014	A+	Lake Elsinore	136	18	41	1	12	301	362	390	752	9	83	0.57	3	1	24	88	4.91
2014	A+	Inland Empire	297	40	97	0	24	327	363	418	781	5	83	0.34	8	6	23	91	5.09

Came over to the Padres in Huston Street trade. Knows how to play game. Now owns a career .300 average. Rarely strikes out and exhibits bat control to put ball in play. Doesn't own a power profile, but should hit for BA. Possesses all requisite tools to become solid defender.

Rosa,Gabriel | 789 | Cincinnati

EXP MLB DEBUT: 2017 | H/W: 6-4 185 | FUT: Starting OF | 8E

Bats R Age 21
2011 (2) HS (PR)
Pwr + + +
BAvg + +
Spd + + +
Def + + +

Year	Lev	Team	AB	R	H	HR	RBI	Avg	OB	Slg	OPS	bb%	ct%	Eye	SB	CS	x/h%	Iso	RC/G
2011	Rk	AZL Reds	106	17	26	2	10	245	298	406	704	7	74	0.29	6	3	38	160	4.25
2012	NCAA	Southern Miss	53	8	11	0	8	208	288	264	552	10	85	0.75	1	0	27	57	2.68
2012	Rk	Billings	78	8	14	0	5	179	190	256	446	1	68	0.04	2	0	43	77	0.50
2013	Rk	Billings	180	29	38	6	23	211	307	339	646	12	74	0.54	13	2	29	128	3.49
2014	A	Dayton	147	13	25	3	12	170	242	279	521	9	69	0.30	9	2	36	109	1.66

Battled injuries yet again in '14. Brings intriguing power/speed/defense combo if he can stay on the field. Struggles to make consistent contact and LD% plummeted, but has improved plate patience. Played solely OF for first time in his career; has enough range and arm to play any OF spot.

Rosario,Amed | 6 | New York (N)

EXP MLB DEBUT: 2018 | H/W: 6-2 170 | FUT: Starting SS | 8D

Bats R Age 19
2013 FA (DR)
Pwr + +
BAvg + + +
Spd + + + +
Def + + + +

Year	Lev	Team	AB	R	H	HR	RBI	Avg	OB	Slg	OPS	bb%	ct%	Eye	SB	CS	x/h%	Iso	RC/G
2013	Rk	Kingsport	212	22	51	3	23	241	278	358	637	5	80	0.26	2	6	29	118	3.24
2014	A-	Brooklyn	266	39	77	1	23	289	332	380	712	6	82	0.36	7	3	22	90	4.28

Played NYPL at 18 years old. Tall and lanky for a SS with quick reactions in the field, plus range, and a plus arm. Shows quick bat, contact approach, and strength projection left in his frame. Swing gets long and pitch recognition a struggle. As much upside as anyone in Mets sytem.

Rosario,Eddie | 4789 | Minnesota

EXP MLB DEBUT: 2015 | H/W: 6-1 180 | FUT: Starting 2B/OF | 8D

Bats L Age 23
2010 (4) HS (PR)
Pwr + + +
BAvg + + +
Spd + + +
Def + +

Year	Lev	Team	AB	R	H	HR	RBI	Avg	OB	Slg	OPS	bb%	ct%	Eye	SB	CS	x/h%	Iso	RC/G
2012	A	Beloit	392	60	116	12	70	296	348	490	837	7	82	0.45	11	11	41	194	5.81
2013	A+	Fort Myers	207	40	68	6	35	329	379	527	906	8	86	0.59	3	6	35	198	6.63
2013	AA	New Britain	289	40	82	4	38	284	332	412	744	7	77	0.31	7	4	32	128	4.71
2014	A+	Fort Myers	30	5	9	0	4	300	382	300	682	12	83	0.80	1	1	0	0	4.19
2014	AA	New Britain	316	40	75	8	36	237	276	396	672	5	78	0.25	8	4	41	158	3.65

Smooth-swinging prospect who missed time after drug suspension. Exhibits plus bat speed and hitting instincts while covering plate well. Dropped off in production during season, but picked up in AFL. Fans frequently and can chase pitches while selling out for pop. Looking for defensive home.

Rosario,Yeremy | 6 | Colorado

EXP MLB DEBUT: 2019 | H/W: 6-0 160 | FUT: Starting SS | 7E

Bats R Age 17
2014 FA (DR)
Pwr + +
BAvg + +
Spd + + +
Def + + +

Year	Lev	Team	AB	R	H	HR	RBI	Avg	OB	Slg	OPS	bb%	ct%	Eye	SB	CS	x/h%	Iso	RC/G
2014		(did not play in the US in 2014)																	

Signed with the Rockies for $800,000 in July 2014. Has a good line-drive approach and should add power as he gains experience. Has plus speed and fluid actions and has a chance to stick at short. Definitely worth keeping an eye on, but is years away from the majors.

Rua,Ryan | 3457 | Texas

EXP MLB DEBUT: 2014 | H/W: 6-2 205 | FUT: Starting 2B/3B | 7A

Bats R Age 25
2011 (17) Lake Erie
Pwr + + +
BAvg + + +
Spd + +
Def + +

Year	Lev	Team	AB	R	H	HR	RBI	Avg	OB	Slg	OPS	bb%	ct%	Eye	SB	CS	x/h%	Iso	RC/G
2013	A	Hickory	367	70	92	29	82	251	339	559	898	12	75	0.54	13	2	59	308	6.70
2013	AA	Frisco	86	19	20	3	9	233	290	384	674	8	72	0.29	1	0	30	151	3.70
2014	AA	Frisco	257	34	77	10	38	300	373	475	848	10	79	0.55	5	3	31	175	6.06
2014	AAA	Round Rock	214	31	67	8	36	313	374	505	879	9	80	0.50	1	2	34	192	6.38
2014	MLB	Texas	105	11	31	2	14	295	308	419	727	2	83	0.11	1	0	29	124	4.13

Versatile, natural hitter who hit at all levels. Hits for nice BA due to bat control and has moderate to above average power to all fields. Can be tough out with smooth, fluid stroke and honed eye at plate. Doesn't run well and poor range and average arm bring future position in doubt.

Ruiz,Rio | 5 | Houston

EXP MLB DEBUT: 2016 | H/W: 6-2 215 | FUT: Starting 3B | 8C

Bats L Age 20
2012 (4) HS (CA)
Pwr + + +
BAvg + + +
Spd + +
Def + +

Year	Lev	Team	AB	R	H	HR	RBI	Avg	OB	Slg	OPS	bb%	ct%	Eye	SB	CS	x/h%	Iso	RC/G
2012	Rk	GCL Astros	85	13	23	0	11	271	361	412	773	12	74	0.55	2	0	43	141	5.58
2012	Rk	Greeneville	50	8	11	1	7	220	278	380	658	7	80	0.40	0	0	45	160	3.67
2013	A	Quad Cities	416	46	108	12	63	260	339	430	769	11	78	0.54	12	3	43	171	5.17
2014	A+	Lancaster	516	76	151	11	77	293	390	436	826	14	82	0.90	4	4	33	143	6.07

Sweet-swinging 3B who has impressive upside and offensive ability. Became more patient with improved approach and leverages plus bat speed to hit for BA and above average pop. Adding strength and can hit LHP. Can be sloppy defender, but has tools to become average infielder.

Russell,Addison | 6 | Chicago (N)

EXP MLB DEBUT: 2015 | H/W: 6-0 195 | FUT: Starting SS | 9C

Bats R Age 21
2012 (1) HS (FL)
Pwr + + + +
BAvg + + + +
Spd + + +
Def + + +

Year	Lev	Team	AB	R	H	HR	RBI	Avg	OB	Slg	OPS	bb%	ct%	Eye	SB	CS	x/h%	Iso	RC/G
2013	A+	Stockton	429	85	118	17	60	275	365	508	873	12	73	0.53	21	3	47	233	6.76
2013	AAA	Sacramento	13	1	1	0	0	77	77	77	154	0	31	0.00	0	0	0	0	-5.10
2014	A+	Stockton	16	0	3	0	1	188	278	188	465	11	63	0.33	1	0	0	0	0.79
2014	AA	Midland	48	7	16	1	8	333	429	500	929	14	83	1.00	3	2	31	167	7.41
2014	AA	Tennessee	194	32	57	12	36	294	325	536	861	4	82	0.26	2	2	40	242	5.72

Multi-talented SS was the centerpiece of the Samardzjia deal. Owns avg to plus tools across board and has strong, athletic frame. Has above-avg power with the ability to hit for high BA due to quick hands and ability to make contact. Hits hard line drives to all fields with simple swing.

Saladino,Tyler | 46 | Chicago (A)

EXP MLB DEBUT: 2015 | H/W: 6-0 200 | FUT: Reserve INF | 6B

Bats R Age 25
2010 (7) Oral Roberts
Pwr + + +
BAvg + +
Spd + + +
Def + + +

Year	Lev	Team	AB	R	H	HR	RBI	Avg	OB	Slg	OPS	bb%	ct%	Eye	SB	CS	x/h%	Iso	RC/G
2011	A+	Winston-Salem	397	75	107	16	55	270	353	501	854	11	77	0.57	7	7	48	232	6.31
2012	AA	Birmingham	418	71	99	4	39	237	353	321	674	15	78	0.82	38	8	23	84	4.21
2012	AAA	Charlotte	49	9	11	0	6	224	283	265	548	8	67	0.25	1	0	18	41	2.09
2013	AA	Birmingham	424	49	97	5	55	229	312	314	625	11	80	0.59	28	8	25	85	3.37
2014	AAA	Charlotte	294	41	91	9	43	310	368	483	851	8	83	0.54	7	1	32	173	6.00

Versatile INF who ended season in July after TJ surgery. Continues to improve with bat, showing increase in BA with emerging pop. Draws walks and gets on base to use average speed. Can play all INF spots with strong arm and fine instincts. Inconsistent performance is befuddling.

Salcedo,Erick | 46 | Los Angeles (A)

EXP MLB DEBUT: 2017 | H/W: 5-10 155 | FUT: Utility player | 7D

Bats B Age 21
2010 FA (Venezuela)
Pwr +
BAvg + +
Spd + + +
Def + + +

Year	Lev	Team	AB	R	H	HR	RBI	Avg	OB	Slg	OPS	bb%	ct%	Eye	SB	CS	x/h%	Iso	RC/G
2013	Rk	AZL Angels	189	27	51	0	22	270	327	365	692	8	83	0.50	10	3	25	95	4.21
2014	A	Burlington	422	48	101	0	24	239	293	265	558	7	86	0.56	21	10	8	26	2.58

Short, lean INF who provides good glove and quickness. Didn't set MWL ablaze in first full season, but thrives on gap-to-gap, contact-oriented approach. Hasn't yet hit HR in pro career and needs to get on base more. Runs well and is shrewd baserunner. Can play either middle infield spot.

Sanchez,Ali — 2 — New York (N)

EXP MLB DEBUT: 2019 | H/W: 6-0 175 | FUT: Starting C | 8D

Bats R Age 18 — 2013 FA (Venezuela) — Pwr ++ | BAvg +++ | Spd ++ | Def ++++

Year	Lev	Team	AB	R	H	HR	RBI	Avg	OB	Slg	OPS	bb%	ct%	Eye	SB	CS	x/h%	Iso	RC/G
2014	Rk	DSL Mets	175	21	53	3	24	303	396	394	790	13	82	0.87	6	6	19	91	5.57

Advanced offensive and defensive skillset for the 18 y/o prospect. Threw out 51% of opposing base runners. Shows strong arm and blocking/receiving skills behind the plate. Exhibits nice bat control with a short path to the ball, though he could benefit from more loft in his swing.

Sanchez,Carlos — 46 — Chicago (A)

EXP MLB DEBUT: 2014 | H/W: 5-11 195 | FUT: Starting 2B/SS | 7B

Bats R Age 22 — 2009 FA (Venezuela) — Pwr ++ | BAvg +++ | Spd +++ | Def ++++

Year	Lev	Team	AB	R	H	HR	RBI	Avg	OB	Slg	OPS	bb%	ct%	Eye	SB	CS	x/h%	Iso	RC/G
2012	AA	Birmingham	119	17	44	0	13	370	419	462	881	8	82	0.45	7	5	23	92	6.47
2012	AAA	Charlotte	39	4	10	0	1	256	256	308	564	0	85	0.00	0	0	20	51	2.18
2013	AAA	Charlotte	432	50	104	0	28	241	289	296	585	6	82	0.38	16	7	21	56	2.76
2014	AAA	Charlotte	437	60	128	7	57	293	347	412	759	8	81	0.43	16	4	25	119	4.88
2014	MLB	Chi White Sox	100	6	25	0	5	250	272	300	572	3	75	0.12	1	1	20	50	2.26

Switch-hitting INF who reached majors after higher BA and HR in 2nd year in AAA. Exhibits above average defense with quick hands and strong arm. Owns solid-average speed and possesses instincts on base. Has enough strength for occasional pull HR and offers quick stroke for BA.

Sanchez,Gary — 2 — New York (A)

EXP MLB DEBUT: 2015 | H/W: 6-3 235 | FUT: Starting C | 8C

Bats R Age 22 — 2009 FA (DR) — Pwr ++++ | BAvg +++ | Spd ++ | Def ++

Year	Lev	Team	AB	R	H	HR	RBI	Avg	OB	Slg	OPS	bb%	ct%	Eye	SB	CS	x/h%	Iso	RC/G
2012	A	CharlestonSC	263	44	78	13	56	297	351	517	868	8	75	0.34	11	4	41	221	6.23
2012	A+	Tampa	172	21	48	5	29	279	319	436	755	5	76	0.24	4	0	33	157	4.69
2013	A+	Tampa	362	38	92	13	61	254	308	420	728	7	80	0.39	3	1	37	166	4.38
2013	AA	Trenton	92	12	23	2	10	250	343	380	723	12	83	0.81	0	0	35	130	4.71
2014	AA	Trenton	429	48	116	13	65	270	337	406	742	9	79	0.47	1	1	28	135	4.66

Bat-first backstop whose power is stagnant, though has plus-plus potential. Produces easy power with simple swing and uses entire field in mature approach. Defense is improving, but footwork and blocking still subpar despite very strong arm. Youth on his side, but needs to step up.

Sandberg,Cord — 78 — Philadelphia

EXP MLB DEBUT: 2018 | H/W: 6-3 215 | FUT: Starting LF | 8D

Bats L Age 20 — 2013 (3) HS (FL) — Pwr +++ | BAvg ++ | Spd ++ | Def ++

Year	Lev	Team	AB	R	H	HR	RBI	Avg	OB	Slg	OPS	bb%	ct%	Eye	SB	CS	x/h%	Iso	RC/G
2013	Rk	GCL Phillies	169	23	35	2	14	207	306	272	578	12	79	0.67	4	3	17	65	2.79
2014	A-	Williamsport	264	33	62	6	24	235	265	345	610	4	79	0.20	8	3	23	110	2.76

Tools are still raw due to his two-sport past, but the smooth swing and above-average power and speed all flash at different times. Anything off-speed can disrupt his timing, though he slowly improved in this area as the season wore on. Defensively, he's likely limited to LF, so he has to hit. Full-season ball will be a test.

Sano,Miguel — 5 — Minnesota

EXP MLB DEBUT: 2015 | H/W: 6-4 235 | FUT: Starting 3B | 9B

Bats R Age 21 — 2009 FA (DR) — Pwr +++++ | BAvg +++ | Spd ++ | Def ++

Year	Lev	Team	AB	R	H	HR	RBI	Avg	OB	Slg	OPS	bb%	ct%	Eye	SB	CS	x/h%	Iso	RC/G
2011	Rk	Elizabethton	267	58	78	20	59	292	348	637	985	8	71	0.30	5	4	58	345	8.03
2012	A	Beloit	457	75	118	28	100	258	369	521	890	15	68	0.56	8	3	51	263	7.12
2013	A+	Fort Myers	206	51	68	16	48	330	413	655	1068	12	70	0.48	9	2	49	325	9.42
2013	AA	New Britain	233	35	55	19	55	236	338	571	909	13	65	0.44	2	1	67	335	7.48
2014		(did not play)																	

Strong 3B who missed season after elbow surgery. Provides mammoth power to all fields and projects to middle-of-order bat. Swings with authority, yet has feel for contact. Hits for BA, though will strike out. Could eventually move to 1B due to fringy feet, though arm is very strong.

Santana,Domingo — 79 — Houston

EXP MLB DEBUT: 2014 | H/W: 6-5 225 | FUT: Starting RF | 8C

Bats R Age 22 — 2009 FA (DR) — Pwr ++++ | BAvg +++ | Spd ++ | Def +++

Year	Lev	Team	AB	R	H	HR	RBI	Avg	OB	Slg	OPS	bb%	ct%	Eye	SB	CS	x/h%	Iso	RC/G
2011	A	Lexington	68	13	26	5	21	382	432	662	1094	8	78	0.40	1	0	35	279	8.93
2012	A+	Lancaster	457	87	138	23	97	302	377	536	913	11	68	0.37	7	1	40	234	7.42
2013	AA	Corpus Christi	416	72	105	25	64	252	327	498	824	10	67	0.33	12	5	48	245	6.05
2014	AAA	Oklahoma City	443	63	131	16	81	296	385	474	859	13	66	0.43	6	4	34	178	6.82
2014	MLB	Houston	17	1	0	0	0	0	56	0	56	6	18	0.07	0	0		0	-10.39

Tall OF who reached HOU and struggled, but has requisite skills to be major contributor. Possesses well above average pop and some BA ability despite aggressive approach. Kills LHP, though has plenty of holes in swing. Won't steal many bases, but is solid corner OF with strong arm.

Schebler,Scott — 79 — Los Angeles (N)

EXP MLB DEBUT: 2015 | H/W: 6-1 208 | FUT: Starting OF | 7D

Bats L Age 24 — 2010 (26) Des Moines CC — Pwr +++ | BAvg ++ | Spd ++ | Def ++

Year	Lev	Team	AB	R	H	HR	RBI	Avg	OB	Slg	OPS	bb%	ct%	Eye	SB	CS	x/h%	Iso	RC/G
2010	Rk	AZL Dodgers	17	3	5	0	1	294	333	529	863	6	71	0.20	1	0	40	235	6.81
2011	Rk	Ogden	295	44	84	13	58	285	315	529	844	4	67	0.13	1	1	45	244	6.25
2012	A	Great Lakes	515	67	134	6	67	260	301	388	689	6	81	0.30	17	11	34	128	3.97
2013	A+	Rancho Cuca	477	95	141	27	91	296	344	581	924	7	71	0.25	16	5	49	285	7.23
2014	AA	Chattanooga	489	82	137	28	73	280	341	556	897	8	78	0.41	10	4	47	276	6.61

Not particularly athletic, but has good bat speed and makes hard contact. An average runner and defender, he is likely limited to LF. His LH power bat is his ticket to the show. Can be overly aggressive at times, which causes his swing to get big and results in lots of swings and misses.

Schwarber,Kyle — 27 — Chicago (N)

EXP MLB DEBUT: 2016 | H/W: 6-0 235 | FUT: Starting LF | 9D

Bats L Age 22 — 2014 (1) Indiana — Pwr ++++ | BAvg ++++ | Spd + | Def ++

Year	Lev	Team	AB	R	H	HR	RBI	Avg	OB	Slg	OPS	bb%	ct%	Eye	SB	CS	x/h%	Iso	RC/G
2013	NCAA	Indiana	235	65	86	18	54	366	462	647	1109	15	84	1.14	4	3	34	281	9.30
2014	NCAA	Indiana	232	66	83	14	48	358	460	659	1120	16	87	1.47	10	3	43	302	9.58
2014	A-	Boise	20	7	12	4	10	600	636	1350	1986	9	90	1.00	0	1	50	750	18.10
2014	A	Kane County	83	17	30	4	15	361	436	602	1039	12	80	0.65	1	1	40	241	8.57
2014	A+	Daytona	159	31	48	10	28	302	400	560	960	14	76	0.68	4	0	42	258	7.70

Impressive debut, a combined .344/.428/.634. Was the most advanced LH college bat in the draft. Saw limited action behind the plate and spent most of the season in LF. Makes consistent hard contact and has good plate discipline. Cubs have said they will continue to work on him as a catcher.

Seager,Corey — 6 — Los Angeles (N)

EXP MLB DEBUT: 2015 | H/W: 6-4 215 | FUT: Starting 3B | 9D

Bats L Age 20 — 2012 (1) HS (NC) — Pwr ++++ | BAvg +++ | Spd ++ | Def +++

Year	Lev	Team	AB	R	H	HR	RBI	Avg	OB	Slg	OPS	bb%	ct%	Eye	SB	CS	x/h%	Iso	RC/G
2012	Rk	Ogden	175	34	54	8	33	309	383	520	903	11	81	0.64	8	2	35	211	6.73
2013	A	Great Lakes	272	45	84	12	57	309	386	529	915	11	79	0.59	9	4	39	221	6.99
2013	A+	Rancho Cuca	100	10	16	4	15	160	250	320	570	11	69	0.39	1	0	44	160	2.31
2014	A+	Rancho Cuca	327	61	115	18	70	352	406	633	1039	8	77	0.39	5	1	47	281	8.50
2014	AA	Chattanooga	148	28	51	2	27	345	386	534	920	6	74	0.26	1	1	41	189	7.21

Plus bat speed that allows him to make hard contact. Was more aggressive, which resulted in better power, but a bit less contact. A move to 3B seems likely where his strong arm and good hands will play. Average runner but his foot speed is not a liability due to athleticism and instincts.

Severino,Pedro — 2 — Washington

EXP MLB DEBUT: 2017 | H/W: 6-1 180 | FUT: Starting C | 7C

Bats R Age 21 — 2010 FA (DR) — Pwr + | BAvg ++ | Spd ++ | Def ++++

Year	Lev	Team	AB	R	H	HR	RBI	Avg	OB	Slg	OPS	bb%	ct%	Eye	SB	CS	x/h%	Iso	RC/G
2011	Rk	GCL Nationals	115	16	21	2	9	183	248	287	535	8	77	0.37	0	0	33	104	2.00
2012	Rk	GCL Nationals	109	9	24	0	8	220	280	266	546	8	92	1.00	0	0	17	46	2.74
2013	A	Hagerstown	282	28	68	1	45	241	275	333	608	4	81	0.24	1	0	32	92	2.93
2014	A+	Potomac	291	41	72	9	36	247	298	399	697	7	80	0.37	2	0	35	151	3.99

Defense-first catcher with lightning release and elite arm strength that shuts down the running game. It's a major-league defensive profile, though there is still work to do with the bat. Progressed with pitch recognition and a power spike in the second half; if that continues, he could be a starter.

Shaffer,Richie — 5 — Tampa Bay

EXP MLB DEBUT: 2015 | H/W: 6-3 218 | FUT: Starting 3B/1B | 8D

Bats R Age 24 — 2012 (1) Clemson — Pwr ++++ | BAvg ++ | Spd ++ | Def ++

Year	Lev	Team	AB	R	H	HR	RBI	Avg	OB	Slg	OPS	bb%	ct%	Eye	SB	CS	x/h%	Iso	RC/G
2011	NCAA	Clemson	222	62	70	13	55	315	429	577	1005	17	76	0.83	8	1	43	261	8.50
2012	NCAA	Clemson	232	49	78	10	46	336	478	573	1051	21	77	1.19	8	2	42	237	9.48
2012	A-	Hudson Valley	117	25	36	4	26	308	391	487	878	12	74	0.52	0	0	31	179	6.74
2013	A+	Charlotte	469	55	119	11	73	254	306	399	704	7	77	0.33	6	0	38	145	4.15
2014	AA	Montgomery	427	58	95	19	64	222	313	440	753	12	72	0.47	4	0	54	218	4.99

Powerful 3B had poor year, but finished strong. Posted high in HR due to all-fields power and exemplary bat speed. Muscles balls out of park, but dwindling BA reduces value. Poor two-strike approach and can chase breaking balls. Likely to move to 1B as he lacks agility and quickness.

Shaw,Travis — 35 — Boston

EXP MLB DEBUT: 2015 | H/W: 6-4 225 | FUT: Starting 1B | 7C

Bats L Age 24 — 2011 (9) Kent State

Pwr +++ | BAvg +++ | Spd ++ | Def +++

Year	Lev	Team	AB	R	H	HR	RBI	Avg	OB	Slg	OPS	bb%	ct%	Eye	SB	CS	x/h%	Iso	RC/G
2012	A+	Salem	354	69	108	16	73	305	404	545	950	14	77	0.73	11	2	46	240	7.69
2012	AA	Portland	110	13	25	3	12	227	351	427	778	16	69	0.62	1	1	64	200	5.75
2013	AA	Portland	444	57	98	16	50	221	337	394	731	15	74	0.67	7	3	42	173	4.82
2014	AA	Portland	177	35	54	11	37	305	403	548	951	14	87	1.26	5	3	37	243	7.37
2014	AAA	Pawtucket	313	43	82	10	41	262	323	431	754	8	76	0.37	2	0	39	169	4.83

Smooth-swinging INF who set career high in HR while improving contact. Brings disciplined eye to plate with solid pitch recognition. Power mostly to pull side, but can hit to opposite field. Doesn't run well and lacks agility to be premium defender, though makes routine plays with good hands.

Shipman,Aaron — 789 — Oakland

EXP MLB DEBUT: 2016 | H/W: 6-0 175 | FUT: Starting OF | 7E

Bats L Age 23 — 2010 (3) HS (GA)

Pwr + | BAvg ++ | Spd ++++ | Def ++++

Year	Lev	Team	AB	R	H	HR	RBI	Avg	OB	Slg	OPS	bb%	ct%	Eye	SB	CS	x/h%	Iso	RC/G
2011	A-	Vermont	201	34	51	0	19	254	383	303	686	17	81	1.08	17	3	18	50	4.56
2012	A	Burlington	360	40	74	0	32	206	319	261	580	14	76	0.70	11	11	22	56	2.93
2013	Rk	AZL Athletics	19	7	8	0	3	421	522	579	1101	17	100		2	0	25	158	9.71
2013	A	Beloit	244	44	68	0	16	279	395	324	719	16	80	0.94	17	8	13	45	4.90
2014	A+	Stockton	178	30	52	1	16	292	411	410	821	17	78	0.92	13	2	25	118	6.32

Sweet-swinging OF who missed time with injury. Hit first career HR and has very little power projection. Premium athlete with plus speed and astute eye at plate. Gets on base, but tends to be passive at plate. Has played all OF positions, including CF, and has plus range and nice arm.

Sierra,Magneuris — 8 — St. Louis

EXP MLB DEBUT: 2019 | H/W: 5-11 160 | FUT: Starting CF | 8D

Bats L Age 18 — 2012 FA (DR)

Pwr ++ | BAvg +++ | Spd +++ | Def +++

Year	Lev	Team	AB	R	H	HR	RBI	Avg	OB	Slg	OPS	bb%	ct%	Eye	SB	CS	x/h%	Iso	RC/G
2013	Rk	DSL Cardinals	212	44	57	1	21	269	357	340	696	12	84	0.88	15	7	18	71	4.46
2014	Rk	GCL Cardinals	202	42	78	2	30	386	431	505	936	7	85	0.53	13	3	22	119	6.99

Athletic OF had an eye-opening US debut. Excellent eye-hand coordination and barrels well. Showed a good understanding of the strike zone and good speed. Doesn't project to have much power, but has speed and arm-strength and was one of the better defenders in the league.

Silva,Juan — 89 — Cincinnati

EXP MLB DEBUT: 2016 | H/W: 5-11 205 | FUT: Starting OF | 7C

Bats L Age 24 — 2009 (8) HS (PR)

Pwr ++ | BAvg +++ | Spd +++ | Def +++

Year	Lev	Team	AB	R	H	HR	RBI	Avg	OB	Slg	OPS	bb%	ct%	Eye	SB	CS	x/h%	Iso	RC/G
2010	Rk	AZL Reds	178	26	41	3	24	230	318	371	689	11	73	0.48	4	1	34	140	4.24
2011	Rk	Billings	150	30	44	4	21	293	404	413	818	16	71	0.65	4	6	18	120	6.13
2012	A	Dayton	380	58	103	8	42	271	383	413	796	15	71	0.63	25	12	34	142	5.90
2013	A+	Bakersfield	336	51	91	8	44	271	383	414	797	15	77	0.80	31	13	31	143	5.78
2014	A+	Bakersfield	252	51	78	4	42	310	420	437	857	16	81	0.98	34	9	27	127	6.63

Despite missing final three months with thumb injury, set career highs in BA and SB (with improved success rate). He's sustained excellent Eye and plate approach while showing pop to all fields. Plays any spot in the OF, but most likely ends up in LF. Needs to repeat success in high minors.

Sisco,Chance — 2 — Baltimore

EXP MLB DEBUT: 2017 | H/W: 6-2 195 | FUT: Starting C | 8D

Bats L Age 20 — 2013 (2) HS (CA)

Pwr ++ | BAvg ++++ | Spd ++ | Def ++

Year	Lev	Team	AB	R	H	HR	RBI	Avg	OB	Slg	OPS	bb%	ct%	Eye	SB	CS	x/h%	Iso	RC/G
2013	Rk	GCL Orioles	97	15	36	1	11	371	465	464	929	15	78	0.81	1	1	17	93	7.54
2013	A-	Aberdeen	5	1	1	0	0	200	333	200	533	17	60	0.50	0	0	0	0	1.98
2014	A	Delmarva	426	56	145	5	63	340	400	448	848	9	81	0.53	1	2	23	108	6.08

Athletic receiver who led SAL in BA and OBP in first full season. Makes easy contact with natural, clean stroke and ability to go to opp field highlights plus BA. Gets on base with selectivity, but could leverage strength more for pop. Still unpolished defensively, but has arm and smarts.

Skole,Matt — 35 — Washington

EXP MLB DEBUT: 2015 | H/W: 6-3 225 | FUT: Starting 1B | 7C

Bats L Age 25 — 2011 (5) Georgia Tech

Pwr +++ | BAvg +++ | Spd ++ | Def +

Year	Lev	Team	AB	R	H	HR	RBI	Avg	OB	Slg	OPS	bb%	ct%	Eye	SB	CS	x/h%	Iso	RC/G
2011	A-	Auburn	272	43	79	5	48	290	385	438	823	13	81	0.81	2	1	37	147	6.05
2012	A	Hagerstown	343	73	98	27	92	286	439	574	1014	22	66	0.81	10	0	46	289	9.27
2012	A+	Potomac	70	11	22	0	12	314	360	486	846	7	76	0.29	1	0	50	171	6.26
2013	AA	Harrisburg	5	1	1	0	2	200	429	400	829	29	60	1.00	0	0	100	200	7.54
2014	AA	Harrisburg	461	58	111	14	68	241	351	399	750	14	72	0.61	3	1	40	158	5.10

Premium eye at the plate makes pitchers work, but doesn't always capitalize when in a hitter's count. Swing is noisy, but has some bat speed and uses whole field. A poor defender, if power does not return (arm injury wiped out much of 2013), he likely won't hit enough to warrant a starter's spot at 1B.

Smith,Dominic — 3 — New York (N)

EXP MLB DEBUT: 2018 | H/W: 6-0 185 | FUT: Starting 1B | 9E

Bats L Age 19 — 2013 (1) HS (CA)

Pwr +++ | BAvg ++++ | Spd + | Def ++++

Year	Lev	Team	AB	R	H	HR	RBI	Avg	OB	Slg	OPS	bb%	ct%	Eye	SB	CS	x/h%	Iso	RC/G
2013	Rk	GCL Mets	167	23	48	3	22	287	377	407	784	13	78	0.65	2	4	27	120	5.49
2013	Rk	Kingsport	6	2	4	0	4	667	750	1333	2083	25	100		0	0	100	667	21.29
2014	A	Savannah	461	52	125	1	44	271	344	338	682	10	83	0.66	5	4	22	67	4.16

Has been a disappointment thus far in power output. Iso and Slg % plummeted in '14. Still just a teenager with very high upside despite recent results. Plus hit tool, advanced approach and pitch recognition. Can drive anything in the zone to all fields while limiting Ks. Plus defender at 1B.

Smith,Dwight — 78 — Toronto

EXP MLB DEBUT: 2015 | H/W: 5-11 180 | FUT: Starting OF | 7B

Bats L Age 22 — 2011 (1-S) HS (GA)

Pwr +++ | BAvg +++ | Spd +++ | Def +++

Year	Lev	Team	AB	R	H	HR	RBI	Avg	OB	Slg	OPS	bb%	ct%	Eye	SB	CS	x/h%	Iso	RC/G
2012	Rk	Bluefield	159	20	36	4	21	226	276	340	616	6	86	0.50	1	1	28	113	3.12
2012	A-	Vancouver	63	5	11	0	8	175	246	254	500	9	83	0.55	0	0	36	79	1.93
2013	A	Lansing	423	57	120	7	46	284	362	388	750	11	81	0.63	25	5	23	104	4.94
2014	A+	Dunedin	472	83	134	12	60	284	362	453	816	11	85	0.84	15	4	36	169	5.79

Advanced hitter who finished 3rd in FSL in SLG. Makes contact with patient approach and has advanced pitch recognition skills. Swing is pure and fast and helped set career high in HR. Doesn't project to plus power, though steals bases with good speed and baserunning instincts.

Smith,Mallex — 8 — Atlanta

EXP MLB DEBUT: 2017 | H/W: 5-9 170 | FUT: Starting CF | 8D

Bats L Age 21 — 2012 (5) HS (FL)

Pwr ++ | BAvg ++++ | Spd ++++ | Def ++++

Year	Lev	Team	AB	R	H	HR	RBI	Avg	OB	Slg	OPS	bb%	ct%	Eye	SB	CS	x/h%	Iso	RC/G
2012	Rk	AZL Padres	96	23	33	1	10	344	376	417	793	5	80	0.26	13	3	12	73	5.09
2012	A-	Eugene	32	6	6	1	5	188	316	281	597	16	75	0.75	4	1	17	94	2.94
2013	A	Fort Wayne	424	81	111	4	29	262	352	340	692	12	80	0.70	64	16	21	78	4.31
2014	A	Fort Wayne	254	56	75	0	15	295	387	394	781	13	78	0.69	48	16	25	98	5.60
2014	A+	Lake Elsinore	223	43	73	5	16	327	409	475	885	12	78	0.65	40	10	30	148	6.76

Monster breakout season, hitting .310 with 88 SB across two levels. Has a quick bat and a balanced approach. Works the count well and has plus strike zone that should allow him to continue to hit as he moves up. Plus, plus speed is his best asset and he an accomplished bunter.

Soler,Jorge — 9 — Chicago (N)

EXP MLB DEBUT: 2014 | H/W: 6-4 215 | FUT: Starting RF | 8A

Bats R Age 23 — 2012 FA (Cuba)

Pwr +++ | BAvg ++++ | Spd +++ | Def +++

Year	Lev	Team	AB	R	H	HR	RBI	Avg	OB	Slg	OPS	bb%	ct%	Eye	SB	CS	x/h%	Iso	RC/G
2013	A+	Daytona	210	38	59	8	35	281	346	467	813	9	82	0.55	5	1	37	186	5.55
2014	Rk	AZL Cubs	25	7	10	1	6	400	483	640	1123	14	72	0.57	0	0	40	240	10.40
2014	AA	Tennessee	65	13	27	6	22	415	506	862	1368	16	77	0.80	0	0	59	446	13.20
2014	AAA	Iowa	110	22	31	8	29	282	378	618	996	13	76	0.65	0	1	65	336	8.17
2014	MLB	Chi Cubs	89	11	26	5	20	292	337	573	910	6	73	0.25	1	0	54	281	6.86

Fast-twitch player who exudes athleticism and is just starting to tap into his potential. Has plus bat speed and continues to show good plate discipline, but can be overly aggressive. He has above-avg speed with a strong arm. There are some concerns about work ethic and durability.

Solorzano,Jesus — 89 — Miami

EXP MLB DEBUT: 2017 | H/W: 6-0 190 | FUT: Starting OF | 7D

Bats R Age 24 — 2009 FA (Venezuela)

Pwr ++ | BAvg +++ | Spd ++++ | Def ++++

Year	Lev	Team	AB	R	H	HR	RBI	Avg	OB	Slg	OPS	bb%	ct%	Eye	SB	CS	x/h%	Iso	RC/G
2011	Rk	GCL Marlins	194	34	58	3	31	299	343	454	797	6	85	0.43	18	7	34	155	5.32
2012	A-	Jamestown	210	36	66	8	27	314	366	519	885	7	77	0.35	7	6	36	205	6.47
2013	A	Greensboro	484	72	138	15	66	285	319	450	769	5	77	0.22	33	4	34	165	4.82
2014	A+	Jupiter	301	27	70	3	19	233	255	316	570	3	74	0.12	18	7	21	83	2.21

Small, athletic OF was slow to recover from hamate surgery. Aggressive approach at the plate caught up to him as he walked just 8 times while striking out 78. Will need to make an adjustment in order to tap into power. Plus runner and defender with good range and can stick in CF.

Sosa,Edmundo | 6 | St. Louis | EXP MLB DEBUT: 2019 | H/W: 5-11 170 | FUT: Starting SS | 7D

Bats R Age 19	Year	Lev	Team	AB	R	H	HR	RBI	Avg	OB	Slg	OPS	bb%	ct%	Eye	SB	CS	x/h%	Iso	RC/G
2012 FA (Panama)																				
Pwr ++																				
BAvg +++	2013	Rk	DSL Cardinals	169	33	53	3	27	314	393	450	842	12	91	1.47	7	5	26	136	6.21
Spd ++	2014	Rk	GCL Cardinals	207	37	57	1	23	275	333	377	710	8	86	0.62	8	5	25	101	4.45
Def ++++	2014	A-	State College	5	0	1	0	0	200	200	200	400	0	60	0.00	0	0	0	0	-0.49

Good all-around skills, and understands how to play the game. Advanced feel for hitting with good patience. Not likely to hit for power, but shows good gap ability. Quick defender with good hands and range, but a below average arm. Good combination of offense and defense.

Soto,Isael | 789 | Miami | EXP MLB DEBUT: 2018 | H/W: 6-0 190 | FUT: Starting OF | 8D

Bats L Age 18	Year	Lev	Team	AB	R	H	HR	RBI	Avg	OB	Slg	OPS	bb%	ct%	Eye	SB	CS	x/h%	Iso	RC/G
2013 FA (DR)																				
Pwr +++																				
BAvg +++																				
Spd ++																				
Def ++	2014	Rk	GCL Marlins	183	26	46	7	23	251	290	426	716	5	74	0.21	1	2	37	175	4.15

Raw, but has good athleticism and played the entire season as a 17-year-old. Has a strong frame and shows plus raw power with good bat speed. He was overly aggressive in debut, walking just 10 times. Projects as an avg runner with a good arm and should settle in as a corner OF.

Souza,Steven | 789 | Tampa Bay | EXP MLB DEBUT: 2014 | H/W: 6-4 225 | FUT: Starting OF | 7B

Bats R Age 25	Year	Lev	Team	AB	R	H	HR	RBI	Avg	OB	Slg	OPS	bb%	ct%	Eye	SB	CS	x/h%	Iso	RC/G
2007 (3) HS (WA)	2013	AA	Harrisburg	273	54	82	15	44	300	392	557	948	13	72	0.54	20	6	48	256	7.75
Pwr ++++	2014	A	Hagerstown	2	0	1	0	1	500	500	500	1000	0	50	0.00	1	0	0	0	11.13
BAvg +++	2014	A+	Potomac	9	0	1	0	1	111	111	111	222	0	56	0.00	1	0	0	0	-3.48
Spd +++	2014	AAA	Syracuse	346	62	121	18	75	350	435	590	1024	13	78	0.69	26	7	37	240	8.48
Def +++	2014	MLB	Washington	23	2	3	2	2	130	231	391	622	12	70	0.43	0	0	67	261	2.77

Tall, physical OF who led IL in BA, OBP, and SLG. Showcased impressive tools, especially power, speed, and arm. Hit for BA with cleaner swing mechanics and higher contact rate. Swing has some length, but has plus bat speed for all-fields pop. Solid corner OF who can play CF in pinch.

Spangenberg,Cory | 45 | San Diego | EXP MLB DEBUT: 2014 | H/W: 6-0 195 | FUT: Starting 2B | 7C

Bats L Age 24	Year	Lev	Team	AB	R	H	HR	RBI	Avg	OB	Slg	OPS	bb%	ct%	Eye	SB	CS	x/h%	Iso	RC/G
2011 (1) Indian River JC	2013	AA	San Antonio	287	35	83	2	20	289	329	366	695	6	79	0.28	19	11	18	77	3.97
Pwr +	2014	Rk	AZL Padres	6	3	1	0	2	167	375	500	875	25	100		0	0	100	333	8.00
BAvg +++	2014	A-	Eugene	25	3	5	0	2	200	200	280	480	0	76	0.00	2	0	20	80	1.04
Spd +++	2014	AA	San Antonio	281	38	93	2	22	331	365	470	835	5	78	0.24	14	9	29	139	5.83
Def +++	2014	MLB	San Diego	62	7	18	2	9	290	313	452	764	3	77	0.14	4	2	28	161	4.63

Missed 2 months with a concussion. Has the ability to hit for BA despite making below avg contact. Bat speed remains an issue, and will likely prevent him from adding much power. Does have a nice gap-to-gap approach and handles the bat well. Has excellent speed and quickness for 2B.

Stamets,Eric | 6 | Los Angeles (A) | EXP MLB DEBUT: 2015 | H/W: 6-0 190 | FUT: Reserve INF | 6A

Bats R Age 23	Year	Lev	Team	AB	R	H	HR	RBI	Avg	OB	Slg	OPS	bb%	ct%	Eye	SB	CS	x/h%	Iso	RC/G
2012 (6) Evansville	2011	NCAA	Evansville	212	51	62	2	21	292	364	382	746	10	84	0.71	27	10	24	90	4.92
Pwr ++	2012	NCAA	Evansville	225	41	71	1	27	316	396	422	818	12	92	1.76	30	7	30	107	6.05
BAvg ++	2012	A	Cedar Rapids	248	34	68	1	20	274	316	347	662	6	86	0.43	7	2	22	73	3.71
Spd +++	2013	A+	Inland Empire	506	80	142	4	53	281	326	375	701	6	87	0.52	16	4	25	95	4.22
Def ++++	2014	AA	Arkansas	344	46	81	4	23	235	285	314	599	7	82	0.39	11	1	22	78	2.87

Athletic INF who is excellent defender with soft, quick hands, strong arm, and keen instincts. Lacks punch in balanced stroke and needs to drive ball more to all fields. Makes easy contact and is tough to strike out. Can steal bases with good speed, but needs to get on base more.

Starling,Bubba | 8 | Kansas City | EXP MLB DEBUT: 2016 | H/W: 6-4 180 | FUT: Starting OF | 8E

Bats R Age 22	Year	Lev	Team	AB	R	H	HR	RBI	Avg	OB	Slg	OPS	bb%	ct%	Eye	SB	CS	x/h%	Iso	RC/G
2011 (1) HS (KS)																				
Pwr ++++																				
BAvg ++	2012	Rk	Burlington	200	35	55	10	33	275	364	485	849	12	65	0.40	10	1	36	210	6.65
Spd ++++	2013	A	Lexington	435	51	105	13	63	241	324	398	721	11	71	0.41	22	3	36	156	4.59
Def ++++	2014	A+	Wilmington	482	67	105	9	54	218	290	338	628	9	69	0.33	17	2	34	120	3.26

Toolsy prospect who looks part, but hasn't produced. Finished 2nd in CAR in Ks and lacks bat control and feel. Swings and misses frequently and has disjointed stroke. Plus bat speed and power give him promise. Plays very good defense in CF with above average speed, range, and arm.

Stassi,Max | 2 | Houston | EXP MLB DEBUT: 2013 | H/W: 5-10 200 | FUT: Starting C | 7B

Bats R Age 24	Year	Lev	Team	AB	R	H	HR	RBI	Avg	OB	Slg	OPS	bb%	ct%	Eye	SB	CS	x/h%	Iso	RC/G
2009 (4) HS (CA)	2012	A+	Stockton	314	48	84	15	45	268	326	468	794	8	74	0.33	3	1	39	201	5.28
Pwr +++	2013	AA	Corpus Christi	289	40	80	17	60	277	321	529	851	6	76	0.28	1	1	48	253	5.86
BAvg ++	2013	MLB	Houston	7	0	2	0	1	286	286	286	571	0	71	0.00	0	0	0	0	1.97
Spd ++	2014	AAA	Oklahoma City	392	49	97	9	45	247	287	378	665	5	74	0.21	1	0	32	130	3.54
Def +++	2014	MLB	Houston	20	2	7	0	4	350	350	450	800	0	70	0.00	0	0	29	100	5.34

Short, stocky backstop who has struggled to stay healthy, but owns impactful raw power. Swings hard early in count and won't draw many walks and BA is in question. Profiles to 15-20 HR. Solid receiver behind plate with clean footwork. Only has average arm, but releases quickly.

Stokes,Troy | 78 | Milwaukee | EXP MLB DEBUT: 2018 | H/W: 5-8 182 | FUT: Starting LF | 7D

Bats R Age 19	Year	Lev	Team	AB	R	H	HR	RBI	Avg	OB	Slg	OPS	bb%	ct%	Eye	SB	CS	x/h%	Iso	RC/G
2014 (4) HS (MD)																				
Pwr ++																				
BAvg +++																				
Spd ++++																				
Def ++	2014	Rk	AZL Brewers	172	29	45	0	18	262	352	331	683	12	73	0.51	19	3	24	70	4.24

4th round pick has as short, but athletic frame. Has a nice line-drive approach at the plate that allows him to utilize his plus speed. Won't hit for much power, but he held his own in his debut, and has some SB ability.

Story,Trevor | 6 | Colorado | EXP MLB DEBUT: 2016 | H/W: 6-1 175 | FUT: Starting SS | 8D

Bats R Age 22	Year	Lev	Team	AB	R	H	HR	RBI	Avg	OB	Slg	OPS	bb%	ct%	Eye	SB	CS	x/h%	Iso	RC/G
2011 (2) HS (TX)	2012	A	Asheville	477	96	132	18	63	277	358	505	863	11	75	0.50	15	3	51	229	6.50
Pwr +++	2013	A+	Modesto	497	71	116	12	65	233	297	394	691	8	63	0.25	23	1	44	161	4.37
BAvg +++	2014	A-	Tri-City	7	2	2	0	0	286	375	429	804	13	57	0.33	0	0	50	143	7.08
Spd +++	2014	A+	Modesto	184	38	61	5	28	332	428	582	1009	14	68	0.53	20	4	48	250	9.30
Def +++	2014	AA	Tulsa	205	29	41	9	20	200	296	380	677	12	60	0.34	3	1	44	180	4.16

Boom-or-bust prospect is a streaky hitter. When going well, he hits for average and power and draws walks. But when he's not, he struggles to make contact and becomes overly aggressive. Can make all of the plays on defense and shows good range and a plus arm. Getting additional work in at 2B and 3B during instructional and AFL.

Susac,Andrew | 2 | San Francisco | EXP MLB DEBUT: 2014 | H/W: 6-1 215 | FUT: Starting C | 7B

Bats R Age 25	Year	Lev	Team	AB	R	H	HR	RBI	Avg	OB	Slg	OPS	bb%	ct%	Eye	SB	CS	x/h%	Iso	RC/G
2011 (2) Oregon State	2011	NCAA	Oregon State	134	31	42	5	32	313	429	552	981	17	76	0.84	0	1	43	239	8.36
Pwr +++	2012	A+	San Jose	361	58	88	9	52	244	344	380	723	13	72	0.55	1	1	32	136	4.70
BAvg ++	2013	AA	Richmond	262	32	67	12	46	256	359	458	817	14	74	0.62	1	0	43	202	5.89
Spd ++	2014	AAA	Fresno	213	34	57	10	32	268	368	451	819	14	77	0.68	0	0	33	183	5.84
Def ++++	2014	MLB	SF Giants	88	13	24	3	19	273	326	466	792	7	68	0.25	0	0	46	193	5.57

Athletic C with plus arm and good receiving skills had impressive season in AAA before finishing the year in San Francisco. Short stroke and improved ct% in the minors give potential for higher BA ceiling. Plus glove paired with good plate discipline and average power will lead to starting CA role in the bigs.

Swanner,William | 23 | Colorado | EXP MLB DEBUT: 2015 | H/W: 6-2 195 | FUT: Starting C | 7D

Bats R Age 23	Year	Lev	Team	AB	R	H	HR	RBI	Avg	OB	Slg	OPS	bb%	ct%	Eye	SB	CS	x/h%	Iso	RC/G
2010 (15) HS (CA)	2011	Rk	Casper	159	33	42	10	24	264	346	553	900	11	62	0.33	1	2	60	289	7.65
Pwr +++	2012	A	Asheville	325	60	98	16	61	302	375	529	904	10	69	0.38	3	2	42	228	7.19
BAvg +++	2013	A+	Modesto	355	52	85	13	51	239	323	425	749	11	64	0.34	7	4	46	186	5.23
Spd ++	2014	A+	Modesto	310	36	81	9	41	261	330	419	750	9	66	0.30	7	5	35	158	5.11
Def ++	2014	AA	Tulsa	104	12	29	4	14	279	306	442	748	4	66	0.11	1	4	31	163	4.74

Strong CA has good bat speed and legit power, but swing can be long and contact rate and pitch recognition is problematic. Can be overly aggressive in his approach and struck out 141 times. Still raw behind the plate and needs to improve on signal calling and blocking and receiving skills.

Sweeney,Darnell — 468 — Los Angeles (N)

EXP MLB DEBUT: 2015 | H/W: 6-1 180 | FUT: Utility player | 7C

Bats B Age 24
2012 (13) Central Florida

Pwr	+++
BAvg	+++
Spd	+++
Def	++

Year	Lev	Team	AB	R	H	HR	RBI	Avg	OB	Sig	OPS	bb%	ct%	Eye	SB	CS	x/h%	Iso	RC/G
2012	NCAA	Central Florida	238	50	62	3	35	261	367	370	737	14	85	1.11	20	8	26	109	5.08
2012	Rk	Ogden	66	12	20	0	10	303	387	379	765	12	88	1.13	10	2	15	76	5.39
2012	A	Great Lakes	199	34	58	5	23	291	368	447	815	11	79	0.59	17	4	29	156	5.76
2013	A+	Rancho Cuca	552	79	152	11	77	275	328	455	782	7	73	0.28	48	20	40	179	5.37
2014	AA	Chattanooga	490	88	141	14	57	288	384	463	848	14	76	0.66	15	16	38	176	6.39

Slender, athletic player remains raw, but has interesting tools. Has good plate discipline and makes consistent contact with moderate power. He has plus speed. Range and arm were below-average at SS, but he was moved to 2B where he profiles better.

Swihart,Blake — 2 — Boston

EXP MLB DEBUT: 2015 | H/W: 6-1 185 | FUT: Starting C | 8B

Bats B Age 23
2011 (1) HS (NM)

Pwr	+++
BAvg	++++
Spd	++
Def	+++

Year	Lev	Team	AB	R	H	HR	RBI	Avg	OB	Sig	OPS	bb%	ct%	Eye	SB	CS	x/h%	Iso	RC/G
2011	Rk	GCL Red Sox	6	0	0	0	0	0	0	0	0	0	67	0.00	0	0		0	-6.12
2012	A	Greenville	344	44	90	7	53	262	314	395	709	7	80	0.38	6	2	31	134	4.22
2013	A+	Salem	376	45	112	2	42	298	367	428	795	10	83	0.65	7	8	34	130	5.58
2014	AA	Portland	347	47	104	12	55	300	354	487	841	8	81	0.45	7	1	37	187	5.84
2014	AAA	Pawtucket	69	6	18	1	9	261	282	377	659	3	78	0.13	1	0	28	116	3.37

Athletic backstop who has vastly improved with glove. Receives ball cleanly and has quick release along with strong arm. More of line drive hitter, though set high in HR. Projects to high BA and puts bat-to-ball with line drive swing. Runs fairly well for catcher and could grow into All-Star.

Szczur,Matt — 789 — Chicago (N)

EXP MLB DEBUT: 2014 | H/W: 6-1 195 | FUT: Backup OF | 6B

Bats R Age 25
2010 (5) Villanova

Pwr	+
BAvg	+++
Spd	++++
Def	+++

Year	Lev	Team	AB	R	H	HR	RBI	Avg	OB	Sig	OPS	bb%	ct%	Eye	SB	CS	x/h%	Iso	RC/G
2012	A+	Daytona	295	68	87	2	34	295	392	407	799	14	83	0.94	38	12	29	112	5.83
2012	AA	Tennessee	143	24	30	2	6	210	280	357	637	9	80	0.48	4	2	43	147	3.51
2013	AA	Tennessee	512	78	144	3	44	281	345	367	712	9	85	0.67	22	12	24	86	4.49
2014	AAA	Iowa	414	52	108	1	24	261	311	312	622	7	81	0.38	30	7	17	51	3.17
2014	MLB	Chi Cubs	62	6	14	2	5	226	273	355	628	6	82	0.36	0	0	29	129	3.09

Speedy OF started well at AAA, earning him a brief look in the majors. Has plus speed and decent strike zone judgment, but walk rate dipped. Isn't likely to develop power due to a slashing swing, but should hit for BA. Continues to improve defensively and should stick in CF.

Tapia,Raimel — 789 — Colorado

EXP MLB DEBUT: 2016 | H/W: 6-2 160 | FUT: Starting OF | 8C

Bats L Age 21
2010 FA (DR)

Pwr	+++
BAvg	+++
Spd	++++
Def	+++

Year	Lev	Team	AB	R	H	HR	RBI	Avg	OB	Sig	OPS	bb%	ct%	Eye	SB	CS	x/h%	Iso	RC/G
2013	Rk	Grand Junction	258	53	92	7	47	357	392	562	954	5	88	0.48	10	9	36	205	7.02
2014	A	Asheville	481	93	157	9	72	326	372	453	825	7	81	0.39	33	16	27	127	5.63

Good approach at the plate. Uses good eye-hand coordination to make contact and hit for BA Also has good plate discipline and a quick LH stroke. Has raw power and it should continue to develop as he matures. Has enough speed to stick in CF.

Taylor,Chuck — 78 — Arizona

EXP MLB DEBUT: 2017 | H/W: 5-9 185 | FUT: Starting CF | 7D

Bats B Age 21
2012 (4) HS (TX)

Pwr	+
BAvg	+++
Spd	+++
Def	+++

Year	Lev	Team	AB	R	H	HR	RBI	Avg	OB	Sig	OPS	bb%	ct%	Eye	SB	CS	x/h%	Iso	RC/G
2012	Rk	AZL Dbacks	205	41	48	0	16	234	302	288	590	9	73	0.36	16	7	19	54	2.78
2013	Rk	Missoula	220	38	64	3	25	291	371	414	785	11	79	0.60	3	5	28	123	5.46
2014	A	South Bend	400	60	114	3	50	285	378	370	748	13	82	0.81	11	6	21	85	5.11

OF has plus speed and is a good defender in CF. He drew a career high 60 walks in '14 and has nice top-of-the-order skills. Given his size and line-drive approach, the switch-hitter isn't likely to hit for power.

Taylor,Michael — 8 — Washington

EXP MLB DEBUT: 2014 | H/W: 6-3 210 | FUT: Starting CF | 8C

Bats R Age 24
2009 (6) HS (FL)

Pwr	+++
BAvg	++
Spd	++++
Def	++++

Year	Lev	Team	AB	R	H	HR	RBI	Avg	OB	Sig	OPS	bb%	ct%	Eye	SB	CS	x/h%	Iso	RC/G
2012	A+	Potomac	384	51	93	3	37	242	314	362	676	9	71	0.35	19	9	41	120	4.05
2013	A+	Potomac	509	79	134	10	87	263	335	426	761	10	74	0.42	51	7	43	163	5.14
2014	AA	Harrisburg	384	74	120	22	61	313	392	539	931	12	66	0.38	34	8	34	227	7.74
2014	AAA	Syracuse	44	7	10	1	3	227	333	409	742	14	68	0.50	3	1	50	182	5.18
2014	MLB	Washington	39	5	8	1	5	205	262	359	621	7	56	0.18	0	2	50	154	3.54

Began to utilize his hefty toolbox and resulted in a huge stats season. Quick-twitch athlete with exciting bat speed, pop, and borderline elite defense. He has become more selective at the plate, though swing-and-miss continues to be a concern, and could hold the rest of the tools hostage at the highest level.

Taylor,Tyrone — 8 — Milwaukee

EXP MLB DEBUT: 2016 | H/W: 6-0 185 | FUT: Starting CF | 8C

Bats R Age 21
2012 (2) HS (CA)

Pwr	+++
BAvg	+++
Spd	+++
Def	+++

Year	Lev	Team	AB	R	H	HR	RBI	Avg	OB	Sig	OPS	bb%	ct%	Eye	SB	CS	x/h%	Iso	RC/G
2012	Rk	Helena	39	11	15	2	5	385	455	641	1096	11	79	0.63	3	2	40	256	9.26
2012	Rk	AZL Brewers	36	11	14	0	6	389	405	694	1100	3	92	0.33	3	1	57	306	8.72
2013	A	Wisconsin	485	69	133	8	57	274	323	400	723	7	87	0.56	19	8	32	126	4.47
2014	A+	Brevard Cnty	507	69	141	6	68	278	330	396	726	7	89	0.67	22	6	32	118	4.59
2014	AA	Huntsville	13	0	1	0	0	77	143	77	220	7	62	0.20	1	0	0	0	-3.22

Athletic OF with 5-tool potential. Has plus bat speed and good raw power. Is aggressive at the plate, but makes good contact. Better plate discipline would allow him to be more selective. A legitimate CF, his plus speed plays up in the field, where he shows plus instincts.

Telis,Tomas — 2 — Texas

EXP MLB DEBUT: 2014 | H/W: 5-8 200 | FUT: Starting C | 7D

Bats B Age 23
2007 FA (Venezuela)

Pwr	++
BAvg	+++
Spd	++
Def	++

Year	Lev	Team	AB	R	H	HR	RBI	Avg	OB	Sig	OPS	bb%	ct%	Eye	SB	CS	x/h%	Iso	RC/G
2012	A+	Myrtle Beach	450	45	111	4	43	247	274	331	605	4	88	0.32	9	2	26	84	2.98
2013	AA	Frisco	348	32	92	4	43	264	285	353	638	3	87	0.22	8	2	25	89	3.23
2014	AA	Frisco	267	31	81	2	33	303	345	401	746	6	89	0.59	7	1	25	97	4.74
2014	AAA	Round Rock	139	18	48	3	17	345	372	489	862	4	91	0.50	1	1	25	144	5.84
2014	MLB	Texas	68	7	17	0	8	250	261	279	540	1	85	0.10	0	0	12	29	1.98

Short, stout C who hits for BA with quiet load in stroke. Smashes line drives to gaps, though long ball power not evident. Can be beaten on outer half of plate. Receives well and can block balls, but inconsistent arm and accuracy mute natural talent. Has decent speed for position and frame.

Tellez,Rowdy — 3 — Toronto

EXP MLB DEBUT: 2018 | H/W: 6-4 220 | FUT: Starting 1B | 8E

Bats L Age 20
2013 (30) HS (CA)

Pwr	++++
BAvg	++
Spd	++
Def	++

Year	Lev	Team	AB	R	H	HR	RBI	Avg	OB	Sig	OPS	bb%	ct%	Eye	SB	CS	x/h%	Iso	RC/G
2013	Rk	GCL Blue Jays	124	10	29	2	20	234	317	371	688	11	79	0.58	1	0	34	137	4.20
2014	Rk	Bluefield	191	26	56	4	36	293	357	424	781	9	86	0.70	3	2	29	131	5.24
2014	A	Lansing	42	6	15	2	7	357	449	500	949	14	76	0.70	0	0	13	143	7.54

Strong 1B with significant raw power to all fields. Started season cold before heating up late. Has patient approach and doesn't K much for profile. Bat-only prospect at present with limited speed and shoddy defense. Has enough range and hands, but makes careless errors.

Thomas,Lane — 578 — Toronto

EXP MLB DEBUT: 2018 | H/W: 6-1 210 | FUT: Starting 3B/OF | 7D

Bats R Age 19
2014 (5) HS (TN)

Pwr	++
BAvg	+++
Spd	+++
Def	+++

Year	Lev	Team	AB	R	H	HR	RBI	Avg	OB	Sig	OPS	bb%	ct%	Eye	SB	CS	x/h%	Iso	RC/G
2014	Rk	Bluefield	65	10	21	1	8	323	380	431	811	8	75	0.38	2	0	24	108	5.64
2014	Rk	GCL Blue Jays	131	21	34	0	11	260	362	382	744	14	75	0.64	7	3	35	122	5.22

Strong, athletic OF who has ability to play both CF and 3B. Has average power potential due to strength and moderate bat speed. Has level swing path and exhibits patience at plate. Runs well for size and ranges well in CF. Strong arm is asset at any position. Room to grow into frame.

Thompson,Trayce — 89 — Chicago (A)

EXP MLB DEBUT: 2015 | H/W: 6-3 210 | FUT: Starting OF | 8E

Bats R Age 24
2009 (2) HS (CA)

Pwr	++++
BAvg	++
Spd	+++
Def	+++

Year	Lev	Team	AB	R	H	HR	RBI	Avg	OB	Sig	OPS	bb%	ct%	Eye	SB	CS	x/h%	Iso	RC/G
2012	A+	Winston-Salem	449	77	114	22	90	254	322	486	807	9	68	0.31	18	3	48	232	5.79
2012	AA	Birmingham	50	10	14	3	6	280	379	520	899	14	68	0.50	2	0	36	240	7.23
2012	AAA	Charlotte	18	1	3	0	0	167	250	278	528	10	67	0.33	1	0	67	111	2.00
2013	AA	Birmingham	507	78	116	15	73	229	310	383	693	11	73	0.43	25	8	37	154	4.15
2014	AA	Birmingham	518	86	123	16	59	237	322	419	741	11	71	0.43	20	5	46	181	4.91

Tall, athletic OF who repeated AA to similar results. Finished 2nd in K in SL due to long swing. Offers intriguing speed/power combo and has plenty of strength and leverage in vicious stroke. Still struggles with reading spin and has low BA potential. Can play any OF spot with average arm.

Tilson,Charlie — 8 — St. Louis

EXP MLB DEBUT: 2015 | H/W: 5-11 175 | FUT: Starting CF | 7C

Bats L Age 22
2011 (2) HS (IL)

- Pwr ++
- BAvg +++
- Spd +++
- Def +++

Year	Lev	Team	AB	R	H	HR	RBI	Avg	OB	Slg	OPS	bb%	ct%	Eye	SB	CS	x/h%	Iso	RC/G
2011	Rk	GCL Cardinals	12	2	2	0	1	167	286	167	452	14	75	0.67	1	0	0	0	1.08
2013	A	Peoria	376	49	114	4	30	303	347	388	735	6	85	0.43	15	6	16	85	4.52
2013	A+	Palm Beach	34	1	9	0	0	265	359	353	712	13	82	0.83	0	0	22	88	4.73
2014	A+	Palm Beach	370	54	114	5	36	308	350	414	764	6	79	0.32	10	7	18	105	4.85
2014	AA	Springfield	139	19	33	2	17	237	269	324	593	4	80	0.21	2	3	21	86	2.60

High-energy CF with a smooth compact LH stroke is willing to drive the ball the opposite way. Puts the ball into play and uses his above-average speed. Can be overly aggressive as shown by low walk rate. Not likely to hit for much power, but has good speed and is a solid defender in CF.

Tocci,Carlos — 8 — Philadelphia

EXP MLB DEBUT: 2017 | H/W: 6-2 160 | FUT: Starting CF | 8D

Bats R Age 19
2011 FA (Venezuela)

- Pwr ++
- BAvg +++
- Spd +++
- Def ++++

Year	Lev	Team	AB	R	H	HR	RBI	Avg	OB	Slg	OPS	bb%	ct%	Eye	SB	CS	x/h%	Iso	RC/G
2012	Rk	GCL Phillies	97	13	27	0	9	278	320	299	619	6	81	0.33	9	2	7	21	3.05
2013	A	Lakewood	421	40	88	0	26	209	248	249	498	5	82	0.29	6	7	19	40	1.60
2014	A	Lakewood	487	59	118	2	30	242	279	324	604	5	80	0.26	10	11	24	82	2.87

Body type is the question: Will he ever be able to add real strength and muscle to his frame? Or is this what he has to work with? Has the defensive chops in CF; glides to the ball and has an adequate arm. Made strides at the plate, but physical growth is coming slowly.

Toles,Andrew — 8 — Tampa Bay

EXP MLB DEBUT: 2016 | H/W: 5-10 185 | FUT: Starting OF | 7C

Bats L Age 22
2012 (3) Chipola JC

- Pwr ++
- BAvg +++
- Spd ++++
- Def +++

Year	Lev	Team	AB	R	H	HR	RBI	Avg	OB	Slg	OPS	bb%	ct%	Eye	SB	CS	x/h%	Iso	RC/G
2012	NCAA	Chipola College	166	41	61	5	33	367	429	554	984	10	100		29	7	31	187	7.66
2012	Rk	Princeton	199	31	56	7	33	281	322	482	805	6	82	0.33	14	5	41	201	5.29
2013	A	Bowling Green	519	79	169	2	57	326	353	466	819	4	80	0.21	62	17	31	141	5.56
2014	Rk	GCL Devil Rays	24	4	7	0	2	292	292	375	667	0	75	0.00	6	0	14	83	3.39
2014	A+	Charlotte	199	28	52	1	13	261	303	337	640	6	84	0.39	18	10	23	75	3.41

Plus athlete who missed time due to disciplinary actions (makeup concerns). Has ideal tools to become impact bat at top of lineup. Drives ball with authority and has premium speed. Can be overly aggressive and is inefficient baserunner. Nice upside, but needs to hustle and stay on field.

Tomas,Yasmany — 79 — Arizona

EXP MLB DEBUT: 2015 | H/W: 6-1 230 | FUT: Starting OF | 8C

Bats R Age 24
2014 FA (Cuba)

- Pwr ++++
- BAvg ++
- Spd ++
- Def +++

Year	Lev	Team	AB	R	H	HR	RBI	Avg	OB	Slg	OPS	bb%	ct%	Eye	SB	CS	x/h%	Iso	RC/G
2011		Cuba	27	4	5	1	3	185	185	370	556	0	70	0.00	0	1	40	185	1.86
2012		Cuba	272	46	81	20	50	298	337	581	918	6	79	0.28	4	2	44	283	6.51
2013		Cuba	277	45	80	15	60	289	367	538	904	11	81	0.65	1	3	45	249	6.75
2014		Cuba	241	28	69	6	36	286	346	444	790	8	80	0.45	6	6	35	158	5.31

Big, strong OF who should compete for starting OF job. Possesses brute raw power from right side with elite bat speed and leverage. May struggle to hit for BA due to long, uppercut stroke and likely to run into strikeouts in MLB. Has been a fine OF with very strong arm, though often doesn't take best routes.

Torrens,Luis — 2 — New York (A)

EXP MLB DEBUT: 2018 | H/W: 6-0 175 | FUT: Starting C | 8D

Bats R Age 18
2012 FA (Venezuela)

- Pwr ++
- BAvg +++
- Spd ++
- Def +++

Year	Lev	Team	AB	R	H	HR	RBI	Avg	OB	Slg	OPS	bb%	ct%	Eye	SB	CS	x/h%	Iso	RC/G
2013	Rk	GCL Yankees 2	174	17	42	1	14	241	343	299	642	13	77	0.68	2	0	19	57	3.69
2014	Rk	GCL Yankees	16	1	4	0	1	250	250	313	563	0	88	0.00	0	0	25	63	2.28
2014	A-	Staten Island	185	27	50	2	18	270	322	405	727	7	78	0.34	1	2	36	135	4.54
2014	A	CharlestonSC	26	4	4	1	3	154	313	269	582	19	73	0.86	0	0	25	115	2.72

Agile catcher who has intriguing tools with bat and glove. Exhibits pure arm strength and continues to improve receiving and throwing accuracy. Shows ability to hit for BA with gap power and quick bat. Can expand strike zone with breaking balls and get pull happy. Power could emerge.

Torres,Gleyber — 6 — Chicago (N)

EXP MLB DEBUT: 2018 | H/W: 6-1 175 | FUT: Starting SS | 8D

Bats R Age 18
2013 FA (Venezuela)

- Pwr +++
- BAvg ++
- Spd ++
- Def ++++

Year	Lev	Team	AB	R	H	HR	RBI	Avg	OB	Slg	OPS	bb%	ct%	Eye	SB	CS	x/h%	Iso	RC/G
2014	Rk	AZL Cubs	154	33	43	1	29	279	380	377	757	14	79	0.76	8	7	23	97	5.28
2014	A-	Boise	28	4	11	1	4	393	469	786	1254	13	75	0.57	2	0	55	393	12.14

Has a short, compact stroke and above-avg bat speed. Makes consistent contact and has an advanced understanding of the strike zone. Doesn't have much power, but instead shoots hard lines drives to all fields. Has decent range, soft hands, and a strong, accurate arm.

Torres,Ramon — 456 — Kansas City

EXP MLB DEBUT: 2016 | H/W: 5-10 155 | FUT: Utility player | 6B

Bats B Age 22
2009 FA (DR)

- Pwr ++
- BAvg +++
- Spd +++
- Def +++

Year	Lev	Team	AB	R	H	HR	RBI	Avg	OB	Slg	OPS	bb%	ct%	Eye	SB	CS	x/h%	Iso	RC/G
2012	Rk	AZL Royals	193	47	61	3	27	316	389	430	819	11	87	0.92	17	8	20	114	5.82
2013	Rk	Burlington	162	24	45	3	20	278	304	420	723	4	93	0.50	5	5	33	142	4.39
2013	A	Lexington	87	4	19	0	5	218	277	264	541	7	80	0.41	1	3	21	46	2.22
2014	A	Lexington	276	46	84	5	26	304	342	428	770	5	86	0.40	15	5	26	123	4.88
2014	A+	Wilmington	149	14	37	0	8	248	296	322	618	6	89	0.63	5	2	22	74	3.38

Short, lean INF with plenty of athleticism and can hit for BA from both sides of plate. Increased strength led to high in HR while balanced swing makes contact. Has good speed for SB and has the range and hands to be asset at any infield spot. Plus arm is best defensive attribute.

Towey,Cal — 259 — Los Angeles (A)

EXP MLB DEBUT: 2016 | H/W: 6-1 215 | FUT: Utility player | 7E

Bats L Age 25
2013 (17) Baylor

- Pwr +++
- BAvg +++
- Spd ++
- Def ++

Year	Lev	Team	AB	R	H	HR	RBI	Avg	OB	Slg	OPS	bb%	ct%	Eye	SB	CS	x/h%	Iso	RC/G
2011	NCAA	Baylor	131	22	32	4	15	244	377	397	774	18	63	0.57	6	5	31	153	5.88
2012	NCAA	Baylor	224	43	66	6	51	295	399	469	868	15	72	0.62	9	7	35	174	6.87
2013	NCAA	Baylor	199	34	58	4	45	291	400	457	857	15	78	0.84	10	2	34	166	6.64
2013	Rk	Orem	230	69	73	8	53	317	471	543	1015	23	74	1.14	13	3	41	226	9.23
2014	A+	Inland Empire	477	72	133	10	63	279	348	417	766	10	71	0.37	21	15	30	138	5.20

Versatile player who played all over diamond, even at catcher. Hits for BA with mature approach and use of entire field. Can stay in against LHP, though strikes out a lot. Steals bases despite fringy speed, though was caught frequently in 2014. Lacks range at 3B and defense choppy.

Trahan,Stryker — 79 — Arizona

EXP MLB DEBUT: 2016 | H/W: 5-11 215 | FUT: Starting RF | 8D

Bats L Age 20
2012 (1) HS (LA)

- Pwr +++
- BAvg ++
- Spd ++
- Def ++

Year	Lev	Team	AB	R	H	HR	RBI	Avg	OB	Slg	OPS	bb%	ct%	Eye	SB	CS	x/h%	Iso	RC/G
2012	Rk	AZL Dbacks	167	29	47	5	25	281	420	473	893	19	71	0.83	8	1	40	192	7.46
2013	Rk	Missoula	236	44	60	10	33	254	323	462	785	9	76	0.42	1	0	45	208	5.26
2014	A-	Hillsboro	113	15	29	6	22	257	344	496	839	12	80	0.65	2	2	48	239	5.99
2014	A	South Bend	368	47	73	13	52	198	259	367	626	8	60	0.21	3	0	48	168	3.32

Has yet to prove he can hit and owns a career slash line of .237/.324/.430. Still has good bat speed and raw power. Struggles to make consistent contact and will need to improve to hit for average. He has a plus arm and moves reasonably well, so the move to RF makes sense.

Travis,Devon — 48 — Toronto

EXP MLB DEBUT: 2015 | H/W: 5-9 195 | FUT: Starting 2B/CF | 8C

Bats R Age 24
2012 (13) Florida State

- Pwr ++
- BAvg ++++
- Spd ++++
- Def +++

Year	Lev	Team	AB	R	H	HR	RBI	Avg	OB	Slg	OPS	bb%	ct%	Eye	SB	CS	x/h%	Iso	RC/G
2012	NCAA	Florida State	268	63	87	8	44	325	393	504	896	10	85	0.75	7	2	37	179	6.66
2012	A-	Connecticut	93	17	26	3	11	280	337	441	777	8	89	0.80	3	1	27	161	5.13
2013	A	West Michigan	290	55	102	6	42	352	422	486	908	11	89	1.09	14	3	25	134	6.84
2013	A+	Lakeland	214	38	75	10	34	350	401	561	962	8	85	0.56	8	1	31	210	7.16
2014	AA	Erie	396	68	118	10	52	298	358	460	818	9	85	0.62	16	5	31	162	5.64

Short, athletic INF who has progressed steadily. High BA hitter with short stroke and disciplined approach. Owns decent pop for size and projects to average pop. Covers plate with compact stroke and is tough out. Plays 2B with average arm and range, but could move to CF to use speed.

Travis,Sam — 3 — Boston

EXP MLB DEBUT: 2017 | H/W: 6-0 195 | FUT: Starting 1B | 7C

Bats R Age 21
2014 (2) Indiana

- Pwr +++
- BAvg +++
- Spd ++
- Def ++

Year	Lev	Team	AB	R	H	HR	RBI	Avg	OB	Slg	OPS	bb%	ct%	Eye	SB	CS	x/h%	Iso	RC/G
2012	NCAA	Indiana	232	41	74	9	50	319	395	509	903	11	85	0.83	4	2	35	190	6.75
2013	NCAA	Indiana	244	53	77	10	57	316	410	545	955	14	86	1.18	4	4	44	230	7.57
2014	NCAA	Indiana	245	55	85	12	58	347	407	576	983	9	89	0.96	8	5	35	229	7.47
2014	A-	Lowell	165	28	55	4	30	333	349	448	798	2	89	0.22	5	1	18	115	4.92
2014	A	Greenville	107	12	31	3	14	290	333	495	829	6	87	0.50	0	1	48	206	5.67

Natural hitter who goes gap to gap with polished approach. Hit over .400 against LHP and contact-making comes easy to him. Mostly pull power at present and could grow into more. Lacks foot speed to steal bases and is relegated to 1B with limited hands. Bat will have to carry him.

Trevino,Jose — 245 — Texas

EXP MLB DEBUT: 2017 | H/W: 5-11 195 | FUT: Starting C | 7D

Bats R Age 22
2014 (6) Oral Roberts
Pwr +++
BAvg ++
Spd +
Def ++

Year	Lev	Team	AB	R	H	HR	RBI	Avg	OB	Slg	OPS	bb%	ct%	Eye	SB	CS	x/h%	Iso	RC/G
2012	NCAA	Oral Roberts	246	44	78	13	57	317	361	573	934	6	86	0.50	3	0	44	256	6.76
2013	NCAA	Oral Roberts	195	32	47	8	37	241	321	410	731	11	85	0.79	0	0	36	169	4.63
2014	NCAA	Oral Roberts	230	37	70	10	43	304	360	491	851	8	89	0.80	4	0	31	187	5.90
2014	A-	Spokane	288	58	74	9	49	257	312	448	760	7	83	0.46	2	0	46	191	4.88

Versatile peformer who TEX likes as C, but can play 2B and 3B. Makes easy contact and has strength for long ball pop. Has nice hitting instincts with aggressive swing. OK eye at the plate, and has limited athleticism and speed. Possesses good hands and natural arm strength.

Tromp,Jiandido — 8 — Philadelphia

EXP MLB DEBUT: 2018 | H/W: 5-11 175 | FUT: Starting LF | 7D

Bats R Age 21
2011 FA (Aruba)
Pwr ++
BAvg ++
Spd +++
Def +++

Year	Lev	Team	AB	R	H	HR	RBI	Avg	OB	Slg	OPS	bb%	ct%	Eye	SB	CS	x/h%	Iso	RC/G
2013	A-	Williamsport	107	9	32	1	8	299	348	430	778	7	77	0.32	6	2	34	131	5.20
2013	A-	Williamsport	107	9	32	1	8	299	348	430	778	7	77	0.32	6	2	34	131	5.20
2013	A	Lakewood	40	2	6	0	3	150	190	275	465	5	60	0.13	0	1	50	125	1.01
2014	A-	Williamsport	259	39	69	14	33	266	317	498	815	7	72	0.26	16	5	43	232	5.56
2014	A	Lakewood	85	11	19	1	9	224	275	329	604	7	65	0.20	3	0	32	106	2.94

His power surfaced for the first time as he set a team-record 14 HR at short-season Williamsport to put him on the prospect map. Even if that regresses, has some of the best OF instincts in the system, is an above-average runner and defender. Challenge will be to hit enough as he rises through the organization.

Tucker,Cole — 6 — Pittsburgh

EXP MLB DEBUT: 2018 | H/W: 6-3 185 | FUT: Starting SS | 8D

Bats B Age 18
2014 (1) HS (AZ)
Pwr ++
BAvg +++
Spd +++
Def +++

Year	Lev	Team	AB	R	H	HR	RBI	Avg	OB	Slg	OPS	bb%	ct%	Eye	SB	CS	x/h%	Iso	RC/G
2014	Rk	GCL Pirates	180	39	48	2	13	267	359	356	715	13	79	0.68	13	5	21	89	4.61

Switch-hitter held his own in his pro debut. Is projectable and could add power as he matures. Has good range, a strong arm, and gets good reads off the bat. As a result, he should be able to stick at short. Swing can get a bit long, but he barrels the ball and is a smart, athletic player.

Tucker,Preston — 379 — Houston

EXP MLB DEBUT: 2015 | H/W: 6-0 215 | FUT: Reserve OF | 6B

Bats L Age 24
2012 (7) Florida
Pwr ++++
BAvg ++
Spd +
Def +

Year	Lev	Team	AB	R	H	HR	RBI	Avg	OB	Slg	OPS	bb%	ct%	Eye	SB	CS	x/h%	Iso	RC/G
2012	A-	Tri City	165	32	53	8	38	321	388	509	897	10	90	1.13	1	2	28	188	6.50
2013	A+	Lancaster	298	61	97	15	74	326	385	544	929	9	85	0.64	3	0	35	218	6.84
2013	AA	Corpus Christi	237	36	62	10	29	262	337	456	793	10	81	0.59	0	1	40	194	5.35
2014	AA	Corpus Christi	261	41	72	17	43	276	341	536	878	9	82	0.57	3	3	47	261	6.21
2014	AAA	Oklahoma City	275	38	79	7	51	287	359	429	789	10	73	0.42	2	0	32	142	5.45

Natural hitter who may not have much athleticism or agility, but hits the ball hard with emerging power. Bat speed fringe average at best, but has good strength and feel. Doesn't have speed for SB and profiles as bat-only performer. Defense is well below average at 1B and OF corners.

Turner,Stuart — 2 — Minnesota

EXP MLB DEBUT: 2015 | H/W: 6-2 230 | FUT: Starting C | 7C

Bats R Age 23
2013 (3) Mississippi
Pwr +++
BAvg ++
Spd ++
Def ++++

Year	Lev	Team	AB	R	H	HR	RBI	Avg	OB	Slg	OPS	bb%	ct%	Eye	SB	CS	x/h%	Iso	RC/G
2012	NCAA	LSU-Eunice	187	52	62	7	49	332	447	529	976	17	88	1.77	6	5	37	198	8.04
2013	NCAA	Mississippi	222	44	83	5	51	374	444	518	962	11	83	0.76	2	4	25	144	7.55
2013	Rk	Elizabethton	121	15	32	3	19	264	331	380	711	9	82	0.55	0	1	25	116	4.30
2013	AA	New Britain	4	1	2	0	0	500	500	500	1000	0	75	0.00	0	0	0	0	7.40
2014	A+	Fort Myers	325	49	81	7	40	249	315	375	690	9	81	0.51	7	0	31	126	4.07

Steady, consistent catcher who is standout behind plate with advanced receiving and blocking skills. Owns strong, accurate arm with quick release and ideal footwork. Projects to average power, but line drive swing limits upside. Long stroke can be exploited and he can get pull happy.

Turner,Trea — 6 — Washington

EXP MLB DEBUT: 2016 | H/W: 6-1 175 | FUT: Starting SS | 8B

Bats R Age 21
2014 (1) North Carolina St
Pwr ++
BAvg +++
Spd +++
Def ++

Year	Lev	Team	AB	R	H	HR	RBI	Avg	OB	Slg	OPS	bb%	ct%	Eye	SB	CS	x/h%	Iso	RC/G
2012	NCAA	NC State	259	72	87	5	43	336	427	459	886	14	85	1.08	57	4	23	124	6.79
2013	NCAA	NC State	228	66	84	7	42	368	459	553	1011	14	86	1.23	30	6	29	184	8.30
2014	NCAA	NC State	215	65	69	8	36	321	421	516	937	15	88	1.48	26	4	33	195	7.40
2014	A-	Eugene	92	14	21	1	2	228	311	283	593	11	79	0.58	9	1	14	54	2.91
2014	A	Fort Wayne	187	31	69	4	22	369	441	529	970	11	74	0.50	14	3	29	160	8.02

13th overall pick made a quick impact. Worked hard to shorten his stroke and put the ball in play. Did a good job of staying back on breaking balls and not expanding the strike zone. Shows good contact ability and surprising pop. Plus speed makes him an ideal top of the order hitter.

Twine,Justin — 6 — Miami

EXP MLB DEBUT: 2019 | H/W: 5-11 205 | FUT: Starting SS | 8D

Bats R Age 19
2014 (2) HS (TX)
Pwr +++
BAvg ++
Spd ++++
Def +++

Year	Lev	Team	AB	R	H	HR	RBI	Avg	OB	Slg	OPS	bb%	ct%	Eye	SB	CS	x/h%	Iso	RC/G
2014	Rk	GCL Marlins	166	19	38	1	16	229	256	355	611	3	69	0.12	5	1	37	127	2.96

43rd overall pick struggled in his debut, striking out 52 times. Was one of the best athletes in the draft and has plus speed and raw strength, but can be overly aggressive and his swing can be long, resulting in poor contact. Range and hands are fringy and a move to the OF seems likely.

Unroe,Riley — 46 — Tampa Bay

EXP MLB DEBUT: 2018 | H/W: 5-10 180 | FUT: Starting SS | 7D

Bats B Age 19
2013 (2) HS (AZ)
Pwr ++
BAvg ++
Spd +++
Def +++

Year	Lev	Team	AB	R	H	HR	RBI	Avg	OB	Slg	OPS	bb%	ct%	Eye	SB	CS	x/h%	Iso	RC/G
2013	Rk	GCL Devil Rays	167	34	41	1	15	246	370	341	711	17	74	0.77	7	2	27	96	4.79
2014	Rk	Princeton	243	32	55	3	19	226	309	325	634	11	81	0.62	7	5	29	99	3.52

Switch-hitting INF who split time between 2B and SS. Brings plus bat speed to plate and enough feel for hitting to improve BA. Understands strike zone and will work counts. Runs very well with above average wheels and may profile better at 2B due to range. Needs to drive ball more.

Urena,Jhoan — 5 — New York (N)

EXP MLB DEBUT: 2018 | H/W: 6-1 200 | FUT: Starting 3B | 7D

Bats B Age 20
2013 FA (DR)
Pwr +++
BAvg +++
Spd ++
Def +++

Year	Lev	Team	AB	R	H	HR	RBI	Avg	OB	Slg	OPS	bb%	ct%	Eye	SB	CS	x/h%	Iso	RC/G
2013	Rk	GCL Mets	157	19	47	0	20	299	353	376	729	8	78	0.38	4	1	19	76	4.59
2014	A-	Brooklyn	283	30	85	5	47	300	361	431	792	9	80	0.47	7	9	31	131	5.38

Switch hitter with a knack for hitting line drives to the gaps. Brings a nice plate approach and potential for more power as he physically matures. Shows advanced pitch recognition and makes hard contact. At 3B, has soft hands and strong arm but size and foot speed could move him to 1B.

Urena,Richard — 46 — Toronto

EXP MLB DEBUT: 2018 | H/W: 6-1 170 | FUT: Starting SS | 8D

Bats L Age 19
2012 FA (DR)
Pwr ++
BAvg ++++
Spd +++
Def +++

Year	Lev	Team	AB	R	H	HR	RBI	Avg	OB	Slg	OPS	bb%	ct%	Eye	SB	CS	x/h%	Iso	RC/G
2013	Rk	GCL Blue Jays	27	3	9	0	3	333	400	407	807	10	78	0.50	0	0	22	74	5.73
2013	Rk	DSL Blue Jays	243	45	72	1	35	296	374	403	777	11	82	0.70	9	5	31	107	5.41
2014	Rk	Bluefield	217	35	69	2	20	318	365	433	798	7	76	0.31	5	4	28	115	5.43
2014	A-	Vancouver	33	3	8	0	5	242	306	364	669	8	85	0.60	1	0	38	121	4.05

Lean, athletic INF with terrific quickness and smooth defensive skills. Soft hands and arm strength are attributes, but can get careless. Runs bases aggressively with average speed. Not much power in stroke, but has feel for hitting and knows strike zone. Can bail on good breaking balls.

Urrutia,Henry — 79 — Baltimore

EXP MLB DEBUT: 2013 | H/W: 6-3 180 | FUT: Starting OF | 7C

Bats B Age 28
2012 FA (Cuba)
Pwr ++
BAvg +++
Spd ++
Def ++

Year	Lev	Team	AB	R	H	HR	RBI	Avg	OB	Slg	OPS	bb%	ct%	Eye	SB	CS	x/h%	Iso	RC/G
2013	AA	Bowie	200	33	73	7	37	365	433	550	983	11	82	0.67	1	1	32	185	7.75
2013	AAA	Norfolk	114	16	36	2	13	316	361	430	790	7	87	0.53	0	0	22	114	5.19
2013	MLB	Baltimore	58	5	16	0	2	276	276	310	586	0	81	0.00	0	0	6	34	2.32
2014	Rk	GCL Orioles	49	4	9	0	2	184	231	204	435	6	78	0.27	0	0	11	20	0.66
2014	AAA	Norfolk	204	14	55	0	17	270	287	338	625	2	75	0.10	2	1	24	69	2.96

Long, lean OF who missed time with hernia. Can hit for BA with level swing path and ideal contact. Has frame to add strength, but doesn't pull ball to realize natural power. Secondary skills lag behind bat as he isn't good runner and is relegated to OF corner due to fringy arm and range.

Urshela,Giovanny — 5 — Cleveland

EXP MLB DEBUT: 2015 | H/W: 6-0 195 | FUT: Starting 3B | **7C**

Bats R | Age 23 | 2008 FA (Colombia)

Pwr +++ | BAvg ++ | Spd ++ | Def ++++

Year	Lev	Team	AB	R	H	HR	RBI	Avg	OB	Slg	OPS	bb%	ct%	Eye	SB	CS	x/h%	Iso	RC/G
2011	A	Lake County	505	57	120	9	46	238	258	347	605	3	86	0.20	3	0	29	109	2.82
2012	A+	Carolina	439	50	122	14	59	278	303	446	750	4	86	0.27	1	1	37	169	4.49
2013	AA	Akron	445	42	120	8	43	270	292	384	676	3	89	0.29	1	1	28	115	3.72
2014	AA	Akron	90	15	27	5	19	300	344	567	910	6	82	0.38	1	1	52	267	6.53
2014	AAA	Columbus	395	63	109	13	65	276	327	473	800	7	87	0.59	0	2	42	197	5.35

Breakout prospect who set highs in doubles and HR while drawing more walks. Plus hand-eye coordination led to contact, but uppercut stroke and expansion of zone brought BA into question. Lacks agility, but is terrific defender with plus range, arm, and instincts. Does not run well.

Valaika,Pat — 46 — Colorado

EXP MLB DEBUT: 2017 | H/W: 5-11 200 | FUT: Utility INF | **7D**

Bats R | Age 22 | 2013 (9) UCLA

Pwr ++ | BAvg +++ | Spd ++ | Def +++

Year	Lev	Team	AB	R	H	HR	RBI	Avg	OB	Slg	OPS	bb%	ct%	Eye	SB	CS	x/h%	Iso	RC/G
2012	NCAA	UCLA	229	37	61	1	39	266	317	362	680	7	86	0.53	5	1	26	96	4.02
2013	NCAA	UCLA	249	32	63	5	48	253	340	394	734	12	82	0.75	8	3	35	141	4.83
2013	A-	Tri-City	146	27	35	1	18	240	343	390	734	14	77	0.70	5	3	51	151	5.04
2014	A	Asheville	127	25	47	4	23	370	412	575	987	7	80	0.35	12	2	36	205	7.66
2014	A+	Modesto	331	46	90	8	47	272	321	417	738	7	69	0.24	7	6	30	145	4.71

Has a good approach at the plate. For the year, Valaika hit .299/.345/.461. Does have some swing-and-miss and can be beat on the outer third. Range and arm strength are light for short, though he does have good instincts and soft hands. Profiles as a utility player at the next level.

Valentin,Jesmuel — 4 — Philadelphia

EXP MLB DEBUT: 2017 | H/W: 5-9 180 | FUT: Starting 2B | **7C**

Bats B | Age 20 | 2012 (S-1) HS (PR)

Pwr ++ | BAvg ++ | Spd +++ | Def +++

Year	Lev	Team	AB	R	H	HR	RBI	Avg	OB	Slg	OPS	bb%	ct%	Eye	SB	CS	x/h%	Iso	RC/G
2012	Rk	AZL Dodgers	152	34	32	2	18	211	358	316	674	19	84	1.46	5	2	31	105	4.52
2013	Rk	Ogden	250	53	71	4	24	284	367	396	763	12	86	0.97	11	7	24	112	5.23
2013	A	Great Lakes	99	12	21	0	5	212	322	293	615	14	72	0.57	4	3	33	81	3.36
2014	A	Great Lakes	407	73	114	7	47	280	342	430	772	9	82	0.53	24	7	33	150	5.14
2014	A+	Clearwater	44	8	9	0	0	205	255	250	505	6	86	0.50	1	1	22	45	1.96

Had an offensive breakout season at Low-A, where he showed more power that you'd think from such a small frame. 2B works better for him than SS—though a strong fielder, his arm is below average. While not a burner, he used his speed to set a season high in SB. He'll set out to prove it 2014 was not a fluke at High-A.

Valera,Breyvic — 4 — St. Louis

EXP MLB DEBUT: 2016 | H/W: 5-11 160 | FUT: Starting 2B | **7C**

Bats B | Age 22 | 2010 FA (Venezuela)

Pwr + | BAvg ++++ | Spd +++ | Def +++

Year	Lev	Team	AB	R	H	HR	RBI	Avg	OB	Slg	OPS	bb%	ct%	Eye	SB	CS	x/h%	Iso	RC/G
2012	A-	Batavia	282	39	89	1	33	316	357	418	775	6	90	0.67	10	6	26	103	5.12
2012	AA	Springfield	5	2	1	0	1	200	200	200	400	0	100		0	0	0	0	1.14
2013	A	Peoria	515	71	159	0	48	309	359	367	726	7	94	1.33	13	7	15	58	4.73
2014	A+	Palm Beach	294	35	98	0	37	333	386	388	773	8	96	1.92	13	10	12	54	5.31
2014	AA	Springfield	227	31	65	0	20	286	331	339	670	6	90	0.68	4	5	15	53	3.94

Short, switch-hitting 2B prospect put up another impressive season, hitting .313 with 40 BB/35 K. Hits well from both sides of the plate and uses the whole field. Doesn't have much power, but has good speed. Solid range and actions at 2B and also saw action at 3B.

Vallot,Chase — 2 — Kansas City

EXP MLB DEBUT: 2018 | H/W: 6-0 215 | FUT: Starting C | **8D**

Bats R | Age 18 | 2014 (1-S) HS (LA)

Pwr ++++ | BAvg ++ | Spd ++ | Def ++

Year	Lev	Team	AB	R	H	HR	RBI	Avg	OB	Slg	OPS	bb%	ct%	Eye	SB	CS	x/h%	Iso	RC/G
2014	Rk	Burlington	186	29	40	7	27	215	311	403	715	12	56	0.32	0	1	53	188	5.16

Young, raw backstop with plenty of potential in bat. Swings hard and has the loft in swing to realize plus power. Draws walks, but long swing and struggles with breaking balls mute BA. Has chance to develop into solid receiver. Good agility and arm, but needs work on release and blocking.

Vasquez,Danry — 79 — Houston

EXP MLB DEBUT: 2016 | H/W: 6-3 175 | FUT: Starting OF | **7D**

Bats L | Age 21 | 2010 FA (Venezuela)

Pwr ++ | BAvg +++ | Spd ++ | Def ++

Year	Lev	Team	AB	R	H	HR	RBI	Avg	OB	Slg	OPS	bb%	ct%	Eye	SB	CS	x/h%	Iso	RC/G
2012	A-	Connecticut	289	36	90	2	35	311	341	401	742	4	84	0.29	6	4	22	90	4.51
2012	A	West Michigan	99	5	16	1	7	162	217	222	439	7	80	0.35	0	0	25	61	0.83
2013	A	Quad Cities	118	12	34	3	20	288	323	398	721	5	87	0.40	2	0	18	110	4.22
2013	A	West Michigan	375	47	106	6	40	283	337	400	737	8	85	0.55	9	8	25	117	4.66
2014	A+	Lancaster	423	67	123	5	47	291	352	407	759	9	84	0.59	1	2	30	116	4.99

Long, lean OF with contact-oriented approach. Showed improved pop in 2nd half and willing to draw walks with strong eye. Smokes line drives and has feel for hitting despite unorthodox swing. Noted struggles with LHP could lead to platoon role. Lacks foot speed and relegated to LF.

Velazquez,Andrew — 6 — Tampa Bay

EXP MLB DEBUT: 2017 | H/W: 5-8 175 | FUT: Starting SS | **7C**

Bats B | Age 20 | 2012 (7) HS (NY)

Pwr ++ | BAvg +++ | Spd ++++ | Def ++++

Year	Lev	Team	AB	R	H	HR	RBI	Avg	OB	Slg	OPS	bb%	ct%	Eye	SB	CS	x/h%	Iso	RC/G
2012	Rk	AZL Dbacks	116	33	37	1	20	319	410	500	910	13	70	0.51	20	3	38	181	7.73
2012	Rk	Missoula	50	9	11	0	4	220	291	300	591	9	76	0.42	2	0	18	80	2.89
2013	A	South Bend	235	23	61	0	16	260	320	336	656	8	75	0.36	7	2	23	77	3.69
2014	A	South Bend	544	94	158	9	56	290	363	428	791	10	75	0.46	50	15	27	138	5.54

Reached base in 74 straight and was traded to Tampa. Switch-hitter has plus-plus speed and is a solid defender with good range and an above-average arm. Should stick at the position, but needs to prove he can hit as he moves up.

Verdugo,Alex — 8 — Los Angeles (N)

EXP MLB DEBUT: 2018 | H/W: 6-0 200 | FUT: Starting RF | **8C**

Bats L | Age 18 | 2014 (2) HS (AZ)

Pwr +++ | BAvg ++++ | Spd +++ | Def +++

Year	Lev	Team	AB	R	H	HR	RBI	Avg	OB	Slg	OPS	bb%	ct%	Eye	SB	CS	x/h%	Iso	RC/G
2014	Rk	AZL Dodgers	170	28	59	3	33	347	416	518	933	11	92	1.43	8	0	34	171	7.19
2014	Rk	Ogden	20	3	8	0	8	400	400	450	850	0	80	0.00	3	0	13	50	5.47

Top two-way player in the draft has a short, compact LH stroke with good bat speed. Showed a good understanding of the strike zone, walking more than he struck out. Has a line-drive approach, but he could develop avg power once he learns to hit with more backspin and loft..

Vettleson,Drew — 9 — Washington

EXP MLB DEBUT: 2016 | H/W: 6-1 185 | FUT: Starting OF | **7C**

Bats L | Age 23 | 2010 (1) HS (WA)

Pwr +++ | BAvg +++ | Spd +++ | Def +++

Year	Lev	Team	AB	R	H	HR	RBI	Avg	OB	Slg	OPS	bb%	ct%	Eye	SB	CS	x/h%	Iso	RC/G
2011	Rk	Princeton	234	33	66	7	40	282	356	462	818	10	77	0.51	20	6	36	179	5.79
2012	A	Bowling Green	505	80	139	15	69	275	342	432	773	9	77	0.44	20	11	32	156	5.12
2013	A+	Charlotte	467	50	128	4	62	274	331	388	719	8	83	0.51	5	7	30	113	4.49
2014	A+	Auburn	22	3	7	0	2	318	400	455	855	12	77	0.60	1	0	29	136	6.58
2014	AA	Harrisburg	248	24	61	8	28	246	278	423	701	4	70	0.15	3	3	41	177	4.07

Pure hitter with short swing and ability to drive the ball to all parts of the field. Missed significant time with broken hand, but should hit for good BA and above-average power. Has the arm for RF, but could use work on routes and focus. Will try to re-establish himself in 2015.

Villalobos,Andres — 6 — Miami

EXP MLB DEBUT: 2019 | H/W: 5-11 160 | FUT: Starting SS | **7E**

Bats B | Age 18 | 2014 FA (Venezuela)

Pwr ++ | BAvg +++ | Spd ++ | Def ++

Year	Lev	Team	AB	R	H	HR	RBI	Avg	OB	Slg	OPS	bb%	ct%	Eye	SB	CS	x/h%	Iso	RC/G
2014	(did not play in the US in 2014)																		

Signed by the Marlins for $350,000 in July 2014. Is a switch-hitter with a good line-drive approach. Could develop average power once he matures. Moves well in the field with good range and hands. Raw talent is years away and has not yet made his U.S. debut.

Villalona,Angel — 3 — San Francisco

EXP MLB DEBUT: 2015 | H/W: 6-3 255 | FUT: Backup 1B | **6C**

Bats R | Age 24 | 2006 FA (DR)

Pwr +++ | BAvg ++ | Spd + | Def +

Year	Lev	Team	AB	R	H	HR	RBI	Avg	OB	Slg	OPS	bb%	ct%	Eye	SB	CS	x/h%	Iso	RC/G
2009	A+	San Jose	292	47	78	9	42	267	289	397	686	3	75	0.12	0	1	26	130	3.61
2013	A+	San Jose	284	37	65	14	42	229	268	433	701	5	73	0.20	0	0	46	204	3.90
2013	AA	Richmond	196	23	46	8	28	235	265	413	678	4	69	0.13	0	0	41	179	3.65
2014	Rk	AZL Giants	22	4	6	0	3	273	273	409	682	0	86	0.00	0	0	50	136	3.72
2014	AA	Richmond	365	35	83	10	54	227	273	381	654	6	74	0.24	1	1	39	153	3.43

Former highly touted prospect continued his downward spiral in 2014, making his future in the bigs a large question mark. Has plus raw power, but only plays average in game. Struggles drawing walks and making consistent contact hinder BA ceiling. Below average defender and runner limited to 1B.

Villanueva,Christian — 5 — Chicago (N)

EXP MLB DEBUT: 2015 | H/W: 5-11 210 | FUT: Starting 3B | 7D

Bats R Age 23 — 2008 FA (Mexico)

Pwr +++ | BAvg ++ | Spd ++ | Def ++++

Year	Lev	Team	AB	R	H	HR	RBI	Avg	OB	Slg	OPS	bb%	ct%	Eye	SB	CS	x/h%	Iso	RC/G
2012	A+	Daytona	84	14	21	4	9	250	330	452	782	11	71	0.42	5	2	43	202	5.31
2012	A+	Myrtle Beach	375	45	107	10	59	285	328	421	750	6	78	0.29	9	9	28	136	4.62
2013	AA	Tennessee	490	60	128	19	72	261	309	469	779	6	76	0.29	5	7	48	208	5.06
2014	AA	Tennessee	234	31	58	4	32	248	304	385	689	8	82	0.45	0	1	41	137	4.06
2014	AAA	Iowa	223	22	47	6	26	211	279	372	651	9	71	0.33	2	1	51	161	3.54

Short, strong-bodied 3B continued to regress, hitting just 10 HR. Short, compact stroke and good bat speed result in above-average power, but aggressive approach continues to cut into BA. Is a plus defender with good hands, range, and strong arm, but not much going on here.

Vogelbach,Dan — 3 — Chicago (N)

EXP MLB DEBUT: 2017 | H/W: 6-0 250 | FUT: Starting 1B | 8D

Bats L Age 22 — 2011 (2) HS (FL)

Pwr ++++ | BAvg +++ | Spd + | Def +

Year	Lev	Team	AB	R	H	HR	RBI	Avg	OB	Slg	OPS	bb%	ct%	Eye	SB	CS	x/h%	Iso	RC/G
2012	Rk	AZL Cubs	102	16	33	7	31	324	395	686	1081	11	86	0.86	1	0	64	363	8.78
2012	A-	Boise	143	23	46	10	31	322	416	608	1024	14	76	0.68	0	1	43	287	8.52
2013	A	Kane County	433	55	123	17	71	284	367	450	818	12	82	0.75	4	4	31	166	5.72
2013	A+	Daytona	50	13	14	2	5	280	455	440	895	24	74	1.23	1	0	29	160	7.47
2014	A+	Daytona	482	71	129	16	76	268	356	429	785	12	81	0.73	4	4	35	162	5.39

Has plus raw power, good plate discipline, and a short, compact stroke. Makes consistent contact for a power hitter, giving him the potential to hit. Is well below-average defensively with limited range and stiff hands. He is likely best suited as a DH down the road.

Waldrop Kyle — 7 — Cincinnati

EXP MLB DEBUT: 2016 | H/W: 6-2 220 | FUT: Starting LF | 7D

Bats L Age 23 — 2010 (12) HS (FL)

Pwr ++++ | BAvg +++ | Spd ++ | Def ++

Year	Lev	Team	AB	R	H	HR	RBI	Avg	OB	Slg	OPS	bb%	ct%	Eye	SB	CS	x/h%	Iso	RC/G
2011	Rk	Billings	278	38	76	5	29	273	299	471	770	3	77	0.15	4	4	47	198	4.96
2012	A	Dayton	416	59	118	8	50	284	344	421	764	8	81	0.49	10	6	30	137	5.00
2013	A+	Bakersfield	504	66	130	21	54	258	302	462	765	6	76	0.26	20	8	44	204	4.82
2014	A+	Bakersfield	256	54	92	6	32	359	410	516	926	8	78	0.39	11	2	29	156	7.02
2014	AA	Pensacola	232	27	73	8	35	315	361	517	879	7	81	0.39	3	4	38	203	6.28

Showed improvement in all aspects of his game. Emphasized more of line-drive approach while using entire field which bumped OBP significantly. Utilizes smooth stroke and ball jumps off his bat. BB% and ct% trending in the right direction. Knows how to steal bases. Decent range in LF.

Walker,Adam — 9 — Minnesota

EXP MLB DEBUT: 2015 | H/W: 6-4 225 | FUT: Starting OF | 8D

Bats R Age 23 — 2012 (3) Jacksonville

Pwr ++++ | BAvg ++ | Spd +++ | Def ++

Year	Lev	Team	AB	R	H	HR	RBI	Avg	OB	Slg	OPS	bb%	ct%	Eye	SB	CS	x/h%	Iso	RC/G
2011	NCAA	Jacksonville	242	65	99	13	74	409	484	682	1166	13	74	0.56	14	0	38	273	10.65
2012	NCAA	Jacksonville	210	44	72	12	42	343	423	581	1004	12	78	0.62	19	1	36	238	8.13
2012	Rk	Elizabethton	232	44	58	14	45	250	307	496	802	8	67	0.25	4	0	43	246	5.60
2013	A	Cedar Rapids	508	83	141	27	109	278	319	526	845	6	77	0.27	10	0	46	248	5.78
2014	A+	Fort Myers	505	78	124	25	94	246	306	436	742	8	69	0.28	9	5	36	190	4.65

Athletic OF with big-time power and led FSL in both HR and K. Chases pitches frequently and pulls head off ball. Improved walk rate, but more due to being pitched around. Has among best raw power in minors, though lacks secondary skills. Improving defender with good speed for size.

Walker,Christian — 3 — Baltimore

EXP MLB DEBUT: 2014 | H/W: 6-0 220 | FUT: Starting 1B | 7B

Bats R Age 24 — 2012 (4) South Carolina

Pwr +++ | BAvg +++ | Spd + | Def +++

Year	Lev	Team	AB	R	H	HR	RBI	Avg	OB	Slg	OPS	bb%	ct%	Eye	SB	CS	x/h%	Iso	RC/G
2013	A+	Frederick	215	25	62	8	35	288	341	479	820	7	81	0.41	2	0	40	191	5.54
2013	AA	Bowie	62	7	15	0	1	242	309	323	631	9	84	0.60	0	0	33	81	3.54
2014	AA	Bowie	366	58	110	20	77	301	366	516	883	9	77	0.46	2	1	34	216	6.40
2014	AAA	Norfolk	166	15	43	6	19	259	332	428	759	10	70	0.37	0	0	37	169	5.04
2014	MLB	Baltimore	18	1	3	1	1	167	211	389	599	5	50	0.11	0	0	67	222	3.47

Instinctual hitter who set easy high in HR. Power emerging due to pulling more and using natural bat speed. Tweaked approach to be more disciplined and focused on OBP. Improved defender with textbook feet and nice hands. Won't steal many bases as he lacks speed and athleticism.

Walker,Jared — 5 — Los Angeles (N)

EXP MLB DEBUT: 2018 | H/W: 6-2 195 | FUT: Starting 3B | 7D

Bats L Age 19 — 2014 (5) HS (GA)

Pwr ++ | BAvg +++ | Spd ++ | Def ++

Year	Lev	Team	AB	R	H	HR	RBI	Avg	OB	Slg	OPS	bb%	ct%	Eye	SB	CS	x/h%	Iso	RC/G
2014	Rk	AZL Dodgers	104	18	24	1	13	231	355	327	682	16	67	0.59	6	4	29	96	4.36

LHH has a good line-drive approach with raw power. Struggled in a brief stint in the AZL and will need time to adjust. Good athlete but actions are a bit stiff at 3B and needs to develop better footwork. Raw talent that needs work and to find a long-term position.

Walker,Keenyn — 89 — Chicago (A)

EXP MLB DEBUT: 2015 | H/W: 6-3 190 | FUT: Starting OF | 7D

Bats B Age 24 — 2011 (1-S) Central AZ JC

Pwr ++ | BAvg ++ | Spd ++++ | Def ++++

Year	Lev	Team	AB	R	H	HR	RBI	Avg	OB	Slg	OPS	bb%	ct%	Eye	SB	CS	x/h%	Iso	RC/G
2012	A	Kannapolis	266	53	75	1	39	282	396	387	783	16	65	0.54	39	11	28	105	6.08
2012	A+	Winston-Salem	143	31	34	3	16	238	347	364	711	14	65	0.48	17	4	32	126	4.74
2013	AA	Birmingham	462	77	93	3	32	201	305	277	582	13	67	0.45	38	15	26	76	2.76
2014	A+	Winston-Salem	230	27	50	0	21	217	294	278	572	10	63	0.29	20	3	22	61	2.60
2014	AA	Birmingham	110	15	17	2	4	155	231	236	468	9	50	0.20	11	2	24	82	0.95

Long, lean OF who can't get past High-A. Demoted in June after major struggles. Strikes out too often for prospect with limited pop. Not much feel for bat control or contact, though has slap and dash approach. Exhibits plus-plus speed and is terrific defender with strong, accurate arm.

Wall,Forrest — 4 — Colorado

EXP MLB DEBUT: 2018 | H/W: 6-0 176 | FUT: Starting 2B | 8D

Bats L Age 19 — 2014 (1) HS (FL)

Pwr ++ | BAvg ++++ | Spd +++ | Def +++

Year	Lev	Team	AB	R	H	HR	RBI	Avg	OB	Slg	OPS	bb%	ct%	Eye	SB	CS	x/h%	Iso	RC/G
2014	Rk	Grand Junction	157	48	50	3	24	318	418	490	909	15	80	0.84	18	5	30	172	7.27

Quick, compact LH stroke generates good bat speed. Stays back and balanced even against off-speed stuff, which allows him to make consistent, hard contact. Currently has more of a line-drive approach, but has the size and swing to hit 15-20 home runs in the majors.

Wallach,Chad — 2 — Cincinnati

EXP MLB DEBUT: 2016 | H/W: 6-3 210 | FUT: Starting C | 7D

Bats R Age 23 — 2013 (5) Cal St Fullerton

Pwr ++ | BAvg +++ | Spd ++ | Def +++

Year	Lev	Team	AB	R	H	HR	RBI	Avg	OB	Slg	OPS	bb%	ct%	Eye	SB	CS	x/h%	Iso	RC/G
2012	NCAA	Cal St. Fullerton	68	7	14	0	7	206	270	265	535	8	82	0.50	1	0	29	59	2.27
2013	NCAA	Cal St. Fullerton	162	24	50	2	32	309	367	444	812	8	90	0.88	2	2	34	136	5.67
2013	A-	Batavia	146	19	33	0	13	226	280	267	547	7	82	0.41	0	0	18	41	2.30
2014	A	Greensboro	271	50	87	7	49	321	427	476	903	16	86	1.28	3	0	31	155	7.10
2014	A+	Jupiter	64	4	21	0	8	328	434	375	809	16	89	1.71	0	0	14	47	6.14

23-year-old backstop had a breakout season. Line-drive approach doesn't figure to translate to plus power, but he controls the strike zone and shoots balls into the gaps. Solid defender with a good arm and should be able stick at CA. A bit old for this level, he'll need to repeat it against better competition.

Ward,Drew — 5 — Washington

EXP MLB DEBUT: 2018 | H/W: 6-4 210 | FUT: Starting 3B/1B | 7C

Bats L Age 20 — 2013 (3) HS (OK)

Pwr ++++ | BAvg +++ | Spd ++ | Def +++

Year	Lev	Team	AB	R	H	HR	RBI	Avg	OB	Slg	OPS	bb%	ct%	Eye	SB	CS	x/h%	Iso	RC/G
2013	Rk	GCL Nationals	168	24	49	1	28	292	383	387	770	13	74	0.57	2	4	29	95	5.45
2014	A	Hagerstown	431	45	116	10	73	269	334	413	747	9	72	0.35	2	2	34	144	4.88

Took on a full-season assignment at 19 years old, and held his own. Evaluators laud his current good approach, and see an above-average BA as well as additional power that is on its way from his smooth LH swing. He may outgrow 3B and move to first, which would put pressure on his bat to perform.

Wates,Austin — 8 — Miami

EXP MLB DEBUT: 2015 | H/W: 6-1 180 | FUT: Backup OF | 6B

Bats R Age 26 — 2010 (3) Virginia Tech

Pwr + | BAvg +++ | Spd ++++ | Def +++

Year	Lev	Team	AB	R	H	HR	RBI	Avg	OB	Slg	OPS	bb%	ct%	Eye	SB	CS	x/h%	Iso	RC/G
2012	AA	Corpus Christi	359	58	109	7	48	304	359	429	788	8	80	0.44	17	11	25	125	5.24
2013	AA	Corpus Christi	87	14	27	1	5	310	406	448	854	14	79	0.78	11	1	26	138	6.54
2013	AAA	Oklahoma City	49	5	15	0	5	306	333	347	680	4	94	0.67	4	0	13	41	3.97
2014	AAA	New Orleans	111	18	28	0	0	252	308	333	642	8	80	0.41	6	2	29	81	3.52
2014	AAA	Oklahoma City	281	44	84	2	30	299	392	381	773	13	84	0.96	31	4	19	82	5.44

Natural-hitting OF bounced back from a broken arm. Was traded to the Marlins in July. Nice balanced swing and bat control. Likes to go to opp field with inside-out stroke and rarely pulls ball. Has 4th OF profile as he lacks power and isn't great defender. Has OK arm and instincts.

Wendle,Joe — 4 — Oakland

EXP MLB DEBUT: 2015 | H/W: 5-11 190 | FUT: Starting 2B | 7D

Bats L Age 24
2012 (6) West Chester
Pwr ++
BAvg +++
Spd +++
Def ++

Year	Lev	Team	AB	R	H	HR	RBI	Avg	OB	Slg	OPS	bb%	ct%	Eye	SB	CS	x/h%	Iso	RC/G
2012	NCAA	West Chester	198	64	79	12	59	399	476	768	1243	13	97	5.80	12	1	51	369	10.57
2012	A-	Mahoning Val	245	32	80	4	37	327	365	469	835	6	90	0.60	4	1	29	143	5.71
2013	A+	Carolina	413	73	122	16	64	295	363	513	877	10	81	0.56	10	2	43	218	6.42
2014	Rk	AZL Indians	22	8	10	0	4	455	538	591	1129	15	82	1.00	1	1	20	136	10.17
2014	AA	Akron	336	46	85	8	50	253	307	414	720	7	83	0.46	4	2	39	161	4.41

Short INF missed time with broken bone in hand. Possesses natural hitting skills with innate feel for contact. Won't hit for ton of power, but can jerk balls out on pull side. Knows limitations in game and uses instincts to advantage. Not a great runner, but good enough and has OK range.

Westbrook,Jamie — 4 — Arizona

EXP MLB DEBUT: 2017 | H/W: 5-9 170 | FUT: Backup 2B | 6C

Bats R Age 19
2013 (5) HS (AZ)
Pwr ++
BAvg ++
Spd ++
Def +++

Year	Lev	Team	AB	R	H	HR	RBI	Avg	OB	Slg	OPS	bb%	ct%	Eye	SB	CS	x/h%	Iso	RC/G
2013	Rk	AZL Dbacks	154	31	45	1	20	292	363	468	830	10	86	0.81	3	3	38	175	6.07
2013	Rk	Missoula	67	12	17	1	13	254	315	343	658	8	70	0.30	1	0	24	90	3.62
2014	A	South Bend	509	69	132	8	49	259	311	375	686	7	81	0.39	6	3	30	116	3.95

Natural hitter has a nice compact RH stroke, but tends to try to pull everything. Despite being just 5-9 he does have some pop and has average speed. Played SS in HS, but the move to 2B was logical given his size and limited range. Defensively he moves well and has good hands.

Wick,Rowan — 9 — St. Louis

EXP MLB DEBUT: 2017 | H/W: 6-3 220 | FUT: Backup OF | 6B

Bats R Age 22
2012 (9) Cypress JC
Pwr +++
BAvg ++
Spd ++
Def ++

Year	Lev	Team	AB	R	H	HR	RBI	Avg	OB	Slg	OPS	bb%	ct%	Eye	SB	CS	x/h%	Iso	RC/G
2012	NCAA	Cypress College	87	15	27	6	22	310	375	586	961	9	82	0.56	1	0	41	276	7.25
2012	Rk	GCL Cardinals	77	9	12	1	8	156	207	273	480	6	73	0.24	1	1	50	117	1.17
2013	Rk	Johnson City	207	28	53	10	35	256	350	464	814	13	66	0.42	2	1	42	208	6.09
2014	A-	State College	119	30	45	14	38	378	468	815	1283	14	71	0.59	1	1	51	437	12.27
2014	A	Peoria	141	21	31	6	22	220	286	433	718	8	57	0.22	4	0	52	213	5.09

Strong-bodied player has some of the best raw power in the system. Killed it in short-season ball, but struggled when moved up. Can be overly aggressive at the plate hunting for power, and is not likely to hit for average. The Cards are attempting to convert him from behind the plate to the OF.

Wilkins,Andy — 3 — Chicago (A)

EXP MLB DEBUT: 2013 | H/W: 6-1 220 | FUT: Starting 1B | 7D

Bats L Age 26
2010 (5) Arkansas
Pwr ++++
BAvg ++
Spd +
Def ++

Year	Lev	Team	AB	R	H	HR	RBI	Avg	OB	Slg	OPS	bb%	ct%	Eye	SB	CS	x/h%	Iso	RC/G
2012	AA	Birmingham	435	68	104	17	69	239	335	425	761	13	78	0.67	6	4	44	186	5.09
2013	AA	Birmingham	243	37	70	10	49	288	384	477	862	14	76	0.66	3	0	37	189	6.47
2013	AAA	Charlotte	215	25	57	7	30	265	310	423	733	6	76	0.27	2	1	35	158	4.42
2014	AAA	Charlotte	491	79	144	30	85	293	339	558	897	6	81	0.37	0	1	48	265	6.34
2014	MLB	Chi White Sox	43	2	6	0	2	140	178	186	364	4	49	0.09	0	0	33	47	-0.81

Big, strong 1B who led IL in HR after slow start. Changed set-up and swing to generate more bat speed and has leverage and loft for plus pop. Can hit LHP, but has aggressive approach and can overswing. Also can be pull-conscious. Limited to 1B with subpar range and has very little speed.

Williams,Justin — 79 — Tampa Bay

EXP MLB DEBUT: 2018 | H/W: 6-2 215 | FUT: Starting LF | 8D

Bats L Age 19
2013 (2) HS (LA)
Pwr +++
BAvg ++
Spd ++
Def ++

Year	Lev	Team	AB	R	H	HR	RBI	Avg	OB	Slg	OPS	bb%	ct%	Eye	SB	CS	x/h%	Iso	RC/G
2013	Rk	Missoula	51	12	21	0	5	412	423	529	952	2	86	0.14	0	0	29	118	6.81
2013	Rk	AZL Dbacks	148	17	51	1	32	345	378	446	824	5	76	0.23	0	1	25	101	5.66
2013	A	South Bend	9	3	1	0	0	111	273	111	384	18	78	1.00	0	0	0	0	0.44
2014	Rk	Missoula	189	31	73	2	23	386	437	471	908	8	77	0.39	1	1	14	85	6.85
2014	A	South Bend	102	16	29	2	23	284	330	461	791	6	77	0.30	0	1	38	176	5.32

Physically mature OF had another impressive season, hitting a combined .351/.403/.467. Was then traded to the Rays. Has good speed and projectable power, but is raw in the OF and power is not yet game-useable. Can be overly aggressive at the plate, but made nice progress in '14.

Williams,Mason — 8 — New York (A)

EXP MLB DEBUT: 2015 | H/W: 6-1 180 | FUT: Starting OF | 7E

Bats L Age 23
2010 (4) HS (FL)
Pwr ++
BAvg ++
Spd ++++
Def ++++

Year	Lev	Team	AB	R	H	HR	RBI	Avg	OB	Slg	OPS	bb%	ct%	Eye	SB	CS	x/h%	Iso	RC/G
2012	A	CharlestonSC	276	55	84	8	28	304	354	489	843	7	88	0.64	19	9	37	185	5.85
2012	A+	Tampa	83	13	23	3	7	277	302	422	724	3	83	0.21	1	4	26	145	4.08
2013	A+	Tampa	406	56	106	3	24	261	326	350	676	9	85	0.64	15	9	25	89	4.03
2013	AA	Trenton	72	7	11	1	4	153	164	264	428	1	75	0.06	0	0	45	111	0.36
2014	AA	Trenton	507	67	113	5	40	223	289	304	593	8	87	0.69	21	8	24	81	3.07

Excellent athlete who has stalled in AA. Still remains a plus defender in CF with excellent range and shrewd instincts. Tracks down balls with plus speed and quickness. Fringy bat speed and inconsistent slap approach limit upside. BA regressing and only has average pop potential.

Williams,Nick — 789 — Texas

EXP MLB DEBUT: 2017 | H/W: 6-3 195 | FUT: Starting OF | 8D

Bats L Age 21
2012 (2) HS (TX)
Pwr +++
BAvg +++
Spd +++
Def +++

Year	Lev	Team	AB	R	H	HR	RBI	Avg	OB	Slg	OPS	bb%	ct%	Eye	SB	CS	x/h%	Iso	RC/G
2012	Rk	AZL Rangers	201	34	63	2	27	313	364	448	812	7	75	0.32	15	2	27	134	5.70
2013	A	Hickory	376	70	110	17	60	293	320	543	862	4	71	0.14	8	5	44	250	6.26
2014	Rk	AZL Rangers	13	3	4	0	2	308	357	462	819	7	85	0.50	0	0	25	154	5.77
2014	A+	Myrtle Beach	377	61	110	13	68	292	326	491	816	5	69	0.16	5	7	41	199	5.76
2014	AA	Frisco	62	4	14	0	4	226	250	290	540	3	66	0.10	1	1	21	65	1.88

Aggressive hitter who continues to struggle with strikeouts, but entices with natural talents. Generates easy bat speed and swing fluidity allows for nice BA despite approach. Rarely walks, though can hit LHP. Could have more SB with higher OBP and could breakout in power department.

Williamson,Mac — 9 — San Francisco

EXP MLB DEBUT: 2016 | H/W: 6-5 240 | FUT: Starting OF | 8D

Bats R Age 24
2012 (3) Wake Forest
Pwr ++++
BAvg +++
Spd +++
Def ++

Year	Lev	Team	AB	R	H	HR	RBI	Avg	OB	Slg	OPS	bb%	ct%	Eye	SB	CS	x/h%	Iso	RC/G
2012	NCAA	Wake Forest	192	42	55	17	52	286	363	589	951	11	79	0.56	12	3	44	302	7.14
2012	Rk	AZL Giants	17	4	3	2	7	176	263	529	793	11	71	0.40	0	0	67	353	5.02
2012	A-	Salem-Kaizer	114	22	39	7	25	342	375	596	971	5	83	0.32	0	0	38	254	7.06
2013	A+	San Jose	520	94	152	25	89	292	356	504	859	9	75	0.39	10	1	38	212	6.20
2014	A+	San Jose	85	16	27	3	11	318	408	506	914	13	84	0.93	6	1	37	188	7.06

Big, physical OF came out of ST, showing improved ct% and better plate discipline in a small sample before TJS ended his season. There is some swing-and-miss in his game, but shows good power to all fields, draws walks, and makes adjustments. He runs well for his size, shows solid range and a strong arm in RF.

Wilson,Austin — 79 — Seattle

EXP MLB DEBUT: 2016 | H/W: 6-4 250 | FUT: Starting OF | 8D

Bats R Age 23
2013 (2) Stanford
Pwr ++++
BAvg ++
Spd +++
Def +++

Year	Lev	Team	AB	R	H	HR	RBI	Avg	OB	Slg	OPS	bb%	ct%	Eye	SB	CS	x/h%	Iso	RC/G
2012	NCAA	Stanford	221	56	63	10	54	285	355	493	848	10	80	0.55	7	0	38	208	6.01
2013	NCAA	Stanford	118	26	34	5	26	288	359	475	833	10	85	0.72	5	2	35	186	5.81
2013	A-	Everett	203	22	49	6	27	241	300	414	714	8	79	0.40	2	4	41	172	4.31
2014	Rk	AZL Mariners	8	3	5	1	1	625	667	1375	2042	11	75	0.50	1	0	60	750	22.33
2014	A	Clinton	261	38	76	12	54	291	355	517	873	9	75	0.40	1	1	42	226	6.42

Powerful, athletic OF who missed most of 2nd half of season with strained Achilles. Provides significant strength and impressive raw tools. Projects to plus power due to additional loft in stroke. Runs very well which enhances RF play. Exhibits plus arm, but routes and jumps are raw.

Wilson,Jacob — 45 — St. Louis

EXP MLB DEBUT: 2015 | H/W: 5-11 180 | FUT: Utility INF | 6B

Bats R Age 24
2012 (10) Memphis
Pwr ++
BAvg +++
Spd ++
Def +++

Year	Lev	Team	AB	R	H	HR	RBI	Avg	OB	Slg	OPS	bb%	ct%	Eye	SB	CS	x/h%	Iso	RC/G
2012	A-	Batavia	160	28	44	6	25	275	329	444	773	8	79	0.39	2	1	32	169	4.95
2013	A	Peoria	348	63	92	15	72	264	340	468	809	10	84	0.74	6	5	43	204	5.56
2013	A+	Palm Beach	117	12	21	3	10	179	284	291	574	13	83	0.85	0	1	33	111	2.85
2014	A+	Palm Beach	121	18	36	0	20	298	361	397	758	9	80	0.50	0	0	33	99	5.07
2014	AA	Springfield	131	15	40	5	21	305	359	519	878	8	82	0.48	3	1	45	214	6.30

Has a good idea of what he is doing at the plate and gets the most of his ability. Hit the ball well, but season was cut short by injury. Bounced back in the AFL and should be ready for the majors. Can be overly aggressive, but makes consistent contact and has good gap power.

Wilson,Marcus — 8 — Arizona

EXP MLB DEBUT: 2018 | H/W: 6-3 175 | FUT: Starting CF | 7E

Bats R Age 18
2014 (2) HS (CA)
Pwr ++
BAvg ++
Spd +++
Def +++

Year	Lev	Team	AB	R	H	HR	RBI	Avg	OB	Slg	OPS	bb%	ct%	Eye	SB	CS	x/h%	Iso	RC/G
2014	Rk	AZL Dbacks	131	15	27	1	22	206	293	275	567	11	69	0.40	4	2	19	69	2.46

Dreadful debut, hitting .208 with no power. Raw, but toolsy OF with of athleticism. Lean and projectable with good bat speed and should add moderate power. Speed is best current tool and gives him the potential to stick in CF. Raw talent, but tons of work to do.

Winker,Jesse

7 | Cincinnati | EXP MLB DEBUT: 2016 | H/W: 6-3 210 | FUT: Starting LF | 8B

Bats L Age 21
2012 (1) HS (FL)

- Pwr ++++
- BAvg ++++
- Spd ++
- Def ++

Year	Lev	Team	AB	R	H	HR	RBI	Avg	OB	Slg	OPS	bb%	ct%	Eye	SB	CS	x/h%	Iso	RC/G
2012	Rk	Billings	228	42	77	5	35	338	437	500	937	15	78	0.80	1	3	31	162	7.64
2013	A	Dayton	417	73	117	16	76	281	375	463	838	13	82	0.84	6	1	33	182	6.09
2014	A+	Bakersfield	205	42	65	13	49	317	429	580	1009	16	78	0.87	5	1	43	263	8.43
2014	AA	Pensacola	77	15	16	2	8	208	330	351	680	15	71	0.64	0	0	44	143	4.18

Crushed High-A pitching and reached AA at 20 y/o before tendon injury cut season short. Disciplined hitter with advanced approach and plus power to all fields. Makes hard contact against LHP and RHP. Plus pitch recognition and strength compensates for average bat speed.

Wisdom,Patrick

5 | St. Louis | EXP MLB DEBUT: 2016 | H/W: 6-2 210 | FUT: Reserve 3B | 6C

Bats R Age 23
2012 (S-1) St. Marys

- Pwr +++
- BAvg ++
- Spd ++
- Def +++

Year	Lev	Team	AB	R	H	HR	RBI	Avg	OB	Slg	OPS	bb%	ct%	Eye	SB	CS	x/h%	Iso	RC/G
2012	NCAA	St. Mary's (CA)	191	39	50	9	24	262	382	476	858	16	77	0.86	4	2	44	215	6.51
2012	A-	Batavia	241	40	68	6	32	282	364	465	829	11	76	0.53	2	1	40	183	6.07
2013	A	Peoria	372	54	86	13	62	231	309	411	720	10	69	0.37	4	1	43	180	4.56
2013	A+	Palm Beach	92	8	23	2	11	250	317	359	676	9	75	0.39	1	0	26	109	3.82
2014	AA	Springfield	452	49	97	14	53	215	277	367	644	8	67	0.26	5	1	38	153	3.41

52nd overall pick from 2012 is looking like a bust. Has average bat speed, moderate power, but approach at the plate has not developed and he struck out a career-high 149 times with a career-low OPS. Has good athleticism, but is a below-average runner and is limited to a corner INF slot.

Wolters,Tony

24 | Cleveland | EXP MLB DEBUT: 2015 | H/W: 5-10 180 | FUT: Utility player | 6B

Bats L Age 22
2010 (3) HS (CA)

- Pwr ++
- BAvg +++
- Spd ++
- Def ++

Year	Lev	Team	AB	R	H	HR	RBI	Avg	OB	Slg	OPS	bb%	ct%	Eye	SB	CS	x/h%	Iso	RC/G
2010	Rk	AZL Indians	19	2	4	0	3	211	286	211	496	10	74	0.40	2	0	0	0	1.44
2011	A-	Mahoning Val	267	50	78	1	20	292	364	363	727	10	82	0.61	19	4	18	71	4.68
2012	A+	Carolina	485	66	126	8	58	260	311	404	715	7	79	0.35	5	9	37	144	4.35
2013	A+	Carolina	289	36	80	3	33	277	367	353	720	12	80	0.71	3	6	20	76	4.66
2014	AA	Akron	341	36	85	1	34	249	319	314	633	9	78	0.47	3	2	21	65	3.42

Improving receiver who can also play middle infield. Moves well behind plate with agility and quickness. Quick release enhances strong arm. Gets on base with mature approach and has feel for bat, but struggles with LHP and has below average pop. Ideal utility player with lefty stroke.

Wong,Kean

4 | Tampa Bay | EXP MLB DEBUT: 2017 | H/W: 5-11 190 | FUT: Starting 2B | 7B

Bats L Age 19
2013 (4) HS (HI)

- Pwr ++
- BAvg ++++
- Spd ++
- Def +++

Year	Lev	Team	AB	R	H	HR	RBI	Avg	OB	Slg	OPS	bb%	ct%	Eye	SB	CS	x/h%	Iso	RC/G
2013	Rk	GCL Devil Rays	177	27	58	0	22	328	367	390	757	6	88	0.50	7	1	16	62	4.83
2014	A	Bowling Green	422	56	129	2	24	306	347	370	717	6	83	0.37	13	7	16	64	4.29

Short, instinctual INF who is tough out and finished 2nd in MWL in BA. Steady defender with sufficient range and hands. Arm best suited for 2B. Possesses ideal bat control for a #2 hitter and makes contact with compact stroke. Not much thunder in stick and isn't much of a runner.

Wren,Kyle

8 | Milwaukee | EXP MLB DEBUT: 2016 | H/W: 5-10 175 | FUT: Starting CF | 7C

Bats L Age 23
2013 (8) Georgia Tech

- Pwr +
- BAvg +++
- Spd +++++
- Def +++

Year	Lev	Team	AB	R	H	HR	RBI	Avg	OB	Slg	OPS	bb%	ct%	Eye	SB	CS	x/h%	Iso	RC/G
2013	Rk	Danville	22	6	9	0	4	409	458	636	1095	8	86	0.67	3	0	44	227	9.15
2013	A	Rome	195	36	64	2	20	328	379	456	836	8	89	0.76	32	6	27	128	5.88
2013	A+	Lynchburg	1	0	0	0	0	0	500	0	500	50	100		0	1		0	4.75
2014	A+	Lynchburg	291	46	86	0	27	296	361	357	719	9	87	0.77	33	9	16	62	4.62
2014	AA	Mississippi	205	28	58	0	16	283	335	376	710	7	80	0.40	13	5	26	93	4.37

Short, fleet-footed OF doesn't have much power and has hit just 2 HR as a pro. Prototypical lead-off hitter who has a patient approach and makes consistent contact. Is a plus runner and stole 46 bases. Covers ground well and takes good routes, but has a below-average arm.

Wright,Ryan

4 | Cincinnati | EXP MLB DEBUT: 2016 | H/W: 6-1 200 | FUT: Starting 2B | 7C

Bats R Age 25
2011 (5) Louisville

- Pwr ++
- BAvg ++
- Spd +++
- Def +++

Year	Lev	Team	AB	R	H	HR	RBI	Avg	OB	Slg	OPS	bb%	ct%	Eye	SB	CS	x/h%	Iso	RC/G
2012	A	Dayton	389	53	111	5	50	285	340	424	764	8	87	0.63	14	1	34	139	5.04
2012	A+	Bakersfield	96	17	26	5	16	271	286	521	807	2	82	0.12	3	1	46	250	5.03
2013	A+	Bakersfield	411	53	109	8	52	265	309	384	693	6	84	0.39	5	3	29	119	3.99
2014	A+	Bakersfield	241	46	75	8	41	311	339	498	837	4	87	0.31	7	1	36	187	5.52
2014	AA	Pensacola	219	23	45	2	17	205	240	288	528	4	77	0.20	2	1	31	82	1.78

Lacks plus tool, but consistent performer. Tools play up due to instincts and work ethic, including HRs despite below-average power and SB with average speed. Ct% dipped at AA but should adjust. Knows the strike zone and utilizes compact stroke and contact-first approach. Solid defender.

Yarbrough,Alex

4 | Los Angeles (A) | EXP MLB DEBUT: 2015 | H/W: 6-0 195 | FUT: Starting 2B | 7C

Bats B Age 23
2012 (4) Mississippi

- Pwr ++
- BAvg +++
- Spd ++
- Def ++

Year	Lev	Team	AB	R	H	HR	RBI	Avg	OB	Slg	OPS	bb%	ct%	Eye	SB	CS	x/h%	Iso	RC/G
2012	NCAA	Mississippi	250	43	95	3	43	380	430	508	938	8	90	0.92	4	0	24	128	7.03
2012	A	Cedar Rapids	244	35	70	0	27	287	315	410	725	4	92	0.50	9	2	30	123	4.53
2012	AA	Arkansas	18	1	2	0	0	111	111	167	278	0	83	0.00	0	0	50	56	-1.10
2013	A+	Inland Empire	582	77	182	11	80	313	343	459	802	4	82	0.25	14	4	29	146	5.22
2014	AA	Arkansas	544	66	155	5	77	285	326	397	723	6	77	0.27	6	6	30	112	4.39

Underrated INF who won TL MVP with solid production with bat and glove. Hits for BA despite aggressive approach and tendency to expand K zone. Produces gap power and has enough speed to leg out extra base hits. Lacks range and arm to be standout defender, but maximizes fringy tools.

Yastrzemski,Mike

789 | Baltimore | EXP MLB DEBUT: 2015 | H/W: 5-11 180 | FUT: Fourth OF | 6A

Bats L Age 24
2013 (14) Vanderbilt

- Pwr ++
- BAvg +++
- Spd +++
- Def +++

Year	Lev	Team	AB	R	H	HR	RBI	Avg	OB	Slg	OPS	bb%	ct%	Eye	SB	CS	x/h%	Iso	RC/G
2014	A	Delmarva	258	52	79	10	44	306	354	554	908	7	75	0.30	12	4	43	248	6.88
2014	A+	Frederick	93	21	29	1	19	312	366	462	829	8	83	0.50	5	0	34	151	5.85
2014	AA	Bowie	184	23	46	3	12	250	303	413	716	7	82	0.41	1	2	43	163	4.42

Breakout prospect who hit well on three levels. Can hit LHP, though lacks long ball pop to profile to everyday player. Smooth, fast bat and natural feel allow for high BA and runs bases with polished instincts despite average speed. May not have standout tool, but has myriad of skills.

Yrizarri,Yeyson

46 | Texas | EXP MLB DEBUT: 2018 | H/W: 6-0 175 | FUT: Starting SS | 7C

Bats R Age 18
2013 FA (Venezuela)

- Pwr ++
- BAvg ++
- Spd +++
- Def +++

Year	Lev	Team	AB	R	H	HR	RBI	Avg	OB	Slg	OPS	bb%	ct%	Eye	SB	CS	x/h%	Iso	RC/G
2014	Rk	DSL Rangers	43	7	13	0	6	302	348	419	766	7	91	0.75	1	1	31	116	5.13
2014	Rk	AZL Rangers	190	23	45	1	19	237	271	332	603	5	81	0.25	5	3	33	95	2.87

Quick, athletic INF with ability to play either middle infield spot. Has room to grow into lean frame, yet still exhibits doubles power at present. Needs to use entire field to take advantage of bat speed. Not the fastest guy, but can steal bases with polished instincts. Owns good feel for glove.

Zagunis,Mark

279 | Chicago (N) | EXP MLB DEBUT: 2017 | H/W: 6-0 205 | FUT: Starting C | 7D

Bats R Age 22
2014 (3) Virginia Tech

- Pwr ++
- BAvg +++
- Spd +++
- Def +++

Year	Lev	Team	AB	R	H	HR	RBI	Avg	OB	Slg	OPS	bb%	ct%	Eye	SB	CS	x/h%	Iso	RC/G
2013	NCAA	Virginia Tech	232	62	79	9	51	341	420	543	964	12	88	1.10	19	5	33	203	7.52
2014	NCAA	Virginia Tech	209	44	69	2	39	330	419	426	845	13	90	1.60	16	3	20	96	6.37
2014	Rk	AZL Cubs	8	1	1	0	1	125	222	250	472	11	75	0.50	0	0	100	125	1.45
2014	A-	Boise	154	32	46	2	27	299	416	422	838	17	80	1.00	11	2	28	123	6.47
2014	A	Kane County	50	11	14	0	4	280	400	440	840	17	82	1.11	5	0	50	160	6.64

Compact, line-drive approach and good plate discipline give him the tools to hit for avg, but not much power. Moves well behind the plate with solid catch and throw skills and blocks balls well. Above-avg runner and split time in the OF at Virginia Tech. Nice pro debut, hitting combined .288 with 16 SB.

Zimmer,Bradley

89 | Cleveland | EXP MLB DEBUT: 2016 | H/W: 6-4 185 | FUT: Starting OF | 8C

Bats L Age 22
2014 (1) San Francisco

- Pwr +++
- BAvg +++
- Spd +++
- Def +++

Year	Lev	Team	AB	R	H	HR	RBI	Avg	OB	Slg	OPS	bb%	ct%	Eye	SB	CS	x/h%	Iso	RC/G
2012	NCAA	San Francisco	153	17	37	0	15	242	261	314	575	3	80	0.13	3	0	27	72	2.40
2013	NCAA	San Francisco	203	48	65	7	37	320	405	512	917	13	85	0.94	19	8	34	192	7.05
2014	NCAA	San Francisco	220	42	81	7	31	368	446	573	1019	12	85	0.91	21	11	30	205	8.30
2014	A-	Mahoning Val	168	32	51	4	30	304	374	464	839	10	82	0.63	11	4	33	161	6.01
2014	A	Lake County	11	4	3	2	2	273	385	909	1294	15	73	0.67	1	0	100	636	11.97

Tall, lean OF with evidence of all five tools. Could be either CF or corner OF depending on development of range and power. Exhibits above average wheels while currently hitting for high BA with gap power. Hits hard line drives to all fields and covers plate with simple, repeatable stroke.

Pitchers are classified as Starters (SP) or Relievers (RP).

THROWS: Handedness — right (RH) or left (LH).

AGE: Pitcher's age, as of April 1, 2015.

DRAFTED: The year, round, and school that the pitcher performed at as an amateur if drafted, or the year and country where the player was signed from, if a free agent.

EXP MLB DEBUT: The year a player is expected to debut in the major leagues.

H/W: The player's height and weight.

FUT: The role that the pitcher is expected to have for the majority of his major league career, not necessarily his greatest upside.

PITCHES: Each pitch that a pitcher throws is graded and designated with a "+", indicating the quality of the pitch, taking into context the pitcher's age and level pitched. Pitches are graded for their velocity, movement, and command. An average pitch will receive three "+" marks. If known, a pitcher's velocity for each pitch is indicated.

FB	fastball
CB	curveball
SP	split-fingered fastball
SL	slider
CU	change-up
CT	cut-fastball
KC	knuckle-curve
KB	knuckle-ball
SC	screwball
SU	slurve

PLAYER STAT LINES: Pitchers receive statistics for the last five teams that they played for (if applicable), including college and the major leagues.

TEAM DESIGNATIONS: Each team that the pitcher performed for during a given year is included.

LEVEL DESIGNATIONS: The level for each team a player performed is included. "AAA" means Triple-A, "AA" means Double-A, "A+" means high Class-A, "A-" means low Class-A and "Rk" means rookie level.

SABERMETRIC CATEGORIES: Descriptions of all the sabermetric categories appear in the glossary.

CAPSULE COMMENTARIES: For each pitcher, a brief analysis of their skills/statistics, and their future potential is provided.

ELIGIBILITY: Eligibility for inclusion is the standard for which Major League Baseball adheres to; 50 innings pitched or 45 days on the 25-man roster, not including the month of September.

POTENTIAL RATINGS: The Potential Ratings are a two-part system in which a player is assigned a number rating based on his upside potential (1-10) and a letter rating based on the probability of reaching that potential (A-E).

Potential

10:	Hall of Famer	5:	MLB reserve
9:	Elite player	4:	Top minor leaguer
8:	Solid regular	3:	Average minor leaguer
7:	Average regular	2:	Minor league reserve
6:	Platoon player	1:	Minor league roster filler

Probability Rating

A:	90% probability of reaching potential
B:	70% probability of reaching potential
C:	50% probability of reaching potential
D:	30% probability of reaching potential
E:	10% probability of reaching potential

FASTBALL: Scouts grade a fastball in terms of both velocity and movement. Movement of a pitch is purely subjective, but one can always watch the hitter to see how he reacts to a pitch or if he swings and misses. Pitchers throw four types of fastballs with varying movement. A two-seam fastball is often referred to as a sinker. A four-seam fastball appears to maintain its plane at high velocities. A cutter can move in different directions and is caused by the pitcher both cutting-off his extension out front and by varying the grip. A split-fingered fastball (forkball) is thrown with the fingers spread apart against the seams and demonstrates violent downward movement. Velocity is often graded on the 20-80 scale and is indicated by the chart below.

Scout Grade	Velocity (mph)
80	96+
70	94-95
60	92-93
50 (avg)	89-91
40	87-88
30	85-86
20	82-84

PITCHER RELEASE TIMES: The speed (in seconds) that a pitcher releases a pitch from the stretch is extremely important in terms of halting the running game and establishing good pitching mechanics. Pitchers are timed from the movement of the front leg until the baseball reaches the catcher's mitt. The phrases "slow to the plate" or "quick to the plate" may often appear in the capsule commentary box.

1.0-1.2	+
1.3-1.4	MLB average
1.5+	−

Adam, Jason — SP — Minnesota

EXP MLB DEBUT: 2015 | H/W: 6-4 225 | FUT: #4 starter | **7C**

Thrws R Age 23
2010 (5) HS (KS)
88-95 FB +++
75-79 CB +++
82-85 CU ++

Year	Lev	Team	W	L	Sv	IP	K	ERA	WHIP	BF/G	OBA	H%	S%	xERA	Ctl	Dom	Cmd	hr/9	BPV
2012	A+	Wilmington	7	12	0	158	123	3.53	1.16	23.3	249	29	73	3.55	2.1	7.0	3.4	1.0	89
2013	AA	NW Arkansas	8	11	0	144	126	5.19	1.44	23.6	274	33	64	4.30	3.4	7.9	2.3	0.8	69
2014	AA	NW Arkansas	4	8	0	98	89	5.05	1.40	21.8	279	34	64	4.34	2.8	8.2	3.0	0.8	91
2014	AAA	Omaha	1	1	0	15	11	2.38	1.39	7.9	285	35	81	3.66	2.4	6.6	2.8	0.0	72
2014	AA	New Britain	0	0	0	7	3	5.14	1.71	15.9	336	37	67	5.30	2.6	3.9	1.5	0.0	18

Tall, durable SP who repeated AA and was slightly better. Doesn't own plus stuff, but succeeds with excellent control and improved, cleaner delivery. Can still have erratic plane to plate, which can leave FB flat. CB has quality promise and CU has moments despite reduced arm speed.

Adams, Austin — RP — Cleveland

EXP MLB DEBUT: 2014 | H/W: 5-11 190 | FUT: Setup RP | **7C**

Thrws R Age 28
2009 (5) Faulkner
93-98 FB ++++
81-83 SL +++
80-82 CU ++
CU ++

Year	Lev	Team	W	L	Sv	IP	K	ERA	WHIP	BF/G	OBA	H%	S%	xERA	Ctl	Dom	Cmd	hr/9	BPV
2010	A-	Kinston	6	1	0	58	51	1.55	1.12	17.6	234	28	92	2.97	2.3	7.9	3.4	0.8	97
2011	AA	Akron	11	10	0	136	131	3.77	1.54	22.8	277	36	75	4.28	4.2	8.7	2.1	0.4	61
2013	AA	Akron	3	2	4	55	76	2.62	1.33	5.1	221	34	81	3.04	4.7	12.4	2.6	0.5	114
2014	AAA	Columbus	3	2	5	54	52	2.50	1.11	5.1	224	29	80	2.73	2.7	8.7	3.3	0.7	102
2014	MLB	Cleveland	0	0	0	7	4	9.00	1.43	5.0	313	34	33	5.40	1.3	5.1	4.0	1.3	76

Short, max-effort pitcher who was moved to bullpen after missing all '12 with shoulder surgery. Spots effective, cutting SL within strike zone and complements with quality SL and fringy CU. Tends to rush delivery, but keeps ball down. Can miss bats with FB up in zone and hard SL.

Adams, Spencer — SP — Chicago (A)

EXP MLB DEBUT: 2018 | H/W: 6-3 170 | FUT: #2 starter | **9D**

Thrws R Age 18
2014 (2) HS (GA)
89-96 FB ++++
82-86 SL +++
82-84 CU +++

Year	Lev	Team	W	L	Sv	IP	K	ERA	WHIP	BF/G	OBA	H%	S%	xERA	Ctl	Dom	Cmd	hr/9	BPV
2014	Rk	AZL White Sox	3	3	0	41	59	3.71	1.29	16.9	297	44	73	4.32	0.9	12.9	14.8	0.9	226

Lean, athletic SP with high upside and solid current stuff. Rarely allows walks, but needs better command within strike zone. Quick arm produces plus FB with electric, late life. Exhibits feel for CU, though can be too firm. Uses FB to set up SL which serves as potential plus K offering.

Agosta, Martin — SP — San Francisco

EXP MLB DEBUT: 2016 | H/W: 6-1 180 | FUT: #4 Starter/Power RP | **7D**

Thrws R Age 24
2012 (2) St. Mary's
89-91 FB +++
78-80 SL +++
80-83 CU +++
CT ++

Year	Lev	Team	W	L	Sv	IP	K	ERA	WHIP	BF/G	OBA	H%	S%	xERA	Ctl	Dom	Cmd	hr/9	BPV
2012	NCAA	St. Mary's (CA)	9	2	0	103	95	2.18	1.11	28.9	230	30	81	2.50	2.4	8.3	3.5	0.3	104
2012	Rk	AZL Giants	0	0	0	19	19	4.41	1.67	9.2	218	45	71	3.34	7.9	16.8	2.1	0.0	105
2013	A	Augusta	9	3	0	91	109	2.07	1.10	19.8	181	26	82	1.92	4.2	10.8	2.5	0.4	97
2014	Rk	AZL Giants	1	0	0	14	19	4.50	1.29	14.4	288	44	61	3.38	1.3	12.2	9.5	0.0	203
2014	A+	San Jose	3	3	0	39	25	9.23	2.18	17.7	317	35	56	7.22	7.8	5.8	0.7	1.2	-90

Undersized RHP took a step back in '14, struggling to find the strike zone. Following stint on DL, showed signs of life with improved Cmd, mixing four pitches. His pitch sequencing allow him to get swings and misses, though more refined secondary pitches will dictate role: either backend SP or power RP.

Alcantara, Raul — SP — Oakland

EXP MLB DEBUT: 2016 | H/W: 6-3 225 | FUT: #3 starter | **8D**

Thrws R Age 22
2009 FA (DR)
90-95 FB +++
80-84 SL +++
77-80 CB ++
80-83 CU +++

Year	Lev	Team	W	L	Sv	IP	K	ERA	WHIP	BF/G	OBA	H%	S%	xERA	Ctl	Dom	Cmd	hr/9	BPV
2011	A-	Lowell	0	3	0	17	14	6.32	1.81	19.8	341	42	61	5.61	3.2	7.4	2.3	0.0	65
2012	A	Burlington	6	11	0	102	57	5.11	1.54	16.5	292	32	68	5.14	3.3	5.0	1.5	1.1	18
2013	A	Beloit	7	1	0	77	58	2.45	1.18	23.7	279	34	80	3.36	0.8	6.8	8.3	0.4	118
2013	A+	Stockton	5	5	0	79	66	3.76	1.14	22.3	247	29	70	3.34	1.9	7.5	3.9	0.9	101
2014	AA	Midland	2	0	0	19	10	2.34	1.15	25.4	239	28	77	2.42	2.3	4.7	2.0	0.0	39

Big, strong SP who started 3 games before being shut down and eventually undergoing TJ surgery in May. When healthy, throws with smooth arm action and locates solid FB to all parts of zone. Mixes in hard SL that flashes plus along with CB and CU. Disappointing K rate given stuff.

Alcantara, Victor — SP — Los Angeles (A)

EXP MLB DEBUT: 2017 | H/W: 6-2 190 | FUT: #4 starter/setupRP | **7D**

Thrws R Age 22
2011 FA (DR)
91-97 FB ++++
81-84 SL ++
83-85 CU ++

Year	Lev	Team	W	L	Sv	IP	K	ERA	WHIP	BF/G	OBA	H%	S%	xERA	Ctl	Dom	Cmd	hr/9	BPV
2013	Rk	Orem	2	5	0	59	48	7.47	1.83	16.1	305	35	60	6.49	5.3	7.3	1.4	1.5	6
2014	A	Burlington	7	6	1	125	117	3.81	1.26	18.9	217	28	69	2.81	4.3	8.4	2.0	0.4	53

Strong-armed SP who fared well in first full season. Induces groundballs with electric and hard sinking FB. Mechanics are a tad crude and needs consistency with below average SL. Has some feel for fading CU and could stand to throw better strikes with smoother delivery and arm slot.

Almonte, Miguel — SP — Kansas City

EXP MLB DEBUT: 2016 | H/W: 6-2 180 | FUT: #3 starter | **8C**

Thrws R Age 22
2010 FA (DR)
90-95 FB +++
76-79 CB ++
83-87 CU ++++

Year	Lev	Team	W	L	Sv	IP	K	ERA	WHIP	BF/G	OBA	H%	S%	xERA	Ctl	Dom	Cmd	hr/9	BPV
2012	Rk	AZL Royals	2	1	0	27	28	2.33	1.00	17.2	224	31	74	1.82	1.7	9.3	5.6	0.0	141
2013	A	Lexington	6	9	0	130	132	3.11	1.16	20.7	239	32	73	2.80	2.5	9.1	3.7	0.4	115
2014	A+	Wilmington	6	8	0	110	101	4.50	1.26	19.5	256	32	65	3.60	2.6	8.3	3.2	0.7	96

Smooth SP who has little bit of everything in arsenal. Throws hard with quick arm action, but also adds deception with ability to hide ball. Has tendency to overthrow, causing FB to flatten, but throws strikes and has standout CU. Exhibits decent break in CB, but below average at present.

Altavilla, Dan — SP — Seattle

EXP MLB DEBUT: 2017 | H/W: 5-11 200 | FUT: #5 starter/setupRP | **7E**

Thrws R Age 22
2014 (5) Mercyhurst
90-94 FB +++
80-82 SL +++
81-82 CU +++

Year	Lev	Team	W	L	Sv	IP	K	ERA	WHIP	BF/G	OBA	H%	S%	xERA	Ctl	Dom	Cmd	hr/9	BPV
2014	A-	Everett	5	3	0	66	66	4.36	1.61	20.9	284	36	75	5.06	4.4	9.0	2.1	1.0	62

Short, stocky SP who was Div II Pitcher of the Year. Likely RP in future with max effort delivery, but has FB to thrive in any role. Gets ample pitch movement with quick arm and keeps RHH at bay with average SL. CU exhibits splitter action and is tough to elevate. Lacks projection.

Alvarado, Jose — SP — Tampa Bay

EXP MLB DEBUT: 2018 | H/W: 6-0 180 | FUT: #3 starter | **8E**

Thrws L Age 19
2012 FA (Venezuela)
91-96 FB ++++
77-82 CB +++
82-87 CU +

Year	Lev	Team	W	L	Sv	IP	K	ERA	WHIP	BF/G	OBA	H%	S%	xERA	Ctl	Dom	Cmd	hr/9	BPV
2014	Rk	GCL Devil Rays	1	5	0	40	46	3.82	1.42	14.2	198	29	71	2.77	6.5	10.3	1.6	0.2	28

Short, powerful SP who couldn't consistently throw strikes in first yr in U.S. but has potential for 2 plus pitches. Uses loose, electric arm to generate plus FB with heavy sink. Notches Ks with both FB and hard CB that features depth. Delivery is erratic and CU can be too firm. Tough to hit.

Alvarez, R.J. — RP — Oakland

EXP MLB DEBUT: 2014 | H/W: 6-1 200 | FUT: Reliever | **8C**

Thrws R Age 23
2012 (3) Florida Atlantic
93-99 FB ++++
86-88 SL +++

Year	Lev	Team	W	L	Sv	IP	K	ERA	WHIP	BF/G	OBA	H%	S%	xERA	Ctl	Dom	Cmd	hr/9	BPV
2012	A	Cedar Rapids	3	2	0	27	38	3.32	1.22	4.8	224	34	74	2.95	3.7	12.6	3.5	0.7	147
2013	A+	Inland Empire	4	2	4	48	79	2.99	1.27	5.3	200	36	76	2.50	5.0	14.8	2.9	0.4	147
2014	AA	Arkansas	0	0	1	27	38	0.33	0.85	4.7	146	25	96	0.53	3.3	12.7	3.8	0.0	156
2014	AA	San Antonio	0	1	6	16	23	2.80	1.18	3.8	261	42	74	2.71	1.7	12.9	7.7	0.0	204
2014	MLB	San Diego	0	0	0	8	9	1.13	1.00	3.1	117	18	88	0.64	5.6	10.1	1.8	0.0	48

Quick-armed reliever who was traded twice in six months can dominate in short stints with heavy FB and knockout SL. Plus arm strength generates quality 93-99 mph FB and a plus hard SL that misses bats. Pitch movement results in Ks and improved control got him to the majors.

Anderson, Chris — SP — Los Angeles (N)

EXP MLB DEBUT: 2016 | H/W: 6-4 215 | FUT: #3 starter | **8D**

Thrws R Age 22
2013 (1) Jacksonville
92-94 FB ++++
83-85 SL ++++
CB ++
CU +++

Year	Lev	Team	W	L	Sv	IP	K	ERA	WHIP	BF/G	OBA	H%	S%	xERA	Ctl	Dom	Cmd	hr/9	BPV
2011	NCAA	Jacksonville	4	2	11	50	39	3.94	1.47	6.0	220	25	75	3.83	6.1	7.0	1.1	0.9	-21
2012	NCAA	Jacksonville	5	4	1	88	69	4.49	1.52	23.9	274	33	70	4.40	4.1	7.0	1.7	0.6	35
2013	NCAA	Jacksonville	7	5	0	104	101	2.50	1.12	29.3	234	31	79	2.67	2.3	8.7	3.7	0.4	112
2013	A	Great Lakes	3	0	0	46	50	1.96	1.22	15.5	198	29	82	2.05	4.7	9.8	2.1	0.0	67
2014	A+	Ranch Cuca	7	7	0	134	146	4.63	1.57	21.8	280	37	71	4.68	4.2	9.8	2.3	0.7	80

Big, durable RHP with good downhill plane, pounding the strike zone with a four-pitch mix. Features a good 92-94 mph FB up to 98 at times. FB-SL combo generates swings and misses. Struggles with control and command took their toll, but he did lead the CAL in strikeouts with 146.

Anderson,Cody

SP | Cleveland | EXP MLB DEBUT: 2015 | H/W: 6-4 220 | FUT: #4 starter | 7B

Thrws R Age 24
2011 (14) Feather River JC

Velo	Pitch	Grade
90-95	FB	+++
79-83	CB	+++
80-83	SL	++
84-88	CU	++

Year	Lev	Team	W	L	Sv	IP	K	ERA	WHIP	BF/G	OBA	H%	S%	xERA	Ctl	Dom	Cmd	hr/9	BPV
2011	A-	Mahoning Val	0	0	0	5	3	1.80	1.60	7.4	221	26	88	3.33	7.2	5.4	0.8	0.0	-79
2012	A	Lake County	4	7	0	98	72	3.21	1.23	16.6	250	29	76	3.45	2.7	6.6	2.5	0.7	65
2013	A+	Carolina	9	4	0	123	112	2.34	1.10	21.0	232	30	80	2.61	2.3	8.2	3.6	0.4	104
2013	AA	Akron	0	0	0	12	10	5.90	2.05	19.8	317	36	74	7.19	6.6	7.4	1.1	1.5	-28
2014	AA	Akron	4	11	0	125	81	5.46	1.49	21.6	285	31	65	5.05	3.2	5.8	1.8	1.2	35

Tall, durable SP with clean, loose arm and athletic delivery. Exhibits mostly power stuff, but K rate declining as he lacks sequencing. Throws good strikes, but can be too passive at times. Repeats slot well and gets depth on power CB. Nice arm speed on CU but doesn't fool LHH (.341 oppBA).

Anderson,Tyler

SP | Colorado | EXP MLB DEBUT: 2015 | H/W: 6-4 215 | FUT: #3 starter | 7C

Thrws L Age 25
2011 (1) Oregon

Velo	Pitch	Grade
89-92	FB	+++
77-80	SL	+++
74-77	CB	++
81-83	CU	++++

Year	Lev	Team	W	L	Sv	IP	K	ERA	WHIP	BF/G	OBA	H%	S%	xERA	Ctl	Dom	Cmd	hr/9	BPV
2011	NCAA	Oregon	8	3	0	107	114	2.35	1.03	27.5	199	28	76	1.74	2.9	9.6	3.3	0.2	111
2012	A	Asheville	12	3	0	120	81	2.47	1.08	23.4	231	27	78	2.50	2.1	6.1	2.9	0.4	71
2013	A-	Tri-City	1	1	0	15	13	0.60	0.80	18.1	175	23	92	0.76	1.8	7.8	4.3	0.0	110
2013	A+	Modesto	3	2	0	74	63	3.27	1.16	22.7	229	26	78	3.43	2.9	7.6	2.6	1.2	77
2014	AA	Tulsa	7	4	0	118	106	1.98	1.11	20.2	215	28	82	2.21	3.0	8.1	2.7	0.2	81

Soft-tossing LHP continues to thrive despite average stuff and now has a career 2.42 ERA. Has a decent 89-92 mph FB, and complements it with a SL, CB, CU. Good command of all pitches and nice deception. Was shut down at the end of the season with an elbow injury.

Andriese,Matt

SP | Tampa Bay | EXP MLB DEBUT: 2015 | H/W: 6-3 210 | FUT: #4 starter | 7C

Thrws R Age 25
2011 (3) UC-Riverside

Velo	Pitch	Grade
89-94	FB	+++
78-80	CB	+++
83-84	CU	+++

Year	Lev	Team	W	L	Sv	IP	K	ERA	WHIP	BF/G	OBA	H%	S%	xERA	Ctl	Dom	Cmd	hr/9	BPV
2011	A-	Eugene	5	1	0	41		1.53	0.95	12.9	200	28	82	1.39	2.2	9.2	4.2	0.0	124
2012	A+	Lake Elsinore	10	8	0	146	131	3.58	1.22	21.8	254	32	71	3.29	2.3	8.1	3.4	0.6	100
2013	AA	San Antonio	8	2	0	76	63	2.37	1.16	20.2	249	31	80	2.89	2.0	7.5	3.7	0.4	98
2013	AAA	Tucson	3	5	0	58	42	4.48	1.31	20.0	281	34	64	3.67	1.9	6.5	3.5	0.3	85
2014	AAA	Durham	11	8	0	162	129	3.78	1.24	23.5	251	29	73	3.73	2.7	7.2	2.7	1.0	75

Consistent, durable SP with exquisite control and command. Allowed more HR than first 3 yrs combined, but generally lives low in zone. Maintains average velocity late in games. CB and CU both thrown for strikes, though neither miss bats. Throws across body, but repeats delivery.

Appel,Mark

SP | Houston | EXP MLB DEBUT: 2015 | H/W: 6-5 225 | FUT: #2 starter | 8C

Thrws R Age 23
2013 (1) Stanford

Velo	Pitch	Grade
93-98	FB	+++
83-87	SL	++++
80-83	CU	+++

Year	Lev	Team	W	L	Sv	IP	K	ERA	WHIP	BF/G	OBA	H%	S%	xERA	Ctl	Dom	Cmd	hr/9	BPV
2013	NCAA	Stanford	10	4	0	106	130	2.12	0.97	28.7	211	32	77	1.73	2.0	11.0	5.7	0.2	164
2013	A-	Tri City	0	0	0	5	6	3.60	1.20	10.1	299	43	67	3.33	0.0	10.8		0.0	212
2013	A	Quad Cities	3	1	0	33	27	3.82	1.18	16.5	244	30	68	3.06	2.5	7.4	3.0	0.5	84
2014	A+	Lancaster	2	5	0	44	40	9.80	1.93	17.4	373	44	49	8.19	2.2	8.2	3.6	1.8	104
2014	AA	Corpus Christi	1	2	0	39	38	3.69	1.23	22.6	241	31	70	3.06	3.0	8.8	2.9	0.5	95

Tall, strong starter who befuddled with poor season, but came on late and was terrific in AFL. Throws with clean, easy arm action that peppers strike zone with velocity. SL misses bats and CU flashes plus. Tends to slow arm on CU, but has pitch mix and smarts to be frontline guy.

Aquino,Jayson

SP | Colorado | EXP MLB DEBUT: 2016 | H/W: 6-1 180 | FUT: #4 starter | 6C

Thrws L Age 22
2009 FA (DR)

Velo	Pitch	Grade
87-92	FB	+++
	CB	+
	CU	++++

Year	Lev	Team	W	L	Sv	IP	K	ERA	WHIP	BF/G	OBA	H%	S%	xERA	Ctl	Dom	Cmd	hr/9	BPV
2012	Rk	Grand Junction	4	0	0	43	36	1.88	1.00	23.5	208	26	83	2.03	2.3	7.5	3.3	0.4	91
2013	A-	Tri-City	0	1	0	23	16	3.13	1.13	22.7	245	29	72	2.81	2.0	6.3	3.2	0.4	78
2013	A	Asheville	0	9	0	64	57	4.78	1.36	24.3	268	33	64	3.84	3.0	8.0	2.7	0.6	83
2014	A+	Modesto	5	10	0	95	74	5.40	1.51	25.7	297	35	63	4.73	2.8	7.0	2.5	0.7	67
2014	AA	Tulsa	0	0	0	12	9	3.00	1.42	25.4	210	27	76	2.72	6.0	6.8	1.1	0.0	-23

Soft-tossing LHP found the sledding tough in the CAL. Has a good 87-91 mph FB that tops out at 92 mph and plus CU that allows him to keep hitters off balance. CB remains below-average and inconsistent. Works his FB well to both corners and keeps the ball down inducing plenty of GB outs.

Arano,Victor

SP | Philadelphia | EXP MLB DEBUT: 2017 | H/W: 6-2 200 | FUT: #4 starter | 7C

Thrws R Age 20
2013 FA (Mexico)

Velo	Pitch	Grade
90-93	FB	+++
77-79	CB	++
84-86	CU	++

Year	Lev	Team	W	L	Sv	IP	K	ERA	WHIP	BF/G	OBA	H%	S%	xERA	Ctl	Dom	Cmd	hr/9	BPV
2013	Rk	AZL Dodgers	3	2	0	49	49	4.22	1.32	15.7	273	35	69	3.98	2.4	9.0	3.8	0.7	115
2014	A	Great Lakes	4	7	3	86	83	4.08	1.26	15.9	266	33	71	4.11	2.1	8.7	4.2	1.2	118

Part of the Roberto Hernandez trade to LA in 2014, he has a mature body at such a young age, along with above-average command of his FB. Breaking pitch wavers between a curve and higher-velo slider, and the CU can flash average. Real nice year as a 19-year-old in a full season league.

Araujo,Victor

RP | Los Angeles (N) | EXP MLB DEBUT: 2017 | H/W: 5-11 171 | FUT: Reliever | 7B

Thrws R Age 22
2009 FA (DR)

Velo	Pitch	Grade
90-93	FB	+++
	SL	+++

Year	Lev	Team	W	L	Sv	IP	K	ERA	WHIP	BF/G	OBA	H%	S%	xERA	Ctl	Dom	Cmd	hr/9	BPV
2012	Rk	AZL Dodgers	4	2	0	53	48	6.94	1.54	17.8	299	35	56	5.66	3.0	8.1	2.7	1.5	82
2012	A	Great Lakes	0	0	0	5	3	5.40	1.40	21.1	221	15	80	6.21	5.4	5.4	1.0	3.6	-31
2013	Rk	Ogden	5	3	0	76	75	6.50	1.45	21.6	295	37	53	4.70	2.4	8.9	3.8	0.8	114
2014	A	Great Lakes	5	2	6	68	74	1.32	0.79	5.9	169	24	85	0.90	2.0	9.8	4.9	0.3	141
2014	A+	Ranch Cuca	0	1	0	5	4	7.20	1.40	4.2	262	28	50	5.03	3.6	7.2	2.0	1.8	50

Short, RH reliever from the D.R. put up impressive numbers in the MWL. Despite his small stature, he comes after hitters with a good 90-93 mph FB that has late life and generates swings and misses. Pairs that with a plus SL. Career Cmd rate of 3.7 gives him potential to contribute in the majors.

Armstrong,Mark

SP | Cincinnati | EXP MLB DEBUT: 2017 | H/W: 6-2 210 | FUT: #4 starter | 7D

Thrws R Age 20
2013 (3) HS (NY)

Velo	Pitch	Grade
88-92	FB	+++
	CB	+++
	CU	+++

Year	Lev	Team	W	L	Sv	IP	K	ERA	WHIP	BF/G	OBA	H%	S%	xERA	Ctl	Dom	Cmd	hr/9	BPV
2013	Rk	AZL Reds	0	0	0	3	2	0.00	0.33	4.7	106	13	100	0.00	0.0	6.0		0.0	126
2014	Rk	AZL Reds	4	3	0	61	56	4.26	1.24	17.8	264	33	65	3.52	2.1	8.2	4.0	0.6	111

Armstrong has a strong, stocky pitcher's frame. CIN has been cautious with innings count due to heavy prep work load but he got some reps in '14. Plus command profile and throws to groundball contact. FB should add velocity as he matures. Throws slightly above-average CB and CU.

Armstrong,Shawn

RP | Cleveland | EXP MLB DEBUT: 2015 | H/W: 6-2 210 | FUT: Middle reliever | 7D

Thrws R Age 24
2011 (18) East Carolina

Velo	Pitch	Grade
89-96	FB	++++
83-87	SL	+++
81-83	CU	++

Year	Lev	Team	W	L	Sv	IP	K	ERA	WHIP	BF/G	OBA	H%	S%	xERA	Ctl	Dom	Cmd	hr/9	BPV
2012	AA	Akron	1	0	3	20	22	0.90	1.19	4.7	175	26	92	1.73	5.4	9.9	1.8	0.0	50
2013	Rk	AZL Indians	0	0	0	4	5	4.50	0.75	4.8	210	24	50	3.11	0.0	11.3		2.3	221
2013	AA	Akron	2	3	0	33	43	4.09	1.61	4.9	256	37	75	4.25	5.7	11.7	2.0	0.5	74
2014	AA	Akron	6	2	15	51	68	2.12	1.14	4.6	213	32	84	2.50	3.4	12.0	3.6	0.5	143
2014	AAA	Columbus	0	0	0	5	4	5.40	1.40	4.2	221	23	67	4.50	5.4	7.2	1.3	1.8	2

Powerful RP with durability and stamina. Delivery suited for bullpen work as he throws across body, though has some deception. Fires plus FB in strike zone and has live arm to add late sink. Uses hard SL as chase pitch and posts low oppBA. Mixes in occasional cutter and CU.

Asher,Alec

SP | Texas | EXP MLB DEBUT: 2015 | H/W: 6-4 225 | FUT: #4 starter | 7B

Thrws R Age 23
2012 (4) Polk County JC

Velo	Pitch	Grade
90-95	FB	+++
84-87	SL	++++
78-81	CB	++
83-85	CU	++

Year	Lev	Team	W	L	Sv	IP	K	ERA	WHIP	BF/G	OBA	H%	S%	xERA	Ctl	Dom	Cmd	hr/9	BPV
2011	NCAA	Santa Fe CC	5	0	1	49	56	2.56	1.20	15.2	249	36	76	2.63	2.4	10.2	4.3	0.0	138
2012	NCAA	Polk State	13	1	0	111	118	1.38	0.91	20.7	191	26	88	1.58	2.2	9.6	4.4	0.4	131
2012	A-	Spokane	2	3	5	35	50	3.09	1.14	6.9	227	34	78	3.15	2.8	12.9	4.5	1.0	173
2013	A+	Myrtle Beach	9	7	0	133	139	2.91	1.20	20.6	242	32	78	3.19	2.7	9.4	3.5	0.7	114
2014	AA	Frisco	11	11	0	154	122	3.80	1.11	21.6	242	28	69	3.34	1.9	7.1	3.8	1.1	96

Big, durable SP who has seen K rate decline and subject to flyballs and HR, but commands and controls zone with FB and can wipe out hitters with plus, hard SL. Uses height for good angle to plate and has three secondary offerings. CB and CU still fringy and delivery can get stiff.

Baez,Angel

RP | Kansas City | EXP MLB DEBUT: 2016 | H/W: 6-3 225 | FUT: Setup RP | 7D

Thrws R Age 24
2008 FA (DR)

Velo	Pitch	Grade
91-97	FB	++++
77-81	CB	++
83-87	CU	++

Year	Lev	Team	W	L	Sv	IP	K	ERA	WHIP	BF/G	OBA	H%	S%	xERA	Ctl	Dom	Cmd	hr/9	BPV
2011	Rk	Burlington	0	6	0	47	41	7.09	2.06	16.4	336	41	64	6.68	5.7	7.9	1.4	0.6	4
2012	A	Kane County	6	5	0	76	83	3.19	1.26	19.4	232	31	76	3.13	3.7	9.8	2.7	0.6	96
2013	Rk	AZL Royals	1	0	0	14	17	2.55	1.42	10.0	299	43	80	3.90	1.9	10.9	5.7	0.0	162
2013	A+	Wilmington	3	1	0	37	35	4.38	1.68	20.8	246	31	75	4.49	6.8	8.5	1.3	0.7	-13
2014	AA	NW Arkansas	1	5	0	62	71	4.65	1.40	7.5	249	32	71	4.37	4.2	10.3	2.4	1.3	90

Max-effort pitcher who was moved to RP in '14. Has pure, electric stuff with plus FB thrown with terrific arm speed. Hasn't yet developed dependable second pitch and struggles with control. Both CB and CU have moments, but are inconsistent. Gets hit hard when pitching up in zone.

Baez,Pedro — RP — Los Angeles (N)

EXP MLB DEBUT: 2014 | H/W: 6-2 230 | FUT: Setup RP | 7C

Thrws R Age 27 — 2007 FA (DR)

Velo	Pitch	Grade
92-96	FB	+++
83-85	SL	+++
	CB	+

Year	Lev	Team	W	L	Sv	IP	K	ERA	WHIP	BF/G	OBA	H%	S%	xERA	Ctl	Dom	Cmd	hr/9	BPV
2013	A+	Ranch Cuca	2	2	2	34	32	3.68	1.64	4.8	298	37	79	5.20	3.9	8.4	2.1	0.8	63
2013	AA	Chattanooga	1	1	0	23	23	4.29	1.47	6.2	285	35	74	4.94	3.1	9.0	2.9	1.2	95
2014	AA	Chattanooga	2	1	6	19	18	2.83	1.26	4.6	218	29	75	2.40	4.2	8.5	2.0	0.0	56
2014	AAA	Albuquerque	0	0	6	22	20	4.86	1.40	4.1	301	35	70	5.42	1.6	8.1	5.0	1.6	120
2014	MLB	LA Dodgers	0	0	0	24	18	2.63	0.88	4.4	191	21	78	2.20	1.9	6.8	3.6	1.1	89

Former 3B looks to have reinvented himself as an effective reliever. Always had a plus arm and good athleticism and now features a plus 92-96 mph FB that hits 99. Has a thick, stocky frame and a short arm action. He keeps his front side firm, which gives him at least average command.

Baker,Dylan — SP — Cleveland

EXP MLB DEBUT: 2016 | H/W: 6-2 215 | FUT: #4 starter/setupRP | 7B

Thrws R Age 23 — 2012 (5) W Nevada JC

Velo	Pitch	Grade
90-95	FB	+++
83-86	SL	+++
78-82	CB	++
80-84	CU	++

Year	Lev	Team	W	L	Sv	IP	K	ERA	WHIP	BF/G	OBA	H%	S%	xERA	Ctl	Dom	Cmd	hr/9	BPV
2012	NCAA	W Nevada JC	13	0	1	84	126	1.92	1.09	18.3	162	27	85	1.80	4.9	13.5	2.7	0.5	128
2012	Rk	AZL Indians	0	1	0	24	30	4.13	1.63	13.3	262	38	74	4.22	5.6	11.3	2.0	0.4	69
2013	A	Lake County	7	6	0	143	117	3.65	1.30	21.8	235	30	70	2.91	3.9	7.4	1.9	0.2	45
2014	Rk	AZL Indians	0	0	0	5	13	1.73	0.58	5.9	120	38	100	1.11	1.7	22.5	13.0	1.7	376
2014	A+	Carolina	3	3	0	46	28	4.09	1.36	21.5	257	29	70	3.75	3.5	5.5	1.6	0.6	22

Athletic, physical SP who missed time with broken ankle. Flown under radar despite excellent FB/SL combo. Quick FB jumps on hitters with late action, though needs to command better. SL has plus potential and can be wipeout pitch. Inconsistent slot and effort may eventually lead to pen.

Ball,Trey — SP — Boston

EXP MLB DEBUT: 2017 | H/W: 6-6 185 | FUT: #2 starter | 9E

Thrws L Age 20 — 2013 (1) HS (IN)

Velo	Pitch	Grade
88-94	FB	+++
74-78	CB	+++
78-82	CU	+++

Year	Lev	Team	W	L	Sv	IP	K	ERA	WHIP	BF/G	OBA	H%	S%	xERA	Ctl	Dom	Cmd	hr/9	BPV
2013	Rk	GCL Red Sox	0	1	0	7	5	6.43	2.29	7.1	336	38	73	7.93	7.7	6.4	0.8	1.3	-75
2014	A	Greenville	5	10	0	100	68	4.68	1.50	19.6	282	32	70	4.66	3.5	6.1	1.7	0.8	33

Long, lean LHP who got better as season progressed. Owns very high upside with potential for 3 above average pitches. Throws downhill with lively FB and has projection to throw harder. Lack of consistent CB and CU make him hittable and needs more time to repeat delivery better.

Balog,Alex — SP — Colorado

EXP MLB DEBUT: 2017 | H/W: 6-5 210 | FUT: #4 starter | 7D

Thrws R Age 22 — 2013 (2-S) San Francisco

Velo	Pitch	Grade
92-95	FB	+++
78-81	CB	++
81-83	SL	+++
78-80	CU	+

Year	Lev	Team	W	L	Sv	IP	K	ERA	WHIP	BF/G	OBA	H%	S%	xERA	Ctl	Dom	Cmd	hr/9	BPV
2011	NCAA	San Francisco	2	2	0	17	5	6.32	1.81	5.0	313	34	61	5.19	4.7	2.6	0.6	0.0	-63
2012	NCAA	San Francisco	4	4	0	78	57	3.45	1.19	20.9	219	26	71	2.70	3.6	6.6	1.8	0.5	40
2013	NCAA	San Francisco	3	4	0	91	67	3.65	1.39	27.4	268	31	75	4.06	3.3	6.6	2.0	0.7	49
2013	Rk	Grand Junction	1	4	0	30	17	9.30	1.97	20.5	376	39	54	8.62	2.4	5.1	2.1	2.1	45
2014	A	Asheville	8	5	1	150	114	3.96	1.33	23.0	272	32	71	3.97	2.5	6.8	2.8	0.7	75

Bounced back nicely from a disastrous pro debut. Has ideal size and a good power arm. FB sits at 92-95 with good late, sinking action and he mixes in a power CB and a hard SL. Low Dom rate is due to underdeveloped CU that will be key to his long-term future.

Banda,Anthony — SP — Arizona

EXP MLB DEBUT: 2017 | H/W: 6-2 190 | FUT: #4 starter | 7D

Thrws L Age 21 — 2012 (10) San Jacinto JC

Velo	Pitch	Grade
89-92	FB	++
	CB	+++
	CU	++

Year	Lev	Team	W	L	Sv	IP	K	ERA	WHIP	BF/G	OBA	H%	S%	xERA	Ctl	Dom	Cmd	hr/9	BPV
2012	NCAA	San Jacinto	6	0	0	64	62	1.96	1.01	20.5	158	22	78	1.10	4.3	8.7	2.0	0.0	57
2012	Rk	AZL Brewers	2	3	0	41	43	5.90	1.89	13.9	317	41	68	6.00	5.2	9.4	1.8	0.7	46
2013	Rk	Helena	3	4	0	60	45	4.49	1.48	18.5	274	31	72	4.69	3.7	6.7	1.8	1.0	38
2014	A	South Bend	3	0	0	35	34	1.54	1.11	23.0	245	32	89	2.86	1.8	8.7	4.9	0.5	127
2014	A	Wisconsin	6	6	2	83	83	3.68	1.47	17.8	264	35	75	3.92	4.1	9.0	2.2	0.4	69

Best offering is a plus hard CB. Also has a decent 88-93 mph FB and a decent CU. Can miss bats, but struggled with Ctl in '14. Was better after the trade from ARI and proflies as a back-end starter.

Bandilla,Bryce — RP — San Francisco

EXP MLB DEBUT: 2015 | H/W: 6-4 235 | FUT: Reliever | 7D

Thrws L Age 25 — 2011 (4) Arizona

Velo	Pitch	Grade
92-95	FB	++++
83-85	SL	++
	CU	+++

Year	Lev	Team	W	L	Sv	IP	K	ERA	WHIP	BF/G	OBA	H%	S%	xERA	Ctl	Dom	Cmd	hr/9	BPV
2012	Rk	AZL Giants	0	0	0	14	20	1.93	0.64	12.1	151	24	75	0.65	1.3	12.9	10.0	0.6	215
2012	A	Augusta	2	4	0	44	48	3.06	1.63	17.9	261	36	80	4.09	5.7	9.8	1.7	0.2	40
2013	A+	San Jose	1	4	5	44	72	3.67	1.16	4.6	173	29	72	2.52	5.1	14.7	2.9	1.0	145
2014	A+	San Jose	0	1	8	34	47	3.17	1.26	3.9	219	33	78	3.13	4.2	12.4	2.9	0.8	127
2014	AA	Richmond	0	2	0	15	10	8.94	2.19	5.0	297	33	58	6.96	8.9	6.0	0.7	1.2	-116

Struggled in his 2nd season since becoming a RP. Has seen hiis Cmd and Ctl both trend in the wrong direction. Dom is still at elite thanks to his mid-to-upper-90s FB that tops out at 97. He complements it with a decent CU and playable SL. Velo plays, but needs to the find consistency with his command.

Banuelos,Manny — SP — Atlanta

EXP MLB DEBUT: 2015 | H/W: 5-10 205 | FUT: #2 starter | 8D

Thrws L Age 24 — 2008 FA (Mexico)

Velo	Pitch	Grade
91-95	FB	+++
74-79	CB	++
80-83	SL	++
83-85	CU	++++

Year	Lev	Team	W	L	Sv	IP	K	ERA	WHIP	BF/G	OBA	H%	S%	xERA	Ctl	Dom	Cmd	hr/9	BPV
2011	AAA	Scranton/WB	2	2	0	34	31	4.22	1.61	21.6	272	34	74	4.51	5.0	8.2	1.6	0.5	30
2012	AAA	Scranton/WB	0	2	0	24	22	4.50	1.63	17.8	300	37	73	5.16	3.8	8.3	2.2	0.8	65
2014	A+	Tampa	0	0	0	12	14	2.95	0.98	9.3	225	33	67	1.78	1.5	10.3	7.0	0.0	164
2014	AA	Trenton	1	3	0	49	44	4.59	1.20	11.6	224	25	67	3.73	3.5	8.1	2.3	1.5	69
2014	AAA	Scranton/WB	1	0	0	15	13	3.60	1.60	16.6	249	29	82	4.79	6.0	7.8	1.3	1.2	-4

Short SP returning to health after TJ surgery in Oct 2012. Velocity and quality of stuff back to normal and added new SL to arsenal. Erratic control hinders present stuff, though should get better with time. CU remains outstanding with deceptive arm speed and late action. Tough on LHH.

Barlow,Scott — SP — Los Angeles (N)

EXP MLB DEBUT: 2017 | H/W: 6-3 170 | FUT: #5 starter | 6B

Thrws R Age 22 — 2011 (6) HS (CA)

Velo	Pitch	Grade
89-93	FB	+++
	CB	++
	SL	+++
83-85	CU	++

Year	Lev	Team	W	L	Sv	IP	K	ERA	WHIP	BF/G	OBA	H%	S%	xERA	Ctl	Dom	Cmd	hr/9	BPV
2011	Rk	AZL Dodgers	0	1	0	1	1	37.50	5.83	5.2	596	63	33	29.97	15.0	7.5	0.5	7.5	-252
2013	Rk	Ogden	4	3	0	69	51	6.24	1.65	20.6	296	32	65	6.05	4.2	6.6	1.6	1.7	25
2014	A	Great Lakes	6	7	1	106	104	4.50	1.40	19.4	274	34	69	4.37	3.0	8.8	3.0	0.9	97

Tall, lanky RH continues to work his way back from TJS. FB sits in the low-90s with the FB, but projectable frame could lead to more. SL is his best secondary, used to get swings and misses, but CB and CU have a chance to play avg. Improved Cmd and Dom hint at the potential.

Barnes,Matt — SP — Boston

EXP MLB DEBUT: 2014 | H/W: 6-4 205 | FUT: #3 starter | 8C

Thrws R Age 24 — 2011 (1) Connecticut

Velo	Pitch	Grade
90-96	FB	+++
74-79	CB	+++
84-86	CU	+++

Year	Lev	Team	W	L	Sv	IP	K	ERA	WHIP	BF/G	OBA	H%	S%	xERA	Ctl	Dom	Cmd	hr/9	BPV
2012	A+	Salem	5	5	0	93	91	3.58	1.18	18.6	245	32	70	3.10	2.4	8.8	3.6	0.6	111
2013	AA	Portland	5	10	0	108	135	4.33	1.46	19.3	269	37	72	4.42	3.8	11.3	2.9	0.9	117
2013	AAA	Pawtucket	1	0	0	5	7	0.00	0.98	19.4	173	29	100	1.14	3.5	12.4	3.5	0.0	145
2014	AAA	Pawtucket	8	9	0	127	103	3.96	1.30	22.8	249	30	69	3.44	3.3	7.3	2.2	0.6	61
2014	MLB	Boston	0	0	0	9	8	4.00	1.44	7.7	302	37	75	4.98	2.0	8.0	4.0	1.0	108

Tall, durable SP with solid arsenal and improving FB command. Arm speed and strength generate good velocity, though has tendency to pitch up in zone. Saw decline in K rate due to inconsistent CB. CU becoming top offering and can baffle LHH. Polishing CB is paramount to success.

Barrett,Jake — RP — Arizona

EXP MLB DEBUT: 2015 | H/W: 6-3 230 | FUT: Setup RP | 8D

Thrws R Age 23 — 2012 (3) Arizona State

Velo	Pitch	Grade
94-96	FB	++++
85-87	SL	++++
78-80	CU	++

Year	Lev	Team	W	L	Sv	IP	K	ERA	WHIP	BF/G	OBA	H%	S%	xERA	Ctl	Dom	Cmd	hr/9	BPV
2012	A	South Bend	0	3	6	24	25	5.95	1.69	4.4	291	38	64	5.18	4.8	9.3	1.9	0.7	55
2013	A+	Visalia	2	1	15	27	37	1.99	1.11	3.8	216	33	86	2.58	3.0	12.3	4.1	0.7	158
2013	AA	Mobile	1	1	14	24	22	0.37	0.87	3.7	209	26	105	2.01	1.1	8.2	7.3	0.7	135
2014	AA	Mobile	1	2	12	26	24	2.41	1.42	4.4	254	34	81	3.26	4.1	8.3	2.0	0.0	55
2014	AAA	Reno	1	0	16	29	23	3.72	1.28	4.0	212	24	74	3.26	4.7	7.1	1.5	0.9	21

Strong-armed reliever comes after hitters with a good 94-96 mph FB that can go as high as 98. Ability to throw strikes took a step back in '14, but he held his own at AA/AAA. Adds in a plus 85-87 mph SL and a CU. He notched 28 saves and is one of the better relief prospects in the NL.

Bassitt,Chris — SP — Oakland

EXP MLB DEBUT: 2014 | H/W: 6-5 210 | FUT: #4 starter | 7C

Thrws R Age 26 — 2011 (16) Akron

Velo	Pitch	Grade
90-94	FB	+++
82-84	SL	+++
77-79	CB	++
81-85	CU	++

Year	Lev	Team	W	L	Sv	IP	K	ERA	WHIP	BF/G	OBA	H%	S%	xERA	Ctl	Dom	Cmd	hr/9	BPV
2013	A+	Winston-Salem	7	2	0	101	101	3.47	1.31	23.2	240	31	76	3.55	3.7	9.0	2.4	0.8	79
2013	AA	Birmingham	4	2	0	47	37	2.29	1.10	23.1	208	26	80	2.26	3.2	7.1	2.2	0.4	57
2014	Rk	AZL White Sox	0	0	0	8	13	4.39	1.46	11.7	280	47	67	3.69	3.3	14.3	4.3	0.0	186
2014	AA	Birmingham	3	1	0	34	36	1.58	1.17	22.7	212	28	89	2.60	3.7	9.5	2.6	0.5	89
2014	MLB	Chi White Sox	1	1	0	29	21	4.01	1.61	21.6	292	36	72	4.31	4.0	6.5	1.6	0.0	26

Consistent, steady SP who began year in June and ended in CHW. Has tall frame, but throws from low 3/4 slot and gets ample movement to 4 pitches. Sinking FB induces groundballs while sweeping SL is best secondary pitch. Fringy CU needs polish in order to retire LHH consistently.

Beck,Christopher | SP | Chicago (A) | EXP MLB DEBUT: 2015 | H/W: 6-3 225 | FUT: #4 starter | 7D

Thrws R Age 24	Year	Lev	Team	W	L	Sv	IP	K	ERA	WHIP	BF/G	OBA	H%	S%	xERA	Ctl	Dom	Cmd	hr/9	BPV
2012 (2) Georgia Southern	2012	Rk	Great Falls	4	3	0	40	36	4.71	1.57	11.7	311	38	70	5.12	2.7	8.1	3.0	0.7	91
89-95 FB +++	2013	A+	Winston-Salem	11	8	0	118	57	3.12	1.35	23.4	260	28	80	3.99	3.2	4.3	1.4	0.8	10
83-86 SL +++	2013	AA	Birmingham	2	2	0	28	22	2.89	1.04	21.6	248	31	69	2.23	1.0	7.1	7.3	0.0	119
CU ++	2014	AA	Birmingham	5	8	0	116	57	3.41	1.27	23.7	261	29	74	3.53	2.4	4.4	1.8	0.5	33
	2014	AAA	Charlotte	1	3	0	33	28	4.08	1.48	20.3	278	35	71	4.03	3.5	7.6	2.2	0.3	60

Competitive, durable SP who has surprisingly low K rate despite solid arsenal. Uses drop-and-drive delivery to spot ball low in zone. Possesses lively FB with good command while hard SL is potent against RHH. CU still below average, but getting better. Mechanics could use overhaul.

Bedrosian,Cam | RP | Los Angeles (A) | EXP MLB DEBUT: 2014 | H/W: 6-0 205 | FUT: Closer | 7B

Thrws R Age 23	Year	Lev	Team	W	L	Sv	IP	K	ERA	WHIP	BF/G	OBA	H%	S%	xERA	Ctl	Dom	Cmd	hr/9	BPV
2010 (1) HS (GA)	2013	A+	Inland Empire	0	0	0	8	9	0.00	1.34	4.9	147	22	100	1.81	7.7	9.9	1.3	0.0	-12
92-97 FB ++++	2014	A+	Inland Empire	0	0	1	5	15	0.00	0.58	3.5	64	151	100	0.00	3.5	26.0	7.5	0.0	392
83-85 SL +++	2014	AA	Arkansas	1	0	15	32	57	1.12	0.62	3.7	99	21	84	0.00	2.8	16.0	5.7	0.3	230
81-83 CU ++	2014	AAA	Salt Lake	1	1	2	7	10	7.71	1.57	3.8	202	34	45	2.96	7.7	12.9	1.7	0.0	41
	2014	MLB	LA Angels	0	1	0	19	20	6.60	1.83	5.2	299	38	64	5.84	5.7	9.4	1.7	0.9	35

Powerful RP who pitched on 4 levels, including majors. Posted very high K rate with plus FB and power SL. Gets lots of pitch movement and is tough to square up. Moved to pen in 2013 due to injury history but stuff plays up in short stints. Can nibble at corners and rarely uses CU.

Beede,Tyler | SP | San Francisco | EXP MLB DEBUT: 2016 | H/W: 6-4 200 | FUT: #2 Starter | 9C

Thrws R Age 21	Year	Lev	Team	W	L	Sv	IP	K	ERA	WHIP	BF/G	OBA	H%	S%	xERA	Ctl	Dom	Cmd	hr/9	BPV
2014 (1) Vanderbilt	2012	NCAA	Vanderbilt	1	5	0	71		4.55	1.54	19.4	280	36	70	4.42	4.0	8.6	2.1	0.5	64
91-94 FB ++++	2013	NCAA	Vanderbilt	14	1	0	101	103	2.32	1.26	24.2	183	25	81	2.24	5.6	9.2	1.6	0.3	32
79-81 CB +++	2014	NCAA	Vanderbilt	8	8	0	113	116	4.06	1.28	24.4	224	30	67	2.83	4.2	9.2	2.2	0.3	70
80-82 CU +++	2014	Rk	AZL Giants	0	1	0	8	11	3.29	1.46	8.8	257	40	75	3.39	4.4	12.1	2.8	0.0	117
	2014	A-	Salem-Kaizer	0	0	0	6	7	2.90	1.77	14.2	314	43	82	5.03	4.4	10.2	2.3	0.0	83

Tall, durable RHP impressed during two stops in '14, showing a FB up to 97, a power CB, and plus CU, all of which he will use in any count. He will need to clean up his delivery that gets out of sync at times, effecting his Ctl, but with the Giants' staff on his side, he has what he takes to reach that of a #2.

Berrios,Jose | SP | Minnesota | EXP MLB DEBUT: 2016 | H/W: 6-0 185 | FUT: #2 starter | 8B

Thrws R Age 20	Year	Lev	Team	W	L	Sv	IP	K	ERA	WHIP	BF/G	OBA	H%	S%	xERA	Ctl	Dom	Cmd	hr/9	BPV
2012 (1-S) HS (PR)	2012	Rk	GCL Twins	1	0	4	16	27	1.11	0.62	7.0	133	27	80	0.00	1.7	15.0	9.0	0.0	243
91-96 FB ++++	2013	A	Cedar Rapids	7	7	0	103	100	4.01	1.41	22.9	265	34	71	3.88	3.5	8.7	2.5	0.5	81
80-83 CB +++	2014	A+	Fort Myers	9	3	0	96	109	1.97	1.05	23.3	223	31	82	2.28	2.2	10.2	4.7	0.4	144
80-82 CU +++	2014	AA	New Britain	3	4	0	40	28	3.58	1.12	19.8	225	27	67	2.59	2.7	6.3	2.3	0.4	58
	2014	AAA	Rochester	0	1	0	3	3	18.00	3.33	18.5	453	56	40	11.74	9.0	9.0	1.0	0.0	-63

Electric SP who dominated High-A before promotion. Advancing quickly with polished nature and ability to change speeds. Aggressively establishes plate with plus FB and mixes in power CB and advanced CU with depth and fade. Limits hard contact with repertoire. Size is only concern.

Berry,Tim | SP | Baltimore | EXP MLB DEBUT: 2015 | H/W: 6-3 180 | FUT: #4 starter | 7B

Thrws L Age 24	Year	Lev	Team	W	L	Sv	IP	K	ERA	WHIP	BF/G	OBA	H%	S%	xERA	Ctl	Dom	Cmd	hr/9	BPV
2009 (50) HS (CA)	2012	A	Delmarva	2	7	0	52	44	5.02	1.48	22.4	290	36	65	4.44	2.9	7.6	2.6	0.5	76
88-94 FB +++	2012	A+	Frederick	5	5	0	75	61	4.32	1.37	21.0	282	34	69	4.23	2.4	7.3	3.1	0.7	85
75-79 CB +++	2012	AA	Bowie	0	1	0	1	4	52.50	7.50	12.4	674	110	22	31.32	15.0	30.0	2.0	0.0	153
78-82 SL ++	2013	A+	Frederick	11	7	0	152	119	3.85	1.29	23.1	267	32	72	3.86	2.4	7.0	3.0	0.8	81
80-82 CU +++	2014	AA	Bowie	6	7	0	133	108	3.52	1.25	23.6	245	29	74	3.52	3.0	7.3	2.4	0.8	67

Lean, steady SP with improved FB command and consistent K rate. Keeps ball down and generates solid pitch movement with loose, fast arm. Uses two breaking balls and counters with nice CU. Hard CB can register Ks, though SL can be too loose. Tough on LHH, but RHH hit him.

Biddle,Jesse | SP | Philadelphia | EXP MLB DEBUT: 2015 | H/W: 6-5 220 | FUT: #3 starter | 8D

Thrws L Age 23	Year	Lev	Team	W	L	Sv	IP	K	ERA	WHIP	BF/G	OBA	H%	S%	xERA	Ctl	Dom	Cmd	hr/9	BPV
2010 (1) HS (PA)	2012	A+	Clearwater	10	6	0	142	151	3.23	1.29	22.5	243	32	76	3.38	3.4	9.6	2.8	0.6	98
90-92 FB +++	2013	AA	Reading	5	14	0	138	154	3.65	1.35	21.3	211	29	74	3.14	5.3	10.0	1.9	0.7	54
70-74 CB +++	2014	Rk	GCL Phillies	0	0	0	2	3	4.50	1.00	7.6	151	0	100	5.17	4.5	13.5	3.0	4.5	140
78-80 CU +++	2014	A+	Clearwater	2	0	0	10	9	0.90	0.90	18.6	96	14	89	0.21	5.4	8.1	1.5	0.0	18
	2014	AA	Reading	3	10	0	82	80	5.04	1.49	22.1	252	31	68	4.54	4.8	8.8	1.8	1.2	46

Bizarre head injury (suffered concussion during a hailstorm) in May clouded entire season. At his best, a sturdy southpaw with 90-92 FB, sharp CB and usable CU, but control history and tendency for difficulties to snowball are valid concerns. Winter-ball elbow issue another factor to monitor. Needs to step forward.

Binford,Christian | SP | Kansas City | EXP MLB DEBUT: 2015 | H/W: 6-6 215 | FUT: #4 starter | 7C

Thrws R Age 22	Year	Lev	Team	W	L	Sv	IP	K	ERA	WHIP	BF/G	OBA	H%	S%	xERA	Ctl	Dom	Cmd	hr/9	BPV
2011 (30) HS (PA)	2012	Rk	Burlington	2	3	0	40	31	2.03	1.10	19.6	262	32	81	2.80	0.9	7.0	7.8	0.2	119
88-93 FB +++	2013	A	Lexington	8	7	0	135	130	2.67	1.14	23.2	253	33	78	2.99	1.7	8.7	5.2	0.5	129
79-82 SL ++	2014	A+	Wilmington	5	4	0	82	92	2.41	1.01	22.5	237	33	75	2.21	1.2	10.1	8.4	0.2	167
79-85 CU +++	2014	AA	NW Arkansas	3	2	0	48	38	3.19	1.06	23.3	250	28	77	3.56	1.1	7.1	6.3	1.3	116
	2014	AAA	Omaha	0	1	0	10	9	5.40	2.10	12.3	362	44	75	7.54	4.5	8.1	1.8	0.9	42

Tall SP with exceptional control and feel for craft. Downhill angle and natural sink to FB lead to groundballs while arm speed brings solid-average CU. Lacks an out pitch and has unorthodox delivery with significant effort. Upside limited and will require better SL to retire big league hitters.

Bird,Zachary | SP | Los Angeles (N) | EXP MLB DEBUT: 2017 | H/W: 6-4 205 | FUT: #4 starter | 7D

Thrws R Age 20	Year	Lev	Team	W	L	Sv	IP	K	ERA	WHIP	BF/G	OBA	H%	S%	xERA	Ctl	Dom	Cmd	hr/9	BPV
2012 (9) HS (MS)																				
88-92 FB +++	2012	Rk	AZL Dodgers	1	2	0	39	46	4.59	1.35	16.4	246	35	65	3.40	3.9	10.6	2.7	0.5	103
70-73 CB ++	2013	Rk	Ogden	2	4	0	43	44	5.83	1.44	20.4	261	34	58	3.99	4.0	9.2	2.3	0.6	76
SL ++	2013	A	Great Lakes	2	5	0	60	50	5.10	1.68	14.2	249	30	70	4.58	6.8	7.5	1.1	0.8	-29
CU ++	2014	A	Great Lakes	6	17	0	118	110	4.26	1.46	19.5	261	33	71	4.13	4.2	8.4	2.0	0.7	56

Tall, lean RHP with projection continues to show signs of raw ability, but has inconsistent mechanics. FB now sits in the low-90s with a tight CB that flashes plus. Delivery is a mess with no repeatability or command of his pitch selection. Repeat of MWL led to modest improvement.

Blach,Ty | SP | San Francisco | EXP MLB DEBUT: 2015 | H/W: 6-1 210 | FUT: #3 starter | 8D

Thrws L Age 24	Year	Lev	Team	W	L	Sv	IP	K	ERA	WHIP	BF/G	OBA	H%	S%	xERA	Ctl	Dom	Cmd	hr/9	BPV
2012 (5) Creighton	2010	NCAA	Creighton	3	3	0	75	58	3.12	1.08	20.9	229	27	74	2.89	2.2	7.0	3.2	0.8	85
90-92 FB +++	2011	NCAA	Creighton	10	3	0	102	100	2.65	1.21	21.6	246	33	78	2.88	2.6	8.8	3.4	0.3	108
78-81 SL +++	2012	NCAA	Creighton	6	6	0	120	83	2.70	1.02	21.9	217	26	74	2.16	2.1	6.2	3.0	0.4	73
80-82 CU +++	2013	A+	San Jose	12	4	0	130	117	2.91	1.09	23.1	253	32	75	2.95	1.2	8.1	6.5	0.6	130
	2014	AA	Richmond	8	8	0	141	91	3.13	1.28	23.1	263	30	76	3.56	2.5	5.8	2.3	0.5	55

Advanced command lefty continued to impress in AA, showing his plus feel for pitching and ability to keep hitters guessing. Works down in zone and generates a good amount of GBs, mixing pitches with ease. May never have huge Dom totals, but pitchability and feel for his arsenal make him a safe mid-rotation SP.

Black,Corey | SP | Chicago (N) | EXP MLB DEBUT: 2016 | H/W: 5-11 175 | FUT: #4 starter | 7C

Thrws R Age 23	Year	Lev	Team	W	L	Sv	IP	K	ERA	WHIP	BF/G	OBA	H%	S%	xERA	Ctl	Dom	Cmd	hr/9	BPV
2012 (4) Faulkner	2012	A-	Staten Island	0	0	0	27	21	2.32	1.10	17.8	223	27	79	2.40	2.6	6.9	2.6	0.3	72
94-96 FB ++++	2012	A	CharlestonSC	2	2	0	23	29	3.88	0.99	17.7	216	33	57	1.68	1.9	11.3	5.8	0.0	168
85-88 SL ++	2013	A+	Daytona	4	0	0	25	28	2.88	1.28	20.5	238	31	83	3.71	3.6	10.1	2.8	1.1	102
80-83 CU ++	2013	A+	Tampa	3	8	0	82	88	4.27	1.51	18.7	254	35	70	3.69	4.9	9.6	2.0	0.2	58
76-78 CB ++	2014	AA	Tennessee	6	7	0	124	119	3.48	1.38	20.0	222	27	78	3.64	5.1	8.6	1.7	0.9	34

Small RH has surprising velocity. Heater sits at 94-96 mph and tops at 100 mph. Also throws a SL, CB, and CU. Shows good feel for CU, but breaking balls remain a work in progress. Works with a quick tempo, but is max-effort and can rush his delivery resulting in below average FB command.

Blackburn,Clayton | SP | San Francisco | EXP MLB DEBUT: 2015 | H/W: 6-2 260 | FUT: #2 Starter | 8D

Thrws R Age 22	Year	Lev	Team	W	L	Sv	IP	K	ERA	WHIP	BF/G	OBA	H%	S%	xERA	Ctl	Dom	Cmd	hr/9	BPV
2011 (16) HS (OK)	2011	Rk	AZL Giants	3	1	0	33	30	1.09	0.57	9.4	146	18	88	0.39	0.8	8.2	10.0	0.5	143
88-91 FB +++	2012	A	Augusta	8	4	0	131	143	2.54	1.02	22.9	239	33	74	2.25	1.2	9.8	7.9	0.2	161
72-74 CB ++++	2013	A+	San Jose	7	5	0	133	138	3.65	1.10	22.7	228	29	69	2.88	2.4	9.3	3.9	0.8	122
78-80 SL ++	2014	Rk	AZL Giants	0	1	0	5	9	3.60	0.80	9.1	221	44	50	1.21	0.0	16.2		0.0	310
80-82 CU ++	2014	AA	Richmond	5	6	0	93	85	3.29	1.23	20.9	264	34	71	3.01	1.9	8.2	4.3	0.1	114

Big, durable RHP continues to carve his way through the Giants' farm system. FB in the low-90s with a SL, CU, and CB that flashes plus and can be manipulated and generates Ks.Clean arm, durable build, and repeatable delivery translate into good Ctl results. Not the velo of an ace, but pitchability will make him a top end SP.

Blackburn,Paul — SP — Chicago (N)

EXP MLB DEBUT: 2017 | H/W: 6-2 185 | FUT: #3 starter | 7C

Thrws R Age 21
2012 (1-S) HS (CA)

Velo	Pitch	Grade
90-94	FB	+++
78-80	CB	+++
	CU	++

Year	Lev	Team	W	L	Sv	IP	K	ERA	WHIP	BF/G	OBA	H%	S%	xERA	Ctl	Dom	Cmd	hr/9	BPV
2012	Rk	AZL Cubs	2	0	0	20	13	3.56	1.49	9.7	288	32	79	4.78	3.1	5.8	1.9	0.9	38
2013	A-	Boise	2	3	0	46	38	3.33	1.52	15.4	240	29	79	3.91	5.7	7.4	1.3	0.6	-1
2014	A	Kane County	9	4	0	117	75	3.23	1.19	19.5	247	29	73	3.05	2.4	5.8	2.4	0.5	57

Strong-armed RH showed signs of improvement. Improved Ctl was key; FB is his bread and butter and it sits at 91-93 mph and now tops out at 95 mph. Secondary offerings include a curve and CU that have potential and showed greater consistency in '14.

Blair,Aaron — SP — Arizona

EXP MLB DEBUT: 2015 | H/W: 6-5 230 | FUT: #3 starter | 8C

Thrws R Age 22
2013 (1-S) Marshall

Velo	Pitch	Grade
92-94	FB	+++
75-79	CB	++
82-85	CU	++++

Year	Lev	Team	W	L	Sv	IP	K	ERA	WHIP	BF/G	OBA	H%	S%	xERA	Ctl	Dom	Cmd	hr/9	BPV
2013	A-	Hillsboro	1	1	0	31	28	2.90	1.23	15.7	222	28	78	2.92	3.8	8.1	2.2	0.6	62
2013	A	South Bend	0	2	0	17	13	3.66	1.34	23.8	281	35	70	3.46	2.1	6.8	3.3	0.0	84
2014	A	South Bend	1	2	0	35	44	4.09	1.11	23.0	201	29	62	2.28	3.6	11.3	3.1	0.5	124
2014	A+	Visalia	4	2	0	72	81	4.37	1.26	22.6	256	34	66	3.59	2.6	10.1	3.9	0.7	129
2014	AA	Mobile	4	1	0	46	46	1.95	1.00	22.0	187	24	86	2.12	3.1	9.0	2.9	0.8	95

Physical RH pitched well at three different levels. Uptick in FB velocity and improved CB fueled the breakout. FB now sits at 92-94 mph, topping out at 95. Turns his back on hitters to generate torque and creates deception. Was 2nd in the minors with 171 K and limited hitters to a .218 BA.

Blazek,Mike — RP — Milwaukee

EXP MLB DEBUT: 2013 | H/W: 6-0 200 | FUT: Reliever | 6C

Thrws R Age 26
2007 (35) HS (NV)

Velo	Pitch	Grade
94-97	FB	+++
73-75	CB	++
	SL	++
	CU	++

Year	Lev	Team	W	L	Sv	IP	K	ERA	WHIP	BF/G	OBA	H%	S%	xERA	Ctl	Dom	Cmd	hr/9	BPV
2013	AA	Springfield	0	0	7	19		0.94	1.09	4.4	169	27	90	1.39	4.7	11.7	2.5	0.0	102
2013	AAA	Memphis	1	2	2	26	27	2.77	1.27	5.6	188	26	78	2.40	5.5	9.3	1.7	0.3	37
2013	MLB	Milwaukee	0	1	0	7	4	3.86	1.29	4.1	233	24	75	3.90	3.9	5.1	1.3	1.3	6
2013	MLB	St. Louis	0	0	0	10	10	7.13	1.98	4.4	260	30	67	6.43	8.9	8.9	1.0	1.8	-62
2014	AAA	Nashville	4	4	1	102	87	4.14	1.43	11.7	269	33	72	4.26	3.5	7.7	2.2	0.8	61

Short, durable RH worked both as a SP and in relief. Came over from the Cards and spent most of '14 at AAA. Has a plus mid-90s FB, a CB, SL, and CU, but lacks a true out pitch. FB has good velo but tends to be straight. Can be effective when he gets his CB over, but is likley limited to relief.

Blewett,Scott — SP — Kansas City

EXP MLB DEBUT: 2018 | H/W: 6-6 210 | FUT: #2 starter | 8D

Thrws R Age 18
2014 (2) HS (NY)

Velo	Pitch	Grade
88-93	FB	+++
75-78	CB	+++
80-82	CU	++

Year	Lev	Team	W	L	Sv	IP	K	ERA	WHIP	BF/G	OBA	H%	S%	xERA	Ctl	Dom	Cmd	hr/9	BPV
2014	Rk	Burlington	1	2	0	28	29	4.82	1.50	15.1	255	32	69	4.38	4.8	9.3	1.9	1.0	56

Quick-armed SP with plus projection and potential. Has chance for three average to plus offerings and will need instruction to smooth out delivery. FB command a bit short, but has good life and potential for more velocity. Loses velocity late in games at present. CB is best secondary.

Bonilla,Lisalverto — RP — Texas

EXP MLB DEBUT: 2014 | H/W: 6-0 175 | FUT: Setup RP | 7C

Thrws R Age 24
2008 FA (DR)

Velo	Pitch	Grade
90-96	FB	+++
78-81	SL	++
82-84	CU	++++

Year	Lev	Team	W	L	Sv	IP	K	ERA	WHIP	BF/G	OBA	H%	S%	xERA	Ctl	Dom	Cmd	hr/9	BPV
2012	AA	Reading	2	1	3	33	46	1.64	1.18	6.3	191	31	87	2.11	4.6	12.5	2.7	0.3	119
2013	AA	Frisco	2	0	6	30	50	0.30	0.83	5.2	159	31	96	0.58	2.7	15.0	5.6	0.0	214
2013	AAA	Round Rock	5	5	0	43	56	7.95	1.77	7.6	300	40	56	6.35	5.0	11.7	2.3	1.7	93
2014	AAA	Round Rock	4	2	1	74	92	4.12	1.32	7.9	259	35	72	4.08	3.0	11.2	3.7	1.1	137
2014	MLB	Texas	3	0	0	20	17	3.12	1.24	16.4	186	22	78	2.82	5.3	7.6	1.4	0.9	10

Short, deceptive pitcher who was SP at end of season with TEX. Mostly RP in career with ability to get grounders and Ks. Pitches off solid-average FB and uses plus CU as K pitch. Below average SL may move him to pen full-time. Has effort in delivery with long arm action.

Borden,Buddy — SP — Tampa Bay

EXP MLB DEBUT: 2017 | H/W: 6-3 210 | FUT: #4 starter | 7D

Thrws R Age 22
2013 (7) Nevada-Las Vegas

Velo	Pitch	Grade
90-93	FB	+++
	CB	+
	CU	+

Year	Lev	Team	W	L	Sv	IP	K	ERA	WHIP	BF/G	OBA	H%	S%	xERA	Ctl	Dom	Cmd	hr/9	BPV
2011	NCAA	UNLV	1	2	0	22	10	10.59	2.26	11.2	391	42	50	8.46	4.1	4.1	1.0	0.8	-19
2012	NCAA	UNLV	2	5	1	54	63	4.98	1.66	15.2	268	36	71	4.83	5.6	10.5	1.9	0.8	54
2013	NCAA	UNLV	8	2	0	100	77	2.60	1.23	27.0	237	29	79	2.92	3.1	6.9	2.2	0.4	58
2013	A-	Jamestown	0	0	0	16	23	1.11	0.93	10.1	180	31	87	1.07	2.8	12.8	4.6	0.0	173
2014	A	West Virginia	7	9	1	128	122	3.16	1.18	19.0	222	27	77	3.11	3.4	8.6	2.5	0.9	81

Athletic RH put up solid numbers in full-season debut and was then traded to Tampa. Has a lively 90-93 mph FB that can hit 95. Also has a decent CU and a CB that needs refinement. Showed solid cmd, walking 48 while striking out 122. Profiles as a back-end starter, but could be more.

Borucki,Ryan — SP — Toronto

EXP MLB DEBUT: 2018 | H/W: 6-4 175 | FUT: #3 starter | 8E

Thrws L Age 21
2012 (15) HS (IL)

Velo	Pitch	Grade
89-94	FB	+++
75-79	CB	++
80-83	CU	+++

Year	Lev	Team	W	L	Sv	IP	K	ERA	WHIP	BF/G	OBA	H%	S%	xERA	Ctl	Dom	Cmd	hr/9	BPV
2012	Rk	GCL Blue Jays	1	0	0	6	10	3.00	0.67	5.2	191	30	67	1.94	0.0	15.0		1.5	288
2014	Rk	Bluefield	2	1	0	33	30	2.72	0.97	15.7	218	27	73	2.18	1.6	8.2	5.0	0.5	121
2014	A-	Vancouver	1	1	1	23	22	1.94	0.69	16.3	166	22	73	0.73	1.2	8.5	7.3	0.4	140

Lanky, projectable LHP who bounced back strong after missing '13 due to TJ surgery. Moves lively FB effectively around strike zone and has refined CB and CU to give varying looks and speeds. Improved delivery to quicken arm speed for ample pitch movement. Very tough on LHH.

Boshers,Buddy — RP — Colorado

EXP MLB DEBUT: 2013 | H/W: 6-3 205 | FUT: Setup RP | 6C

Thrws L Age 26
2008 (4) Calhoun CC

Velo	Pitch	Grade
91-94	FB	++
77-80	CB	+++
80-82	CU	++

Year	Lev	Team	W	L	Sv	IP	K	ERA	WHIP	BF/G	OBA	H%	S%	xERA	Ctl	Dom	Cmd	hr/9	BPV
2013	AA	Arkansas	3	2	1	28	35	3.19	1.17	4.0	201	30	72	2.25	4.1	11.2	2.7	0.3	107
2013	AAA	Salt Lake	1	0	1	19	26	3.75	1.56	5.3	250	38	76	3.98	5.6	12.2	2.2	0.5	86
2013	MLB	LA Angels	0	0	0	15	13	4.77	1.39	2.5	234	31	62	2.94	4.8	7.7	1.6	0.0	29
2014	AA	Arkansas	2	3	0	61	70	2.66	1.21	8.5	215	31	77	2.37	4.0	10.3	2.6	0.1	96
2014	AAA	Salt Lake	1	0	0	13	12	6.23	1.77	5.4	214	27	64	4.30	9.0	8.3	0.9	0.7	-75

Tall, deceptive RP who continues to spotlight excellent CB that retires LHH consistently. Arm action can be tough to pick up, though has difficulty throwing consistent strikes. When behind in count, CB isn't as impactful. Gets fair share of grounders and keeps HR to minimum.

Bostick,Akeem — SP — Texas

EXP MLB DEBUT: 2017 | H/W: 6-4 180 | FUT: #3 starter | 8E

Thrws R Age 19
2013 (2) HS (SC)

Velo	Pitch	Grade
88-94	FB	+++
78-82	CB	++
80-83	CU	++

Year	Lev	Team	W	L	Sv	IP	K	ERA	WHIP	BF/G	OBA	H%	S%	xERA	Ctl	Dom	Cmd	hr/9	BPV
2013	Rk	AZL Rangers	4	1	1	41	33	2.85	1.31	12.1	266	34	76	3.18	2.6	7.2	2.8	0.0	77
2014	A	Hickory	5	6	0	92	64	5.18	1.37	18.4	274	31	63	4.36	2.7	6.3	2.3	1.0	57

Raw, athletic SP who was aggresively placed at Low-A. Has clean arm action, though can have inconsistent delivery. Uses height well and has projection remaining. Throws downhill with solid FB with cutting action. LHH hit him as he doesn't use CU often and only has average CB.

Boyd,Matt — SP — Toronto

EXP MLB DEBUT: 2016 | H/W: 6-3 215 | FUT: #4 starter | 7E

Thrws L Age 24
2013 (6) Oregon State

Velo	Pitch	Grade
88-94	FB	+++
81-85	SL	+++
80-83	CU	++

Year	Lev	Team	W	L	Sv	IP	K	ERA	WHIP	BF/G	OBA	H%	S%	xERA	Ctl	Dom	Cmd	hr/9	BPV
2013	NCAA	Oregon State	11	4	1	132	122	2.04	0.95	24.9	198	26	79	1.70	2.2	8.3	3.7	0.3	107
2013	A	Lansing	0	1	0	14	12	0.64	0.57	9.5	151	20	88	0.00	0.6	7.7	12.0	0.0	140
2013	A+	Dunedin	0	2	0	10	11	5.40	1.00	12.7	199	23	50	3.20	2.7	9.9	3.7	1.8	123
2014	A+	Dunedin	5	3	0	90	103	1.40	0.94	21.2	204	29	88	1.79	2.0	10.3	5.2	0.4	149
2014	AA	New Hampshire	1	4	0	42	44	7.04	1.61	18.7	316	40	56	5.66	2.8	9.4	3.4	1.1	112

Command-oriented LHP who bounced back and forth between High-A and AA. Dominates LHH with FB/SL combo and could move into bullpen. Throws with deceptive angle to plate, but can leave SL up in zone. Registers Ks more with tricky delivery than natural stuff. Lacks feel for CU.

Bradley,Archie — SP — Arizona

EXP MLB DEBUT: 2015 | H/W: 6-4 235 | FUT: #1 starter | 9C

Thrws R Age 22
2011 (1) HS (OK)

Velo	Pitch	Grade
93-96	FB	+++++
80-83	CB	++++
83-85	CU	++

Year	Lev	Team	W	L	Sv	IP	K	ERA	WHIP	BF/G	OBA	H%	S%	xERA	Ctl	Dom	Cmd	hr/9	BPV
2013	A+	Visalia	2	0	0	28	43	1.28	1.13	22.3	217	37	90	2.32	3.2	13.7	4.3	0.3	179
2013	AA	Mobile	12	5	0	123	119	1.97	1.23	23.8	211	28	85	2.60	4.3	8.7	2.0	0.4	58
2014	Rk	AZL Dbacks	0	0	0	4	6	4.50	1.50	17.3	307	49	67	4.19	2.3	13.5	6.0	0.0	200
2014	AA	Mobile	2	3	0	54	46	4.15	1.49	19.5	227	29	71	3.44	6.0	7.6	1.3	0.3	-6
2014	AAA	Reno	1	4	0	24	23	5.23	1.58	21.2	277	37	63	3.98	4.5	8.6	1.9	0.0	52

Tall, athletic RH missed two months of action and didn't dominate the way many anticipated. Is physically mature and generates easy velocity with a plus 93-96 mph FB. CB, once considered plus, was less effective in '14, and his CU remains a work in progress, but both pitches show potential.

Bradley, Jed — SP — Milwaukee

EXP MLB DEBUT: 2016 H/W: 6-4 225 FUT: #4 starter **7D**

Thrws L Age 24
2011 (1) Georgia Tech
89-93 FB +++
83-85 SL ++
80-83 CU +++

Year	Lev	Team	W	L	Sv	IP	K	ERA	WHIP	BF/G	OBA	H%	S%	xERA	Ctl	Dom	Cmd	hr/9	BPV
2011	NCAA	Georgia Tech	7	3	0	98	106	3.49	1.22	24.8	244	34	69	2.72	2.8	9.7	3.4	0.1	116
2012	A+	Brevard Cnty	5	10	0	107	60	5.55	1.67	24.1	310	34	66	5.47	3.6	5.0	1.4	0.8	11
2013	A+	Brevard Cnty	4	4	0	78	58	4.15	1.54	21.3	269	32	74	4.44	4.5	6.7	1.5	0.7	17
2014	A+	Brevard Cnty	5	2	0	60	53	3.00	1.06	23.3	242	30	73	2.78	1.5	7.9	5.3	0.6	120
2014	AA	Huntsville	5	8	0	87	71	4.55	1.63	22.8	302	36	73	5.28	3.7	7.3	2.0	0.8	50

15th overall pick in 2011 has yet to get past AA. Started the year well, but looked more pedestrian when moved up. FB now sits at 89-93 mph with a mid-80s SL and an above-avg CU. Still has potential, but so far this bonus baby has been a bust. Look for a jump to AAA, but he needs to show more.

Brady, Sean — SP — Cleveland

EXP MLB DEBUT: 2017 H/W: 6-0 175 FUT: #4 starter **7D**

Thrws L Age 20
2013 (5) HS (FL)
87-92 FB ++
77-80 CB +++
80-82 CU +++

Year	Lev	Team	W	L	Sv	IP	K	ERA	WHIP	BF/G	OBA	H%	S%	xERA	Ctl	Dom	Cmd	hr/9	BPV
2013	Rk	AZL Indians	0	1	0	32	30	1.97	0.94	12.0	210	27	82	2.03	1.7	8.4	5.0	0.6	124
2014	A-	Mahoning Val	2	4	0	71	44	2.79	1.34	21.1	254	30	78	3.33	3.4	5.6	1.6	0.3	26
2014	A	Lake County	0	1	0	2	2	16.36	3.64	14.2	492	49	67	21.24	8.2	8.2	1.0	8.2	-56

Advanced pitcher with nice current stuff, but lacks projection and velocity. Can be tough on LHH with CB that has plus potential and CU that shows fade. Commands FB well down in zone and will need to live there as he lacks height. Mixes efficiently, but doesn't project to high K rate.

Brault, Steven — SP — Baltimore

EXP MLB DEBUT: 2016 H/W: 6-1 175 FUT: #4 starter **7D**

Thrws L Age 22
2013 (11) Regis
89-93 FB +++
80-82 SL ++
75-78 CB ++
CU +++

Year	Lev	Team	W	L	Sv	IP	K	ERA	WHIP	BF/G	OBA	H%	S%	xERA	Ctl	Dom	Cmd	hr/9	BPV
2013	A-	Aberdeen	1	2	0	43	38	2.09	1.09	14.0	224	29	80	2.26	2.5	8.0	3.2	0.2	93
2014	A	Delmarva	9	8	0	130	115	3.05	1.04	22.8	226	29	69	2.21	1.9	8.0	4.1	0.3	109
2014	A+	Frederick	2	0	0	16	9	0.56	0.56	18.1	134	16	89	0.00	1.1	5.0	4.5	0.0	78

Command-oriented SP who repeats delivery consistently and hides ball to keep hitters off guard. Tough to hit at lower levels, but K rate disappointing. Lacks knockout offering, though mixes four pitches effectively. Keeps ball down in zone and rarely allows walks. Very tough on LHH.

Brice, Austin — SP — Miami

EXP MLB DEBUT: 2016 H/W: 6-4 205 FUT: #3 starter **7D**

Thrws R Age 22
2010 (9) HS (NC)
92-95 FB ++++
80-82 CB ++++
CU +++

Year	Lev	Team	W	L	Sv	IP	K	ERA	WHIP	BF/G	OBA	H%	S%	xERA	Ctl	Dom	Cmd	hr/9	BPV
2010	Rk	GCL Marlins	0	1	0	8	8	4.44	1.73	6.1	235	32	71	3.79	7.8	8.9	1.1	0.0	-32
2011	Rk	GCL Marlins	6	0	0	48	55	2.99	1.35	18.3	191	27	78	2.64	6.2	10.3	1.7	0.4	36
2012	A	Greensboro	8	6	0	109	122	4.37	1.50	18.9	238	31	74	4.26	5.6	10.1	1.8	1.1	48
2013	A	Greensboro	8	11	0	113	111	5.73	1.77	19.9	270	34	68	5.20	6.5	8.8	1.4	0.9	1
2014	A+	Jupiter	8	9	0	127	109	3.61	1.33	21.1	241	30	72	3.22	3.9	7.7	2.0	0.4	52

Tall, projectable RH put in a solid year of work at High-A in the FSL. Works with a 92-94 FB, curve that flashes plus, and a show-me CU that flashes average. Pure stuff allows him to dominate at times, but after repeated control issues, his mechanics will need work in order to succeed.

Briceno, Endrys — SP — Detroit

EXP MLB DEBUT: 2017 H/W: 6-5 170 FUT: #3 starter **8E**

Thrws R Age 23
2009 FA (Venezula)
89-95 FB +++
81-84 SL ++
80-83 CU +++

Year	Lev	Team	W	L	Sv	IP	K	ERA	WHIP	BF/G	OBA	H%	S%	xERA	Ctl	Dom	Cmd	hr/9	BPV
2011	Rk	GCL Tigers	2	5	0	59	49	5.34	1.54	21.4	302	37	63	4.57	2.9	7.5	2.6	0.3	74
2012	A-	Connecticut	4	3	0	57	30	5.19	1.43	20.3	271	30	62	4.02	3.5	4.7	1.4	0.5	10
2013	A	West Michigan	7	9	0	116	65	4.49	1.51	20.1	262	31	69	4.17	4.0	5.0	1.3	0.4	2
2014	A+	Lakeland	0	0	0	16	7	3.38	1.19	21.4	262	28	72	3.37	1.7	3.9	2.3	0.6	43

Lean, projectable SP who underwent TJ surgery early and will return mid-'15. Creates good leverage with arm action and adds quality sink to hard FB. Velocity comes easy and free, but FB can lose life at higher ticks. SL flashes plus at times, but slows arm on rudimentary CU.

Brickhouse, Bryan — SP — Kansas City

EXP MLB DEBUT: 2017 H/W: 6-0 195 FUT: #4 starter **7D**

Thrws R Age 22
2011 (3) HS (TX)
90-95 FB +++
75-79 CB +++
82-83 CU ++

Year	Lev	Team	W	L	Sv	IP	K	ERA	WHIP	BF/G	OBA	H%	S%	xERA	Ctl	Dom	Cmd	hr/9	BPV
2012	Rk	Idaho Falls	0	0	0	1	1	52.50	6.67	11.4	596	63	14	32.07	22.5	7.5	0.3	7.5	-455
2012	A	Kane County	3	3	0	51	40	5.64	1.43	21.7	258	31	59	3.85	4.1	7.0	1.7	0.5	35
2013	A	Lexington	4	4	0	60	49	2.25	1.25	22.2	242	30	83	3.12	3.2	7.4	2.3	0.5	65
2014	Rk	Idaho Falls	1	2	0	27	22	4.96	1.47	13.0	281	33	68	4.72	3.3	7.3	2.2	1.0	60

Short, stocky SP who returned in mid '14 after TJ surgery in '13. Gets natural sink and movement with hard, heavy FB and mixes in decent CB and CU. Key is to stay healthy as he lacks frontline size and arm strength. Doesn't repeat delivery, though has some natural deception.

Bridwell, Parker — SP — Baltimore

EXP MLB DEBUT: 2016 H/W: 6-4 190 FUT: #3 starter **8E**

Thrws R Age 23
2010 (9) HS (TX)
87-94 FB ++++
80-82 CB ++
80-83 CU ++

Year	Lev	Team	W	L	Sv	IP	K	ERA	WHIP	BF/G	OBA	H%	S%	xERA	Ctl	Dom	Cmd	hr/9	BPV
2011	A-	Aberdeen	2	5	0	53	57	4.57	1.47	19.0	272	37	67	3.94	3.7	9.6	2.6	0.3	91
2011	A	Delmarva	0	3	0	21	13	7.22	1.70	19.2	278	33	53	4.33	5.5	5.5	1.0	0.4	-32
2012	A	Delmarva	5	9	0	114	71	5.99	1.62	22.0	275	30	64	5.21	5.0	5.6	1.1	1.2	-15
2013	A	Delmarva	8	9	0	142	144	4.75	1.41	23.1	260	34	65	3.85	3.7	9.1	2.4	0.6	81
2014	A+	Frederick	7	10	0	141	142	4.46	1.37	22.7	236	30	68	3.56	4.5	9.1	2.0	0.7	60

Tall, athletic SP who finished 2nd in CAR in Ks. Strong K rate predicated on frontline stuff and lively FB with late sink. Eats innings with strong arm and durability. Uses height well, but pitches up in zone and can hang below-average CB. Tends to rush delivery and needs to throw more strikes.

Brigham, Jeff — SP — Los Angeles (N)

EXP MLB DEBUT: 2018 H/W: 6-0 200 FUT: #4 starter **7D**

Thrws R Age 23
2014 (4) Washington
92-94 FB +++
SL ++
CU +

Year	Lev	Team	W	L	Sv	IP	K	ERA	WHIP	BF/G	OBA	H%	S%	xERA	Ctl	Dom	Cmd	hr/9	BPV
2011	NCAA	Washington	4	1	2	51	30	4.76	1.57	9.3	265	29	66	4.16	3.2	5.3	1.7	0.9	28
2012	NCAA	Washington	0	2	0	33	11	4.35	1.36	12.6	267	28	67	3.86	3.0	3.0	1.0	0.5	-9
2014	NCAA	Washington	7	4	0	90	45	2.90	1.13	22.2	237	27	74	2.65	2.3	4.5	2.0	0.3	37
2014	Rk	Ogden	0	3	0	32	33	3.63	1.49	12.6	261	34	76	4.06	4.5	9.2	2.1	0.6	63

Short, stocky RH has a good 90-94 mph FB, maxing out at 97, but throws with effort and can rush his delivery. Flashes a decent, but inconsistent SL that shows good late break and a below-avg CU. Keeps the ball at the bottom of the zone and gave up just 2 HR. Profiles as a back-end guy.

Britton, Drake — RP — Boston

EXP MLB DEBUT: 2013 H/W: 6-2 215 FUT: Setup RP **7D**

Thrws L Age 25
2007 (23) HS (TX)
88-95 FB +++
74-78 SL +++
81-84 CU ++

Year	Lev	Team	W	L	Sv	IP	K	ERA	WHIP	BF/G	OBA	H%	S%	xERA	Ctl	Dom	Cmd	hr/9	BPV
2013	AA	Portland	7	6	0	97	80	3.52	1.34	23.8	256	31	74	3.54	3.3	7.4	2.2	0.5	61
2013	AAA	Pawtucket	0	1	0	5	5	8.82	2.16	25.4	410	52	55	7.78	1.8	8.8	5.0	0.0	129
2013	MLB	Boston	1	1	0	21	17	3.86	1.33	4.8	262	32	70	3.58	3.0	7.3	2.4	0.4	68
2014	AAA	Pawtucket	2	3	5	58	37	5.89	1.98	6.2	320	35	72	6.84	5.9	5.7	1.0	1.2	-38
2014	MLB	Boston	0	0	0	6	4	0.00	1.13	3.5	242	27	100	2.16	2.9	6.0	2.0	0.0	44

Lived-armed RP who has been in role since mid '13. Had good April, but no other month below 6.35 ERA. Stingy against LHH with solid SL and potent FB. Allows HR despite groundball rate and struggles to throw strikes with regressing FB command. Still hope if swing-and-miss stuff returns.

Brown, Mitch — SP — Cleveland

EXP MLB DEBUT: 2017 H/W: 6-1 195 FUT: #3 starter **8E**

Thrws R Age 20
2012 (2) HS (MN)
89-95 FB +++
84-86 SL ++
77-79 CB +++
81-84 CU ++

Year	Lev	Team	W	L	Sv	IP	K	ERA	WHIP	BF/G	OBA	H%	S%	xERA	Ctl	Dom	Cmd	hr/9	BPV
2012	Rk	AZL Indians	2	0	0	27	26	3.64	1.10	13.3	207	25	70	2.81	3.3	8.6	2.6	1.0	84
2013	Rk	AZL Indians	2	4	0	52	48	5.37	1.65	19.4	280	36	65	4.55	5.0	8.3	1.7	0.3	32
2013	A	Lake County	1	1	0	15	18	11.84	2.11	15.0	329	41	43	8.32	6.5	10.7	1.6	2.4	34
2014	A	Lake County	8	8	0	138	127	3.32	1.22	20.7	225	29	72	2.75	3.6	8.3	2.3	0.4	70

Durable, strong SP who was spectacular late in breakout season. Realized potential by showing cleaner and more consistent delivery. Spots FB to all quadrants of zone and keeps ball down despite lack of height. Can cut FB as well. CB can be very good and has feel for fringy CU.

Bundy, Dylan — SP — Baltimore

EXP MLB DEBUT: 2012 H/W: 6-1 195 FUT: #1 starter **9B**

Thrws R Age 22
2011 (1) HS (OK)
91-97 FB ++++
77-82 CB ++++
79-84 CU +++

Year	Lev	Team	W	L	Sv	IP	K	ERA	WHIP	BF/G	OBA	H%	S%	xERA	Ctl	Dom	Cmd	hr/9	BPV
2012	A+	Frederick	6	3	0	57	66	2.84	1.18	19.8	230	31	79	3.02	2.8	10.4	3.7	0.8	129
2012	AA	Bowie	2	0	0	16	13	3.33	1.36	22.6	235	28	76	3.40	4.4	7.2	1.6	0.6	28
2012	MLB	Baltimore	0	0	0	1	0	0.00	1.67	2.7	228	23	100	3.64	7.5	0.0	0.0	0.0	-185
2014	A-	Aberdeen	0	1	0	15	22	0.60	0.87	18.4	191	33	92	1.05	1.8	13.2	7.3	0.0	207
2014	A+	Frederick	1	2	0	26	15	4.83	1.57	19.1	276	32	66	3.99	4.5	5.2	1.2	0.0	-10

Athletic, strong SP who missed '13 and returned in June '14 after TJS. Regaining plus velocity along with big-breaking CB. Has frontline potential if all pitches work in tandem. CU flashes plus with deceptive arm speed and has well above average FB to blow ball by hitters. Just needs health.

Burawa,Dan

RP | New York (A) | EXP MLB DEBUT: 2015 | H/W: 6-2 210 | FUT: Setup RP | 7E

Thrws R Age 26
2010 (12) St. John's

Velo	Pitch	Grade
90-96	FB	++++
80-85	SL	++
83-88	CU	++

Year	Lev	Team	W	L	Sv	IP	K	ERA	WHIP	BF/G	OBA	H%	S%	xERA	Ctl	Dom	Cmd	hr/9	BPV
2011	A	CharlestonSC	3	2	3	44	35	3.67	1.15	9.2	224	25	73	3.38	3.1	7.1	2.3	1.2	64
2011	A+	Tampa	2	2	2	39	31	3.68	1.28	8.0	271	34	68	3.17	2.1	7.1	3.4	0.0	91
2013	AA	Trenton	6	3	4	66	66	2.59	1.35	6.0	202	28	80	2.56	5.7	9.0	1.6	0.1	25
2014	AA	Trenton	0	0	1	17	18	1.59	1.00	5.9	213	30	82	1.69	2.1	9.5	4.5	0.0	132
2014	AAA	Scranton/WB	3	1	3	42	55	5.99	1.73	6.2	284	41	64	5.05	5.6	11.8	2.1	0.6	80

Power-armed RP who is tough on RHH with plus FB and sweeping SL. Throws from high 3/4 angle, but has lots of effort in delivery. Possesses erratic control thanks to inconsistent release point. When throwing strikes, can be very difficult to make hard contact against. Below average CU.

Burdi,Nick

RP | Minnesota | EXP MLB DEBUT: 2016 | H/W: 6-5 215 | FUT: Closer | 8D

Thrws R Age 22
2014 (2) Louisville

Velo	Pitch	Grade
93-98	FB	++++
85-88	SL	+++
84-88	CU	+

Year	Lev	Team	W	L	Sv	IP	K	ERA	WHIP	BF/G	OBA	H%	S%	xERA	Ctl	Dom	Cmd	hr/9	BPV
2012	NCAA	Louisville	1	2	0	22	14	5.68	1.71	7.7	309	36	65	5.22	4.1	5.7	1.4	0.4	11
2013	NCAA	Louisville	3	3	16	35	62	0.77	1.08	4.7	201	40	92	1.68	3.3	15.9	4.8	0.0	214
2014	NCAA	Louisville	3	1	18	37	65	0.49	0.76	4.1	147	30	96	0.50	2.4	15.8	6.5	0.2	237
2014	A	Cedar Rapids	0	0	4	13	26	4.15	1.23	4.1	179	43	63	1.79	5.5	18.0	3.3	0.0	192
2014	A+	Fort Myers	2	0	1	7	12	0.00	0.99	3.9	200	38	100	1.43	2.5	15.2	6.0	0.0	223

Power RP with tantalizing arm strength and plus FB. Posts very high K rate and keeps ball on ground when contact made. Violent delivery generates fast arm action and has two swing-and-miss offerings in FB and SL. Has durability to pitch in back-to-back games while holding velocity.

Burgos,Enrique

RP | Arizona | EXP MLB DEBUT: 2016 | H/W: 6-4 200 | FUT: Setup RP | 7C

Thrws R Age 24
2007 FA (Panama)

Velo	Pitch	Grade
94-96	FB	++++
80-83	CU	++
89-91	SL	++

Year	Lev	Team	W	L	Sv	IP	K	ERA	WHIP	BF/G	OBA	H%	S%	xERA	Ctl	Dom	Cmd	hr/9	BPV
2011	Rk	Missoula	4	4	0	46		6.62	1.84	21.5	304	38	63	5.79	5.5	8.4	1.5	0.8	22
2011	A	South Bend	0	2	0	3	4	22.50	3.44	10.0	399	50	30	13.40	14.1	11.3	0.8	2.8	-159
2012	A-	Yakima	2	3	4	38	40	2.36	1.23	6.2	207	29	80	2.42	4.5	9.4	2.1	0.2	67
2013	A	South Bend	2	2	17	46	50	3.90	1.69	4.2	182	26	75	3.25	9.6	9.8	1.0	0.2	-65
2014	A+	Visalia	3	3	29	54	83	2.49	1.16	3.9	195	31	83	2.61	4.3	13.8	3.2	0.8	150

Tall, thick-bodied RP saw an uptick velo when he moved to relief and now comes after hiters with a plus 94-96 mph FB, maxing out at 98. Also throws a short SL that is serviceable. Dominated the competition in the CAL with 29 saves.

Butler,Eddie

SP | Colorado | EXP MLB DEBUT: 2014 | H/W: 6-2 180 | FUT: #2 starter | 9D

Thrws R Age 24
2012 (1-S) Radford

Velo	Pitch	Grade
92-95	FB	++++
84-87	SL	++
71-74	CB	+
87-88	CU	+++

Year	Lev	Team	W	L	Sv	IP	K	ERA	WHIP	BF/G	OBA	H%	S%	xERA	Ctl	Dom	Cmd	hr/9	BPV
2013	AA	Tulsa	1	0	0	27	25	0.66	0.70	16.0	145	20	89	0.18	2.0	8.3	4.2	0.0	113
2014	A+	Modesto	0	0	0	4	2	6.75	1.00	15.3	151	18	25	1.03	4.5	4.5	1.0	0.0	-23
2014	AA	Tulsa	6	9	0	108	63	3.58	1.26	24.5	255	28	74	3.69	2.7	5.3	2.0	0.8	41
2014	AAA	Colorado Springs	0	1	0	5	4	10.59	2.16	25.4	357	44	45	6.76	5.3	7.1	1.3	0.0	2
2014	MLB	Colorado	1	1	0	16	3	6.75	1.88	25.0	338	33	64	6.81	3.9	1.7	0.4	1.1	-58

Took a huge step back in '14, raising concerns about long-term potential. Regressed across the board with a drop in dominance. Shoulder soreness limited him in the 2nd half. When healthy, featured a heavy 92-95 mph FB, a hard SL and an improved CU, giving him three plus offerings.

Butler,Keith

RP | St. Louis | EXP MLB DEBUT: 2013 | H/W: 6-0 170 | FUT: Reliever | 6C

Thrws R Age 26
2009 (24) Wabash Valley CC

Velo	Pitch	Grade
88-91	FB	++
73-75	CB	++
	CU	++

Year	Lev	Team	W	L	Sv	IP	K	ERA	WHIP	BF/G	OBA	H%	S%	xERA	Ctl	Dom	Cmd	hr/9	BPV
2013	AA	Springfield	0	0	7	13	21	0.68	0.76	3.6	177	30	100	1.25	1.4	14.3	10.5	0.7	239
2013	AAA	Memphis	3	2	2	27	28	3.65	1.11	5.3	216	27	70	2.92	3.0	9.3	3.1	1.0	105
2013	MLB	St. Louis	0	0	0	20	16	4.05	1.20	5.0	187	24	63	1.91	5.0	7.2	1.5	0.0	14
2014	AAA	Memphis	1	0	0	10	13	0.88	0.98	4.3	218	34	90	1.67	1.8	11.5	6.5	0.0	177
2014	MLB	St. Louis	0	0	0	2	2	27.00	3.50	6.3	515	62	14	13.93	4.5	9.0	2.0	0.0	59

Had TJS in May and was limted to just 12.2 IP. Prior to the injury showed the ability to keep hitters off balance with an 88-91 mph FB, low-70s CB, and a good CU. Has a career 11.2 Dom rate despite a rather pedestrian FB. Assuming a full recovery he should settle in as a reliever.

Cabrera,Mauricio

SP | Atlanta | EXP MLB DEBUT: 2017 | H/W: 6-2 180 | FUT: Setup RP | 8E

Thrws R Age 21
2010 FA (DR)

Velo	Pitch	Grade
93-97	FB	++++
81-85	SL	+++
88-91	CU	++

Year	Lev	Team	W	L	Sv	IP	K	ERA	WHIP	BF/G	OBA	H%	S%	xERA	Ctl	Dom	Cmd	hr/9	BPV
2012	Rk	Danville	2	2	0	57	48	2.99	1.19	19.1	218	28	74	2.53	3.6	7.6	2.1	0.3	56
2013	A	Rome	3	8	0	131	107	4.19	1.44	23.3	242	30	69	3.37	4.9	7.3	1.5	0.2	19
2014	Rk	GCL Braves	0	0	0	4	3	6.75	1.25	5.4	210	27	40	2.30	4.5	6.8	1.5	0.0	18
2014	A+	Lynchburg	1	1	0	29	28	5.59	1.48	6.6	227	30	60	3.37	5.9	8.7	1.5	0.3	15

22-year-old missed almost two months with a forearm strain. Throws across his body and struggles to maintain a consistent release point, but his raw stuff remains electric. FB sits at 95-98 with good life and can reach 100. Also has decent feel for a CU, but his SL remains a work in progress.

Cabrera,Wander

SP | Chicago (N) | EXP MLB DEBUT: 2019 | H/W: 6-2 190 | FUT: #4 starter | 7E

Thrws L Age 17
2014 FA (DR)

Velo	Pitch	Grade
88-91	FB	+++
	SL	++
	CU	++

Year	Lev	Team	W	L	Sv	IP	K	ERA	WHIP	BF/G	OBA	H%	S%	xERA	Ctl	Dom	Cmd	hr/9	BPV
2014		(did not play in the US in 2014)																	

Tall, loose-armed Dominican hurler was signed by the Cubs for $250,00. Projectable LH already has good 88-91 mph velocity and could gain more as he matures. Breaking ball and CU are still rudimentary, but he has nice long-term potential. Look for him to make his state-side debut in 2015.

Caminero,Arquimedes

RP | Miami | EXP MLB DEBUT: 2013 | H/W: 6-4 250 | FUT: Reliever | 7D

Thrws R Age 27
2005 FA (DR)

Velo	Pitch	Grade
89-98	FB	++++
80-82	SL	+++
	CT	++

Year	Lev	Team	W	L	Sv	IP	K	ERA	WHIP	BF/G	OBA	H%	S%	xERA	Ctl	Dom	Cmd	hr/9	BPV
2013	AA	Jacksonville	5	2	5	52	68	3.63	1.06	4.8	188	28	67	2.15	3.6	11.7	3.2	0.7	131
2013	AAA	New Orleans	1	0	0	2	1	0.00	0.00	5.6	0	0		0.00	0.0	4.5		0.0	99
2013	MLB	Miami	0	0	0	13	12	2.77	1.00	3.8	214	24	82	3.01	2.1	8.3	4.0	1.4	111
2014	AAA	New Orleans	4	1	10	63	79	4.86	1.59	6.6	283	39	71	5.01	4.3	11.3	2.6	1.0	105
2014	MLB	Miami	0	1	0	6	8	11.61	1.94	4.9	314	39	40	8.15	5.8	11.6	2.0	2.9	70

Tall, thick-bodied RP regressed in '14. Struggles with control were the culprit and he walked 30 in 63 IP at AAA. Possesses a plus mid-90s FB, a cutter, and an inconsistent SL. Did notch 10 sv and has the raw stuff to close out games, but needs to refine his mechanics and release point.

Campos,Jose

SP | New York (A) | EXP MLB DEBUT: 2016 | H/W: 6-4 195 | FUT: #2 starter | 8E

Thrws R Age 22
2009 FA (Venezuela)

Velo	Pitch	Grade
90-95	FB	+++
77-80	CB	++
80-83	CU	+++

Year	Lev	Team	W	L	Sv	IP	K	ERA	WHIP	BF/G	OBA	H%	S%	xERA	Ctl	Dom	Cmd	hr/9	BPV
2011	A-	Everett	5	5	0	81	85	2.33	0.97	22.0	224	30	77	2.17	1.4	9.4	6.5	0.4	149
2012	A	CharlestonSC	3	0	0	24	26	4.09	1.16	19.2	227	30	65	2.94	3.0	9.7	3.3	0.7	112
2013	A	CharlestonSC	4	2	2	87	77	3.41	1.13	13.2	251	31	70	2.98	1.7	8.0	4.8	0.5	117
2014		(did not play in 2014)																	

Tall, deceptive SP who missed entire season after TJ surgery. Tough to hit with solid pitch mix, highlighted by FB that can be plus. Spots ball low in zone with impeccable location and induces grounders. Trying to find consistency in breaking ball and CU. Has some feel for changing speeds.

Campos,Leonel

RP | San Diego | EXP MLB DEBUT: 2014 | H/W: 6-3 185 | FUT: Reliever | 6C

Thrws R Age 27
2010 FA (Venezuela)

Velo	Pitch	Grade
93-95	FB	+++
80-83	CB	+++
	CU	+

Year	Lev	Team	W	L	Sv	IP	K	ERA	WHIP	BF/G	OBA	H%	S%	xERA	Ctl	Dom	Cmd	hr/9	BPV
2013	A	Fort Wayne	2	1	5	36	63	2.24	1.14	5.1	157	30	82	1.80	5.5	15.7	2.9	0.5	153
2013	AA	San Antonio	1	0	2	30	43	0.89	0.99	4.4	141	25	90	0.84	4.8	12.8	2.7	0.0	120
2014	AA	San Antonio	2	7	1	72	95	5.62	1.48	10.0	253	37	61	4.10	4.7	11.9	2.5	0.7	103
2014	AAA	El Paso	0	0	0	10	13	11.70	3.30	5.6	415	54	65	12.43	11.7	11.7	1.0	1.8	-87
2014	MLB	San Diego	0	0	0	7	9	5.14	1.86	5.5	313	46	69	5.21	5.1	11.6	2.3	0.0	87

Has a 93-96 mph FB that hits 98 with good arm-side run. Also has a good CB and a below-avg CU. Was dominant in 2014, whiffing over 11 per nine between AA and AAA, but also walking 51 in 82.1 IP. Still has the stuff to be an impact reliever in the majors.

Cash,Ralston

RP | Los Angeles (N) | EXP MLB DEBUT: 2015 | H/W: 6-3 215 | FUT: Reliever | 7D

Thrws R Age 23
2010 (2) HS (GA)

Velo	Pitch	Grade
88-92	FB	+++
75-77	CB	++
	CU	++

Year	Lev	Team	W	L	Sv	IP	K	ERA	WHIP	BF/G	OBA	H%	S%	xERA	Ctl	Dom	Cmd	hr/9	BPV
2012	A	Great Lakes	1	6	0	40	29	6.49	1.72	20.3	284	33	62	5.30	5.4	6.5	1.2	0.9	-10
2013	Rk	AZL Dodgers	0	0	0	2	5	0.00	0.50	6.6	151	61	100	0.00	0.0	22.5		0.0	423
2013	A	Great Lakes	4	3	0	53	56	3.21	1.37	13.9	210	28	78	3.23	5.6	9.5	1.7	0.7	38
2014	A	Great Lakes	3	1	1	50	62	2.87	1.10	6.8	189	29	72	1.79	3.9	11.1	2.8	0.2	112
2014	AA	Chattanooga	0	0	0	8	10	3.33	1.36	5.6	180	28	73	2.18	6.7	11.1	1.7	0.0	38

RP had a solid season in a repeat of Low-A. FB control remains an issue but is balanced by a high Dom rate and he struck out 72 in 59 IP. Arm action is clean, though he needs to learn to repeat mechanics better. CB is showing better depth while CU is becoming a more usable third offering.

Castellani,Ryan — SP — Colorado

EXP MLB DEBUT: 2019 | H/W: 6-3 193 | FUT: #3 starter | 8D

Thrws R Age 19
2014 (2) HS (AZ)

Velo	Pitch	Grade
89-92	FB	+++
73-75	CB	++
79-83	CU	++
77-80	SL	++

Year	Lev	Team	W	L	Sv	IP	K	ERA	WHIP	BF/G	OBA	H%	S%	xERA	Ctl	Dom	Cmd	hr/9	BPV
2014	A-	Tri-City	1	2	0	37	25	3.65	1.19	14.8	251	29	69	3.13	2.2	6.1	2.8	0.5	68

Durable RH has a plus sinking FB that currently sits at 88-92 mph, but he has a lean, projectable frame and could add velo at maturity. Throws downhill, keeping the ball on the ground. Mixes in a CB, SL, and CU, but none project as above-avg. Does pound the strike zone.

Castro,Miguel — SP — Toronto

EXP MLB DEBUT: 2017 | H/W: 6-5 190 | FUT: #2 starter | 9D

Thrws R Age 20
2012 FA (DR)

Velo	Pitch	Grade
92-97	FB	++++
80-83	SL	+++
82-84	CU	+++

Year	Lev	Team	W	L	Sv	IP	K	ERA	WHIP	BF/G	OBA	H%	S%	xERA	Ctl	Dom	Cmd	hr/9	BPV
2013	Rk	DSL Blue Jays	5	2	0	53	71	1.36	0.98	18.3	211	34	85	1.59	2.0	12.1	5.9	0.0	180
2013	Rk	GCL Blue Jays	1	0	1	15	14	2.40	0.87	18.4	206	28	69	1.28	1.2	8.4	7.0	0.0	137
2014	A-	Vancouver	6	2	0	50	53	2.16	1.12	19.7	203	28	81	2.20	3.6	9.5	2.7	0.4	92
2014	A	Lansing	1	1	0	21	20	3.82	0.80	19.2	143	17	53	1.22	3.0	8.5	2.9	0.8	91
2014	A+	Dunedin	1	0	0	8	5	3.29	0.85	15.1	147	10	80	2.68	3.3	5.5	1.7	2.2	28

Tall, wiry SP with extreme projection. Clean delivery for youth and generates velocity and pitch movement with low 3/4 slot. FB is ultra quick and gets in on hitters while sweeping SL serves as K pitch. Repeats arm speed and slot on CU and can become above average. High upside arm.

Cease,Dylan — SP — Chicago (N)

EXP MLB DEBUT: 2019 | H/W: 6-2 180 | FUT: #3 starter | 8D

Thrws R Age 19
2014 (6) HS (GA)

Velo	Pitch	Grade
92-95	FB	++++
74-77	CB	+++
78-80	CU	+

Year	Lev	Team	W	L	Sv	IP	K	ERA	WHIP	BF/G	OBA	H%	S%	xERA	Ctl	Dom	Cmd	hr/9	BPV
2014	(did not play in the US in 2014)																		

6th round pick has decent potential. Best offering is a good 92-95 mph FB that has arm-side run. Tends to leave FB up in the zone and needs to finish the pitch. CB flashes plus at times, but he tends to get on the side of the ball. CU is below-average. Torn UCL in March kept him out of action.

Cederoth,Michael — SP — Minnesota

EXP MLB DEBUT: 2017 | H/W: 6-6 195 | FUT: #3 starter/setupRP | 8E

Thrws R Age 22
2014 (3) San Diego State

Velo	Pitch	Grade
93-98	FB	++++
83-85	SL	+++
77-80	CB	+++
83-86	CU	++

Year	Lev	Team	W	L	Sv	IP	K	ERA	WHIP	BF/G	OBA	H%	S%	xERA	Ctl	Dom	Cmd	hr/9	BPV
2012	NCAA	San Diego State	4	4	0	67	62	4.16	1.56	19.6	231	30	73	3.72	6.4	8.3	1.3	0.4	-6
2013	NCAA	San Diego State	3	9	0	95	109	4.26	1.26	25.9	212	30	65	2.67	4.5	10.3	2.3	0.4	81
2014	NCAA	San Diego State	6	2	20	51	55	2.29	1.25	6.5	200	28	82	2.49	4.9	9.7	2.0	0.4	59
2014	Rk	Elizabethton	4	2	0	45	42	3.58	1.31	17.0	243	32	71	3.03	3.6	8.4	2.3	0.2	72

Long, lean pitcher who was SP in pro debut. Has tantalizing upside with raw arm strength. Uses electric FB in combination with impressive hard SL to miss bats. FB has tendency to be flat despite high arm slot. Lacks deception with long arm action and will need better CU to stick as SP.

Church,Andrew — SP — New York (N)

EXP MLB DEBUT: 2018 | H/W: 6-2 190 | FUT: #4 starter | 7E

Thrws R Age 20
2013 (2) HS (NV)

Velo	Pitch	Grade
91-93	FB	+++
73-76	CB	+++
	CU	++

Year	Lev	Team	W	L	Sv	IP	K	ERA	WHIP	BF/G	OBA	H%	S%	xERA	Ctl	Dom	Cmd	hr/9	BPV
2013	Rk	GCL Mets	3	3	0	35	19	5.91	1.63	17.3	332	37	62	5.49	2.1	4.9	2.4	0.5	50
2014	Rk	Kingsport	3	5	0	52	31	4.66	1.67	21.3	332	38	70	5.25	2.4	5.3	2.2	0.2	49

Young pitcher with nice upside. Still learning finer points of pitching. Shows good projection on all three offerings. FB should hold enough velocity and curve flashes plus. FB gets flat and finds lots of bats. Needs to shore up mechanics, release point, and get more movement on his pitches.

Clarkin,Ian — SP — New York (A)

EXP MLB DEBUT: 2017 | H/W: 6-2 190 | FUT: #3 starter | 8C

Thrws L Age 20
2013 (1) HS (CA)

Velo	Pitch	Grade
90-95	FB	+++
71-75	CB	+++
80-83	CU	+++

Year	Lev	Team	W	L	Sv	IP	K	ERA	WHIP	BF/G	OBA	H%	S%	xERA	Ctl	Dom	Cmd	hr/9	BPV
2013	Rk	GCL Yankees	0	2	0	5	4	10.80	1.80	7.7	262	23	43	7.73	7.2	7.2	1.0	3.6	-47
2014	A	CharlestonSC	3	3	0	70	71	3.21	1.23	17.7	245	31	76	3.39	2.8	9.1	3.2	0.8	106
2014	A+	Tampa	1	0	0	5	4	1.80	1.60	22.1	332	41	88	4.91	1.8	7.2	4.0	0.0	99

Aggressive, smooth SP who has nice feel for stuff and good velocity. High release point gives FB some bite and freezes RHH with big-breaking, slow CB. Drops CB in for strikes and can use as chase pitch. CU continues to improve and will need to battle LHH. Should add strength as he ages.

Claudio,Alex — RP — Texas

EXP MLB DEBUT: 2014 | H/W: 6-3 160 | FUT: Setup RP | 6B

Thrws L Age 23
2010 (27) HS (PR)

Velo	Pitch	Grade
83-88	FB	++
76-78	SL	++
64-70	CU	++++

Year	Lev	Team	W	L	Sv	IP	K	ERA	WHIP	BF/G	OBA	H%	S%	xERA	Ctl	Dom	Cmd	hr/9	BPV
2013	AA	Frisco	1	5	0	31	29	2.88	1.25	6.0	241	31	78	3.22	3.2	8.4	2.6	0.6	83
2014	A+	Myrtle Beach	4	0	4	49	56	1.10	0.96	10.9	215	30	91	1.94	1.6	10.3	6.2	0.4	158
2014	AA	Frisco	2	2	0	37	22	2.18	0.89	17.2	229	27	75	1.86	0.5	5.3	11.0	0.2	101
2014	AAA	Round Rock	0	1	0	5	6	3.53	1.57	11.2	294	42	75	4.20	3.5	10.6	3.0	0.0	113
2014	MLB	Texas	0	0	0	12	14	2.98	1.49	3.5	291	41	78	3.95	3.0	10.4	3.5	0.0	125

Very lean sidearmer who fools hitters with plus-plus deception and knockout CU. Has very little velocity, but keeps ball down to induce ton of groundballs. Has a lot of moving parts in delivery, though is tough to pick ball up out of hand. No pitch is straight and is ideal RP to get out of jams.

Clevinger,Michael — SP — Cleveland

EXP MLB DEBUT: 2016 | H/W: 6-4 220 | FUT: #4 starter | 7D

Thrws R Age 24
2011 (4) Seminole State JC

Velo	Pitch	Grade
89-93	FB	+++
81-83	SL	+++
77-80	CB	++
81-84	CU	++

Year	Lev	Team	W	L	Sv	IP	K	ERA	WHIP	BF/G	OBA	H%	S%	xERA	Ctl	Dom	Cmd	hr/9	BPV
2013	Rk	AZL Angels	0	0	0	3	3	3.00	1.33	6.2	191	27	75	2.27	6.0	9.0	1.5	0.0	18
2013	Rk	Orem	0	1	0	2	2	20.45	3.64	14.2	492	59	38	13.55	8.2	8.2	1.0	0.0	-56
2014	A	Burlington	3	0	0	24	27	1.88	0.88	17.7	191	26	84	1.81	1.9	10.1	5.4	0.8	150
2014	A+	Inland Empire	1	3	0	55	58	5.39	1.54	18.5	272	34	68	5.05	4.4	9.5	2.1	1.3	69
2014	A+	Carolina	0	1	0	20	15	4.90	1.53	17.6	260	31	67	4.08	4.9	6.7	1.4	0.4	6

Tall SP who returned after missing most of '12 and '13 with TJ surgery. Has durable frame with four potential average pitches. Uses height to pitch on downward angle and can locate average FB fairly well. Uses both SL and CB and may eventually scrap one. Throws with lots of effort.

Cole,A.J. — SP — Washington

EXP MLB DEBUT: 2015 | H/W: 6-5 200 | FUT: #3 starter | 8B

Thrws R Age 23
2010 (4) HS (FL)

Velo	Pitch	Grade
92-95	FB	++++
77-79	SL	++
80-82	CU	+++

Year	Lev	Team	W	L	Sv	IP	K	ERA	WHIP	BF/G	OBA	H%	S%	xERA	Ctl	Dom	Cmd	hr/9	BPV
2012	A+	Stockton	0	7	0	38	31	7.82	1.84	22.1	359	41	59	7.55	2.4	7.3	3.1	1.7	86
2013	A+	Potomac	6	3	0	97	102	4.26	1.23	21.8	260	33	68	3.89	2.1	9.5	4.4	1.1	131
2013	AA	Harrisburg	4	2	0	45	49	2.20	0.91	24.0	196	26	79	1.81	2.0	9.8	4.9	0.6	140
2014	AA	Harrisburg	6	3	0	71	61	2.92	1.32	21.0	283	36	76	3.56	1.9	7.7	4.1	0.1	106
2014	AAA	Syracuse	7	0	0	63	50	3.43	1.37	24.0	280	32	81	4.72	2.4	7.1	2.9	1.3	81

Posted good numbers at most levels due to ability to command his 92-95 mph FB. CU is plus, but an average SL caps his upside. Knows how to sequence and set up hitters, and arm explodes through otherwise deliberate delivery. Has a frame to eat innings, though would benefit from more Triple-A time.

Cole,Taylor — SP — Toronto

EXP MLB DEBUT: 2015 | H/W: 6-1 190 | FUT: #5 starter | 6B

Thrws R Age 25
2011 (29) Brigham Young

Velo	Pitch	Grade
88-92	FB	+++
80-83	SL	++
81-83	CU	+++

Year	Lev	Team	W	L	Sv	IP	K	ERA	WHIP	BF/G	OBA	H%	S%	xERA	Ctl	Dom	Cmd	hr/9	BPV
2012	A-	Vancouver	6	0	0	66	57	0.82	0.80	20.0	162	22	89	0.62	2.3	7.8	3.4	0.0	95
2013	A	Lansing	7	11	0	132	101	4.02	1.52	22.0	275	33	72	4.14	4.0	6.9	1.7	0.3	33
2013	A+	Dunedin	0	1	0	5	2	1.80	1.60	22.1	299	33	88	4.41	3.6	3.6	1.0	0.0	-14
2014	A+	Dunedin	8	9	0	132	171	3.07	1.16	21.9	234	35	72	2.58	2.7	11.7	4.4	0.3	156
2014	AA	New Hampshire	0	2	0	12	10	7.44	1.57	26.6	260	31	50	4.44	5.2	7.4	1.4	0.7	11

Finesse RHP with advanced feel for craft. Lacks out pitch and is far from overpowering, but sequences average offerings. Likes to use CU with quality fade and throws nice FB with late movement. Spots pitches well in lower half of strike zone. Has to keep ball down to succeed.

Colome,Alex — SP — Tampa Bay

EXP MLB DEBUT: 2013 | H/W: 6-2 210 | FUT: #3 starter | 8B

Thrws R Age 26
2007 FA (DR)

Velo	Pitch	Grade
90-95	FB	++++
77-79	CB	++++
81-86	SL	+++
80-84	CU	++

Year	Lev	Team	W	L	Sv	IP	K	ERA	WHIP	BF/G	OBA	H%	S%	xERA	Ctl	Dom	Cmd	hr/9	BPV
2013	AAA	Durham	4	6	0	70	72	3.08	1.31	20.7	242	32	78	3.43	3.7	9.2	2.5	0.6	84
2013	MLB	Tampa Bay	1	1	0	16	12	2.25	1.44	22.7	237	27	90	4.17	5.1	6.8	1.3	1.1	3
2014	A+	Charlotte	0	1	0	11	10	1.64	1.09	14.3	184	25	83	1.59	4.1	8.2	2.0	0.0	55
2014	AAA	Durham	7	6	0	86	73	3.77	1.33	23.8	257	33	70	3.28	3.1	7.6	2.4	0.2	71
2014	MLB	Tampa Bay	2	0	0	23	13	2.72	1.25	18.9	225	26	79	2.87	3.9	5.0	1.3	0.4	4

Electric SP who is now realizing potential. Started year late after suspension and durability in question due to injury history. Owns two plus pitches in FB and tight CB while hard SL and CU showing improvement. Better FB command could lead to higher K rate. Has cleaned up delivery.

Conley,Adam — SP — Miami
EXP MLB DEBUT: 2015 | H/W: 6-3 215 | FUT: #3 starter | 8D

Thrws L Age 24 — 2011 (2) Washington State
- 88-95 FB ++++
- SL +++
- CU ++++

Year	Lev	Team	W	L	Sv	IP	K	ERA	WHIP	BF/G	OBA	H%	S%	xERA	Ctl	Dom	Cmd	hr/9	BPV
2012	A	Greensboro	7	3	0	74	84	2.79	1.11	20.8	217	30	76	2.45	2.9	10.2	3.5	0.5	123
2012	A+	Jupiter	4	2	0	52	51	4.48	1.49	18.8	286	38	67	3.91	3.3	8.8	2.7	0.0	88
2013	AA	Jacksonville	11	7	0	138	129	3.26	1.17	21.2	243	31	72	2.93	2.4	8.4	3.5	0.5	104
2014	A+	Jupiter	0	1	0	5	2	5.29	2.16	25.4	385	42	73	7.32	3.5	3.5	1.0	0.0	-14
2014	AAA	New Orleans	3	5	0	60	48	6.00	1.52	21.7	278	34	58	4.28	3.9	7.2	1.8	0.5	42

Lean, lanky LH struggled with tendinitis and was limited to 65.1 IP. When on the mound, he lacked the velocity and command. Healthy now and has a nice 88-93 mph FB, an above-avg CU and a good SL. Breaking ball will need to make progress and there are still concerns about his durability.

Connaughton,Pat — SP — Baltimore
EXP MLB DEBUT: 2016 | H/W: 6-5 215 | FUT: #4 starter | 7D

Thrws R Age 22 — 2014 (4) Notre Dame
- 88-94 FB +++
- 77-80 CB ++
- 82-84 CU +

Year	Lev	Team	W	L	Sv	IP	K	ERA	WHIP	BF/G	OBA	H%	S%	xERA	Ctl	Dom	Cmd	hr/9	BPV
2012	NCAA	Notre Dame	4	4	0	45	40	3.19	1.51	16.3	270	35	76	3.72	4.2	8.0	1.9	0.0	49
2013	NCAA	Notre Dame	4	2	0	47	29	1.72	1.63	21.0	269	32	88	4.06	5.4	5.5	1.0	0.0	-27
2014	NCAA	Notre Dame	3	5	0	62	36	3.92	1.50	26.8	233	28	71	3.23	5.8	5.2	0.9	0.0	-45
2014	A-	Aberdeen	0	1	0	14	10	2.54	1.13	9.3	245	30	75	2.44	1.9	6.3	3.3	0.0	81

Tall, athletic SP who is raw, but has upside if he focuses on baseball. Possesses exemplary arm strength that produces quality velocity at present, but has potential for more. FB features riding life and tail, but doesn't command it. CB shows some promise, but lacks feel for changing speeds.

Constante,Jacob — SP — Cincinnati
EXP MLB DEBUT: 2018 | H/W: 6-4 215 | FUT: #4 starter | 8E

Thrws L Age 21 — 2012 FA (DR)
- 92-94 FB +++
- 80-83 SL +++
- 83-84 CU ++

Year	Lev	Team	W	L	Sv	IP	K	ERA	WHIP	BF/G	OBA	H%	S%	xERA	Ctl	Dom	Cmd	hr/9	BPV
2013	Rk	DSL Reds	0	1	0	38	55	1.88	1.31	13.1	206	35	84	2.34	5.2	13.0	2.5	0.0	111
2014	Rk	AZL Reds	0	5	0	33	31	4.09	1.61	13.3	311	39	75	5.08	3.0	8.5	2.8	0.5	89

First body of work in U.S. showed promising results. Good life on his plus FB. Continued to strike out batters at a good clip while greatly reducing walks. Works down in the zone with easy arm action and racks up groundball outs. Can get hitters to chase his improving slider.

Contreras,Carlos — RP — Cincinnati
EXP MLB DEBUT: 2014 | H/W: 5-11 205 | FUT: Setup RP | 7C

Thrws R Age 24 — 2008 FA (DR)
- 92-95 FB ++++
- 80-83 CU ++++
- 80-81 SL ++

Year	Lev	Team	W	L	Sv	IP	K	ERA	WHIP	BF/G	OBA	H%	S%	xERA	Ctl	Dom	Cmd	hr/9	BPV
2012	A+	Bakersfield	1	0	4	10	12	2.70	1.40	4.7	242	33	85	3.89	4.5	10.8	2.4	0.9	91
2013	A+	Bakersfield	5	7	0	90	96	3.80	1.23	20.3	216	28	72	3.15	4.1	9.6	2.3	0.9	80
2013	AA	Pensacola	3	2	0	42	26	2.78	1.35	22.0	233	27	80	3.26	4.5	5.6	1.2	0.4	-3
2014	AA	Pensacola	2	1	0	20	27	2.70	1.30	9.2	210	34	77	2.38	5.0	12.2	2.5	0.0	103
2014	MLB	Cincinnati	0	1	0	19	19	6.60	1.88	5.3	261	33	65	5.42	8.0	9.0	1.1	0.9	-37

Moved back to pen and responded with career high Dom. Control still problematic thanks to inconsistent release point. Throws plus FB (though it gets flat) and CU as well as a developing slider. CU can neutralize righties. Would do well in setup role if SL progresses and keeps the ball down.

Cooney,Harrison — SP — Los Angeles (A)
EXP MLB DEBUT: 2016 | H/W: 6-2 175 | FUT: #4 starter | 7E

Thrws R Age 23 — 2013 (6) Florida Gulf Coast
- 89-93 FB +++
- 81-84 SL +++
- CU ++

Year	Lev	Team	W	L	Sv	IP	K	ERA	WHIP	BF/G	OBA	H%	S%	xERA	Ctl	Dom	Cmd	hr/9	BPV
2011	NCAA	Florida GC	3	2	2	37	26	5.84	1.70	8.0	306	35	65	5.44	4.1	6.3	1.5	0.7	20
2012	NCAA	Florida GC	4	3	2	35	28	5.11	1.51	8.0	292	35	65	4.53	3.1	7.2	2.3	0.5	64
2013	NCAA	Florida GC	6	6	5	66	59	3.26	1.31	13.0	234	29	76	3.26	4.1	8.0	2.0	0.5	52
2013	Rk	Orem	1	2	2	30	18	5.10	1.30	8.8	249	29	58	3.21	3.3	5.4	1.6	0.3	26
2014	A	Burlington	9	8	1	129	91	2.65	1.23	20.9	229	27	79	2.82	3.6	6.3	1.8	0.3	36

Deceptive SP who is tough to make hard contact against. Is menace to RHH with strong sinker and SL. Keeps ball low in zone, but won't profile to K pitcher. Maintains velocity late in games due to pure arm strength, but doesn't blow ball by hitters nor have a true swing and miss pitch.

Cooney,Tim — SP — St. Louis
EXP MLB DEBUT: 2015 | H/W: 6-3 195 | FUT: #4 starter | 7B

Thrws L Age 24 — 2012 (3) Wake Forest
- 88-92 FB ++
- 75-77 CB ++
- 82-85 SL +++
- CT ++

Year	Lev	Team	W	L	Sv	IP	K	ERA	WHIP	BF/G	OBA	H%	S%	xERA	Ctl	Dom	Cmd	hr/9	BPV
2012	NCAA	Wake Forest	6	7	0	99	90	3.82	1.38	27.7	262	33	72	3.72	3.5	8.2	2.4	0.5	72
2012	A-	Batavia	3	3	0	55	43	3.42	1.16	16.9	265	32	72	3.39	1.3	7.0	5.4	0.7	109
2013	A+	Palm Beach	3	3	0	36	23	2.75	1.17	23.9	272	32	76	3.15	1.0	5.8	5.8	0.3	95
2013	AA	Springfield	7	10	0	118	125	3.81	1.27	24.2	284	37	70	3.88	1.4	9.5	6.9	0.6	152
2014	AAA	Memphis	14	6	0	158	119	3.47	1.30	25.0	262	30	78	4.21	2.7	6.8	2.5	1.2	68

LH from has a good feel for pitching, keeping hitters off-balance. His FB sits at 89-93 with good late life and mixes in a mid-70s CB, CT, and CU. Locates all offerings well and does a good job of changing speed. Drop in dominance after he moved up to AAA and 21 HR allowed are red flags.

Corcino,Daniel — SP — Cincinnati
EXP MLB DEBUT: 2014 | H/W: 5-11 210 | FUT: #4 starter/RP | 8D

Thrws R Age 24 — 2008 FA (DR)
- 91-95 FB ++++
- 75-78 SL ++++
- 84-85 CU +++

Year	Lev	Team	W	L	Sv	IP	K	ERA	WHIP	BF/G	OBA	H%	S%	xERA	Ctl	Dom	Cmd	hr/9	BPV
2012	AA	Pensacola	8	8	0	143	126	3.02	1.23	22.3	216	27	77	2.84	4.1	7.9	1.9	0.6	50
2013	AAA	Louisville	7	14	0	129	90	5.86	1.66	20.6	279	31	66	5.36	5.1	6.3	1.2	1.2	-6
2014	AA	Pensacola	10	11	0	143	113	4.15	1.35	23.0	233	27	72	3.78	4.4	7.1	1.6	1.0	27
2014	AAA	Louisville	0	1	0	5	6	7.20	1.40	21.1	175	0	75	7.32	7.2	10.8	1.5	5.4	18
2014	MLB	Cincinnati	0	2	0	18	15	4.45	1.26	14.9	202	23	67	3.17	4.9	7.4	1.5	1.0	18

High-upside prospect with power arsenal despite subpar production. Made 3 big league starts with mixed results. FB has good velo and life, above-average SL is out pitch, but doesn't use CU much. Adds deception with shifting arm slot but creates control issues. Needs to throw more strikes.

Cosart,Jake — SP — Boston
EXP MLB DEBUT: 2018 | H/W: 6-2 175 | FUT: #3 starter | 8E

Thrws R Age 21 — 2014 (3) Seminole State JC
- 90-95 FB +++
- 74-77 CB ++
- 79-83 SL +
- 81-83 CU ++

Year	Lev	Team	W	L	Sv	IP	K	ERA	WHIP	BF/G	OBA	H%	S%	xERA	Ctl	Dom	Cmd	hr/9	BPV
2014	Rk	GCL Red Sox	0	1	0	16	16	2.25	1.13	9.0	134	19	78	1.14	6.2	9.0	1.5	0.0	13

Lean, athletic SP with upside and projection. Velocity improving with cleaner mechanics and two breaking balls have potential, but both in infancy stage. Generates quality FB with plus arm speed. Key will be to repeat delivery consistently to enhance look and feel of promising CU.

Covey,Dylan — SP — Oakland
EXP MLB DEBUT: 2016 | H/W: 6-2 195 | FUT: #4 starter | 7C

Thrws R Age 23 — 2013 (4) San Diego
- 89-95 FB +++
- 80-82 CB +++
- 81-83 CU ++

Year	Lev	Team	W	L	Sv	IP	K	ERA	WHIP	BF/G	OBA	H%	S%	xERA	Ctl	Dom	Cmd	hr/9	BPV
2013	NCAA	San Diego	5	4	1	76	65	5.08	1.75	19.3	295	37	69	4.91	5.1	7.7	1.5	0.2	19
2013	A-	Vermont	0	0	0	12	15	0.00	0.83	11.0	210	32	100	1.21	0.8	11.3	15.0	0.0	200
2013	A	Beloit	1	1	0	47	31	4.78	1.72	21.4	325	37	73	5.83	3.2	5.9	1.8	0.8	37
2014	A	Beloit	4	9	0	101	70	4.81	1.24	22.8	258	31	58	3.14	2.3	6.2	2.7	0.3	68
2014	A+	Stockton	3	5	0	39	22	7.15	1.64	21.7	308	35	53	5.08	3.5	5.1	1.5	0.5	16

Promising SP who remains inconsistent but has upside with three decent pitches. Induces groundballs with nice FB thrown downhill with sink. Can be effective against LHH with power CB and OK CU thrown with good arm speed. Doesn't miss many bats and can be inefficient when nibbling.

Crawford,Jonathon — SP — Cincinnati
EXP MLB DEBUT: 2016 | H/W: 6-2 205 | FUT: #3 starter | 8D

Thrws R Age 23 — 2013 (1) Florida
- 90-96 FB ++++
- 82-87 SL +++
- 83-86 CU ++

Year	Lev	Team	W	L	Sv	IP	K	ERA	WHIP	BF/G	OBA	H%	S%	xERA	Ctl	Dom	Cmd	hr/9	BPV
2011	NCAA	Florida	0	0	0	3	4	5.63	2.19	3.2	399	50	83	10.25	2.8	11.3	4.0	2.8	145
2012	NCAA	Florida	6	2	0	77	73	3.15	1.28	16.7	256	34	74	3.18	2.8	8.5	3.0	0.2	96
2013	NCAA	Florida	3	6	0	86	69	3.86	1.36	24.0	248	30	71	3.43	3.9	7.2	1.9	0.4	43
2013	A-	Connecticut	0	2	0	19	21	1.89	1.26	9.7	219	32	83	2.41	4.3	9.9	2.3	0.0	82
2014	A	West Michigan	8	3	0	123	85	2.85	1.16	21.3	211	26	74	2.31	3.7	6.2	1.7	0.2	31

Strong-armed SP who was consistent all season, but stayed in Low-A. Tough to square up pitches and can deftly change speeds to keep hitters off-balance. Throws with lots of effort, meaning move to pen could come. Maintains velocity on plus, sinking FB and hard SL misses bats.

Crick,Kyle — SP — San Francisco
EXP MLB DEBUT: 2015 | H/W: 6-2 220 | FUT: #2 Starter | 9D

Thrws R Age 22 — 2011 (1) HS (TX)
- 93-97 FB ++++
- 82-84 SL +++
- 87-89 CU ++
- 88-91 CT ++

Year	Lev	Team	W	L	Sv	IP	K	ERA	WHIP	BF/G	OBA	H%	S%	xERA	Ctl	Dom	Cmd	hr/9	BPV
2011	Rk	AZL Giants	1	0	0	7	8	6.43	2.43	5.2	313	43	71	6.66	10.3	10.3	1.0	0.0	-75
2012	A	Augusta	7	6	0	111	128	2.51	1.28	19.8	193	29	79	2.22	5.4	10.4	1.9	0.1	58
2013	A+	San Jose	3	1	0	68	95	1.58	1.28	20.0	200	33	87	2.31	5.1	12.5	2.4	0.1	105
2014	AA	Richmond	6	7	0	90	111	3.80	1.54	17.1	235	33	77	3.96	6.1	11.1	1.8	0.7	53

Big, strong RHP racked up plent of Ks using his mid-90s FB, up to 98, and plus SL. Explosive arm action, but inconsistent delivery led to horrid Ctl issues. At 21, he is still raw, and with added time to tighten his Cmd and refine his delivery, he has the potential to reach that of a frontline starter.

Curtis,Zac
RP | Arizona | EXP MLB DEBUT: 2017 | H/W: 5-9 179 | FUT: Setup RP | 7C

Thrws L Age 22
2014 (6) Middle Tennessee State

Velo	Pitch	Grade
88-92	FB	+++
	SL	+++
	CB	++
	CU	++

Year	Lev	Team	W	L	Sv	IP	K	ERA	WHIP	BF/G	OBA	H%	S%	xERA	Ctl	Dom	Cmd	hr/9	BPV
2013	NCAA	Middle Tenn St	5	4	0	80	74	4.94	1.34	23.8	252	32	62	3.67	3.5	8.3	2.4	0.7	74
2014	NCAA	Middle Tenn St	6	2	0	82	98	2.08	1.05	28.9	222	33	79	2.00	2.2	10.7	4.9	0.1	152
2014	A-	Hillsboro	2	1	14	27	42	1.00	1.11	4.4	191	35	90	1.66	4.0	14.0	3.5	0.0	162

Short, collegiate LH is not overpowering, but knows how to pitch. FB tops out at 92 mph, but gets swings-and-misses from a plus SL. CB and CU are also serviceable.

Danish,Tyler
SP | Chicago (A) | EXP MLB DEBUT: 2016 | H/W: 6-0 205 | FUT: #4 starter | 7B

Thrws R Age 20
2013 (2) HS (FL)

Velo	Pitch	Grade
89-94	FB	++++
80-84	SL	+++
79-82	CU	++

Year	Lev	Team	W	L	Sv	IP	K	ERA	WHIP	BF/G	OBA	H%	S%	xERA	Ctl	Dom	Cmd	hr/9	BPV
2013	Rk	Bristol	1	0	0	26	22	1.38	0.77	7.2	170	21	84	0.95	1.7	7.6	4.4	0.3	108
2013	A	Kannapolis	0	0	0	4	6	0.00	0.50	6.6	151	27	100	0.00	0.0	13.5		0.0	261
2014	A	Kannapolis	3	0	0	38	25	0.71	1.00	20.7	207	25	92	1.65	2.4	5.9	2.5	0.0	61
2014	A+	Winston-Salem	5	3	0	91	78	2.66	1.21	20.4	253	31	81	3.37	2.3	7.7	3.4	0.7	95

Advanced pitcher who thrives with sinker and plus command. Doesn't have ideal size and has effort in delivery, but spots pitches with precision with sinker/slider combo. Keeps ball in yard and has SL with big, late break. CU isn't yet effective as he can telegraph pitch when slowing arm.

Darnell,Logan
SP | Minnesota | EXP MLB DEBUT: 2014 | H/W: 6-2 210 | FUT: #5 starter | 6B

Thrws L Age 26
2010 (6) Kentucky

Velo	Pitch	Grade
88-92	FB	+++
75-79	CB	++
81-82	SL	++
80-83	CU	+++

Year	Lev	Team	W	L	Sv	IP	K	ERA	WHIP	BF/G	OBA	H%	S%	xERA	Ctl	Dom	Cmd	hr/9	BPV
2012	AA	New Britain	11	12	0	156		5.08	1.54	24.3	305	33	70	5.53	2.7	5.7	2.1	1.3	47
2013	AA	New Britain	6	6	0	96	77	2.62	1.24	26.0	261	32	79	3.28	2.2	7.2	3.3	0.4	90
2013	AAA	Rochester	4	4	0	57	43	4.26	1.49	20.5	282	33	73	4.60	3.5	6.8	2.0	0.8	46
2014	AAA	Rochester	7	6	0	115	90	3.60	1.37	20.9	250	28	79	4.27	3.8	7.0	1.8	1.3	41
2014	MLB	Minnesota	0	2	0	24	22	7.13	1.63	15.2	314	36	59	6.43	3.0	8.3	2.8	1.9	86

Savvy LHP who has limited upside, but thrives with deep arsenal. Lacks frontline velocity and does not have put-away pitch. Throws strikes with fringy FB and two breaking balls. Keeps hitters off-guard with strong CU that he can use in any count. Induces grounders by working down.

Davies,Zach
SP | Baltimore | EXP MLB DEBUT: 2015 | H/W: 6-0 150 | FUT: #4 starter | 7A

Thrws R Age 22
2011 (26) HS (AZ)

Velo	Pitch	Grade
86-91	FB	+++
73-75	CB	+++
79-82	SL	++
80-85	CU	++++

Year	Lev	Team	W	L	Sv	IP	K	ERA	WHIP	BF/G	OBA	H%	S%	xERA	Ctl	Dom	Cmd	hr/9	BPV
2012	A	Delmarva	5	7	1	114	91	3.87	1.36	19.1	253	30	74	3.93	3.6	7.2	2.0	0.9	49
2013	A+	Frederick	7	9	0	148	132	3.70	1.23	23.1	258	32	71	3.43	2.3	8.0	3.5	0.6	100
2014	AA	Bowie	10	7	0	110	109	3.35	1.25	21.3	255	33	75	3.48	2.6	8.9	3.4	0.7	108

Short, slight pitcher with advanced command and pitch mix. Throws consistent strikes with 4 pitches, highlighted by plus CU with impressive arm speed. May not have top-shelf velocity, but sequences with precision and repeats athletic delivery. Pitches down in zone and has been durable.

Dayton,Grant
RP | Miami | EXP MLB DEBUT: 2015 | H/W: 6-1 205 | FUT: Reliever | 7D

Thrws L Age 27
2010 (11) Auburn

Velo	Pitch	Grade
91-94	FB	+++
81-84	SL	+++
	CU	++

Year	Lev	Team	W	L	Sv	IP	K	ERA	WHIP	BF/G	OBA	H%	S%	xERA	Ctl	Dom	Cmd	hr/9	BPV
2012	A+	Jupiter	2	5	2	60	71	2.10	1.10	7.6	221	32	80	2.16	2.7	10.7	3.9	0.2	137
2012	AA	Jacksonville	2	1	0	13	19	4.15	1.23	7.5	247	36	71	3.95	2.8	13.2	4.8	1.4	180
2013	AA	Jacksonville	4	4	1	38	56	2.37	1.18	5.1	235	36	85	3.28	2.8	13.3	4.7	0.9	180
2014	AA	Jacksonville	0	1	3	16	18	1.12	1.30	6.0	272	38	90	3.22	2.2	10.1	4.5	0.0	139
2014	AAA	New Orleans	2	2	1	55	61	3.75	1.36	5.9	254	31	80	4.64	3.6	9.9	2.8	1.6	100

Strong, durable LH continues to thrive since being moved to relief. FB sits 92-94 with late life and hitters struggle to pick it up. Complements it with a low-80s SL and below-avg CU, though it has decent fade and keeps RHH at bay. Continues to show good command of all his pitches.

De Jong,Chase
SP | Toronto | EXP MLB DEBUT: 2017 | H/W: 6-4 200 | FUT: #4 starter | 7C

Thrws R Age 21
2012 (2) HS (CA)

Velo	Pitch	Grade
87-94	FB	+++
74-78	CB	+++
80-81	CU	+++

Year		Team	W	L	Sv	IP	K	ERA	WHIP	BF/G	OBA	H%	S%	xERA	Ctl	Dom	Cmd	hr/9	BPV
2012	Rk	GCL Blue Jays	1	0	0	12	15	1.50	0.67	7.0	171	27	75	0.35	0.8	11.3	15.0	0.0	200
2013	Rk	Bluefield	2	3	0	56	66	3.05	1.21	17.4	269	38	74	3.24	1.6	10.6	6.6	0.3	166
2014	A	Lansing	1	6	0	97	73	4.82	1.39	17.8	292	33	67	4.81	2.0	6.8	3.3	1.1	85

Large, durable SP who has repertoire to be solid, but allows too many hits and struggles with LHH. Inconsistent secondaries have been issue, though has quality FB with potential for more velocity. CU can be plus pitch and repeats delivery well. Tends to overthrow, leaving FB straight.

de la Rosa,Edgar
SP | Detroit | EXP MLB DEBUT: 2016 | H/W: 6-8 235 | FUT: #4 starter | 7C

Thrws R Age 24
2009 FA (DR)

Velo	Pitch	Grade
89-97	FB	++++
81-85	SL	++
84-88	CU	++

Year	Lev	Team	W	L	Sv	IP	K	ERA	WHIP	BF/G	OBA	H%	S%	xERA	Ctl	Dom	Cmd	hr/9	BPV
2011	Rk	GCL Tigers	2	4	0	67	50	3.21	1.31	23.1	270	32	77	3.86	2.4	6.7	2.8	0.7	73
2012	A-	Connecticut	4	4	0	72	54	3.12	1.40	20.3	245	30	78	3.47	4.4	6.7	1.5	0.4	21
2013	A	West Michigan	8	6	0	120	78	5.62	1.51	20.8	292	34	61	4.49	3.1	5.8	1.9	0.4	40
2014	A+	Lakeland	7	9	0	139	91	3.30	1.22	21.6	228	25	76	3.24	3.4	5.9	1.7	0.8	31

Hulking, strong-armed, aggressive pitcher who hits triple digits with electric FB. Much improved from Low-A in '13, but still lacks command and strikeouts. Uses height very well and shows touch for changing speeds with FB, but lacks secondary pitch. Throws with loose arm, but leaves balls up frequently.

De Leon,Jose
SP | Los Angeles (N) | EXP MLB DEBUT: 2018 | H/W: 6-2 185 | FUT: #3 starter | 9D

Thrws R Age 22
2013 (24) Southern

Velo	Pitch	Grade
94-96	FB	++++
80-83	SL	+++
	CU	++

Year	Lev	Team	W	L	Sv	IP	K	ERA	WHIP	BF/G	OBA	H%	S%	xERA	Ctl	Dom	Cmd	hr/9	BPV
2013	NCAA	Southern	4	3	0	82	73	2.85	1.13	27.0	211	28	72	2.01	3.4	8.0	2.4	0.0	70
2013	Rk	Ogden	1	2	0	19	18	12.25	1.89	18.4	394	46	36	9.24	1.4	8.5	6.0	2.4	133
2013	Rk	AZL Dodgers	2	3	0	33	35	4.07	1.51	16.0	255	35	71	3.74	4.9	9.5	1.9	0.3	57
2014	Rk	Ogden	5	0	0	54	77	2.66	1.16	21.6	224	36	77	2.51	3.2	12.8	4.1	0.3	163
2014	A	Great Lakes	2	0	0	22	42	1.22	0.72	19.7	183	39	87	0.93	0.8	17.0	21.0	0.4	303

Late-developing hurler took a big step forward. Attacks hitters with a good 91-94 mph FB. Also showed an improved slurve and an avg CU. Improved conditioning and a mechanical adjustment fueled the breakout. Had attention-grabbing strikeout-to-walk ratio of 42/2 with a sub-Mendoza oppBA in MWL.

DeCarr,Austin
SP | New York (A) | EXP MLB DEBUT: 2017 | H/W: 6-3 215 | FUT: #4 starter | 7D

Thrws R Age 20
2014 (3) HS (CT)

Velo	Pitch	Grade
88-94	FB	+++
78-82	CB	++
83-87	CU	+++

Year	Lev	Team	W	L	Sv	IP	K	ERA	WHIP	BF/G	OBA	H%	S%	xERA	Ctl	Dom	Cmd	hr/9	BPV
2014	Rk	GCL Yankees	2	1	0	23	24	4.68	1.17	8.4	235	32	58	2.75	2.7	9.4	3.4	0.4	113

Tall, strong SP who has projectable arm strength and potential for plus FB. Throws from high 3/4 slot and makes it tough for hitters to elevate ball. Has tendency to overthrow and can leave CB up. Uses hard CU that features late action and CB has potential to become third solid pitch.

DeSclafani,Anthony
SP | Cincinnati | EXP MLB DEBUT: 2014 | H/W: 6-1 190 | FUT: #3 starter | 8C

Thrws R Age 24
2011 (6) Florida

Velo	Pitch	Grade
90-96	FB	++++
81-85	SL	++++
84-87	CU	+++

Year	Lev	Team	W	L	Sv	IP	K	ERA	WHIP	BF/G	OBA	H%	S%	xERA	Ctl	Dom	Cmd	hr/9	BPV
2013	A+	Jupiter	4	2	0	54	53	1.67	1.06	17.4	240	31	87	2.63	1.5	8.8	5.9	0.5	137
2013	AA	Jacksonville	5	4	0	75	62	3.36	1.17	23.0	259	31	74	3.52	1.7	7.4	4.4	0.8	107
2014	AA	Jacksonville	3	4	0	43	38	4.19	1.28	22.0	271	33	69	3.94	2.1	8.0	3.8	0.8	105
2014	AAA	New Orleans	3	3	0	59	59	3.50	1.17	19.6	224	30	69	2.52	3.2	9.0	2.8	0.3	93
2014	MLB	Miami	2	2	0	33	26	6.27	1.36	10.6	301	35	54	4.84	1.4	7.1	5.2	1.1	109

Continues to improve game utilizing plus control and a deep arsenal. Works off plus FB/SL combo and mixes in good CU. He's aggressive going after hitters and pounds lower half of zone with strikes before going to SL as out pitch. Commands all his pitches to both sides of plate.

Diaz,Chris
SP | Atlanta | EXP MLB DEBUT: 2017 | H/W: 6-0 195 | FUT: #4 starter | 7D

Thrws L Age 21
2014 (5) Miami

Velo	Pitch	Grade
88-92	FB	+++
80-83	CU	++
	SL	++

Year	Lev	Team	W	L	Sv	IP	K	ERA	WHIP	BF/G	OBA	H%	S%	xERA	Ctl	Dom	Cmd	hr/9	BPV
2012	NCAA	Miami	2	1	0	32	20	4.21	1.50	6.0	279	33	69	3.84	3.6	5.6	1.5	0.0	21
2013	NCAA	Miami	7	5	0	109	78	1.65	1.17	27.2	247	30	85	2.65	2.2	6.4	2.9	0.1	74
2014	NCAA	Miami	9	1	0	101	86	2.41	1.28	25.9	236	30	80	2.77	3.7	7.7	2.1	0.1	57
2014	A	Rome	0	0	0	33	36	2.99	1.27	13.5	184	26	76	2.27	5.7	9.8	1.7	0.3	40

5th round pick is a short, compact LH is not overpowering. His FB sits at 87-90 mph but he gets late sinking action that makes it tough to square up. Also has an average SL and CU. Succeeds despite a lack of velocity due to the sinker. Walked 5.7 per nine, but held batters to a terrible BA.

Diaz,Edwin — SP — Seattle

EXP MLB DEBUT: 2017 | H/W: 6-2 180 | FUT: #3 starter | 8D

Thrws R Age 21
2012 (3) HS (PR)

Velo	Pitch	Grade
90-95	FB	++++
74-77	CB	+++
81-84	SL	+++
82-85	CU	++

Year	Lev	Team	W	L	Sv	IP	K	ERA	WHIP	BF/G	OBA	H%	S%	xERA	Ctl	Dom	Cmd	hr/9	BPV
2012	Rk	AZL Mariners	2	1	0	19	20	5.21	1.53	9.2	183	23	67	3.55	8.1	9.5	1.2	0.9	-29
2013	Rk	Pulaski	5	2	0	69	79	1.43	0.91	19.8	188	26	90	1.77	2.3	10.3	4.4	0.7	140
2014	A	Clinton	6	8	0	116	111	3.33	1.19	19.4	227	30	71	2.70	3.3	8.6	2.6	0.4	85

High upside SP who finished strong in first full year. Tough to make hard contact against with four pitches, including plus FB with advanced location. Gets ahead in count with FB and complements with two breakers and developing CU. Loses velocity late in games and needs strength.

Diaz,Jairo — RP — Colorado

EXP MLB DEBUT: 2014 | H/W: 6-0 195 | FUT: Closer | 8E

Thrws R Age 23
2007 FA (Venezuela)

Velo	Pitch	Grade
94-99	FB	++++
86-89	SL	+++
84-88	CU	+

Year	Lev	Team	W	L	Sv	IP	K	ERA	WHIP	BF/G	OBA	H%	S%	xERA	Ctl	Dom	Cmd	hr/9	BPV
2013	A	Burlington	0	3	8	34	28	3.97	1.12	4.2	220	26	66	2.83	2.9	7.4	2.5	0.8	73
2013	A+	Inland Empire	0	2	0	22	21	8.96	2.35	8.8	379	46	61	8.79	5.7	8.6	1.5	1.2	18
2014	A+	Inland Empire	2	3	4	32	37	4.78	1.28	4.5	256	35	62	3.46	2.8	10.4	3.7	0.6	129
2014	AA	Arkansas	2	1	11	32	48	2.24	1.24	4.8	248	40	84	3.23	2.8	13.4	4.8	0.6	184
2014	MLB	LA Angels	0	0	0	5	8	3.46	1.35	4.3	214	38	71	2.53	5.2	13.8	2.7	0.0	127

Overpowering RP who moved to pen in 2013. Throws strikes from high 3/4 slot and uses plus arm strength to fire FB by hitters. All offerings are hard, including average SL and iffy CU. Max effort delivery hinders command, though exhibits decent control and keeps ball on ground.

Diaz,Miguel — RP — Milwaukee

EXP MLB DEBUT: 2018 | H/W: 6-1 180 | FUT: #3 starter/Setup RP | 7C

Thrws R Age 20
2011 FA (DR)

Velo	Pitch	Grade
94-96	FB	++++
75-78	SL	++
85-87	CT	++
	CU	++

Year	Lev	Team	W	L	Sv	IP	K	ERA	WHIP	BF/G	OBA	H%	S%	xERA	Ctl	Dom	Cmd	hr/9	BPV
2013	Rk	DSL Brewers	3	2	0	48	34	2.43	1.18	17.5	209	26	77	2.13	3.9	6.3	1.6	0.0	26
2014	Rk	AZL Brewers	4	2	0	47	53	4.21	1.32	15.0	241	33	68	3.37	3.8	10.1	2.7	0.6	97

Quick-armed Dominican hurler impressed in his U.S debut. Features a plus 94-96 mph FB with arm-side run. Mixes in a mid-70s SL and a mid-80s CU, both of which need work. Remains raw, but has the velo and arm strength to pitch in the majors, whether as a starter or in relief.

Diaz,Miller — SP — New York (N)

EXP MLB DEBUT: 2017 | H/W: 6-1 210 | FUT: Reliever | 6C

Thrws R Age 22
2009 FA (Venezuela)

Velo	Pitch	Grade
92-94	FB	+++
80-82	SL	++
	CU	++

Year	Lev	Team	W	L	Sv	IP	K	ERA	WHIP	BF/G	OBA	H%	S%	xERA	Ctl	Dom	Cmd	hr/9	BPV
2011	Rk	Kingsport	1	1	1	33	22	5.42	1.81	17.1	294	35	68	5.10	5.7	6.0	1.0	0.3	-28
2012	Rk	Kingsport	2	1	0	43	45	3.56	1.26	15.9	229	31	71	2.92	3.8	9.4	2.5	0.4	86
2012	A	Savannah	0	1	0	4	8	6.43	1.90	19.8	371	65	63	6.28	2.1	17.1	8.0	0.0	269
2013	A-	Brooklyn	7	3	0	66	87	2.04	1.16	20.3	191	30	82	1.94	4.5	11.8	2.6	0.1	110
2014	A	Savannah	6	1	2	68	79	2.25	1.04	20.2	187	27	79	1.85	3.6	10.5	2.9	0.4	110

Put together most complete season in '14. Improved bb% while maintaining high number of Ks and groundballs. Throws from a 3/4 arm slot. FB/SL combo misses lots of bats and he limits hard contact. Profiles long-term as reliever due to the effort in his delivery and lack of third reliable pitch.

Dickey,Robbie — SP — Washington

EXP MLB DEBUT: 2017 | H/W: 6-3 205 | FUT: #4 starter | 7C

Thrws R Age 21
2014 (4) Blinn JC (TX)

Velo	Pitch	Grade
91-93	FB	+++
	SL	++
	CT	++
	CU	++

Year	Lev	Team	W	L	Sv	IP	K	ERA	WHIP	BF/G	OBA	H%	S%	xERA	Ctl	Dom	Cmd	hr/9	BPV
2014	Rk	GCL Nationals	0	2	0	5	5	13.85	2.69	9.6	429	53	43	9.54	5.2	8.7	1.7	0.0	34
2014	A-	Auburn	0	2	0	20	13	2.25	1.05	15.5	242	29	76	2.21	1.4	5.9	4.3	0.0	87
2014	A	Hagerstown	1	0	0	9	5	3.00	1.67	20.2	283	33	80	4.33	5.0	5.0	1.0	0.0	-27

Though his high-strikeout ways from junior college didn't carry over to his intial pro experience, scouts like his smooth delivery that produces a FB that tops out at 95 mph. Secondary pitches are still developing, but his arm strength is there. Has competitive demeanor that could be an asset out of the bullpen.

Dickson,Cody — SP — Pittsburgh

EXP MLB DEBUT: 2016 | H/W: 6-3 180 | FUT: #4 starter | 7D

Thrws L Age 22
2013 (4) Sam Houston State

Velo	Pitch	Grade
91-93	FB	+++
	CB	+++
	CU	++

Year	Lev	Team	W	L	Sv	IP	K	ERA	WHIP	BF/G	OBA	H%	S%	xERA	Ctl	Dom	Cmd	hr/9	BPV
2011	NCAA	Sam Houston St	4	1	0	45	52	4.38	1.59	14.2	230	33	70	3.56	6.8	10.4	1.5	0.2	22
2012	NCAA	Sam Houston St	4	5	0	72	46	3.25	1.47	17.2	251	29	78	3.86	4.8	5.8	1.2	0.5	-7
2013	NCAA	Sam Houston St	9	5	0	95	91	4.26	1.18	21.1	185	24	62	2.18	4.8	8.6	1.8	0.4	43
2013	A-	Jamestown	2	0	0	57	59	2.37	1.16	16.2	207	28	81	2.46	3.8	9.3	2.5	0.5	83
2014	A	West Virginia	7	9	0	129	104	3.90	1.52	20.7	275	33	76	4.54	4.0	7.3	1.8	0.8	39

Tall, lean LH had a solid year in his full-season debut. Has a good 91-93 mph FB. His curve and CU both show solid potential, but lacks consistency and he sometimes struggles to throw strikes. Can rush delivery resulting in inconsistent command.

Diplan,Marcos — SP — Texas

EXP MLB DEBUT: 2018 | H/W: 6-0 160 | FUT: #3 starter | 8E

Thrws R Age 18
2013 FA (DR)

Velo	Pitch	Grade
90-95	FB	+++
77-79	CB	+++
83-86	CU	++

Year	Lev	Team	W	L	Sv	IP	K	ERA	WHIP	BF/G	OBA	H%	S%	xERA	Ctl	Dom	Cmd	hr/9	BPV
2014	Rk	DSL Rangers	7	2	0	64	57	1.54	1.06	19.1	150	20	86	1.41	5.1	8.0	1.6	0.3	26

Loose-armed SP who showcases promising pitch mix. Has limited projection in delivery that has effort. Throws hard now with quick arm, though FB lacks life. CB is best secondary offering with nice, late break, but needs to improve CU that can be too firm. Tough to hit when he's on.

Dominguez,Jose — RP — Tampa Bay

EXP MLB DEBUT: 2013 | H/W: 6-0 200 | FUT: Reliever | 6C

Thrws R Age 24
2007 FA (DR)

Velo	Pitch	Grade
96-100	FB	+++++
	SL	+++
	CU	+++

Year	Lev	Team	W	L	Sv	IP	K	ERA	WHIP	BF/G	OBA	H%	S%	xERA	Ctl	Dom	Cmd	hr/9	BPV
2013	AAA	Albuquerque	1	0	0	8	12	0.00	0.75	3.6	42	9	100	0.00	5.6	13.5	2.4	0.0	109
2013	MLB	LA Dodgers	0	0	0	8	4	2.22	1.73	4.1	325	37	86	5.15	3.3	4.4	1.3	0.0	8
2014	Rk	Ogden	0	0	0	1	2	16.36	1.82	2.6	244	48	0	4.06	8.2	16.4	2.0	0.0	92
2014	AAA	Albuquerque	1	2	10	33	39	3.26	1.48	4.6	249	36	77	3.60	4.9	10.6	2.2	0.3	77
2014	MLB	LA Dodgers	0	0	0	6	8	11.80	1.64	5.4	289	35	25	7.06	4.4	11.8	2.7	3.0	111

Undersized RP overpowers hitters with a plus FB that sits in the upper 90s, maxing out at 100 mph. All-out delivery continues to result in control problems and he walked 18 in 33.1 IP. Offers a solid average SL that complements the heater well. Was traded to the Rays as part of the Peralta deal.

Drake,Oliver — RP — Baltimore

EXP MLB DEBUT: 2015 | H/W: 6-4 215 | FUT: Setup RP | 6B

Thrws R Age 28
2008 (43) Navy

Velo	Pitch	Grade
89-94	FB	+++
82-85	SP	++
84-87	SL	+++

Year	Lev	Team	W	L	Sv	IP	K	ERA	WHIP	BF/G	OBA	H%	S%	xERA	Ctl	Dom	Cmd	hr/9	BPV
2011	AA	Bowie	3	5	0	64	47	5.20	1.58	23.5	299	34	69	5.39	3.4	6.6	2.0	1.1	46
2011	AAA	Norfolk	0	0	0	2	2	0.00	1.00	7.6	151	22	100	0.99	4.5	9.0	2.0	0.0	59
2012	AA	Bowie	1	1	0	18	15	1.50	0.67	20.9	136	16	82	0.48	2.0	7.5	3.8	0.5	99
2013	AA	Bowie	3	0	8	31	38	1.74	1.03	6.3	179	27	84	1.62	3.8	11.0	2.9	0.3	115
2014	AA	Bowie	2	4	31	52	71	3.10	1.11	4.1	218	34	71	2.32	2.9	12.2	4.2	0.3	159

Aggressive RP who led EL in saves in first full year since '11. Shoulder surgery wiped out most of '12 and '13, but has come back strong with solid-average FB that induces groundballs. Uses splitter as chase pitch and SL, though inconsistent, can miss bats. Converted to RP in '13.

Driver,Dustin — SP — Oakland

EXP MLB DEBUT: 2018 | H/W: 6-2 210 | FUT: #3 starter | 8E

Thrws R Age 20
2013 (7) HS (WA)

Velo	Pitch	Grade
90-96	FB	+++
77-80	CB	++
81-84	CU	++

Year	Lev	Team	W	L	Sv	IP	K	ERA	WHIP	BF/G	OBA	H%	S%	xERA	Ctl	Dom	Cmd	hr/9	BPV
2014		(did not play in 2014)																	

Big, physical SP who did not pitch due to back issue. Has very strong arm that occasionally pumps mid-90s FB into zone. Very raw secondary pitches, but show promise. Struggles to repeat delivery and slot and will need to stay consistent for CB. Tends to telegraph CU with slower arm.

Drummond,Calvin — RP — Detroit

EXP MLB DEBUT: 2016 | H/W: 6-3 200 | FUT: Middle reliever | 7D

Thrws R Age 25
2013 (6) Arizona Christian

Velo	Pitch	Grade
91-96	FB	+++
84-88	SL	+++
74-80	CB	++
82-85	CU	++

Year	Lev	Team	W	L	Sv	IP	K	ERA	WHIP	BF/G	OBA	H%	S%	xERA	Ctl	Dom	Cmd	hr/9	BPV
2011	NCAA	San Diego	3	4	0	76	55	3.31	1.44	23.2	254	30	77	3.68	4.4	6.5	1.5	0.4	17
2012	NCAA	San Diego	8	6	0	86	80	3.45	1.53	22.1	287	37	77	4.42	3.5	8.4	2.4	0.4	73
2013	Rk	GCL Tigers	1	0	0	2	2	0.00	0.50	3.3	151	22	100	0.00	0.0	9.0		0.0	180
2013	A	West Michigan	3	2	1	40	47	2.24	0.97	6.6	169	25	76	1.31	3.6	10.5	2.9	0.2	111
2014	A+	Lakeland	3	3	1	45	65	3.99	1.71	5.8	257	39	78	4.74	6.6	13.0	2.0	0.8	74

Max-effort RP who has enough FB velocity and movement to be effective, but may not have command or control to advance. Keeps ball down in zone from throwing on downhill angle and mixes in quality SL that serves as out pitch. Must find consistent arm slot to improve CB and CU.

Duffey,Tyler — SP — Minnesota

EXP MLB DEBUT: 2016 | H/W: 6-3 230 | FUT: #4 starter | 7D

Thrws R Age 24
2012 (5) Rice

Velo	Pitch	Grade
88-94	FB	+++
79-82	CB	+++
79-84	CU	++

Year	Lev	Team	W	L	Sv	IP	K	ERA	WHIP	BF/G	OBA	H%	S%	xERA	Ctl	Dom	Cmd	hr/9	BPV
2013	A	Cedar Rapids	3	2	0	58	47	2.79	0.95	24.3	230	27	74	2.51	0.9	7.3	7.8	0.8	124
2013	A+	Fort Myers	4	5	0	62	44	4.49	1.35	17.3	276	33	65	3.84	2.5	6.4	2.6	0.4	66
2014	A+	Fort Myers	3	0	0	22	13	2.85	1.22	22.3	261	31	74	2.90	2.0	5.3	2.6	0.0	58
2014	AA	New Britain	8	3	0	111	84	3.81	1.11	24.2	249	28	70	3.50	1.5	6.8	4.4	1.1	99
2014	AAA	Rochester	2	0	0	16	16	3.94	1.38	22.4	262	31	79	4.85	3.4	9.0	2.7	1.7	89

Big-bodied SP who earned time on three levels and can be innings eater. Velocity doesn't match body type, but can still leverage natural strength. Exhibits plus control and average command with three pitches. CB is tough on RHH while CU needs polish in order to retire LHH consistently.

Eades,Ryan — SP — Minnesota

EXP MLB DEBUT: 2016 | H/W: 6-2 200 | FUT: #4 starter | 7D

Thrws R Age 23
2013 (2) Louisiana State

Velo	Pitch	Grade
88-95	FB	+++
79-83	CB	+++
80-82	CU	++

Year	Lev	Team	W	L	Sv	IP	K	ERA	WHIP	BF/G	OBA	H%	S%	xERA	Ctl	Dom	Cmd	hr/9	BPV
2011	NCAA	LSU	4	1	0	43	31	4.81	1.56	10.5	288	33	70	4.90	3.8	6.5	1.7	0.8	33
2012	NCAA	LSU	5	3	0	94	63	3.83	1.44	23.5	288	33	75	4.53	2.7	6.0	2.3	0.8	54
2013	NCAA	LSU	8	1	0	100	78	2.79	1.33	24.4	264	32	78	3.45	2.9	7.0	2.4	0.3	67
2013	Rk	Elizabethton	0	0	0	15	13	4.74	1.64	6.8	233	30	68	3.57	7.1	7.7	1.1	0.0	-35
2014	A	Cedar Rapids	10	11	0	133	98	5.14	1.48	22.0	282	33	65	4.53	3.4	6.6	2.0	0.7	46

Lean SP with athleticism and frame to add strength. Pitches to contact with two-seamer, but has power CB that is used as chase pitch. Throws downhill, but struggles with FB command. Improved CU, but can telegraph pitch by slowing arm. Inconsistent mechanics need to be ironed out.

Edwards,C.J. — SP — Chicago (N)

EXP MLB DEBUT: 2015 | H/W: 6-2 155 | FUT: #3 starter | 9D

Thrws R Age 23
2011 (48) HS (SC)

Velo	Pitch	Grade
92-95	FB	++++
75-78	CB	++++
80-83	SL	++
82-85	CU	++

Year	Lev	Team	W	L	Sv	IP	K	ERA	WHIP	BF/G	OBA	H%	S%	xERA	Ctl	Dom	Cmd	hr/9	BPV
2012	A-	Spokane	2	3	0	47		2.11	0.96	17.8	164	26	76	1.00	3.6	11.5	3.2	0.0	127
2013	A	Hickory	8	2	0	93	122	1.84	1.03	19.9	191	31	80	1.48	3.3	11.8	3.6	0.0	142
2013	A+	Daytona	0	0	0	23	33	1.96	0.91	14.3	178	29	80	1.39	2.7	12.9	4.7	0.4	176
2014	Rk	AZL Cubs	0	0	0	5	8	1.73	1.15	10.3	120	23	83	1.02	6.9	13.8	2.0	0.0	80
2014	AA	Tennessee	1	2	0	48	46	2.44	1.06	18.6	181	25	76	1.66	3.9	8.6	2.2	0.2	67

Athletic RH gets serious torque from his 6-2, 155 frame. FB sits at 92-95 mph. Heater has good cutting action and he complements it with a quality 12-6 curve. Also mixes in a SL and an improved CU. Concerns about durability cut into his long-term potential and he missed three months of action.

Eflin,Zach — SP — Philadelphia

EXP MLB DEBUT: 2016 | H/W: 6-4 200 | FUT: #3 starter | 8D

Thrws R Age 20
2012 (1-S) HS (FL)

Velo	Pitch	Grade
92-94	FB	+++
	CB	+
81-83	CU	+++

Year	Lev	Team	W	L	Sv	IP	K	ERA	WHIP	BF/G	OBA	H%	S%	xERA	Ctl	Dom	Cmd	hr/9	BPV
2012	Rk	AZL Padres	0	1	0	7	4	7.71	1.71	7.9	313	36	50	4.91	3.9	5.1	1.3	0.0	6
2013	A	Fort Wayne	7	6	0	118	86	2.74	1.19	21.6	248	29	78	3.14	2.4	6.5	2.8	0.5	72
2014	A+	Lake Elsinore	10	7	0	128	93	3.80	1.32	22.1	277	32	72	3.95	2.2	6.5	3.0	0.6	77

Athletic SP held his own in the CAL. Still has some projection left and throws from a ¾ arm slot and likes to change speeds by cutting and sinking plus FB. Has feel for pitching and throws lots of strikes, but fails to adequately drop CB in the zone. His strikeout rate is a bit low and is a FB pitcher.

Eickhoff,Jared — SP — Texas

EXP MLB DEBUT: 2015 | H/W: 6-4 240 | FUT: #4 starter | 7D

Thrws R Age 24
2011 (15) Olney Central JC

Velo	Pitch	Grade
90-95	FB	+++
81-84	SL	++
78-82	CB	+++
82-85	CU	++

Year	Lev	Team	W	L	Sv	IP	K	ERA	WHIP	BF/G	OBA	H%	S%	xERA	Ctl	Dom	Cmd	hr/9	BPV
2011	A-	Spokane	1	1	2	14	18	2.55	0.78	5.1	167	24	70	1.19	1.9	11.5	6.0	0.6	173
2012	A	Hickory	13	7	0	126	90	4.71	1.35	20.2	271	29	70	4.81	2.7	6.4	2.4	1.6	60
2013	A+	Myrtle Beach	7	3	0	116	80	3.41	1.17	22.1	252	29	72	3.30	2.0	6.2	3.1	0.7	75
2013	AA	Frisco	1	1	0	29	13	7.45	1.66	21.6	294	29	57	6.22	4.3	4.0	0.9	1.9	-27
2014	AA	Frisco	10	9	0	154	144	4.09	1.17	22.8	229	28	68	3.26	3.0	8.4	2.8	1.0	87

Large-framed SP who led TL in Ks. Maintains solid velocity deep into games and uses heavy sinker to get outs. K rate increased as both breaking balls improved, though may ditch SL in favor of CB full-time. Allows HR when leaves balls up. Repeats arm speed on CU, but not much movement.

Ellis,Chris — SP — Los Angeles (A)

EXP MLB DEBUT: 2016 | H/W: 6-4 190 | FUT: #4 starter | 7C

Thrws R Age 22
2014 (3) Mississippi

Velo	Pitch	Grade
90-94	FB	+++
83-86	SL	+++
80-83	CU	++

Year	Lev	Team	W	L	Sv	IP	K	ERA	WHIP	BF/G	OBA	H%	S%	xERA	Ctl	Dom	Cmd	hr/9	BPV
2012	NCAA	Mississippi	4	0	0	31	29	2.88	1.06	6.4	221	29	72	2.21	2.3	8.4	3.6	0.3	106
2013	NCAA	Mississippi	1	2	0	21	16	5.57	2.00	7.8	344	40	73	6.93	4.7	6.9	1.5	0.9	14
2014	NCAA	Mississippi	10	3	0	116	67	2.56	1.32	25.3	253	29	82	3.55	3.3	5.2	1.6	0.5	24
2014	Rk	Orem	0	1	0	15	16	7.11	1.64	7.5	284	36	57	5.36	4.7	9.5	2.0	1.2	61

Long, lean, SP with room to add strength, but offers solid arsenal and could ascend quickly. Uses height and arm slot to throw downhill and owns two pitches that can miss bats. CU and SL are inconsistent, but show glimpses while FB can be straight at times. Could use better command.

Emanuel,Kent — SP — Houston

EXP MLB DEBUT: 2016 | H/W: 6-3 225 | FUT: #4 starter | 7D

Thrws L Age 22
2013 (3) North Carolina

Velo	Pitch	Grade
87-92	FB	+++
76-79	CB	++
82-84	SL	+++
76-79	CU	+++

Year	Lev	Team	W	L	Sv	IP	K	ERA	WHIP	BF/G	OBA	H%	S%	xERA	Ctl	Dom	Cmd	hr/9	BPV
2012	NCAA	North Carolina	8	4	0	110	100	1.96	1.04	25.0	227	30	81	2.19	1.9	8.2	4.3	0.2	114
2013	NCAA	North Carolina	11	5	1	131	98	3.16	1.17	24.9	246	30	73	3.00	2.2	6.7	3.1	0.5	80
2013	Rk	GCL Astros	0	0	0	9	8	0.00	0.89	8.3	191	26	100	1.16	2.0	8.0	4.0	0.0	108
2014	A	Quad Cities	0	2	0	22	17	2.45	1.09	14.3	244	27	86	3.48	1.6	7.0	4.3	1.2	99
2014	A+	Lancaster	9	5	2	102	76	4.59	1.27	19.9	278	32	66	4.26	1.7	6.7	4.0	1.1	93

Big, strong SP who profiles as back-end rotation guy. Throws pinpoint strikes at will and throws with quality angle to plate. Can be hittable with lack of plus stuff. Provides some deception with rigid delivery and attacks hitters early in count. Keeps ball on ground with sinking FB and CU.

Escobar,Edwin — SP — Boston

EXP MLB DEBUT: 2014 | H/W: 6-1 185 | FUT: #3 starter | 7B

Thrws L Age 22
2008 FA (Venezuela)

Velo	Pitch	Grade
88-94	FB	+++
82-85	SL	+++
83-85	CU	+++

Year	Lev	Team	W	L	Sv	IP	K	ERA	WHIP	BF/G	OBA	H%	S%	xERA	Ctl	Dom	Cmd	hr/9	BPV
2013	A+	San Jose	3	4	0	74	92	2.91	1.15	18.4	245	36	74	2.78	2.1	11.2	5.4	0.4	163
2013	AA	Richmond	5	4	0	54	54	2.67	1.06	20.9	224	30	75	2.28	2.2	9.0	4.2	0.3	122
2014	AAA	Fresno	3	8	0	111	96	5.11	1.49	23.9	290	34	68	5.18	3.0	7.8	2.6	1.3	77
2014	AAA	Pawtucket	0	2	0	27	20	4.32	1.51	23.5	302	35	74	5.15	2.7	6.6	2.5	1.0	66
2014	MLB	Boston	0	0	0	2	2	4.50	0.50	3.3	151	22	0	0.00	0.0	9.0		0.0	180

Durable SP who has intriguing mix of command and ability to change speeds. Struggles with RHH and was hittable despite good pitch mix. Strong, fast arm generates FB that he locates well. Misses bats with SL which neutralizes LHH. Repeats arm speed on CU though can be too firm.

Farmer,Buck — SP — Detroit

EXP MLB DEBUT: 2014 | H/W: 6-4 225 | FUT: #4 starter | 7B

Thrws R Age 24
2013 (5) Georgia Tech

Velo	Pitch	Grade
88-95	FB	++++
80-84	SL	+++
83-87	CU	++

Year	Lev	Team	W	L	Sv	IP	K	ERA	WHIP	BF/G	OBA	H%	S%	xERA	Ctl	Dom	Cmd	hr/9	BPV
2013	A-	Connecticut	0	3	0	32	33	3.09	1.22	10.8	262	35	74	3.13	2.0	9.3	4.7	0.3	132
2014	A	West Michigan	10	5	0	103	116	2.62	1.11	22.6	238	33	78	2.77	2.1	10.1	4.8	0.5	144
2014	AA	Erie	1	0	0	12	11	3.00	1.17	23.9	228	28	77	3.01	3.0	8.3	2.8	0.8	86
2014	AAA	Toledo	1	1	0	7	2	10.14	2.11	17.5	355	36	50	7.83	5.1	2.5	0.5	1.3	-73
2014	MLB	Detroit	0	1	0	9	11	11.87	1.87	10.7	319	41	33	7.19	4.9	10.9	2.2	2.0	80

Surprising pitcher who reached majors in breakout. Repeats delivery consistently giving him solid control of three pitch mix. Long arm action means little deception, but has natural stuff to compete. Combines plus FB with very good SL to register Ks and only needs more consistent CU.

Faulkner,Andrew — SP — Texas

EXP MLB DEBUT: 2016 | H/W: 6-3 180 | FUT: #4 starter | 7C

Thrws L Age 22
2011 (14) HS (SC)

Velo	Pitch	Grade
89-93	FB	+++
77-79	CB	++
81-84	CU	++++

Year	Lev	Team	W	L	Sv	IP	K	ERA	WHIP	BF/G	OBA	H%	S%	xERA	Ctl	Dom	Cmd	hr/9	BPV
2011	Rk	AZL Rangers	0	2	0	25	27	2.16	0.84	7.6	194	27	75	1.39	1.4	9.7	6.8	0.4	154
2012	A	Hickory	5	5	0	94	74	4.31	1.50	14.0	268	33	69	3.86	4.2	7.1	1.7	0.2	32
2013	A	Hickory	6	5	0	111	84	3.48	1.44	22.5	282	33	77	4.34	3.0	6.8	2.3	0.6	60
2014	A+	Myrtle Beach	10	1	1	104	100	2.07	1.12	19.6	227	31	80	2.25	2.7	8.6	3.2	0.1	101
2014	AA	Frisco	2	4	0	30	33	5.07	1.39	18.2	247	32	64	3.94	4.2	9.8	2.4	0.9	82

Breakout performer who is ascending quickly with advanced stuff. CU is best pitch and is good enough to get upper level hitters out. Lives in lower half of strike zone with FB that he commands well. Can cut and sink FB and uses SPL and slow CB to advantage. Throws across body.

Fedde,Erick — SP — Washington

EXP MLB DEBUT: 2018 | H/W: 6-4 180 | FUT: #2 starter | 9E

Thrws R Age 22
2014 (1) Nevada-Las Vegas

Velo	Pitch	Grade
92-94	FB	+++++
85-88	SL	++++
83-84	CU	+++

Year	Lev	Team	W	L	Sv	IP	K	ERA	WHIP	BF/G	OBA	H%	S%	xERA	Ctl	Dom	Cmd	hr/9	BPV
2014		(did not play in 2014)																	

Likely single-digit pick in 2014 dropped in draft after spring Tommy John surgery. Skills are electric: mid-90s sinking FB that can reach 98, plus-plus SL and usable CU. Generates tons of groundballs, and has room to add bulk to current slight frame. Could be draft steal if the TJS recovery goes smoothly.

Feliz,Michael

SP | Houston | EXP MLB DEBUT: 2017 | H/W: 6-4 210 | FUT: #3 starter | 8D

Thrws R Age 21
2010 FA (DR)

- 91-96 FB ++++
- 84-87 SL +++
- 79-83 CU ++

Year	Lev	Team	W	L	Sv	IP	K	ERA	WHIP	BF/G	OBA	H%	S%	xERA	Ctl	Dom	Cmd	hr/9	BPV
2011	Rk	GCL Astros	0	3	0	50	44	4.32	1.48	17.9	273	34	69	4.03	3.8	7.9	2.1	0.4	59
2012	Rk	GCL Astros	5	0	0	38	35	1.65	0.89	20.2	189	24	84	1.58	2.1	8.3	3.9	0.5	109
2012	Rk	Greeneville	1	1	0	26	28	5.17	1.61	19.3	276	37	66	4.36	4.8	9.7	2.0	0.3	61
2013	A-	Tri City	4	2	1	69	78	1.96	0.96	18.6	214	30	80	1.82	1.7	10.2	6.0	0.3	155
2014	A	Quad Cities	8	6	0	102	111	4.05	1.38	17.2	265	36	70	3.81	3.3	9.8	3.0	0.5	106

Breakout prospect who appeared in Futures Game in first full season. Keeps ball down with plus FB thrown with great arm speed. Exhibits fine control, though FB command needs work. SL is out pitch with potental to be plus while he needs to improve CU to better attack LHH.

Fernandez,Jeffry

SP | Boston | EXP MLB DEBUT: 2017 | H/W: 6-3 180 | FUT: #3 starter | 8E

Thrws R Age 22
2011 FA (DR)

- 92-96 FB ++++
- 81-86 SL ++
- 84-88 CU ++

Year	Lev	Team	W	L	Sv	IP	K	ERA	WHIP	BF/G	OBA	H%	S%	xERA	Ctl	Dom	Cmd	hr/9	BPV
2012	Rk	GCL Red Sox	0	0	0	6	3	5.90	2.13	15.1	368	41	69	6.91	4.4	4.4	1.0	0.0	-22
2014	Rk	GCL Red Sox	1	1	0	36	22	4.74	1.02	15.4	233	27	50	2.27	1.5	5.5	3.7	0.2	76
2014	A-	Lowell	0	3	0	18	4	5.44	1.54	19.8	300	30	65	5.23	3.0	2.0	0.7	1.0	-27

Tall, live-armed SP who produces easy velocity and throws with effective angle to plate. Missed '13 after TJ surgery, but velocity has returned. FB exhibits nasty late life and can counter with hard SL. Struggles to command secondary pitches and low K rate doesn't tell story of stuff.

Fernandez,Junior

SP | St. Louis | EXP MLB DEBUT: 2019 | H/W: 6-1 180 | FUT: #3 starter | 7D

Thrws R Age 18
2014 FA (DR)

- 90-92 FB +++
- 72-74 CB ++
- 78-81 CU ++

Year	Lev	Team	W	L	Sv	IP	K	ERA	WHIP	BF/G	OBA	H%	S%	xERA	Ctl	Dom	Cmd	hr/9	BPV
2014	(did not play in the US in 2014)																		

Athletic hurler was signed for $400,000. Features a 90-92 mph FB with room for a bit of projection. Also shows some feel for a CB and CU, but both need refinement. Throws with some effort and in showcase events struggled with command, but the raw tools are there for a good mid-rotation SP.

Fernandez,Pedro

SP | Kansas City | EXP MLB DEBUT: 2017 | H/W: 6-0 175 | FUT: #4 starter | 7C

Thrws R Age 20
2011 FA (DR)

- 90-94 FB ++++
- 82-84 SL +++
- 81-84 CU +++

Year	Lev	Team	W	L	Sv	IP	K	ERA	WHIP	BF/G	OBA	H%	S%	xERA	Ctl	Dom	Cmd	hr/9	BPV
2013	Rk	DSL Royals	0	0	0	12	15	0.75	0.67	10.5	129	21	88	0.00	2.3	11.3	5.0	0.0	160
2013	Rk	AZL Royals	0	1	0	34	38	1.84	1.05	16.6	225	30	88	2.70	2.1	10.0	4.8	0.8	141
2014	A	Lexington	1	8	3	61	60	5.01	1.36	16.0	225	28	64	3.57	4.9	8.8	1.8	0.9	46

Short, advanced SP with clean arm and delivery. Has potential for three average-to-plus offerings with FB best bet of the lot. Doesn't have the stamina to hold velocity late in games, but shows decent touch on SL and CU. Control regressed in '14, but lives in lower half of strike zone.

Finnegan,Brandon

SP | Kansas City | EXP MLB DEBUT: 2014 | H/W: 5-11 185 | FUT: #3 starter / Closer | 8C

Thrws L Age 21
2014 (1) Texas Christian

- 91-97 FB ++++
- 82-84 SL +++
- 84-86 CU ++

Year	Lev	Team	W	L	Sv	IP	K	ERA	WHIP	BF/G	OBA	H%	S%	xERA	Ctl	Dom	Cmd	hr/9	BPV
2013	NCAA	TCU	0	8	0	79	86	3.19	1.38	20.8	249	34	76	3.41	4.0	9.8	2.5	0.3	87
2014	NCAA	TCU	9	3	0	105	134	2.05	1.03	23.8	210	32	80	1.94	2.5	11.5	4.6	0.3	157
2014	A+	Wilmington	0	1	0	15	13	0.60	0.47	9.9	106	12	100	0.00	1.2	7.8	6.5	0.6	126
2014	AA	NW Arkansas	0	3	0	12	13	2.25	1.42	6.4	307	38	93	5.43	1.5	9.8	6.5	1.5	153
2014	MLB	Kansas City	0	1	0	7	10	1.29	1.00	3.8	233	38	86	1.90	1.3	12.9	10.0	0.0	215

Short, live-armed pitcher who was on World Series roster. Could return to rotation to maximize value. Throws with violent arm action to generate plus velocity, yet keeps ball within strike zone. SL is swing-and-miss pitch while CU has moments of effectiveness. Likes to challenge hitters inside.

Finnegan,Kyle

SP | Oakland | EXP MLB DEBUT: 2016 | H/W: 6-2 170 | FUT: #4 starter. | 7D

Thrws R Age 23
2013 (6) Texas State

- 89-95 FB +++
- 79-82 CB +++
- 81-82 CU ++

Year	Lev	Team	W	L	Sv	IP	K	ERA	WHIP	BF/G	OBA	H%	S%	xERA	Ctl	Dom	Cmd	hr/9	BPV
2013	NCAA	Texas State	5	3	1	65	64	4.69	1.69	15.5	287	36	75	5.44	5.0	8.8	1.8	1.1	43
2013	A-	Vermont	3	3	0	50	35	2.70	1.10	17.8	234	29	73	2.22	2.2	6.3	2.9	0.0	73
2013	A	Beloit	1	1	0	7	5	10.14	2.54	19.0	375	42	59	9.23	7.6	6.3	0.8	1.3	-73
2014	A	Beloit	7	9	0	119	55	3.70	1.27	21.2	228	24	73	3.44	3.9	4.2	1.1	0.9	-13
2014	AA	Midland	0	1	0	5	6	12.35	2.16	25.4	410	46	50	12.74	1.8	10.6	6.0	5.3	161

Lean, athletic SP who started strong, but faded late. Has better stuff than numbers suggest, particularly low K rate. Learning how to sequence and change speeds with all pitches. Developing CU and inconsistent CB leaves FB as go-to pitch. Has good velocity with potential for more.

Flaherty,Jack

SP | St. Louis | EXP MLB DEBUT: 2019 | H/W: 6-4 205 | FUT: #3 starter | 8D

Thrws R Age 19
2014 (1) HS (CA)

- 90-92 FB +++
- 73-75 CB ++
- 77-80 SL +++
- 80-83 CU ++++

Year	Lev	Team	W	L	Sv	IP	K	ERA	WHIP	BF/G	OBA	H%	S%	xERA	Ctl	Dom	Cmd	hr/9	BPV
2014	Rk	GCL Cardinals	1	1	0	22	28	1.62	0.99	10.6	223	33	86	2.15	1.6	11.4	7.0	0.4	179

Rare high school hurler that already features a good four-pitch mix. His FB tops out at 93 mph and mixes in a SL, CB, and CU, all of which have the potential to be at least average. Has good athleticism and easy, repeatable mechanics, though his arm slot on breaking balls needs to be more consistent.

Flexen,Chris

SP | New York (N) | EXP MLB DEBUT: 2018 | H/W: 6-3 215 | FUT: #2/#3 starter | 7C

Thrws R Age 20
2012 (14) HS (CA)

- 90-92 FB +++
- SL +++
- CB ++
- CU +++

Year	Lev	Team	W	L	Sv	IP	K	ERA	WHIP	BF/G	OBA	H%	S%	xERA	Ctl	Dom	Cmd	hr/9	BPV
2012	Rk	Kingsport	1	3	0	32	26	5.63	1.63	20.3	296	36	64	4.93	3.9	7.3	1.9	0.6	43
2013	Rk	Kingsport	8	1	0	69	62	2.09	0.94	23.6	214	26	83	2.30	1.6	8.1	5.2	0.8	121
2014	A	Savannah	3	5	0	69	46	4.83	1.62	23.6	278	32	70	4.76	4.8	6.0	1.2	0.7	-4

Struggled prior to being shut down for TJS and should miss all of 2015. When healthy, throws with good command of arsenal and a hard-breaking slider that flashes plus. He can throw all his pitches for strikes and each has projection left. Durable frame and works deep into games.

Flores,Kendry

SP | Miami | EXP MLB DEBUT: 2016 | H/W: 6-2 175 | FUT: #4 Starter | 7C

Thrws R Age 23
2009 FA (DR)

- 90-93 FB +++
- 79-81 CB +++
- 89-91 CT ++
- 83-85 CU +++

Year	Lev	Team	W	L	Sv	IP	K	ERA	WHIP	BF/G	OBA	H%	S%	xERA	Ctl	Dom	Cmd	hr/9	BPV
2010	Rk	AZL Giants	5	4	0	55	56	3.60	1.13	16.7	240	32	67	2.65	2.1	9.2	4.3	0.3	126
2011	A-	Salem-Kaizer	4	3	0	48	47	5.06	1.52	17.4	304	38	68	5.12	2.6	8.8	3.4	0.9	106
2012	A-	Salem-Kaizer	1	3	0	42	34	4.49	1.31	17.4	270	32	67	4.03	2.4	7.3	3.1	0.9	85
2013	A	Augusta	10	6	0	141	137	2.74	0.92	24.0	221	28	73	2.25	1.1	8.7	8.1	0.7	146
2014	A+	San Jose	4	6	0	105	112	4.11	1.26	21.5	254	32	71	3.99	2.7	9.6	3.5	1.2	117

Strong Cmd RHP continued to make strides in high-A, showing plus pitchability and ability to miss bats. Uses a four pitch mix: FB up to 95, above average CU, hard CB, and serviceable CT. Repeats delivery well, pounding the strike zone. Not a ton of projection left, but aptitude and Cmd to thrive in backend of rotation.

Flynn,Brian

SP | Kansas City | EXP MLB DEBUT: 2013 | H/W: 6-7 250 | FUT: #3 starter | 7C

Thrws L Age 24
2011 (7) Wichita State

- 88-95 FB ++++
- SL ++++
- CU +++
- CB +++

Year	Lev	Team	W	L	Sv	IP	K	ERA	WHIP	BF/G	OBA	H%	S%	xERA	Ctl	Dom	Cmd	hr/9	BPV
2013	AA	Jacksonville	1	1	0	23	25	1.57	0.91	21.5	217	29	89	2.25	1.2	9.8	8.3	0.8	162
2013	AAA	New Orleans	6	11	0	138	122	2.80	1.21	24.2	246	31	78	3.07	2.6	8.0	3.1	0.5	91
2013	MLB	Miami	0	2	0	18	15	8.50	2.22	22.7	347	39	64	8.62	6.5	7.5	1.2	2.0	-23
2014	AAA	New Orleans	8	10	0	139	104	4.07	1.57	24.5	301	35	76	5.14	3.2	6.7	2.1	0.8	52
2014	MLB	Miami	0	1	0	7	6	9.00	2.14	17.4	378	47	53	7.10	3.9	7.7	2.0	0.0	53

Big-bodied LH made two appearances in Miami, but was relegated to a full-season at AAA. Does have a nice four pitch mix. Works with his low-90s FB and hard SL, mixing in a CU and CB on occassion. Uses size well to work downhill, repeating mechanics and getting solid ground ball rates.

Foltynewicz,Mike

SP | Houston | EXP MLB DEBUT: 2014 | H/W: 6-4 220 | FUT: #3 starter | 8B

Thrws R Age 23
2010 (1) HS (SC)

- 90-99 FB ++++
- 77-80 CB +++
- 82-85 SL +++
- 79-83 CU ++

Year	Lev	Team	W	L	Sv	IP	K	ERA	WHIP	BF/G	OBA	H%	S%	xERA	Ctl	Dom	Cmd	hr/9	BPV
2012	A	Lexington	14	4	0	152	125	3.14	1.36	23.5	253	31	79	3.73	3.7	7.4	2.0	0.7	52
2013	A+	Lancaster	1	0	0	26	29	3.81	1.73	16.9	297	38	83	5.96	4.8	10.0	2.1	1.4	68
2013	AA	Corpus Christi	5	3	3	103	95	2.88	1.23	18.2	205	26	79	2.84	4.5	8.3	1.8	0.7	45
2014	AAA	Oklahoma City	7	7	0	102	102	5.11	1.47	20.9	254	32	66	4.21	4.6	9.0	2.0	0.9	56
2014	MLB	Houston	0	1	0	18	14	5.44	1.65	5.1	309	35	70	6.06	3.5	6.9	2.0	1.5	49

Power-armed starter who was inconsistent, but reached HOU. FB touches triple-digits and started to sequence better to increase K rate. Uses height to throw downhill and keep ball on ground. FB exhibits sink at lower velocity and mixes in effective CB and SL. Needs better CU for LHH.

Franco,Enderson — SP — Tampa Bay

EXP MLB DEBUT: 2017 | H/W: 6-2 170 | FUT: #4 starter | 7D

Thrws R Age 22
2009 FA (Venezuela)

Velo	Pitch	Grade
91-96	FB	+++
77-81	SL	++
83-85	CU	+++

Year	Lev	Team	W	L	Sv	IP	K	ERA	WHIP	BF/G	OBA	H%	S%	xERA	Ctl	Dom	Cmd	hr/9	BPV
2011	Rk	GCL Astros	1	2	0	47	26	4.40	1.55	20.6	297	34	69	4.44	3.3	5.0	1.5	0.2	20
2012	Rk	GCL Astros	3	2	0	50	37	4.86	1.54	21.8	329	39	67	5.05	1.4	6.7	4.6	0.4	99
2013	Rk	Greeneville	2	5	0	51	41	5.10	1.48	18.4	287	34	65	4.57	3.2	7.2	2.3	0.7	62
2014	A-	Hudson Valley	7	3	0	68	50	3.30	1.20	21.1	278	33	73	3.57	1.1	6.6	6.3	0.5	108

Lean, hard-throwing RHP who has never pitched in full-season, but shows potential. Has advanced command for raw arm and provides enough deception with arm action for pitches to play up. FB is best pitch with plus sink and average CU is effective against LHP. Lacks feel for SL.

Freeland,Kyle — SP — Colorado

EXP MLB DEBUT: 2017 | H/W: 6-3 170 | FUT: #3 starter | 9D

Thrws L Age 21
2014 (1) Evansville

Velo	Pitch	Grade
92-95	FB	++++
83-86	SL	+++
	CT	++
	CU	++

Year	Lev	Team	W	L	Sv	IP	K	ERA	WHIP	BF/G	OBA	H%	S%	xERA	Ctl	Dom	Cmd	hr/9	BPV
2012	NCAA	Evansville	4	5	0	91	70	4.55	1.25	26.5	264	31	65	3.84	2.2	6.9	3.2	0.9	84
2013	NCAA	Evansville	4	8	0	93	84	4.35	1.43	28.3	290	37	68	4.16	2.5	8.1	3.2	0.4	96
2014	NCAA	Evansville	10	2	0	99	128	1.91	0.93	26.6	220	34	77	1.57	1.2	11.6	9.8	0.0	195
2014	Rk	Grand Junction	1	0	0	17	15	1.58	1.05	13.2	249	33	83	2.29	1.1	7.9	7.5	0.0	132
2014	A	Asheville	2	0	0	21	18	0.85	0.85	15.6	190	24	94	1.45	1.7	7.6	4.5	0.4	110

Projectable LH logged 39 innings in debut, but showed plus command, walking just 6 while striking out 33. Fast arm generates low-to-mid 90s velocity and can mix in a CT, SL, and good CU. Is especially tough on LHH with the CU. Spots his FB to all parts of the plate and has a high pitching IQ.

Frias,Carlos — RP — Los Angeles (N)

EXP MLB DEBUT: 2014 | H/W: 6-4 170 | FUT: Reliever | 6C

Thrws R Age 25
2007 FA (DR)

Velo	Pitch	Grade
90-93	FB	++
80-83	SL	+++
	CU	+

Year	Lev	Team	W	L	Sv	IP	K	ERA	WHIP	BF/G	OBA	H%	S%	xERA	Ctl	Dom	Cmd	hr/9	BPV
2013	A+	Ranch Cuca	2	3	0	46		4.11	1.37	24.1	286	37	71	4.32	2.2	9.4	4.4	0.8	129
2013	AA	Chattanooga	1	1	0	16	8	3.94	1.38	8.4	250	26	75	4.20	3.9	4.5	1.1	1.1	-7
2014	AA	Chattanooga	2	1	0	32	14	3.38	1.34	26.6	274	30	76	3.93	2.5	3.9	1.6	0.6	21
2014	AAA	Albuquerque	8	4	0	91	65	5.03	1.48	24.5	307	36	64	4.59	2.1	6.4	3.1	0.4	78
2014	MLB	LA Dodgers	1	1	0	32	29	6.17	1.25	8.7	267	32	50	4.07	2.0	8.1	4.1	1.1	111

Tall Dominican reliever made his MLB debut. Features a low-90s sinking FB that tops out at 95, a plus breaking ball and an inconsistent CU. Improved control since moving to relief while maintaining solid Dom, walking 7 while striking out 29 with the Dodgers. Nothing more than a solid middle RP.

Fried,Max — SP — Atlanta

EXP MLB DEBUT: 2017 | H/W: 6-4 185 | FUT: #2 starter | 9C

Thrws L Age 21
2012 (1) HS (CA)

Velo	Pitch	Grade
90-94	FB	+++
74-78	CB	+++
80-83	CU	++

Year	Lev	Team	W	L	Sv	IP	K	ERA	WHIP	BF/G	OBA	H%	S%	xERA	Ctl	Dom	Cmd	hr/9	BPV
2012	Rk	AZL Padres	0	1	0	17	17	3.66	1.16	6.9	224	29	68	2.72	3.1	8.9	2.8	0.5	93
2013	A	Fort Wayne	6	7	0	118	100	3.50	1.38	21.6	243	30	75	3.53	4.3	7.6	1.8	0.5	40
2014	Rk	AZL Padres	0	0	0	5	8	5.40	2.20	8.4	362	57	73	6.88	5.4	14.4	2.7	0.0	131
2014	A	Fort Wayne	0	1	0	5	2	5.19	1.73	11.8	323	32	75	6.76	3.5	3.5	1.0	1.7	-13

Projectable LH was limited to just 10.2 innings and had TJS in August. Best pitch is hard CB that he can throw for strikes, followed by a plus 95 mph FB. Struggled with control and needs to return to health and improve his CU. Was traded to ATL as part of the Justin Upton deal.

Fry,Jace — SP — Chicago (A)

EXP MLB DEBUT: 2017 | H/W: 6-1 190 | FUT: #5 starter / RP | 6B

Thrws L Age 21
2014 (3) Oregon State

Velo	Pitch	Grade
87-92	FB	+++
80-83	SL	+++
75-78	CB	++
81-83	CU	++

Year	Lev	Team	W	L	Sv	IP	K	ERA	WHIP	BF/G	OBA	H%	S%	xERA	Ctl	Dom	Cmd	hr/9	BPV
2012	NCAA	Oregon State	5	3	0	88	53	2.45	1.17	27.0	215	26	77	2.27	3.6	5.4	1.5	0.1	19
2013	NCAA	Oregon State	0	1	0	7	2	5.00	1.11	4.7	228	25	50	2.22	2.5	2.5	1.0	0.0	-5
2014	NCAA	Oregon State	11	2	0	120	98	1.80	0.94	28.2	197	25	80	1.50	2.2	7.3	3.3	0.1	89
2014	Rk	Great Falls	1	0	0	9	10	2.93	1.09	5.1	212	31	70	1.89	2.9	9.8	3.3	0.0	115

Strong-framed SP who repeats delivery and generally throws strikes with nifty FB/SL combo. Gets good sink on lively FB and can register Ks with solid-average SL. Gives hitters different look with slow CB and middling CU. Doesn't have eye-popping stuff and needs to sequence better.

Fulenchek,Garrett — SP — Atlanta

EXP MLB DEBUT: 2018 | H/W: 6-4 205 | FUT: #2 starter | 8D

Thrws R Age 18
2014 (2) HS (TX)

Velo	Pitch	Grade
89-93	FB	+++
85-86	SL	++
	CU	++

Year	Lev	Team	W	L	Sv	IP	K	ERA	WHIP	BF/G	OBA	H%	S%	xERA	Ctl	Dom	Cmd	hr/9	BPV
2014	Rk	GCL Braves	0	7	0	37	29	4.84	1.51	13.4	245	30	67	3.83	5.3	7.0	1.3	0.5	1

2nd rounder has good size and comes after hitters with a 89-93 mph FB with arm-side run from a low ¾ arm slot. FB tops out at 95 mph with room for projection. SL and CU show potential, but need polish. Needs a more consistent release point and he walked 22 in 37.2 innings.

Fulmer,Michael — SP — New York (N)

EXP MLB DEBUT: 2016 | H/W: 6-3 200 | FUT: #3 starter/Setup RP | 8D

Thrws R Age 22
2011 (1) HS (OK)

Velo	Pitch	Grade
92-95	FB	++++
83-85	SL	++++
	CU	++

Year	Lev	Team	W	L	Sv	IP	K	ERA	WHIP	BF/G	OBA	H%	S%	xERA	Ctl	Dom	Cmd	hr/9	BPV
2012	A	Savannah	7	6	0	108	101	2.75	1.20	20.7	232	30	78	2.91	3.2	8.4	2.7	0.5	84
2013	Rk	GCL Mets	1	1	0	12	13	3.00	0.83	21.9	210	30	60	1.22	0.8	9.8	13.0	0.0	173
2013	A+	St. Lucie	2	2	0	34	29	3.44	1.24	19.7	200	26	71	2.39	4.8	7.7	1.6	0.3	28
2014	A+	St. Lucie	6	10	0	95	86	3.97	1.50	21.6	295	37	74	4.69	2.9	8.1	2.8	0.7	85
2014	AA	Binghamton	0	1	0	3	1	17.42	2.90	17.7	407	39	38	12.38	8.7	2.9	0.3	2.9	-165

2014 was a better season than numbers suggest. Stayed healthy and progressed with CU. Uses plus FB/SL combo for plenty of Ks and ground balls. FB has downward plane and SL tight, hard break. Exhibits solid mound demeanor and work ethic. Could land in pen depending on progress of CU.

Gagnon,Drew — SP — Milwaukee

EXP MLB DEBUT: 2016 | H/W: 6-4 195 | FUT: #4 starter | 7D

Thrws R Age 24
2011 (3) Long Beach State

Velo	Pitch	Grade
90-92	FB	+++
82-85	SL	++
85-86	CU	++
78-82	CB	++

Year	Lev	Team	W	L	Sv	IP	K	ERA	WHIP	BF/G	OBA	H%	S%	xERA	Ctl	Dom	Cmd	hr/9	BPV
2012	A	Wisconsin	6	1	0	82	65	2.85	1.05	22.7	224	27	75	2.58	2.1	7.1	3.4	0.7	90
2012	A+	Brevard Cnty	1	2	0	67	49	2.82	1.10	23.9	229	27	75	2.55	2.4	6.6	2.7	0.4	71
2013	A+	Brevard Cnty	3	4	0	45	50	5.19	1.35	18.8	266	36	59	3.62	3.0	10.0	3.3	0.4	117
2013	AA	Huntsville	4	9	0	84	58	5.57	1.62	23.3	284	31	68	5.43	4.5	6.2	1.4	1.3	8
2014	AA	Huntsville	11	6	0	154	118	3.97	1.28	22.6	237	27	72	3.69	3.6	6.9	1.9	1.1	44

RH had a nice bounceback. Not overpowering with a low 90s FB, but complements it with an avg CU and a developing CB. Attacks the zone with decent control. Mechanics are solid, but overall command needs refinement. Looks to be stuck in neutral for now and his upside is as a back-end SP.

Garcia,Jarlin — SP — Miami

EXP MLB DEBUT: 2017 | H/W: 6-2 170 | FUT: #4 starter | 8D

Thrws L Age 22
2010 FA (DR)

Velo	Pitch	Grade
90-95	FB	+++
	CB	++
	CU	++

Year	Lev	Team	W	L	Sv	IP	K	ERA	WHIP	BF/G	OBA	H%	S%	xERA	Ctl	Dom	Cmd	hr/9	BPV
2012	Rk	GCL Marlins	1	3	0	40	32	3.60	1.30	13.7	252	31	72	3.38	3.2	7.2	2.3	0.5	63
2013	A-	Batavia	2	3	0	69	74	3.12	1.10	18.1	229	30	75	2.98	2.3	9.6	4.1	0.9	128
2014	A	Greensboro	10	5	0	133	111	4.39	1.30	21.9	288	34	68	4.28	1.4	7.5	5.3	0.9	115

Lanky LH from the D.R. had a solid debut. Isn't overpowering, but has a nice mix that includes a 90-95 mph FB, a CU, and a power SL. FB is relatively straight, but he locates it well. Breaking ball and CU have potential, but are inconsistent. Has a bit of projection left and pounds the strike zone.

Garcia,Onelki — RP — Chicago (A)

EXP MLB DEBUT: 2013 | H/W: 6-3 225 | FUT: Reliever | 6C

Thrws L Age 25
2012 (3) HS (CA)

Velo	Pitch	Grade
90-95	FB	++++
	CB	+++
	SL	++
	CU	+

Year	Lev	Team	W	L	Sv	IP	K	ERA	WHIP	BF/G	OBA	H%	S%	xERA	Ctl	Dom	Cmd	hr/9	BPV
2012	A+	Ranch Cuca	0	0	0	2	4	0.00	0.00	5.6	0	0		0.00	0.0	18.0		0.0	342
2013	AA	Chattanooga	2	3	1	52	53	2.76	1.40	8.8	218	29	81	3.25	5.5	9.2	1.7	0.5	34
2013	AAA	Albuquerque	0	1	0	9	14	3.91	0.98	3.5	188	33	56	1.29	2.9	13.7	4.7	0.0	185
2013	MLB	LA Dodgers	0	0	0	1	1	16.36	4.55	2.7	244	0	75	18.71	32.7	8.2	0.3	8.2	-718
2014	A+	Ranch Cuca	0	1	0	0	0	90.00	15.00	3.6	780	78	33	61.58	45.0	0.0	0.0	0.0	-1197

Cuban RP was limited with a season-long elbow injury and was slow to recover. Prior to the injury showed a good FB in low-to-mid 90s, a good 12-6 CB, SL, and a well below average CU. Mechanics have always been an issue, resulting in below-average control and injury.

Garcia,Yimi — RP — Los Angeles (N)

EXP MLB DEBUT: 2014 | H/W: 6-1 175 | FUT: Setup RP | 7C

Thrws R Age 24
2009 FA (DR)

Velo	Pitch	Grade
92-96	FB	+++
80-83	SL	+++
83-85	CU	+

Year	Lev	Team	W	L	Sv	IP	K	ERA	WHIP	BF/G	OBA	H%	S%	xERA	Ctl	Dom	Cmd	hr/9	BPV
2012	A	Great Lakes	4	4	14	41	60	3.06	1.43	4.4	266	43	76	3.41	3.7	13.1	3.5	0.0	154
2012	A+	Ranch Cuca	2	1	2	10	22	2.65	1.18	4.5	196	51	75	1.82	4.4	19.4	4.4	0.0	248
2013	AA	Chattanooga	4	6	19	60	85	2.55	0.82	4.5	171	24	80	1.97	2.1	12.7	6.1	1.3	191
2014	AAA	Albuquerque	4	2	5	61	69	3.10	1.25	5.3	252	34	77	3.49	2.7	10.2	3.8	0.7	130
2014	MLB	LA Dodgers	0	0	0	10	9	1.80	0.70	4.4	175	17	100	2.20	0.9	8.1	9.0	1.8	140

Strong-armed hurler was impressive in big-league debut. Comes after hitters with a 91-94 mph FB that tops out at 97 mph with late life. Complements the heat with a good hard SL that has tight spin and late break. Pitches down in the zone and repeats his mechanics well.

Garrett,Amir — SP — Cincinnati

EXP MLB DEBUT: 2017 | H/W: 6-5 210 | FUT: #3 starter | 8D

Thrws L Age 22
2011 (22) HS (NV)

Velo	Pitch	Grade
92-94	FB	+++
83-85	SL	++
80-82	CU	+

Year	Lev	Team	W	L	Sv	IP	K	ERA	WHIP	BF/G	OBA	H%	S%	xERA	Ctl	Dom	Cmd	hr/9	BPV
2012	Rk	Billings	0	0	0	6	5	0.00	0.83	11.0	191	25	100	1.03	1.5	7.5	5.0	0.0	113
2012	Rk	AZL Reds	0	2	0	14	13	5.79	1.86	9.4	262	33	68	5.09	7.7	8.4	1.1	0.6	-40
2013	Rk	Billings	1	1	0	23	17	2.72	1.38	19.5	252	31	78	3.16	3.9	6.6	1.7	0.0	32
2013	A	Dayton	1	3	0	34	15	6.88	1.65	19.0	294	31	58	5.46	4.2	4.0	0.9	1.1	-25
2014	A	Dayton	7	8	0	133	127	3.65	1.25	20.0	235	30	72	3.28	3.4	8.6	2.5	0.7	79

Stretches of dominance made decision to pursue baseball full-time easier. Didn't miss rotation turn and pitched deep into many games. SL took huge step forward and a nice out pitch following plus fastball. CU showing improvement. Needs reps and consistency with mechanics. Huge upside.

Garvin,Grayson — SP — Tampa Bay

EXP MLB DEBUT: 2015 | H/W: 6-6 225 | FUT: #4 starter | 7C

Thrws L Age 25
2011 (1-S) Vanderbilt

Velo	Pitch	Grade
88-94	FB	+++
82-85	SL	++
79-81	CU	+++

Year	Lev	Team	W	L	Sv	IP	K	ERA	WHIP	BF/G	OBA	H%	S%	xERA	Ctl	Dom	Cmd	hr/9	BPV
2011	NCAA	Vanderbilt	13	2	0	112	101	2.49	1.10	24.4	236	29	81	2.98	2.0	8.1	4.0	0.8	110
2012	A+	Charlotte	2	4	0	46	37	5.08	1.39	17.6	257	33	59	3.25	3.7	7.2	1.9	0.0	48
2013	Rk	GCL Devil Rays	0	1	0	11	12	2.41	1.34	7.8	258	34	86	3.87	3.2	9.6	3.0	0.8	105
2013	A+	Charlotte	0	1	0	16	12	1.11	0.74	11.5	149	19	83	0.34	2.2	6.7	3.0	0.0	78
2014	AA	Montgomery	1	8	0	74	60	3.77	1.23	15.0	267	32	70	3.55	1.8	7.3	4.0	0.6	100

Tall SP who is getting back to speed after TJ surgery in mid '12. Hasn't yet been stretched out, but has good feel and command quickly returned. Uses height to thrown on solid angle and repeats effortless delivery. Cuts and sinks FB effectively and good CU is best secondary pitch.

Gatto,Joe — SP — Los Angeles (A)

EXP MLB DEBUT: 2018 | H/W: 6-3 205 | FUT: #2 starter | 8D

Thrws R Age 19
2014 (2) HS (NJ)

Velo	Pitch	Grade
89-94	FB	+++
79-82	CB	+++
	CU	++

Year	Lev	Team	W	L	Sv	IP	K	ERA	WHIP	BF/G	OBA	H%	S%	xERA	Ctl	Dom	Cmd	hr/9	BPV
2014	Rk	AZL Angels	2	1	0	25	15	5.40	1.68	11.3	319	37	66	5.25	3.2	5.4	1.7	0.4	28
2014	Rk	Orem	0	0	0	2	1	4.50	1.50	8.6	347	30	100	9.18	0.0	4.5		4.5	99

Tall, athletic SP who thrives with clean, athletic delivery. Possesses durable frame and throws with good angle to plate. Lively FB induces high amount of groundballs and power CB is putaway pitch. Present CU is below average, but uses good arm speed and offers some deception.

German,Domingo — SP — New York (A)

EXP MLB DEBUT: 2017 | H/W: 6-2 175 | FUT: #3 starter | 7C

Thrws R Age 22
2009 FA (DR)

Velo	Pitch	Grade
91-95	FB	+++
	SL	++
	CU	++

Year	Lev	Team	W	L	Sv	IP	K	ERA	WHIP	BF/G	OBA	H%	S%	xERA	Ctl	Dom	Cmd	hr/9	BPV
2012	Rk	GCL Marlins	2	0	0	22	29	1.63	1.49	7.3	214	34	88	2.92	6.5	11.8	1.8	0.0	55
2013	Rk	GCL Marlins	3	0	0	26	27	1.38	0.77	18.7	170	23	84	0.93	1.7	9.3	5.4	0.3	140
2013	A-	Batavia	2	3	0	41	34	1.76	0.93	19.2	222	29	79	1.63	1.1	7.5	6.8	0.0	123
2014	A	Greensboro	9	3	0	123	113	2.49	1.15	19.5	250	32	79	2.95	1.8	8.3	4.5	0.4	117

RH whiffed Kris Bryant and Joey Gallo in the Futures game. Has a good 91-95 mph sinking FB that can hit 97. Has an easy delivery and keeps the ball down. Mixes in a SL and a good mph CU. Pounds the strike zone, but doesn't get great marks for picthability and throws with some effort.

Gibson,Daniel — RP — Arizona

EXP MLB DEBUT: 2016 | H/W: 6-2 220 | FUT: Setup RP | 7C

Thrws L Age 23
2013 (7) Florida

Velo	Pitch	Grade
92-95	FB	++++
	SL	+++
	CB	+
	CU	+

Year	Lev	Team	W	L	Sv	IP	K	ERA	WHIP	BF/G	OBA	H%	S%	xERA	Ctl	Dom	Cmd	hr/9	BPV
2013	NCAA	Florida	2	1	0	38	31	4.48	1.47	5.1	250	30	70	4.02	4.7	7.3	1.6	0.7	22
2013	A-	Hillsboro	1	0	3	20	22	0.45	1.25	5.8	232	33	96	2.54	3.6	9.9	2.8	0.0	99
2013	A	South Bend	0	1	0	8	5	1.11	0.99	5.1	208	25	88	1.63	2.2	5.6	2.5	0.0	58
2014	A	South Bend	3	2	3	36	45	1.99	1.14	3.9	210	31	83	2.20	3.5	11.2	3.2	0.2	126
2014	A+	Visalia	4	3	0	22	22	9.32	1.94	5.0	331	41	50	6.87	4.9	8.9	1.8	1.2	47

Lefty reliever looked dominant in the MWL, with 14 BB/45 K, but then got hammered when he moved up. Comes after hitters with a plus 92-95 mph FB and quality SL. Also featues a CB and CU, but both are below-avg. Smooth easy delivery with good control.

Gilmartin,Sean — SP — New York (N)

EXP MLB DEBUT: 2015 | H/W: 6-2 190 | FUT: #4 starter | 7C

Thrws L Age 24
2011 (1) Florida State

Velo	Pitch	Grade
89-92	FB	+++
80-84	SL	++
83-84	CU	+++

Year	Lev	Team	W	L	Sv	IP	K	ERA	WHIP	BF/G	OBA	H%	S%	xERA	Ctl	Dom	Cmd	hr/9	BPV
2013	Rk	GCL Braves	0	0	0	9	11	0.00	0.11	8.8	38	7	100	0.00	0.0	11.0		0.0	216
2013	A	Rome	1	0	0	5	5	1.80	0.80	18.1	221	31	75	1.28	0.0	9.0		0.0	180
2013	AAA	Gwinnett	3	8	0	91	65	5.74	1.59	23.6	304	34	65	5.56	3.3	6.4	2.0	1.2	46
2014	AA	New Britain	7	3	0	72	74	3.13	1.28	24.6	272	36	74	3.40	2.0	9.3	4.6	0.3	131
2014	AAA	Rochester	2	4	0	73	59	4.30	1.33	21.7	251	30	69	3.81	3.4	7.3	2.1	0.9	56

Finesse LHP who took step back to AA in '14. Limited upside with fringy velocity and FB, but knows how to pitch and sequence. Has deceptive motion and commands plate with repeatable delivery. Is very tough on LHH with late-breaking SL and CU flashes plus at times. Good control.

Giolito,Lucas — SP — Washington

EXP MLB DEBUT: 2016 | H/W: 6-6 255 | FUT: #1 starter | 9B

Thrws R Age 20
2012 (1) HS (CA)

Velo	Pitch	Grade
93-97	FB	+++++
79-81	CB	++++
81-83	CU	+++

Year	Lev	Team	W	L	Sv	IP	K	ERA	WHIP	BF/G	OBA	H%	S%	xERA	Ctl	Dom	Cmd	hr/9	BPV
2012	Rk	GCL Nationals	0	0	0	2	1	4.50	1.00	7.6	262	30	50	2.36	0.0	4.5		0.0	99
2013	Rk	GCL Nationals	1	1	0	22	25	2.84	1.31	11.5	233	34	76	2.69	4.1	10.1	2.5	0.0	91
2013	A-	Auburn	1	0	0	14	14	0.64	0.93	17.5	186	24	100	1.79	2.6	9.0	3.5	0.6	111
2014	A	Hagerstown	10	2	0	98	110	2.20	1.00	18.7	202	27	81	2.15	2.6	10.1	3.9	0.6	130

Simply the top RHP prospect in the game, and the training wheels have yet to come off after 2012 Tommy John surgery. Pairs two elite pitches—mid-90s FB with tons of life and a sharp, tight 11-5 CB—with a usable CU. Has the mental makeup of an ace, too, and will move quickly as long as he stays healthy.

Glasnow,Tyler — SP — Pittsburgh

EXP MLB DEBUT: 2016 | H/W: 6-7 195 | FUT: #1 starter | 9C

Thrws R Age 21
2011 (5) HS (CA)

Velo	Pitch	Grade
93-95	FB	++++
75-78	CB	+++
	CU	+++

Year	Lev	Team	W	L	Sv	IP	K	ERA	WHIP	BF/G	OBA	H%	S%	xERA	Ctl	Dom	Cmd	hr/9	BPV
2012	Rk	GCL Pirates	0	3	0	34	40	2.11	1.03	11.9	165	22	84	1.93	4.2	10.6	2.5	0.8	94
2012	A-	State College	0	0	0	4	4	0.00	1.25	16.3	262	35	100	2.95	2.3	9.0	4.0	0.0	119
2013	A	West Virginia	9	3	0	111	164	2.19	1.04	17.8	147	23	83	1.68	4.9	13.3	2.7	0.7	124
2014	A+	Bradenton	12	5	0	124	157	1.74	1.06	20.9	175	27	84	1.56	4.1	11.4	2.8	0.2	111

RH has emerged as one of the best pitching prospects in the NL.Dominated the FSL, leading the league in ERA, WHIP, and oppBAA. Has a plus-plus 93-95 mph FB that tops out 98 with good downhill tilt. His upper-70s CB is now above-average. Throws effort and sometimes doesn't finish.

Goforth,David — RP — Milwaukee

EXP MLB DEBUT: 2015 | H/W: 5-10 205 | FUT: Closer | 7C

Thrws R Age 26
2011 (7) Mississippi

Velo	Pitch	Grade
93-97	FB	++++
89-91	SL	+++
90-93	CB	++
	CU	++

Year	Lev	Team	W	L	Sv	IP	K	ERA	WHIP	BF/G	OBA	H%	S%	xERA	Ctl	Dom	Cmd	hr/9	BPV
2011	Rk	Helena	0	4	2	40	42	4.48	1.34	8.8	280	35	69	4.48	2.2	9.4	4.2	1.1	127
2012	A	Wisconsin	10	8	0	150	93	4.67	1.44	22.9	267	29	69	4.44	3.8	5.6	1.5	1.0	16
2013	A+	Brevard Cnty	7	5	0	78	58	3.11	1.22	22.5	233	28	75	2.94	3.2	6.7	2.1	0.5	51
2013	AA	Huntsville	4	3	5	46	36	3.31	1.08	9.0	197	25	67	1.91	3.5	7.0	2.0	0.2	50
2014	AA	Huntsville	5	4	27	64	46	3.79	1.39	5.0	249	30	71	3.40	4.1	6.4	1.6	0.3	24

92-95 mph FB and a quality SL. Also featues a CB and CU when starting, but both are below-average. Smooth easy delivery with good control. Could move up quickly.

Gohara,Luiz — SP — Seattle

EXP MLB DEBUT: 2018 | H/W: 6-3 210 | FUT: #3 starter | 8E

Thrws L Age 18
2012 FA (Brazil)

Velo	Pitch	Grade
90-95	FB	++++
77-79	CB	++
81-84	SL	++
	CU	+++

Year	Lev	Team	W	L	Sv	IP	K	ERA	WHIP	BF/G	OBA	H%	S%	xERA	Ctl	Dom	Cmd	hr/9	BPV
2013	Rk	Pulaski	1	2	0	21	27	4.25	1.46	15.1	269	39	70	3.95	3.8	11.5	3.0	0.4	121
2014	Rk	AZL Mariners	1	1	0	12	16	2.21	1.07	23.7	242	37	77	2.19	1.5	11.8	8.0	0.0	191
2014	A-	Everett	0	6	0	37	37	8.25	1.89	15.9	305	37	56	6.56	5.8	9.0	1.5	1.5	22

Large-framed SP who owns clean mechanics and can miss bats with natural, plus stuff. Had trouble finding strike zone with inconsistent CB and SL. CU can be potent given repeatable arm speed, but lacks the feel for breaking stuff. Has high upside and needs significant polish to advance.

Gonsalves,Stephen — SP — Minnesota

EXP MLB DEBUT: 2017 | H/W: 6-5 190 | FUT: #3 starter | 8E

Thrws L Age 20
2013 (4) HS (CA)

Velo	Pitch	Grade
88-93	FB	+++
77-80	CB	++
81-83	CU	+++

Year	Lev	Team	W	L	Sv	IP	K	ERA	WHIP	BF/G	OBA	H%	S%	xERA	Ctl	Dom	Cmd	hr/9	BPV
2013	Rk	Elizabethton	1	1	0	14	21	1.29	1.00	17.8	202	35	86	1.51	2.6	13.5	5.3	0.0	192
2013	Rk	GCL Twins	1	0	0	14	18	0.64	1.06	11.0	167	27	93	1.30	4.5	11.5	2.6	0.0	104
2014	Rk	Elizabethton	2	0	0	29	26	2.79	1.14	19.1	220	28	75	2.41	3.1	8.1	2.6	0.3	79
2014	A	Cedar Rapids	2	3	0	36	44	3.23	1.16	18.0	233	34	71	2.55	2.7	10.9	4.0	0.2	141

Tall, projectable LHP with advanced ability to command FB early in count. Still unpolished secondary offerings, but has repeatable delivery and slot to improve. Spike CB can register Ks and average CU getting better. Allows flyballs consistently, but hasn't been victim of long balls.

Gonzales,Marco — SP — St. Louis

EXP MLB DEBUT: 2014 | H/W: 6-1 195 | FUT: #3 starter | 8A

Thrws L Age 23
2013 (1) Gonzaga

88-92	FB	+++
75-77	CB	++
85-86	SL	++
77-79	CU	++++

Year	Lev	Team	W	L	Sv	IP	K	ERA	WHIP	BF/G	OBA	H%	S%	xERA	Ctl	Dom	Cmd	hr/9	BPV
2013	A+	Palm Beach	0	0	0	16	13	1.67	0.93	15.2	180	22	86	1.65	2.8	7.2	2.6	0.6	73
2014	A+	Palm Beach	2	2	0	37	32	1.45	1.13	24.5	245	31	88	2.65	1.9	7.7	4.0	0.2	105
2014	AA	Springfield	3	2	0	38	46	2.36	1.13	21.5	235	33	80	2.69	2.4	10.8	4.6	0.5	149
2014	AAA	Memphis	4	1	0	45	39	3.38	1.15	22.4	252	29	78	3.89	1.8	7.8	4.3	1.4	109
2014	MLB	St. Louis	4	2	0	34	31	4.21	1.55	14.9	249	30	76	4.53	5.5	8.2	1.5	1.1	16

LH pitched at four levels and logged important post-season innings. Has a fluid, clean arm action that leads to plus control. FB sits at 88-92 mph and isn't overpowering, but he locates it well. Best offering is a plus CU that he will throw in any count. It keeps hitters off his below-average FB.

Gonzalez,Alex — SP — Texas

EXP MLB DEBUT: 2015 | H/W: 6-2 195 | FUT: #2 starter | 8B

Thrws R Age 23
2013 (1) Oral Roberts

90-94	FB	++++
83-87	SL	++++
79-81	CB	++
84-86	CU	+++

Year	Lev	Team	W	L	Sv	IP	K	ERA	WHIP	BF/G	OBA	H%	S%	xERA	Ctl	Dom	Cmd	hr/9	BPV
2013	NCAA	Oral Roberts	9	5	0	113	126	1.83	0.97	28.6	206	29	83	1.90	2.1	10.0	4.7	0.4	140
2013	A-	Spokane	0	4	0	23	20	4.66	1.59	11.4	314	39	69	4.97	2.7	7.8	2.9	0.4	84
2013	A+	Myrtle Beach	0	0	0	19	15	2.84	1.26	15.5	219	27	78	2.88	4.3	7.1	1.7	0.5	31
2014	A+	Myrtle Beach	5	2	0	65	49	2.63	1.11	23.2	234	28	77	2.62	2.2	6.8	3.1	0.4	80
2014	AA	Frisco	7	4	0	73	64	2.71	1.26	19.9	245	31	79	3.10	3.1	7.9	2.6	0.4	77

Lean, projectable SP with exciting pitch mix, highlighted by plus sinking FB and wipeout SL. Changes speeds effectively and hitters rarely make hard contact due to pitch movement. Lacks premium velocity, but offers deception with fading CU. Spots FB to all quadrants of strike zone.

Gonzalez,Brian — SP — Baltimore

EXP MLB DEBUT: 2017 | H/W: 6-3 230 | FUT: #4 starter | 7C

Thrws L Age 19
2014 (3) HS (FL)

87-92	FB	+++
75-78	CB	+++
80-83	CU	+++

Year	Lev	Team	W	L	Sv	IP	K	ERA	WHIP	BF/G	OBA	H%	S%	xERA	Ctl	Dom	Cmd	hr/9	BPV
2014	Rk	GCL Orioles	0	0	0	24	25	0.00	0.79	10.9	139	20	100	0.32	3.0	9.3	3.1	0.0	105
2014	A-	Aberdeen	0	1	0	9	11	5.00	1.33	18.7	283	41	58	3.43	2.0	11.0	5.5	0.0	162

Durable prospect with above average stuff for age. Pitches downhill and gets good leverage to plate. Keeps walks to minimum by commanding average FB with late sink. Can be tough to square up, especially with nifty CU. Throws strikes with CB, yet can use to get hitters to chase.

Gonzalez,Miguel — SP — Philadelphia

EXP MLB DEBUT: 2014 | H/W: 6-3 200 | FUT: #4 starter/RP | 7C

Thrws R Age 28
2013 FA (Cuba)

91-94	FB	+++
78-80	SP	++
78-82	CU	++
73-75	CB	++

Year	Lev	Team	W	L	Sv	IP	K	ERA	WHIP	BF/G	OBA	H%	S%	xERA	Ctl	Dom	Cmd	hr/9	BPV
2014	A+	Clearwater	0	2	0	15	11	4.77	1.92	8.9	320	39	72	5.52	5.4	6.6	1.2	0.0	-9
2014	AA	Reading	0	2	5	14	24	3.19	1.21	5.2	201	34	80	3.20	4.5	15.3	3.4	1.3	173
2014	AAA	Lehigh Valley	0	0	2	16	19	1.67	1.23	5.5	180	27	85	1.87	5.6	10.6	1.9	0.0	58
2014	MLB	Philadelphia	0	1	0	5	5	7.06	2.35	4.4	385	46	73	9.42	5.3	8.8	1.7	1.8	34

Role is biggest question: Given chance to start in spring 2014; floundered, but then found success out of bullpen at AA and AAA. May be given chance to start again in 2015, where vast array of pitches (FB, SP, CU, CB, CT) could work if he can command them. Otherwise, bullpen is a likely destination.

Gonzalez,Rayan — RP — Colorado

EXP MLB DEBUT: 2017 | H/W: 6-3 175 | FUT: Setup RP | 7C

Thrws R Age 24
2012 (21) Bethune Cookman

92-95	FB	+++
	CT	++++
	CU	+++

Year	Lev	Team	W	L	Sv	IP	K	ERA	WHIP	BF/G	OBA	H%	S%	xERA	Ctl	Dom	Cmd	hr/9	BPV
2011	NCAA	BethneColkmn	0	3	0	46	49	4.88	1.78	21.2	309	40	73	5.69	4.7	9.6	2.0	0.8	64
2012	NCAA	BethneColkmn	9	2	0	92	82	2.15	1.10	24.0	236	31	78	2.23	2.1	8.0	3.9	0.0	107
2012	Rk	Grand Junction	0	3	0	24	27	6.75	2.00	5.3	328	42	67	6.88	5.6	10.1	1.8	1.1	48
2013	A	Asheville	2	3	12	53	70	2.71	1.35	4.5	254	39	78	3.07	3.6	11.8	3.3	0.0	135
2014	A+	Modesto	4	5	11	56	64	4.01	1.55	4.9	291	41	71	4.11	3.5	10.3	2.9	0.0	108

Lanky RH from PR has a plus 92-95 mph sinker that he uses to get tons of GB outs—3.3 gb/fb ratio; one of the best in the minors. Also has an above-average CU that he uses with great effect vs. LHB.

Gonzalez,Severino — SP — Philadelphia

EXP MLB DEBUT: 2015 | H/W: 6-1 153 | FUT: #4/#5 starter | 7C

Thrws R Age 22
2011 FA (Panama)

88-91	FB	+++
75-77	CB	++
82-84	SL	++
83-86	CU	++

Year	Lev	Team	W	L	Sv	IP	K	ERA	WHIP	BF/G	OBA	H%	S%	xERA	Ctl	Dom	Cmd	hr/9	BPV
2013	A	Lakewood	3	0	0	21	31	1.71	0.62	18.1	144	24	75	0.31	1.3	13.2	10.3	0.4	221
2013	A+	Clearwater	3	5	0	75	82	2.03	1.13	14.9	237	32	84	2.76	2.3	9.8	4.3	0.5	133
2013	AA	Reading	1	0	0	6	6	2.90	1.29	25.5	314	41	75	3.82	0.0	8.7		0.0	175
2014	AA	Reading	9	13	0	158	115	4.61	1.28	24.0	275	31	68	4.46	1.9	6.5	3.4	1.3	84

Rough stat line in 2014, but mandated to work on CU at expense of cutter. Maintained very good control, which will be imperative since the stuff only average and doesn't have a consistent bat-missing pitch. Athletic and some projection left, but still just tops out as a back-end starter.

Gossett,Daniel — RP — Oakland

EXP MLB DEBUT: 2017 | H/W: 6-2 185 | FUT: Setup RP | 7D

Thrws R Age 22
2014 (2) Clemson

88-95	FB	+++
81-83	CB	+++
79-82	CU	++

Year	Lev	Team	W	L	Sv	IP	K	ERA	WHIP	BF/G	OBA	H%	S%	xERA	Ctl	Dom	Cmd	hr/9	BPV
2012	NCAA	Clemson	6	3	2	77	87	4.32	1.31	16.7	222	31	66	3.01	4.6	10.2	2.2	0.5	78
2013	NCAA	Clemson	10	4	0	98	91	2.57	1.18	24.5	220	28	81	2.84	3.5	8.3	2.4	0.6	74
2014	NCAA	Clemson	7	2	0	107	107	1.93	1.01	27.3	205	28	82	1.93	2.5	9.0	3.6	0.3	112
2014	A-	Vermont	1	0	0	24	25	2.25	0.71	7.1	191	26	69	1.04	0.4	9.4	25.0	0.4	177

Quick-armed RP who should advance quickly with excellent sinker and occasional above average CB. Hides ball well in delivery, though doesn't repeat consistently. Throws effective strikes with three pitches. FB can be straight and will need to add durability and stamina for multiple innings.

Gott,Trevor — RP — Los Angeles (A)

EXP MLB DEBUT: 2015 | H/W: 6-0 190 | FUT: Setup RP | 7B

Thrws R Age 22
2013 (6) Kentucky

90-95	FB	++++
81-83	SL	++
82-83	CU	++

Year	Lev	Team	W	L	Sv	IP	K	ERA	WHIP	BF/G	OBA	H%	S%	xERA	Ctl	Dom	Cmd	hr/9	BPV
2013	A-	Eugene	0	0	0	4	8	2.20	1.71	4.6	257	53	86	3.95	6.6	17.6	2.7	0.0	156
2013	A	Fort Wayne	2	2	4	31	33	2.60	1.12	4.6	207	29	76	2.19	3.5	9.5	2.8	0.3	96
2014	A+	Lake Elsinore	2	4	16	31	31	3.18	1.19	4.3	242	31	76	3.34	2.6	9.0	3.4	0.9	109
2014	AA	Arkansas	2	1	2	17	18	1.57	1.05	5.1	185	27	83	1.47	3.7	9.4	2.6	0.0	89
2014	AA	San Antonio	0	0	0	11	11	4.82	1.79	5.2	258	35	70	4.25	7.2	8.8	1.2	0.0	-18

Short RP who has flown under radar despite closer experience and K rate. Generates easy, plus velocity with quick arm and rarely allows HR due to vicious sinking action on FB. Can get on side of SL, but mixes efficiently along with occasional CU. Needs better command within strike zone.

Graham,J.R. — SP — Minnesota

EXP MLB DEBUT: 2015 | H/W: 6-0 195 | FUT: #4 starter | 7D

Thrws R Age 25
2011 (4) Santa Clara

92-95	FB	++++
82-85	SL	+++
	CU	++

Year	Lev	Team	W	L	Sv	IP	K	ERA	WHIP	BF/G	OBA	H%	S%	xERA	Ctl	Dom	Cmd	hr/9	BPV
2011	Rk	Danville	5	2	0	57	52	1.73	1.14	17.4	244	32	83	2.43	2.0	8.2	4.0	0.0	110
2012	A+	Lynchburg	9	1	0	102	68	2.64	1.03	23.1	234	27	76	2.54	1.5	6.0	4.0	0.5	85
2012	AA	Mississippi	3	1	0	45	42	3.19	1.15	19.9	216	28	72	2.49	3.4	8.4	2.5	0.4	77
2013	AA	Mississippi	1	3	0	35	28	4.09	1.39	18.5	282	35	67	3.61	2.6	7.2	2.8	0.0	78
2014	AA	Mississippi	1	5	0	71	50	5.57	1.48	11.3	283	34	59	4.08	3.3	6.3	1.9	0.3	43

RH has made just 27 starts since '12 due a lingering shoulder injury. When healthy has a plus 92-95 FB and SL. CU is average and attacks hitters low in the strike zone, inducing plenty of gb. The Twins will have to have him on their active roster all season in order to keep him.

Graveman,Kendall — SP — Oakland

EXP MLB DEBUT: 2014 | H/W: 6-2 195 | FUT: #4 starter | 7D

Thrws R Age 24
2013 (8) Mississippi State

87-92	FB	+++
75-78	CB	++
79-83	SL	++
82-84	CU	+++

Year	Lev	Team	W	L	Sv	IP	K	ERA	WHIP	BF/G	OBA	H%	S%	xERA	Ctl	Dom	Cmd	hr/9	BPV
2014	A	Lansing	2	0	0	26	25	0.34	0.65	22.7	130	18	94	0.00	2.1	8.6	4.2	0.0	117
2014	A+	Dunedin	8	4	0	96	64	2.25	1.11	23.6	247	30	78	2.52	1.7	6.0	3.6	0.1	80
2014	AA	New Hampshire	1	0	0	6	4	1.50	1.67	26.9	321	38	90	4.91	3.0	6.0	2.0	0.0	45
2014	AAA	Buffalo	3	2	0	38	22	1.89	1.02	24.4	240	28	82	2.35	1.2	5.2	4.4	0.2	80
2014	MLB	Toronto	0	0	0	4	4	4.29	0.95	3.2	252	34	50	2.07	0.0	8.6		0.0	172

Durable sinkerballer with exceptional command and pitched on 5 levels. Knows how to pitch and get hitters to chase ordinary stuff. Added cutter into arsenal which can befuddle hitters, but lacks bat-missing breaking ball. Must rely on throwing strikes and inducing grounders.

Graves,Brett — SP — Oakland

EXP MLB DEBUT: 2017 | H/W: 6-1 170 | FUT: #4 starter | 7D

Thrws R Age 22
2014 (3) Missouri

91-95	FB	+++
78-80	CB	+++
80-81	SL	++
81-83	CU	+

Year	Lev	Team	W	L	Sv	IP	K	ERA	WHIP	BF/G	OBA	H%	S%	xERA	Ctl	Dom	Cmd	hr/9	BPV
2012	NCAA	Missouri	4	5	0	47	28	6.32	1.83	12.1	297	34	63	5.31	5.7	5.4	0.9	0.4	-41
2013	NCAA	Missouri	2	5	0	71	32	3.80	1.39	21.4	280	29	77	4.69	2.7	4.1	1.5	1.1	19
2014	NCAA	Missouri	3	6	0	93	64	3.87	1.25	27.0	272	32	68	3.47	1.7	6.2	3.6	0.4	82
2014	Rk	AZL Athletics	0	0	0	1	1	0.00	1.00	3.8	0	0	100	0.00	9.0	9.0	1.0	0.0	-63
2014	A-	Vermont	3	2	0	21	18	6.86	1.43	11.2	288	36	48	4.19	2.6	7.7	3.0	0.4	87

Very athletic SP who lacks top-of-rotation size and stuff, but gets by with average pitch mix. Lives in lower half of zone by repeating smooth delivery. Lively FB induces grounders while CB has plus potential. Command issues have plagued him at times and needs to polish poor CU.

Gray, Jonathan — SP — Colorado

EXP MLB DEBUT: 2015 H/W: 6-4 235 FUT: #1 starter **9C**

Thrws R Age 23
2013 (1) Oklahoma

95-97	FB	++++
85-88	SL	++++
81-84	CU	++

Year	Lev	Team	W	L	Sv	IP	K	ERA	WHIP	BF/G	OBA	H%	S%	xERA	Ctl	Dom	Cmd	hr/9	BPV
2012	NCAA	Oklahoma	8	4	0	102	104	3.17	1.39	23.9	258	34	76	3.49	3.7	9.2	2.5	0.3	83
2013	NCAA	Oklahoma	10	3	0	126	147	1.64	0.85	27.2	189	28	79	1.08	1.7	10.5	6.1	0.1	161
2013	Rk	Grand Junction	0	0	0	13	15	4.12	1.30	13.5	289	41	65	3.44	1.4	10.3	7.5	0.0	166
2013	A+	Modesto	4	0	0	24	36	0.75	0.67	16.7	129	24	88	0.00	2.3	13.5	6.0	0.0	200
2014	AA	Tulsa	10	5	0	124	113	3.92	1.19	20.7	234	29	68	3.12	3.0	8.2	2.8	0.7	85

Attacks hitters with a plus-plus 95-97 mph FB that hits 100. Holds velocity deep into games and commands FB well to both sides. ERA is not indicative of long-term potential. Low strand rate and xERA suggest he was unlucky in '14. SL is a true swing-and-miss offering with good late break.

Green, Hunter — SP — Los Angeles (A)

EXP MLB DEBUT: 2018 H/W: 6-4 175 FUT: #3 starter **8D**

Thrws L Age 19
2013 (2) HS (KY)

85-93	FB	+++
76-79	CB	+++
78-80	CU	++

Year	Lev	Team	W	L	Sv	IP	K	ERA	WHIP	BF/G	OBA	H%	S%	xERA	Ctl	Dom	Cmd	hr/9	BPV
2013	Rk	AZL Angels	0	1	0	16	11	4.44	1.98	9.7	259	32	75	4.77	8.9	6.1	0.7	0.0	-112
2014		(did not play in 2014)																	

Tall, lanky, and projectable prospect who did not pitch in 2014 due to back issue. Fringy velocity now, but should add more once he gains strength. FB features sink and tail while mixing in solid CB with good shape and depth. A consistent arm slot would improve command and control.

Gregorio, Joan — SP — San Francisco

EXP MLB DEBUT: 2016 H/W: 6-7 180 FUT: #4 Starter **7D**

Thrws R Age 23
2010 FA (DR)

91-93	FB	++++
82-85	SL	+++
84-86	CU	+

Year	Lev	Team	W	L	Sv	IP	K	ERA	WHIP	BF/G	OBA	H%	S%	xERA	Ctl	Dom	Cmd	hr/9	BPV
2011	Rk	AZL Giants	3	0	0	50		2.34	1.18	16.7	233	30	79	2.57	2.9	7.7	2.7	0.2	79
2012	A-	Salem-Kaizer	7	7	0	76	69	5.56	1.42	20.2	284	34	62	4.69	2.7	8.2	3.0	1.1	91
2013	A	Augusta	6	3	0	69	84	4.03	1.18	19.8	250	36	65	2.97	2.2	10.9	4.9	0.4	155
2014	A	Augusta	2	7	1	68	65	3.57	1.13	20.7	207	27	67	2.20	3.6	8.6	2.4	0.5	76
2014	A+	San Jose	2	0	0	22	27	6.89	1.80	17.1	301	41	61	5.65	5.3	10.9	2.1	0.8	73

Tall, lean SP saw his Ctl and Cmd take a large step back in '14, though he continued to miss bats. Relies heavily on his low-90s FB up to 97, with a mid-80s SL that flashes average and a well below CU that he rarely uses. Arm is clean but 6-7 frame make repeating his delivery troublesome, which contributes to Ctl issues.

Griffin, Foster — SP — Kansas City

EXP MLB DEBUT: 2018 H/W: 6-3 200 FUT: #3 starter **8D**

Thrws L Age 19
2014 (1) HS (FL)

88-94	FB	+++
75-79	CB	++
81-82	CU	+++

Year	Lev	Team	W	L	Sv	IP	K	ERA	WHIP	BF/G	OBA	H%	S%	xERA	Ctl	Dom	Cmd	hr/9	BPV
2014	Rk	Burlington	0	2	0	28	19	3.21	1.11	10.0	194	22	72	2.36	3.9	6.1	1.6	0.6	24

Tall, strong SP who possesses solid present mix with chance to add more velocity down road. Good arm speed and strength and uses height for potent angle to plate. Advanced CU could become go-to offering and CB projects to average. Spots lively FB well to both sides of plate.

Grosser, Alec — SP — Atlanta

EXP MLB DEBUT: 2018 H/W: 6-2 190 FUT: #4 starter **7D**

Thrws R Age 20
2013 (11) HS (VA)

91-93	FB	+++
81-84	SL	++++
83-85	CU	++

Year	Lev	Team	W	L	Sv	IP	K	ERA	WHIP	BF/G	OBA	H%	S%	xERA	Ctl	Dom	Cmd	hr/9	BPV
2013	Rk	GCL Braves	1	3	0	29	23	2.16	0.93	8.4	128	17	74	0.59	4.6	7.1	1.5	0.0	21
2014	Rk	Danville	4	3	0	63	63	3.70	1.30	20.0	252	34	68	2.93	3.1	9.0	2.9	0.0	95

Has a good 91-93 mph FB with good arm-side run and sink, and can push it up to 95 mph. Also has a good SL with late movement and a below-average CU. Smooth and repeatable mechanics with deception. Isn't physical and his velocity tends to fade later in games. Showed decent command.

Gsellman, Robert — SP — New York (N)

EXP MLB DEBUT: 2017 H/W: 6-4 200 FUT: #4 starter **7C**

Thrws R Age 21
2011 (13) HS (CA)

89-92	FB	+++
79-82	CB	+++
81-84	CU	+++

Year	Lev	Team	W	L	Sv	IP	K	ERA	WHIP	BF/G	OBA	H%	S%	xERA	Ctl	Dom	Cmd	hr/9	BPV
2011	Rk	GCL Mets	0	0	1	13	8	4.15	1.31	7.7	290	33	69	4.18	1.4	5.5	4.0	0.7	80
2012	Rk	Kingsport	1	3	0	43	33	3.96	1.39	16.5	256	31	72	3.83	3.8	6.9	1.8	0.6	41
2013	A-	Brooklyn	3	3	0	70	64	2.06	1.01	22.4	230	30	80	2.18	1.5	8.2	5.3	0.3	124
2013	A	Savannah	2	3	0	29	14	3.72	1.41	24.6	300	33	74	4.54	1.9	4.3	2.3	0.6	46
2014	A	Savannah	10	6	0	116	92	2.56	1.34	24.2	271	34	80	3.48	2.6	7.1	2.7	0.2	75

Excellent year including 4 CG and 2.6 Ctl. Strikeouts lag behind the quality of his stuff. Repeats low-effort delivery and maintains arm speed on secondary pitches. Throws across his body with some deception. Good velo and command with FB; CB and CU flash solid-average but inconsistent.

Guduan, Reymin — SP — Houston

EXP MLB DEBUT: 2017 H/W: 6-4 185 FUT: #4 starter **8E**

Thrws L Age 23
2009 FA (DR)

91-97	FB	++++
82-85	SL	+++
	CU	+

Year	Lev	Team	W	L	Sv	IP	K	ERA	WHIP	BF/G	OBA	H%	S%	xERA	Ctl	Dom	Cmd	hr/9	BPV
2012	Rk	GCL Astros	1	1	0	18	16	5.47	2.32	11.6	337	42	76	7.28	8.0	8.0	1.0	0.5	-54
2013	Rk	GCL Astros	0	1	0	20	28	4.46	1.44	8.6	250	36	73	4.48	4.5	12.5	2.8	1.3	122
2013	AAA	Oklahoma City	0	0	0	2	4	4.29	1.90	9.9	144	34	75	3.12	12.9	17.1	1.3	0.0	-21
2014	Rk	Greeneville	2	5	0	44	58	4.49	1.81	15.7	299	43	74	5.26	5.5	11.8	2.1	0.4	82

Quick-armed SP who has yet to get out of short-season. Generates plus velocity with ease, exhibiting balanced and athletic delivery. Complements plus FB with hard SL that features nice break. Fails to command plate and lacks touch for changing speeds. High risk/high reward.

Gueller, Mitch — SP — Philadelphia

EXP MLB DEBUT: 2017 H/W: 6-3 210 FUT: #4/#5 starter **7D**

Thrws R Age 21
2012 (1) HS (WA)

89-91	FB	+++
81-84	SL	++
	CU	++

Year	Lev	Team	W	L	Sv	IP	K	ERA	WHIP	BF/G	OBA	H%	S%	xERA	Ctl	Dom	Cmd	hr/9	BPV
2012	Rk	GCL Phillies	1	5	0	27	19	5.31	1.40	14.3	254	31	58	3.25	4.0	6.3	1.6	0.0	24
2013	A-	Williamsport	3	8	0	58	35	5.89	1.88	19.5	336	38	68	6.28	4.0	5.4	1.3	0.6	7
2014	A-	Williamsport	5	5	0	63	31	4.71	1.49	20.9	268	30	66	3.94	4.1	4.4	1.1	0.3	-14

Small signs of improvement in a repeat of short-season ball, but still walks too many and strikeout rate trend is scary, even in the minors. Fastball command is the place to start, but he's had trouble with that since being a first-rounder in 2012.

Guerrero, Alberto — SP — Miami

EXP MLB DEBUT: 2019 H/W: 6-3 190 FUT: #4 starter **7D**

Thrws R Age 18
2014 FA (Panama)

85-88	FB	++
	CB	++
	CU	++

Year	Lev	Team	W	L	Sv	IP	K	ERA	WHIP	BF/G	OBA	H%	S%	xERA	Ctl	Dom	Cmd	hr/9	BPV
2014		(did not play in the US in 2014)																	

Signed with the Marlins for $300,000. Has good size and some projection left. Already has a good 85-88 mph FB with room for growth and has shown some ability to spin a breaking ball. CU is a work in progress and he will likely make his pro debut in 2015.

Guerrero, Tayron — RP — San Diego

EXP MLB DEBUT: 2018 H/W: 6-7 189 FUT: Setup RP **8E**

Thrws R Age 24
2009 FA (Colombia)

95-98	FB	++++
87-88	SL	+++

Year	Lev	Team	W	L	Sv	IP	K	ERA	WHIP	BF/G	OBA	H%	S%	xERA	Ctl	Dom	Cmd	hr/9	BPV
2013	Rk	AZL Padres	1	0	0	4	5	6.43	1.19	5.6	297	42	40	3.28	0.0	10.7		0.0	211
2013	A-	Eugene	1	4	0	32	35	4.50	1.53	9.3	210	29	69	3.25	7.0	9.8	1.4	0.3	5
2013	A	Fort Wayne	0	1	0	3	4	8.44	5.00	6.3	470	61	81	16.36	22.5	11.3	0.5	0.0	-387
2014	A	Fort Wayne	6	1	1	36	42	1.00	0.94	5.4	178	25	94	1.60	3.0	10.5	3.5	0.5	126
2014	A+	Lake Elsinore	0	0	3	13	14	2.73	1.36	3.9	212	28	82	3.22	5.5	9.5	1.8	0.7	43

The 6-7 RH has a blazing FB that tops out at 100 mph and could add a tick more velocity as he matures. Also has an inconsistent, but plus hard SL. Given his size it is not surprising that he struggles with mechanics and command. He's walked 6.4 per nine, but he also proven very difficult to hit.

Guerrieri, Taylor — SP — Tampa Bay

EXP MLB DEBUT: 2016 H/W: 6-3 195 FUT: #2 starter **9D**

Thrws R Age 22
2011 (1) HS (SC)

90-95	FB	+++
77-81	CB	++++
80-83	CU	++

Year	Lev	Team	W	L	Sv	IP	K	ERA	WHIP	BF/G	OBA	H%	S%	xERA	Ctl	Dom	Cmd	hr/9	BPV
2012	A-	Hudson Valley	1	2	0	52	45	1.04	0.77	15.6	193	26	85	0.88	0.9	7.8	9.0	0.0	135
2013	A	Bowling Green	6	2	0	67	51	2.01	0.99	18.2	222	26	84	2.42	1.6	6.9	4.3	0.7	98
2014	Rk	GCL Devil Rays	0	0	0	9	10	0.00	0.99	6.9	214	31	100	1.67	2.0	9.9	5.0	0.0	143

Tall, lean SP who only pitched briefly in July after TJ surgery in 2013. When healthy, has ultra arm strength that generates hard FB with late action. Big-breaking CB is best pitch and misses bats consistently. Pitches to both sides of plate and keeps walks to minimum. CU needs work.

Guillon,Ismael — SP — Cincinnati

EXP MLB DEBUT: 2017 | H/W: 6-2 210 | FUT: #3 starter | **7D**

Thrws L Age 23
2008 FA (Venezuela)

Velo	Pitch	Grade
88-93	FB	+++
	CU	+++
	CB	++

Year	Lev	Team	W	L	Sv	IP	K	ERA	WHIP	BF/G	OBA	H%	S%	xERA	Ctl	Dom	Cmd	hr/9	BPV
2012	Rk	Billings	4	1	0	51	63	2.29	1.24	18.8	213	32	81	2.43	4.2	11.1	2.6	0.2	104
2012	A	Dayton	2	0	0	24	27	2.60	1.20	24.3	244	33	81	3.26	2.6	10.0	3.9	0.7	128
2013	A	Dayton	7	8	0	121	134	4.76	1.57	19.7	218	28	72	4.14	7.1	10.0	1.4	1.0	7
2014	A	Dayton	4	1	0	65	69	3.18	1.04	19.4	183	25	69	1.83	3.7	9.5	2.6	0.4	89
2014	A+	Bakersfield	1	6	0	58	45	6.82	1.65	21.7	293	32	63	6.32	4.3	7.0	1.6	2.0	26

Strikes out or walks one-third of batters faced. Excellent swing-and-miss stuff but continued trouble with command and throwing strikes. Showed an improved delivery in '14 and more confidence in improving CB. FB and CU solid offerings with deception. 13 HR in 58 IP after promotion to High-A.

Gunkel,Joe — SP — Boston

EXP MLB DEBUT: 2016 | H/W: 6-5 225 | FUT: #5 starter | **6B**

Thrws R Age 23
2013 (18) West Chester

Velo	Pitch	Grade
87-92	FB	+++
79-82	SL	++
81-83	CU	++

Year	Lev	Team	W	L	Sv	IP	K	ERA	WHIP	BF/G	OBA	H%	S%	xERA	Ctl	Dom	Cmd	hr/9	BPV
2013	NCAA	West Chester	7	4	0	77	76	2.45	0.95	26.4	222	30	71	1.66	1.3	8.9	6.9	0.0	143
2013	Rk	GCL Red Sox	0	0	0	1	1	0.00	0.00	2.8	0	0		0.00	0.0	9.0		0.0	180
2013	A-	Lowell	3	0	5	20	32	1.35	0.55	4.8	124	25	73	0.00	1.4	14.4	10.7	0.0	241
2014	A	Greenville	3	0	2	51	62	2.29	0.72	10.7	153	22	71	0.79	1.9	10.9	5.6	0.5	162
2014	A+	Salem	3	5	0	52	39	4.66	1.44	22.2	297	35	67	4.44	2.2	6.7	3.0	0.5	79

Deceptive sinkerballer who was better out of pen in Low-A than as SP in High-A. Tough to hit with near sidearm delivery. Lives in lower half of strike zone and can command average FB at will. Sweepy SL doesn't miss many bats and CU hasn't been effective against LHH.

Gustave,Jandel — SP — Kansas City

EXP MLB DEBUT: 2017 | H/W: 6-2 160 | FUT: #3 starter | **8E**

Thrws R Age 22
2010 FA (DR)

Velo	Pitch	Grade
92-98	FB	++++
84-88	SL	++
	CU	++

Year	Lev	Team	W	L	Sv	IP	K	ERA	WHIP	BF/G	OBA	H%	S%	xERA	Ctl	Dom	Cmd	hr/9	BPV
2012	Rk	GCL Astros	2	1	0	28	22	5.79	1.82	13.0	233	30	65	4.03	8.7	7.1	0.8	0.0	-89
2013	Rk	Greeneville	2	3	0	43	49	2.71	1.41	18.3	238	33	81	3.41	4.8	10.2	2.1	0.4	72
2014	A	Quad Cities	5	5	2	79	82	5.01	1.56	15.0	297	39	66	4.54	3.3	9.3	2.8	0.3	97

Long, lean SP who showed drastic improvement in control. Has pure, electric stuff, but has been remarkably hittable. Lacks separation between FB and CU while pitches can be straight. Explosive FB thrown with ease and has repeatable delivery to add polish to below average CU and SL.

Hader,Josh — SP — Houston

EXP MLB DEBUT: 2016 | H/W: 6-3 160 | FUT: #4 starter | **7C**

Thrws L Age 20
2012 (19) HS (MD)

Velo	Pitch	Grade
89-93	FB	+++
75-78	CB	+++
83-85	CU	+++

Year	Lev	Team	W	L	Sv	IP	K	ERA	WHIP	BF/G	OBA	H%	S%	xERA	Ctl	Dom	Cmd	hr/9	BPV
2012	A-	Aberdeen	0	0	0	8	13	0.00	0.49	5.4	81	17	100	0.00	2.2	14.4	6.5	0.0	218
2013	A	Delmarva	3	6	0	85	79	2.65	1.28	20.5	218	28	80	2.87	4.4	8.4	1.9	0.4	48
2013	A	Quad Cities	2	0	0	22	16	3.26	1.18	17.7	183	23	69	1.81	4.9	6.5	1.3	0.0	3
2014	A+	Lancaster	9	2	2	103	112	2.71	1.11	18.4	207	27	79	2.61	3.3	9.8	2.9	0.8	104
2014	AA	Corpus Christi	1	1	0	20	24	6.30	1.60	17.7	221	30	60	4.12	7.2	10.8	1.5	0.9	18

Tall, lean SP with deceptive delivery and clean arm action. Tough to square up due to ability to hide ball. Improving control despite moving parts in delivery. Found success in hitters haven by mixing three average pitches. Changes speeds and can effectively vary arm angle.

Haley,Justin — SP — Boston

EXP MLB DEBUT: 2016 | H/W: 6-5 230 | FUT: #4 starter | **7C**

Thrws R Age 23
2012 (6) Fresno State

Velo	Pitch	Grade
88-95	FB	+++
77-81	SL	+++
82-84	CU	+++

Year	Lev	Team	W	L	Sv	IP	K	ERA	WHIP	BF/G	OBA	H%	S%	xERA	Ctl	Dom	Cmd	hr/9	BPV
2012	NCAA	Fresno State	7	4	0	93	94	3.19	1.45	18.1	268	36	76	3.62	3.8	9.1	2.4	0.1	80
2012	A-	Lowell	0	1	0	33	33	1.90	1.18	10.2	198	27	84	2.21	4.4	9.0	2.1	0.3	62
2013	A	Greenville	7	11	0	124	124	3.70	1.38	20.0	217	28	75	3.36	5.4	9.0	1.7	0.7	35
2014	A+	Salem	7	4	1	92	74	2.83	1.08	18.9	228	28	74	2.48	2.2	7.2	3.2	0.4	87
2014	AA	Portland	3	2	0	37	33	1.21	1.24	25.2	222	28	93	2.86	3.9	8.0	2.1	0.5	57

Workhorse SP who eats innings and has ideal stamina and durability to stick in rotation. Uses height effectively and limits oppBA with heavy FB. Improved command and control by spotting SL better in zone, though still somewhat erratic. CU has become average with depth and fade.

Harris,Greg — SP — Tampa Bay

EXP MLB DEBUT: 2019 | H/W: 6-2 170 | FUT: Reliever | **6C**

Thrws R Age 20
2013 (17) HS (CA)

Velo	Pitch	Grade
86-90	FB	++
	CB	++
	CU	++

Year	Lev	Team	W	L	Sv	IP	K	ERA	WHIP	BF/G	OBA	H%	S%	xERA	Ctl	Dom	Cmd	hr/9	BPV
2013	Rk	AZL Dodgers	2	3	0	34	22	5.29	1.24	13.8	256	28	58	3.86	2.4	5.8	2.4	1.1	59
2014	A	Great Lakes	7	6	0	87	92	4.45	1.33	16.4	264	35	67	3.86	2.9	9.5	3.3	0.7	111

Harris worked primarily as a starter in the MWL and put up solid numbers. Is not overpowering and his FB sits at 88-91 mph with a below-average curve and CU. He does throw strikes, but will likely move to relief down the road.

Harvey,Hunter — SP — Baltimore

EXP MLB DEBUT: 2017 | H/W: 6-3 175 | FUT: #2 starter | **8C**

Thrws R Age 20
2013 (1) HS (NC)

Velo	Pitch	Grade
91-96	FB	++++
74-80	CB	++++
81-84	CU	++

Year	Lev	Team	W	L	Sv	IP	K	ERA	WHIP	BF/G	OBA	H%	S%	xERA	Ctl	Dom	Cmd	hr/9	BPV
2013	Rk	GCL Orioles	0	0	0	13	18	1.37	0.92	9.8	213	35	83	1.44	1.4	12.4	9.0	0.0	203
2013	A-	Aberdeen	0	1	0	12	15	2.25	1.25	16.3	245	37	80	2.78	3.0	11.3	3.8	0.0	140
2014	A	Delmarva	7	5	0	87	106	3.20	1.14	20.3	212	30	72	2.48	3.4	10.9	3.2	0.5	123

Projectable SP who dominated first 2 months before succumbing to elbow inflammation. Clean, quick arm action produces plus velocity and movement. Mixes pitches efficiently with plus CB and CU that should become average. Should add strength with age and has consistent mechanics to boot.

Healy,Tucker — RP — Oakland

EXP MLB DEBUT: 2015 | H/W: 6-1 195 | FUT: Setup RP | **6A**

Thrws R Age 24
2012 (23) Ithaca

Velo	Pitch	Grade
90-95	FB	+++
82-84	SL	+++
	CU	+

Year	Lev	Team	W	L	Sv	IP	K	ERA	WHIP	BF/G	OBA	H%	S%	xERA	Ctl	Dom	Cmd	hr/9	BPV
2013	A	Beloit	0	1	2	28	43	0.96	0.89	5.8	201	33	96	1.81	1.6	13.7	8.6	0.6	222
2013	A+	Stockton	1	1	3	19	31	1.88	0.94	4.8	194	32	88	2.15	2.4	14.6	6.2	0.9	217
2014	A+	Stockton	2	1	3	17	29	1.05	0.76	4.7	157	29	92	0.89	2.1	15.3	7.3	0.5	236
2014	AA	Midland	0	1	4	19	29	2.36	1.20	6.4	240	39	82	2.93	2.8	13.7	4.8	0.5	188
2014	AAA	Sacramento	1	1	0	24	28	8.22	1.87	5.6	313	40	56	6.65	5.2	10.5	2.0	1.5	65

Unheralded RP who pitched on 3 levels and racked up Ks with very deceptive low arm angle. Pitches aggressively off hard sinking FB and complements with promising SL. Throws good strikes, though SL can be loose and subject to flyballs. Steady mechanics positively impact command.

Heaney,Andrew — SP — Los Angeles (A)

EXP MLB DEBUT: 2014 | H/W: 6-2 185 | FUT: #2 starter | **9C**

Thrws L Age 23
2012 (1) Oklahoma State

Velo	Pitch	Grade
91-97	FB	++++
	SL	++++
	CU	++++

Year	Lev	Team	W	L	Sv	IP	K	ERA	WHIP	BF/G	OBA	H%	S%	xERA	Ctl	Dom	Cmd	hr/9	BPV
2013	A+	Jupiter	5	2	0	61	66	0.88	1.01	18.0	207	29	93	1.91	2.5	9.7	3.9	0.3	125
2013	AA	Jacksonville	4	1	0	33	23	2.98	1.20	22.3	249	29	76	3.19	2.4	6.2	2.6	0.5	64
2014	AA	Jacksonville	4	2	0	53	52	2.37	1.09	23.1	231	30	79	2.45	2.2	8.8	4.0	0.3	117
2014	AAA	New Orleans	5	4	0	83	91	3.89	1.18	22.2	242	31	70	3.41	2.5	9.8	4.0	1.0	128
2014	MLB	Miami	0	3	0	29	20	5.88	1.34	17.3	281	30	61	5.21	2.2	6.2	2.9	1.9	71

LH came in as one of the more advanced prospects in the NL and was traded to the Angels. Comes at hitters with a low-90s FB up to 97, hard SL, and CU that freezes RHH. Commands all pitches well and improved his pitch sequencing. Easy, clean arm action with repeatable mechanics.

Hellweg,Johnny — SP — Milwaukee

EXP MLB DEBUT: 2013 | H/W: 6-9 210 | FUT: #3 starter/Setup RP | **8E**

Thrws R Age 26
2008 (16) Florida CC

Velo	Pitch	Grade
94-97	FB	+++++
	CB	++
	CU	++

Year	Lev	Team	W	L	Sv	IP	K	ERA	WHIP	BF/G	OBA	H%	S%	xERA	Ctl	Dom	Cmd	hr/9	BPV
2012	AA	Huntsville	2	1	0	20	17	2.70	1.55	12.5	221	29	81	3.18	6.8	7.7	1.1	0.0	-27
2013	A	Wisconsin	1	0	0	6	4	3.00	1.17	23.9	228	28	71	2.32	3.0	6.0	2.0	0.0	45
2013	AAA	Nashville	12	5	0	125	89	3.16	1.47	23.4	226	27	79	3.46	5.8	6.4	1.1	0.4	-24
2013	MLB	Milwaukee	1	4	0	30	9	6.85	2.19	18.9	320	33	68	7.07	7.7	2.7	0.3	0.9	-143
2014	AAA	Nashville	1	2	0	20	12	4.95	1.80	23.1	271	31	71	4.92	6.8	5.4	0.8	0.5	-67

Despite having good size and velo, mechanics continue to be an issue. Mid-90s FB maxes out at 98 mph and is complimented with an avg CB and CU. Works downhill to get good gb rates while pounding his FB to generate swing-and-misses. Has dominant stuff, but future may be as a reliever.

Hembree,Heath — RP — Boston

EXP MLB DEBUT: 2013 | H/W: 6-4 210 | FUT: Closer | **7C**

Thrws R Age 26
2010 (5) College of Charleston

Velo	Pitch	Grade
91-96	FB	++++
84-88	SL	+++

Year	Lev	Team	W	L	Sv	IP	K	ERA	WHIP	BF/G	OBA	H%	S%	xERA	Ctl	Dom	Cmd	hr/9	BPV
2013	AAA	Fresno	1	4	31	55	63	4.08	1.27	4.2	258	34	71	4.01	2.6	10.3	3.9	1.1	133
2013	MLB	SF Giants	0	0	0	7	12	0.00	0.83	2.9	165	33	100	0.66	2.5	15.0	6.0	0.0	221
2014	AAA	Fresno	1	3	18	39	46	3.91	1.36	4.0	266	35	75	4.34	3.0	10.6	3.5	1.2	128
2014	AAA	Pawtucket	0	1	2	6	9	2.90	1.61	3.9	222	37	80	3.31	7.3	13.1	1.8	0.0	57
2014	MLB	Boston	0	0	0	10	6	4.50	1.60	7.4	281	31	73	4.97	4.5	5.4	1.2	0.9	-6

Big, strong RP who posts high K rate from closer role. Gets swings and misses with FB/SL combo. Very stingy against RHH with improved location of power SL. Pitches up with plus FB and has velocity to do so, but can get hurt due to flyballs. Lacks touch and feel for changing speeds.

Hensley, Ty — SP — New York (A) — EXP MLB DEBUT: 2017 — H/W: 6-4 220 — FUT: #2 starter — 8D

Thrws R Age 21
2012 (1) HS (OK)

90-95	FB	+++
77-79	CB	+++
78-81	CU	++

Year	Lev	Team	W	L	Sv	IP	K	ERA	WHIP	BF/G	OBA	H%	S%	xERA	Ctl	Dom	Cmd	hr/9	BPV
2012	Rk	GCL Yankees	1	2	0	12	14	3.00	1.25	9.8	191	26	79	2.75	5.3	10.5	2.0	0.8	65
2014	Rk	GCL Yankees	0	0	0	19	23	2.37	1.32	11.2	230	31	87	3.56	4.3	10.9	2.6	0.9	99
2014	A-	Staten Island	0	0	0	11	17	4.02	1.16	11.1	258	43	62	2.63	1.6	13.7	8.5	0.0	221

Tall pitcher who has yet to pitch in full-season ball. DNP in '13 due to injured hip. Needs innings in order to develop command for power arsenal. FB thrown with easy arm action to produce velocity and sink. CB features big, late break, though can be left up in zone. Needs to polish CU.

Hentges, Sam — SP — Cleveland — EXP MLB DEBUT: 2018 — H/W: 6-6 220 — FUT: #3 starter — 8E

Thrws L Age 18
2014 (4) HS (MN)

86-92	FB	+++
75-78	CB	++
79-82	CU	++

Year	Lev	Team	W	L	Sv	IP	K	ERA	WHIP	BF/G	OBA	H%	S%	xERA	Ctl	Dom	Cmd	hr/9	BPV
2014	Rk	AZL Indians	1	0	0	13	10	0.69	0.69	5.7	98	13	89	0.00	3.5	6.9	2.0	0.0	49

Tall, projectable SP who has arm and build to dream on. Has fringe velocity now, but has potential for lot more. Needs to refine mechanics to take advantage of loose,quick arm. Very raw feel for secondary pitches, though gets good break on CB. Repeats arm speed on middling CU.

Heredia, Luis — SP — Pittsburgh — EXP MLB DEBUT: 2017 — H/W: 6-6 205 — FUT: #2 starter — 8E

Thrws R Age 20
2010 FA (Mexico)

90-93	FB	++++
	CB	++
83-85	CU	++
	SL	++

Year	Lev	Team	W	L	Sv	IP	K	ERA	WHIP	BF/G	OBA	H%	S%	xERA	Ctl	Dom	Cmd	hr/9	BPV
2011	Rk	GCL Pirates	1	2	0	30	23	4.78	1.56	11.0	248	29	70	4.41	5.7	6.9	1.2	0.9	-12
2012	A-	State College	4	2	0	66	40	2.72	1.10	18.5	221	26	75	2.34	2.7	5.4	2.0	0.3	43
2013	A	West Virginia	7	3	0	65	55	3.05	1.37	19.5	221	27	80	3.38	5.1	7.6	1.5	0.7	17
2014	A	West Virginia	2	4	0	89	43	4.15	1.35	20.6	257	27	71	4.04	3.3	4.3	1.3	0.9	6

Missed 2 months with shoulder soreness and never seemed to regain his form. Still has a good 90-93 mph FB, but it lacks the zip it once had. His CB, SL, and CU are below-avg and he has yet to log more than 89 IP. Mechanics have become inconsistent, leading to struggles with control.

Heston, Chris — SP — San Francisco — EXP MLB DEBUT: 2014 — H/W: 6-4 185 — FUT: #5 Starter — 6C

Thrws R Age 26
2009 (12) East Carolina

87-89	FB	++
	CB	+++
	SL	++
	CU	++

Year	Lev	Team	W	L	Sv	IP	K	ERA	WHIP	BF/G	OBA	H%	S%	xERA	Ctl	Dom	Cmd	hr/9	BPV
2011	A+	San Jose	12	4	0	151	131	3.16	1.22	25.4	253	31	75	3.31	2.4	7.8	3.3	0.6	94
2012	AA	Richmond	9	8	0	148	116	2.25	1.11	23.3	229	30	78	2.27	2.4	8.2	3.4	0.1	100
2013	AAA	Fresno	7	6	0	108	97	5.82	1.62	25.3	297	36	65	5.49	3.8	8.1	2.1	1.2	60
2014	AAA	Fresno	12	9	0	173	125	3.38	1.17	24.7	238	27	74	3.24	2.7	6.5	2.5	0.8	63
2014	MLB	SF Giants	0	0	0	5	4	5.29	1.76	7.8	294	37	67	4.73	5.3	7.1	1.3	0.0	2

Finese RH got a cup of coffee with SF after a rebound season in AAA. Knows his role and continues to do what he does best, pounding upper-80s with a FB which sink down in the zone to generate GBs. Mixes in a CB which flashes average, and a below average CU and SL. Uses height well to repeat his delivery, control the zone and walks.

Hinsz, Gage — SP — Pittsburgh — EXP MLB DEBUT: 2019 — H/W: 6-4 210 — FUT: #3 starter — 7D

Thrws R Age 18
2014 (11) HS (MT)

90-93	FB	+++
	CB	++
	CU	++

Year	Lev	Team	W	L	Sv	IP	K	ERA	WHIP	BF/G	OBA	H%	S%	xERA	Ctl	Dom	Cmd	hr/9	BPV
2014	Rk	GCL Pirates	0	0	0	8	7	3.38	1.50	11.5	262	34	75	3.59	4.5	7.9	1.8	0.0	38

Pirates went over budget to sign him for $580,000 and he has good size and some projection. Already saw his velo jump for the mid-80s to 90-93 mph. Has an easy high 3/4 arm slot and throws downhill, keeping the ball down. Breaking ball and CU need work but show decent potential.

Hockin, Grant — SP — Cleveland — EXP MLB DEBUT: 2018 — H/W: 6-4 200 — FUT: #4 starter — 7C

Thrws R Age 19
2014 (2) HS (CA)

88-94	FB	+++
81-83	SL	+++
76-79	CB	+++
81-82	CU	+++

Year	Lev	Team	W	L	Sv	IP	K	ERA	WHIP	BF/G	OBA	H%	S%	xERA	Ctl	Dom	Cmd	hr/9	BPV
2014	Rk	AZL Indians	0	0	0	21	19	3.86	1.19	9.4	262	33	67	3.21	1.7	8.1	4.8	0.4	118

Tall, durable SP with delivery that produces easy velocity. Not much projection left, but has strong existing pitch mix. Gets late movement to solid-average FB that he throws downhill. Varies speeds with two breaking balls and has some feel for CU. Lacks true K pitch, but gets job done.

Hoffman, Jeff — SP — Toronto — EXP MLB DEBUT: 2017 — H/W: 6-4 185 — FUT: #3 starter — 8C

Thrws R Age 22
2014 (1) East Carolina

91-96	FB	++++
83-87	SL	+++
78-82	CB	++
84-87	CU	+++

Year	Lev	Team	W	L	Sv	IP	K	ERA	WHIP	BF/G	OBA	H%	S%	xERA	Ctl	Dom	Cmd	hr/9	BPV
2014		(did not play in 2014)																	

Athletic, lanky SP who underwent TJ surgery in May. Should return mid-year. When healthy, has electric pitch mix with dominant FB, two-seamer, and hard SL. Command comes and goes and may take awhile to improve. Needs to sequence better, but has clean delivery and quick arm.

Holland, Neil — RP — Washington — EXP MLB DEBUT: 2015 — H/W: 6-0 190 — FUT: Reliever — 7B

Thrws R Age 26
2010 (11) Louisville

87-89	FB	+++
	SL	++
	CU	++

Year	Lev	Team	W	L	Sv	IP	K	ERA	WHIP	BF/G	OBA	H%	S%	xERA	Ctl	Dom	Cmd	hr/9	BPV
2012	A+	Potomac	7	1	4	60	44	1.65	0.97	5.8	206	25	85	1.96	2.1	6.6	3.1	0.4	80
2012	AAA	Syracuse	0	0	0	1	0	0.00	0.00	2.8	0	0		0.00	0.0	0.0		0.0	18
2013	AA	Harrisburg	1	4	1	50	63	2.87	1.18	4.9	253	36	77	3.12	2.0	11.3	5.7	0.5	168
2014	AA	Harrisburg	6	3	1	67	60	3.22	1.15	6.6	232	29	73	2.81	2.7	8.1	3.0	0.5	91
2014	AAA	Syracuse	1	1	0	9	3	4.89	1.63	6.8	316	30	77	6.61	2.9	2.9	1.0	2.0	-8

Sinker/slider sidearmer that throws strikes and induces groundballs. Can pitch multiple innings and is equally effecitve vs righties and lefties. Didn't fare well in a late-season promotion to Triple-A; will need to conquer that level before get his MLB chance.

Holmberg, David — SP — Cincinnati — EXP MLB DEBUT: 2013 — H/W: 6-3 225 — FUT: #4 starter — 7C

Thrws L Age 23
2009 (2) HS (FL)

88-92	FB	+++
	SL	++
80-83	CU	++++

Year	Lev	Team	W	L	Sv	IP	K	ERA	WHIP	BF/G	OBA	H%	S%	xERA	Ctl	Dom	Cmd	hr/9	BPV
2012	AA	Mobile	5	5	0	95	67	3.60	1.34	26.3	280	32	75	4.15	2.2	6.3	2.9	0.8	73
2013	AA	Mobile	5	8	0	157	116	2.75	1.20	24.3	238	28	80	3.16	2.9	6.6	2.3	0.7	60
2013	MLB	Arizona	0	0	0	3	0	8.44	2.81	18.0	399	40	67	9.30	8.4	0.0	0.0	0.0	-210
2014	AAA	Louisville	2	6	0	92	56	4.69	1.65	22.9	314	36	70	5.12	3.2	5.5	1.7	0.4	29
2014	MLB	Cincinnati	2	2	0	30	18	4.80	1.43	18.2	242	22	77	5.43	4.8	5.4	1.1	2.4	-14

Lost command and feel for strike zone until September and was roughed up initially in CIN. When he's right, shows plus command and pitch sequencing while leveraging height to pound low in the zone and force groundballs. Throws good sinking FB, plus CU, and average SL.

Holmes, Brian — SP — Houston — EXP MLB DEBUT: 2016 — H/W: 6-4 210 — FUT: #5 starter — 6C

Thrws L Age 24
2012 (13) Wake Forest

87-90	FB	+++
75-79	CB	++
80-82	SL	+++
81-82	CU	+++

Year	Lev	Team	W	L	Sv	IP	K	ERA	WHIP	BF/G	OBA	H%	S%	xERA	Ctl	Dom	Cmd	hr/9	BPV
2012	NCAA	Wake Forest	7	3	0	82	81	2.85	1.35	24.5	211	27	80	3.06	5.4	8.9	1.7	0.5	33
2012	A-	Tri City	7	2	0	66	65	2.58	0.97	19.3	173	22	75	1.65	3.4	8.8	2.6	0.5	85
2013	Rk	GCL Astros	0	0	0	10	17	0.00	0.50	11.2	95	21	100	0.00	1.8	15.1	8.5	0.0	243
2013	A	Quad Cities	5	3	0	61	62	2.50	1.16	16.2	232	30	81	2.88	2.8	9.1	3.3	0.6	107
2014	A+	Lancaster	5	2	2	87	82	4.55	1.25	17.7	259	31	68	4.18	2.4	8.5	3.6	1.3	106

Tall, durable SP who commands plate with solid-average FB, though lacks velocity. Can cut and sink, but often lives up in zone with secondary offerings. SL can miss bats and is best secondary pitch. CB may be shelved while CU has some polish and fade. May be best in bullpen.

Holmes, Clay — SP — Pittsburgh — EXP MLB DEBUT: 2018 — H/W: 6-5 230 — FUT: #4 starter — 7D

Thrws R Age 22
2011 (9) HS (AL)

90-93	FB	++++
	CB	++
	CU	++

Year	Lev	Team	W	L	Sv	IP	K	ERA	WHIP	BF/G	OBA	H%	S%	xERA	Ctl	Dom	Cmd	hr/9	BPV
2012	A-	State College	5	3	0	59	34	2.28	1.08	17.7	174	20	78	1.62	4.4	5.2	1.2	0.2	-8
2013	A	West Virginia	5	6	0	119	90	4.08	1.47	19.6	240	29	72	3.73	5.2	6.8	1.3	0.5	0
2014		(did not play in 2014)																	

Had TJS and missed all of '14. Should be 100% by 2015. When healthy he has a good 90-93 mph FB that has good downhill tilt and generates plenty of groundball outs—1.7 gb/fb ratio in his career. Scrapped his SL in favor or a more consistently effective CB and a CU that still needs works.

Holmes,Grant — SP — Los Angeles (N)

EXP MLB DEBUT: 2019 | H/W: 6-1 215 | FUT: #2 starter | **9D**

Thrws R Age 19
2014 (1) HS (SC)

Velo	Pitch	Grade
92-96	FB	++++
83-85	CB	+++
	CU	++

Year	Lev	Team	W	L	Sv	IP	K	ERA	WHIP	BF/G	OBA	H%	S%	xERA	Ctl	Dom	Cmd	hr/9	BPV
2014	Rk	Ogden	1	1	0	18	25	4.97	1.38	19.0	271	41	63	3.84	3.0	12.4	4.2	0.5	161
2014	Rk	AZL Dodgers	1	2	0	30	33	3.00	0.90	15.9	191	26	68	1.73	2.1	9.9	4.7	0.6	140

Strong-bodied hurler showed some of the best velocity in the draft. FB sits at 93-96 mph and tops out at 100 mph. He also has a plus power CB and a CU that shows potential. Lacks projection and his body isn't fluid. Showed impressive FB command in his debut, which bodes well long-term.

Honeywell,Brent — SP — Tampa Bay

EXP MLB DEBUT: 2017 | H/W: 6-2 180 | FUT: #3 starter | **8D**

Thrws R Age 20
2014 (2-S) Walters State

Velo	Pitch	Grade
88-94	FB	+++
81-84	SL	+++
75-79	CB	++
81-85	CU	++

Year	Lev	Team	W	L	Sv	IP	K	ERA	WHIP	BF/G	OBA	H%	S%	xERA	Ctl	Dom	Cmd	hr/9	BPV
2014	Rk	Princeton	2	1	0	33	40	1.08	0.75	13.2	169	25	88	0.79	1.6	10.8	6.7	0.3	169

Athletic, projectable SP who needs to add strength, but has solid pitches and feel. Velocity increasing with tweaks to delivery and learning to sequence better. Uses occasional screwball to keep hitters guessing. Quick arm generates FB movement, but needs to find consistency in CB.

Houser,Adrian — SP — Houston

EXP MLB DEBUT: 2017 | H/W: 6-4 225 | FUT: #4 starter | **7D**

Thrws R Age 22
2011 (2) HS (OK)

Velo	Pitch	Grade
88-94	FB	+++
76-78	CB	+++
79-83	CU	++

Year	Lev	Team	W	L	Sv	IP	K	ERA	WHIP	BF/G	OBA	H%	S%	xERA	Ctl	Dom	Cmd	hr/9	BPV
2011	Rk	GCL Astros	1	2	0	22		4.07	1.54	16.1	278	39	71	3.89	4.1	10.2	2.5	0.0	91
2011	Rk	Greeneville	1	2	0	25	19	4.64	1.59	18.5	260	32	69	4.13	5.4	6.8	1.3	0.4	-5
2012	Rk	Greeneville	3	4	0	58	54	4.19	1.31	21.8	245	32	65	3.02	3.6	8.4	2.3	0.2	72
2013	A-	Tri City	0	4	0	50	39	3.42	1.34	14.9	288	35	73	3.73	1.8	7.0	3.9	0.2	96
2014	A	Quad Cities	5	6	0	108	93	4.16	1.26	17.6	245	31	66	3.14	3.1	7.7	2.5	0.4	74

Tall sinkerballer who pitched in full season for first time. Tough to elevate pitches with solid-average FB thrown on downhill plane. Cuts FB effectively while staying tall in delivery. Uses decent CB to RHH, but slows arm on fringy CU. Has ideal frame, but lacks durability and stamina.

Howard,Nick — SP — Cincinnati

EXP MLB DEBUT: 2017 | H/W: 6-3 215 | FUT: #3/4 starter/ RP | **8D**

Thrws R Age 22
2014 (1) Virginia

Velo	Pitch	Grade
90-94	FB	+++
77-79	CB	++++
83-86	SL	++
85-86	CU	+++

Year	Lev	Team	W	L	Sv	IP	K	ERA	WHIP	BF/G	OBA	H%	S%	xERA	Ctl	Dom	Cmd	hr/9	BPV
2012	NCAA	Virginia	3	0	0	41	37	2.84	1.12	8.5	226	29	73	2.36	2.6	8.1	3.1	0.2	93
2013	NCAA	Virginia	6	4	0	61	52	3.39	1.34	19.6	280	35	74	3.72	2.2	7.7	3.5	0.3	96
2014	NCAA	Virginia	2	2	20	37	60	1.94	0.99	4.6	180	31	85	1.92	3.4	14.5	4.3	0.7	188
2014	A	Dayton	2	1	0	33	23	3.80	1.17	12.1	230	25	71	3.39	3.0	6.2	2.1	1.1	50

College closer converted to SP. Positive results from Dayton in commanding and mixing four-pitch arsenal. Good FB with movement, plus CB, developing SL and CU. Pitches to both sides of plate and induces groundball outs. Fluid motion and mechanics bode well for sticking as SP.

Howard,Sam — SP — Colorado

EXP MLB DEBUT: 2018 | H/W: 6-3 170 | FUT: #5 starter | **6C**

Thrws L Age 22
2014 (3) Georgia Southern

Velo	Pitch	Grade
88-92	FB	++
	SL	++
	CB	++
	CU	++

Year	Lev	Team	W	L	Sv	IP	K	ERA	WHIP	BF/G	OBA	H%	S%	xERA	Ctl	Dom	Cmd	hr/9	BPV
2012	NCAA	GA Southern	3	1	0	24	22	5.23	1.83	9.3	306	36	75	6.46	5.2	8.2	1.6	1.5	25
2013	NCAA	GA Southern	6	7	0	84	87	5.56	1.66	16.4	307	40	65	5.05	3.7	9.3	2.5	0.4	84
2014	NCAA	GA Southern	7	6	0	95	94	2.36	1.08	23.2	232	30	80	2.57	2.1	8.9	4.3	0.5	122
2014	Rk	Grand Junction	1	3	0	53	42	5.42	1.56	16.6	328	38	66	5.70	1.7	7.1	4.2	1.0	100

3rd round pick struggled in his debut, but some was bad luck as he had a .381 BABIP. LH has a FB that sits at 88-91 mph, topping out at 94 mph with a decent SL, CB, and some feel for a CU. He has good size and a bit of projection left, but looks like a back-end starter at this point.

Hoyt,James — RP — Atlanta

EXP MLB DEBUT: 2015 | H/W: 6-5 220 | FUT: Reliever | **6B**

Thrws R Age 28
2012 FA Centenary

Velo	Pitch	Grade
94-96	FB	++++
	SL	++

Year	Lev	Team	W	L	Sv	IP	K	ERA	WHIP	BF/G	OBA	H%	S%	xERA	Ctl	Dom	Cmd	hr/9	BPV
2012	Ind	Edinburg	0	0	1	17	19	1.05	1.35	5.9	212	31	91	2.54	5.3	10.0	1.9	0.0	56
2013	A+	Lynchburg	3	2	0	49	72	4.94	1.30	11.9	219	35	61	3.00	4.6	13.2	2.9	0.5	132
2013	AA	Mississippi	0	1	1	32	33	2.52	0.93	5.5	158	22	72	1.15	3.6	9.2	2.5	0.3	86
2014	AA	Mississippi	2	2	6	31	43	1.15	0.93	4.2	178	29	89	1.34	2.9	12.4	4.3	0.3	163
2014	AAA	Gwinnett	1	1	1	28	34	5.46	1.86	5.5	325	43	73	6.61	4.5	10.9	2.4	1.3	93

Strong-armed RP dominated at AA, but got hit hard when moved up. FB sits at 94-96 mph with good movement and mixes in a swing-and-miss SL. Is a bit of a late bloomer and pitched in Indy ball until he was 25. Since turning pro he's struck out 11.7 per nine with a 3.48 ERA,

Huijer,Lars — SP — Seattle

EXP MLB DEBUT: 2017 | H/W: 6-4 200 | FUT: #4 starter | **7D**

Thrws R Age 21
2011 FA (Netherlands)

Velo	Pitch	Grade
86-91	FB	+++
74-77	CB	+++
77-79	CU	+++

Year	Lev	Team	W	L	Sv	IP	K	ERA	WHIP	BF/G	OBA	H%	S%	xERA	Ctl	Dom	Cmd	hr/9	BPV
2011	Rk	AZL Mariners	0	1	0	15	9	5.40	1.40	12.7	310	34	63	5.20	1.2	5.4	4.5	1.2	83
2012	Rk	Pulaski	1	2	2	32	21	3.91	1.65	7.2	300	35	75	4.80	3.9	5.9	1.5	0.3	18
2013	A-	Everett	8	2	0	71	61	3.04	1.13	20.0	221	28	72	2.35	2.9	7.7	2.7	0.3	78
2014	A	Clinton	4	5	0	71	44	4.04	1.31	18.4	227	27	67	2.90	4.3	5.6	1.3	0.3	2
2014	A+	High Desert	2	4	0	52	32	6.56	1.84	20.2	320	35	66	6.63	4.7	5.5	1.2	1.4	-8

Polished RHP who was hit hard in High-A upon promotion. Has room to grow into long frame, but doesn't throw hard and arm action provides little projection. Keeps ball low in zone with all pitches and is sufficient mixer. Deceptive CU is most effective offering while CB thrown for strikes.

Hultzen,Danny — SP — Seattle

EXP MLB DEBUT: 2015 | H/W: 6-3 210 | FUT: #3 starter | **8D**

Thrws L Age 25
2011 (1) Virginia

Velo	Pitch	Grade
90-95	FB	+++
80-84	SL	+++
83-87	CU	++++

Year	Lev	Team	W	L	Sv	IP	K	ERA	WHIP	BF/G	OBA	H%	S%	xERA	Ctl	Dom	Cmd	hr/9	BPV
2012	AA	Jackson	8	3	0	75	79	1.20	0.93	21.7	152	21	88	1.05	3.8	9.5	2.5	0.2	85
2012	AAA	Tacoma	1	4	0	48	57	5.98	1.91	19.0	265	37	67	4.98	8.0	10.6	1.3	0.4	-7
2013	Rk	AZL Mariners	1	0	0	5	8	1.80	0.60	17.1	175	33	67	0.19	0.0	14.4		0.0	277
2013	AAA	Tacoma	4	1	0	30	34	2.09	0.86	18.5	182	26	76	1.25	2.1	10.1	4.9	0.3	144
2014		(did not play in 2014)																	

Tall and injury-prone SP did not pitch in '14 due to shoulder surgery. Didn't pitch in winter ball either. Has been successful in limited pro innings with very deceptive delivery and plus CU thrown with same arm speed as solid FB. Mechanics could use overhaul and needs hard SL to return.

Hursh,Jason — SP — Atlanta

EXP MLB DEBUT: 2016 | H/W: 6-3 200 | FUT: #3 starter/Setup RP | **8C**

Thrws R Age 23
2013 (1) Oklahoma State

Velo	Pitch	Grade
92-94	FB	++++
74-78	SL	++
80-82	CU	++

Year	Lev	Team	W	L	Sv	IP	K	ERA	WHIP	BF/G	OBA	H%	S%	xERA	Ctl	Dom	Cmd	hr/9	BPV
2011	NCAA	Oklahoma State	1	1	0	29	10	2.77	1.61	12.9	298	33	81	4.44	3.7	3.1	0.8	0.0	-26
2013	NCAA	Oklahoma State	6	5	0	106	86	2.80	1.25	27.0	260	32	78	3.26	2.4	7.3	3.1	0.3	85
2013	A	Rome	1	1	0	27	15	0.67	1.11	11.8	208	24	97	2.26	3.3	5.0	1.5	0.3	18
2014	AA	Mississippi	11	7	0	148	83	3.59	1.31	22.7	266	30	71	3.47	2.6	5.0	1.9	0.3	38

RH is a better prospect than his surface numbers indicate. Has a good 91-93 mph FB that hitters beat into the ground. Can get a little extra on the FB when needed, but prefers to pitch to contact. CB has nice depth and break, but can be inconsistent Had TJS but has been healthy since.

Iglesias,Raisel — SP — Cincinnati

EXP MLB DEBUT: 2016 | H/W: 6-2 165 | FUT: #4 starter/Setup RP | **8D**

Thrws R Age 25
2014 FA (Cuba)

Velo	Pitch	Grade
94-96	FB	++++
81-85	SL	+++
79-80	CB	+
82-84	CU	+++

Year	Lev	Team	W	L	Sv	IP	K	ERA	WHIP	BF/G	OBA	H%	S%	xERA	Ctl	Dom	Cmd	hr/9	BPV
2014		(did not play in the US in 2014)																	

Signed June '14 and debuted in AFL. Being stretched from reliever to starter after year off. Plus FB with movement, SL that flashes plus, average and improving CU, and developing CB. High-effort delivery with deception from varying arm slots. Knows how to pitch, needs to prove durability.

Imhof,Matt — SP — Philadelphia

EXP MLB DEBUT: 2017 | H/W: 6-5 220 | FUT: #4 starter | **7C**

Thrws L Age 21
2014 (2) Cal Poly

Velo	Pitch	Grade
89-91	FB	++
75-80	CB	+++
81-83	CU	++

Year	Lev	Team	W	L	Sv	IP	K	ERA	WHIP	BF/G	OBA	H%	S%	xERA	Ctl	Dom	Cmd	hr/9	BPV
2013	NCAA	Cal Poly	7	3	0	101	95	2.76	1.24	25.6	250	32	78	3.17	2.7	8.4	3.2	0.4	98
2014	NCAA	Cal Poly	10	4	0	99	124	2.45	1.09	25.8	189	29	76	1.78	3.9	11.3	2.9	0.2	115
2014	Rk	GCL Phillies	0	0	0	3	2	0.00	1.00	11.5	191	24	100	1.46	3.0	6.0	2.0	0.0	45
2014	A-	Williamsport	1	0	0	12	11	0.75	0.83	14.6	151	21	90	0.58	3.0	8.3	2.8	0.0	86
2014	A	Lakewood	0	2	0	27	27	4.32	1.40	16.3	295	37	71	4.75	2.0	9.0	4.5	1.0	126

Height allows him to work on a big downward plane that benefits both his 89-91 FB and his overhand CB. Has the ability to spot the FB, and a deceptive delivery benefits all of his pitches, including an average CU. Continued development of secondary pitches will hold the key to his future.

Jackson,Luke — SP — Texas — EXP MLB DEBUT: 2015 — H/W: 6-2 205 — FUT: #2 starter — 8C

Thrws R Age 23	Year	Lev	Team	W	L	Sv	IP	K	ERA	WHIP	BF/G	OBA	H%	S%	xERA	Ctl	Dom	Cmd	hr/9	BPV
2010 (1-S) HS (FL)	2012	A+	Myrtle Beach	5	2	0	65	74	4.42	1.52	21.8	267	37	69	3.94	4.4	10.2	2.3	0.3	83
91-97 FB ++++	2013	A+	Myrtle Beach	9	4	0	101	104	2.41	1.25	21.6	217	29	83	2.86	4.2	9.3	2.2	0.5	72
83-87 SL ++	2013	AA	Frisco	2	0	0	27	30	0.67	0.93	16.9	146	22	92	0.74	4.0	10.0	2.5	0.0	90
79-83 CB ++	2014	AA	Frisco	8	2	1	83	83	3.03	0.99	21.1	198	26	70	1.99	2.6	9.0	3.5	0.5	110
83-85 CU ++	2014	AAA	Round Rock	1	3	0	40	43	10.35	2.10	17.9	332	40	51	8.05	6.3	9.7	1.5	2.0	22

Aggressive, strong SP who dominated AA, but struggled in AAA. Can fire FB by hitters up in zone with velocity and movement, but can overthrow. Has two breaking pitches at disposal, but erratic control hinders effectiveness. Mechanics are sufficient to log innings and has feel for CU.

Jaime,Juan — RP — Atlanta — EXP MLB DEBUT: 2014 — H/W: 6-2 250 — FUT: Setup RP — 7C

Thrws R Age 27	Year	Lev	Team	W	L	Sv	IP	K	ERA	WHIP	BF/G	OBA	H%	S%	xERA	Ctl	Dom	Cmd	hr/9	BPV
2004 FA (DR)	2009	A	Hagerstown	3	1	0	31	40	2.31	1.22	15.7	200	29	83	2.60	4.6	11.5	2.5	0.6	101
95-98 FB ++++	2012	A+	Lynchburg	1	3	18	51	73	3.17	1.25	5.0	177	28	77	2.53	5.8	12.9	2.2	0.7	93
CB +	2013	AA	Mississippi	2	5	0	42	70	4.07	1.38	5.0	202	37	68	2.66	6.0	15.0	2.5	0.2	126
CU +	2014	AAA	Gwinnett	1	0	18	41	63	3.51	1.54	4.2	189	33	76	2.92	7.9	13.8	1.8	0.2	54
	2014	MLB	Atlanta	0	0	0	12	18	5.95	1.90	3.6	291	45	68	5.66	6.7	13.4	2.0	0.7	78

RP had another solid season and held his own in MLB debut. FB maxes out at 100 mph and he mixes in a decent SL and CU. Continues to struggle with consistency and control and now has a career 6.2 Ctl ratio, but he can bring the heat and miss bats in the majors.

James,Chad — SP — Texas — EXP MLB DEBUT: 2015 — H/W: 6-3 180 — FUT: #3 starter — 8E

Thrws L Age 24	Year	Lev	Team	W	L	Sv	IP	K	ERA	WHIP	BF/G	OBA	H%	S%	xERA	Ctl	Dom	Cmd	hr/9	BPV
2009 (1) HS (OK)	2011	A+	Jupiter	5	15	0	149		3.80	1.50	23.9	292	35	76	4.70	3.1	7.5	2.4	0.7	70
90-93 FB ++++	2012	A+	Jupiter	6	10	0	114	80	4.89	1.65	21.3	300	35	70	5.19	3.9	6.3	1.6	0.7	25
80-82 SL ++	2013	A	Greensboro	2	6	0	53	57	5.76	1.60	18.1	276	35	65	4.97	4.7	9.7	2.0	1.0	64
78-80 CU +++	2014	A+	Myrtle Beach	4	3	0	42	35	2.77	1.37	22.1	232	28	82	3.49	4.7	7.5	1.6	0.6	26
	2014	Ind	Evansville Otters	4	2	0	46	67	5.08	1.50	22.1	198	32	65	3.26	7.2	13.1	1.8	0.6	58

Former 1st round pick put up better results, but was limited to 8 starts and the Rangers snagged him as a minor league FA. The LH still has a decent 90-93 mph FB with good movement. SL and CU have potential, but are inconsistent. At this point, a move to relief would seem the obvious.

Jenkins,Tyrell — SP — Atlanta — EXP MLB DEBUT: 2016 — H/W: 6-4 204 — FUT: #2 starter — 8D

Thrws R Age 22	Year	Lev	Team	W	L	Sv	IP	K	ERA	WHIP	BF/G	OBA	H%	S%	xERA	Ctl	Dom	Cmd	hr/9	BPV
2010 (1-S) HS (TX)	2011	Rk	Johnson City	4	2	0	56	55	3.86	1.36	21.3	285	37	71	4.00	2.1	8.8	4.2	0.5	121
93-94 FB ++++	2012	A	Quad Cities	4	4	0	82	80	5.15	1.46	18.5	266	34	63	4.06	3.9	8.8	2.2	0.5	69
76-78 CB +++	2013	A	Peoria	4	4	0	49	34	4.77	1.53	21.3	269	31	69	4.46	4.4	6.2	1.4	0.7	11
80-82 CU ++	2013	A+	Palm Beach	0	0	0	10	6	4.50	1.40	14.1	316	37	64	4.16	0.9	5.4	6.0	0.0	91
	2014	A+	Palm Beach	6	5	0	74	41	3.28	1.31	23.5	262	29	77	3.82	2.8	5.0	1.8	0.7	32

Due to shoulder problems, including lat surgery in '13, he has yet to log more than 90 IP in a season. Was healthy in 2nd half and posted a 3.28 ERA. Competes well with a 92-94 mph FB and a good 1-7 CB and a nice CU. Comes at hitters with a low 3/4 delivery with and good movement on his FB.

Jensen,Chris — SP — Oakland — EXP MLB DEBUT: 2015 — H/W: 6-4 200 — FUT: #5 starter — 6B

Thrws R Age 24	Year	Lev	Team	W	L	Sv	IP	K	ERA	WHIP	BF/G	OBA	H%	S%	xERA	Ctl	Dom	Cmd	hr/9	BPV
2011 (6) San Diego	2011	NCAA	San Diego	3	7	2	82	73	3.95	1.41	19.3	257	33	70	3.41	4.0	8.0	2.0	0.1	56
90-94 FB +++	2011	A-	Tri-City	2	1	0	37	28	2.67	1.00	17.7	205	25	72	1.84	2.4	6.8	2.8	0.2	75
81-82 CB +++	2012	A	Asheville	12	3	0	145	95	4.28	1.37	24.3	266	30	70	4.14	3.1	5.9	1.9	0.9	40
CU ++	2013	A+	Modesto	5	8	0	152	136	4.56	1.31	22.5	273	33	66	4.11	2.3	8.0	3.5	0.9	101
	2014	AA	Midland	12	8	0	160	94	3.15	1.31	25.4	246	29	74	3.06	3.5	5.3	1.5	0.2	19

Tall, durable pitcher who had best pro season to date. K rate dropped considerably while LHH continue to hit him hard, but commands plate with sinking FB. Mostly uses FB to keep ball low in zone and rarely allows HR. Mixes in average, hard CB for strikes and fringy CU has potential.

Jimenez,Joe — RP — Detroit — EXP MLB DEBUT: 2018 — H/W: 6-3 220 — FUT: Setup RP — 8E

Thrws R Age 20	Year	Lev	Team	W	L	Sv	IP	K	ERA	WHIP	BF/G	OBA	H%	S%	xERA	Ctl	Dom	Cmd	hr/9	BPV
2013 NDFA HS (PR)																				
92-97 FB ++++																				
83-85 SL +++																				
74-78 CB ++	2013	Rk	GCL Tigers	3	0	1	18	24	0.50	0.83	8.2	151	25	93	0.54	3.0	12.0	4.0	0.0	153
81-82 CU ++	2014	A-	Connecticut	3	2	4	26	41	2.75	1.07	4.4	229	39	74	2.33	2.1	14.1	6.8	0.3	216

Big, physical RP with impressive upside predicated on hard arsenal. Uses height to pitch on downward angle and spots plus FB to both sides of plate. SL showing vast improvement while he has some feel for CU. Will stay in pen with rigid delivery and arm action and has struggled with LHH.

Johansen,Jake — SP — Washington — EXP MLB DEBUT: 2016 — H/W: 6-6 235 — FUT: setup/closer — 8D

Thrws R Age 24	Year	Lev	Team	W	L	Sv	IP	K	ERA	WHIP	BF/G	OBA	H%	S%	xERA	Ctl	Dom	Cmd	hr/9	BPV
2013 (2) Dallas Baptist	2012	NCAA	Dallas Baptist	3	1	1	46	40	5.48	1.72	10.4	266	32	69	5.11	6.3	7.8	1.3	1.0	-10
92-94 FB ++++	2013	NCAA	Dallas Baptist	7	6	0	88	75	5.41	1.53	25.6	305	38	62	4.59	2.7	7.7	2.9	0.3	84
86-90 SL +++	2013	A-	Auburn	1	1	0	42	44	1.07	0.95	15.9	156	22	90	1.12	3.8	9.4	2.4	0.2	83
77-89 CB ++	2013	A	Hagerstown	0	2	0	9	7	5.93	1.98	21.8	336	39	71	6.87	4.9	6.9	1.4	1.0	9
86-90 CU ++	2014	A	Hagerstown	5	6	0	100	89	5.21	1.75	15.8	298	38	68	4.98	4.9	8.0	1.6	0.3	29

A tough year in the stat line, but fastball and slider are both plus pitches. Needs to continue to work on fastball command, and mechanics and delivery are far from polished. Ended the season with 10 straight relief appearances, which is where many think he'll end up as an impact reliever.

Johnson,Brian — SP — Boston — EXP MLB DEBUT: 2015 — H/W: 6-3 225 — FUT: #4 starter — 7A

Thrws L Age 24	Year	Lev	Team	W	L	Sv	IP	K	ERA	WHIP	BF/G	OBA	H%	S%	xERA	Ctl	Dom	Cmd	hr/9	BPV
2012 (1) Florida	2013	Rk	GCL Red Sox	0	0	0	5	7	0.00	0.60	8.6	66	12	100	0.00	3.6	12.6	3.5	0.0	148
88-93 FB +++	2013	A	Greenville	1	6	0	69	69	2.87	1.13	18.2	204	27	76	2.40	3.7	9.0	2.5	0.5	81
80-83 SL ++	2013	A+	Salem	1	0	0	11	8	1.64	1.27	22.5	225	28	86	2.54	4.1	6.5	1.6	0.0	25
76-79 CB +++	2014	A+	Salem	3	1	0	25	33	3.93	1.19	20.2	245	38	63	2.54	2.5	11.8	4.7	0.0	163
83-86 CU +++	2014	AA	Portland	10	2	0	118	99	1.75	0.93	22.1	190	24	84	1.69	2.4	7.6	3.1	0.5	88

Advanced, savvy SP who led EL in ERA. Toys with hitters by sequencing, changing speeds, and commanding four pitches. Velocity isn't great, but gets good movement to solid-average FB. Uses both CB and SL and mixes in very good CU. Keeps ball in park and induces groundballs.

Johnson,Chase — RP — San Francisco — EXP MLB DEBUT: 2017 — H/W: 6-3 185 — FUT: #4 Starter — 7C

Thrws R Age 23	Year	Lev	Team	W	L	Sv	IP	K	ERA	WHIP	BF/G	OBA	H%	S%	xERA	Ctl	Dom	Cmd	hr/9	BPV
2013 (3) Cal Poly	2012	NCAA	Cal Poly	3	4	8	35	31	3.34	1.20	5.6	227	30	69	2.37	3.3	8.0	2.4	0.0	71
91-94 FB ++++	2013	NCAA	Cal Poly	0	0	0	23	21	2.34	1.26	6.3	235	31	79	2.61	3.5	8.2	2.3	0.0	71
CB ++	2013	Rk	AZL Giants	1	0	0	5	7	1.76	1.18	6.8	258	40	83	2.67	1.8	12.4	7.0	0.0	193
SL ++	2013	A-	Salem-Kaizer	3	2	0	41	37	4.17	1.17	16.4	237	30	64	3.05	2.6	8.1	3.1	0.7	93
CU +++	2014	A	Augusta	4	7	0	110	94	4.58	1.37	20.1	263	33	65	3.67	3.3	7.7	2.4	0.4	68

Tall, athletic RH had an up-and-down season in '14, but good frame, clean arm action, and a respectable arsenal show promise for future in the rotation. Sits in the low-90s with the FB up to 97, complemented by an average CU that gets swings-and-misses and a usable, but below average, CB and SL. Someone to keep an eye on in 2015.

Johnson,Chris — SP — San Francisco — EXP MLB DEBUT: 2017 — H/W: 6-4 205 — FUT: #5 Starter — 7D

Thrws R Age 23	Year	Lev	Team	W	L	Sv	IP	K	ERA	WHIP	BF/G	OBA	H%	S%	xERA	Ctl	Dom	Cmd	hr/9	BPV
2012 (17) Portland	2011	NCAA	Portland	3	5	0	83	58	3.57	1.23	24.0	254	30	71	3.33	2.4	6.3	2.6	0.5	67
89-91 FB ++	2012	NCAA	Portland	4	4	0	76	57	3.08	1.34	21.1	274	33	78	3.82	2.5	6.8	2.7	0.5	72
CB +++	2012	A-	Salem-Kaizer	2	4	0	48	47	6.91	1.39	12.7	292	36	50	4.96	2.1	8.8	4.3	1.3	121
SL ++	2013	A-	Salem-Kaizer	6	3	0	83	78	2.49	0.88	20.5	217	29	69	1.54	0.9	8.5	9.8	0.1	147
CU ++	2014	A	Augusta	0	1	0	2	0	9.00	2.50	10.6	347	35	60	7.51	9.0	0.0	0.0	0.0	-225

Tall, durable SP was sidelined all but two innings in 2014 with an injury. Will look to get back on track and replicate his 2013 success in which he had a 78:8 K:BB ratio. FB sits in the upper-80s-low-90s with sinking action, complemented by an average CB and below average SL and CU. Arm is clean and he repeats his delivery well.

Johnson,Pierce — SP — Chicago (N) — EXP MLB DEBUT: 2016 — H/W: 6-3 170 — FUT: #3 starter — 8D

Thrws R Age 23	Year	Lev	Team	W	L	Sv	IP	K	ERA	WHIP	BF/G	OBA	H%	S%	xERA	Ctl	Dom	Cmd	hr/9	BPV
2012 (1-S) Missouri State	2012	A-	Boise	0	0	0	8	12	4.50	1.63	8.9	307	49	69	4.51	3.4	13.5	4.0	0.0	170
91-93 FB ++++	2013	A	Kane County	5	5	0	69	74	3.12	1.30	21.9	258	35	77	3.51	2.9	9.6	3.4	0.5	114
86-88 CT ++	2013	A+	Daytona	6	1	0	48	50	2.24	1.29	19.8	232	32	82	2.81	3.9	9.3	2.4	0.2	80
82-84 CU ++	2014	A	Kane County	0	1	0	11	8	2.45	0.64	19.0	114	12	67	0.50	2.5	6.5	2.7	0.8	70
80-83 CB +++	2014	AA	Tennessee	5	4	0	91	91	2.57	1.25	20.6	189	24	83	2.78	5.3	9.0	1.7	0.8	36

RH comes after hitters with a good 91-93 mph FB that has late life and hits 95. Also has a plus CB that gets swings and misses, but CU remains inconsistent. Below-avg control and spent over a month on the DL with a hamstring injury, but was lights-out after returning to action, posting 1.80 ERA.

Johnson,Stephen — RP — San Francisco

EXP MLB DEBUT: 2016 | H/W: 6-4 205 | FUT: Reliever | 7D

Thrws R Age 24
2012 (6) St. Edward's

Velo	Pitch	Grade
91-95	FB	+++
	CB	++

Year	Lev	Team	W	L	Sv	IP	K	ERA	WHIP	BF/G	OBA	H%	S%	xERA	Ctl	Dom	Cmd	hr/9	BPV
2012	Rk	AZL Giants	0	0	0	2	2	4.50	1.50	4.3	151	22	67	2.25	9.0	9.0	1.0	0.0	-63
2012	A-	Salem-Kaizer	0	2	2	19	19	4.71	1.62	5.0	261	33	72	4.76	5.7	9.0	1.6	0.9	26
2013	A	Augusta	5	1	8	52	71	3.63	1.36	4.8	218	34	72	2.96	5.2	12.3	2.4	0.3	99
2014	A+	San Jose	7	4	1	69	77	3.65	1.42	6.0	242	33	75	3.71	4.7	10.0	2.1	0.7	72

Tall RH RP comes at hitters with low-to-mid-90s FB. Pairs it with a slightly below average CB that he uses for punchouts. Funky arm action hinder his ability to command his pitches, leading to less than stellar Ctl, though it has improved every year since going pro. Dom numbers are promising, but needs to throw strikes.

Jokisch,Eric — SP — Chicago (N)

EXP MLB DEBUT: 2014 | H/W: 6-2 185 | FUT: #5 starter | 6B

Thrws L Age 25
2010 (11) Northwestern

Velo	Pitch	Grade
86-90	FB	++
	CB	++
	CU	+++

Year	Lev	Team	W	L	Sv	IP	K	ERA	WHIP	BF/G	OBA	H%	S%	xERA	Ctl	Dom	Cmd	hr/9	BPV
2012	A+	Daytona	3	4	0	54	52	3.49	1.31	24.8	265	34	75	3.78	2.7	8.7	3.3	0.7	102
2012	AA	Tennessee	7	2	0	105	63	2.91	1.13	23.1	225	25	76	2.77	2.8	5.4	1.9	0.6	39
2013	AA	Tennessee	11	13	0	160	137	3.43	1.24	24.1	242	29	74	3.39	3.0	7.7	2.5	0.8	75
2014	AAA	Iowa	9	10	0	158	143	3.59	1.18	24.3	258	32	71	3.36	1.8	8.1	4.6	0.7	117
2014	MLB	Chi Cubs	0	0	0	14	10	1.91	1.56	15.4	312	34	100	6.29	2.6	6.4	2.5	1.9	64

24-year-old doesn't blow people away but throws strikes and made him MLB deubt. FB rarely breaks 90 mph, but he mixes in a plus CU and a CB. 4.6 Cmd ratio gives him the potential to carve out a role at the backend of a rotation.

Jones,Brent — SP — Arizona

EXP MLB DEBUT: 2018 | H/W: 6-3 215 | FUT: #5 starter/mid reliever | 6C

Thrws R Age 22
2014 (4) Cornell

Velo	Pitch	Grade
93-96	FB	++++
79-82	CB	++
80-83	SL	++

Year	Lev	Team	W	L	Sv	IP	K	ERA	WHIP	BF/G	OBA	H%	S%	xERA	Ctl	Dom	Cmd	hr/9	BPV
2012	NCAA	Cornell	4	2	0	48		4.50	1.54	19.0	289	36	68	4.26	3.6	7.5	2.1	0.2	57
2013	NCAA	Cornell	4	1	1	36	25	3.49	1.47	17.2	267	33	74	3.59	4.0	6.2	1.6	0.0	22
2014	NCAA	Cornell	2	3	0	50	47	2.51	1.16	22.1	242	32	77	2.62	2.3	8.4	3.6	0.2	107
2014	A-	Hillsboro	2	1	0	27	18	3.97	1.18	18.1	223	25	67	2.90	3.3	6.0	1.8	0.7	36
2014	A	South Bend	5	2	0	35	27	2.82	1.51	19.0	293	36	81	4.31	3.1	6.9	2.3	0.3	60

He is fully developed and has good arm strength. Arsenal includes a good 92-94 mph FB that hits 97, a hard CB, and a rudimentary CU. The FB/CB combination give him a chance to remain a starer if the CU can develop. Profiles as a durable back-end starter or a middle-reliever.

Jones,Cory — SP — St. Louis

EXP MLB DEBUT: 2018 | H/W: 6-5 225 | FUT: Reliever | 6C

Thrws R Age 23
2012 (5) JC of the Canyons

Velo	Pitch	Grade
90-94	FB	+++
80-83	CB	++
	CU	+

Year	Lev	Team	W	L	Sv	IP	K	ERA	WHIP	BF/G	OBA	H%	S%	xERA	Ctl	Dom	Cmd	hr/9	BPV
2010	NCAA	Pepperdine	0	1	0	7	6	19.29	3.86	5.8	477	57	44	13.70	11.6	7.7	0.7	0.0	-156
2012	Rk	Johnson City	0	2	0	17	15	7.37	1.87	16.0	303	35	62	6.61	5.8	7.9	1.4	1.6	4
2013	A	Peoria	8	2	0	66	52	2.04	1.03	23.1	218	26	83	2.35	2.2	7.1	3.3	0.5	87
2014	A+	Palm Beach	1	0	0	18	13	7.00	1.83	16.8	262	30	61	5.38	7.5	6.5	0.9	1.0	-68

Collegiate RH took a step back and managed to get into only 5 G. When healthy, uses his big frame well to generate 90-93 mph velocity on his FB. Also features a slurvy CB and a below-avg CU. Fared well in the MWL, but given the lack of a CU and injury history a move to relief seems likely.

Jones,Tyler — RP — Minnesota

EXP MLB DEBUT: 2015 | H/W: 6-4 250 | FUT: Setup RP | 6B

Thrws R Age 25
2011 (11) Louisiana State

Velo	Pitch	Grade
90-95	FB	++++
83-87	SL	+++
81-83	CU	++

Year	Lev	Team	W	L	Sv	IP	K	ERA	WHIP	BF/G	OBA	H%	S%	xERA	Ctl	Dom	Cmd	hr/9	BPV
2011	Rk	Elizabethton	0	0	0	7	8	12.86	2.57	9.4	448	54	50	12.09	2.6	10.3	4.0	2.6	134
2012	A	Beloit	5	5	0	86	102	4.70	1.45	20.4	270	38	67	4.04	3.7	10.6	2.9	0.5	111
2013	A	Cedar Rapids	4	3	9	37	44	1.94	0.94	5.8	154	24	77	0.86	3.9	10.7	2.8	0.0	105
2013	A+	Fort Myers	1	3	4	15	22	4.20	1.47	5.4	299	47	68	3.98	2.4	13.2	5.5	0.0	191
2014	A+	Fort Myers	3	3	13	50	53	3.76	1.43	5.3	257	35	73	3.68	4.1	9.5	2.3	0.4	78

Large-bodied RP with imposing frame and power stuff. Exceptional FB that features cut and sink is K pitch. Has trouble commanding due to late action, but has consistent break in SL as quality second pitch. Uses occasional CU with fade, but has long struggled to keep LHH at bay.

Jorge,Felix — SP — Minnesota

EXP MLB DEBUT: 2017 | H/W: 6-2 170 | FUT: #3 starter | 8D

Thrws R Age 21
2011 FA (DR)

Velo	Pitch	Grade
90-93	FB	+++
78-82	CB	+++
81-84	CU	++

Year	Lev	Team	W	L	Sv	IP	K	ERA	WHIP	BF/G	OBA	H%	S%	xERA	Ctl	Dom	Cmd	hr/9	BPV
2012	Rk	GCL Twins	0	3	1	34	37	2.37	1.23	11.5	237	34	79	2.56	3.2	9.7	3.1	0.0	108
2013	Rk	Elizabethton	2	2	0	61	72	2.95	1.21	20.5	246	35	75	2.90	2.7	10.6	4.0	0.3	138
2014	Rk	Elizabethton	4	2	0	66	61	2.59	1.09	21.5	238	31	76	2.49	1.9	8.3	4.4	0.3	116
2014	A	Cedar Rapids	2	5	0	39	23	9.00	1.97	15.6	341	36	56	7.99	4.6	5.3	1.2	2.1	-11

Lean, athletic SP who had tough start in Low-A prior to demotion. Spots three pitches well within strike zone and rarely walks hitters. Needs better pitch to combat LHH and needs to add strength to inconsistent delivery. Sinking FB is solid-average and impressive CB misses bats often.

Julio,Erick — SP — Colorado

EXP MLB DEBUT: 2018 | H/W: 6-1 150 | FUT: #3 starter | 7D

Thrws R Age 18
2013 FA (Colombia)

Velo	Pitch	Grade
87-90	FB	+++
	CB	+++
	CU	++

Year	Lev	Team	W	L	Sv	IP	K	ERA	WHIP	BF/G	OBA	H%	S%	xERA	Ctl	Dom	Cmd	hr/9	BPV
2014	Rk	DSL Rockies	2	5	0	66	45	2.45	0.94	19.1	215	26	73	1.84	1.5	6.1	4.1	0.3	88

Columbian hurler has yet to make his U.S. debut, but fared well in the DSL, going 2-5 with a 2.45 ERA. FB sits in the 88-91 range with the potential for more. Shows the ability to spin a breaking ball and some feel for a CU.

Jungmann,Taylor — SP — Milwaukee

EXP MLB DEBUT: 2015 | H/W: 6-6 210 | FUT: #3 starter | 7C

Thrws R Age 25
2011 (1) Texas

Velo	Pitch	Grade
90-92	FB	+++
76-78	SL	+++
	CU	++

Year	Lev	Team	W	L	Sv	IP	K	ERA	WHIP	BF/G	OBA	H%	S%	xERA	Ctl	Dom	Cmd	hr/9	BPV
2011	NCAA	Texas	13	3	0	141	126	1.60	0.83	27.1	169	22	81	1.01	2.3	8.0	3.5	0.3	101
2012	A+	Brevard Cnty	11	6	0	153	99	3.53	1.34	24.5	269	31	73	3.69	2.7	5.8	2.2	0.4	50
2013	AA	Huntsville	10	10	0	139	82	4.34	1.37	22.4	230	25	69	3.52	4.7	5.3	1.1	0.7	-14
2014	AA	Huntsville	4	4	0	52	46	2.77	1.29	23.7	262	32	81	3.70	2.6	8.0	3.1	0.7	91
2014	AAA	Nashville	8	6	0	101	101	4.00	1.32	22.1	236	31	70	3.37	4.1	9.0	2.2	0.6	69

Has a good 90-92 mph sinking FB with downhill tilt and his sinker generates GB outs. Control abandoned him when he moved to AAA. Mixes in a good SL and an average CU that lacks separation. Mechanics are herky-jerky and throws across his body, partially explaining the lack of command.

Kaminsky,Rob — SP — St. Louis

EXP MLB DEBUT: 2017 | H/W: 5-11 191 | FUT: #3 starter | 8C

Thrws L Age 20
2013 (1) HS (NJ)

Velo	Pitch	Grade
88-92	FB	+++
76-79	CB	++++
80-83	CU	+++

Year	Lev	Team	W	L	Sv	IP	K	ERA	WHIP	BF/G	OBA	H%	S%	xERA	Ctl	Dom	Cmd	hr/9	BPV
2013	Rk	GCL Cardinals	0	3	0	22	28	3.68	1.45	11.8	270	39	74	3.94	3.7	11.5	3.1	0.4	125
2014	A	Peoria	8	2	0	100	79	1.89	1.02	21.4	201	25	81	1.77	2.8	7.1	2.5	0.2	71

LH had a huge breakout in his full-season debut. Isn't overpowering and his FB sits at 88-92 mph with good life. Backs it up with a plus CB that generates plenty of swings and misses and an improved CU. Thrives by keeping hitters off balance and locating his FB to both sides of the plate.

Karns,Nate — SP — Tampa Bay

EXP MLB DEBUT: 2013 | H/W: 6-3 230 | FUT: #4 starter | 7B

Thrws R Age 27
2009 (12) Texas Tech

Velo	Pitch	Grade
90-96	FB	+++
80-83	CB	++++
81-85	CU	++

Year	Lev	Team	W	L	Sv	IP	K	ERA	WHIP	BF/G	OBA	H%	S%	xERA	Ctl	Dom	Cmd	hr/9	BPV
2012	A+	Potomac	8	4	0	71	87	2.28	1.03	21.1	190	29	76	1.58	3.3	11.0	3.3	0.1	127
2013	AA	Harrisburg	10	6	0	132	155	3.27	1.19	23.0	226	30	76	3.20	3.3	10.6	3.2	1.0	120
2013	MLB	Washington	0	1	0	12	11	7.50	1.92	18.9	334	34	72	9.26	4.5	8.3	1.8	3.8	45
2014	AAA	Durham	9	9	0	145	153	5.09	1.41	22.7	258	33	65	4.21	3.8	9.5	2.5	1.0	85
2014	MLB	Tampa Bay	1	1	0	12	13	4.50	0.92	22.4	171	16	63	3.11	3.0	9.8	3.3	2.3	113

Aggressive, durable SP who led IL in K. Not much deception with long arm action, but has arm strength to generate power arsenal. High K rate with multiple pitches, including plus, hard CB and dynamic sinker. CU shows potential and has fair command. Struggles to keep CB in strike zone.

Kela,Keone — RP — Texas

EXP MLB DEBUT: 2015 | H/W: 6-1 225 | FUT: Setup RP | 7C

Thrws R Age 21
2012 (12) Everett CC

Velo	Pitch	Grade
93-99	FB	++++
82-86	SL	++
80-82	CB	+++
	CU	+

Year	Lev	Team	W	L	Sv	IP	K	ERA	WHIP	BF/G	OBA	H%	S%	xERA	Ctl	Dom	Cmd	hr/9	BPV
2013	Rk	AZL Rangers	2	0	0	3	6	8.44	3.44	6.7	470	73	73	12.36	8.4	16.9	2.0	0.0	94
2013	A-	Spokane	1	2	2	16	26	3.89	1.42	5.7	271	45	73	3.97	3.3	14.4	4.3	0.6	188
2013	A	Hickory	2	2	1	18	20	2.47	1.32	6.3	260	36	79	3.08	3.0	9.9	3.3	0.0	116
2014	A+	Myrtle Beach	0	1	5	10	13	2.67	1.29	5.2	240	37	77	2.72	3.6	11.6	3.3	0.0	130
2014	AA	Frisco	2	1	5	38	55	1.88	1.28	4.4	170	28	85	2.08	6.4	13.0	2.0	0.2	79

Dynamic RP who is on fast track. Can dominate with plus FB and hard CB. Either gets groundball outs or Ks as evidenced by high Dom. Adds deception by fast arm speed and hiding ball in delivery. SL can be a bit short and FB often lacks movement at higher velocities. Closer stuff.

Keller,Brad

SP | **Arizona** | EXP MLB DEBUT: 2018 | H/W: 6-5 230 | FUT: #4 starter | **7D**

Thrws R Age 19
2013 (8) HS (GA)

Velo	Pitch	Grade
90-93	FB	+++
	SL	+++
	CU	++

Year	Lev	Team	W	L	Sv	IP	K	ERA	WHIP	BF/G	OBA	H%	S%	xERA	Ctl	Dom	Cmd	hr/9	BPV
2013	Rk	AZL Dbacks	7	3	0	56	61	2.24	1.41	18.3	251	34	84	3.48	4.2	9.8	2.3	0.3	81
2013	Rk	Missoula	0	0	0	6	4	4.50	1.67	13.5	262	32	70	4.03	6.0	6.0	1.0	0.0	-36
2014	Rk	AZL Dbacks	4	0	0	31	20	2.32	1.25	21.1	255	29	84	3.44	2.6	5.8	2.2	0.6	52
2014	Rk	Missoula	1	4	0	33	30	7.05	2.05	20.2	348	41	68	7.84	4.9	8.1	1.7	1.6	33
2014	A-	Hillsboro	1	0	0	6	8	0.00	0.33	18.9	56	10	100	0.00	1.5	12.0	8.0	0.0	194

Good size paired with a low-90s FB. Also has a hard SL and a decent CU. Keller struggled in the Pioneer League, but recovered when sent to the AZL. Isn't overpowering, but does throw strikes and has the size and stuff to develop into a back-end starter.

Keller,Jon

RP | **Baltimore** | EXP MLB DEBUT: 2016 | H/W: 6-5 210 | FUT: Setup RP | **7C**

Thrws R Age 22
2013 (22) Tampa

Velo	Pitch	Grade
91-96	FB	++++
81-85	SL	+++
	CU	+

Year	Lev	Team	W	L	Sv	IP	K	ERA	WHIP	BF/G	OBA	H%	S%	xERA	Ctl	Dom	Cmd	hr/9	BPV
2013	NCAA	Tampa	6	3	0	66	47	3.95	1.42	21.5	247	30	69	3.21	4.5	6.4	1.4	0.0	12
2013	Rk	GCL Orioles	1	2	0	15	18	4.17	1.26	10.3	285	41	63	3.28	1.2	10.7	9.0	0.0	179
2013	A-	Aberdeen	1	0	0	3	2	3.00	0.67	10.5	106	13	50	0.00	3.0	6.0	2.0	0.0	45
2014	A	Delmarva	3	0	5	56	66	1.60	0.94	8.8	197	29	83	1.49	2.2	10.6	4.7	0.2	148
2014	A+	Frederick	0	0	0	4	5	8.78	3.66	13.3	409	55	73	11.52	15.4	11.0	0.7	0.0	-199

Large-framed RP who took to new role after starting in college. Induces ton of groundballs with plus, sinking FB. Pitches tough to elevate due to height, arm slot, and movement. Stingy against RHH with strong SL that hitters chase. Throws good strikes, though can struggle to repeat slot.

Keller,Mitch

SP | **Pittsburgh** | EXP MLB DEBUT: 2019 | H/W: 6-3 195 | FUT: #3 starter | **8D**

Thrws R Age 19
2014 (2) HS (IA)

Velo	Pitch	Grade
90-93	FB	+++
	CB	++
	CU	++

Year	Lev	Team	W	L	Sv	IP	K	ERA	WHIP	BF/G	OBA	H%	S%	xERA	Ctl	Dom	Cmd	hr/9	BPV
2014	Rk	GCL Pirates	0	0	0	27	29	1.99	1.18	12.0	199	29	81	1.97	4.3	9.6	2.2	0.0	75

2nd round pick is a good athlete with a low-90s FB that maxes at 95. Has easy arm action and repeatable mechanics. Gets good life on his FB and keeps the ball down in the zone. Second best offering is a hard CB that has potential, but lacks consistency. CU showed solid potential in debut.

Kelliher,Branden

SP | **Oakland** | EXP MLB DEBUT: 2018 | H/W: 5-11 175 | FUT: #4 starter | **7D**

Thrws R Age 19
2014 (8) HS (WA)

Velo	Pitch	Grade
88-94	FB	+++
74-78	CB	++
80-83	CU	++

Year	Lev	Team	W	L	Sv	IP	K	ERA	WHIP	BF/G	OBA	H%	S%	xERA	Ctl	Dom	Cmd	hr/9	BPV
2014	Rk	AZL Athletics	1	4	0	28	37	4.82	1.93	12.1	240	37	72	4.34	9.3	11.9	1.3	0.0	-20

Short SP who throws hard and gets pitch movement due to fast arm action. Looks to work quickly, but has control issues. Has difficulty repeating delivery which impacts pitch mix. CB has potential to become plus, but needs consistent release point. Shows feel for CU, but needs work.

Kelly,Casey

SP | **San Diego** | EXP MLB DEBUT: 2012 | H/W: 6-3 210 | FUT: #3 starter | **8D**

Thrws R Age 25
2008 (1) HS (FL)

Velo	Pitch	Grade
90-94	FB	++++
76-79	CB	++++
80-84	CU	+++

Year	Lev	Team	W	L	Sv	IP	K	ERA	WHIP	BF/G	OBA	H%	S%	xERA	Ctl	Dom	Cmd	hr/9	BPV
2012	AA	San Antonio	0	1	0	16	18	3.89	0.86	19.9	194	27	54	1.63	1.7	10.0	6.0	0.6	153
2012	AAA	Tucson	0	0	0	12	14	2.25	1.00	22.9	262	38	75	2.30	0.0	10.5		0.0	207
2012	MLB	San Diego	2	3	0	29	26	6.21	1.69	21.8	323	38	66	6.44	3.1	8.1	2.6	1.6	79
2014	A+	Lake Elsinore	0	0	0	8	9	4.44	1.73	18.4	380	50	71	6.07	0.0	10.0		0.0	198
2014	AA	San Antonio	1	0	0	12	8	0.75	1.00	22.9	245	30	92	2.12	0.8	6.0	8.0	0.0	106

Missed all of '13 with TJS and was shut down with a sore elbow; has logged 87 innings since '11. When he's right he has a three-pitch mix that includes a low-90s sinking FB with arm-side run, a plus CB, and a good CU. Commands all three offerings well and incudes plenty of GB outs.

Kickham,Mike

SP | **Chicago (NL)** | EXP MLB DEBUT: 2013 | H/W: 6-4 205 | FUT: #5 starter/RP | **6C**

Thrws L Age 26
2010 (6) Missouri State

Velo	Pitch	Grade
90-92	FB	+++
80-83	SL	+++
80-82	CU	+

Year	Lev	Team	W	L	Sv	IP	K	ERA	WHIP	BF/G	OBA	H%	S%	xERA	Ctl	Dom	Cmd	hr/9	BPV
2012	AA	Richmond	11	10	0	150	137	3.06	1.29	22.1	219	28	77	2.96	4.5	8.2	1.8	0.5	44
2013	AAA	Fresno	7	7	0	110	90	4.33	1.40	23.2	253	30	70	3.90	4.0	7.4	1.8	0.7	42
2013	MLB	SF Giants	0	3	0	28	29	10.25	1.99	11.3	367	43	50	8.91	3.2	9.3	2.9	2.6	99
2014	AAA	Fresno	8	8	0	148	131	4.44	1.59	24.2	290	36	71	4.67	3.9	8.0	2.0	0.5	56
2014	MLB	SF Giants	0	0	0	2	1	22.50	4.50	7.3	587	60	50	23.38	4.5	4.5	1.0	4.5	-23

Physical LH has good low-90s FB that induces lots of GBs, average SL he uses to generate swing-and-misses, and a below average CU. Gets good downhill plane and keep the ball down, though he struggles to repeat his delivery and has Ctl issues. Cmd trending in the right direction, but at 26, his future role is in question.

Kilome,Franklyn

SP | **Philadelphia** | EXP MLB DEBUT: 2018 | H/W: 6-6 198 | FUT: #2 starter | **9E**

Thrws R Age 19
2013 FA (D.R.)

Velo	Pitch	Grade
90-93	FB	+++
78-80	CB	+++
80-83	CU	++

Year	Lev	Team	W	L	Sv	IP	K	ERA	WHIP	BF/G	OBA	H%	S%	xERA	Ctl	Dom	Cmd	hr/9	BPV
2014	Rk	GCL Phillies	3	1	0	40	25	3.14	1.17	14.6	241	28	73	2.93	2.5	5.6	2.3	0.4	52

This one's all about projection. A reworked delivery resulted in better use of his huge frame and excellent athleticism. Low-90s FB could tick up with added strength; breaking pitch and CU both above average now and just need consistency. A long way off, but ingredients are there for #2 starter.

Kime,Dace

SP | **Cleveland** | EXP MLB DEBUT: 2016 | H/W: 6-4 200 | FUT: #4 starter/setupRP | **7C**

Thrws R Age 23
2013 (3) Louisville

Velo	Pitch	Grade
90-94	FB	+++
81-84	SL	+++
78-82	CB	+++
	CU	++

Year	Lev	Team	W	L	Sv	IP	K	ERA	WHIP	BF/G	OBA	H%	S%	xERA	Ctl	Dom	Cmd	hr/9	BPV
2011	NCAA	Louisville	1	2	0	25	25	3.96	1.40	7.0	246	33	71	3.45	4.3	9.0	2.1	0.4	63
2012	NCAA	Louisville	1	0	0	40	42	4.93	1.37	6.2	225	31	61	2.97	4.9	9.4	1.9	0.2	54
2013	NCAA	Louisville	6	1	1	69	83	3.00	1.22	10.3	247	36	73	2.77	2.6	10.8	4.2	0.1	142
2013	A-	Mahoning Val	0	2	0	24	26	2.98	1.45	11.5	218	31	77	2.86	6.0	9.7	1.6	0.0	31
2014	A	Lake County	7	14	0	136	108	5.22	1.50	21.0	278	33	65	4.57	3.7	7.1	1.9	0.8	47

Durable SP who struggled in first full season. Lack of pitch movement hurts ability to miss bats and can be hit hard. Throws with clean arm action and does nice job of mixing pitches. Command comes and goes and needs to improve CU. Can overuse CB, limiting its effectiveness.

Kingham,Nick

SP | **Pittsburgh** | EXP MLB DEBUT: 2015 | H/W: 6-5 220 | FUT: #3 starter | **8C**

Thrws R Age 23
2010 (4) HS (NV)

Velo	Pitch	Grade
90-93	FB	++++
83-85	CB	+++
	CU	+++

Year	Lev	Team	W	L	Sv	IP	K	ERA	WHIP	BF/G	OBA	H%	S%	xERA	Ctl	Dom	Cmd	hr/9	BPV
2012	A	West Virginia	6	8	0	127	117	4.39	1.19	18.9	243	29	65	3.55	2.6	8.3	3.3	1.1	98
2013	A+	Bradenton	6	3	0	70	75	3.09	0.99	20.5	218	29	71	2.43	1.8	9.6	5.4	0.8	143
2013	AA	Altoona	3	3	0	73	69	2.71	1.37	21.9	253	33	79	3.25	3.7	8.5	2.3	0.1	71
2014	AA	Altoona	1	7	0	71	54	3.04	1.35	24.7	262	32	77	3.58	3.2	6.8	2.2	0.4	56
2014	AAA	Indianapolis	5	4	0	88	65	3.58	1.10	24.7	220	26	68	2.63	2.8	6.6	2.4	0.6	63

FB sits in the 90-93 mph range and tops out at 95 with arm-side run. His CB/SL is an above-average offering and his CU continues to improve though it can still be firm. Stands tall in his delivery, but has consistent mechanics and release point, which lead to decent command.

Klein,Phil

RP | **Texas** | EXP MLB DEBUT: 2014 | H/W: 6-7 260 | FUT: Setup RP | **6B**

Thrws R Age 25
2011 (30) Youngstown State

Velo	Pitch	Grade
89-93	FB	+++
81-85	SL	+++
	CU	+

Year	Lev	Team	W	L	Sv	IP	K	ERA	WHIP	BF/G	OBA	H%	S%	xERA	Ctl	Dom	Cmd	hr/9	BPV
2013	A+	Myrtle Beach	1	0	0	13	12	2.05	0.68	6.6	139	19	67	0.07	2.0	8.2	4.0	0.0	110
2013	AA	Frisco	5	1	0	53	74	2.54	1.67	8.2	231	36	86	4.04	7.4	12.5	1.7	0.5	42
2014	AA	Frisco	3	0	10	33	42	0.82	0.88	5.1	138	23	90	0.53	3.8	11.4	3.0	0.0	121
2014	AAA	Round Rock	0	0	0	18	28	0.00	0.72	7.1	121	23	100	0.00	3.0	13.9	4.7	0.0	188
2014	MLB	Texas	1	2	0	19	23	2.84	1.11	4.4	170	21	83	2.78	4.7	10.9	2.3	1.4	86

Tall, strong RP who uses height and high arm slot to thrive. Held RHH to under .100 BA and posts great numbers with FB/SL combo. Can struggle to throw strikes due to moving levers in delivery, but has clean arm action. Hard SL is K pitch while FB only shows average velocity.

Kline,Branden

SP | **Baltimore** | EXP MLB DEBUT: 2015 | H/W: 6-3 210 | FUT: #3 starter/setupRP | **8E**

Thrws R Age 23
2012 (2) Virginia

Velo	Pitch	Grade
88-93	FB	+++
81-84	SL	+++
80-83	CU	++

Year	Lev	Team	W	L	Sv	IP	K	ERA	WHIP	BF/G	OBA	H%	S%	xERA	Ctl	Dom	Cmd	hr/9	BPV
2012	NCAA	Virginia	7	3	0	93	94	3.57	1.37	24.4	244	32	73	3.38	4.2	9.1	2.2	0.4	69
2012	A-	Aberdeen	0	0	0	12	12	4.50	1.33	12.5	262	33	67	3.86	3.0	9.0	3.0	0.8	99
2013	A	Delmarva	1	2	0	35	32	5.90	1.57	22.0	293	36	63	5.16	3.6	8.2	2.3	1.0	69
2014	A+	Frederick	8	6	0	126	95	3.85	1.39	23.1	287	34	73	4.27	2.3	6.8	3.0	0.6	78
2014	AA	Bowie	0	2	0	16	9	6.11	1.79	24.9	283	32	64	5.16	6.1	5.0	0.8	0.6	-57

Athletic SP who returned after breaking ankle in '13. Prospect status dimmed, but still has solid pitch mix. FB can be straight at times, but arm slot used to throw on good angle to plate. Needs better offspeed pitch to retire LHH. SL has moments of plus action, but tends to get on side of it.

Knebel,Corey — RP — Texas

EXP MLB DEBUT: 2014 | H/W: 6-3 195 | FUT: Setup RP / Closer | 7B

Thrws R Age 23
2013 (1-S) Texas

- 91-96 FB ++++
- 80-83 CB +++
- 84-86 CU ++

Year	Lev	Team	W	L	Sv	IP	K	ERA	WHIP	BF/G	OBA	H%	S%	xERA	Ctl	Dom	Cmd	hr/9	BPV
2013	A	West Michigan	2	1	15	31	41	0.87	0.77	3.6	138	23	88	0.26	2.9	11.9	4.1	0.0	154
2014	AA	Erie	3	0	1	15	23	1.20	1.07	5.3	159	27	93	1.76	4.8	13.8	2.9	0.6	137
2014	AAA	Toledo	1	1	2	18	20	1.99	0.83	4.7	105	16	73	0.10	4.5	9.9	2.2	0.0	76
2014	AAA	Round Rock	1	0	0	12	20	3.75	1.17	5.3	210	34	75	3.42	3.8	15.0	4.0	1.5	187
2014	MLB	Detroit	0	0	0	8	11	6.59	1.71	4.6	322	48	57	4.97	3.3	12.1	3.7	0.0	146

Max-effort RP who has pitch mix and aggressiveness to pitch in late innings. Establishes plate early with lively, hard FB and complements with power CB that features plus break. Doesn't use CU much, though shows flashes of becoming average. Keeps ball down and throws downhill.

Kohler,Chris — SP — Oakland

EXP MLB DEBUT: 2018 | H/W: 6-3 210 | FUT: #3 starter | 7E

Thrws L Age 19
2013 (3-S) HS (CA)

- 88-93 FB +++
- 77-79 CB +++
- CU ++

Year	Lev	Team	W	L	Sv	IP	K	ERA	WHIP	BF/G	OBA	H%	S%	xERA	Ctl	Dom	Cmd	hr/9	BPV
2014		(did not play in 2014)																	

Quick-armed SP who did not pitch due to minor elbow concern. Has potential to throw harder once he adds strength. Succeeds with solid secondary pitches, led by CB that has wicked bend. Possesses good feel for pitching and commands plate well for age. Needs time to develop.

Kolek,Tyler — SP — Miami

EXP MLB DEBUT: 2018 | H/W: 6-5 260 | FUT: #1 starter | 9C

Thrws R Age 19
2014 (1) HS (TX)

- 96-98 FB ++++
- 85-87 SL +++
- CB ++
- CU +

Year	Lev	Team	W	L	Sv	IP	K	ERA	WHIP	BF/G	OBA	H%	S%	xERA	Ctl	Dom	Cmd	hr/9	BPV
2014	Rk	GCL Marlins	0	3	0	22	18	4.50	1.59	10.8	262	33	69	3.82	5.3	7.4	1.4	0.0	7

Physically mature RH had the best velocity in the draft. Prior to the draft hit 102 mph, but FB sat at 92-94 post-draft. FB also has good late life to it and projects as a plus-plus offering. Throws both a SL and a CB, but both remain inconsistent. Rarely needed to use his CU in HS.

Kopech,Michael — SP — Boston

EXP MLB DEBUT: 2019 | H/W: 6-3 195 | FUT: #2 starter | 9E

Thrws R Age 18
2014 (1) HS (TX)

- 89-94 FB +++
- 80-83 SL +++
- CU ++

Year	Lev	Team	W	L	Sv	IP	K	ERA	WHIP	BF/G	OBA	H%	S%	xERA	Ctl	Dom	Cmd	hr/9	BPV
2014	Rk	GCL Red Sox	0	1	0	13	16	4.77	1.52	7.2	228	34	65	3.15	6.1	10.9	1.8	0.0	49

Tall, athletic SP who is all about projection. Long ways from majors, but has very high ceiling. Struggles to repeat delivery and slot, but has athleticism to improve. Quick arm creates FB movement with late life. Has feel for both SL and CU and SL could evolve into legitimate K pitch.

Krehbiel,Joseph — RP — Arizona

EXP MLB DEBUT: 2017 | H/W: 6-2 185 | FUT: Reliever | 7C

Thrws R Age 22
2011 (12) HS (FL)

- 91-93 FB +++
- SL ++
- CU +

Year	Lev	Team	W	L	Sv	IP	K	ERA	WHIP	BF/G	OBA	H%	S%	xERA	Ctl	Dom	Cmd	hr/9	BPV
2012	Rk	Orem	2	2	0	31	34	5.19	1.54	6.2	302	40	65	4.78	2.9	9.8	3.4	0.6	117
2013	A	Burlington	6	5	1	65	70	2.76	1.18	5.4	210	29	77	2.49	3.9	9.7	2.5	0.4	88
2014	A	Burlington	0	0	5	14	17	1.93	1.00	4.1	168	26	79	1.16	3.9	10.9	2.8	0.0	111
2014	A+	Visalia	1	0	3	25	28	1.43	0.88	4.2	155	22	86	1.05	3.2	10.0	3.1	0.4	112
2014	A+	Inland Empire	0	0	0	4	6	2.25	0.75	3.6	151	16	100	2.43	2.3	13.5	6.0	2.3	200

RH reliever had an impressive season, posting a 1.66 ERA and 11 Sv. Was traded from the Angels in July. FB sits a 91-93 mph and he comes after hitters from a low 3/4 arm slot that gives his stuff movement. Can be tough against both LHB and RHB and posted an oppBAA of .151.

Kubitza,Austin — SP — Detroit

EXP MLB DEBUT: 2017 | H/W: 6-5 225 | FUT: #4 starter | 7C

Thrws R Age 23
2013 (4) Rice

- 88-92 FB +++
- 81-85 SL +++
- 86-89 CT ++

Year	Lev	Team	W	L	Sv	IP	K	ERA	WHIP	BF/G	OBA	H%	S%	xERA	Ctl	Dom	Cmd	hr/9	BPV
2012	NCAA	Rice	6	5	0	80	73	2.70	1.22	20.2	210	28	76	2.33	4.3	8.2	1.9	0.1	50
2013	NCAA	Rice	8	4	0	109	134	2.06	1.09	23.7	188	29	79	1.60	4.0	11.1	2.8	0.0	110
2013	Rk	GCL Tigers	0	0	0	8	5	2.22	0.74	4.8	180	22	67	0.68	1.1	5.6	5.0	0.0	88
2013	A+	Lakeland	0	1	0	17	14	5.82	1.53	9.2	250	32	58	3.51	5.3	7.4	1.4	0.0	8
2014	A	West Michigan	10	2	0	131	140	2.34	1.08	22.2	210	29	79	2.16	3.0	9.6	3.3	0.3	111

Tall SP who finished 2nd in MWL in ERA. Was very good all year and succeeded with plus pitch movement. Mostly works with sinking FB and mixes in SL and occasional cutter. K rate likely to decline without wipeout pitch, but groundball rate very high. Can struggle with command at times.

Kukuk,Cody — SP — Boston

EXP MLB DEBUT: 2016 | H/W: 6-4 200 | FUT: #3 starter | 8D

Thrws L Age 21
2011 (7) HS (KS)

- 89-95 FB +++
- 81-83 SL +++
- 80-83 CU ++

Year	Lev	Team	W	L	Sv	IP	K	ERA	WHIP	BF/G	OBA	H%	S%	xERA	Ctl	Dom	Cmd	hr/9	BPV
2012	Rk	GCL Red Sox	2	0	0	10	16	0.90	0.60	6.8	96	20	83	0.00	2.7	14.4	5.3	0.0	204
2013	A	Greenville	4	13	1	107	113	4.63	1.48	17.7	203	28	67	3.16	6.8	9.5	1.4	0.4	5
2014	A	Greenville	3	0	0	24	29	1.88	1.25	19.5	210	31	86	2.62	4.5	10.9	2.4	0.4	92
2014	A+	Salem	4	7	0	78	87	5.29	1.82	18.1	244	34	69	4.33	8.2	10.0	1.2	0.2	-22

Athletic, powerful SP with off-field issues, but has upside. Tough to make hard contact against and has pitch mix to miss bats. Hard SL serves as wipeout pitch and offers enough velocity to pitch up. Significant control problems stem from inconsistent mechanics and slot. Could move to pen.

Labourt,Jairo — SP — Toronto

EXP MLB DEBUT: 2017 | H/W: 6-4 205 | FUT: #3 starter | 8D

Thrws L Age 21
2011 FA (DR)

- 91-96 FB +++
- 82-85 SL +++
- 81-83 CU +++

Year	Lev	Team	W	L	Sv	IP	K	ERA	WHIP	BF/G	OBA	H%	S%	xERA	Ctl	Dom	Cmd	hr/9	BPV
2012	Rk	GCL Blue Jays	0	3	0	38	39	3.79	1.61	14.0	262	35	76	4.28	5.4	9.2	1.7	0.5	37
2013	Rk	Bluefield	2	2	0	51	45	1.93	1.04	16.4	213	27	84	2.28	2.5	7.9	3.2	0.5	94
2014	A-	Vancouver	5	3	0	71	82	1.77	1.18	19.0	190	28	83	1.86	4.7	10.4	2.2	0.0	78
2014	A	Lansing	0	0	0	14	11	6.43	2.50	12.4	275	33	74	6.91	12.9	7.1	0.6	0.6	-202

Quick-armed SP who led NWL in ERA after demotion. Induces tons of groundballs with above average, sinking FB. Gets great extension in high delivery to pitch downhill. Lacks feel for consistent slot and delivery. Tough to make hard contact against FB and SL that flash plus.

Lail,Brady — SP — New York (A)

EXP MLB DEBUT: 2017 | H/W: 6-2 175 | FUT: #4 starter | 7D

Thrws R Age 21
2012 (18) HS (UT)

- 86-92 FB +++
- 77-80 CB +++
- 83-86 CU ++

Year	Lev	Team	W	L	Sv	IP	K	ERA	WHIP	BF/G	OBA	H%	S%	xERA	Ctl	Dom	Cmd	hr/9	BPV
2012	Rk	GCL Yankees	1	0	0	12	10	1.48	0.82	8.9	189	25	80	0.96	1.5	7.4	5.0	0.0	111
2013	Rk	GCL Yankees	4	1	0	54	51	2.33	0.81	16.4	204	28	68	1.12	0.8	8.5	10.2	0.0	149
2013	A+	Tampa	1	0	0	7	5	7.50	2.36	18.7	408	46	69	9.46	3.8	6.3	1.7	1.3	29
2014	A	CharlestonSC	8	4	0	97	95	3.71	1.27	22.0	279	36	71	3.76	1.6	8.8	5.6	0.6	134
2014	A+	Tampa	3	1	0	37	21	3.40	1.05	20.5	223	25	68	2.43	2.2	5.1	2.3	0.5	51

Command-oriented sinkerballer who throws with effort and long arm action, but gets job done with variety of pitches. Has tall, lean frame and works down in zone. No swing-and-miss pitch in arsenal, but CB can be thrown for strikes. CU can be too firm and hit hard by LHH.

Lamb,John — SP — Kansas City

EXP MLB DEBUT: 2015 | H/W: 6-4 205 | FUT: #4 starter | 7D

Thrws L Age 24
2008 (5) HS (CA)

- 87-93 FB +++
- 77-79 CB +++
- 78-81 CU +++

Year	Lev	Team	W	L	Sv	IP	K	ERA	WHIP	BF/G	OBA	H%	S%	xERA	Ctl	Dom	Cmd	hr/9	BPV
2012	Rk	Idaho Falls	0	1	0	7	8	7.61	1.55	15.5	310	37	56	6.78	2.5	10.1	4.0	2.5	132
2012	Rk	AZL Royals	0	0	0	5	6	6.92	1.54	5.7	290	41	50	4.07	3.5	10.4	3.0	0.0	111
2013	A+	Wilmington	4	12	0	92	76	5.66	1.39	20.4	295	34	61	4.99	1.9	7.4	4.0	1.3	101
2013	AAA	Omaha	1	2	0	16	10	6.75	1.38	22.4	250	29	48	3.66	3.9	5.6	1.4	0.6	13
2014	AAA	Omaha	8	10	0	138	131	3.98	1.48	22.0	260	31	77	4.68	4.4	8.5	1.9	1.2	52

Tall SP who is back at full strength after missing most of '11 and '12 with TJ surgery. Command isn't as good as before, but still has plus potential. Lively FB used early in count to set up average CB and CU that shows glimpses of becoming plus offering. Flyball pitcher subject to HR.

Langfield,Dan — SP — Cincinnati

EXP MLB DEBUT: 2016 | H/W: 6-2 195 | FUT: Setup RP | 7C

Thrws R Age 24
2012 (3) Memphis

- 92-95 FB +++
- SL +++
- CB ++
- CU ++

Year	Lev	Team	W	L	Sv	IP	K	ERA	WHIP	BF/G	OBA	H%	S%	xERA	Ctl	Dom	Cmd	hr/9	BPV
2010	NCAA	Memphis	4	4	1	39	47	4.62	1.67	10.3	313	41	76	6.03	3.5	10.8	3.1	1.4	120
2011	NCAA	Memphis	3	3	0	85	94	4.34	1.48	24.4	243	33	70	3.76	5.2	9.9	1.9	0.5	57
2012	NCAA	Memphis	7	6	0	93	111	2.80	1.26	25.3	210	31	77	2.55	4.5	10.7	2.4	0.3	88
2012	Rk	Billings	3	0	0	37	54	2.68	1.19	9.9	206	34	77	2.26	4.1	13.1	3.2	0.2	143
2014	A	Dayton	3	2	0	60	81	4.64	1.46	12.3	210	30	70	3.77	6.4	12.1	1.9	1.0	62

Missed '13 with injury and rebuilt stamina in pen prior to nine 2H starts. Piled up strikeouts with swing-and-miss stuff but struggled with BB and HR. Best pitches are mid-90s FB and a hard SL. FB/SL combo better in short stints as FB will flatten out, but probably gets another chance to start.

Law,Derek — RP — San Francisco

EXP MLB DEBUT: 2016 | H/W: 6-2 210 | FUT: Setup RP | **7B**

Thrws R Age 24
2011 (9) Miami Dade CC

Velo	Pitch	Grade
92-95	FB	++++
80-82	CB	++++

Year	Lev	Team	W	L	Sv	IP	K	ERA	WHIP	BF/G	OBA	H%	S%	xERA	Ctl	Dom	Cmd	hr/9	BPV
2012	A	Augusta	5	2	2	55	67	2.93	1.23	7.0	224	31	81	3.31	3.8	10.9	2.9	1.0	113
2013	Rk	AZL Giants	1	0	0	5	9	3.46	0.96	3.9	214	41	60	1.54	1.7	15.6	9.0	0.0	252
2013	A	Augusta	0	3	3	35	48	2.31	1.06	7.1	215	34	78	2.06	2.6	12.3	4.8	0.3	171
2013	A+	San Jose	4	0	11	25	45	2.14	0.83	4.2	220	42	75	1.61	0.4	16.1	45.0	0.4	298
2014	AA	Richmond	2	0	13	28	29	2.57	1.18	4.1	194	26	78	2.21	4.5	9.3	2.1	0.3	64

His season was cut short due to TJS. His FB took a tick forward sitting in the mid-90s up to 98 paired with a plus, power CB, generating plenty of Ks. In a small smaple in '14, his Ctl and Cmd took a step back but he has the making of a high leverage RP.

Leal,Erick — SP — Chicago (N)

EXP MLB DEBUT: 2018 | H/W: 6-3 180 | FUT: #4 starter | **7D**

Thrws R Age 20
2011 FA (Venezuela)

Velo	Pitch	Grade
88-91	FB	++
75-77	CB	++
	CU	++

Year	Lev	Team	W	L	Sv	IP	K	ERA	WHIP	BF/G	OBA	H%	S%	xERA	Ctl	Dom	Cmd	hr/9	BPV
2013	Rk	AZL Cubs	3	2	1	48	52	2.80	1.20	14.9	269	36	77	3.27	1.5	9.7	6.5	0.4	152
2014	A-	Boise	6	2	0	62	31	3.76	1.38	20.1	279	30	76	4.52	2.6	4.5	1.7	1.0	28

Continues to hold his own despite the lack of an overpowering FB. Heater sits at 88-91, topping out at 93 mph and he mixes in a decent mid-70s curve and a CU that remains a work in progress.

Leathersich,Jack — RP — New York (N)

EXP MLB DEBUT: 2015 | H/W: 5-11 200 | FUT: Reliever | **7C**

Thrws L Age 24
2011 (5) U Mass - Lowell

Velo	Pitch	Grade
91-93	FB	+++
78-81	CB	+++
	CU	++

Year	Lev	Team	W	L	Sv	IP	K	ERA	WHIP	BF/G	OBA	H%	S%	xERA	Ctl	Dom	Cmd	hr/9	BPV
2012	A+	St. Lucie	2	5	1	48		4.13	1.35	7.7	232	39	69	3.30	4.5	14.3	3.2	0.6	153
2013	AA	Binghamton	2	0	3	29	55	1.55	1.20	4.9	188	40	88	2.12	4.9	17.0	3.4	0.3	191
2013	AAA	Las Vegas	2	0	0	29	47	7.76	2.10	5.1	281	46	61	5.90	9.0	14.6	1.6	0.6	38
2014	AA	Binghamton	3	3	1	46	79	2.93	1.28	5.1	227	42	76	2.68	4.1	15.5	3.8	0.2	185
2014	AAA	Las Vegas	0	0	0	8	14	5.56	1.85	3.4	259	40	77	6.45	7.8	15.6	2.0	2.2	88

Outstanding Dom rates continue thanks to deception more than velo. Plus movement on FB that can cut in or run away from hitters. Also throws big-breaking CB and below-average CU. There's deception in his high-effort delivery, but can get too fine with location and behind in counts.

Leclerc,Jose — RP — Texas

EXP MLB DEBUT: 2016 | H/W: 6-0 165 | FUT: Setup RP | **7E**

Thrws R Age 21
2010 FA (DR)

Velo	Pitch	Grade
91-96	FB	+++
84-87	SL	+++
74-76	CB	++
83-86	CU	++

Year	Lev	Team	W	L	Sv	IP	K	ERA	WHIP	BF/G	OBA	H%	S%	xERA	Ctl	Dom	Cmd	hr/9	BPV
2013	A	Hickory	3	4	5	59	77	3.36	1.25	6.2	242	36	72	2.95	3.2	11.7	3.7	0.3	143
2014	A+	Myrtle Beach	4	1	14	57	79	3.31	1.33	5.6	195	27	81	3.46	5.8	12.5	2.1	1.3	85

Fast-armed RP who started strong, but ran out of gas late. Needs to work on command as his pure stuff is quite good. Arm action adds late life to solid-average FB and uses hard-breaking SL to miss bats. Lacks strength in smallish frame. K rate has increased at each level of minors.

Lee,Zach — SP — Los Angeles (N)

EXP MLB DEBUT: 2015 | H/W: 6-3 195 | FUT: #4 starter | **8D**

Thrws R Age 23
2010 (1) HS (TX)

Velo	Pitch	Grade
89-93	FB	+++
75-78	CB	+++
81-84	SL	+++
	CU	+++

Year	Lev	Team	W	L	Sv	IP	K	ERA	WHIP	BF/G	OBA	H%	S%	xERA	Ctl	Dom	Cmd	hr/9	BPV
2011	A	Great Lakes	9	6	0	109	91	3.47	1.22	18.3	247	30	73	3.39	2.6	7.5	2.8	0.7	82
2012	A+	Ranch Cuca	2	3	0	55	52	4.57	1.27	18.8	279	33	69	4.62	1.6	8.5	5.2	1.5	127
2012	AA	Chattanooga	4	3	0	65	51	4.28	1.40	21.1	273	32	71	4.27	3.0	7.0	2.3	0.8	63
2013	AA	Chattanooga	10	10	0	142	131	3.23	1.17	20.3	248	31	75	3.34	2.2	8.3	3.7	0.8	107
2014	AAA	Albuquerque	7	13	0	150	97	5.39	1.54	23.4	295	33	66	5.19	3.2	5.8	1.8	1.1	35

Still has a good low-90s FB that tops out at 95 with life and a four-pitch mix, but a drop in Dom and struggles with control doomed him. When he's on his FB generates good ground ball rates, and complements it with a SL, CU, and CB that he uses in any count. Gave up a career high 18 HR.

Leibrandt,Brandon — SP — Philadelphia

EXP MLB DEBUT: 2017 | H/W: 6-4 190 | FUT: #4 starter/RP | **7D**

Thrws L Age 22
2014 (6) Florida State

Velo	Pitch	Grade
85-88	FB	++
	SL	++
	CU	++++

Year	Lev	Team	W	L	Sv	IP	K	ERA	WHIP	BF/G	OBA	H%	S%	xERA	Ctl	Dom	Cmd	hr/9	BPV
2012	NCAA	Florida State	8	3	0	99	83	2.82	1.19	20.9	242	30	76	2.89	2.6	7.5	2.9	0.4	83
2013	NCAA	Florida State	10	4	0	89	77	3.44	1.34	23.1	262	32	76	3.84	3.0	7.8	2.6	0.7	76
2014	NCAA	Florida State	4	1	0	39	30	1.84	1.02	25.0	219	27	84	2.28	2.1	6.9	3.3	0.5	86
2014	Rk	GCL Phillies	1	2	1	19	22	4.22	1.15	15.2	270	37	62	3.22	0.9	10.3	11.0	0.5	178
2014	A-	Williamsport	2	3	0	41	45	2.20	0.90	21.8	201	28	75	1.49	1.8	9.9	5.6	0.2	148

All pitchability, he can locate his below-average FB with precision, even pitching inside, that sets up a monster CU. His SL is also a tick above average, but it's his overall moxie that gives him a chance. Young enough that if he'd find a couple mph on his fastball, his MLB future would be more secure.

Lemond,Zach — SP — San Diego

EXP MLB DEBUT: 2016 | H/W: 6-1 170 | FUT: Setup RP | **7D**

Thrws R Age 22
2014 (3) Rice

Velo	Pitch	Grade
91-93	FB	+++
80-83	CB	+++
81-84	SL	+
	CU	+

Year	Lev	Team	W	L	Sv	IP	K	ERA	WHIP	BF/G	OBA	H%	S%	xERA	Ctl	Dom	Cmd	hr/9	BPV
2012	NCAA	Rice	1	0	1	35	32	2.56	1.19	9.4	214	29	76	2.19	3.8	8.2	2.1	0.0	62
2013	NCAA	Rice	7	2	14	75	71	2.03	1.02	9.0	209	28	79	1.81	2.5	8.5	3.4	0.1	103
2014	NCAA	Rice	4	1	3	53	52	1.35	1.05	13.7	210	28	89	2.11	2.7	8.8	3.3	0.3	103
2014	A-	Eugene	2	3	0	38	34	3.79	1.16	13.7	267	34	65	3.01	1.2	8.1	6.8	0.2	131
2014	AA	San Antonio	0	0	0	4	2	0.00	0.25	12.3	81	10	100	0.00	0.0	4.5		0.0	99

3rd round pick worked as both a closer and a starter in college. Used as a starter in debut with good results. FB sits in the 91-93 mph, but jumps up to 94-96 mph in relief. Also has a CB and a below-avg SL and CU. Has simple and repeatable mechanics and walked just 5 in 42 innings of work.

Leon,Arnold — SP — Oakland

EXP MLB DEBUT: 2014 | H/W: 6-1 205 | FUT: #5 starter | **6A**

Thrws R Age 26
2008 FA (Mexico)

Velo	Pitch	Grade
89-94	FB	+++
75-79	CB	++
79-83	SL	+++
80-81	CU	+++

Year	Lev	Team	W	L	Sv	IP	K	ERA	WHIP	BF/G	OBA	H%	S%	xERA	Ctl	Dom	Cmd	hr/9	BPV
2012	AA	Midland	1	0	1	15	18	2.37	1.32	6.3	284	41	80	3.41	1.8	10.7	6.0	0.0	162
2012	AAA	Sacramento	3	0	0	35	31	1.79	1.16	6.4	208	24	92	3.01	3.8	7.9	2.1	1.0	57
2013	AA	Midland	4	5	0	72	48	3.86	1.36	23.2	299	33	75	4.84	1.4	6.0	4.4	1.1	89
2013	AAA	Sacramento	5	3	0	71	49	4.43	1.32	24.5	288	34	66	4.00	1.6	6.2	3.8	0.5	85
2014	AAA	Sacramento	10	7	0	145	128	4.97	1.52	23.3	294	36	67	4.80	3.2	7.9	2.5	0.7	76

Strong pitcher who has spent 3 yrs in AAA. Converted to SP in '13 to take advantage of deep repertoire. Can be very hittable and doesn't miss bats as pitches can be straight. CU may be best pitch with fast arm speed and fade. Can throw slow CB for strikes and generally commands FB.

Liberatore,Adam — RP — Los Angeles (N)

EXP MLB DEBUT: 2015 | H/W: 6-3 235 | FUT: Situational reliever | **6B**

Thrws L Age 27
2010 (21) Tennessee Tech

Velo	Pitch	Grade
89-94	FB	+++
80-82	SL	++
84-88	CU	+++

Year	Lev	Team	W	L	Sv	IP	K	ERA	WHIP	BF/G	OBA	H%	S%	xERA	Ctl	Dom	Cmd	hr/9	BPV
2012	AA	Montgomery	3	4	8	52	27	2.94	1.40	6.7	265	29	81	4.08	3.5	4.7	1.4	0.7	9
2012	AAA	Durham	1	1	1	21	21	1.29	1.24	5.3	233	32	88	2.54	3.4	9.0	2.6	0.0	87
2013	AA	Montgomery	0	0	1	2	3	0.00	0.50	6.6	151	27	100	0.00	0.0	13.5		0.0	261
2013	AAA	Durham	5	3	0	60	69	3.59	1.25	5.7	228	33	69	2.62	3.7	10.3	2.8	0.1	103
2014	AAA	Durham	6	1	4	65	86	1.66	0.89	4.5	190	30	81	1.25	2.1	11.9	5.7	0.1	176

Large-framed RP who repeated AAA to great success. Keeps oppBA low with FB that features heavy, late sink. Fools hitters with very good, deceptive CU. Breaking ball is rudimentary, but can throw for strikes. Rarely allows HR and could become setup RP with groundball tendencies.

Lindgren,Jacob — RP — New York (A)

EXP MLB DEBUT: 2015 | H/W: 5-11 180 | FUT: Closer | **8C**

Thrws L Age 22
2014 (2) Mississippi State

Velo	Pitch	Grade
89-94	FB	++++
82-86	SL	++++
80-83	CU	++

Year	Lev	Team	W	L	Sv	IP	K	ERA	WHIP	BF/G	OBA	H%	S%	xERA	Ctl	Dom	Cmd	hr/9	BPV
2014	NCAA	MississippiSt	6	1	3	55	100	0.82	0.87	7.8	129	29	90	0.37	4.1	16.3	4.0	0.0	202
2014	Rk	GCL Yankees	0	0	0	1	2	0.00	2.00	4.8	415	71	100	7.40	0.0	18.0		0.0	342
2014	A	CharlestonSC	1	0	1	5	11	1.80	0.20	3.8	66	24	0	0.00	0.0	19.8		0.0	374
2014	A+	Tampa	0	0	0	7	17	0.00	0.99	4.5	130	50	100	0.62	5.1	21.5	4.3	0.0	269
2014	AA	Trenton	1	1	0	11	18	4.02	1.34	5.8	160	31	67	1.88	7.2	14.5	2.0	0.0	83

Short, aggressive RP with dominating pitch mix. Projects as ideal closer with two plus pitches. FB may not be quickest, but has late, vicious life that makes it tough to elevate. Hard SL has significant shape and makes hitters look foolish. Needs to clean up control and command.

Lively,Ben — SP — Philadelphia

EXP MLB DEBUT: 2016 | H/W: 6-4 190 | FUT: #4 starter | **7C**

Thrws R Age 23
2013 (4) Central Florida

Velo	Pitch	Grade
92-93	FB	+++
84-86	SL	+++
80-82	CB	+++
	CU	++

Year	Lev	Team	W	L	Sv	IP	K	ERA	WHIP	BF/G	OBA	H%	S%	xERA	Ctl	Dom	Cmd	hr/9	BPV
2013	NCAA	Central FL	7	5	0	106	101	2.04	1.09	27.7	227	30	81	2.27	2.4	8.6	3.6	0.2	108
2013	Rk	Billings	0	3	0	37	49	0.73	0.89	11.4	168	28	91	0.87	2.9	11.9	4.1	0.0	154
2013	A	Dayton	0	1	0	4	7	2.25	0.75	14.3	151	32	67	0.29	2.3	15.8	7.0	0.0	241
2014	A+	Bakersfield	10	1	0	79	95	2.28	0.92	22.8	204	29	79	2.01	1.8	10.8	5.9	0.7	164
2014	AA	Pensacola	3	6	0	72	76	3.88	1.33	23.0	228	29	73	3.53	4.5	9.5	2.1	0.9	68

Relies on deceptive delivery, advanced feel for pitching, and quality pitch mix to keep hitters off balance. Has struck out more than a batter per inning at each stop while showing great durability. Works down in the zone; limits line drives and HR. Solid mechanics and delivery.

Lobstein, Kyle — SP — Detroit
EXP MLB DEBUT: 2014 | H/W: 6-3 200 | FUT: #5 starter | 6B

Thrws L | Age 25 | 2008 (2) HS (AZ)
85-90 FB ++ | 80-83 CB +++ | 77-79 SL ++ | 81-82 CU +++

Year	Lev	Team	W	L	Sv	IP	K	ERA	WHIP	BF/G	OBA	H%	S%	xERA	Ctl	Dom	Cmd	hr/9	BPV
2012	AA	Montgomery	8	7	0	144	129	4.06	1.45	22.8	256	32	73	4.09	4.3	8.1	1.9	0.8	47
2013	AA	Erie	7	4	0	95	83	3.12	1.25	25.8	255	32	76	3.41	2.6	7.9	3.1	0.6	90
2013	AAA	Toledo	6	3	0	72	65	3.50	1.36	23.2	264	34	73	3.50	3.1	8.1	2.6	0.2	80
2014	AAA	Toledo	9	11	0	146	127	4.07	1.48	24.1	297	37	73	4.62	2.6	7.8	3.0	0.6	89
2014	MLB	Detroit	1	2	0	39	27	4.37	1.25	22.8	241	28	65	3.35	3.2	6.2	1.9	0.7	43

Loose, tall SP who works down in zone and gets hitters to bury ball in ground. Ordinary stuff leads to high oppBA and can lack movement to pitches with limited arm speed. Locates FB well and commands CU that features both depth and fade. CB better than SL, but still not out pitch.

Lopez, Adam — SP — Chicago (A)
EXP MLB DEBUT: 2016 | H/W: 6-5 195 | FUT: #4 starter/setupRP | 7D

Thrws R | Age 25 | 2012 (21) Virginia Military
88-94 FB +++ | 81-85 SL +++ | CU ++ | CT ++

Year	Lev	Team	W	L	Sv	IP	K	ERA	WHIP	BF/G	OBA	H%	S%	xERA	Ctl	Dom	Cmd	hr/9	BPV
2012	Rk	Bristol	1	0	0	11	14	3.27	1.82	4.6	311	45	80	5.08	4.9	11.5	2.3	0.0	92
2012	A	Kannapolis	0	0	1	3	6	0.00	0.00	4.4	0	0		0.00	0.0	17.4		0.0	332
2013	A	Kannapolis	5	3	3	99	129	2.54	1.20	12.5	231	35	78	2.65	3.2	11.7	3.7	0.3	143
2014	Rk	AZL White Sox	0	0	0	4	8	0.00	1.67	6.3	202	44	100	3.16	8.6	17.1	2.0	0.0	95
2014	A+	Winston-Salem	0	1	0	7	9	5.14	1.29	7.2	168	27	56	1.87	6.4	11.6	1.8	0.0	53

Tall, lean SP who began year in August due to knee and elbow issues. Throws with excellent angle to plate and stuff plays up as result. Doesn't repeat delivery or arm slot consistently and impacts command and control. Uses cutter and SL to register Ks and CU has some potential.

Lopez, Eduar — SP — Los Angeles (A)
EXP MLB DEBUT: 2018 | H/W: 6-0 180 | FUT: #4 starter | 7D

Thrws R | Age 20 | 2012 FA (DR)
90-94 FB +++ | 78-82 CB +++ | 83-84 CU +

Year	Lev	Team	W	L	Sv	IP	K	ERA	WHIP	BF/G	OBA	H%	S%	xERA	Ctl	Dom	Cmd	hr/9	BPV
2013	Rk	DSL Angels	6	3	0	62	83	1.88	1.11	17.4	134	23	81	1.06	6.1	12.0	2.0	0.0	70
2014	Rk	AZL Angels	0	3	0	42	53	4.70	1.57	16.8	257	38	68	3.85	5.3	11.3	2.1	0.2	78

Short SP who flashed dominance in 1st year in U.S. Throws with excellent arm speed from quick, clean delivery to produce velocity and has some gas left in tank. Lacks height, but keeps ball down in zone to induce groundballs. Tough on RHH with breaking ball, but owns poor CU.

Lopez, Jorge — SP — Milwaukee
EXP MLB DEBUT: 2016 | H/W: 6-4 165 | FUT: #3 starter | 7D

Thrws R | Age 22 | 2011 (2) HS (PR)
88-92 FB +++ | CB +++ | CU +++

Year	Lev	Team	W	L	Sv	IP	K	ERA	WHIP	BF/G	OBA	H%	S%	xERA	Ctl	Dom	Cmd	hr/9	BPV
2011	Rk	AZL Brewers	0	0	0	12	10	2.25	1.33	12.5	278	35	81	3.39	2.3	7.5	3.3	0.0	92
2012	Rk	AZL Brewers	1	3	2	25	20	5.38	1.55	15.7	276	33	65	4.60	4.3	7.2	1.7	0.7	31
2013	A	Wisconsin	7	8	2	117	92	5.23	1.44	19.9	267	31	65	4.44	3.7	7.1	1.9	1.0	46
2014	A+	Brevard Cnty	10	10	0	137	119	4.59	1.38	23.1	271	33	67	4.17	3.0	7.8	2.6	0.8	77

Nice three-pitch mix features a good 90-94 mph sinking FB, a CB that flashes plus, and a below avg CU. FB command is average and he frequently misses his spots. Gets good spin on the breaker and keeps it down in the zone and CU remains average.

Lopez, Reynaldo — SP — Washington
EXP MLB DEBUT: 2017 | H/W: 6-0 185 | FUT: #2 starter | 9C

Thrws R | Age 21 | 2012 FA (DR)
93-96 FB ++++ | 76-78 CB +++ | 84-86 CU +++

Year	Lev	Team	W	L	Sv	IP	K	ERA	WHIP	BF/G	OBA	H%	S%	xERA	Ctl	Dom	Cmd	hr/9	BPV
2013	A-	Auburn	0	1	0	1	0	57.27	6.36	10.1	693	69	0	30.16	0.0	0.0		0.0	18
2013	A	Hagerstown	0	0	0	4	4	6.75	2.25	20.3	415	49	75	10.24	2.3	9.0	4.0	2.3	119
2014	A-	Auburn	3	2	0	36	31	0.75	0.83	18.8	129	18	90	0.36	3.8	7.8	2.1	0.0	56
2014	A	Hagerstown	4	1	0	47	39	1.34	0.81	19.0	169	22	84	0.89	2.1	7.5	3.5	0.2	95

Athletic starter blew up over two levels in 2014, let by explosive FB, hard-biting CB and a passable CU. Still needs to refine command and continue to develop secondaries, as well as prove he can withstand the rigors of a full season. But the package of his arsenal and athleticism is exciting.

Lorenzen, Michael — SP — Cincinnati
EXP MLB DEBUT: 2016 | H/W: 6-3 195 | FUT: #3 starter/closer | 8D

Thrws R | Age 23 | 2013 (1) Cal State Fullerton
92-96 FB ++++ | 81-83 CB +++ | 83-85 SL ++ | 80-82 CU +++

Year	Lev	Team	W	L	Sv	IP	K	ERA	WHIP	BF/G	OBA	H%	S%	xERA	Ctl	Dom	Cmd	hr/9	BPV
2013	Rk	AZL Reds	0	0	0	1	1	0.00	1.00	3.8	262	35	100	2.32	0.0	9.0		0.0	180
2013	A	Dayton	1	0	2	8	7	0.00	1.11	3.5	235	31	100	2.25	2.2	7.8	3.5	0.0	98
2013	A+	Bakersfield	0	1	2	5	6	6.92	2.12	5.1	290	37	70	7.15	8.7	10.4	1.2	1.7	-29
2013	AA	Pensacola	0	0	0	6	5	4.50	2.00	4.1	262	30	82	6.26	9.0	7.5	0.8	1.5	-90
2014	AA	Pensacola	4	6	0	120	84	3.14	1.30	20.6	248	29	78	3.54	3.3	6.3	1.9	0.7	42

Converted OF/RP fared well in first season as SP. Plus arm, athleticism, and feel for pitching aided transition straight to AA. Added SL and CU to his arsenal that helps neutralize lefties. Works down in zone, limits HRs, and can get hitters to chase. Needs to build arm strength.

Loux, Barret — SP — Chicago (N)
EXP MLB DEBUT: 2015 | H/W: 6-5 230 | FUT: #4 starter | 7D

Thrws R | Age 26 | 2010 (1) Texas A&M
89-94 FB +++ | 78-81 CB ++ | 82-84 SL +++ | CU +++

Year	Lev	Team	W	L	Sv	IP	K	ERA	WHIP	BF/G	OBA	H%	S%	xERA	Ctl	Dom	Cmd	hr/9	BPV
2010	NCAA	Texas A&M	11	2	0	105	136	2.83	1.07	24.0	209	31	75	2.34	2.9	11.7	4.0	0.6	149
2011	A+	Myrtle Beach	8	5	0	109	127	3.80	1.28	21.3	256	36	70	3.41	2.8	10.5	3.7	0.5	131
2012	AA	Frisco	14	1	0	127	100	3.47	1.27	20.8	251	30	74	3.53	2.9	7.1	2.4	0.7	67
2013	AAA	Iowa	4	6	0	80	76	4.84	1.64	18.8	274	35	69	4.51	5.2	8.6	1.7	0.5	32
2014		(did not play in 2014)																	

Tall RH has failed to live up to expectations and missed the season with TJS. Should be ready to resume action in '15 but his clock is ticking. Prior to the injury his FB was at 90-92 with a decent curve, an average SL, and a CU. Struggled with Ctl, but has potential. A move to relief seems likely.

Lugo, Luis — SP — Cleveland
EXP MLB DEBUT: 2017 | H/W: 6-5 200 | FUT: #4 starter | 7C

Thrws L | Age 21 | 2011 FA (Venezuela)
88-93 FB +++ | 74-77 CB ++ | 79-82 CU +++

Year	Lev	Team	W	L	Sv	IP	K	ERA	WHIP	BF/G	OBA	H%	S%	xERA	Ctl	Dom	Cmd	hr/9	BPV
2011	Rk	AZL Indians	0	2	0	7	8	6.34	2.54	12.7	333	43	76	8.45	10.1	10.1	1.0	1.3	-73
2012	Rk	AZL Indians	2	4	0	42	51	4.50	1.40	16.1	243	34	69	3.87	4.5	10.9	2.4	0.9	93
2013	A-	Mahoning Val	1	4	0	50	30	1.98	1.00	17.4	216	25	80	1.93	2.0	5.4	2.7	0.2	62
2013	A	Lake County	0	1	0	14	14	3.83	1.35	19.6	260	34	72	3.77	3.2	8.9	2.8	0.6	93
2014	A	Lake County	10	9	0	126	146	4.92	1.30	19.2	259	34	64	4.09	2.9	10.4	3.7	1.1	128

Big, physical SP who finished season on high note. Misses bats with variety of pitches, including quick FB. Uses advanced command and control to get ahead in count and use excellent CU to retire hitters. More of a flyball pitcher and will need better CB to keep hitters honest.

Magill, Matt — RP — Cincinnati
EXP MLB DEBUT: 2013 | H/W: 6-3 210 | FUT: Reliever | 7C

Thrws R | Age 25 | 2008 (31) HS (CA)
89-94 FB +++ | SL +++ | CU ++

Year	Lev	Team	W	L	Sv	IP	K	ERA	WHIP	BF/G	OBA	H%	S%	xERA	Ctl	Dom	Cmd	hr/9	BPV
2012	AA	Chattanooga	11	8	0	146	168	3.76	1.29	23.1	236	33	71	3.14	3.8	10.3	2.8	0.5	103
2013	Rk	AZL Dodgers	0	0	0	3	3	0.00	0.33	9.5	106	15	100	0.00	0.0	9.0		0.0	180
2013	AAA	Albuquerque	6	2	0	85	101	3.49	1.43	20.1	231	32	77	3.67	5.3	10.7	2.0	0.7	67
2013	MLB	LA Dodgers	0	2	0	27	26	6.62	2.02	22.0	260	29	71	6.74	9.3	8.6	0.9	2.0	-77
2014	AAA	Albuquerque	7	6	0	84	70	5.24	1.65	10.5	252	30	69	4.64	6.3	7.5	1.2	0.9	-18

RH stalled at AAA upon moving to relief. Gets good downhill plane on his four-pitch mix that features a low-90s FB up to 95, a wipeout SL, and a below average CU and CB. Very aggressive on the mound, showing good pitch sequencing. Lack of control continues to be the culprit.

Magnifico, Damien — SP — Milwaukee
EXP MLB DEBUT: 2015 | H/W: 6-1 185 | FUT: Setup RP | 7C

Thrws R | Age 23 | 2009 (5) Oklahoma
95-99 FB +++++ | SL +++ | CU ++

Year	Lev	Team	W	L	Sv	IP	K	ERA	WHIP	BF/G	OBA	H%	S%	xERA	Ctl	Dom	Cmd	hr/9	BPV
2012	NCAA	Oklahoma	3	1	2	51	34	3.70	1.59	10.7	280	33	75	4.24	4.4	6.0	1.4	0.2	7
2012	Rk	Helena	0	3	0	21	25	5.94	1.70	10.6	260	35	65	4.83	6.4	10.6	1.7	0.8	37
2013	A	Wisconsin	5	1	0	54	46	3.83	1.39	20.7	251	31	73	3.79	4.0	7.7	1.9	0.7	48
2013	A+	Brevard Cnty	0	2	0	26	17	6.18	1.87	12.3	302	35	66	5.77	5.8	5.8	1.0	0.7	-35
2014	A+	Brevard Cnty	8	6	0	120	76	3.75	1.27	22.3	245	27	73	3.59	3.2	5.7	1.8	0.8	34

Plus FB continues to be his calling card and has some of the best velo in the minors. FB sits in the mid-90s, topping out at 100 and backs it up with a SL and below-average CU. Lack of quality secondary offering limits his upside. At 23, he just completed High-A. so a move to relief is possible.

Manaea, Sean — SP — Kansas City
EXP MLB DEBUT: 2015 | H/W: 6-5 235 | FUT: #2 starter | 8C

Thrws L | Age 23 | 2013 (1-S) Indiana State
88-95 FB ++++ | 82-85 SL +++ | 84-87 CU ++

Year	Lev	Team	W	L	Sv	IP	K	ERA	WHIP	BF/G	OBA	H%	S%	xERA	Ctl	Dom	Cmd	hr/9	BPV
2011	NCAA	Indiana State	5	5	0	83	82	4.33	1.42	23.5	230	30	70	3.57	5.2	8.9	1.7	0.6	37
2012	NCAA	Indiana State	5	3	0	105	115	3.34	1.25	25.1	241	33	74	3.14	3.2	9.9	3.1	0.5	110
2013	NCAA	Indiana State	5	4	0	73	93	1.48	1.04	21.7	192	29	88	1.86	3.3	11.5	3.4	0.4	134
2014	A+	Wilmington	7	8	0	121	146	3.12	1.29	19.9	230	33	75	2.95	4.0	10.8	2.7	0.4	105

Big-framed LHP who made pro debut and led CAR in K while dominating last 2 months of season. Tough to make hard contact against with power arsenal and natural deception from low 3/4 slot. Control can be erratic at times due to inconsistent release point. Keeps ball down in zone.

Maples,Dillon — SP — Chicago (N)

Thrws R | Age 22 | 2011 (14) HS (NC)
EXP MLB DEBUT: 2017 | H/W: 6-2 195 | FUT: #3 starter | 8E

Velo	Pitch	Grade
93-95	FB	++++
75-78	CB	+++
80-83	CU	+++

Year	Lev	Team	W	L	Sv	IP	K	ERA	WHIP	BF/G	OBA	H%	S%	xERA	Ctl	Dom	Cmd	hr/9	BPV
2012	Rk	AZL Cubs	0	1	0	10	12	4.46	1.58	7.4	174	27	69	2.69	8.9	10.7	1.2	0.0	-30
2013	A-	Boise	5	2	0	42	41	2.14	1.33	17.4	238	32	82	2.84	4.1	8.8	2.2	0.0	66
2013	A	Kane County	0	2	1	34	34	8.42	1.87	14.6	255	34	51	4.67	8.2	8.9	1.1	0.3	-41
2014	Rk	AZL Cubs	0	2	0	10	10	3.56	1.19	10.1	174	25	67	1.71	5.3	8.9	1.7	0.0	34
2014	A-	Boise	0	2	0	17	13	12.56	2.85	16.3	374	45	51	8.82	10.5	6.8	0.7	0.0	-142

Slow to develop due to a rib injury that took longer to recover from than anticapted. Has a plus 93-95 mph FB with movement and a plus CB. Mechanics remain a work in progress and he has struggled to throw strikes. In 115 career innings, has walked 86 and has a WHIP of 1.71.

Mariot,Michael — RP — Kansas City

Thrws R | Age 26 | 2010 (8) Nebraska
EXP MLB DEBUT: 2014 | H/W: 6-0 190 | FUT: Middle reliever | 6B

Velo	Pitch	Grade
91-96	FB	++++
82-84	SL	+++
77-79	CB	++
80-84	CU	+

Year	Lev	Team	W	L	Sv	IP	K	ERA	WHIP	BF/G	OBA	H%	S%	xERA	Ctl	Dom	Cmd	hr/9	BPV
2012	AA	NW Arkansas	6	3	1	113	81	3.42	1.25	14.8	258	29	76	3.80	2.4	6.4	2.7	1.0	70
2012	AAA	Omaha	0	0	0	8	3	2.25	1.13	15.8	210	23	78	2.02	3.4	3.4	1.0	0.0	-12
2013	AAA	Omaha	4	5	11	60	66	3.59	1.40	5.4	258	35	75	3.81	3.7	9.9	2.6	0.6	95
2014	AAA	Omaha	2	1	2	20	25	4.95	1.30	5.9	252	35	63	3.76	3.2	11.3	3.6	0.9	135
2014	MLB	Kansas City	1	0	0	25	21	6.48	1.72	6.7	305	37	61	5.46	4.3	7.6	1.8	0.7	37

Aggressive RP who was up and down between KC and AAA. Has deep arsenal for RP and has good velocity. Doesn't have imposing figure, but has pure arm strength. Throws good strikes and uses two breaking balls as chase pitches. FB shows late movement while SL is best secondary.

Martes,Francis — SP — Houston

Thrws R | Age 19 | 2012 FA (DR)
EXP MLB DEBUT: 2018 | H/W: 6-0 170 | FUT: #3 starter/setupRP | 7D

Velo	Pitch	Grade
90-94	FB	+++
82-84	SL	++
80-82	CU	+++

Year	Lev	Team	W	L	Sv	IP	K	ERA	WHIP	BF/G	OBA	H%	S%	xERA	Ctl	Dom	Cmd	hr/9	BPV
2013	Rk	DSL Marlins	3	3	0	50	33	3.05	1.30	17.2	265	32	75	3.31	2.5	5.9	2.4	0.2	57
2014	Rk	GCL Astros	1	1	0	11	12	0.82	0.73	9.8	139	21	88	0.17	2.5	9.8	4.0	0.0	128
2014	Rk	GCL Marlins	2	2	0	33	33	5.18	1.48	17.8	238	33	61	3.22	5.5	9.0	1.7	0.0	33

Undersized SP with power arsenal and upside, but far away from majors. Can register Ks with quick arm and lively FB. Has alternated between CB and SL, though both need significant work. CU can flash above average and thrown with quick arm. Not much projection left in short frame.

Martin,Cody — SP — Atlanta

Thrws R | Age 25 | 2011 (7) Gonzaga
EXP MLB DEBUT: 2015 | H/W: 6-3 230 | FUT: #4 starter | 7C

Velo	Pitch	Grade
90-94	FB	+++
83-85	SL	+++
	CB	++
	CU	++

Year	Lev	Team	W	L	Sv	IP	K	ERA	WHIP	BF/G	OBA	H%	S%	xERA	Ctl	Dom	Cmd	hr/9	BPV
2011	A	Rome	1	0	6	24	35	1.49	0.91	6.4	209	33	90	2.08	1.5	13.1	8.8	0.7	213
2012	A+	Lynchburg	12	7	0	107	123	2.94	1.19	19.5	235	32	77	2.97	2.9	10.3	3.6	0.6	127
2013	AA	Mississippi	3	3	0	67	71	2.82	1.34	17.4	250	34	79	3.40	3.6	9.5	2.6	0.4	92
2013	AAA	Gwinnett	3	4	1	69	66	3.51	1.30	21.9	232	29	75	3.42	4.0	8.6	2.1	0.8	64
2014	AAA	Gwinnett	7	8	1	156	142	3.52	1.33	24.0	256	31	77	3.98	3.2	8.2	2.5	1.0	78

Features a good 91-94 mph FB that has late life and a swing-and-miss SL. Also has a curve and CU, both of which could develop into average offerings. Maintained the control improvements he made in 2013, but never got the chance to show what he can do in the majors.

Martin,Jarrett — RP — Milwaukee

Thrws L | Age 25 | 2009 (18) Bakersfield JC
EXP MLB DEBUT: 2015 | H/W: 6-3 230 | FUT: Reliever | 6B

Velo	Pitch	Grade
92-94	FB	+++
83-85	SL	+++
80-83	CU	+

Year	Lev	Team	W	L	Sv	IP	K	ERA	WHIP	BF/G	OBA	H%	S%	xERA	Ctl	Dom	Cmd	hr/9	BPV
2012	A	Great Lakes	4	5	0	77	78	4.31	1.44	20.5	224	30	69	3.37	5.6	9.1	1.6	0.5	31
2012	A+	Ranch Cuca	0	1	0	3	2	14.06	2.19	8.0	307	22	40	11.29	8.4	5.6	0.7	5.6	-109
2013	A+	Ranch Cuca	6	7	2	85	95	4.65	1.58	12.9	261	35	72	4.57	5.3	10.0	1.9	0.8	56
2013	AA	Chattanooga	0	0	0	10	11	1.76	2.25	4.7	277	38	91	5.68	10.6	9.7	0.9	0.0	-93
2014	AA	Chattanooga	1	1	7	54	64	3.32	1.51	5.1	182	27	77	2.76	8.0	10.6	1.3	0.2	-6

Raw stuff is not overpowering, but he misses bats with a plus, late breaking SL. FB tops out at 92 mph, but his mechanics and control are well below average. He walked 48 in 54.2 innings, but still managed to post a 3.29 ERA. Profiles as a fringy reliver, but one who racks up tons of Ks.

Martinez,Jose — SP — Arizona

Thrws R | Age 20 | 2011 FA (DR)
EXP MLB DEBUT: 2018 | H/W: 6-1 160 | FUT: #2 starter/RP | 8E

Velo	Pitch	Grade
92-95	FB	++++
76-79	CB	+++
81-84	SL	+
78-81	CU	+

Year	Lev	Team	W	L	Sv	IP	K	ERA	WHIP	BF/G	OBA	H%	S%	xERA	Ctl	Dom	Cmd	hr/9	BPV
2012	A-	Yakima	0	1	0	10	8	4.41	1.37	21.4	218	25	69	3.53	5.3	7.1	1.3	0.9	2
2013	A-	Hillsboro	2	3	0	38	30	4.03	1.18	15.2	157	18	67	2.21	5.9	7.1	1.2	0.7	-14
2014	A	South Bend	1	1	0	6	3	6.00	2.00	14.5	321	33	73	7.18	6.0	4.5	0.8	1.5	-63

Athletic hurler was limited to just 6 IP with an elbow injury. When heatlhy has a 93-95 mph FB. Uses plus arm-speed to generate easy velocity. Mechanics and release point are inconsistent. Currently relies heavily on FB, but also has a plus hard CB, a SL, and a seldom used CU.

Mateo,Luis — RP — New York (N)

Thrws R | Age 25 | 2011 FA (DR)
EXP MLB DEBUT: 2017 | H/W: 6-3 185 | FUT: #3 starter/RP | 8D

Velo	Pitch	Grade
92-95	FB	+++
86-89	SL	++++
	CU	+

Year	Lev	Team	W	L	Sv	IP	K	ERA	WHIP	BF/G	OBA	H%	S%	xERA	Ctl	Dom	Cmd	hr/9	BPV
2012	A-	Brooklyn	4	5	0	73	85	2.46	0.90	22.7	217	31	72	1.70	1.1	10.5	9.4	0.2	176
2013	A+	St. Lucie	1	1	0	8	11	4.39	1.59	12.0	302	43	75	5.37	3.3	12.1	3.7	1.1	146
2013	AA	Binghamton	0	1	0	3	2	12.00	3.00	17.5	415	44	63	12.86	9.0	6.0	0.7	3.0	-117
2014	Rk	GCL Mets	0	0	1	5	6	1.76	0.98	4.8	218	26	100	3.34	1.8	10.6	6.0	1.8	161
2014	A-	Brooklyn	0	0	0	5	4	7.20	1.60	5.5	332	37	57	6.60	1.8	7.2	4.0	1.8	99

Dynamic arsenal but ongoing elbow issues have hindered development. Age (25), extensive injury history, and 3 IP above A-ball indicates bullpen the likely path. Throws FB that touches 95 and a hard SL with plus command. CU has a ways to go, but FB/SL enough to rack up Ks out of the pen.

Matz,Steven — SP — New York (N)

Thrws L | Age 23 | 2009 (2) HS (NY)
EXP MLB DEBUT: 2016 | H/W: 6-2 200 | FUT: #2 starter | 8C

Velo	Pitch	Grade
92-95	FB	++++
75-79	CB	+++
84-86	CU	++

Year	Lev	Team	W	L	Sv	IP	K	ERA	WHIP	BF/G	OBA	H%	S%	xERA	Ctl	Dom	Cmd	hr/9	BPV
2012	Rk	Kingsport	2	1	0	29	34	1.55	1.14	19.1	164	24	88	1.75	5.3	10.6	2.0	0.3	65
2013	A	Savannah	5	6	0	106	121	2.63	1.17	20.2	223	32	78	2.54	3.2	10.3	3.2	0.3	116
2014	A+	St. Lucie	4	4	0	69	62	2.21	1.26	23.5	253	33	80	2.86	2.7	8.1	3.0	0.0	90
2014	AA	Binghamton	6	5	0	71	69	2.28	1.13	23.4	248	32	81	2.80	1.8	8.7	4.9	0.4	127

Missed '09-'11 to TJS, but has more than proven fully recovered. Hasn't missed rotation turn in two seasons and is unhittable for stretches. Leads with plus FB that can hit 98 coupled with CB that flashes plus and solid-average CU. Needs to refine command, but very high ceiling.

May,Trevor — SP — Minnesota

Thrws R | Age 25 | 2008 (4) HS (WA)
EXP MLB DEBUT: 2014 | H/W: 6-5 215 | FUT: #3 starter | 8D

Velo	Pitch	Grade
90-95	FB	+++
76-79	CB	+++
82-85	SL	++
81-84	CU	+++

Year	Lev	Team	W	L	Sv	IP	K	ERA	WHIP	BF/G	OBA	H%	S%	xERA	Ctl	Dom	Cmd	hr/9	BPV
2011	A+	Clearwater	10	8	0	151	208	3.63	1.24	22.7	221	34	71	2.82	4.0	12.4	3.1	0.5	133
2012	AA	Reading	10	13	0	149	151	4.89	1.45	22.8	248	30	70	4.53	4.7	9.1	1.9	1.3	55
2013	AA	New Britain	9	9	0	151	159	4.52	1.43	23.8	259	34	69	4.14	4.0	9.5	2.4	0.8	81
2014	AAA	Rochester	8	6	0	98	94	2.84	1.16	21.7	213	28	75	2.45	3.6	8.6	2.4	0.4	77
2014	MLB	Minnesota	3	6	0	45	44	7.96	1.79	20.8	316	38	55	6.43	4.4	8.8	2.0	1.4	57

Big, durable SP who reached majors. Cleaner delivery led to improved control and power arsenal becoming effective with efficient sequencing. FB command needs attention, though has good velocity and late movement. Downer CB is ahead of SL and owns solid CU.

Mayers,Mike — SP — St. Louis

Thrws R | Age 23 | 2013 (3) Mississippi
EXP MLB DEBUT: 2016 | H/W: 6-4 185 | FUT: #4 starter | 7C

Velo	Pitch	Grade
92-94	FB	+++
82-84	SL	+++
78-81	CU	++

Year	Lev	Team	W	L	Sv	IP	K	ERA	WHIP	BF/G	OBA	H%	S%	xERA	Ctl	Dom	Cmd	hr/9	BPV
2013	Rk	GCL Cardinals	1	0	0	12	13	1.50	1.00	9.2	151	19	91	1.69	4.5	9.8	2.2	0.8	72
2013	A	Peoria	0	3	0	24	14	3.73	1.41	20.4	299	33	75	4.63	1.9	5.2	2.8	0.7	62
2014	A+	Palm Beach	2	7	0	72	61	3.74	1.34	25.1	292	36	73	4.21	1.6	7.6	4.7	0.6	111
2014	AA	Springfield	6	5	0	76	52	2.84	1.37	24.5	274	33	78	3.66	2.7	6.1	2.3	0.2	55
2014	AAA	Memphis	0	0	0	5	4	7.20	2.00	24.1	390	41	75	10.36	1.8	7.2	4.0	3.6	99

Tall SP had another solid season. Has three average to above-average offerings including a good 90-93 mph FB. Lack of overpowering FB is compensated by an ability to throw strikes and a good SL. CU will need to improve as he moves up.

Mazzoni,Cory — SP — New York (N)

Thrws R | Age 25 | 2011 (2) North Carolina State
EXP MLB DEBUT: 2015 | H/W: 6-1 200 | FUT: #4 starter/RP | 7D

Velo	Pitch	Grade
90-94	FB	++++
72-75	CB	+++
	SP	++

Year	Lev	Team	W	L	Sv	IP	K	ERA	WHIP	BF/G	OBA	H%	S%	xERA	Ctl	Dom	Cmd	hr/9	BPV
2013	AA	Binghamton	5	3	0	66	74	4.36	1.35	21.2	273	37	67	3.86	2.6	10.1	3.9	0.5	130
2014	Rk	GCL Mets	0	1	0	4	7	4.50	1.50	17.3	307	54	67	4.17	2.3	15.8	7.0	0.0	241
2014	A+	St. Lucie	0	0	0	9	9	5.00	1.56	19.7	302	40	64	4.31	3.0	9.0	3.0	0.0	99
2014	AA	Binghamton	2	0	0	12	10	4.50	1.17	23.9	228	30	57	2.31	3.0	7.5	2.5	0.0	72
2014	AAA	Las Vegas	5	1	0	52	49	4.67	1.27	23.6	269	33	65	4.08	2.1	8.5	4.1	1.0	115

Endured yet another injury-shortened season. Stuff keeps improving year-over-year. FB can hit 97, but sits at 90-94. Arsenal also includes hard-breaking curve and inconsistent splitter. Shows good feel for pitching and above-average control. Move to pen very likely due to max-effort delivery.

McAvoy, Kevin — SP — Boston

EXP MLB DEBUT: 2017 | H/W: 6-4 210 | FUT: #4 starter | 7C

Thrws R Age 21
2014 (4) Bryant

89-94	FB	+++	
79-83	SL	++	
82-85	CU	++	

Year	Lev	Team	W	L	Sv	IP	K	ERA	WHIP	BF/G	OBA	H%	S%	xERA	Ctl	Dom	Cmd	hr/9	BPV
2012	NCAA	Bryant Univ	5	1	0	70	41	2.95	1.36	20.9	275	32	77	3.55	2.6	5.3	2.1	0.1	43
2013	NCAA	Bryant Univ	7	2	0	81	56	3.44	1.19	23.3	237	28	70	2.81	2.9	6.2	2.2	0.3	52
2014	NCAA	Bryant Univ	9	1	0	99	94	2.63	1.06	25.6	216	29	72	1.87	2.5	8.5	3.4	0.0	103
2014	A-	Lowell	0	2	0	28	23	1.92	0.93	9.6	225	29	77	1.66	1.0	7.4	7.7	0.0	125

Strike-throwing sinkerballer who may lack an out pitch, but lives in lower half of zone and is tough to elevate. FB velocity only average, but gets plus late movement. Rarely walks hitters despite pitch action. Slows arm on CU and fringy SL lacks power to miss bats. Has been tough on RHH.

McCullers, Lance — SP — Houston

EXP MLB DEBUT: 2016 | H/W: 6-2 205 | FUT: #2 starter / Closer | 8C

Thrws R Age 21
2012 (1-S) HS (FL)

91-96	FB	++++	
81-85	CB	++++	
82-84	CU	+	

Year	Lev	Team	W	L	Sv	IP	K	ERA	WHIP	BF/G	OBA	H%	S%	xERA	Ctl	Dom	Cmd	hr/9	BPV
2012	Rk	GCL Astros	0	1	0	11	12	1.64	1.09	10.8	244	34	83	2.29	1.6	9.8	6.0	0.0	151
2012	Rk	Greeneville	0	3	0	15	17	4.80	1.33	15.6	191	24	67	3.39	6.0	10.2	1.7	1.2	40
2013	A	Quad Cities	6	5	0	104	117	3.20	1.35	17.4	238	33	75	3.13	4.2	10.1	2.4	0.3	86
2014	A+	Lancaster	3	6	4	97	115	5.47	1.56	17.0	258	33	69	5.22	5.2	10.7	2.1	1.7	70

Max-effort pitcher who could move to RP. Has exceptional FB with plus life down in zone and wipes out hitters with both FB and power CB. Allowed HR, though can be attributed to home park. Generally keeps ball down, though CU is too firm. Needs FB command and CU to stick as SP.

McCullough, Mason — RP — Arizona

EXP MLB DEBUT: 2018 | H/W: 6-4 245 | FUT: Setup RP | 7D

Thrws R Age 22
2014 (5) Lander

93-96	FB	+++	
83-85	SL	+	

Year	Lev	Team	W	L	Sv	IP	K	ERA	WHIP	BF/G	OBA	H%	S%	xERA	Ctl	Dom	Cmd	hr/9	BPV
2012	NCAA	North Carolina	0	0	0	9	8	3.96	1.87	2.7	260	34	76	4.48	7.9	7.9	1.0	0.0	-53
2013	NCAA	North Carolina	0	1	0	12	14	0.74	0.91	2.7	105	17	91	0.29	5.2	10.4	2.0	0.0	65
2014	A-	Hillsboro	1	0	1	12	16	3.69	1.48	4.0	149	25	72	2.14	8.9	11.8	1.3	0.0	-9

Has an athletic frame, had as much velocity as any player in the draft. Attacks hitters with a good 93-96 mph FB that hits 100. Secondary offerings lack consistency and are highlighted by a mid-80s SL. Has little finese to his mechanics and at this point is just an all-out thrower.

McGowin, Kyle — SP — Los Angeles (A)

EXP MLB DEBUT: 2016 | H/W: 6-3 180 | FUT: #4 starter | 7D

Thrws R Age 23
2013 (5) Savannah State

86-93	FB	+++	
82-84	SL	+++	
83-85	CU	++	

Year	Lev	Team	W	L	Sv	IP	K	ERA	WHIP	BF/G	OBA	H%	S%	xERA	Ctl	Dom	Cmd	hr/9	BPV
2013	NCAA	Savannah State	12	2	2	120	134	2.02	1.10	27.7	230	32	81	2.34	2.3	10.0	4.3	0.2	136
2013	Rk	Orem	1	1	0	14	12	6.38	1.21	6.3	232	26	47	3.65	3.2	7.7	2.4	1.3	70
2014	Rk	AZL Angels	0	0	0	2	2	0.00	1.50	8.6	262	35	100	3.58	4.5	9.0	2.0	0.0	59
2014	A+	Inland Empire	1	5	0	58	48	2.94	1.15	23.1	237	29	76	2.97	2.5	7.4	3.0	0.6	85
2014	AA	Arkansas	0	1	0	5	3	5.40	1.20	20.1	299	31	60	5.08	0.0	5.4		1.8	115

Tall, savvy SP who ended season early due to elbow soreness. Exhibits athleticism in delivery and does nice job of varying speeds with multiple pitches. Won't miss many bats, but induces weak contact. CU is currently below average, but has potential to be better with sufficient arm speed.

McGrath, Daniel — SP — Boston

EXP MLB DEBUT: 2017 | H/W: 6-3 205 | FUT: #5 starter | 6B

Thrws L Age 20
2012 FA (Australia)

85-89	FB	+++	
71-75	CB	++	
77-82	CU	+++	

Year	Lev	Team	W	L	Sv	IP	K	ERA	WHIP	BF/G	OBA	H%	S%	xERA	Ctl	Dom	Cmd	hr/9	BPV
2013	Rk	GCL Red Sox	0	1	0	20	30	1.35	0.70	17.6	124	19	92	0.77	2.7	13.5	5.0	0.9	188
2013	A-	Lowell	3	3	0	33	35	4.89	1.27	16.9	237	32	60	3.17	3.5	9.5	2.7	0.5	94
2014	A	Greenville	6	6	0	97	81	4.08	1.36	21.4	226	27	72	3.55	4.8	7.5	1.6	0.8	23

Lean, tall SP who succeeds with limited velocity, but premium CU and pitch movement. Sequences with precision and commands plate early in count. Stiff delivery needs to be corrected to add velocity. CB is below average at present and can be too slow. Needs to throw more strikes.

McWilliams, Sam — SP — Philadelphia

EXP MLB DEBUT: 2019 | H/W: 6-7 190 | FUT: #3 starter | 8E

Thrws R Age 19
2014 (8) HS (TN)

88-92	FB	++	
	CB	++	
	CU	++	

Year	Lev	Team	W	L	Sv	IP	K	ERA	WHIP	BF/G	OBA	H%	S%	xERA	Ctl	Dom	Cmd	hr/9	BPV
2014	Rk	GCL Phillies	2	3	0	25	10	5.40	1.36	11.6	284	31	58	3.93	2.2	3.6	1.7	0.4	24

Lottery ticket because of his size and lack of history, his fastball velocity can vary from start to start. But it's a projectable body that is not near done filling out, and the hope is that he adds some velocity along with strength, and can develop consistent secondary stuff along with a cleaner delivery.

Mecias, Yoel — SP — Philadelphia

EXP MLB DEBUT: 2017 | H/W: 6-2 160 | FUT: #3 starter | 8D

Thrws L Age 21
2010 FA (Venezuela)

90-92	FB	+++	
78-80	SL	++	
80-82	CU	+++	

Year	Lev	Team	W	L	Sv	IP	K	ERA	WHIP	BF/G	OBA	H%	S%	xERA	Ctl	Dom	Cmd	hr/9	BPV
2012	Rk	GCL Phillies	0	2	2	41	34	2.18	1.04	11.4	216	25	85	2.67	2.4	7.4	3.1	0.9	87
2013	A	Lakewood	4	3	1	57	70	3.79	1.37	18.4	248	36	72	3.48	3.9	11.1	2.8	0.5	110
2014	Rk	GCL Phillies	0	1	0	17	10	4.76	1.59	18.7	284	33	67	4.15	4.2	5.3	1.3	0.0	-1
2014	A	Lakewood	3	3	0	33	23	3.25	1.14	18.8	236	28	72	2.88	2.4	6.2	2.6	0.5	64

On his way back from 2013 Tommy John surgery, showed glimpses of his mid-rotation upside. Thin but athletic, uses a low-90s FB with some movement, and pairs it with an excellent fading CU. His SL still needs refinement. Still young and growing into his body; is agressive but could enhance overall approach.

Medeiros, Kodi — SP — Milwaukee

EXP MLB DEBUT: 2019 | H/W: 6-2 180 | FUT: #2 starter | 9E

Thrws L Age 18
2014 (1) HS (HI)

92-94	FB	++++	
	SL	++++	
	CU	++	

Year	Lev	Team	W	L	Sv	IP	K	ERA	WHIP	BF/G	OBA	H%	S%	xERA	Ctl	Dom	Cmd	hr/9	BPV
2014	Rk	AZL Brewers	0	2	1	17	26	7.33	2.15	9.5	331	49	66	7.20	6.8	13.6	2.0	1.0	79

HS lefty was the 12th pick in draft. Unorthodox delivery from a very low ¾ arm slot. Does throw with effort and pumps his FB in at 92-94 mph. Also features a plus CB and with a wipeout SL. Because of his size and delivery there is risk here, but also the potential for an effective big leaguer.

Meisner, Casey — SP — New York (N)

EXP MLB DEBUT: 2018 | H/W: 6-7 190 | FUT: #4 starter | 7D

Thrws R Age 19
2013 (3) HS (TX)

92-94	FB	++++	
75-76	CB	+++	
80-82	CU	+	

Year	Lev	Team	W	L	Sv	IP	K	ERA	WHIP	BF/G	OBA	H%	S%	xERA	Ctl	Dom	Cmd	hr/9	BPV
2013	Rk	GCL Mets	1	3	0	35	28	3.08	1.17	14.0	238	30	71	2.45	2.6	7.2	2.8	0.0	78
2014	A-	Brooklyn	5	3	0	62	67	3.77	1.37	20.0	277	37	73	3.99	2.6	9.7	3.7	0.6	122

Impressive command profile given age and height. Puts up impressive Dom/Cmd numbers with plenty more projection. Throws plus FB with downward plane and a solid-average CB. Arm action is easy but delivery requires effort and lacks deception. Needs CU to become reliable option.

Mejia, Adalberto — SP — San Francisco

EXP MLB DEBUT: 2015 | H/W: 6-3 195 | FUT: #4 Starter | 7B

Thrws L Age 21
2011 FA (DR)

90-92	FB	+++	
81-84	SL	+++	
82-85	CU	++	
85-87	CT	++	

Year	Lev	Team	W	L	Sv	IP	K	ERA	WHIP	BF/G	OBA	H%	S%	xERA	Ctl	Dom	Cmd	hr/9	BPV
2012	A	Augusta	10	7	0	106	79	3.98	1.35	14.7	289	35	69	3.92	1.8	6.7	3.8	0.3	90
2013	A+	San Jose	7	4	0	87	89	3.31	1.13	21.5	234	29	76	3.34	2.4	9.2	3.9	1.1	119
2013	AAA	Fresno	0	0	0	5	2	3.60	1.40	21.1	262	20	100	6.76	3.6	3.6	1.0	3.6	-14
2014	AA	Richmond	7	9	0	108	82	4.67	1.39	20.7	281	33	67	4.29	2.6	6.8	2.6	0.8	71

Lanky, advanced LHP struggled in 2014, but made progress with mechanics and arsenal. He features a four-pitch mix, utilizing the fastball-slider combo to get swings-and-misses. He does not overpower hitters or rack up Dom numbers, but his pitchability and advance Cmd will allow him to flourish in the middle of a rotation

Mejia, Jefferson — RP — Arizona

EXP MLB DEBUT: 2018 | H/W: 6-7 195 | FUT: Reliever | 7C

Thrws R Age 20
2013 FA (DR)

90-93	FB	+++	
73-75	CB	++	
	CU	+++	

Year	Lev	Team	W	L	Sv	IP	K	ERA	WHIP	BF/G	OBA	H%	S%	xERA	Ctl	Dom	Cmd	hr/9	BPV
2013	Rk	DSL Cubs	0	0	0	9	6	3.00	1.00	11.5	191	24	67	1.46	3.0	6.0	2.0	0.0	45
2014	Rk	AZL Cubs	2	4	0	40	48	2.48	1.18	13.3	210	30	78	2.29	3.8	10.1	2.6	0.2	97

Tall, lanky RH reliever was part of the M. Montero deal. At 6-7, 190 he has some projectability left and already has a 90-93 mph FB. Also has a good CU and a CB with potential. Needs to figure out mechanics and learn to throw strikes, but he had an impressive state-side debut.

Mella,Keury — SP — San Francisco

EXP MLB DEBUT: 2017 | H/W: 6-2 200 | FUT: #3 Starter | 9D

Thrws R | Age 21 | 2012 FA (DR)

Velo	Pitch	Grade
91-95	FB	++++
75-78	CB	+++
79-81	CU	++

Year	Lev	Team	W	L	Sv	IP	K	ERA	WHIP	BF/G	OBA	H%	S%	xERA	Ctl	Dom	Cmd	hr/9	BPV
2013	Rk	AZL Giants	3	2	0	36	41	2.25	1.25	14.7	251	36	80	2.79	2.8	10.3	3.7	0.0	128
2014	A-	Salem-Kaizer	1	1	0	19	20	1.88	1.15	12.7	228	32	82	2.24	2.8	9.4	3.3	0.0	111
2014	A	Augusta	3	3	0	66	63	3.95	1.24	22.4	270	36	65	3.17	1.8	8.6	4.8	0.1	125

Strong RHP from the DR continued to make strides in 2014. Strong longer half and effort in his delivery generate plus velocity, but he repeats well and commands his pitches. FB up to 98 with sink, a CB that generates Ks, and a usable CU. Some see RP due to delivery, but he continues to make strides as a SP.

Melotakis,Mason — RP — Minnesota

EXP MLB DEBUT: 2016 | H/W: 6-2 205 | FUT: Setup RP | 6B

Thrws L | Age 23 | 2012 (2) Northwestern State

Velo	Pitch	Grade
88-94	FB	+++
81-84	SL	+++
80-83	CU	+

Year	Lev	Team	W	L	Sv	IP	K	ERA	WHIP	BF/G	OBA	H%	S%	xERA	Ctl	Dom	Cmd	hr/9	BPV
2012	Rk	Elizabethton	1	1	0	6	10	1.45	0.65	3.1	103	21	75	0.00	2.9	14.5	5.0	0.0	201
2012	A	Beloit	3	1	1	17	24	2.11	1.11	5.2	237	33	94	3.72	2.1	12.6	6.0	1.6	189
2013	A	Cedar Rapids	11	4	1	111	84	3.16	1.31	19.1	253	30	76	3.45	3.2	6.8	2.2	0.5	55
2014	A+	Fort Myers	3	1	1	47	45	3.45	1.57	8.3	274	35	79	4.48	4.6	8.6	1.9	0.6	49
2014	AA	New Britain	1	0	2	16	17	2.25	1.25	5.0	274	38	80	3.11	1.7	9.6	5.7	0.0	145

Tall, strong RP who returned to pen after SP in '13. Underwent TJ surgery in October and likely out for all '15. When healthy, combines decent velocity and strong SL from high 3/4 slot to add deception. Can miss bats as well as induce groundballs. Inconsistent control has been problem.

Mercedes,Melvin — RP — Detroit

EXP MLB DEBUT: 2014 | H/W: 6-3 250 | FUT: Setup RP | 7C

Thrws R | Age 24 | 2008 FA (DR)

Velo	Pitch	Grade
91-98	FB	++++
85-88	SL	+++
	CU	+

Year	Lev	Team	W	L	Sv	IP	K	ERA	WHIP	BF/G	OBA	H%	S%	xERA	Ctl	Dom	Cmd	hr/9	BPV
2012	A+	Lakeland	0	0	0	1		0.00	2.00	4.8	262	26	100	4.93	9.0	0.0	0.0	0.0	-225
2013	A+	Lakeland	3	1	11	28	17	0.96	1.00	4.5	226	26	93	2.18	1.6	5.5	3.4	0.3	73
2013	AA	Erie	2	1	12	25	19	1.44	1.28	3.9	246	28	97	3.85	3.2	6.8	2.1	1.1	54
2014	AAA	Toledo	0	3	3	60	31	4.94	1.41	5.5	289	31	68	4.92	2.4	4.6	1.9	1.2	37
2014	MLB	Detroit	0	0	0	2	2	0.00	0.00	5.6	0	0		0.00	0.0	9.0		0.0	180

Big, imposing RP who continues to make progress with control and command. Fires electric FB into zone, and SL has flashes of plus offering, but doesn't get many Ks. Lacks deception in max-effort delivery and can overthrow. Doesn't have feel for changing speeds, but doesn't need CU.

Mercedes,Simon — SP — Boston

EXP MLB DEBUT: 2017 | H/W: 6-4 230 | FUT: #4 starter/setupRP | 7D

Thrws R | Age 23 | 2012 FA (DR)

Velo	Pitch	Grade
91-97	FB	++++
78-83	SL	++
78-81	CB	++
82-85	CU	+

Year	Lev	Team	W	L	Sv	IP	K	ERA	WHIP	BF/G	OBA	H%	S%	xERA	Ctl	Dom	Cmd	hr/9	BPV
2013	A-	Lowell	2	2	1	63	57	3.14	1.25	19.8	258	33	74	3.18	2.4	8.1	3.4	0.3	99
2014	A-	Lowell	0	0	0	11	5	1.64	1.45	15.7	295	33	88	3.99	2.5	4.1	1.7	0.0	25
2014	A+	Salem	5	10	1	85	74	4.76	1.45	19.1	262	32	67	4.05	4.0	7.8	1.9	0.6	50

Big, angular SP who bypassed Low-A in aggressive assignment. Lacks stamina so could move to pen where heavy FB and power stuff could play up. Pitches inside and challenges hitters with FB while generating late sink due to arm action. Lacks consistency in secondary offerings.

Merejo,Luis — SP — Atlanta

EXP MLB DEBUT: 2018 | H/W: 6-0 175 | FUT: #3 starter | 7D

Thrws L | Age 20 | 2011 FA (DR)

Velo	Pitch	Grade
88-91	FB	+++
	CB	++
	CU	+

Year	Lev	Team	W	L	Sv	IP	K	ERA	WHIP	BF/G	OBA	H%	S%	xERA	Ctl	Dom	Cmd	hr/9	BPV
2012	Rk	GCL Braves	0	5	0	41	53	4.61	1.15	16.3	247	37	57	2.67	2.0	11.6	5.9	0.2	174
2013	Rk	Danville	1	0	0	10	11	0.00	1.30	13.7	221	32	100	2.53	4.5	9.9	2.2	0.0	75
2013	Rk	GCL Braves	0	0	0	6	1	0.00	1.33	12.5	191	20	100	2.35	6.0	1.5	0.3	0.0	-117
2014		(did not play in 2014)																	

Short Dominican lefty has a modest 89-91 mph fastball that tops out at 94. Also has a good, sharp-breaking CB, and an improved CU. Might be better suited in a relief role. Missed all of 2014 with TJS, but should be back on the mound in 2015.

Merritt,Ryan — SP — Cleveland

EXP MLB DEBUT: 2016 | H/W: 6-0 165 | FUT: #5 starter | 6B

Thrws L | Age 23 | 2011 (16) McLennan CC

Velo	Pitch	Grade
85-89	FB	+++
74-78	CB	++
79-82	CU	+++

Year	Lev	Team	W	L	Sv	IP	K	ERA	WHIP	BF/G	OBA	H%	S%	xERA	Ctl	Dom	Cmd	hr/9	BPV
2011	Rk	AZL Indians	0	0	1	8	10	1.11	1.48	8.7	304	44	92	4.13	2.2	11.1	5.0	0.0	158
2012	A-	Mahoning Val	3	4	0	66	40	4.09	1.50	20.4	306	35	72	4.64	2.3	5.5	2.4	0.4	54
2013	A	Lake County	6	9	0	126	91	3.43	1.27	21.5	285	33	75	4.02	1.3	6.5	5.1	0.7	100
2013	A+	Carolina	0	0	0	9	6	5.00	0.89	16.7	216	24	43	2.42	1.0	6.0	6.0	1.0	99
2014	A+	Carolina	13	3	0	160	127	2.59	0.96	24.2	221	26	76	2.32	1.4	7.1	5.1	0.7	109

Consistent SP with limited upside, but finished 3rd in CAR in ERA. Pitches aggressively with FB that he commands to all quadrants of strike zone. CB needs work, but spins well and can throw for strikes. Athletic delivery provides some deception on CU, but lacks size, velocity, and K pitch.

Meyer,Alex — SP — Minnesota

EXP MLB DEBUT: 2015 | H/W: 6-9 220 | FUT: #2 starter | 9D

Thrws R | Age 25 | 2011 (1) Kentucky

Velo	Pitch	Grade
93-97	FB	++++
83-87	SL	++++
81-83	CU	++

Year	Lev	Team	W	L	Sv	IP	K	ERA	WHIP	BF/G	OBA	H%	S%	xERA	Ctl	Dom	Cmd	hr/9	BPV
2012	A	Hagerstown	7	4	0	90	107	3.10	1.13	19.8	211	30	72	2.36	3.4	10.7	3.1	0.4	119
2012	A+	Potomac	3	2	0	39	32	2.31	1.03	21.4	209	26	79	2.15	2.5	7.4	2.9	0.5	82
2013	Rk	GCL Twins	0	0	0	8	16	1.11	1.23	10.9	235	51	90	2.46	3.3	17.8	5.3	0.0	248
2013	AA	New Britain	4	3	0	70	84	3.21	1.27	22.0	233	33	74	2.96	3.7	10.8	2.9	0.4	112
2014	AAA	Rochester	7	7	0	130	153	3.53	1.38	20.3	240	33	76	3.63	4.4	10.6	2.4	0.7	89

Tall, angular RHP who led IL in Ks. Holds plus velocity late in games and continues to post high K rate with power repertoire. Plus-plus FB thrown on downhill angle to plate to induce grounders and has improved hard SL to throw for strikes. CU can be effective at times, though lacks deception.

Mitchell,Andrew — RP — Chicago (A)

EXP MLB DEBUT: 2016 | H/W: 6-3 205 | FUT: Setup RP | 7E

Thrws R | Age 23 | 2013 (4) Texas Christian

Velo	Pitch	Grade
91-97	FB	+++
80-82	CB	++++
	CU	+

Year	Lev	Team	W	L	Sv	IP	K	ERA	WHIP	BF/G	OBA	H%	S%	xERA	Ctl	Dom	Cmd	hr/9	BPV
2011	NCAA	TCU	6	1	2	76	73	2.84	1.09	13.5	195	25	76	2.27	3.7	8.6	2.4	0.6	74
2012	NCAA	TCU	5	3	0	77	101	3.74	1.31	18.7	202	30	73	2.97	5.4	11.8	2.2	0.7	85
2013	NCAA	TCU	1	2	1	49	57	3.49	1.53	10.7	233	34	76	3.43	6.1	10.5	1.7	0.2	43
2013	Rk	Great Falls	1	3	0	56	47	4.50	1.55	17.5	265	31	73	4.68	4.8	7.6	1.6	1.0	24
2014	A	Kannapolis	4	3	0	65	83	5.39	1.81	9.7	217	32	69	4.15	9.3	11.5	1.2	0.4	-26

Hard-throwing RP who has right demeanor, velocity, and breaking ball to pitch in late innings, but can't throw strikes. Throws from low 3/4 angle and pitches exhibit nasty movement. Rushes delivery and inconsistent release point results in unacceptable walk rate. CB is dynamic pitch.

Mitchell,Bryan — SP — New York (A)

EXP MLB DEBUT: 2014 | H/W: 6-3 205 | FUT: #4 starter | 7C

Thrws R | Age 23 | 2009 (16) HS (NC)

Velo	Pitch	Grade
90-95	FB	++++
80-84	CB	+++
85-89	CT	+++
82-86	CU	+

Year	Lev	Team	W	L	Sv	IP	K	ERA	WHIP	BF/G	OBA	H%	S%	xERA	Ctl	Dom	Cmd	hr/9	BPV
2013	A+	Tampa	4	11	0	126	104	5.13	1.56	23.0	288	36	65	4.45	3.8	7.4	2.0	0.4	49
2013	AA	Trenton	0	0	0	18	16	1.98	1.04	23.4	214	28	79	1.82	2.5	7.9	3.2	0.0	94
2014	AA	Trenton	2	5	0	61	60	4.86	1.52	19.0	271	34	69	4.59	4.3	8.8	2.1	0.9	62
2014	AAA	Scranton/WB	4	2	0	41	34	3.71	1.48	19.7	279	33	79	4.81	3.5	7.4	2.1	1.1	57
2014	MLB	NY Yankees	0	1	0	11	7	2.45	1.18	14.7	244	29	77	2.56	2.5	5.7	2.3	0.0	55

Big, durable SP who has impressive arsenal, but can be too hittable. Struggles with release point and can overthrow at times, causing plus FB to flatten. At best when locating pitches down in zone and using CB as swing and miss pitch. Added CT to repertoire and still developing CU.

Molina,Marcos — SP — New York (N)

EXP MLB DEBUT: 2018 | H/W: 6-3 190 | FUT: #3 starter | 8D

Thrws R | Age 20 | 2012 FA (DR)

Velo	Pitch	Grade
94-96	FB	++++
	SL	++
84-86	CU	+++

Year	Lev	Team	W	L	Sv	IP	K	ERA	WHIP	BF/G	OBA	H%	S%	xERA	Ctl	Dom	Cmd	hr/9	BPV
2013	Rk	GCL Mets	4	3	0	53	43	4.41	1.32	20.0	272	33	66	3.76	2.4	7.3	3.1	0.5	85
2014	A-	Brooklyn	7	3	0	76	91	1.77	0.84	23.2	177	26	79	1.07	2.1	10.8	5.1	0.2	154

Breakout season in '14 NYPL. Athletic frame, repeats mechanics well, solid demeanor, and throws all three pitches for strikes. FB hits 96 with good life. CU flashes plus with nice sink and fade; SL is developing but can already miss bats. Needs to learn finer points of pitching as he advances.

Moll,Sam — RP — Colorado

EXP MLB DEBUT: 2017 | H/W: 5-10 185 | FUT: Reliever | 7C

Thrws L | Age 23 | 2013 (3) Memphis

Velo	Pitch	Grade
93-95	FB	+++
84-86	CB	+++
	SL	++

Year	Lev	Team	W	L	Sv	IP	K	ERA	WHIP	BF/G	OBA	H%	S%	xERA	Ctl	Dom	Cmd	hr/9	BPV
2011	NCAA	Memphis	3	1	1	40	48	2.69	1.22	14.7	226	34	76	2.39	3.6	10.8	3.0	0.0	115
2012	NCAA	Memphis	5	5	1	95	59	3.50	1.42	25.2	253	30	74	3.55	4.2	5.6	1.3	0.3	6
2013	NCAA	Memphis	9	3	0	94	106	2.30	1.04	24.2	199	29	76	1.62	3.1	10.1	3.3	0.0	118
2013	A-	Tri-City	3	1	0	30	29	1.80	1.00	11.5	191	26	80	1.43	3.0	8.7	2.9	0.0	94
2014	A-	Tri-City	0	1	0	13	7	4.15	1.62	6.4	317	35	75	5.38	2.8	4.8	1.8	0.7	30

Short LH reliever from Memphis was limited to just 13 IP. In relief FB showed an uptick in velocity, sitting at 92-94. He mixes in a power curve and shelved his below average CU. Mechanics and release point need to be more consistent and at 22 he has yet to make it above short-season ball.

Montas,Francellis — SP — Chicago (A)

EXP MLB DEBUT: 2016 | H/W: 6-2 185 | FUT: #2 starter | 8D

Thrws R Age 22
2009 FA (DR)

Velo	Pitch	Grade
91-98	FB	++++
83-87	SL	+++
84-88	CU	++

Year	Lev	Team	W	L	Sv	IP	K	ERA	WHIP	BF/G	OBA	H%	S%	xERA	Ctl	Dom	Cmd	hr/9	BPV
2013	A	Kannapolis	3	2	0	25	31	4.64	1.51	21.8	220	32	68	3.36	6.4	11.1	1.7	0.4	44
2013	A	Greenville	2	9	0	85	96	5.71	1.48	19.3	281	37	62	4.79	3.4	10.2	3.0	1.1	109
2014	Rk	AZL White Sox	1	0	0	14	23	1.29	0.93	13.1	132	23	92	1.16	4.5	14.8	3.3	0.6	163
2014	A+	Winston-Salem	4	0	0	62	56	1.60	0.95	23.4	205	27	84	1.75	2.0	8.1	4.0	0.3	109
2014	AA	Birmingham	0	0	0	5	1	0.00	0.40	16.1	66	7	100	0.00	1.8	1.8	1.0	0.0	2

Tall, thin pitcher who had breakout year, but missed time late after knee surgery. Showed improved command with hard, plus FB that has vicious late movement. Average SL becoming more consistent and can throw for strikes or use as chase pitch. Development of CU key to future role.

Montero,Rafael — SP — New York (N)

EXP MLB DEBUT: 2014 | H/W: 6-0 185 | FUT: #3 starter | 8C

Thrws R Age 24
2011 FA (DR)

Velo	Pitch	Grade
91-93	FB	+++
80-83	SL	++++
	CU	++

Year	Lev	Team	W	L	Sv	IP	K	ERA	WHIP	BF/G	OBA	H%	S%	xERA	Ctl	Dom	Cmd	hr/9	BPV
2013	AAA	Las Vegas	5	4	0	88	78	3.06	1.25	22.4	255	32	75	3.24	2.6	8.0	3.1	0.4	92
2014	Rk	GCL Mets	0	0	0	2	3	4.50	1.50	8.6	347	53	67	4.86	0.0	13.5		0.0	261
2014	A+	St. Lucie	0	0	0	4	4	0.00	0.75	14.3	151	22	100	0.36	2.3	9.0	4.0	0.0	119
2014	AAA	Las Vegas	6	4	0	80	80	3.60	1.29	20.5	234	31	72	3.10	3.8	9.0	2.4	0.5	77
2014	MLB	NY Mets	1	3	0	44	42	4.08	1.52	19.1	261	30	80	5.16	4.7	8.6	1.8	1.6	46

Struggled with Ctl during MLB debut but solid Dom. Due to size and FB velo, must rely on plus command, movement, and sequencing to succeed. Three-quarters arm angle creates deception in delivery. Slider is best overall pitch. Repeats mechanics, good mound presence, and maximizes arsenal.

Montgomery,Jordan — SP — New York (A)

EXP MLB DEBUT: 2017 | H/W: 6-4 225 | FUT: #4 starter | 7D

Thrws L Age 22
2014 (4) South Carolina

Velo	Pitch	Grade
88-92	FB	+++
72-76	CB	++
77-81	CU	+++

Year	Lev	Team	W	L	Sv	IP	K	ERA	WHIP	BF/G	OBA	H%	S%	xERA	Ctl	Dom	Cmd	hr/9	BPV
2012	NCAA	South Carolina	6	1	0	74		3.64	1.06	19.2	248	30	65	2.77	1.2	6.9	5.7	0.5	110
2013	NCAA	South Carolina	6	1	0	79	60	1.48	1.04	23.4	223	28	86	2.14	2.1	6.8	3.3	0.2	86
2014	NCAA	South Carolina	8	5	0	100	95	3.42	1.22	25.3	248	32	73	3.28	2.6	8.6	3.3	0.6	101
2014	Rk	GCL Yankees 2	0	1	0	5	5	5.19	1.35	7.2	254	34	57	3.09	3.5	8.7	2.5	0.0	80
2014	A-	Staten Island	1	0	0	13	15	3.44	1.15	7.4	229	33	67	2.24	2.7	10.3	3.8	0.0	129

Tall, advanced SP who could move quicky on basis of command, control, and above average CU. Doesn't throw hard and lacks power put-away offering, but mixes well and changes speeds. Varies shape of CB, though inconsistent. Throws all pitches for strikes and pitches downhill.

Montgomery,Mark — RP — New York (A)

EXP MLB DEBUT: 2015 | H/W: 5-11 205 | FUT: Setup RP | 7C

Thrws R Age 24
2011 (11) Longwood

Velo	Pitch	Grade
87-92	FB	+++
82-85	SL	+++
81-83	CU	+

Year	Lev	Team	W	L	Sv	IP	K	ERA	WHIP	BF/G	OBA	H%	S%	xERA	Ctl	Dom	Cmd	hr/9	BPV
2013	Rk	GCL Yankees	0	0	0	3	8	5.81	1.29	6.4	314	84	50	3.68	0.0	23.2		0.0	436
2013	Rk	GCL Yankees 2	0	0	0	2	2	0.00	0.50	3.3	151	22	100	0.00	0.0	9.0		0.0	180
2013	AAA	Scranton/WB	2	3	0	40	49	3.38	1.53	7.0	242	33	81	4.20	5.6	11.0	2.0	0.9	65
2014	AA	Trenton	1	0	2	21	17	0.85	0.99	4.8	179	22	95	1.68	3.4	7.2	2.1	0.4	56
2014	AAA	Scranton/WB	1	1	2	29	34	3.08	1.34	5.5	203	28	78	2.98	5.5	10.5	1.9	0.6	57

Short, deceptive RP who has seen velocity drop and SL become less crisp. Used to have plus-plus SL, but has regressed in last two years. Still used as K pitch, but effectiveness due more to crossfire delivery. FB shows running life, but lacks command, and he has a long arm action. Owns fringy CU.

Montgomery,Mike — SP — Tampa Bay

EXP MLB DEBUT: 2015 | H/W: 6-4 200 | FUT: #4 starter | 7D

Thrws L Age 25
2008 (1-S) HS (CA)

Velo	Pitch	Grade
88-94	FB	+++
74-78	CB	++
81-83	CU	+++

Year	Lev	Team	W	L	Sv	IP	K	ERA	WHIP	BF/G	OBA	H%	S%	xERA	Ctl	Dom	Cmd	hr/9	BPV
2012	AA	NW Arkansas	2	6	0	58	44	6.67	1.55	25.4	297	32	60	5.98	3.3	6.8	2.1	1.9	53
2012	AAA	Omaha	3	6	0	91	67	5.72	1.68	24.1	300	34	67	5.71	4.2	6.6	1.6	1.2	22
2013	A+	Charlotte	0	1	0	8	10	6.59	1.46	17.6	280	41	50	3.72	3.3	11.0	3.3	0.0	127
2013	AAA	Durham	7	8	0	108	77	4.74	1.47	23.2	267	31	68	4.30	4.0	6.4	1.6	0.7	25
2014	AAA	Durham	10	5	0	126	98	4.29	1.31	20.8	248	30	67	3.53	3.4	7.0	2.0	0.6	51

Tall SP who has spent 4 yrs in AAA and '14 was best of the lot. Induces groundballs with FB that he locates better than before. Still encounters mechanical problems at times which limits effectiveness of fringy CB. Most consistent pitch is CU that he trusts and uses in any count.

Mooneyham,Brett — SP — Washington

EXP MLB DEBUT: 2016 | H/W: 6-5 235 | FUT: #5 starter/RP | 7E

Thrws L Age 25
2012 (3) Stanford

Velo	Pitch	Grade
90-92	FB	+++
	SL	++
	CU	++

Year	Lev	Team	W	L	Sv	IP	K	ERA	WHIP	BF/G	OBA	H%	S%	xERA	Ctl	Dom	Cmd	hr/9	BPV
2013	A	Hagerstown	10	3	0	93	79	1.94	0.98	20.8	160	20	83	1.50	4.0	7.6	1.9	0.5	48
2013	A+	Potomac	0	3	0	11	6	13.78	2.70	20.4	352	37	46	9.58	10.5	4.9	0.5	1.6	-179
2014	A-	Auburn	0	0	0	4	3	6.75	2.00	9.6	262	27	71	6.97	9.0	6.8	0.8	2.3	-104
2014	A	Hagerstown	2	0	0	29	26	4.01	1.71	18.9	247	32	76	4.21	7.1	8.0	1.1	0.3	-29
2014	A+	Potomac	2	4	0	33	18	7.36	2.12	16.3	273	31	63	5.86	9.5	4.9	0.5	0.5	-151

Heralded pick from 2012 hasn't been able to get over the High-A hump; demotions likewise were unsuccessful. Consistency issues in delivery are ongoing, and have affected his ability to throw strikes. Size and left-handedness will provide more chances, but the window is closing.

Morales,Andrew — SP — St. Louis

EXP MLB DEBUT: 2018 | H/W: 6-0 185 | FUT: Reliever | 6B

Thrws R Age 22
2014 (2-S) UC-Irvine

Velo	Pitch	Grade
88-91	FB	++
79-82	SL	+++
	CU	++

Year	Lev	Team	W	L	Sv	IP	K	ERA	WHIP	BF/G	OBA	H%	S%	xERA	Ctl	Dom	Cmd	hr/9	BPV
2012	NCAA	Rio Hondo CC	12	1	0	103	78	2.01	1.07	25.0	230	28	81	2.34	2.0	6.8	3.4	0.3	86
2013	NCAA	UC Irvine	10	0	0	95	85	1.89	1.04	21.6	225	29	81	2.13	2.0	8.0	4.0	0.2	109
2014	NCAA	UC Irvine	11	2	0	135	141	1.53	0.90	26.5	189	27	82	1.22	2.2	9.4	4.3	0.1	128
2014	Rk	GCL Cardinals	0	1	0	5	6	3.60	1.00	6.4	124	11	75	2.40	5.4	10.8	2.0	1.8	67
2014	A+	Palm Beach	1	0	0	7	6	1.27	0.28	11.0	91	12	50	0.00	0.0	7.6		0.0	155

Short RH has a good idea of how to pitch and gets outs with a good 88-91 mph FB, CU, and a plus SL. Fared well in his limited pro debut, striking out 8.8 per nine. He profiles better as a RP down the road.

Moreno,Erling — SP — Chicago (N)

EXP MLB DEBUT: 2019 | H/W: 6-3 200 | FUT: #3 starter | 7D

Thrws R Age 18
2013 FA (Colombia)

Velo	Pitch	Grade
87-91	FB	++
73-76	CB	++
	CU	++

Year	Lev	Team	W	L	Sv	IP	K	ERA	WHIP	BF/G	OBA	H%	S%	xERA	Ctl	Dom	Cmd	hr/9	BPV
2014	Rk	DSL Cubs	0	1	0	8	6	1.11	1.11	8.0	208	26	89	1.93	3.3	6.7	2.0	0.0	48

Tall RH from Colombia signed for $650,000 and has yet to make his U.S. debut. He did log 11.1 IP between the VSL and the DSL. FB currently sits at 87-91, but could add velocity as he matures. Already has a good CU and a CB that has potential. Shows good feel for pitching.

Morgan,Adam — RP — Philadelphia

EXP MLB DEBUT: 2015 | H/W: 6-1 195 | FUT: #4 starter | 7D

Thrws L Age 25
2011 (3) Alabama Tuscaloosa

Velo	Pitch	Grade
90-93	FB	++++
84-86	SL	++++
75-78	CB	+++
80-82	CU	++

Year	Lev	Team	W	L	Sv	IP	K	ERA	WHIP	BF/G	OBA	H%	S%	xERA	Ctl	Dom	Cmd	hr/9	BPV
2012	A+	Clearwater	4	10	0	123	140	3.29	1.07	22.8	229	32	69	2.52	2.0	10.2	5.0	0.5	147
2012	AA	Reading	4	1	0	35	29	3.58	1.28	24.0	255	31	72	3.42	2.8	7.4	2.6	0.5	76
2013	Rk	GCL Phillies	0	1	0	7	8	2.57	0.86	12.9	233	34	67	1.56	0.0	10.3		0.0	203
2013	AAA	Lehigh Valley	2	7	0	71	49	4.05	1.55	19.4	295	33	78	5.39	3.3	6.2	1.9	1.3	41
2014		(did not play in 2014)																	

Shoulder injury wiped out 2014 regular season; he pitched some in the AFL but the velocity was not all the way back. If it can return, there's promise here as a four-pitch lefty with very good command and clean, repeatable delivery—and the club will have rotation openings to win. Spring training will be the test.

Morimando,Shawn — SP — Cleveland

EXP MLB DEBUT: 2016 | H/W: 5-11 195 | FUT: #5 starter | 6B

Thrws L Age 22
2011 (19) HS (VA)

Velo	Pitch	Grade
90-94	FB	+++
79-83	CB	+++
	CU	++

Year	Lev	Team	W	L	Sv	IP	K	ERA	WHIP	BF/G	OBA	H%	S%	xERA	Ctl	Dom	Cmd	hr/9	BPV
2011	Rk	AZL Indians	0	0	0	6	8	3.00	1.17	8.0	228	36	71	2.26	3.0	12.0	4.0	0.0	153
2012	A	Lake County	7	6	0	110	69	3.60	1.34	20.8	236	26	76	3.72	4.3	5.6	1.3	0.9	5
2013	A+	Carolina	8	13	0	135	102	3.73	1.41	21.2	232	28	74	3.49	5.1	6.8	1.3	0.5	4
2014	A+	Carolina	8	3	0	96	70	3.00	1.21	21.0	210	24	75	2.58	3.3	6.6	2.0	0.7	48
2014	AA	Akron	2	6	0	56	38	3.85	1.43	23.8	285	34	72	4.05	2.7	6.1	2.2	0.3	54

Athletic SP who succeeds despite lack of height. Doesn't have plus pitch at disposal, but works efficiently with three quality pitches. CU still in development phase, but has good separation from sneaky FB. Throws with little effort and gets good break on tight CB. Still needs more power.

Moscot,Jon — SP — Cincinnati

EXP MLB DEBUT: 2016 | H/W: 6-4 205 | FUT: #5 starter | 7C

Thrws R Age 23
2012 (4) Pepperdine

Velo	Pitch	Grade
90-93	FB	+++
	SL	++
	CU	++

Year	Lev	Team	W	L	Sv	IP	K	ERA	WHIP	BF/G	OBA	H%	S%	xERA	Ctl	Dom	Cmd	hr/9	BPV
2012	Rk	AZL Reds	0	1	0	2	1	0.00	3.81	7.0	336	38	100	10.58	21.4	4.3	0.2	0.0	-483
2013	A+	Bakersfield	2	14	0	115	112	4.61	1.26	21.4	251	30	67	4.07	2.8	8.8	3.1	1.3	100
2013	AA	Pensacola	2	1	0	31	28	3.19	1.48	22.2	280	34	81	4.62	3.5	8.1	2.3	0.9	70
2014	AA	Pensacola	7	10	0	149	111	3.14	1.26	24.3	256	30	77	3.55	2.6	6.7	2.6	0.7	69
2014	AAA	Louisville	1	1	0	17	9	5.79	1.29	23.4	237	20	65	5.23	3.7	4.7	1.3	2.6	4

Command pitcher with proven durability. Heady player with strong work ethi— knows how to get the most out of average arsenal. Keeps hitters on their toes with precise location and advanced sequencing; misses surprising number of bats with low-90s FB and average secondary stuff.

Munson,Kevin — RP — Arizona

EXP MLB DEBUT: 2015 | H/W: 6-1 215 | FUT: Reliever | 6C

Thrws R Age 26
2010 (4) James Madison

Velo	Pitch	Grade
92-95	FB	++++
	SL	++

Year	Lev	Team	W	L	Sv	IP	K	ERA	WHIP	BF/G	OBA	H%	S%	xERA	Ctl	Dom	Cmd	hr/9	BPV
2011	AA	Mobile	0	0	0	3	2	0.00	1.33	6.2	262	32	100	3.19	3.0	6.0	2.0	0.0	45
2012	AA	Mobile	3	5	3	53	64	6.28	1.55	5.3	269	38	57	4.25	4.6	10.9	2.4	0.5	90
2013	AA	Mobile	2	2	13	31	39	3.46	1.03	4.1	162	20	74	2.50	4.3	11.3	2.6	1.4	104
2013	AAA	Reno	0	2	1	23	27	5.09	1.39	4.0	278	39	61	3.88	2.7	10.6	3.9	0.4	134
2014	AAA	Reno	4	3	2	62	82	2.61	1.14	4.4	219	32	80	2.77	3.2	11.9	3.7	0.7	146

Short RH reliever spent his second full season at AAA where he impressed. Has a nice two-pitch FB/SL mix. FB sits in the 90-94 range and can top out at 95 mph. SL has nice swing and miss potential and good late depth. Has the ability to dominate, but gives up too many walks.

Musgrove,Joe — SP — Houston

EXP MLB DEBUT: 2017 | H/W: 6-5 230 | FUT: #3 starter | 8D

Thrws R Age 22
2011 (1-S) HS (CA)

Velo	Pitch	Grade
90-95	FB	+++
77-80	CB	+++
82-83	CU	++

Year	Lev	Team	W	L	Sv	IP	K	ERA	WHIP	BF/G	OBA	H%	S%	xERA	Ctl	Dom	Cmd	hr/9	BPV
2011	Rk	GCL Blue Jays	0	1	0	21	16	4.67	0.99	10.1	221	27	50	2.19	1.7	6.8	4.0	0.4	94
2012	Rk	Bluefield	0	0	0	8	9	1.13	0.63	13.8	181	27	80	0.36	0.0	10.1		0.0	200
2012	Rk	Greeneville	0	1	0	9	10	7.00	2.00	10.8	356	48	61	6.30	4.0	10.0	2.5	0.0	90
2013	Rk	GCL Astros	1	3	0	32	30	4.47	1.46	12.5	321	41	67	4.63	1.1	8.4	7.5	0.3	139
2014	A-	Tri City	7	1	0	77	67	2.81	0.96	19.4	228	29	71	2.22	1.2	7.8	6.7	0.5	127

Tall, physical SP who has spent 4 yrs in rookie and short-season ball. Uses height well and keeps ball down with heavy FB featuring plus, late life. Doesn't dominate, but mixes in nice CB that misses bats. Can be inconsistent, but locates pitches with aplomb. CU with splitter action improving. Potential breakout.

Nesbitt,Angel — RP — Detroit

EXP MLB DEBUT: 2015 | H/W: 6-1 235 | FUT: Middle reliever | 6B

Thrws R Age 24
2009 FA (Venezuela)

Velo	Pitch	Grade
92-97	FB	+++
83-87	SL	++
84-88	CT	+++
83-85	CU	++

Year	Lev	Team	W	L	Sv	IP	K	ERA	WHIP	BF/G	OBA	H%	S%	xERA	Ctl	Dom	Cmd	hr/9	BPV
2012	A-	Connecticut	4	3	0	36	23	4.74	1.66	8.1	325	38	69	5.20	2.7	5.7	2.1	0.2	47
2013	A	West Michigan	3	4	3	67	54	3.22	1.21	5.2	241	29	75	3.21	2.8	7.3	2.6	0.7	72
2014	A+	Lakeland	2	0	14	34	36	0.79	0.91	5.3	193	28	90	1.22	2.1	9.5	4.5	0.0	132
2014	AA	Erie	1	0	6	32	36	2.24	1.09	5.2	181	24	84	2.32	4.2	10.1	2.4	0.8	86

Breakout RP who finished 2nd in FSL in saves despite midseason promotion to AA. Improved K rate based upon emerging command of 4-pitch arsenal. Establishes plate with solid-average FB and has added cutter to repertoire. Throws with lot of effort and will stay in pen long-term.

Newcomb,Sean — SP — Los Angeles (A)

EXP MLB DEBUT: 2016 | H/W: 6-5 240 | FUT: #3 starter | 8D

Thrws L Age 21
2014 (1) Hartford

Velo	Pitch	Grade
90-94	FB	++++
80-82	SL	+++
77-80	CB	++
80-83	CU	++

Year	Lev	Team	W	L	Sv	IP	K	ERA	WHIP	BF/G	OBA	H%	S%	xERA	Ctl	Dom	Cmd	hr/9	BPV
2013	NCAA	Hartford	5	4	0	72	92	3.75	1.25	22.5	207	31	68	2.45	4.6	11.5	2.5	0.3	100
2014	NCAA	Hartford	8	2	0	93	106	1.26	0.96	25.1	163	25	85	0.99	3.7	10.2	2.8	0.0	103
2014	Rk	AZL Angels	0	0	0	3	3	3.00	1.33	6.2	262	27	100	5.98	3.0	9.0	3.0	3.0	99
2014	A	Burlington	0	1	0	11	15	7.23	1.61	12.4	292	42	53	5.00	4.0	12.1	3.0	0.8	126

Big, imposing SP who has advanced pitchability and impressive velocity. Could throw harder, but FB features electric life down in zone. Repeats delivery and adds hint of deception. Uses two breaking balls, neither of which are dominant at present. CU could become best secondary.

Newell,Ryan — SP — Miami

EXP MLB DEBUT: 2018 | H/W: 6-2 215 | FUT: #5 starter | 6C

Thrws R Age 23
2012 (7) Shorter

Velo	Pitch	Grade
90-93	FB	++
82-84	SL	++
82-84	CU	++
77-80	CB	++

Year	Lev	Team	W	L	Sv	IP	K	ERA	WHIP	BF/G	OBA	H%	S%	xERA	Ctl	Dom	Cmd	hr/9	BPV
2012	NCAA	Shorter College	9	4	0	81	110	3.55	1.28	23.9	170	27	72	2.32	6.4	12.2	1.9	0.4	64
2012	Rk	GCL Marlins	0	3	0	10	11	2.70	1.50	8.6	221	32	80	3.04	6.3	9.9	1.6	0.0	26
2012	A-	Jamestown	2	2	0	17	16	5.29	1.76	7.8	226	29	69	4.28	8.5	8.5	1.0	0.5	-58
2013	A-	Batavia	5	4	0	82	75	2.09	0.99	22.3	206	27	78	1.68	2.3	8.2	3.6	0.1	104
2014	A	Greensboro	8	7	0	109	94	3.38	1.20	23.1	263	32	73	3.47	1.7	7.7	4.5	0.7	111

Polished RH starter from NAIA succeeds without overpowering stuff. Posted solid numbers, commanding a 90-93 mph FB, a SL, CB, and a CU, all of which grade as average. Does a good job of changing speeds, but will be hard pressed to duplicate these results.

Nicolino,Justin — SP — Miami

EXP MLB DEBUT: 2015 | H/W: 6-3 190 | FUT: #2 starter | 8B

Thrws L Age 23
2010 (2) HS (FL)

Velo	Pitch	Grade
88-94	FB	++++
	CU	++++
75-78	CB	+++

Year	Lev	Team	W	L	Sv	IP	K	ERA	WHIP	BF/G	OBA	H%	S%	xERA	Ctl	Dom	Cmd	hr/9	BPV
2011	A	Lansing	1	1	0	8	9	3.29	1.59	12.0	322	44	77	4.69	2.2	9.9	4.5	0.0	137
2012	A	Lansing	10	4	0	124	119	2.47	1.07	17.2	242	31	78	2.65	1.5	8.6	5.7	0.4	132
2013	A+	Jupiter	5	2	0	96	64	2.25	1.11	21.0	247	29	81	2.78	1.7	6.0	3.6	0.4	80
2013	AA	Jacksonville	3	2	0	45	31	4.99	1.66	22.5	331	39	68	5.44	2.4	6.2	2.6	0.4	65
2014	AA	Jacksonville	14	4	0	170	81	2.86	1.07	23.6	252	28	74	2.91	1.1	4.3	4.1	0.5	67

LH has a plus feel for pitching. Held his own at AA, but drop in dominance is a red flag. Has a sinking FB that sits in the low-90s.Complements it with a plus CU that generates swing and misses, and a solid CB. Is able to keep the ball down and locate to both sides of the plate with ease.

Nola,Aaron — SP — Philadelphia

EXP MLB DEBUT: 2015 | H/W: 6-1 195 | FUT: #3 starter | 8B

Thrws R Age 21
2014 (1) LSU

Velo	Pitch	Grade
90-93	FB	++++
76-80	SL	+++
	CU	+++

Year	Lev	Team	W	L	Sv	IP	K	ERA	WHIP	BF/G	OBA	H%	S%	xERA	Ctl	Dom	Cmd	hr/9	BPV
2012	NCAA	LSU	7	4	0	89	89	3.63	1.07	18.2	259	33	69	3.30	0.7	9.0	12.7	0.9	161
2013	NCAA	LSU	12	1	0	126	122	1.57	0.80	26.8	189	25	81	1.18	1.3	8.7	6.8	0.3	140
2014	NCAA	LSU	11	1	0	116	134	1.47	0.83	26.5	174	25	84	1.08	2.1	10.4	5.0	0.3	148
2014	A+	Clearwater	2	3	0	31	30	3.18	0.93	16.7	215	26	72	2.63	1.4	8.7	6.0	1.2	135
2014	AA	Reading	2	0	0	24	15	2.63	1.25	19.5	270	29	88	4.50	1.9	5.6	3.0	1.5	69

Comes as a highly-polished college product who is not that far away. Low 3/4 arm slot produces good fastball movement. Slider and change-up grade as average pitches, and boasts impeccable command of all three. Some deception in delivery, and has a heavy ground-ball lean.

Nolin,Sean — SP — Oakland

EXP MLB DEBUT: 2013 | H/W: 6-4 230 | FUT: #4 starter | 7C

Thrws L Age 25
2010 (6) San Jacinto JC

Velo	Pitch	Grade
88-94	FB	+++
79-82	CB	++
81-84	SL	+++
80-82	CU	+++

Year	Lev	Team	W	L	Sv	IP	K	ERA	WHIP	BF/G	OBA	H%	S%	xERA	Ctl	Dom	Cmd	hr/9	BPV
2013	MLB	Toronto	0	1	0	1	0	49.09	7.27	11.1	693	66	29	40.14	8.2	0.0	0.0	8.2	-203
2014	Rk	GCL Blue Jays	0	0	0	2	5	0.00	0.48	6.9	144	52	100	0.00	0.0	21.4		0.0	404
2014	A+	Dunedin	0	1	0	7	9	3.80	1.13	14.0	167	27	63	1.45	5.1	11.4	2.3	0.0	86
2014	AAA	Buffalo	4	6	0	87	74	3.51	1.25	20.9	232	28	73	3.15	3.6	7.6	2.1	0.6	58
2014	MLB	Toronto	0	0	0	1	0	9.00	1.00	3.8	262	0		10.87	0.0	0.0		9.0	18

Durable SP who is stingy against LHH and exhibits above average command with deep arsenal. Establishes plate early with average FB thrown from high 3/4 slot. Not much life to FB, though deceptive CU can be very good. Hard SL is best of two breaking balls and hits spots with both.

Norris,Daniel — SP — Toronto

EXP MLB DEBUT: 2014 | H/W: 6-2 180 | FUT: #2 starter | 9C

Thrws L Age 21
2011 (2) HS (TN)

Velo	Pitch	Grade
91-96	FB	++++
83-87	SL	++++
70-75	CB	+++
82-86	CU	+++

Year	Lev	Team	W	L	Sv	IP	K	ERA	WHIP	BF/G	OBA	H%	S%	xERA	Ctl	Dom	Cmd	hr/9	BPV
2013	A+	Dunedin	1	0	0	5	1	0.00	0.60	17.1	66	7	100	0.00	3.6	1.8	0.5	0.0	-47
2014	A+	Dunedin	6	0	0	66	76	1.23	1.03	19.6	212	31	87	1.73	2.5	10.3	4.2	0.0	138
2014	AA	New Hampshire	3	1	0	35	49	4.60	1.39	18.5	244	35	70	4.23	4.3	12.5	2.9	1.3	126
2014	AAA	Buffalo	3	1	0	22	38	3.24	0.99	16.9	183	33	70	2.01	3.2	15.4	4.8	0.8	208
2014	MLB	Toronto	0	0	0	6	4	5.81	1.61	5.5	222	23	67	4.74	7.3	5.8	0.8	1.5	-73

Dominant SP who pitched on 4 levels in '14. Posts high K rate with exciting FB and SL. Generates velocity from high slot and quick arm adds late sink. Hard SL becoming consistent and misses bats. Mixes in solid-average CB and CU with depth. Command and stamina should improve.

Northcraft,Aaron — SP — San Diego

EXP MLB DEBUT: 2015 | H/W: 6-4 230 | FUT: #5 starter | 7C

Thrws R Age 24
2009 (10) HS (CA)

Velo	Pitch	Grade
88-92	FB	++
73-75	CB	+++
80-83	CU	+++

Year	Lev	Team	W	L	Sv	IP	K	ERA	WHIP	BF/G	OBA	H%	S%	xERA	Ctl	Dom	Cmd	hr/9	BPV
2011	A	Rome	7	8	0	113	88	3.34	1.32	20.3	253	30	76	3.61	3.3	7.0	2.1	0.6	56
2012	A+	Lynchburg	10	11	0	151	160	3.99	1.30	23.1	251	34	67	3.14	3.2	9.5	3.0	0.2	104
2013	AA	Mississippi	8	8	0	137	121	3.42	1.28	21.6	243	31	73	3.20	3.4	7.9	2.4	0.5	71
2014	AA	Mississippi	7	3	0	65	62	2.90	1.24	20.4	237	31	76	2.86	3.3	8.6	2.6	0.3	83
2014	AAA	Gwinnett	0	7	0	64	51	6.59	1.82	22.9	322	38	63	6.10	4.3	7.1	1.6	0.8	29

Finesse RH started well, but hit a wall when moved up top AAA and was traded to the Padres as part of the Upton deal. Has a decent 87-92 sinking FB that he locates well. Also has a good CU and an avg CB. Keeps the ball down in the zone. The move to PETCO gives him a chance.

Oberg,Scott — RP — Colorado

EXP MLB DEBUT: 2015 | H/W: 6-2 205 | FUT: Reliever | 7B

Thrws R Age 25
2012 (15) Connecticut

Velo	Pitch	Grade
93-95	FB	+++
	CB	+++
	CU	+

Year	Lev	Team	W	L	Sv	IP	K	ERA	WHIP	BF/G	OBA	H%	S%	xERA	Ctl	Dom	Cmd	hr/9	BPV
2010	NCAA	Connecticut	5	2	1	46	30	1.95	1.04	5.9	235	29	79	2.10	1.6	5.9	3.8	0.0	81
2012	NCAA	Connecticut	5	0	9	36	36	1.00	0.89	6.1	157	22	88	0.77	3.2	9.0	2.8	0.0	92
2012	Rk	Grand Junction	0	2	13	27	29	2.33	0.96	4.1	208	28	79	2.15	2.0	9.7	4.8	0.7	138
2013	A+	Modesto	1	6	33	53	61	1.86	1.15	3.8	185	25	88	2.36	4.6	10.3	2.3	0.7	81
2014	AA	Tulsa	0	1	15	27	21	2.66	1.03	3.9	224	27	74	2.23	2.0	7.0	3.5	0.3	90

15th round pick continued his development, but had season-ending surgery. Has a good low-90s FB can hit 95 mph. Also has a swing-and-miss CB and a decent CU. Struggles with control at times, but was being groomed as a future closer and has 61 saves in the past three seasons.

Ogando,Jochi

SP | **Seattle** | EXP MLB DEBUT: 2016 | H/W: 6-5 210 | FUT: #3 starter/setupRP | **8E**

Thrws R Age 21
2009 FA (DR)

Velo	Pitch	Grade
92-95	FB	++++
81-84	CB	++
78-80	SL	++
84-88	CU	+

Year	Lev	Team	W	L	Sv	IP	K	ERA	WHIP	BF/G	OBA	H%	S%	xERA	Ctl	Dom	Cmd	hr/9	BPV
2011	Rk	AZL Mariners	1	4	0	24	15	5.95	1.98	14.5	252	29	68	5.05	9.3	5.6	0.6	0.4	-133
2012	Rk	Pulaski	2	3	0	49	39	4.21	1.46	17.6	261	32	70	3.83	4.2	7.1	1.7	0.4	33
2013	A	Clinton	1	3	3	59	56	3.34	1.44	7.6	241	32	75	3.28	4.9	8.5	1.8	0.2	40
2014	A+	High Desert	4	2	0	58	52	7.13	1.86	12.4	305	37	61	6.00	5.6	8.1	1.4	0.9	12
2014	AA	Jackson	0	3	0	13	14	5.54	2.38	16.9	329	44	74	6.82	9.0	9.7	1.1	0.0	-51

Long, lean pitcher with plenty of upside, but very raw. Poor command; lack of second pitch needs immediate attention. Throws plus FB with whippy arm from low 3/4 slot. Arm speed is terrific. Cannot find strike zone and has little faith in secondary pitches. Hard CB and SL have potential.

Ogando,Nefi

RP | **Philadelphia** | EXP MLB DEBUT: 2015 | H/W: 6-2 185 | FUT: Setup RP | **8C**

Thrws R Age 25
2010 FA (D.R)

Velo	Pitch	Grade
96-98	FB	+++++
87-89	SL	+++

Year	Lev	Team	W	L	Sv	IP	K	ERA	WHIP	BF/G	OBA	H%	S%	xERA	Ctl	Dom	Cmd	hr/9	BPV
2011	A-	Lowell	1	5	0	57	38	2.84	1.47	16.3	248	29	80	3.64	4.9	6.0	1.2	0.3	-6
2012	A	Greenville	4	4	2	75	54	3.72	1.41	8.4	254	30	73	3.61	4.1	6.5	1.6	0.4	24
2013	A+	Salem	2	3	3	55	44	4.09	1.38	7.0	240	28	72	3.77	4.4	7.2	1.6	0.8	28
2014	AA	Reading	5	1	7	56	57	6.27	1.64	5.2	288	36	62	5.22	4.5	9.2	2.0	1.0	61

Velocity jumped after 2013 trade from BOS, touched 100 mph on occasion. Command of it still needs work, but has good movement. Pairs heater with a high-80s SL and occasional CU. The arsenal, with additional refinement, is back-end-of-the-bullpen stuff. Likely to make his debut in 2015.

Okert,Steven

RP | **San Francisco** | EXP MLB DEBUT: 2015 | H/W: 6-3 210 | FUT: Setup RP | **7C**

Thrws L Age 23
2012 (4) Grayson County College

Velo	Pitch	Grade
91-94	FB	++++
81-84	SL	+++
	CU	+

Year	Lev	Team	W	L	Sv	IP	K	ERA	WHIP	BF/G	OBA	H%	S%	xERA	Ctl	Dom	Cmd	hr/9	BPV
2012	Rk	AZL Giants	0	0	0	2		0.00	1.50	4.3	262	122	100	3.40	4.5	27.0	6.0	0.0	383
2012	A-	Salem-Kaizer	2	0	0	26	22	2.40	1.41	7.4	260	33	81	3.35	3.8	7.6	2.0	0.0	52
2013	A	Augusta	2	2	2	60	59	2.99	1.31	5.7	245	32	78	3.30	3.6	8.8	2.5	0.4	80
2014	A+	San Jose	1	2	19	35	54	1.54	1.25	4.3	250	41	90	3.23	2.8	13.8	4.9	0.5	191
2014	AA	Richmond	1	0	5	33	38	2.73	1.06	5.3	205	28	78	2.50	3.0	10.4	3.5	0.8	124

Athletic LH comes at hitters with plus FB up to 96, complemented with an average SL that generates swings and misses. Ctl and Cmd both trending in the right direction the past three seasons with Dom taking a huge leap forward (12.1). Clean arm action and smooth delivery. Has the tools to be an impactful late-inning RP.

Oliver,Chris

SP | **Philadelphia** | EXP MLB DEBUT: 2018 | H/W: 6-4 180 | FUT: #3 starter | **8E**

Thrws R Age 21
2014 (4) Arkansas

Velo	Pitch	Grade
90-94	FB	++++
	SL	+++
	CU	++

Year	Lev	Team	W	L	Sv	IP	K	ERA	WHIP	BF/G	OBA	H%	S%	xERA	Ctl	Dom	Cmd	hr/9	BPV
2012	NCAA	Arkansas	1	0	0	16	14	3.91	1.43	6.2	272	32	76	4.61	3.4	7.8	2.3	1.1	68
2013	NCAA	Arkansas	2	2	0	20	21	2.25	1.10	5.6	199	25	85	2.61	3.6	9.5	2.6	0.9	91
2014	NCAA	Arkansas	9	4	0	93	59	2.51	1.12	22.9	206	24	77	2.20	3.5	5.7	1.6	0.3	27
2014	Rk	GCL Phillies	0	1	0	3	4	14.06	2.81	9.0	399	54	44	9.18	8.4	11.3	1.3	0.0	-7
2014	A-	Williamsport	0	1	0	14	6	7.71	2.79	11.2	325	34	73	9.02	12.9	3.9	0.3	1.3	-260

Has pure present stuff, led by an explosive FB that he has trouble controlling, and two secondary pitches that flash average. He will work on his delivery and release, with hopes of corraling the FB without sacrificing movement. Could also add some bulk to his lanky frame. Upside, but needs coaching and innings.

Olmos,Edgar

RP | **Seattle** | EXP MLB DEBUT: 2013 | H/W: 6-4 220 | FUT: Reliever | **6C**

Thrws L Age 24
2008 (3) HS (CA)

Velo	Pitch	Grade
92-97	FB	++++
	SL	+++
	CU	++

Year	Lev	Team	W	L	Sv	IP	K	ERA	WHIP	BF/G	OBA	H%	S%	xERA	Ctl	Dom	Cmd	hr/9	BPV
2012	AA	Jacksonville	0	1	0	16	13	0.56	1.48	7.7	149	20	96	2.20	8.9	7.2	0.8	0.0	-92
2013	AA	Jacksonville	4	2	1	50	41	2.51	1.48	5.7	250	31	82	3.54	4.9	7.4	1.5	0.2	20
2013	MLB	Miami	0	1	0	5	2	7.20	2.00	4.8	332	29	75	9.34	5.4	3.6	0.7	3.6	-63
2014	AA	Jacksonville	1	0	2	26	16	4.48	1.34	6.0	230	23	73	4.41	4.5	5.5	1.2	1.7	-4
2014	AAA	New Orleans	2	3	1	51	44	3.87	1.29	6.4	254	31	71	3.62	3.0	7.7	2.6	0.7	77

Big, strong reliever stagnated in 2014, going 3-3 with a 4.06 ERA and was claimed on waivers by the Mariners in November. Still has good FB velo sitting at 92-95 mph. He pairs the heat with a mid-80s SL, both of which generate swings and misses.

Oramas,Juan

SP | **Toronto** | EXP MLB DEBUT: 2015 | H/W: 5-10 220 | FUT: #4 starter | **7C**

Thrws L Age 24
2006 FA (Mexico)

Velo	Pitch	Grade
89-92	FB	+++
	CB	++
	CU	++

Year	Lev	Team	W	L	Sv	IP	K	ERA	WHIP	BF/G	OBA	H%	S%	xERA	Ctl	Dom	Cmd	hr/9	BPV
2012	AA	San Antonio	3	4	0	35	33	6.41	1.57	19.2	283	34	60	5.25	4.1	8.5	2.1	1.3	60
2013	Rk	AZL Padres	0	0	0	7	15	1.29	1.14	13.9	233	56	88	2.19	2.6	19.3	7.5	0.0	296
2013	AA	San Antonio	3	2	0	55	64	3.10	1.23	18.6	250	34	77	3.34	2.6	10.4	4.0	0.7	135
2014	AA	San Antonio	3	0	0	25	23	1.07	1.19	25.3	252	33	90	2.68	2.1	8.2	3.8	0.0	108
2014	AAA	El Paso	7	7	0	110	93	5.64	1.63	21.3	303	36	67	5.60	3.7	7.6	2.1	1.1	55

Short SP hit a wall when promoted to AAA, going 7-7 with a 5.61 ERA. He was then claimed off waivers by the Blue Jays. Works both sides of plate with FB and has been able to post high Dom despite lack of true out pitch. Has tendency to leave balls up and could be subject to HR.

Ortega,Jose

RP | **Colorado** | EXP MLB DEBUT: 2012 | H/W: 5-11 185 | FUT: Setup RP | **7D**

Thrws R Age 26
2006 FA (Venezuela)

Velo	Pitch	Grade
91-98	FB	++++
82-86	SL	+++
82-84	CU	+

Year	Lev	Team	W	L	Sv	IP	K	ERA	WHIP	BF/G	OBA	H%	S%	xERA	Ctl	Dom	Cmd	hr/9	BPV
2012	MLB	Detroit	0	0	0	2	4	4.09	1.82	5.1	326	48	100	9.11	4.1	16.4	4.0	4.1	202
2013	AAA	Toledo	4	3	4	48	56	1.87	1.27	4.9	171	25	86	2.22	6.2	10.5	1.7	0.4	40
2013	MLB	Detroit	0	2	0	11	10	4.02	1.43	4.3	240	27	79	4.63	4.8	8.0	1.7	1.6	32
2014	AAA	Toledo	2	2	1	58	48	3.57	1.48	5.8	234	28	77	3.76	5.6	7.4	1.3	0.6	1
2014	MLB	Detroit	0	1	0	1	1	32.73	3.64	7.1	0	0	0	6.31	32.7	8.2	0.3	0.0	-718

Short RP who has appeared in majors last 3 seasons. More thrower than pitcher with violent delivery, but produces plus velocity. Lots of life to heater with heavy, late action. Tough to square up, especially when SL working at full capacity. Rarely changes speeds and has control problems.

Ortiz,Braulio

RP | **Chicago (A)** | EXP MLB DEBUT: 2016 | H/W: 6-5 205 | FUT: Setup RP | **7E**

Thrws R Age 23
2011 FA (DR)

Velo	Pitch	Grade
90-97	FB	++++
84-87	SL	++
	CU	+

Year	Lev	Team	W	L	Sv	IP	K	ERA	WHIP	BF/G	OBA	H%	S%	xERA	Ctl	Dom	Cmd	hr/9	BPV
2013	A	Kannapolis	0	4	3	62	74	3.47	1.32	11.7	197	28	73	2.69	5.6	10.7	1.9	0.4	58
2013	A+	Winston-Salem	1	3	0	27	29	6.97	1.92	21.4	268	35	62	5.34	8.0	9.6	1.2	0.7	-24
2014	A+	Winston-Salem	0	8	3	51	51	5.10	1.89	12.1	307	40	72	5.73	5.8	9.0	1.5	0.5	23
2014	AA	Birmingham	0	2	1	18	25	9.00	2.56	6.5	240	38	61	5.91	15.0	12.5	0.8	0.0	-162

Versatile arm who can start or relieve. Has upside to be late-innings guy, but maintaining delivery has been big problem. FB produces above average velocity and sink. Brute arm strength generates hard, wipeout SL, but can rarely throw it for strikes. Allows lots of flyballs.

Ortiz,Luis

SP | **Texas** | EXP MLB DEBUT: 2018 | H/W: 6-3 230 | FUT: #2 starter | **8D**

Thrws R Age 19
2014 (1) HS (CA)

Velo	Pitch	Grade
90-95	FB	+++
81-84	SL	+++
78-80	CB	++
80-84	CU	++

Year	Lev	Team	W	L	Sv	IP	K	ERA	WHIP	BF/G	OBA	H%	S%	xERA	Ctl	Dom	Cmd	hr/9	BPV
2014	Rk	AZL Rangers	1	1	0	13	15	2.06	1.15	8.7	245	35	80	2.44	2.1	10.3	5.0	0.0	148
2014	A	Hickory	0	0	1	7	4	1.29	1.00	8.9	168	16	100	2.42	3.9	5.1	1.3	1.3	6

High-upside arm with big frame and natural arm strength. Generates easy velocity with arm speed and throws from high arm slot. Locates FB with precision and can register Ks with multiple pitches. Pitch sequencing is crude and needs to maintain delivery and arm slot. Needs better CU.

Osuna,Roberto

SP | **Toronto** | EXP MLB DEBUT: 2017 | H/W: 6-2 230 | FUT: #3 starter | **8C**

Thrws R Age 20
2011 FA (Mexico)

Velo	Pitch	Grade
90-96	FB	++++
80-82	SL	++
84-85	CU	+++

Year	Lev	Team	W	L	Sv	IP	K	ERA	WHIP	BF/G	OBA	H%	S%	xERA	Ctl	Dom	Cmd	hr/9	BPV
2012	Rk	Bluefield	1	0	0	24	24	1.50	1.00	13.1	210	28	87	2.00	2.3	9.0	4.0	0.4	119
2012	A-	Vancouver	1	0	0	19	25	3.28	1.20	15.4	205	31	73	2.51	4.2	11.7	2.8	0.5	115
2013	A	Lansing	3	5	0	42	51	5.56	1.19	16.9	247	33	55	3.78	2.4	10.9	4.6	1.3	151
2014	Rk	GCL Blue Jays	0	0	0	1	2	0.00	0.00	2.8	0	0		0.00	0.0	18.0		0.0	342
2014	A+	Dunedin	0	2	0	22	30	6.55	1.68	14.1	311	44	62	5.88	3.7	12.3	3.3	1.2	140

Large-framed SP who returned in August after TJ surgery in July '13. Throws with little effort in delivery and offers deceptive CU with impressive arm speed. Throws hard with all offerings and keeps ball low in zone while posting high K rate. Shows feel for stuff despite limited experience.

Overton,Dillon

SP | **Oakland** | EXP MLB DEBUT: 2016 | H/W: 6-2 170 | FUT: #3 starter | **7B**

Thrws L Age 23
2013 (2) Oklahoma

Velo	Pitch	Grade
87-94	FB	+++
76-79	CB	+++
81-84	CU	+++

Year	Lev	Team	W	L	Sv	IP	K	ERA	WHIP	BF/G	OBA	H%	S%	xERA	Ctl	Dom	Cmd	hr/9	BPV
2011	NCAA	Oklahoma	8	4	0	74	59	2.31	1.42	13.7	256	32	83	3.42	4.0	7.2	1.8	0.1	39
2012	NCAA	Oklahoma	6	3	0	122	126	3.17	1.24	22.5	269	36	74	3.43	1.8	9.3	5.3	0.4	137
2013	NCAA	Oklahoma	9	3	0	92	79	3.03	1.24	23.4	259	33	74	3.08	2.2	7.7	3.4	0.2	96
2014	Rk	AZL Athletics	0	2	0	22	31	1.64	1.00	12.0	234	38	82	1.92	1.2	12.7	10.3	0.0	213
2014	A-	Vermont	0	1	0	15	22	2.40	0.80	10.9	206	35	67	1.06	0.6	13.2	22.0	0.0	239

Lean, polished SP who returned from TJ surgery in June. Has quality pitch mix and velocity gas returned, along with break on improving CB. Keeps ball down in zone and keeps hitters off-guard with location and ability to change speeds. Needs to stay healthy to mute durability concerns.

Owens,Henry — SP — Boston

EXP MLB DEBUT: 2015 | H/W: 6-6 205 | FUT: #3 starter | 8A

Thrws L Age 22
2011 (1-S) HS (CA)

Velo	Pitch	Grade
88-94	FB	++++
74-78	CB	+++
78-83	CU	++++

Year	Lev	Team	W	L	Sv	IP	K	ERA	WHIP	BF/G	OBA	H%	S%	xERA	Ctl	Dom	Cmd	hr/9	BPV
2012	A	Greenville	12	5	0	101	130	4.89	1.45	18.8	259	37	67	4.23	4.2	11.6	2.8	0.9	113
2013	A+	Salem	8	5	0	104	123	2.94	1.14	20.6	183	26	75	2.17	4.6	10.6	2.3	0.5	86
2013	AA	Portland	3	1	0	30	46	1.79	1.10	19.6	175	28	90	2.29	4.5	13.8	3.1	0.9	144
2014	AA	Portland	14	4	0	121	126	2.60	1.12	23.9	207	28	78	2.34	3.5	9.4	2.7	0.4	92
2014	AAA	Pawtucket	3	1	0	38	44	4.03	1.16	25.2	230	31	68	3.17	2.8	10.4	3.7	0.9	129

Tall, lanky LHP who was EL pitcher of year after leading circuit in Ks. Posts high Dom and gets grounders with impressive, deceptive FB and CU. Can dominate at times, though command can be erratic despite improved control. Development of CB will ultimately dictate future success.

Parsons,Wes — SP — Atlanta

EXP MLB DEBUT: 2017 | H/W: 6-5 190 | FUT: #4 starter | 7C

Thrws R Age 22
2012 FA Jackson State CC

Velo	Pitch	Grade
90-93	FB	+++
80-83	CB	+++
	CU	++

Year	Lev	Team	W	L	Sv	IP	K	ERA	WHIP	BF/G	OBA	H%	S%	xERA	Ctl	Dom	Cmd	hr/9	BPV
2013	A	Rome	7	7	0	109	101	2.64	1.03	22.1	228	29	75	2.33	1.7	8.3	4.8	0.4	121
2014	A+	Lynchburg	4	7	0	113	96	5.01	1.35	20.5	272	33	63	4.10	2.7	7.6	2.8	0.8	82

NDFA had a solid debut, but was unable to duplicate the results in 2014. Low-90s FB tends to be fairly straight and hitable. Mixes in an average curve and CU. Throws strikes, but without premium velocity or a true swing-and-miss offering he has limited upside.

Patton,Spencer — RP — Texas

EXP MLB DEBUT: 2014 | H/W: 6-1 185 | FUT: Setup RP | 6B

Thrws R Age 27
2011 (24) SIU-Edwardsville

Velo	Pitch	Grade
90-93	FB	+++
82-84	SL	+++
78-80	CU	++

Year	Lev	Team	W	L	Sv	IP	K	ERA	WHIP	BF/G	OBA	H%	S%	xERA	Ctl	Dom	Cmd	hr/9	BPV
2013	A+	Wilmington	5	2	2	64		1.97	1.08	10.0	213	30	86	2.53	2.8	10.7	3.8	0.7	134
2013	AA	NW Arkansas	0	0	0	18	27	1.50	0.83	5.5	151	25	86	0.99	3.0	13.5	4.5	0.5	180
2014	AAA	Omaha	4	3	14	46	60	4.10	1.04	5.2	167	20	69	2.89	4.3	11.7	2.7	1.8	113
2014	AAA	Round Rock	1	1	4	16	25	3.38	1.19	4.3	262	43	72	3.27	1.7	14.1	8.3	0.6	226
2014	MLB	Texas	1	0	0	9	8	0.99	0.88	3.7	190	25	88	1.12	2.0	7.9	4.0	0.0	107

Deceptive RP who reached TEX in first year above AA. Hides ball in tricky delivery that allows pitches to play up. More numbers over stuff as pitch mix is average at best. Can be hit by LHH, though generally lives down in zone. Posts high K rate and throws decent strikes with 3 pitches.

Payano,Victor — SP — Texas

EXP MLB DEBUT: 2017 | H/W: 6-5 185 | FUT: #3 starter | 7E

Thrws L Age 22
2010 FA (DR)

Velo	Pitch	Grade
88-95	FB	+++
72-75	CB	++
80-82	CU	++

Year	Lev	Team	W	L	Sv	IP	K	ERA	WHIP	BF/G	OBA	H%	S%	xERA	Ctl	Dom	Cmd	hr/9	BPV
2011	A-	Spokane	2	5	0	48	43	5.44	1.67	14.4	281	33	70	5.51	5.1	8.1	1.6	1.3	26
2012	A	Hickory	6	8	1	105	97	4.63	1.51	18.2	247	31	70	4.06	5.3	8.3	1.6	0.7	24
2013	A+	Myrtle Beach	5	7	0	87	96	6.30	1.63	17.6	257	33	62	4.90	5.9	9.9	1.7	1.1	38
2014	A+	Myrtle Beach	5	8	0	125	86	4.60	1.70	19.5	258	30	74	4.81	6.5	6.2	1.0	0.8	-45

Long, lean SP who repeated High-A, but still struggled with walks and saw K rate decline. Generates easy plus FB with quick arm and athletic delivery. Can leave FB up in zone too often and needs better command. Has RP profile unless he can polish tight CB and sinking CU.

Pena,Ariel — SP — Milwaukee

EXP MLB DEBUT: 2015 | H/W: 6-3 240 | FUT: #4 starter/Setup RP | 7C

Thrws R Age 25
2007 FA (DR)

Velo	Pitch	Grade
92-95	FB	++++
84-86	SL	+++
	CU	+

Year	Lev	Team	W	L	Sv	IP	K	ERA	WHIP	BF/G	OBA	H%	S%	xERA	Ctl	Dom	Cmd	hr/9	BPV
2011	AAA	Salt Lake	0	0	0	4	3	2.25	2.75	22.3	383	46	91	8.74	9.0	6.8	0.8	0.0	-104
2012	AA	Arkansas	6	6	0	114	111	3.00	1.20	24.1	228	28	80	3.42	3.3	8.8	2.6	1.1	86
2012	AA	Huntsville	0	2	0	32	29	7.29	1.96	21.9	306	36	64	6.72	6.4	8.1	1.3	1.4	-10
2013	AA	Huntsville	8	9	0	142	131	3.74	1.37	22.0	223	27	76	3.75	5.0	8.3	1.7	1.1	32
2014	AAA	Nashville	9	8	0	128	140	4.57	1.33	21.3	210	28	67	3.28	5.3	9.8	1.9	0.8	53

Hard throwing RH has plus velo, but below average control continues to thwart his development. Attacks hitters with a mid-90s FB and a power SL, both of which get swings and misses. CU remains below average. Inconsistent mechanics and varying release points are the main culprit.

Pena,Richelson — SP — Texas

EXP MLB DEBUT: 2018 | H/W: 6-1 170 | FUT: #4 starter | 7D

Thrws R Age 21
2011 FA (DR)

Velo	Pitch	Grade
89-92	FB	+++
77-80	CB	++
81-85	CU	+++

Year	Lev	Team	W	L	Sv	IP	K	ERA	WHIP	BF/G	OBA	H%	S%	xERA	Ctl	Dom	Cmd	hr/9	BPV
2013	Rk	DSL Rangers	9	1	0	74	76	2.30	0.92	16.3	214	30	73	1.60	1.3	9.2	6.9	0.1	148
2014	A-	Spokane	5	5	0	72	67	3.37	1.15	20.5	251	32	70	2.90	1.9	8.4	4.5	0.4	118

Aggressive SP who fared well in first year in U.S. Possesses great arm and advanced ability to pepper strike zone with quality pitches. Not much strength or stamina and could live in middle innings. Lacks consistency in CB, but can be average pitch. Throws deceptive CU with depth.

Peralta,Ofelky — SP — Baltimore

EXP MLB DEBUT: 2018 | H/W: 6-5 195 | FUT: #2 starter | 8E

Thrws R Age 17
2013 FA (DR)

Velo	Pitch	Grade
89-95	FB	+++
81-85	SL	++
77-79	CB	++
	CU	++

Year	Lev	Team	W	L	Sv	IP	K	ERA	WHIP	BF/G	OBA	H%	S%	xERA	Ctl	Dom	Cmd	hr/9	BPV
2014	Rk	DSL Orioles	0	4	0	43	33	3.13	1.51	17.0	187	24	77	2.69	7.7	6.9	0.9	0.0	-67

Long, projectable pitcher who has yet to pitch in U.S. Shows surprising feel for deep arsenal despite raw ability. More thrower than pitcher at present, but has high upside. Lacks command of quality FB and rarely knows where it will go. Possesses feel for two breaking balls and CU.

Perez,Felipe — SP — Arizona

EXP MLB DEBUT: 2018 | H/W: 6-3 200 | FUT: #4 starter | 6C

Thrws R Age 21
2012 FA HS (CA)

Velo	Pitch	Grade
91-93	FB	+++
	CB	+++
	CU	+++

Year	Lev	Team	W	L	Sv	IP	K	ERA	WHIP	BF/G	OBA	H%	S%	xERA	Ctl	Dom	Cmd	hr/9	BPV
2013	Rk	Missoula	7	5	0	89	50	4.55	1.34	24.7	285	31	67	4.39	1.9	5.1	2.6	0.9	57
2014	Rk	AZL Dbacks	0	1	0	20	14	5.35	1.73	15.3	345	41	66	5.48	2.2	6.2	2.8	0.0	70
2014	A-	Hillsboro	3	0	0	21	12	2.14	1.19	21.1	252	30	80	2.71	2.1	5.1	2.4	0.0	53

Has good size and throws tons of strikes. FB has only average velocity, sitting at 90-93 with run and sink. Mixes in a decent CB and a CU that has good fade. Throws all three offerings for strikes and has walked just 29 batters in two years. Profiles as a decent back-end starter.

Perry,Christopher — RP — St. Louis

EXP MLB DEBUT: 2017 | H/W: 6-2 215 | FUT: Reliever | 7C

Thrws R Age 24
2012 (17) Methodist

Velo	Pitch	Grade
90-93	FB	++++
	CB	+++
	CU	++

Year	Lev	Team	W	L	Sv	IP	K	ERA	WHIP	BF/G	OBA	H%	S%	xERA	Ctl	Dom	Cmd	hr/9	BPV
2013	A-	State College	2	0	0	22	15	1.63	1.00	21.1	214	26	82	1.72	2.0	6.1	3.0	0.0	73
2013	A	Peoria	2	4	0	48	40	3.93	1.35	22.3	269	33	71	3.85	2.8	7.5	2.7	0.6	77
2014	A	Peoria	4	0	3	49	80	2.20	0.90	6.5	173	30	80	1.61	2.8	14.7	5.3	0.7	208
2014	A+	Palm Beach	1	1	5	14	18	1.93	0.86	4.0	132	19	82	1.02	3.9	11.6	3.0	0.6	122

Came late to pitching and started his career as a catcher. Moved to the mound at NCAA Div III Methodist. Comes after hitters with a live 90-93 mph FB and an above-average, but inconsistent CB. Mechanics are not ideal and he has struggled with control, but also struck out 98 in 63 IP in 2014.

Petree,Nick — SP — St. Louis

EXP MLB DEBUT: 2017 | H/W: 6-1 195 | FUT: #5 starter / RP | 6C

Thrws R Age 24
2013 (9) Missouri State

Velo	Pitch	Grade
87-90	FB	++
	CB	+++
	CU	++++

Year	Lev	Team	W	L	Sv	IP	K	ERA	WHIP	BF/G	OBA	H%	S%	xERA	Ctl	Dom	Cmd	hr/9	BPV
2013	NCAA	Missouri State	8	1	0	100	111	1.62	0.98	27.2	219	31	82	1.78	1.7	10.0	5.8	0.1	152
2013	A-	State College	3	1	0	55	46	1.63	1.12	18.1	228	29	87	2.50	2.6	7.5	2.9	0.3	83
2014	A	Peoria	2	0	0	21	24	1.29	1.19	21.1	202	27	96	2.83	4.3	10.3	2.4	0.9	87
2014	A+	Palm Beach	6	5	0	103	80	2.44	1.16	24.2	252	31	80	3.03	1.9	7.0	3.6	0.4	92
2014	AA	Springfield	0	0	0	4	2	10.71	2.62	22.8	458	50	55	10.11	2.1	4.3	2.0	0.0	37

Finesse RH rarely breaks 90 mph with his FB, but does a good job of keeping hittrers off-balance. Gets good deception from a funky delivery and mixes in a good CB and CU. Keeps the ball down in the zone and limits damage against.

Petrick,Zach — SP — St. Louis

EXP MLB DEBUT: 2016 | H/W: 6-3 195 | FUT: #5 starter / RP | 7D

Thrws R Age 25
2012 FA Northwestern Ohio

Velo	Pitch	Grade
90-93	FB	+++
	SL	++
	CU	+++

Year	Lev	Team	W	L	Sv	IP	K	ERA	WHIP	BF/G	OBA	H%	S%	xERA	Ctl	Dom	Cmd	hr/9	BPV
2013	A	Peoria	1	0	7	32	46	0.84	0.99	7.7	209	34	94	1.85	2.2	12.9	5.8	0.3	189
2013	A+	Palm Beach	3	0	1	33	32	0.27	0.76	13.1	184	26	96	0.73	1.1	8.7	8.0	0.0	145
2013	AA	Springfield	3	3	0	47	44	4.01	1.25	21.3	249	32	68	3.32	2.9	8.4	2.9	0.6	92
2014	AA	Springfield	2	0	0	18	15	0.49	0.77	21.8	149	20	93	0.41	2.5	7.4	3.0	0.0	85
2014	AAA	Memphis	7	6	1	115	82	4.62	1.35	20.0	268	30	69	4.49	2.8	6.4	2.3	1.3	57

NDFA took a step back in 2014, though the results weren't as bad as they seem. Features plus command and control of his arsenal that includes a 90-93 mph FB, SL, and above-avg CU. Has a strong frame, but there are concerns about his durability.

Pike,Tyler

SP | Seattle | EXP MLB DEBUT: 2017 | H/W: 6-0 180 | FUT: #4 starter | 7D

Thrws L Age 21
2012 (3) HS (FL)

Velo	Pitch	Grade
88-91	FB	+++
73-78	CB	++
80-83	CU	+++

Year	Lev	Team	W	L	Sv	IP	K	ERA	WHIP	BF/G	OBA	H%	S%	xERA	Ctl	Dom	Cmd	hr/9	BPV
2012	Rk	AZL Mariners	2	1	0	50	57	1.79	1.10	17.9	194	28	83	1.86	3.8	10.2	2.7	0.2	100
2013	A	Clinton	7	4	0	110	90	2.37	1.18	20.0	190	24	81	2.28	4.7	7.4	1.6	0.4	25
2014	A+	High Desert	2	4	0	61	57	5.74	1.67	19.6	245	29	68	5.17	6.8	8.4	1.2	1.5	-14
2014	AA	Jackson	3	4	0	49	33	7.35	1.86	17.6	292	33	59	5.80	6.2	6.1	1.0	0.9	-42

Short, athletic SP who couldn't match breakout from '13. Can nibble at corners instead of attacking. Significant control issues are prevalent and has been harmed by HR. FB lacks velocity, but has life while slow CB can be effective K offering. Advanced CU is most potent pitch in arsenal.

Pineyro,Ivan

SP | Chicago (N) | EXP MLB DEBUT: 2016 | H/W: 6-1 200 | FUT: #4 starter | 6C

Thrws R Age 23
2010 FA (DR)

Velo	Pitch	Grade
90-93	FB	+++
73-77	CB	++
	CU	+++

Year	Lev	Team	W	L	Sv	IP	K	ERA	WHIP	BF/G	OBA	H%	S%	xERA	Ctl	Dom	Cmd	hr/9	BPV
2013	A	Hagerstown	5	3	0	66	65	3.14	1.12	20.0	234	30	73	2.77	2.3	8.9	3.8	0.5	115
2013	A+	Daytona	3	1	0	45	38	3.40	1.18	22.5	257	32	71	3.09	1.8	7.6	4.2	0.4	106
2013	A+	Potomac	1	0	0	14	8	3.80	1.34	19.7	259	29	72	3.76	3.2	5.1	1.6	0.6	24
2014	Rk	AZL Cubs	0	2	0	11	9	5.68	1.53	12.1	324	39	63	5.37	1.6	7.3	4.5	0.8	106
2014	AA	Tennessee	0	4	0	48	41	5.60	1.68	19.7	299	35	69	5.81	4.3	7.7	1.8	1.3	40

Dominican hurler scuffled, going combined 0-6 with a 5.55 ERA in 2014. Lack of control was the culprit and too often he fell behind and was then hammered when he got too much of the plate. Opposing hitters swatted .298 against him. FB sits at 91-93 with a CB and CU, none of which project as above-avg.

Pivetta,Nic

SP | Washington | EXP MLB DEBUT: 2017 | H/W: 6-5 220 | FUT: #3 starter | 8C

Thrws R Age 22
2013 (4) New Mexico JC

Velo	Pitch	Grade
90-93	FB	+++
78-81	CB	+++
	CU	++

Year	Lev	Team	W	L	Sv	IP	K	ERA	WHIP	BF/G	OBA	H%	S%	xERA	Ctl	Dom	Cmd	hr/9	BPV
2012	NCAA	New Mexico JC	4	1	0	54		4.83	1.57	19.8	293	34	66	4.25	3.7	4.8	1.3	0.0	6
2013	NCAA	New Mexico JC	6	1	0	75	49	3.35	1.12	26.9	237	28	70	2.77	2.2	5.9	2.7	0.5	65
2013	Rk	GCL Nationals	1	0	0	12	8	2.21	1.07	11.9	242	29	77	2.25	1.5	5.9	4.0	0.0	84
2013	A-	Auburn	0	1	0	21	17	3.41	1.42	17.9	242	30	76	3.53	4.7	7.3	1.5	0.4	22
2014	A	Hagerstown	13	8	0	132	98	4.22	1.37	21.3	276	32	72	4.43	2.7	6.7	2.5	1.0	66

Put together fine first full season, and still has some projection left in his lanky frame. FB already touches 95 mph, CB is weapon, and CU continues to improve. Has good present command and gets a lot of ground balls. Looks like a future rotation piece in need of more innings.

Plutko,Adam

SP | Cleveland | EXP MLB DEBUT: 2016 | H/W: 6-3 195 | FUT: #4 starter | 7D

Thrws R Age 23
2013 (11) UCLA

Velo	Pitch	Grade
87-92	FB	+++
77-80	CB	+++
82-84	SL	+++
81-82	CU	+++

Year	Lev	Team	W	L	Sv	IP	K	ERA	WHIP	BF/G	OBA	H%	S%	xERA	Ctl	Dom	Cmd	hr/9	BPV
2011	NCAA	UCLA	7	4	0	107	92	2.01	0.90	25.0	195	25	78	1.48	2.0	7.7	3.8	0.3	103
2012	NCAA	UCLA	12	3	0	119	99	2.49	1.16	26.3	213	26	80	2.60	3.5	7.5	2.1	0.5	57
2013	NCAA	UCLA	10	3	0	124	81	2.25	0.98	24.8	208	24	78	2.03	2.2	5.9	2.7	0.4	65
2014	A	Lake County	3	1	0	52	66	3.97	1.17	20.8	250	37	63	2.72	2.1	11.4	5.5	0.2	167
2014	A+	Carolina	4	9	0	97	78	4.08	1.21	21.7	266	31	69	3.87	1.7	7.2	4.3	1.0	103

Smart, command-oriented SP with athletic, repeatable delivery. Sequences four average pitches, though none stand out as wipeout offering. Gets ahead with FB and adds sink at lower velocities. Mixes in two breaking balls and potent CU that fools LHH. Flyball pitcher who gives up HR.

Portillo,Adys

RP | San Diego | EXP MLB DEBUT: 2015 | H/W: 6-3 235 | FUT: Setup RP | 7C

Thrws R Age 23
2008 FA (Venezuela)

Velo	Pitch	Grade
94-96	FB	++++
76-79	SL	+++
	CU	++

Year	Lev	Team	W	L	Sv	IP	K	ERA	WHIP	BF/G	OBA	H%	S%	xERA	Ctl	Dom	Cmd	hr/9	BPV
2011	A	Fort Wayne	3	11	0	82	97	7.13	1.75	16.3	278	37	59	5.45	6.0	10.6	1.8	1.1	47
2012	A	Fort Wayne	6	6	0	91	81	1.88	1.09	19.8	174	22	83	1.74	4.4	8.0	1.8	0.3	42
2012	AA	San Antonio	2	5	0	35	26	7.20	1.69	19.7	256	29	56	4.96	6.4	6.7	1.0	1.0	-35
2013	A	Fort Wayne	0	1	0	9	10	4.95	1.98	14.6	353	47	72	6.20	4.0	9.9	2.5	0.0	89
2014	AA	San Antonio	1	4	0	55	68	3.26	1.58	5.3	220	32	79	3.51	7.0	11.1	1.6	0.3	28

Big-framed hurler returned to action after missing most of '13. Worked exclusively in relief with mixed results. FB now sits at 92-94. Inconsistent mechanics and release point continues to result in poor command. Was left exposed in the Rule 5 draft, but was not selected.

Povse,Max

SP | Atlanta | EXP MLB DEBUT: 2017 | H/W: 6-8 185 | FUT: #4 starter/Setup RP | 7D

Thrws R Age 21
2014 (3) UNC Greensboro

Velo	Pitch	Grade
91-93	FB	+++
	SL	++
	CU	++

Year	Lev	Team	W	L	Sv	IP	K	ERA	WHIP	BF/G	OBA	H%	S%	xERA	Ctl	Dom	Cmd	hr/9	BPV
2012	NCAA	UNC-Greensboro	2	6	0	57	47	6.61	1.59	16.8	274	33	56	4.59	4.7	7.4	1.6	0.6	24
2013	NCAA	UNC-Greensboro	4	4	0	77	81	4.78	1.41	23.3	259	34	67	4.07	3.8	9.4	2.5	0.8	84
2014	NCAA	UNC-Greensboro	6	4	0	79	81	5.01	1.55	23.1	301	40	65	4.39	3.1	9.2	3.0	0.1	101
2014	Rk	Danville	4	2	0	47	37	3.44	1.13	15.5	240	30	67	2.54	2.1	7.1	3.4	0.2	89

Huge but lean frame, so has some projection left. Has a 90-93 mph FB that tops out at 95 mph. Complements the heat with a SL and CU, both of which need work. Has surprising control for his size and walked just 12 while striking out 37. Definitely a player worth watching.

Purke,Matt

SP | Washington | EXP MLB DEBUT: 2016 | H/W: 6-4 215 | FUT: #3 starter | 7D

Thrws L Age 24
2011 (3) TCU

Velo	Pitch	Grade
91-93	FB	+++
78-81	SL	++
80-82	CU	+++

Year	Lev	Team	W	L	Sv	IP	K	ERA	WHIP	BF/G	OBA	H%	S%	xERA	Ctl	Dom	Cmd	hr/9	BPV
2011	NCAA	TCU	5	1	0	52	61	1.72	1.07	18.5	197	28	85	1.98	3.4	10.5	3.1	0.3	114
2012	A	Hagerstown	0	2	0	15	14	5.96	1.79	23.2	260	33	65	4.85	7.2	8.3	1.2	0.6	-25
2013	A	Hagerstown	1	1	0	29	41	2.48	1.10	19.0	234	35	83	3.05	2.2	12.7	5.9	0.9	188
2013	A+	Potomac	5	3	0	61	41	4.43	1.39	21.4	280	33	67	4.01	2.7	6.0	2.3	0.4	55
2014	AA	Harrisburg	1	6	0	31	22	8.10	1.93	18.5	324	36	58	6.97	5.2	6.4	1.2	1.4	-8

Health woes continued to dog him; shoulder and now elbow problems have limited his IP each season. Latest setback was Tommy John surgery in May after disastrous eight starts in Double-A. Lively fastball and bat-missing change-up among his attributes—but durability concerns are a never-ending issue.

Ramirez,Jose

RP | New York (A) | EXP MLB DEBUT: 2014 | H/W: 6-3 190 | FUT: #3 starter | 8D

Thrws R Age 25
2007 FA (DR)

Velo	Pitch	Grade
92-97	FB	+++
82-85	SL	++
83-85	CU	++++

Year	Lev	Team	W	L	Sv	IP	K	ERA	WHIP	BF/G	OBA	H%	S%	xERA	Ctl	Dom	Cmd	hr/9	BPV
2012	A+	Tampa	7	6	0	98	94	3.21	1.24	19.0	249	32	76	3.37	2.7	8.6	3.1	0.6	99
2013	AA	Trenton	1	3	1	42	50	2.78	1.02	18.0	191	23	83	2.87	3.2	10.7	3.3	1.5	124
2013	AAA	Scranton/WB	1	3	0	31	28	4.92	1.61	17.2	248	30	70	4.49	6.1	8.1	1.3	0.9	0
2014	AAA	Scranton/WB	3	0	1	12	16	1.49	1.90	6.3	276	42	91	4.75	7.4	11.9	1.6	0.0	31
2014	MLB	NY Yankees	0	2	0	10	10	5.40	1.80	5.8	281	33	75	6.29	6.3	9.0	1.4	1.8	10

Tall, lean pitcher who moved to pen in '14. Missed significant time with various ailments and durability is a question. Possesses explosive FB with electric life and CU remains plus offering that can miss bats. Fails to repeat delivery and has trouble harnessing arm strength. Upside still there.

Ramirez,Noe

RP | Boston | EXP MLB DEBUT: 2015 | H/W: 6-3 185 | FUT: Middle reliever | 6A

Thrws R Age 25
2011 (4) Cal St Fullerton

Velo	Pitch	Grade
89-93	FB	+++
77-83	SL	++
81-84	CU	++++

Year	Lev	Team	W	L	Sv	IP	K	ERA	WHIP	BF/G	OBA	H%	S%	xERA	Ctl	Dom	Cmd	hr/9	BPV
2011	NCAA	Cal St Fullerton	8	3	0	82	91	1.75	0.85	23.2	183	27	77	0.96	2.0	10.0	5.1	0.0	144
2012	A	Greenville	2	7	0	84	82	4.17	1.28	21.6	273	33	72	4.39	2.0	8.8	4.3	1.3	121
2013	A+	Salem	2	1	1	47	44	2.11	1.06	8.7	236	32	78	2.14	1.7	8.4	4.9	0.0	123
2013	AA	Portland	1	1	5	28	31	2.87	1.06	7.3	217	27	81	3.08	2.6	9.9	3.9	1.3	127
2014	AA	Portland	2	1	18	67	56	2.15	1.07	6.2	228	30	78	2.07	2.1	7.5	3.5	0.0	95

Command-oriented RP who deceives hitters with clever delivery. Did not allow HR in '14 due to potent sinker that he locates to both sides of plate. Can pitch multiple innings and has solid feel for CU with fast arm speed. In control on mound and succeeds without premium velocity or SL.

Ranaudo,Anthony

SP | Boston | EXP MLB DEBUT: 2014 | H/W: 6-7 230 | FUT: #3 starter | 8C

Thrws R Age 25
2010 (1-S) LSU

Velo	Pitch	Grade
88-96	FB	+++
78-82	CB	+++
81-83	CU	+++

Year	Lev	Team	W	L	Sv	IP	K	ERA	WHIP	BF/G	OBA	H%	S%	xERA	Ctl	Dom	Cmd	hr/9	BPV
2012	AA	Portland	1	3	0	37	27	6.77	1.83	19.2	281	32	63	5.61	6.5	6.5	1.0	1.0	-41
2013	AA	Portland	8	4	0	109	106	2.97	1.10	22.5	206	26	76	2.55	3.3	8.7	2.7	0.7	86
2013	AAA	Pawtucket	3	1	0	30	21	2.99	1.30	20.6	274	33	76	3.54	2.1	6.3	3.0	0.3	75
2014	AAA	Pawtucket	14	4	0	138	111	2.61	1.20	23.1	223	27	80	2.90	3.5	7.2	2.1	0.6	53
2014	MLB	Boston	4	3	0	39	15	4.83	1.41	23.6	261	23	76	5.55	3.7	3.5	0.9	2.3	-19

Very strong SP who led IL in ERA. Reached majors and struggled with HR; flyball nature could be issue. Uses height to throw on excellent plane to plate and can be overpowering with strong FB. All about power with CB; CU has nice depth and fade. Needs to improve control.

Ravenelle,Adam

RP | Detroit | EXP MLB DEBUT: 2016 | H/W: 6-3 185 | FUT: Setup RP | 7C

Thrws R Age 22
2014 (4) Vanderbilt

Velo	Pitch	Grade
92-96	FB	+++
80-85	SL	+++
	CU	+

Year	Lev	Team	W	L	Sv	IP	K	ERA	WHIP	BF/G	OBA	H%	S%	xERA	Ctl	Dom	Cmd	hr/9	BPV
2012	NCAA	Vanderbilt	0	0	0	5	9	1.80	1.80	3.9	175	37	89	3.20	10.8	16.2	1.5	0.0	18
2013	NCAA	Vanderbilt	0	0	0	17	9	3.18	1.24	6.3	213	25	71	2.33	4.2	4.8	1.1	0.0	-11
2014	NCAA	Vanderbilt	3	2	3	40	37	1.35	0.83	6.1	144	19	84	0.70	3.2	8.3	2.6	0.2	83
2014	Rk	GCL Tigers	0	0	0	1	1	0.00	0.00	2.8	0	0		0.00	0.0	9.0		0.0	180
2014	A	West Michigan	0	0	1	3	5	0.00	0.00	4.2	0	0		0.00	0.0	15.0		0.0	288

Athletic, lean RP who could advance quickly with advanced approach. May not have plus pitch, but has lively FB featuring late sink and a SL that can miss bats. Has room to fill out, yet already has polished mechanics and arm motion. If SL gains consistency, could be late-innings guy.

Ray,Robbie — SP — Arizona

EXP MLB DEBUT: 2014 | H/W: 6-2 195 | FUT: #4 starter | 7B

Thrws L Age 23
2010 (12) HS (TN)

Velo	Pitch	Grade
91-96	FB	+++
75-80	SL	++
80-83	CU	+++

Year	Lev	Team	W	L	Sv	IP	K	ERA	WHIP	BF/G	OBA	H%	S%	xERA	Ctl	Dom	Cmd	hr/9	BPV
2012	A+	Potomac	4	12	0	105	86	6.59	1.63	21.3	291	34	60	5.46	4.2	7.4	1.8	1.2	37
2013	A+	Potomac	6	3	0	84	100	3.11	1.20	21.1	202	27	78	2.96	4.4	10.7	2.4	1.0	92
2013	AA	Harrisburg	5	2	0	58	60	3.72	1.33	21.9	255	33	73	3.63	3.3	9.3	2.9	0.6	98
2014	AAA	Toledo	7	6	0	100	75	4.23	1.50	21.6	273	33	72	4.26	4.0	6.7	1.7	0.5	33
2014	MLB	Detroit	1	4	0	28	19	8.30	1.91	14.8	351	39	57	7.54	3.5	6.1	1.7	1.6	32

Lean, loose SP with steady progression and durability. Offers some deception and FB can look sneaky quick. Slurvy SL can be too loose and declining K rate is a concern. CU shows nice promise and has arsenal and moxie to keep LHH at bay. Owns nice tools and pitchability to be factor.

Reed,Chris — SP — Los Angeles (N)

EXP MLB DEBUT: 2015 | H/W: 6-4 195 | FUT: #4 starter | 8D

Thrws L Age 24
2011 (1) Stanford

Velo	Pitch	Grade
89-95	FB	++++
	SL	+++
	CU	++

Year	Lev	Team	W	L	Sv	IP	K	ERA	WHIP	BF/G	OBA	H%	S%	xERA	Ctl	Dom	Cmd	hr/9	BPV
2012	A+	Ranch Cuca	1	4	0	35	38	3.09	1.11	19.7	202	28	71	2.08	3.6	9.8	2.7	0.3	97
2012	AA	Chattanooga	0	4	0	35	29	4.87	1.45	12.5	238	29	65	3.64	5.1	7.4	1.5	0.5	13
2013	AA	Chattanooga	4	11	0	137	106	3.87	1.39	19.9	249	30	73	3.70	4.1	7.0	1.7	0.6	32
2014	AA	Chattanooga	4	8	0	137	116	3.22	1.23	24.1	228	28	75	3.09	3.6	7.6	2.1	0.7	58
2014	AAA	Albuquerque	0	3	0	21	18	11.09	2.27	21.5	383	44	51	9.55	4.7	7.7	1.6	2.1	30

Tall LH put up solid numbers at AA, but was overmatched when moved up. FBs sits in the low-90s with plus sink. Complements it with a plus SL and a below avg CU. Swings and misses will never be a huge part of his game, though he does well at pitch sequencing and inducing weak contact.

Reed,Cody — SP — Arizona

EXP MLB DEBUT: 2019 | H/W: 6-3 245 | FUT: #3 starter | 8D

Thrws L Age 18
2014 (2) HS (AL)

Velo	Pitch	Grade
94-96	FB	++++
75-78	CB	++
82-84	SL	+++
	CU	+

Year	Lev	Team	W	L	Sv	IP	K	ERA	WHIP	BF/G	OBA	H%	S%	xERA	Ctl	Dom	Cmd	hr/9	BPV
2014	Rk	AZL Dbacks	0	1	0	20	26	2.23	1.09	7.9	230	35	77	2.09	2.2	11.6	5.2	0.0	166
2014	Rk	Missoula	0	1	0	12	14	2.25	0.83	11.0	81	9	78	0.59	5.3	10.5	2.0	0.8	65

HS lefty had a solid debut, going 0-2 with a 2.20 ERA. Has a good 91-95 mph FB and a nice four-pitch mix. His CB, SL, and CU all need work, but show average potential. Does a good job of keeping hitters off-balance. Repeats his mechanics well and comes after hitters with FBs up in the zone.

Reed,Cody A. — SP — Kansas City

EXP MLB DEBUT: 2017 | H/W: 6-5 220 | FUT: #3 starter/setupRP | 8E

Thrws L Age 21
2013 (2) NW Mississippi CC

Velo	Pitch	Grade
89-94	FB	+++
82-84	SL	++
80-83	CU	++

Year	Lev	Team	W	L	Sv	IP	K	ERA	WHIP	BF/G	OBA	H%	S%	xERA	Ctl	Dom	Cmd	hr/9	BPV
2012	NCAA	NW Mississippi CC	8	2	0	64	65	3.79	1.37	20.7	237	33	69	2.92	4.5	9.1	2.0	0.0	61
2013	NCAA	NW Mississippi CC	8	3	0	73	96	3.08	1.29	25.0	208	32	75	2.55	4.9	11.8	2.4	0.2	98
2013	Rk	Idaho Falls	0	1	0	29	25	6.16	1.85	9.1	274	35	63	4.63	7.1	7.7	1.1	0.0	-35
2014	A	Lexington	3	9	0	84	58	5.46	1.68	19.9	307	36	66	5.22	3.9	6.2	1.6	0.5	26

Tall, raw SP who had inconsistent season. Locates FB down in strike zone to induce groundballs. Rarely allows HR, though can be hit hard with lack of plus pitch. Throws with a lot of effort which impacts command. Will likely move to bullpen unless he can firm up CU and throw strikes.

Reed,Jake — RP — Minnesota

EXP MLB DEBUT: 2016 | H/W: 6-2 190 | FUT: Setup RP | 7C

Thrws R Age 22
2014 (5) Oregon

Velo	Pitch	Grade
91-95	FB	++++
81-83	SL	+++
	CU	++

Year	Lev	Team	W	L	Sv	IP	K	ERA	WHIP	BF/G	OBA	H%	S%	xERA	Ctl	Dom	Cmd	hr/9	BPV
2012	NCAA	Oregon	8	4	0	114	67	2.92	1.17	26.7	221	26	74	2.46	3.3	5.3	1.6	0.2	24
2013	NCAA	Oregon	6	6	0	100	65	3.51	1.23	23.8	248	29	71	3.16	2.7	5.8	2.2	0.4	50
2014	NCAA	Oregon	4	1	13	37	34	1.95	1.00	4.6	174	23	81	1.47	3.6	8.3	2.3	0.2	68
2014	Rk	Elizabethton	0	0	3	6	8	0.00	0.17	4.5	56	10	100	0.00	0.0	12.0		0.0	234
2014	A	Cedar Rapids	3	0	5	25	31	0.36	0.52	5.2	124	20	92	0.00	1.1	11.2	10.3	0.0	190

Athletic pitcher with quick delivery who could move from RP to SP in '15. Posts very low oppBA due to deceptive mechanics and arm action. Adds late sink to plus FB that he generally locates well and mixes in SL that he throws for strikes. If he can maintain velocity, has upside as SP.

Reid-Foley,Sean — SP — Toronto

EXP MLB DEBUT: 2018 | H/W: 6-3 220 | FUT: #2 starter | 8D

Thrws R Age 19
2014 (2) HS (FL)

Velo	Pitch	Grade
90-95	FB	+++
82-86	SL	+++
84-87	CU	++

Year	Lev	Team	W	L	Sv	IP	K	ERA	WHIP	BF/G	OBA	H%	S%	xERA	Ctl	Dom	Cmd	hr/9	BPV
2014	Rk	GCL Blue Jays	1	2	0	22	25	4.86	1.40	10.4	251	36	61	3.16	4.1	10.1	2.5	0.0	91

Big, durable SP who may take time to develop, but has pitch mix and sequencing ability. Needs to clean up max-effort delivery and find consistency in secondary offerings. Generates easy velocity and gets movement on solid FB. Locates pitches fairly well and has feel for changing speeds.

Reininger,Zac — RP — Detroit

EXP MLB DEBUT: 2016 | H/W: 6-3 170 | FUT: Setup RP | 7D

Thrws R Age 22
2013 (8) Hill JC

Velo	Pitch	Grade
88-93	FB	+++
78-80	SL	+++
80-82	CU	++

Year	Lev	Team	W	L	Sv	IP	K	ERA	WHIP	BF/G	OBA	H%	S%	xERA	Ctl	Dom	Cmd	hr/9	BPV
2013	A-	Connecticut	1	2	10	27	32	1.00	0.85	4.5	183	28	87	0.94	2.0	10.7	5.3	0.0	156
2014	A	West Michigan	4	4	11	56	58	2.56	1.05	6.6	209	28	77	2.22	2.7	9.3	3.4	0.5	112

Loose-armed, projectable RP who has flown under radar. Has some closing experience with right demeanor and pitch mix. Works with heavy FB low in zone and limits contact to hitters from both sides with solid-average SL. Will mix in occasional CU. Tough on RHH and keeps ball down.

Reyes,Alexander — SP — St. Louis

EXP MLB DEBUT: 2017 | H/W: 6-3 185 | FUT: #2 starter | 9D

Thrws R Age 20
2012 FA (DR)

Velo	Pitch	Grade
94-96	FB	++++
75-78	CB	+++
83-87	CU	+++

Year	Lev	Team	W	L	Sv	IP	K	ERA	WHIP	BF/G	OBA	H%	S%	xERA	Ctl	Dom	Cmd	hr/9	BPV
2013	Rk	Johnson City	6	4	0	58	68	3.41	1.41	20.5	248	36	74	3.29	4.3	10.5	2.4	0.2	90
2014	A	Peoria	7	7	0	109	137	3.63	1.31	21.5	210	31	72	2.88	5.0	11.3	2.2	0.5	86

Dynamic Dominican hurler has the most upside of any player in the system. Has a good three-pitch mix highlighted by a plus mid-90s FB. Also has a good hard CB and a CU that has potential. Has good size and is physically strong, so he should hold up well once he fills out his 6-3 frame.

Rhame,Jacob — RP — Los Angeles (N)

EXP MLB DEBUT: 2017 | H/W: 6-1 190 | FUT: Reliever | 7D

Thrws R Age 22
2013 (6) Grayson Country CC

Velo	Pitch	Grade
91-94	FB	++++
	CB	++
	CU	++

Year	Lev	Team	W	L	Sv	IP	K	ERA	WHIP	BF/G	OBA	H%	S%	xERA	Ctl	Dom	Cmd	hr/9	BPV
2012	NCAA	Oklahoma	1	0	0	10	7	7.20	1.70	7.5	347	40	56	6.28	1.8	6.3	3.5	0.9	83
2013	NCAA	Grayson Cty Col	2	0	0	75	58	2.16	1.00	23.9	232	29	78	2.17	1.3	7.0	5.3	0.2	108
2013	Rk	Ogden	1	2	8	19	21	4.69	1.46	4.1	260	34	69	4.32	4.2	9.8	2.3	0.9	81
2014	A	Great Lakes	5	4	9	67	90	2.01	0.92	4.9	202	31	80	1.72	1.9	12.1	6.4	0.4	185

6th rounder looked very impressive and was 5-4 with a 2.00 ERA and 14 BB/90 K. Thrives with a plus 90-93 mph sinking FB that is difficult to sqaure up and mixes in a decent CU and a get-me-over CB. Doesn't get the attention he should and has the stuff to be an effective reliever.

Rhoades,Jeremy — SP — Los Angeles (A)

EXP MLB DEBUT: 2017 | H/W: 6-4 225 | FUT: #4 starter | 7D

Thrws R Age 22
2014 (4) Illinois State

Velo	Pitch	Grade
90-94	FB	+++
81-83	SL	+++
	CU	+

Year	Lev	Team	W	L	Sv	IP	K	ERA	WHIP	BF/G	OBA	H%	S%	xERA	Ctl	Dom	Cmd	hr/9	BPV
2013	NCAA	Illinois State	2	1	6	41	37	1.54	1.05	5.9	222	30	84	1.93	2.2	8.1	3.7	0.0	105
2014	NCAA	Illinois State	6	4	4	76	92	2.36	1.17	16.0	229	34	78	2.29	3.0	10.9	3.7	0.0	134
2014	Rk	Orem	2	1	0	38	40	4.48	1.52	11.8	285	37	71	4.61	3.5	9.4	2.7	0.7	92

Strong, aggressive SP who may profile better in bullpen. Likes to pitch inside with lively FB and counter with hard SL that can miss bats. Can be inefficient when going for Ks and can overuse SL at times. Needs more effective CU to last as starter. FB can be straight at higher velocity.

Riefenhauser,C.J. — RP — Tampa Bay

EXP MLB DEBUT: 2014 | H/W: 6-0 180 | FUT: Situational reliever | 6A

Thrws L Age 25
2010 (20) Chipola JC

Velo	Pitch	Grade
88-93	FB	+++
80-83	SL	+++
80-83	CU	+++

Year	Lev	Team	W	L	Sv	IP	K	ERA	WHIP	BF/G	OBA	H%	S%	xERA	Ctl	Dom	Cmd	hr/9	BPV
2012	AA	Montgomery	1	1	0	18	15	3.48	1.27	8.2	227	23	84	4.43	4.0	7.5	1.9	2.0	45
2013	AA	Montgomery	4	0	11	53	48	0.51	0.74	5.5	158	20	100	0.88	1.9	8.2	4.4	0.5	114
2013	AAA	Durham	2	1	0	20	22	3.12	1.09	4.6	197	26	75	2.55	3.6	9.8	2.8	0.9	98
2014	AAA	Durham	3	3	1	57	53	1.42	1.15	5.8	203	26	90	2.40	3.9	8.3	2.1	0.5	62
2014	MLB	Tampa Bay	0	0	0	5	2	8.82	1.76	3.3	294	33	44	4.77	5.3	3.5	0.7	0.0	-61

Short pitcher who has been RP since '12. Very tough on LHH (.111 oppBA) with aggressive FB. Likes to pitch inside and use natural movement to fool hitters. Repeats delivery and arm slot, giving consistentcy to fading CU. Uses tight SL as K pitch. Hasn't been effective against RHH.

Rivero,Armando — RP — Chicago (N)

EXP MLB DEBUT: 2015 | H/W: 6-4 190 | FUT: Reliever | 8C

Thrws R Age 27
2013 FA (Cuba)

94-97	FB	++++
83-85	SL	++
	CU	++

Year	Lev	Team	W	L	Sv	IP	K	ERA	WHIP	BF/G	OBA	H%	S%	xERA	Ctl	Dom	Cmd	hr/9	BPV
2013	A	Kane County	0	0	1	18	28	5.47	1.55	7.2	271	39	71	5.65	4.5	13.9	3.1	2.0	148
2013	A+	Daytona	0	0	1	3	5	2.90	0.97	3.9	255	44	67	2.09	0.0	14.5		0.0	279
2013	AA	Tennessee	0	1	0	8	12	2.20	1.34	5.7	257	42	82	3.07	3.3	13.2	4.0	0.0	166
2014	AA	Tennessee	2	1	10	34	54	1.58	0.99	5.0	157	27	88	1.49	4.2	14.2	3.4	0.5	160
2014	AAA	Iowa	3	0	1	30	46	2.99	1.23	5.3	228	35	82	3.52	3.6	13.8	3.8	1.2	169

Cuban fireballer signed with the Cubs for $3.1 million. Pumps his FB in at 93-95 mph, maxing out at 97. Keeps hitters honest with a plus hard SL and a decent CU. Locates all three offerings well. Is aggressive on the mound and dominated at AA/AAA going 5-1 with a 2.22 ERA and 100 K in 65 IP.

Rivero,Felipe — SP — Washington

EXP MLB DEBUT: 2015 | H/W: 6-2 195 | FUT: #4 starter | 7C

Thrws L Age 23
2008 FA (Venezuela)

90-95	FB	+++
75-78	CB	++
81-83	CU	+++

Year	Lev	Team	W	L	Sv	IP	K	ERA	WHIP	BF/G	OBA	H%	S%	xERA	Ctl	Dom	Cmd	hr/9	BPV
2012	A	Bowling Green	8	8	0	113	98	3.42	1.27	17.1	265	33	73	3.43	2.3	7.8	3.4	0.4	96
2013	A+	Charlotte	9	7	0	127	91	3.40	1.37	21.3	254	30	75	3.63	3.7	6.4	1.8	0.5	35
2014	Rk	GCL Nationals	0	0	0	6	6	0.00	0.83	7.3	191	27	100	1.01	1.5	9.0	6.0	0.0	140
2014	A	Hagerstown	0	0	0	4	6	0.00	0.75	14.3	210	36	100	0.98	0.0	13.5		0.0	261
2014	AA	Harrisburg	2	7	0	43	38	4.17	1.46	18.5	270	33	73	4.37	3.8	7.9	2.1	0.8	59

Struggled and missed time with elbow injury in first half, but finished season strong at Double-A. At his best, attacks hitters with lively mid-90s FB and hard-breaking CB, but CU is best secondary pitch. But too often battles mechanical issues that lead to poor control. Sufficient arm strength to move to the bullpen if necessary.

Rodon,Carlos — SP — Chicago (A)

EXP MLB DEBUT: 2015 | H/W: 6-3 235 | FUT: #2 starter | 9C

Thrws L Age 22
2014 (1) North Carolina State

92-97	FB	++++
84-88	SL	++++
81-85	CU	+++

Year	Lev	Team	W	L	Sv	IP	K	ERA	WHIP	BF/G	OBA	H%	S%	xERA	Ctl	Dom	Cmd	hr/9	BPV
2013	NCAA	NC State	10	3	0	132		3.00	1.05	26.9	201	31	73	2.16	3.1	12.5	4.1	0.5	161
2014	NCAA	NC State	6	7	0	98	117	2.02	1.17	28.0	233	34	82	2.52	2.8	10.7	3.8	0.2	134
2014	Rk	AZL White Sox	0	0	0	3	5	6.00	1.33	6.2	321	54	50	3.98	0.0	15.0		0.0	288
2014	A+	Winston-Salem	0	0	0	9	15	1.96	1.30	9.5	212	39	83	2.39	4.9	14.7	3.0	0.0	150
2014	AAA	Charlotte	0	0	0	12	18	3.00	1.42	16.9	210	36	76	2.66	6.0	13.5	2.3	0.0	99

Durable SP with massive arm strength and power stuff to succeed in any role. Has top-of-rotation stuff with plus FB andwipeout SL that borders on plus-plus. Pitches aggressively to both sides of plate. CU with arm speed is solid-average and keeps RHH off-guard.

Rodriguez,Eduardo — SP — Boston

EXP MLB DEBUT: 2015 | H/W: 6-2 200 | FUT: #3 starter | 8C

Thrws L Age 21
2010 FA (Venezuela)

90-95	FB	+++
80-84	SL	++
82-84	CU	++++

Year	Lev	Team	W	L	Sv	IP	K	ERA	WHIP	BF/G	OBA	H%	S%	xERA	Ctl	Dom	Cmd	hr/9	BPV
2012	A	Delmarva	5	7	0	107	73	3.70	1.24	19.8	254	30	69	3.17	2.5	6.1	2.4	0.3	60
2013	A+	Frederick	6	4	0	85	66	2.86	1.21	24.5	245	30	77	3.04	2.6	7.0	2.6	0.4	72
2013	AA	Bowie	4	3	0	59	59	4.26	1.30	22.2	241	31	68	3.51	3.6	9.0	2.5	0.8	81
2014	AA	Bowie	3	7	0	82	69	4.82	1.45	21.9	280	34	66	4.22	3.2	7.6	2.4	0.5	68
2014	AA	Portland	3	1	0	37	39	0.97	1.02	23.8	223	31	92	2.09	1.9	9.5	4.9	0.2	136

Young, improving SP who had dominant August and saw K rate increase while continuing to keep ball on ground. Pitch movement is terrific with locatable FB and improving SL. Repeats delivery and adds deception to plus CU giving him weapon against RHH. Could add polish to SL.

Rodriguez,Helmis — SP — Colorado

EXP MLB DEBUT: 2019 | H/W: 5-11 155 | FUT: #4 starter | 7E

Thrws L Age 20
2010 FA (Venezuela)

87-91	FB	+++
80-83	CU	+++
	CB	+

Year	Lev	Team	W	L	Sv	IP	K	ERA	WHIP	BF/G	OBA	H%	S%	xERA	Ctl	Dom	Cmd	hr/9	BPV
2013	Rk	Grand Junction	2	4	0	54	36	5.15	1.40	15.3	282	32	63	4.42	2.7	6.0	2.3	0.8	54
2014	A-	Tri-City	4	7	0	91	41	1.98	1.10	23.8	242	27	82	2.53	1.8	4.1	2.3	0.2	43

Short Venezuelan LH was a strike throwing machine in short-season ball. Best offering is a 87-90 mph sinking FB that he pounds down in the zone. CU is a second above-avg offering, but his breaking ball is inconsistent. Could struggle as he moves up, but good control and ability to induce gb.

Rodriguez,Joely — SP — Philadelphia

EXP MLB DEBUT: 2015 | H/W: 6-1 175 | FUT: #5 starter/RP | 7C

Thrws L Age 23
2009 FA (D.R)

89-93	FB	+++
84-86	SL	+++
81-83	CU	++

Year	Lev	Team	W	L	Sv	IP	K	ERA	WHIP	BF/G	OBA	H%	S%	xERA	Ctl	Dom	Cmd	hr/9	BPV
2011	A-	State College	0	1	0	5	3	5.40	2.60	13.6	460	52	77	10.10	1.8	5.4	3.0	0.0	67
2012	A-	State College	3	4	0	64	32	4.50	1.39	19.2	291	33	66	4.02	2.1	4.5	2.1	0.3	42
2013	A	West Virginia	5	5	0	72	57	2.74	1.37	21.6	280	34	81	3.99	2.5	7.1	2.9	0.5	79
2013	A+	Bradenton	4	3	0	67	44	2.68	1.22	22.6	250	29	79	3.25	2.5	5.9	2.3	0.5	55
2014	AA	Altoona	6	11	1	134	73	4.84	1.45	19.1	286	32	66	4.45	2.9	4.9	1.7	0.7	28

Consistency is the key, as he's been both effective and not in stretches. Throws hard from left side, but control has been a problem, though has shown a sharp breaking pitch. Good AFL and winter league and December trade to PHI sets him up for 2015. Must miss more bats to succeed at highest level.

Rogers,Taylor — SP — Minnesota

EXP MLB DEBUT: 2015 | H/W: 6-3 175 | FUT: #5 starter | 6B

Thrws L Age 24
2012 (11) Kentucky

89-93	FB	+++
78-82	SL	+++
79-83	CU	++

Year	Lev	Team	W	L	Sv	IP	K	ERA	WHIP	BF/G	OBA	H%	S%	xERA	Ctl	Dom	Cmd	hr/9	BPV
2012	Rk	Elizabethton	2	1	0	30	39	1.80	0.83	18.3	191	28	83	1.55	1.5	11.7	7.8	0.6	188
2012	A	Beloit	2	2	0	33	35	2.72	1.36	15.4	261	32	88	4.49	3.3	9.5	2.9	1.4	101
2013	A	Cedar Rapids	0	1	0	10	10	7.20	1.80	15.4	332	42	59	6.24	3.6	9.0	2.5	0.9	83
2013	A+	Fort Myers	11	6	0	130	83	2.56	1.16	23.6	245	29	78	2.85	2.2	5.7	2.6	0.3	62
2014	AA	New Britain	11	6	0	145	113	3.29	1.29	24.8	268	33	73	3.39	2.3	7.0	3.1	0.2	82

Lean, wiry SP who was outstanding every month after April. Lacks upside with dwindling K rate and CU needs improvement. Knows how to pitch and works aggressively with lively FB. Challenges hitters inside and moves ball around plate. Exhibits pinpoint location in bottom half of zone.

Romano,Sal — SP — Cincinnati

EXP MLB DEBUT: 2017 | H/W: 6-4 250 | FUT: #5 starter/RP | 7C

Thrws R Age 21
2011 (23) HS (CT)

91-94	FB	+++
82-85	CB	++
	CU	++

Year	Lev	Team	W	L	Sv	IP	K	ERA	WHIP	BF/G	OBA	H%	S%	xERA	Ctl	Dom	Cmd	hr/9	BPV
2012	Rk	Billings	5	6	0	64	52	5.34	1.51	18.5	290	36	61	4.17	3.2	7.3	2.3	0.1	62
2013	A	Dayton	7	11	0	120	89	4.87	1.59	21.2	283	33	70	4.84	4.3	6.7	1.6	0.7	23
2014	A	Dayton	8	11	0	148	128	4.13	1.42	22.5	288	36	71	4.28	2.6	7.8	3.0	0.5	89

Velocity and Cmd improved during repeat year at Dayton. Utilizes durable frame to work downhill (49% GB%). FB now sits 91-95 with tailing action and hard-breaking curve keeps progressing. Improved CU will allow him to fare better against LHB and improve chances of landing rotation spot.

Romero,Enny — SP — Tampa Bay

EXP MLB DEBUT: 2013 | H/W: 6-3 210 | FUT: #3 starter | 8D

Thrws L Age 24
2008 FA (DR)

88-96	FB	+++
82-86	SL	++++
80-83	CU	++

Year	Lev	Team	W	L	Sv	IP	K	ERA	WHIP	BF/G	OBA	H%	S%	xERA	Ctl	Dom	Cmd	hr/9	BPV
2012	A+	Charlotte	5	7	0	126	107	3.93	1.31	20.8	200	25	69	2.66	5.4	7.6	1.4	0.4	9
2013	AA	Montgomery	11	7	0	140	110	2.76	1.31	21.4	218	26	80	3.08	4.7	7.1	1.5	0.6	19
2013	AAA	Durham	0	0	0	8	2	0.00	0.75	28.6	151	16	100	0.43	2.3	2.3	1.0	0.0	-2
2013	MLB	Tampa Bay	0	0	0	4	0	0.00	1.19	16.8	78	8	100	0.86	8.6	0.0	0.0	0.0	-213
2014	AAA	Durham	5	11	0	126	117	4.50	1.43	21.4	265	33	70	4.32	3.7	8.4	2.3	0.9	68

Live-armed SP who was hittable in '14—unlike previous years. Inconsistent release point hinders command, though has groundball-inducing sinker and arm speed to generate plus velocity and movement. When on, SL is plus pitch with vicious break. Posted reverse splits in first year in AAA.

Romero,Fernando — SP — Minnesota

EXP MLB DEBUT: 2018 | H/W: 6-0 215 | FUT: #3 starter | 8E

Thrws R Age 20
2011 FA (DR)

91-97	FB	++++
78-82	CB	++
84-87	CU	++

Year	Lev	Team	W	L	Sv	IP	K	ERA	WHIP	BF/G	OBA	H%	S%	xERA	Ctl	Dom	Cmd	hr/9	BPV
2013	Rk	GCL Twins	2	0	0	45	47	1.60	1.00	14.3	201	29	82	1.54	2.6	9.4	3.6	0.0	117
2014	A	Cedar Rapids	0	0	0	12	9	3.00	1.50	17.3	278	33	82	4.52	3.8	6.8	1.8	0.8	38

Short, strong SP who underwent TJ surgery in July and will miss most of '15. When healthy, throws with little effort to generate plus velocity and has power CB that serves as weapon to hitters from both sides. Works fast and efficiently, but will need time to develop raw CU that has depth.

Ross,Joe — SP — Washington

EXP MLB DEBUT: 2016 | H/W: 6-4 205 | FUT: #3 starter | 9D

Thrws R Age 21
2011 (1) HS (CA)

91-94	FB	++++
78-82	CB	+++
	CU	+++

Year	Lev	Team	W	L	Sv	IP	K	ERA	WHIP	BF/G	OBA	H%	S%	xERA	Ctl	Dom	Cmd	hr/9	BPV
2012	A-	Eugene	0	2	0	26	28	2.06	0.95	12.4	178	25	79	1.48	3.1	9.6	3.1	0.3	108
2012	A	Fort Wayne	0	2	0	27	27	6.31	1.62	20.1	302	39	60	5.09	3.7	9.0	2.5	0.7	81
2013	A	Fort Wayne	5	8	0	122	79	3.76	1.34	22.1	265	31	72	3.74	2.9	5.8	2.0	0.5	43
2014	A+	Lake Elsinore	8	6	0	101	87	4.00	1.27	21.8	261	32	68	3.52	2.5	7.7	3.1	0.5	90
2014	AA	San Antonio	2	0	0	20	19	3.60	1.20	20.1	290	36	73	4.07	0.5	8.6	19.0	0.9	160

Comes after hitters with a plus 92-94 mph FB that tops out at 96 mph. Mixes in a power SL, but CU remains a work in progress. Keeps ball down in the zone and hitters bury them into the ground. A move the bullpen remains possible if his CU doesn't progress, but it showed promise in '14.

Rucinski,Drew

SP | Los Angeles (A) | EXP MLB DEBUT: 2014 | H/W: 6-2 190 | FUT: Middle reliever | 6B

Thrws R Age 26
2011 FA (Ohio State)

Velo	Pitch	Grade
91-94	FB	+++
84-87	SP	+++
81-82	SL	++
	CU	+

Year	Lev	Team	W	L	Sv	IP	K	ERA	WHIP	BF/G	OBA	H%	S%	xERA	Ctl	Dom	Cmd	hr/9	BPV
2012	Ind	Rockford	7	4	1	103	91	3.14	1.18	18.8	248	30	76	3.34	2.3	7.9	3.5	0.8	100
2013	A+	Inland Empire	2	2	0	29	21	1.86	1.14	23.0	262	32	82	2.69	1.2	6.5	5.3	0.0	102
2013	Ind	Rockford	4	6	0	100	101	2.88	1.13	26.3	234	31	74	2.61	2.4	9.1	3.7	0.4	116
2014	AA	Arkansas	10	6	0	148	140	3.16	1.23	23.1	254	33	74	3.20	2.5	8.5	3.4	0.4	104
2014	MLB	LA Angels	0	0	0	7	8	5.07	1.55	10.3	310	43	64	4.40	2.5	10.1	4.0	0.0	132

Surprising SP who finished 2nd in TL in Ks. Pitched in indy leagues in past and returned to affiliated ball with better command and more polished arsenal. Has two solid-average pitches in 4-seamer with late movement and hard splitter. Will need to add polish to secondary pitches.

Ryan,Kyle

SP | Detroit | EXP MLB DEBUT: 2014 | H/W: 6-5 180 | FUT: #5 starter | 6C

Thrws L Age 23
2010 (12) HS (FL)

Velo	Pitch	Grade
88-92	FB	++
80-82	SL	++
75-78	CB	+++
78-82	CU	++

Year	Lev	Team	W	L	Sv	IP	K	ERA	WHIP	BF/G	OBA	H%	S%	xERA	Ctl	Dom	Cmd	hr/9	BPV
2011	A	West Michigan	6	10	0	137	99	3.15	1.28	23.4	273	33	74	3.38	2.0	6.5	3.3	0.2	82
2013	A+	Lakeland	12	7	0	142	90	3.17	1.19	23.7	248	28	76	3.36	2.3	5.7	2.4	0.8	57
2014	AA	Erie	7	10	0	126	78	4.56	1.36	25.1	282	31	69	4.56	2.3	5.6	2.4	1.1	57
2014	AAA	Toledo	3	0	0	33	20	1.64	0.79	23.8	184	22	77	0.85	1.4	5.5	4.0	0.0	79
2014	MLB	Detroit	2	0	0	10	4	2.67	1.19	6.7	260	29	75	2.82	1.8	3.6	2.0	0.0	34

Lanky LHP with below average FB, but ability to work efficiently with four pitches. Throws from low 3/4 slot which enhances sinker. CB is best secondary pitch and can drop in zone for strikes. Very low K rate limits upside, but could slot in at end of rotation to provide innings and groundballs.

Sadler,Casey

RP | Pittsburgh | EXP MLB DEBUT: 2014 | H/W: 6-4 215 | FUT: Reliever | 6C

Thrws R Age 24
2010 (25) Western Okla St JC

Velo	Pitch	Grade
89-93	FB	+++
	CT	++
	SL	+++

Year	Lev	Team	W	L	Sv	IP	K	ERA	WHIP	BF/G	OBA	H%	S%	xERA	Ctl	Dom	Cmd	hr/9	BPV
2012	A+	Bradenton	4	6	2	130		3.74	1.23	16.5	254	30	69	3.27	2.4	6.4	2.7	0.5	68
2013	AA	Altoona	11	7	0	130	67	3.32	1.21	22.8	240	26	75	3.33	2.9	4.6	1.6	0.8	23
2013	AAA	Indianapolis	0	0	0	6	5	4.50	1.33	24.9	293	33	71	5.02	1.5	7.5	5.0	1.5	113
2014	AAA	Indianapolis	11	4	0	124	77	3.04	1.19	23.7	261	29	77	3.58	1.7	5.6	3.2	0.8	71
2014	MLB	Pittsburgh	0	1	0	10	7	8.02	1.68	7.6	296	36	47	4.56	4.5	6.2	1.4	0.0	10

Tall RH from OK worked his way to the majors despite rather pedestrian stuff. Comes after hitters with a side-arm delivery and busts them down in the zone with a 90-92 mph. Gets plenty of GB outs and uses his above-average SL as an effective second offering. Struggled a bit in his MLB debut.

Sampson,Adrian

SP | Pittsburgh | EXP MLB DEBUT: 2015 | H/W: 6-3 200 | FUT: #4 starter | 7D

Thrws R Age 23
2012 (5) Bellevue CC

Velo	Pitch	Grade
90-94	FB	+++
	CB	+++
	CU	+++

Year	Lev	Team	W	L	Sv	IP	K	ERA	WHIP	BF/G	OBA	H%	S%	xERA	Ctl	Dom	Cmd	hr/9	BPV
2012	NCAA	Bellevue CC	11	0	0	79	107	1.37	0.94	22.9	174	28	86	1.26	3.1	12.2	4.0	0.2	154
2012	A-	State College	0	1	0	42	44	2.99	1.30	15.8	242	32	77	3.21	3.6	9.4	2.6	0.4	89
2013	A+	Bradenton	5	8	0	140	85	5.14	1.42	23.8	310	34	66	5.20	1.4	5.5	3.9	1.2	78
2014	AA	Altoona	10	5	0	148	99	2.55	1.05	23.8	230	27	78	2.62	1.8	6.0	3.3	0.6	77
2014	AAA	Indianapolis	1	1	0	19	10	6.16	1.89	22.4	351	39	66	6.46	3.3	4.7	1.4	0.5	14

Compact starter had a nice bounce-back after a rough 2013. Has a decent 88-92 mph FB and an inconsistent CU. Does have a plus, sharp downer CB that generates plenty of swings and misses. Shows good control, but doesn't miss many bats. Profiles as a solid back-end starter.

Sanburn,Nolan

RP | Chicago (A) | EXP MLB DEBUT: 2015 | H/W: 6-0 175 | FUT: Setup RP | 7C

Thrws R Age 23
2012 (2) Arkansas

Velo	Pitch	Grade
91-96	FB	++++
83-85	SL	+++
77-79	CB	++
81-82	CU	++

Year	Lev	Team	W	L	Sv	IP	K	ERA	WHIP	BF/G	OBA	H%	S%	xERA	Ctl	Dom	Cmd	hr/9	BPV
2012	NCAA	Arkansas	4	1	0	40	49	2.46	1.27	7.5	204	31	78	2.23	4.9	11.0	2.2	0.0	82
2012	A-	Vermont	0	1	0	18	19	3.96	1.59	11.5	309	39	78	5.44	3.0	9.4	3.2	1.0	107
2013	Rk	AZL Athletics	0	0	0	4	6	2.25	1.00	7.6	210	36	75	1.61	2.3	13.5	6.0	0.0	200
2013	A	Beloit	1	3	0	26	20	1.38	1.00	7.1	188	23	88	1.74	3.1	6.9	2.2	0.3	59
2014	A+	Stockton	3	1	6	71	73	3.29	1.45	7.2	280	36	79	4.41	3.2	9.2	2.9	0.8	99

Athletic hurler who pitched out of bullpen. Durability in question due to injury history. When on, has four pitch mix highlighted by plus, electric FB with late life. Spots ball to bottom half of zone with all pitches and SL acts as K offering. Lacks depth on CB and may shelve in short stints.

Sanchez,Aaron

SP | Toronto | EXP MLB DEBUT: 2014 | H/W: 6-4 200 | FUT: #2 starter / Closer | 9C

Thrws R Age 22
2010 (1-S) HS (CA)

Velo	Pitch	Grade
92-98	FB	++++
78-83	CB	++++
81-84	CU	+++

Year	Lev	Team	W	L	Sv	IP	K	ERA	WHIP	BF/G	OBA	H%	S%	xERA	Ctl	Dom	Cmd	hr/9	BPV
2012	A	Lansing	8	5	0	90	97	2.50	1.28	14.8	201	28	80	2.52	5.1	9.7	1.9	0.3	55
2013	A+	Dunedin	4	5	0	86	75	3.34	1.20	15.7	206	26	72	2.50	4.2	7.8	1.9	0.4	46
2014	AA	New Hampshire	3	4	0	66	57	3.82	1.39	19.9	218	28	71	3.01	5.5	7.8	1.4	0.3	11
2014	AAA	Buffalo	0	3	0	34	27	4.22	1.55	18.6	272	32	76	4.87	4.5	7.1	1.6	1.1	25
2014	MLB	Toronto	2	2	3	33	27	1.09	0.70	4.8	131	16	86	0.30	2.5	7.4	3.0	0.3	84

Athletic pitcher who worked out of pen in majors. Possesses dynamic stuff thrown with easy delivery. Tough to hit heavy FB and gets ample movement on two-seamer. Plus CB can be dynamite and CU shows above average potential. Walk rate and declining K rate should be watched.

Sanchez,Ricardo

SP | Atlanta | EXP MLB DEBUT: 2018 | H/W: 5-11 170 | FUT: #2 starter | 8D

Thrws L Age 17
2013 FA (Venezuela)

Velo	Pitch	Grade
89-93	FB	+++
77-81	CB	+++
82-85	CU	++

Year	Lev	Team	W	L	Sv	IP	K	ERA	WHIP	BF/G	OBA	H%	S%	xERA	Ctl	Dom	Cmd	hr/9	BPV
2014	Rk	AZL Angels	2	2	0	38	43	3.53	1.62	14.1	271	38	76	4.00	5.2	10.1	2.0	0.0	60

Short, lean prospect who combines smooth delivery and very fast arm to achieve success. Struggles to throw consistent strikes, but has potential for three average to plus offerings. FB features late sink and CB projects to plus pitch with velocity and shape. Needs to develop CU.

Sanchez,Victor

SP | Seattle | EXP MLB DEBUT: 2017 | H/W: 6-0 255 | FUT: #3 starter | 8D

Thrws R Age 20
2011 FA (Venezuela)

Velo	Pitch	Grade
88-94	FB	+++
77-79	CB	++
81-83	CU	+++

Year	Lev	Team	W	L	Sv	IP	K	ERA	WHIP	BF/G	OBA	H%	S%	xERA	Ctl	Dom	Cmd	hr/9	BPV
2012	A-	Everett	6	2	0	85	69	3.18	1.13	22.4	224	27	73	2.66	2.9	7.3	2.6	0.5	72
2013	A	Clinton	6	6	0	113	79	2.79	1.10	22.1	249	30	74	2.72	1.4	6.3	4.4	0.3	92
2014	AA	Jackson	7	6	0	124	97	4.20	1.30	22.3	268	30	72	4.34	2.5	7.0	2.9	1.2	78

Young, strong prospect who has huge, muscular frame and advanced pitchability. Bypassed High-A and showed impressive pitch mix despite mediocre K rate. Throws quality strikes from downhill angle, though can be subject to HR when FB flattens. CB only OK, though CU flashes plus.

Sands,Carson

SP | Chicago (N) | EXP MLB DEBUT: 2019 | H/W: 6-3 195 | FUT: #3 starter | 8D

Thrws L Age 20
2014 (4) HS (FL)

Velo	Pitch	Grade
91-93	FB	+++
73-75	CB	+++
76-78	CU	++

Year	Lev	Team	W	L	Sv	IP	K	ERA	WHIP	BF/G	OBA	H%	S%	xERA	Ctl	Dom	Cmd	hr/9	BPV
2014	Rk	AZL Cubs	3	1	0	19	20	1.89	1.16	8.4	219	31	82	2.15	3.3	9.5	2.9	0.0	99

Big, strong LH. He has a good low-90s FB with good life. Also has a good CB and a promising CU. In HS had a violent delivery with some late head jerk that caused him to slide out of the 1st round. He has quieted down his delivery some, but it also provides deception.

Sappington,Mark

SP | Tampa Bay | EXP MLB DEBUT: 2016 | H/W: 6-5 210 | FUT: #3 starter/setupRP | 7E

Thrws R Age 24
2012 (5) Rockhurst

Velo	Pitch	Grade
90-95	FB	+++
80-83	SL	+++
81-84	CU	++

Year	Lev	Team	W	L	Sv	IP	K	ERA	WHIP	BF/G	OBA	H%	S%	xERA	Ctl	Dom	Cmd	hr/9	BPV
2012	Rk	Orem	1	1	0	36	34	5.22	1.30	9.9	233	29	59	3.39	4.0	8.5	2.1	0.7	63
2013	A+	Inland Empire	11	4	0	130	110	3.39	1.27	24.2	219	27	75	3.10	4.3	7.6	1.8	0.7	39
2013	AA	Arkansas	1	1	0	25	26	3.93	1.71	22.8	245	33	76	4.20	7.1	9.3	1.3	0.4	-8
2014	A+	Inland Empire	3	7	5	70	80	5.78	1.75	9.7	288	37	70	5.91	5.5	10.3	1.9	1.4	54
2014	AA	Arkansas	1	4	0	43	34	6.47	1.86	22.4	266	32	63	4.94	7.5	7.1	0.9	0.4	-57

Hard-throwing RHP who struggled in rotation at AA before demotion to pen at High-A. Was OK last 2 months in new role which allowed him to rear back and fire FB. Gets good late action, but pitches up often. Can overthrow and has inconsistent slot. Hard SL can show plus potential.

Schultz,Jaime

SP | Tampa Bay | EXP MLB DEBUT: 2016 | H/W: 5-10 200 | FUT: #4 starter | 7C

Thrws R Age 23
2013 (14) High Point

Velo	Pitch	Grade
89-95	FB	+++
82-84	SL	++
77-81	CB	+++
80-84	CU	+++

Year	Lev	Team	W	L	Sv	IP	K	ERA	WHIP	BF/G	OBA	H%	S%	xERA	Ctl	Dom	Cmd	hr/9	BPV
2012	NCAA	High Point	4	3	6	43	49	3.14	1.49	8.1	229	33	78	3.30	5.9	10.3	1.8	0.2	44
2013	NCAA	High Point	1	6	0	60	59	3.59	1.30	17.7	198	27	70	2.40	5.4	8.8	1.6	0.1	31
2013	A-	Hudson Valley	1	2	0	44	55	3.06	1.38	10.9	205	29	79	3.11	5.9	11.2	1.9	0.6	60
2014	A	Bowling Green	2	1	0	37	58	1.95	1.11	16.1	206	35	85	2.28	3.4	14.1	4.1	0.5	180
2014	A+	Charlotte	2	0	0	23	21	3.13	1.48	19.8	227	30	76	3.07	5.9	8.2	1.4	0.0	7

Short, compact SP with little projection, but has impactful pitch mix thrown with electric arm. Very little effort in athletic delivery and hides ball well, making sneaky quick FB play up. Varies speed and shape with two breaking balls and CU has some late action. Very tough on RHH (under .200).

Selman,Sam — SP — Kansas City

EXP MLB DEBUT: 2015 | H/W: 6-3 195 | FUT: #3 starter/setupRP | 8D

Thrws L Age 24
2012 (2) Vanderbilt

Velo	Pitch	Grade
89-95	FB	++++
80-85	SL	+++
78-81	CB	++
82-84	CU	++

Year	Lev	Team	W	L	Sv	IP	K	ERA	WHIP	BF/G	OBA	H%	S%	xERA	Ctl	Dom	Cmd	hr/9	BPV
2012	NCAA	Vanderbilt	9	3	0	76	80	3.55	1.43	19.0	235	32	74	3.28	5.1	9.5	1.9	0.2	51
2012	Rk	Idaho Falls	5	4	0	60	89	2.10	1.11	18.2	210	35	80	2.03	3.3	13.3	4.0	0.1	169
2013	A+	Wilmington	11	9	0	125	128	3.38	1.38	19.5	200	27	74	2.69	6.1	9.2	1.5	0.2	19
2014	AA	NW Arkansas	4	6	0	93	87	3.87	1.40	14.0	236	30	73	3.62	4.7	8.4	1.8	0.7	42
2014	AAA	Omaha	0	0	0	4	7	13.50	3.50	5.1	383	62	57	10.54	15.8	15.8	1.0	0.0	-124

Long-limbed LHP who moved to pen in July and may be future role. Misses bats with solid FB/SL combination and stuff is tough to elevate. Delivery remains inconsistent, negatively impacting command. Improving CU, but still not up to snuff. Varies speeds on two distinct breaking balls.

Senzatela,Antonio — SP — Colorado

EXP MLB DEBUT: 2018 | H/W: 6-1 180 | FUT: #4 starter | 7D

Thrws R Age 20
2011 FA (Venezuela)

Velo	Pitch	Grade
90-94	FB	+++
	CB	++
	CU	++

Year	Lev	Team	W	L	Sv	IP	K	ERA	WHIP	BF/G	OBA	H%	S%	xERA	Ctl	Dom	Cmd	hr/9	BPV
2013	Rk	DSL Rockies	6	1	0	51	46	1.76	0.69	22.4	182	24	74	0.71	0.5	8.1	15.3	0.2	150
2013	A-	Tri-City	2	4	0	42	20	3.85	1.45	22.5	288	32	72	4.07	2.8	4.3	1.5	0.2	20
2014	A	Asheville	15	2	0	144	89	3.12	1.18	22.2	248	28	75	3.26	2.2	5.6	2.5	0.7	57

Short, stocky Venezuelan RH put up solid numbers in his full-sesaon debut in the SAL. Comes after hitters from a high 3/4 arm slot and gets a bit of late run on his 92-95 mph FB. Throws a nice splitter and a below-avg CU and CB.

Severino,Luis — SP — New York (A)

EXP MLB DEBUT: 2016 | H/W: 6-0 195 | FUT: #3 starter | 9C

Thrws R Age 21
2011 FA (DR)

Velo	Pitch	Grade
91-97	FB	++++
82-86	SL	+++
83-85	CU	+++

Year	Lev	Team	W	L	Sv	IP	K	ERA	WHIP	BF/G	OBA	H%	S%	xERA	Ctl	Dom	Cmd	hr/9	BPV
2013	Rk	GCL Yankees	3	1	0	26		1.38	0.84	15.9	179	28	82	0.87	2.1	11.0	5.3	0.0	161
2013	A	CharlestonSC	1	1	0	17	21	4.19	1.45	18.4	302	42	71	4.52	2.1	11.0	5.3	0.5	159
2014	A	CharlestonSC	3	2	0	67	70	2.81	1.15	19.0	247	33	75	2.73	2.0	9.4	4.7	0.3	133
2014	A+	Tampa	1	1	0	20	28	1.34	0.84	18.5	162	28	82	0.67	2.7	12.5	4.7	0.0	170
2014	AA	Trenton	2	2	0	25	29	2.52	1.04	16.1	221	31	76	2.21	2.2	10.4	4.8	0.4	148

Breakout SP who dominated three levels despite youth and inexperience. All about Ks and groundballs with plus raw stuff and loose, electric arm. Delivery conducive to keeping ball down despite lack of height, and peppers zone with plus FB and hard SL. Changes speeds well for age.

Shane,Casey — SP — Cleveland

EXP MLB DEBUT: 2018 | H/W: 6-4 200 | FUT: #3 starter | 8E

Thrws R Age 19
2013 (6) HS (TX)

Velo	Pitch	Grade
87-93	FB	+++
80-82	SL	+++
74-78	CB	+
	CU	+++

Year	Lev	Team	W	L	Sv	IP	K	ERA	WHIP	BF/G	OBA	H%	S%	xERA	Ctl	Dom	Cmd	hr/9	BPV
2013	Rk	AZL Indians	1	1	1	29	22	6.52	1.69	11.9	288	35	58	4.73	5.0	6.8	1.4	0.3	7
2014	Rk	AZL Indians	5	0	0	46	40	2.73	1.15	18.3	226	29	75	2.42	2.9	7.8	2.7	0.2	79
2014	A-	Mahoning Val	1	0	0	11	5	0.82	0.82	20.0	205	24	89	1.18	0.8	4.1	5.0	0.0	70

Live-armed SP who has long time to develop nuances of craft. Very raw with mixing pitches, though has assets in athleticism and loose delivery. Velocity is inconsistent and will need strength to maintain deep into games. Has potential for plus CU and SL while CB remains in infancy stage.

Sheffield,Justus — SP — Cleveland

EXP MLB DEBUT: 2018 | H/W: 5-10 195 | FUT: #3 starter | 8D

Thrws L Age 18
2014 (1) HS (TN)

Velo	Pitch	Grade
89-94	FB	+++
75-78	CB	+++
80-83	CU	+++

Year	Lev	Team	W	L	Sv	IP	K	ERA	WHIP	BF/G	OBA	H%	S%	xERA	Ctl	Dom	Cmd	hr/9	BPV
2014	Rk	AZL Indians	3	1	0	20	29	4.90	1.63	11.2	296	46	67	4.37	4.0	12.9	3.2	0.0	142

Very athletic SP with plus arm strength that generates easy velocity. Lack of height could be concern, but compensates with impressive feel and pitch movement. Sinking FB is sneaky quick and CB shows potential for plus, K pitch. Can overthrow at times and erratic arm slot needs work.

Sherfy,Jimmie — RP — Arizona

EXP MLB DEBUT: 2016 | H/W: 6-0 175 | FUT: Setup RP | 7C

Thrws R Age 23
2013 (10) Oregon

Velo	Pitch	Grade
93-94	FB	+++
82-85	SL	+++

Year	Lev	Team	W	L	Sv	IP	K	ERA	WHIP	BF/G	OBA	H%	S%	xERA	Ctl	Dom	Cmd	hr/9	BPV
2013	NCAA	Oregon	2	0	21	40	55	2.25	1.18	4.2	226	36	79	2.26	3.2	12.4	3.9	0.0	156
2013	A-	Hillsboro	0	0	5	9	17	0.00	0.44	3.3	106	26	100	0.00	1.0	17.0	17.0	0.0	297
2013	A	South Bend	1	1	2	8	12	2.22	1.60	4.0	304	48	85	4.42	3.3	13.3	4.0	0.0	168
2014	A+	Visalia	2	0	6	11	23	3.27	1.00	3.8	162	33	78	2.55	4.1	18.8	4.6	1.6	246
2014	AA	Mobile	3	1	1	38	45	4.97	1.37	4.3	241	33	65	3.84	4.3	10.7	2.5	0.9	95

Funky low ¾ delivery is tough to watch, but he is effectively wild. Quick arm action generates solid velocity. FB sits at 93-94 mph. Best pitch is SL that has swing-and-miss action. Arm slot and nasty SL are lethal vs. RHH. Could get MLB hitters out right now, but needs to show better command.

Shipley,Braden — SP — Arizona

EXP MLB DEBUT: 2016 | H/W: 6-3 190 | FUT: #2 starter | 9D

Thrws R Age 23
2013 (1) Nevada

Velo	Pitch	Grade
92-94	FB	++++
78-80	CB	+++
83-86	CU	++++

Year	Lev	Team	W	L	Sv	IP	K	ERA	WHIP	BF/G	OBA	H%	S%	xERA	Ctl	Dom	Cmd	hr/9	BPV
2013	A-	Hillsboro	0	2	0	19	24	7.58	1.89	11.2	359	50	57	6.53	2.8	11.4	4.0	0.5	146
2013	A	South Bend	0	1	0	20	16	2.67	1.09	19.7	197	23	80	2.58	3.6	7.1	2.0	0.9	50
2014	A	South Bend	4	2	0	45	41	3.78	1.26	23.1	265	34	68	3.22	2.2	8.2	3.7	0.2	106
2014	A+	Visalia	2	4	0	60	68	4.04	1.30	24.7	252	33	72	3.90	3.1	10.2	3.2	1.0	116
2014	AA	Mobile	1	2	0	20	18	3.60	1.20	20.1	199	22	76	3.30	4.5	8.1	1.8	1.4	42

Plus FB sits at 92-94 mph maxing out at 99. Also has a good, hard CB, and an above-average CU that is his best offering. FB can flatten out when overthrown and needs to improve FB command. Repeatable mechanics makes his curve and CU more effective.

Shreve,Chasen — RP — New York (A)

EXP MLB DEBUT: 2014 | H/W: 6-3 190 | FUT: Setup RP | 7C

Thrws L Age 24
2010 (11) Coll of So. Nevada CC

Velo	Pitch	Grade
93-96	FB	++++
	CU	++

Year	Lev	Team	W	L	Sv	IP	K	ERA	WHIP	BF/G	OBA	H%	S%	xERA	Ctl	Dom	Cmd	hr/9	BPV
2013	A+	Lynchburg	0	1	2	19	15	2.81	1.20	5.5	217	26	77	2.69	3.8	7.0	1.9	0.5	43
2013	AA	Mississippi	3	1	0	42	28	4.48	1.54	5.1	265	32	69	3.96	4.7	6.0	1.3	0.2	-1
2014	AA	Mississippi	3	2	7	54	76	2.50	0.94	5.7	216	34	73	1.85	1.5	12.6	8.4	0.3	205
2014	AAA	Gwinnett	2	1	2	9	11	3.91	1.30	3.8	258	32	80	4.85	2.9	10.8	3.7	2.0	132
2014	MLB	Atlanta	0	0	0	12	15	0.74	1.07	3.1	227	34	92	2.02	2.2	11.2	5.0	0.0	159

Early in his career attempted to be a command and control LH, but it caught up at AA. Re-worked his approach and started firing the ball in the mid-90s. Dominated hitters at AA, striking out 30 of 59 batters in May. Continued to impress in two stints with the Braves, posting a 0.73 ERA.

Sims,Lucas — SP — Atlanta

EXP MLB DEBUT: 2016 | H/W: 6-2 195 | FUT: #2 starter | 9D

Thrws R Age 20
2012 (1) HS (GA)

Velo	Pitch	Grade
92-95	FB	++++
77-79	CB	+++
83-85	CU	++

Year	Lev	Team	W	L	Sv	IP	K	ERA	WHIP	BF/G	OBA	H%	S%	xERA	Ctl	Dom	Cmd	hr/9	BPV
2012	Rk	Danville	2	4	0	27	29	4.33	1.41	14.3	255	34	69	3.86	4.0	9.7	2.4	0.7	84
2012	Rk	GCL Braves	0	0	0	7	10	1.29	0.43	7.6	92	9	100	0.15	1.3	12.9	10.0	1.3	215
2013	A	Rome	12	4	0	116	134	2.63	1.11	16.3	202	29	75	2.04	3.6	10.4	2.9	0.2	109
2014	A+	Lynchburg	8	11	0	156	107	4.21	1.30	23.0	249	29	68	3.57	3.3	6.2	1.9	0.7	40

Was one of the youngest players in the CAR. FB sits at 92-95 mph with good life. Mixes in an improved CB that has depth. CU is his weakest offering and will need to improve. Started slowly but finished strong with a 2.88 ERA in August. Is effective against both RHH and LHH.

Skoglund,Eric — SP — Kansas City

EXP MLB DEBUT: 2017 | H/W: 6-7 200 | FUT: #4 starter | 7D

Thrws L Age 22
2014 (3) Central Florida

Velo	Pitch	Grade
88-93	FB	+++
78-81	SL	+++
77-81	CU	++

Year	Lev	Team	W	L	Sv	IP	K	ERA	WHIP	BF/G	OBA	H%	S%	xERA	Ctl	Dom	Cmd	hr/9	BPV
2012	NCAA	Central FL	5	3	0	47	45	3.24	1.63	12.4	303	39	79	4.70	3.6	8.6	2.4	0.2	75
2013	NCAA	Central FL	1	4	0	56	26	5.12	1.55	17.5	268	29	66	4.43	4.6	4.2	0.9	0.6	-32
2014	NCAA	Central FL	9	3	0	110	94	2.54	1.03	28.2	217	28	73	1.89	2.2	7.7	3.5	0.1	97
2014	Rk	Idaho Falls	0	2	0	23	25	5.09	1.70	11.5	316	41	70	5.60	3.5	9.8	2.8	0.8	99

Very tall SP who throws with easy arm action to generate average velocity and life with FB. Shows advanced delivery that he repeats consistently. Command can come and go and should add strength as pro. Uses height to pitch downhill and has solid SL that misses bats.

Skulina,Tyler — SP — Chicago (N)

EXP MLB DEBUT: 2017 | H/W: 6-5 255 | FUT: #5 starter | 6C

Thrws R Age 23
2013 (4) Kent State

Velo	Pitch	Grade
91-94	FB	+++
	SL	+++
	CB	++
	CU	++

Year	Lev	Team	W	L	Sv	IP	K	ERA	WHIP	BF/G	OBA	H%	S%	xERA	Ctl	Dom	Cmd	hr/9	BPV
2013	NCAA	Kent State	6	4	0	93	102	3.38	1.16	24.7	220	30	71	2.61	3.3	9.8	3.0	0.5	107
2013	A-	Boise	0	0	0	15	10	1.20	0.80	6.8	175	22	83	0.78	1.8	6.0	3.3	0.0	77
2013	A	Kane County	0	2	0	9	9	9.78	2.17	11.5	350	43	53	7.58	5.9	8.8	1.5	1.0	18
2014	A	Kane County	4	7	0	89	68	3.23	1.19	19.9	220	27	72	2.55	3.5	6.9	1.9	0.3	46
2014	A+	Daytona	0	2	0	8	7	7.68	2.44	14.4	322	41	65	6.86	9.9	7.7	0.8	0.0	-110

Tall, thick-bodied RH from Kent State held his own in 17 starts in the MWL. FB typically sits in the low-90s, topping out at 96 mph with a plus curve. CU is below average. Despite his size he isn't overpowering and will have to work hard to remain in a starting role.

Slegers,Aaron — SP — Minnesota

EXP MLB DEBUT: 2016 | H/W: 6-10 245 | FUT: #5 starter | 7D

Thrws R Age 22
2013 (5) Indiana

Velo	Pitch	Grade
87-93	FB	+++
80-82	SL	+++
80-82	CU	++

Year	Lev	Team	W	L	Sv	IP	K	ERA	WHIP	BF/G	OBA	H%	S%	xERA	Ctl	Dom	Cmd	hr/9	BPV
2012	NCAA	Indiana	0	1	1	7	5	6.34	1.83	6.6	310	37	62	5.15	5.1	6.3	1.3	0.0	-5
2013	NCAA	Indiana	9	2	0	106	59	2.04	1.18	23.6	265	31	81	2.94	1.4	5.0	3.5	0.1	69
2013	Rk	Elizabethton	0	0	3	19	18	0.47	0.95	8.0	230	31	94	1.77	0.9	8.5	9.0	0.0	146
2014	A	Cedar Rapids	7	7	0	113	90	4.54	1.22	22.8	270	33	62	3.53	1.6	7.2	4.5	0.6	104
2014	A+	Fort Myers	2	1	0	19	12	3.32	0.95	23.9	207	22	69	2.41	1.9	5.7	3.0	0.9	69

Very tall RHP with athleticism and can surprisingly repeat delivery despite long levers. Throws with more touch and feel than velocity and pitches to contact. FB is rather pedestrian without much movement and average SL is go-to offering. Lacks deception in delivery and CU.

Smith,Burch — SP — Tampa Bay

EXP MLB DEBUT: 2013 | H/W: 6-4 215 | FUT: #4 starter | 7C

Thrws R Age 24
2011 (14) Oklahoma

Velo	Pitch	Grade
92-96	FB	++++
	CU	++
	CB	++

Year	Lev	Team	W	L	Sv	IP	K	ERA	WHIP	BF/G	OBA	H%	S%	xERA	Ctl	Dom	Cmd	hr/9	BPV
2012	A+	Lake Elsinore	9	6	0	128	137	3.86	1.20	19.8	260	34	69	3.52	1.9	9.6	5.1	0.8	140
2013	AA	San Antonio	1	2	0	31	37	1.16	0.74	18.5	162	24	86	0.71	1.7	10.7	6.2	0.3	164
2013	AAA	Tucson	5	1	0	61	65	3.39	1.20	20.4	246	33	72	3.14	2.5	9.6	3.8	0.6	123
2013	MLB	San Diego	1	3	0	36	46	6.48	1.66	16.2	277	35	67	6.28	5.2	11.5	2.2	2.2	83
2014	AAA	El Paso	0	2	0	5	3	19.41	3.53	16.2	475	49	44	16.16	8.8	5.3	0.6	3.5	-125

Tall, strong-bodied righty from Oklahoma attacks hitters with a plus 92-96 mph FB that tops out at 98. Missed most of 2014 with a forearm injury, but did not need surgery and was in action in the AFL. Fringy CB, CU cloud future role and injury history could result in a move to relief. Was traded to TAM as part of the Wil Myers deal.

Smith,Caleb — SP — New York (A)

EXP MLB DEBUT: 2017 | H/W: 6-2 175 | FUT: #4 starter | 7E

Thrws L Age 23
2013 (14) Sam Houston State

Velo	Pitch	Grade
89-94	FB	+++
79-83	SL	++
82-85	CU	+++

Year	Lev	Team	W	L	Sv	IP	K	ERA	WHIP	BF/G	OBA	H%	S%	xERA	Ctl	Dom	Cmd	hr/9	BPV
2013	NCAA	Sam Houston St	7	5	0	89		3.44	1.42	20.9	208	26	74	2.79	6.1	6.9	1.1	0.1	-22
2013	A-	Staten Island	1	2	0	47	52	1.91	1.02	13.9	199	29	79	1.55	2.9	9.9	3.5	0.0	119
2013	AA	Trenton	0	0	0	3	5	2.81	1.25	13.0	250	43	75	2.73	2.8	14.1	5.0	0.0	195
2014	A	CharlestonSC	5	7	0	78	80	3.11	1.22	17.5	214	29	75	2.68	4.0	9.2	2.3	0.5	75
2014	A+	Tampa	5	2	0	39	36	4.83	1.28	17.8	261	33	60	3.45	2.5	8.3	3.3	0.5	99

Lean, strong SP who posted reverse splits in first full season. Flyballs abound, as likes to pitch up in zone and can have poor location. FB shows plus glimpses, but below average SL needs lot of work. CU is second best offering and can feature depth and fade with fast arm speed.

Smith,Carson — RP — Seattle

EXP MLB DEBUT: 2014 | H/W: 6-6 215 | FUT: Setup RP / Closer | 7B

Thrws R Age 25
2011 (8) Texas State

Velo	Pitch	Grade
90-94	FB	++++
84-87	SL	++++

Year	Lev	Team	W	L	Sv	IP	K	ERA	WHIP	BF/G	OBA	H%	S%	xERA	Ctl	Dom	Cmd	hr/9	BPV
2011	NCAA	Texas State	9	3	0	113	129	1.99	1.22	26.9	220	32	83	2.46	3.8	10.3	2.7	0.2	100
2012	A+	High Desert	5	1	15	62	77	2.90	1.32	5.2	236	35	78	3.04	4.1	11.2	2.8	0.3	109
2013	AA	Jackson	1	3	15	50	71	1.80	1.00	4.3	190	31	82	1.54	3.1	12.8	4.2	0.2	165
2014	AAA	Tacoma	1	3	10	43	45	2.93	1.33	4.6	266	36	77	3.39	2.7	9.4	3.5	0.2	114
2014	MLB	Seattle	1	0	0	8	10	0.00	0.62	3.1	81	13	100	0.00	3.3	11.1	3.3	0.0	128

Tall, strong RP who reached majors and remains effective with two pitches and low arm slot. Slings ball to plate and is extreme groundball pitcher due to plus sinking FB. Hard SL is dependable secondary, though he has trouble commanding. Throws with max effort, but repeats it consistently.

Smith,Kyle — SP — Houston

EXP MLB DEBUT: 2016 | H/W: 6-0 170 | FUT: #4 starter | 6B

Thrws R Age 22
2011 (4) HS (FL)

Velo	Pitch	Grade
87-91	FB	+++
77-80	CB	+++
79-82	CU	++

Year	Lev	Team	W	L	Sv	IP	K	ERA	WHIP	BF/G	OBA	H%	S%	xERA	Ctl	Dom	Cmd	hr/9	BPV
2012	A	Kane County	4	3	0	67	87	2.95	1.22	20.9	247	37	76	3.02	2.7	11.7	4.4	0.4	156
2013	A+	Lancaster	1	1	0	23	21	7.40	1.52	20.0	285	33	52	5.42	3.5	8.2	2.3	1.6	71
2013	A+	Wilmington	5	4	0	104	96	2.85	1.17	21.9	241	30	79	3.20	2.5	8.3	3.3	0.8	100
2014	A+	Lancaster	4	0	0	27	31	2.65	1.10	15.2	190	25	81	2.60	4.0	10.3	2.6	1.0	95
2014	AA	Corpus Christi	5	5	0	95	96	4.35	1.23	18.3	255	31	69	4.05	2.4	9.1	3.8	1.3	118

Aggressive RHP with below average velocity, but above average feel and clean delivery. Tight CB is best pitch and can throw for strikes in any count. Repeats quick delivery, though lacks deception. More of a flyball pitcher who has allowed HR. Must improve fringy CU to get to next level.

Smith,Nate — SP — Los Angeles (A)

EXP MLB DEBUT: 2015 | H/W: 6-3 200 | FUT: Middle reliever | 6B

Thrws L Age 23
2013 (8) Furman

Velo	Pitch	Grade
89-94	FB	+++
76-78	CB	+++
	CU	++

Year	Lev	Team	W	L	Sv	IP	K	ERA	WHIP	BF/G	OBA	H%	S%	xERA	Ctl	Dom	Cmd	hr/9	BPV
2012	NCAA	Furman	4	5	0	74	67	5.58	1.66	22.1	323	40	65	5.36	2.8	8.1	2.9	0.5	89
2013	NCAA	Furman	7	4	0	100	98	3.60	1.38	24.7	269	33	80	4.64	3.1	8.8	2.9	1.3	94
2013	Rk	Orem	2	2	0	35	31	3.86	1.17	9.3	256	31	70	3.65	1.8	8.0	4.4	1.0	113
2014	A+	Inland Empire	6	3	0	55	51	3.10	1.00	21.1	208	27	69	2.09	2.3	8.3	3.6	0.5	106
2014	AA	Arkansas	5	3	0	62	67	2.90	1.26	23.0	215	29	77	2.76	4.3	9.7	2.2	0.4	75

Command-oriented SP who ended season in July. Can be tough to hit, especially RHH, with impressive CB with late break. Generates aveage velocity with clean, loose arm. Locates FB and CB well in strike zone. Not overpowering and is flyball pitcher. Could be better as RP.

Smoral,Matt — SP — Toronto

EXP MLB DEBUT: 2017 | H/W: 6-8 220 | FUT: #2 starter | 9E

Thrws L Age 21
2012 (1-S) HS (OH)

Velo	Pitch	Grade
89-95	FB	++++
80-85	SL	+++
82-84	CU	+

Year	Lev	Team	W	L	Sv	IP	K	ERA	WHIP	BF/G	OBA	H%	S%	xERA	Ctl	Dom	Cmd	hr/9	BPV
2013	Rk	GCL Blue Jays	0	2	0	25	27	7.14	1.90	7.9	236	32	60	4.59	9.3	9.6	1.0	0.4	-59
2014	Rk	Bluefield	2	3	0	33	51	3.52	1.48	15.8	249	42	73	3.29	4.9	13.8	2.8	0.0	135
2014	A-	Vancouver	2	0	0	20	19	2.70	1.45	17.1	199	27	79	2.66	6.8	8.6	1.3	0.0	-10

Very tall SP with long levers and ability to pitch downhill and induce groundballs. Hasn't pitched in full-season ball and has limited experience due to injuries. Has plus potential in lively FB and SL combo, though controlling both has been a problem. Developing CU still in beginner mode and long arm action offers little deception.

Sneed,Cy — SP — Milwaukee

EXP MLB DEBUT: 2018 | H/W: 6-4 185 | FUT: #5 starter | 6C

Thrws R Age 22
2014 (3) Dallas Baptist

Velo	Pitch	Grade
90-92	FB	++
	SL	++
	CU	++
	SP	++

Year	Lev	Team	W	L	Sv	IP	K	ERA	WHIP	BF/G	OBA	H%	S%	xERA	Ctl	Dom	Cmd	hr/9	BPV
2012	NCAA	Dallas Baptist	8	5	0	85	71	4.45	1.39	21.0	275	34	68	4.09	2.9	7.5	2.6	0.6	76
2013	NCAA	Dallas Baptist	4	4	0	83	54	4.87	1.61	23.0	303	34	70	5.20	3.5	5.8	1.7	0.8	30
2014	NCAA	Dallas Baptist	8	3	0	104	82	3.55	1.30	26.8	252	31	72	3.28	3.1	7.1	2.3	0.3	62
2014	Rk	Helena	0	2	1	38	31	5.92	1.68	15.6	318	38	65	5.78	3.3	7.3	2.2	0.9	61

3rd round pick and scuffled in his pro debut. Big, physical kid can hit 94 mph with FB, but it sits at 90-92. Mixes in a solid change, a splitter, and a fringy slurve. Has good mound pressence and should fare better once he reaches full-season ball in 2015.

Snell,Blake — SP — Tampa Bay

EXP MLB DEBUT: 2016 | H/W: 6-4 180 | FUT: #3 starter | 8D

Thrws L Age 22
2011 (1-S) HS (WA)

Velo	Pitch	Grade
88-94	FB	+++
80-83	SL	+++
77-80	CB	++
82-85	CU	+++

Year	Lev	Team	W	L	Sv	IP	K	ERA	WHIP	BF/G	OBA	H%	S%	xERA	Ctl	Dom	Cmd	hr/9	BPV
2011	Rk	GCL Devil Rays	1	2	0	26	26	3.10	1.57	10.4	290	39	78	4.15	3.8	9.0	2.4	0.0	77
2012	Rk	Princeton	5	1	0	47	53	2.10	1.08	16.7	204	27	85	2.49	3.2	10.1	3.1	0.8	113
2013	A	Bowling Green	4	9	0	99	106	4.27	1.65	19.2	244	32	75	4.38	6.6	9.6	1.5	0.7	12
2014	A	Bowling Green	3	2	0	40	42	1.80	1.12	19.8	187	26	84	1.90	4.3	9.4	2.2	0.2	73
2014	A+	Charlotte	5	6	0	75	77	3.95	1.41	19.9	246	34	70	3.25	4.4	9.2	2.1	0.1	64

Tall, lean SP who oozes projection. Repeated Low-A to start season before dominating level and moving up. Combines solid sinker with two breaking balls and promising CU that could evolve into legitimate plus weapon. Has trouble repeating delivery which limits control. Big upside.

Snodgress,Scott — SP — Los Angeles (A)

EXP MLB DEBUT: 2014 | H/W: 6-6 225 | FUT: #4 starter / RP | 7D

Thrws L Age 25
2011 (5) Stanford

Velo	Pitch	Grade
87-93	FB	+++
80-82	CB	++++
80-83	CU	++

Year	Lev	Team	W	L	Sv	IP	K	ERA	WHIP	BF/G	OBA	H%	S%	xERA	Ctl	Dom	Cmd	hr/9	BPV
2012	A+	Winston-Salem	4	0	0	42	44	1.50	0.98	19.9	180	24	87	1.64	3.2	9.4	2.9	0.4	101
2013	AA	Birmingham	11	11	0	143	90	4.71	1.43	23.4	266	30	66	4.02	3.7	5.7	1.5	0.6	20
2014	AA	Birmingham	6	7	0	122	79	3.90	1.40	24.6	257	29	73	3.91	3.8	5.8	1.5	0.7	19
2014	AAA	Charlotte	0	1	0	16	16	5.03	1.30	8.3	272	31	71	5.33	2.2	8.9	4.0	2.2	119
2014	MLB	Chi White Sox	0	0	0	2	1	17.14	5.24	4.2	575	59	70	24.53	12.9	4.3	0.3	4.3	-252

Tall, deceptive lefty who repeated AA to start before moving to pen in AAA. Continues to showcase tight CB that he can drop in zone for strikes. Overthrows and doesn't repeat release point. FB is average at best and features cutting action. CU has moments, but is distant 3rd pitch.

Sobotka,Chad — RP — Atlanta

EXP MLB DEBUT: 2018 | H/W: 6-7 200 | FUT: Setup RP | 7D

Thrws R Age 21
2014 (4) So Carolina/Upstate

Velo	Pitch	Grade
92-94	FB	+++
83-85	SL	++
	CU	++

Year	Lev	Team	W	L	Sv	IP	K	ERA	WHIP	BF/G	OBA	H%	S%	xERA	Ctl	Dom	Cmd	hr/9	BPV
2014		(did not play in 2014)																	

4th round pick out of S. Carolina-Upstate. Missed all of his junior season due to a back injury. When healthy, features a good mid-90s FB and a decent SL. His CU needs significant work, which means he could end up in relief down the road. Will make his pro debut in 2015.

Solis,Sammy — SP — Washington

EXP MLB DEBUT: 2015 | H/W: 6-5 250 | FUT: #5 starter/RP | 7D

Thrws L Age 26
2010 (2) San Diego

Velo	Pitch	Grade
92-94	FB	++++
78-80	CB	++++
80-82	CU	++

Year	Lev	Team	W	L	Sv	IP	K	ERA	WHIP	BF/G	OBA	H%	S%	xERA	Ctl	Dom	Cmd	hr/9	BPV
2013	A+	Potomac	2	1	0	57	40	3.46	1.35	18.3	264	31	74	3.70	3.0	6.3	2.1	0.5	51
2014	Rk	GCL Nationals	0	0	0	3	5	0.00	0.63	5.5	100	20	100	0.00	2.8	14.1	5.0	0.0	195
2014	A	Hagerstown	1	0	0	6	7	0.00	0.67	20.9	191	29	100	0.58	0.0	10.5		0.0	207
2014	A+	Potomac	1	0	0	5	4	1.76	1.57	22.4	327	40	88	4.76	1.8	7.1	4.0	0.0	97
2014	AA	Harrisburg	0	1	0	3	1	23.23	3.23	18.7	507	54	20	13.04	2.9	2.9	1.0	0.0	-8

Injuries keep following him: After Tommy John surgery in 2012 and a cameo in 2013, was expected to compete for WAS bullpen job in 2014. Back issue, then more elbow discomfort limted him to 18 IP. Lefties with two pitches as good as his are hard to find, but needs to prove can stay on the field first.

Sparkman,Glenn — SP — Kansas City

EXP MLB DEBUT: 2016 | H/W: 6-2 210 | FUT: #5 starter | 6B

Thrws R Age 22
2013 (20) Wharton JC

Velo	Pitch	Grade
88-94	FB	+++
79-83	SL	+++
75-77	CB	+++
80-82	CU	++

Year	Lev	Team	W	L	Sv	IP	K	ERA	WHIP	BF/G	OBA	H%	S%	xERA	Ctl	Dom	Cmd	hr/9	BPV
2013	Rk	Idaho Falls	1	0	2	36	47	1.74	0.97	6.9	197	30	82	1.62	2.5	11.7	4.7	0.2	161
2014	A+	Wilmington	8	3	1	121	117	1.56	0.98	15.9	216	29	84	1.82	1.9	8.7	4.7	0.1	124

Breakout SP who started in pen before moving to rotation in May. Led CAR in ERA and was pitcher of year. Exhibits impeccable control and FB command despite inconsistent mechanics. Throws strikes with both SL and CB and has useful CU for LHH. Allows flyballs, but very few HR.

Spomer,Kurt — RP — Los Angeles (A)

EXP MLB DEBUT: 2015 | H/W: 6-2 215 | FUT: Situational reliever | 6B

Thrws R Age 25
2012 FA (Creighton)

Velo	Pitch	Grade
85-88	FB	+++
74-78	CB	++
	CU	+

Year	Lev	Team	W	L	Sv	IP	K	ERA	WHIP	BF/G	OBA	H%	S%	xERA	Ctl	Dom	Cmd	hr/9	BPV
2012	Rk	AZL Angels	5	0	0	34		3.16	1.43	7.3	303	37	79	4.52	1.8	7.6	4.1	0.5	106
2013	A	Burlington	4	3	6	65	45	2.49	1.08	5.5	218	26	76	2.23	2.6	6.2	2.4	0.3	59
2014	A+	Inland Empire	3	2	8	40	28	1.80	1.02	4.8	198	23	85	2.02	2.9	6.3	2.2	0.4	52
2014	AA	Arkansas	3	3	0	24	10	3.73	1.37	6.3	236	26	72	3.31	4.5	3.7	0.8	0.4	-36
2014	AAA	Salt Lake	1	1	0	10	4	0.00	1.40	10.6	242	27	100	3.11	4.5	3.6	0.8	0.0	-39

Deceptive RP who bounced around 3 levels in '14. Delivers ball with sidewinder action and throws across body making it tough for hitters to pick up pitches. Keeps ball low and generally throws strikes. Can be inconsistent with delivery and doesn't have velocity to make mistakes.

Stanek,Ryne — SP — Tampa Bay

EXP MLB DEBUT: 2016 | H/W: 6-4 180 | FUT: #3 starter / Closer | 8D

Thrws R Age 23
2013 (1) Arkansas

Velo	Pitch	Grade
90-96	FB	++++
82-86	SL	+++
83-88	CU	++

Year	Lev	Team	W	L	Sv	IP	K	ERA	WHIP	BF/G	OBA	H%	S%	xERA	Ctl	Dom	Cmd	hr/9	BPV
2012	NCAA	Arkansas	8	4	0	92	83	2.83	1.20	21.8	224	29	75	2.53	3.5	8.1	2.3	0.2	69
2013	NCAA	Arkansas	10	2	0	97	79	1.39	1.16	24.2	208	26	91	2.49	3.8	7.3	1.9	0.5	47
2014	Rk	GCL Devil Rays	0	0	0	1	0	0.00	0.00	2.8	0	0		0.00	0.0	0.0		0.0	18
2014	A	Bowling Green	3	4	0	44	46	3.67	1.36	20.5	274	36	72	3.76	2.6	9.4	3.5	0.4	115
2014	A+	Charlotte	1	1	0	13	4	5.54	1.38	18.2	262	28	56	3.35	3.5	2.8	0.8	0.0	-26

Power pitcher who made pro debut, but missed time with shoulder fatigue. Has ingredients to become top arm, though bullpen role is a possiblity also. Throws everything hard, including plus FB with incredible arm speed and late-breaking SL. Shows feel for CU, but elevates pitches frequently.

Stankiewicz,Teddy — SP — Boston

EXP MLB DEBUT: 2017 | H/W: 6-4 200 | FUT: #3 starter | 8E

Thrws R Age 21
2013 (2) Seminole State JC

Velo	Pitch	Grade
89-94	FB	+++
78-83	SL	+++
75-78	CB	++
81-83	CU	++

Year	Lev	Team	W	L	Sv	IP	K	ERA	WHIP	BF/G	OBA	H%	S%	xERA	Ctl	Dom	Cmd	hr/9	BPV
2013	NCAA	Seminole St Col	4	5	0	60	70	2.54	1.00	20.9	228	31	78	2.54	1.5	10.5	7.0	0.7	166
2013	A-	Lowell	0	0	0	19	15	2.34	0.99	8.1	239	29	78	2.44	0.9	7.0	7.5	0.5	119
2014	A	Greenville	11	8	0	140	102	3.73	1.21	22.6	263	31	70	3.44	1.9	6.6	3.5	0.6	86

Athletic SP who looks part of bulldog and growing into frame. Velocity increasing and learning to repeat drop and drive delivery. Precise location of FB key to early success, though inconsistent SL leaves him vulnerable. Doesn't miss many bats now, but has K rate projection.

Steele,Justin — SP — Chicago (N)

EXP MLB DEBUT: 2019 | H/W: 6-1 180 | FUT: #4 starter | 6C

Thrws L Age 19
2014 (5) HS (MS)

Velo	Pitch	Grade
90-93	FB	++
75-78	SL	++
	CU	+

Year	Lev	Team	W	L	Sv	IP	K	ERA	WHIP	BF/G	OBA	H%	S%	xERA	Ctl	Dom	Cmd	hr/9	BPV
2014	Rk	AZL Cubs	0	0	0	18	25	2.97	1.26	8.3	226	36	74	2.48	4.0	12.4	3.1	0.0	134

Athletic LH was the Cubs 5th round pick. FB velocity varied throughout the year, causing him to fall in the draft, but his debut was excellent, posting a 2.89 ERA with 8 BB/25 K. Low-90s FB is his best offering and has been as high as 95. CU and breaking ball are inconsistent, but show potential.

Stephens,Jackson — SP — Cincinnati

EXP MLB DEBUT: 2018 | H/W: 6-3 205 | FUT: #4 starter/RP | 7D

Thrws R Age 20
2012 (18) HS (AL)

Velo	Pitch	Grade
91-93	FB	+++
	CB	++
	SL	++
	CU	+

Year	Lev	Team	W	L	Sv	IP	K	ERA	WHIP	BF/G	OBA	H%	S%	xERA	Ctl	Dom	Cmd	hr/9	BPV
2012	Rk	AZL Reds	1	1	2	21	22	4.69	1.23	4.3	279	36	63	3.94	1.3	9.4	7.3	0.9	152
2013	A	Dayton	3	7	1	64	55	4.63	1.51	19.9	304	37	70	5.02	2.5	7.7	3.1	0.8	89
2014	A	Dayton	2	7	0	67	54	4.83	1.37	20.1	270	31	67	4.39	3.0	7.2	2.5	1.1	69

Athletic frame and four pitches that project at least average. FB has added velocity but can be overthrown. Breaking pitches are inconsistent and stay out over plate. CU slower to develop but gaining consistency. Has stuff to become reliable starter if he can improve feel and command.

Stephenson,Niklas — SP — Kansas City

EXP MLB DEBUT: 2017 | H/W: 6-2 195 | FUT: #4 starter/setupRP | 7D

Thrws R Age 21
2012 NDFA HS (CA)

Velo	Pitch	Grade
88-95	FB	+++
78-82	CB	++
80-83	CU	++

Year	Lev	Team	W	L	Sv	IP	K	ERA	WHIP	BF/G	OBA	H%	S%	xERA	Ctl	Dom	Cmd	hr/9	BPV
2012	Rk	AZL Royals	0	0	0	8	3	5.63	1.75	5.2	328	34	69	6.31	3.4	3.4	1.0	1.1	-12
2013	Rk	Burlington	0	0	0	23	15	8.18	2.12	9.5	362	41	60	7.50	4.7	5.8	1.3	0.8	-3
2014	Rk	Burlington	3	3	0	59	47	2.14	0.92	20.0	213	26	77	1.78	1.4	7.2	5.2	0.3	110
2014	A	Lexington	1	0	0	9	4	4.00	1.56	19.7	302	34	71	4.36	3.0	4.0	1.3	0.0	9

Raw SP who cleaned up mechanics and added significant velocity. Improved arm speed and strength added new dimension to arsenal. Hasn't used CU much and will need to develop it for third average pitch. Can hang CB, but generally keeps ball down. Intriguing arm to follow.

Stephenson,Robert — SP — Cincinnati

EXP MLB DEBUT: 2016 | H/W: 6-3 195 | FUT: #2 starter | 9C

Thrws R Age 22
2011 (1) HS (CA)

Velo	Pitch	Grade
94-97	FB	++++
73-75	CB	++++
78-80	CU	+++

Year	Lev	Team	W	L	Sv	IP	K	ERA	WHIP	BF/G	OBA	H%	S%	xERA	Ctl	Dom	Cmd	hr/9	BPV
2013	A	Dayton	5	3	0	77	96	2.57	0.99	20.9	205	30	76	2.09	2.3	11.2	4.8	0.6	157
2013	A+	Bakersfield	2	2	0	20	22	3.12	1.04	19.5	250	31	78	3.51	0.9	9.8	11.0	1.3	170
2013	AA	Pensacola	0	2	0	16	18	5.00	1.85	18.9	271	35	75	5.63	7.2	10.0	1.4	1.1	3
2014	AA	Pensacola	7	10	0	136	140	4.76	1.38	21.2	229	28	68	3.96	4.9	9.3	1.9	1.2	52

Disappointing season but still possesses high ceiling thanks to plus FB/CB combo and above-average CU. Has effortless, elite velocity and attacks hitters. FB can flatten out at upper velocity, and he abandons secondary pitches when he gets in trouble. Must improve pitch sequencing.

Stewart,Kohl — SP — Minnesota

EXP MLB DEBUT: 2017 | H/W: 6-3 195 | FUT: #2 starter | 8C

Thrws R Age 20
2013 (1) HS (TX)

Velo	Pitch	Grade
90-96	FB	++++
83-87	SL	+++
75-79	CB	++
	CU	++

Year	Lev	Team	W	L	Sv	IP	K	ERA	WHIP	BF/G	OBA	H%	S%	xERA	Ctl	Dom	Cmd	hr/9	BPV
2013	Rk	Elizabethton	0	0	0	4	8	0.00	0.50	13.3	81	23	100	0.00	2.3	18.0	8.0	0.0	281
2013	Rk	GCL Twins	0	0	0	16	16	1.69	0.94	10.0	210	29	80	1.49	1.7	9.0	5.3	0.0	134
2014	A	Cedar Rapids	3	5	0	87	62	2.59	1.14	18.1	234	28	78	2.71	2.5	6.4	2.6	0.4	66

Strong, athletic SP who missed time late after shoulder inflammation. Throws with clean arm and smooth delivery to produce impressive velocity. Induces weak contact with four pitch mix and can register Ks with sinking FB and hard SL. K rate low due to focus on efficiency and CU.

Stilson,John — RP — Toronto

EXP MLB DEBUT: 2015 | H/W: 6-3 205 | FUT: Setup RP | 6B

Thrws R Age 24
2011 (3) Texas A&M

Velo	Pitch	Grade
91-96	FB	+++
84-87	SL	++
80-82	CU	+++

Year	Lev	Team	W	L	Sv	IP	K	ERA	WHIP	BF/G	OBA	H%	S%	xERA	Ctl	Dom	Cmd	hr/9	BPV
2012	A+	Dunedin	3	0	0	54	47	2.83	1.39	17.5	269	34	79	3.71	3.2	7.8	2.5	0.3	73
2012	AA	New Hampshire	2	4	1	50	44	5.04	1.54	12.8	277	33	69	4.91	4.1	7.9	1.9	1.1	49
2013	AA	New Hampshire	0	0	1	2	6	4.29	1.43	4.5	336	103	67	4.37	0.0	25.7		0.0	481
2013	AAA	Buffalo	6	2	4	47	47	2.10	1.08	5.6	213	28	83	2.44	2.9	9.0	3.1	0.6	102
2014	AAA	Buffalo	2	0	1	34	32	3.18	1.62	6.0	278	35	81	4.61	4.8	8.5	1.8	0.5	42

Max-effort RP who ended season in June and eventually underwent shoulder surgery. Moved to pen in mid '12 and has explosive FB with terrific late action. Walk rate increased and has trouble harnessing natural strength. Commands good CU, though SL velocity and shape erratic.

Stinnett,Jake — SP — Chicago (N)

EXP MLB DEBUT: 2018 | H/W: 6-4 202 | FUT: #4 starter/Setup RP | 8D

Thrws R Age 22
2014 (2) Maryland

Velo	Pitch	Grade
92-95	FB	+++
78-80	SL	++
	CU	+

Year	Lev	Team	W	L	Sv	IP	K	ERA	WHIP	BF/G	OBA	H%	S%	xERA	Ctl	Dom	Cmd	hr/9	BPV
2012	NCAA	Maryland	0	0	0	13	13	3.44	1.83	7.6	245	33	79	4.19	8.2	8.9	1.1	0.0	-44
2013	NCAA	Maryland	6	5	2	63	48	2.85	1.11	15.5	205	26	71	1.89	3.4	6.8	2.0	0.0	49
2014	NCAA	Maryland	8	6	1	118	132	2.67	0.97	26.3	203	28	75	2.07	2.3	10.1	4.4	0.6	137
2014	Rk	AZL Cubs	0	1	0	4	3	8.57	2.14	6.9	432	50	56	8.26	0.0	6.4		0.0	134
2014	A-	Boise	0	0	0	6	7	2.95	0.82	11.1	149	16	75	1.88	3.0	10.3	3.5	1.5	124

2nd round pick has a strong, durable frame and generates good velocity. Best offering is a good 92-95 mph FB, but he frequently pitches up in the zone. Also has a 78-80 mph SL that can have good late break. Needs to develop a more consistent release point and refine his approach.

Stoppelman,Lee — RP — St. Louis

EXP MLB DEBUT: 2015 | H/W: 6-2 210 | FUT: Reliever | 6C

Thrws L Age 24
2012 (24) Central Missouri

Velo	Pitch	Grade
92-95	FB	+++
	SL	+++

Year	Lev	Team	W	L	Sv	IP	K	ERA	WHIP	BF/G	OBA	H%	S%	xERA	Ctl	Dom	Cmd	hr/9	BPV
2013	A+	Palm Beach	2	1	0	24	26	1.50	1.08	6.2	191	28	85	1.63	3.8	9.8	2.6	0.0	92
2013	AA	Springfield	3	1	6	40	50	1.35	0.85	4.0	151	21	90	1.22	3.2	11.3	3.6	0.7	135
2013	AAA	Memphis	1	1	0	2	2	4.50	3.00	3.9	415	52	83	10.01	9.0	9.0	1.0	0.0	-63
2014	AA	Springfield	1	2	4	36	45	5.00	1.42	4.1	262	37	65	4.05	3.8	11.3	3.0	0.8	119
2014	AAA	Memphis	0	1	0	13	12	6.87	1.60	5.8	213	24	58	4.51	7.6	8.2	1.1	1.4	-38

Strong-armed reliever from Central Missouri was a bit unlucky in 2014 posting a 5.00 ERA at Double-A and a .347 BABIP. Has a good mid-90s FB and a good late breaking SL. Has a career Dom of 11.0, but does struggle with control. Decent relief prospect and look for better results in 2015.

Stratton,Chris — SP — San Francisco

EXP MLB DEBUT: 2015 | H/W: 6-3 186 | FUT: #3 Starter | 8D

Thrws R Age 24
2012 (1) Mississippi State

Velo	Pitch	Grade
90-93	FB	++++
81-83	SL	+++
82-84	CU	++
77-79	CB	++

Year	Lev	Team	W	L	Sv	IP	K	ERA	WHIP	BF/G	OBA	H%	S%	xERA	Ctl	Dom	Cmd	hr/9	BPV
2012	NCAA	MississippiSt	11	2	1	109		2.39	1.00	24.5	214	30	78	2.23	2.1	10.5	5.1	0.6	151
2012	A-	Salem-Kaizer	0	1	0	16	16	2.80	1.49	8.7	236	31	83	3.73	5.6	8.9	1.6	0.6	28
2013	A	Augusta	9	3	0	132	123	3.27	1.33	24.9	256	33	75	3.38	3.2	8.4	2.6	0.3	82
2014	A+	San Jose	7	8	0	99	102	5.09	1.40	22.0	269	34	66	4.54	3.3	9.3	2.8	1.2	96
2014	AA	Richmond	1	1	0	23	18	3.52	1.78	21.2	309	37	82	5.74	4.7	7.0	1.5	0.8	18

Athletic RHP with ideal frame uses size to work down in the zone with a four-pitch mix. FB in the low-90s up to 95, mixing in a SL that flashes plus, CU that will be average, and a show-me CB. Struggled with control at times in '14, but continued to show his ability to command the strike zone and miss bats regularly.

Streich,Seth — SP — San Diego

EXP MLB DEBUT: 2016 | H/W: 6-3 210 | FUT: #3 starter | 8E

Thrws R Age 24
2012 (6) Ohio

Velo	Pitch	Grade
89-94	FB	+++
78-81	CB	+++
81-83	CU	+++

Year	Lev	Team	W	L	Sv	IP	K	ERA	WHIP	BF/G	OBA	H%	S%	xERA	Ctl	Dom	Cmd	hr/9	BPV
2012	NCAA	Ohio	4	7	0	75	62	4.43	1.56	25.3	277	34	70	4.28	4.3	7.4	1.7	0.4	35
2012	Rk	AZL Athletics	0	0	0	2	6	4.09	0.91	4.1	139	83	50	0.48	4.1	24.5	6.0	0.0	349
2012	A-	Vermont	4	1	0	34	42	2.63	1.26	9.3	212	31	79	2.55	4.5	11.1	2.5	0.3	96
2013	A	Beloit	10	6	0	110	82	3.84	1.41	22.2	268	33	71	3.61	3.3	6.7	2.0	0.2	48
2014	A+	Stockton	9	6	0	114	116	3.16	1.16	20.6	255	33	74	3.14	1.7	9.2	5.3	0.6	136

Improving SP who led CAL in ERA despite not pitching after July due to shoulder woes. Uses height effectively to throw on downward angle and minimal effort. FB appears quicker than it seems and exhibits late sink. CB gaining consistency and CU showed drastic improvement.

Stripling,Ross — SP — Los Angeles (N)

EXP MLB DEBUT: 2016 | H/W: 6-3 190 | FUT: #4 starter | 7C

Thrws R Age 25
2012 (5) Texas A&M

Velo	Pitch	Grade
88-94	FB	+++
73-75	CB	+++
	SL	+++
	CU	++

Year	Lev	Team	W	L	Sv	IP	K	ERA	WHIP	BF/G	OBA	H%	S%	xERA	Ctl	Dom	Cmd	hr/9	BPV
2012	NCAA	Texas A&M	10	4	0	125	120	3.09	0.99	29.8	229	30	69	2.34	1.4	8.6	6.3	0.5	136
2012	Rk	Ogden	1	0	0	36	37	1.25	0.89	9.6	203	29	84	1.28	1.5	9.2	6.2	0.0	144
2013	A+	Rancho Cuca	2	0	0	33	34	2.98	1.05	21.4	204	28	71	1.97	3.0	9.2	3.1	0.3	103
2013	AA	Chattanooga	6	4	1	94	83	2.78	1.17	17.9	256	32	76	3.03	1.8	7.9	4.4	0.4	112
2014		(did not play in 2014)																	

Missed all of 2014 with TJS. With clean arm action and repeatable mechanics, he pounds the zone with low-90s FB and solid off-speed. His 12-6 CB and tight SL both get high praise and have swing-and-miss potential. Plus command and control will allow him to make an impact sooner rather than later.

Suero,Wander — SP — Washington

EXP MLB DEBUT: 2016 | H/W: 6-3 175 | FUT: #5 starter/RP | 6B

Thrws R Age 23
2010 FA (DR)

Velo	Pitch	Grade
90-93	FB	++
	CB	+++
	CU	++

Year	Lev	Team	W	L	Sv	IP	K	ERA	WHIP	BF/G	OBA	H%	S%	xERA	Ctl	Dom	Cmd	hr/9	BPV
2013	Rk	GCL Nationals	8	1	0	49	46	1.65	0.82	13.7	163	21	82	1.01	2.4	8.4	3.5	0.4	106
2014	A	Hagerstown	4	1	3	72	62	2.13	0.97	16.1	225	28	79	2.13	1.4	7.8	5.6	0.4	120
2014	A+	Potomac	2	1	0	27	21	7.64	1.59	10.0	302	34	51	5.64	3.3	7.0	2.1	1.3	54

Slightly-built, he makes up for average stuff with an aggressive mound demeanor that results in a lot of ground balls. Hard, tight CB his best pitch, but CU development (or lack thereof) will determine his future role. Stretched out as a starter by season's end, Washington likely to leave him there until he proves otherwise.

Suggs,Colby — RP — Miami

EXP MLB DEBUT: 2016 | H/W: 5-11 235 | FUT: Setup RP | 7B

Thrws R Age 23
2013 (2-S) Arkansas

Velo	Pitch	Grade
93-98	FB	++++
78-83	CB	++++

Year	Lev	Team	W	L	Sv	IP	K	ERA	WHIP	BF/G	OBA	H%	S%	xERA	Ctl	Dom	Cmd	hr/9	BPV
2013	NCAA	Arkansas	0	0	13	20	29	1.78	1.34	3.7	149	26	85	1.78	7.6	12.9	1.7	0.0	46
2013	Rk	GCL Marlins	0	0	0	1	1	9.00	3.00	5.8	262	35	67	7.36	18.0	9.0	0.5	0.0	-306
2013	A-	Batavia	1	0	3	8	11	1.13	0.88	4.2	181	30	86	0.97	2.3	12.4	5.5	0.0	180
2013	A+	Jupiter	1	3	0	18	26	3.98	1.27	5.3	150	26	65	1.62	7.0	12.9	1.9	0.0	63
2014	A+	Jupiter	1	6	3	58	47	5.11	1.45	5.4	265	32	63	3.93	3.9	7.3	1.9	0.5	44

Strocky RP uses lower half to generate mid-90s FB up to 98. Pairs it with a power CB with tight spin and sharp downward action. Generates plus Dom results, though his max effort delivery has led to huge Ctl issues. Arsenal has closer potential, but he need smoother mechanics.

Sulbaran,J.C. — SP — Kansas City

EXP MLB DEBUT: 2015 | H/W: 6-2 220 | FUT: #4 starter | 8E

Thrws R Age 25
2008 (30) HS (FL)

Velo	Pitch	Grade
89-94	FB	+++
78-81	CB	+++
82-85	CU	+

Year	Lev	Team	W	L	Sv	IP	K	ERA	WHIP	BF/G	OBA	H%	S%	xERA	Ctl	Dom	Cmd	hr/9	BPV
2012	AA	NW Arkansas	0	4	0	26	24	7.62	2.12	21.4	310	35	69	8.13	7.6	8.3	1.1	2.4	-38
2012	AA	Pensacola	7	7	0	104	111	4.06	1.49	23.6	256	31	78	4.84	4.7	9.6	2.1	1.5	65
2013	A+	Wilmington	1	3	0	34	29	5.03	1.56	18.6	289	34	69	5.12	3.7	7.7	2.1	1.1	56
2013	AA	NW Arkansas	3	4	0	46	26	7.03	1.63	8.2	266	27	59	5.64	5.5	5.1	0.9	1.8	-38
2014	AA	NW Arkansas	8	10	0	127	116	3.26	1.43	21.6	263	33	80	4.16	3.8	8.2	2.1	0.8	63

Big, strong SP who has spent most of last 3 years in AA. Posts high K rate with positive sinker and CB. Throws across body to add deception, but has trouble with CB. Allows fair share of HR in flyball nature, but he throws strikes and limits walks. Has improved mechanics last two years.

Supak,Trey — SP — Pittsburgh

EXP MLB DEBUT: 2019 | H/W: 6-5 210 | FUT: #3 starter | 7D

Thrws R Age 18
2014 (2-S) HS (TX)

Velo	Pitch	Grade
90-93	FB	+++
73-75	CB	+++
	SL	++
	CU	

Year	Lev	Team	W	L	Sv	IP	K	ERA	WHIP	BF/G	OBA	H%	S%	xERA	Ctl	Dom	Cmd	hr/9	BPV
2014	Rk	GCL Pirates	1	3	0	24	21	4.88	1.58	13.2	285	33	74	5.54	4.1	7.9	1.9	1.5	48

FB currently sits at 90-93 mph and gets good downhill tilt from a high ¾ arm slot. Throws with effort and his FB command is currently below average. He also features a good mid-70s CB and a SL and CU that need refinement, but show potential.

Syndergaard,Noah — SP — New York (N)

EXP MLB DEBUT: 2015 | H/W: 6-6 240 | FUT: #2 starter | 9B

Thrws R Age 22
2010 (1) HS (TX)

Velo	Pitch	Grade
92-98	FB	++++
82-85	SL	++++
80-82	CB	+++
81-85	CU	+++

Year	Lev	Team	W	L	Sv	IP	K	ERA	WHIP	BF/G	OBA	H%	S%	xERA	Ctl	Dom	Cmd	hr/9	BPV
2011	A	Lansing	0	0	0	9	9	3.00	1.11	17.7	240	33	70	2.30	2.0	9.0	4.5	0.0	126
2012	A	Lansing	8	5	1	103	122	2.62	1.09	14.9	218	32	75	2.19	2.7	10.6	3.9	0.3	137
2013	A+	St. Lucie	3	3	0	63	64	3.13	1.22	21.3	255	34	74	3.17	2.3	9.1	4.0	0.4	121
2013	AA	Binghamton	6	1	0	54	69	3.00	1.07	19.1	232	31	80	3.34	2.0	11.5	5.8	1.3	171
2014	AAA	Las Vegas	9	7	0	133	145	4.60	1.48	22.0	291	38	69	4.64	2.9	9.8	3.4	0.7	116

Dominant FB and plus four-pitch arsenal. First half struggles partly due to emphasis on developing CU. Improved secondary pitches and sequencing while maintaining Dom/Ctl. Height, frame, and demeanor project well for his future as front-line starter. Throws strikes with all of his pitches.

Taillon,Jameson — SP — Pittsburgh

EXP MLB DEBUT: 2015 | H/W: 6-5 245 | FUT: #1 starter | 9D

Thrws R Age 23
2010 (1) HS (TX)

Velo	Pitch	Grade
93-97	FB	++++
83-85	CB	++++
83-86	CU	+++
	SL	++

Year	Lev	Team	W	L	Sv	IP	K	ERA	WHIP	BF/G	OBA	H%	S%	xERA	Ctl	Dom	Cmd	hr/9	BPV
2012	A+	Bradenton	6	8	0	125	98	3.82	1.17	21.7	236	28	68	3.09	2.7	7.1	2.6	0.7	73
2012	AA	Altoona	3	0	0	17	18	1.59	0.71	20.0	187	27	75	0.63	0.5	9.5	18.0	0.0	175
2013	AA	Altoona	4	7	0	110	106	3.68	1.34	22.9	265	34	74	3.85	2.9	8.7	2.9	0.7	95
2013	AAA	Indianapolis	1	3	0	37	37	3.89	1.27	25.2	229	31	67	2.79	3.9	9.0	2.3	0.2	75
2014		(did not play in 2014)																	

RH had TJS. Prior to the injury had a plus 93-97 mph sinking FB that toped out at 99. Also had a power CB that was his go-to breaking pitch. Flashed a potentially plus CU. Taillon has the size and power frame to dominate. Gets good downhill tilt that makes his FB difficult to elevate.

Tapia,Domingo — SP — New York (N)

EXP MLB DEBUT: 2016 | H/W: 6-4 185 | FUT: #3 starter/Setup RP | 7C

Thrws R Age 23 — 2009 FA (DR)

Velo	Pitch	Grade
95-98	FB	++++
	CB	++
	CU	+

Year	Lev	Team	W	L	Sv	IP	K	ERA	WHIP	BF/G	OBA	H%	S%	xERA	Ctl	Dom	Cmd	hr/9	BPV
2011	Rk	Kingsport	5	5	0	50	30	3.78	1.32	18.8	262	30	71	3.67	2.9	5.4	1.9	0.5	37
2011	A-	Brooklyn	1	0	0	6	6	0.00	0.83	21.9	228	31	100	1.45	0.0	9.0		0.0	180
2012	A	Savannah	6	5	0	108	101	3.99	1.15	21.5	232	31	62	2.45	2.7	8.4	3.2	0.2	97
2013	A+	St. Lucie	3	9	0	101	89	4.63	1.48	18.9	234	30	67	3.43	5.6	7.9	1.4	0.3	9
2014	A+	St. Lucie	6	8	0	109	56	3.96	1.42	22.0	253	28	71	3.69	4.2	4.6	1.1	0.4	-12

Repeated High-A to fix Ctl issues and Dom dipped below 5 despite FB that hits triple digits. FB and CU both have sinking action which accounts for >50% GB%. CB is a continued work-in-progress. Whip-like arm action creates nice movement on pitches but has trouble repeating mechanics.

Tarpley,Stephen — SP — Baltimore

EXP MLB DEBUT: 2017 | H/W: 6-1 180 | FUT: #3 starter | 8D

Thrws L Age 22 — 2013 (3) Scottsdale CC

Velo	Pitch	Grade
88-95	FB	+++
78-80	CB	+++
82-84	SL	++
	CU	+++

Year	Lev	Team	W	L	Sv	IP	K	ERA	WHIP	BF/G	OBA	H%	S%	xERA	Ctl	Dom	Cmd	hr/9	BPV
2012	NCAA	USC	5	4	0	78	67	3.23	1.28	22.9	244	32	72	2.79	3.3	7.7	2.3	0.0	67
2013	NCAA	Scottsdale CC	3	2	0	92	108	2.35	1.11	22.6	193	28	80	2.08	3.9	10.6	2.7	0.4	103
2013	Rk	GCL Orioles	0	1	0	21	25	2.14	1.10	11.7	252	37	78	2.41	1.3	10.7	8.3	0.0	176
2014	A-	Aberdeen	3	5	0	66	60	3.68	1.41	21.5	270	34	74	3.98	3.3	8.2	2.5	0.5	77

Short, athletic SP with high ceiling based upon current stuff and projection. Got better as season progressed, though still has yet to see full season ball. Induces grounders with lively FB and mixes in sound secondaries. Velocity varies too much and has erratic release point and slot.

Taylor,Blake — SP — New York (N)

EXP MLB DEBUT: 2018 | H/W: 6-3 220 | FUT: #3 starter | 7C

Thrws L Age 19 — 2013 (2) HS (CA)

Velo	Pitch	Grade
88-94	FB	+++
76-78	CB	++++
84-86	CU	++

Year	Lev	Team	W	L	Sv	IP	K	ERA	WHIP	BF/G	OBA	H%	S%	xERA	Ctl	Dom	Cmd	hr/9	BPV
2013	Rk	GCL Pirates	0	2	0	21	13	2.57	0.76	9.4	106	13	63	0.00	3.9	5.6	1.4	0.0	14
2014	Rk	GCL Mets	2	0	0	10	10	0.00	0.78	12.3	34	5	100	0.00	6.2	8.8	1.4	0.0	10
2014	Rk	Kingsport	2	1	0	30	20	5.38	2.13	18.6	326	38	73	6.43	6.9	6.0	0.9	0.3	-60

Command issues stemmed from inability to control FB. Young and talented enough to get back on track in '15. FB can hit 94 mph and should add velo as he matures. CB is his best pitch; needs to mix in CU more. Does a nice job working down in the zone to force groundballs.

Thompson,Jake — SP — Texas

EXP MLB DEBUT: 2016 | H/W: 6-4 235 | FUT: #3 starter | 8C

Thrws R Age 21 — 2012 (2) HS (TX)

Velo	Pitch	Grade
88-94	FB	+++
84-87	SL	++++
77-80	CB	+++
80-83	CU	+++

Year	Lev	Team	W	L	Sv	IP	K	ERA	WHIP	BF/G	OBA	H%	S%	xERA	Ctl	Dom	Cmd	hr/9	BPV
2012	Rk	GCL Tigers	1	2	0	28	31	1.92	0.85	14.7	150	21	78	0.91	3.2	9.9	3.1	0.3	110
2013	A	West Michigan	3	3	0	83	91	3.14	1.34	20.3	252	34	77	3.43	3.5	9.9	2.8	0.4	102
2014	A+	Lakeland	6	4	0	83	79	3.14	1.20	20.9	243	32	73	2.89	2.7	8.6	3.2	0.3	99
2014	AA	Erie	1	0	0	11	7	2.45	1.27	22.5	244	29	79	2.79	3.3	5.7	1.8	0.0	33
2014	AA	Frisco	3	1	0	35	44	3.32	1.31	20.8	220	31	77	3.24	4.6	11.3	2.4	0.8	96

Durable, strong SP who is developing quickly. Spots solid-average FB to bottom half of zone and can add cut and sink at will. Hard SL is true plus offering and can throw for strikes or use as chase. Has struggled with LHH despite quality CU. May not dominate, but sequences 4 pitches well.

Thompson,Jeff — SP — Detroit

EXP MLB DEBUT: 2016 | H/W: 6-6 245 | FUT: #4 starter | 7D

Thrws R Age 23 — 2013 (3) Louisville

Velo	Pitch	Grade
89-94	FB	+++
81-83	SL	+++
80-84	CU	++

Year	Lev	Team	W	L	Sv	IP	K	ERA	WHIP	BF/G	OBA	H%	S%	xERA	Ctl	Dom	Cmd	hr/9	BPV
2011	NCAA	Louisville	2	1	1	39	43	2.76	1.48	9.3	266	35	84	4.23	4.1	9.9	2.4	0.7	84
2012	NCAA	Louisville	9	4	0	78	73	4.03	1.47	22.4	259	34	71	3.68	4.4	8.4	1.9	0.2	51
2013	NCAA	Louisville	11	2	0	107	113	2.19	0.94	23.7	182	24	80	1.73	2.9	9.5	3.3	0.6	112
2013	A	West Michigan	2	2	1	45	42	3.80	1.33	13.4	244	31	72	3.49	3.8	8.4	2.2	0.6	67
2014	A	West Michigan	0	0	0	8	10	6.75	2.38	13.9	307	42	72	7.48	10.1	11.3	1.1	1.1	-53

Large-framed SP who ended season in May with shoulder tendinitis. Has both size and athleticism and uses height effectively. Adds cutting action to quality FB and can be tough to make hard contact against. FB flattens at higher velocity and lacks off-speed pitch. Hides ball in delivery.

Thompson,Taylor — RP — Oakland

EXP MLB DEBUT: 2014 | H/W: 6-5 225 | FUT: Middle reliever | 6C

Thrws R Age 27 — 2009 (44) Auburn

Velo	Pitch	Grade
90-93	FB	+++
81-84	SL	+++
84-88	SP	++

Year	Lev	Team	W	L	Sv	IP	K	ERA	WHIP	BF/G	OBA	H%	S%	xERA	Ctl	Dom	Cmd	hr/9	BPV
2012	A+	Winston-Salem	2	1	12	44	57	2.45	0.88	5.0	173	26	73	1.29	2.7	11.6	4.4	0.4	156
2013	AA	Birmingham	4	2	12	50	46	2.16	0.94	5.9	194	26	74	1.31	2.3	8.3	3.5	0.0	104
2013	AAA	Charlotte	1	2	1	16	16	7.88	1.69	6.0	347	43	52	6.43	1.7	9.0	5.3	1.1	134
2014	AAA	Charlotte	3	0	7	59	68	2.14	1.31	6.2	224	31	85	3.01	4.4	10.4	2.3	0.5	85
2014	MLB	Chi White Sox	0	0	0	5	4	10.59	2.55	5.5	385	44	58	9.93	7.1	7.1	1.0	1.8	-46

Low-upside RP with large frame and ability to induce grounders by using height. Mixes pitches well and has deep repertoire to start. Stamina, though, keeps him in pen and lacks plus stuff. Struggles to throw consistent strikes as long levers make repeating delivery difficult. Has decent SL.

Thorpe,Lewis — SP — Minnesota

EXP MLB DEBUT: 2017 | H/W: 6-2 215 | FUT: #3 starter | 8D

Thrws L Age 19 — 2012 FA (Australia)

Velo	Pitch	Grade
89-94	FB	++++
78-80	CB	+++
81-83	SL	++
80-83	CU	+++

Year	Lev	Team	W	L	Sv	IP	K	ERA	WHIP	BF/G	OBA	H%	S%	xERA	Ctl	Dom	Cmd	hr/9	BPV
2013	Rk	GCL Twins	4	1	0	44	64	2.05	0.86	13.5	205	33	78	1.59	1.2	13.1	10.7	0.4	221
2014	A	Cedar Rapids	3	2	0	71	80	3.54	1.38	18.7	236	31	77	3.74	4.6	10.1	2.2	0.9	77

Long, tough LHP who finished year strong before succumbing to sprained elbow ligament. Despite average velocity, FB is among tops in org with plus, vicious action. Tough to throw for consistent strikes, but equally tough for hitters to elevate. CB more effective at lower velocities.

Thurman,Andrew — SP — Houston

EXP MLB DEBUT: 2016 | H/W: 6-3 225 | FUT: #4 starter | 7D

Thrws R Age 23 — 2013 (2) UC-Irvine

Velo	Pitch	Grade
90-94	FB	+++
78-81	SL	+++
73-76	CB	++
81-83	CU	+++

Year	Lev	Team	W	L	Sv	IP	K	ERA	WHIP	BF/G	OBA	H%	S%	xERA	Ctl	Dom	Cmd	hr/9	BPV
2011	NCAA	UC Irvine	3	3	1	66	58	3.82	1.32	13.0	276	35	69	3.59	2.2	7.9	3.6	0.3	101
2012	NCAA	UC Irvine	8	3	0	98	69	2.66	0.93	24.5	197	24	70	1.52	2.1	6.3	3.0	0.2	75
2013	NCAA	UC Irvine	6	4	0	100	91	3.24	1.04	27.6	231	31	66	2.11	1.7	8.2	4.8	0.1	119
2013	A-	Tri City	4	2	1	39	43	3.90	1.38	13.7	280	36	76	4.59	2.5	9.9	3.9	1.1	128
2014	A	Quad Cities	7	9	1	115	107	5.40	1.41	18.7	273	34	61	4.17	3.1	8.4	2.7	0.7	84

Durable SP who has been inconsistent in career despite average pitch mix. Exhibits decent control with all pitches, though hasn't yet mastered breaking ball. Lively FB thrown for strikes from clean delivery and repeatable slot. Has good CU, but LHH hit him hard and he lacks plus pitch.

Tirado,Alberto — SP — Toronto

EXP MLB DEBUT: 2017 | H/W: 6-0 180 | FUT: #3 starter | 8D

Thrws R Age 20 — 2011 FA (DR)

Velo	Pitch	Grade
92-96	FB	++++
82-84	SL	+++
81-82	CU	+++

Year	Lev	Team	W	L	Sv	IP	K	ERA	WHIP	BF/G	OBA	H%	S%	xERA	Ctl	Dom	Cmd	hr/9	BPV
2012	Rk	Bluefield	2	0	0	11	5	2.45	0.82	13.3	114	13	67	0.22	4.1	4.1	1.0	0.0	-19
2012	Rk	GCL Blue Jays	1	2	0	37	34	2.68	1.08	13.1	212	28	73	1.88	2.9	8.3	2.8	0.0	88
2013	Rk	Bluefield	3	0	0	48	44	1.68	1.27	16.4	232	30	87	2.78	3.7	8.2	2.2	0.2	65
2014	A-	Vancouver	1	0	0	35	36	3.58	1.51	9.0	201	28	75	3.06	7.2	9.2	1.3	0.3	-10
2014	A	Lansing	1	2	1	40	40	6.30	2.10	15.1	285	37	69	6.05	8.8	9.0	1.0	0.7	-57

Short, thin SP with loose arm that rarely results in straight pitches. Struggles to maintain delivery and needs strength for stamina. Control issues prevalent, though changes speeds well and can fire FB by hitters. SL can be plus pitch and CU could be third above average offering.

Torrez,Daury — SP — Chicago (N)

EXP MLB DEBUT: 2018 | H/W: 6-3 170 | FUT: #4 starter | 6C

Thrws R Age 21 — 2010 FA (DR)

Velo	Pitch	Grade
92-94	FB	+++
85-88	SL	+++
	CU	+

Year	Lev	Team	W	L	Sv	IP	K	ERA	WHIP	BF/G	OBA	H%	S%	xERA	Ctl	Dom	Cmd	hr/9	BPV
2013	Rk	AZL Cubs	4	2	1	49	49	3.31	1.10	16.0	262	35	69	2.92	0.9	9.0	9.8	0.4	155
2013	A	Kane County	0	1	0	5	2	5.40	1.20	20.1	262	25	60	4.57	1.8	3.6	2.0	1.8	34
2014	A	Kane County	11	7	0	131	81	2.75	1.00	21.8	229	26	74	2.44	1.4	5.6	3.9	0.5	79

Had his best season as a pro in his second stint in the MWL. Torrez has a good 91-93 mph FB and an above-average 85-88 mph SL, but doesn't rack up a ton of strikeouts because of a below-avg CU. Throws tons of strikes but profiles as a back-end starter.

Toussaint,Touki — SP — Arizona

EXP MLB DEBUT: 2018 | H/W: 6-3 185 | FUT: #2 starter | 9E

Thrws R Age 18 — 2014 (1) HS (FL)

Velo	Pitch	Grade
92-96	FB	++++
76-80	CB	++++
	CU	++
86-88	CT	++

Year	Lev	Team	W	L	Sv	IP	K	ERA	WHIP	BF/G	OBA	H%	S%	xERA	Ctl	Dom	Cmd	hr/9	BPV
2014	Rk	AZL Dbacks	1	1	0	15	17	4.80	1.73	9.8	249	36	69	3.97	7.2	10.2	1.4	0.0	7
2014	Rk	Missoula	1	3	0	13	15	12.95	2.27	13.4	392	46	44	10.89	4.1	10.2	2.5	3.4	92

Struggled with consistency and control. Lightning-quick arm can generate a good 92-95 mph FB. His CB has the potential to be a true wipeout offering, while his CU develops. Poor front-side mechanics and an inconsistent release point need to be addressed for him to be effective as a SP.

Travieso,Nick — SP — Cincinnati

EXP MLB DEBUT: 2017 | H/W: 6-2 215 | FUT: #3 starter | 8C

Thrws R Age 21
2012 (1) HS (FL)

- 91-94 FB ++++
- 82-85 SL +++
- CU +++

Year	Lev	Team	W	L	Sv	IP	K	ERA	WHIP	BF/G	OBA	H%	S%	xERA	Ctl	Dom	Cmd	hr/9	BPV
2012	Rk	AZL Reds	0	2	0	21	14	4.71	1.19	10.5	252	27	64	3.91	2.1	6.0	2.8	1.3	68
2013	A	Dayton	7	4	0	81	61	4.66	1.35	19.9	266	31	66	4.02	3.0	6.8	2.3	0.8	59
2014	A	Dayton	14	5	0	142	114	3.04	1.17	21.8	235	28	76	3.01	2.8	7.2	2.6	0.6	73

Hit rough patch in May/June but rest of season was outstanding. Extreme competitor on mound. Plus FB hits 94 with downward action, SL and CU trending towards plus offerings. Easy arm action, durable, repeatable mechanics, and improved command/control bodes well for future.

Tropeano,Nick — SP — Los Angeles (A)

EXP MLB DEBUT: 2014 | H/W: 6-4 200 | FUT: #3 starter | 8D

Thrws R Age 24
2011 (5) Stony Brook

- 90-94 FB +++
- 81-83 SL ++
- 81-85 CU ++++

Year	Lev	Team	W	L	Sv	IP	K	ERA	WHIP	BF/G	OBA	H%	S%	xERA	Ctl	Dom	Cmd	hr/9	BPV
2012	A	Lexington	6	4	0	87	97	2.79	1.18	23.2	239	33	76	2.75	2.7	10.0	3.7	0.3	126
2012	A+	Lancaster	6	3	0	70	69	3.33	1.32	24.2	267	33	79	4.17	2.7	8.8	3.3	1.0	105
2013	AA	Corpus Christi	7	10	5	133	130	4.12	1.34	19.8	272	34	72	4.27	2.6	8.8	3.3	1.0	105
2014	AAA	Oklahoma City	9	5	0	124	120	3.04	0.99	20.6	204	26	72	2.31	2.4	8.7	3.6	0.8	110
2014	MLB	Houston	1	3	0	21	13	4.67	1.32	21.9	241	29	61	2.88	3.8	5.5	1.4	0.0	14

Big, aggressive SP who led PCL in Ks. Steady progression culminated in big league trial and will compete for job in ST. CU is legitimate plus pitch and thrown with conviction. Tough on LHH (.156 oppBA) and has FB to keep hitters at bay. Needs better SL and can often leave balls up.

Tseng,Jen-Ho — SP — Chicago (N)

EXP MLB DEBUT: 2017 | H/W: 6-1 210 | FUT: #3 starter | 8D

Thrws R Age 20
2013 FA (Taiwan)

- 90-93 FB +++
- 75-78 CB +++
- 80-82 CU +++

Year	Lev	Team	W	L	Sv	IP	K	ERA	WHIP	BF/G	OBA	H%	S%	xERA	Ctl	Dom	Cmd	hr/9	BPV
2014	A	Kane County	6	1	0	105	85	2.40	0.87	20.4	204	25	75	1.83	1.3	7.3	5.7	0.6	114

Throws with effort to his delivery, but does have a good 90-93 mph FB, CB, and a plus CU. Hides the ball well and locates all three offerings. Comes inside effectively vs. RHH, but has a slow tempo and throws with effort. He fared well in the MWL.

Tuivailala,Samuel — RP — St. Louis

EXP MLB DEBUT: 2014 | H/W: 6-3 195 | FUT: Closer | 7D

Thrws R Age 22
2010 (3) HS (CA)

- 95-97 FB ++++
- CB +++
- CU ++

Year	Lev	Team	W	L	Sv	IP	K	ERA	WHIP	BF/G	OBA	H%	S%	xERA	Ctl	Dom	Cmd	hr/9	BPV
2013	A	Peoria	0	3	1	35	50	5.38	1.45	5.4	238	39	59	3.11	5.1	12.8	2.5	0.0	110
2014	A+	Palm Beach	0	1	3	37	64	3.63	1.26	5.2	217	41	70	2.56	4.4	15.5	3.6	0.2	179
2014	AA	Springfield	2	1	1	21	30	2.57	1.29	5.1	233	38	78	2.62	3.9	12.9	3.3	0.0	145
2014	AAA	Memphis	0	0	1	1	3	0.00	0.91	2.1	244	91	100	1.69	0.0	24.5		0.0	460
2014	MLB	St. Louis	0	0	0	1	1	36.00	7.00	4.9	639	62	60	44.98	18.0	9.0	0.5	18.0	-306

Converted infielder has established himself as one of the best relief prospects in the organization. Dominates with a blazing upper-90s FB that has good late life and tops out at 100. Improved CB fueled the breakout. Strong, stocky body with thick legs gives him an ideal pitching frame.

Turley,Josh — SP — Detroit

EXP MLB DEBUT: 2016 | H/W: 6-0 185 | FUT: #5 starter | 6B

Thrws L Age 24
2012 (16) Baylor

- 85-90 FB ++
- 77-80 CB +++
- 80-85 CT +++
- CU +++

Year	Lev	Team	W	L	Sv	IP	K	ERA	WHIP	BF/G	OBA	H%	S%	xERA	Ctl	Dom	Cmd	hr/9	BPV
2012	NCAA	Baylor	9	1	0	110	79	1.96	1.05	25.1	234	28	81	2.35	1.7	6.5	3.8	0.2	88
2012	A-	Connecticut	4	0	0	34	25	1.06	0.82	10.3	193	24	86	1.04	1.3	6.6	5.0	0.0	101
2013	A	West Michigan	8	4	2	77	79	2.10	1.05	5.9	227	30	83	2.53	2.0	9.2	4.6	0.6	130
2014	A+	Lakeland	7	1	0	97	81	1.85	0.96	20.4	204	26	80	1.66	2.1	7.5	3.5	0.2	96
2014	AA	Erie	3	4	0	50	28	3.78	1.38	23.3	273	28	79	4.83	2.9	5.0	1.8	1.4	31

Advanced pitcher who moved to rotation to solid results. Uses variety of pitches to keep hitters off guard. Lacks frontline velocity and doesn't own knockout offering. Likes to change speeds with terrific CU and is menace to LHH. Mixes in occasional knuckler while cutting and sinking FB.

Turnbull,Kylin — SP — Washington

EXP MLB DEBUT: 2016 | H/W: 6-5 205 | FUT: Reliever | 6D

Thrws L Age 25
2011 (4) Santa Barbara CC

- 88-92 FB ++
- 80-84 SL ++
- CU +

Year	Lev	Team	W	L	Sv	IP	K	ERA	WHIP	BF/G	OBA	H%	S%	xERA	Ctl	Dom	Cmd	hr/9	BPV
2013	A	Hagerstown	6	5	0	83	67	3.58	1.36	21.7	293	34	78	4.71	1.7	7.3	4.2	1.1	102
2013	A+	Potomac	0	3	0	10	3	15.15	2.77	18.8	413	43	41	10.28	7.1	2.7	0.4	0.9	-126
2014	Rk	GCL Nationals	0	0	0	2	0	0.00	1.00	7.6	262	26	100	2.41	0.0	0.0		0.0	18
2014	A	Hagerstown	0	0	0	5	3	3.60	1.40	21.1	299	31	83	5.58	1.8	5.4	3.0	1.8	67
2014	A+	Potomac	3	3	0	49	37	4.41	1.57	11.3	330	40	70	4.98	1.7	6.8	4.1	0.2	96

Tall lefty battled injury issues in 2014, but again showed good strike-throwing ability. Tends to give up lots of base hits, and limited arsenal is best suited to short stints. Lack of a platoon split also works against him.

Turnbull,Spencer — SP — Detroit

EXP MLB DEBUT: 2017 | H/W: 6-3 215 | FUT: #3 starter/setupRP | 8D

Thrws R Age 22
2014 (2) Alabama

- 90-95 FB ++++
- 83-87 SL +++
- CU +

Year	Lev	Team	W	L	Sv	IP	K	ERA	WHIP	BF/G	OBA	H%	S%	xERA	Ctl	Dom	Cmd	hr/9	BPV
2012	NCAA	Alabama	2	6	0	53	45	5.60	1.51	15.3	265	33	61	4.14	4.4	7.6	1.7	0.5	36
2013	NCAA	Alabama	4	3	0	90	51	3.70	1.44	25.6	266	31	73	3.72	3.8	5.1	1.3	0.2	7
2014	NCAA	Alabama	5	7	0	93	61	2.22	1.16	24.7	189	22	81	2.11	4.5	5.9	1.3	0.3	1
2014	Rk	GCL Tigers	0	0	0	3	4	3.00	1.00	11.5	191	18	100	4.22	3.0	12.0	4.0	3.0	153
2014	A-	Connecticut	0	2	0	28	19	4.48	1.60	11.3	281	33	70	4.43	4.5	6.1	1.4	0.3	6

Powerful pitcher with clean delivery and solid FB/SL combo. Arm action may lead him to pen where hard stuff could play up. Misses bats with effective, lively FB thrown from high 3/4 slot. Complements with power SL that he can vary speeds with. Needs CU to last as SP, but is tough to hit.

Ubiera,Andry — SP — Atlanta

EXP MLB DEBUT: 2017 | H/W: 6-0 170 | FUT: #4 starter | 6C

Thrws R Age 21
2010 FA (DR)

- 92-93 FB +++
- CB ++
- CU ++

Year	Lev	Team	W	L	Sv	IP	K	ERA	WHIP	BF/G	OBA	H%	S%	xERA	Ctl	Dom	Cmd	hr/9	BPV
2012	Rk	GCL Braves	2	2	0	49	48	4.04	1.45	17.4	281	37	71	4.06	3.1	8.8	2.8	0.4	92
2013	Rk	Danville	3	2	0	53	51	3.74	1.43	20.5	269	34	75	4.15	3.6	8.7	2.4	0.7	78
2013	A	Rome	0	0	0	3	2	2.90	1.29	12.7	0	0	75	0.42	11.6	5.8	0.5	0.0	-191
2014	Rk	Danville	4	3	0	63	56	3.70	1.31	18.7	242	30	72	3.39	3.7	8.0	2.2	0.6	62
2014	A	Rome	0	4	0	19	16	9.95	1.89	17.9	282	32	45	6.20	7.1	7.6	1.1	1.4	-37

Short Dominican RH has a good low-90s heater that occassionally hits 95 mph, a decent curve, and an average CU. Struggles with control have stalled his development and at 21 he yet to pitch extensively above rookie ball. Lack of control makes a move to relief likely.

Underwood,Duane — SP — Chicago (N)

EXP MLB DEBUT: 2017 | H/W: 6-2 205 | FUT: #3 starter | 8D

Thrws R Age 20
2012 (2) HS (GA)

- 93-96 FB ++++
- 73-75 CB ++
- CU ++

Year	Lev	Team	W	L	Sv	IP	K	ERA	WHIP	BF/G	OBA	H%	S%	xERA	Ctl	Dom	Cmd	hr/9	BPV
2012	Rk	AZL Cubs	0	1	0	8	7	5.49	1.59	7.2	232	27	67	4.45	6.6	7.7	1.2	1.1	-22
2013	A-	Boise	3	4	0	54	36	4.99	1.65	17.3	289	33	69	4.98	4.5	6.0	1.3	0.7	5
2014	A	Kane County	6	4	0	100	84	2.51	1.21	18.3	231	27	84	3.29	3.2	7.5	2.3	0.9	67

Strong-armed RH put up solid numbers in his full season debut, posting a 2.50 ERA. Features a 90-94 mph FB, a good CU, and a decent CB ball. Has an easy delivery and good athleticism, but an inconsistent release point results in poor command within the zone.

Unsworth,Dylan — SP — Seattle

EXP MLB DEBUT: 2016 | H/W: 6-1 175 | FUT: #5 starter | 6C

Thrws R Age 22
2009 FA (South Africa)

- 85-90 FB +++
- 74-78 CB +++
- 80-81 CU ++

Year	Lev	Team	W	L	Sv	IP	K	ERA	WHIP	BF/G	OBA	H%	S%	xERA	Ctl	Dom	Cmd	hr/9	BPV
2011	Rk	Pulaski	6	5	0	61	46	5.16	1.36	21.3	298	34	63	4.74	1.5	6.8	4.6	1.0	100
2012	A-	Everett	7	2	0	85	67	3.91	1.12	23.9	241	28	67	3.24	2.0	7.1	3.5	1.0	91
2013	Rk	AZL Mariners	0	0	0	6	10	4.50	0.67	7.0	191	30	33	1.94	0.0	15.0		1.5	288
2013	A	Clinton	4	1	0	66	46	2.32	0.91	22.4	238	29	74	2.05	0.3	6.3	23.0	0.3	124
2014	A+	High Desert	6	9	0	119	119	5.89	1.44	19.5	313	39	61	5.40	1.4	9.0	6.3	1.3	141

Lean SP with exceptional control of three pitch repertoire. Keeps ball down, but was victimized by home environment. Drops CB in zone for strikes and registers Ks more on deception and sequencing than natural stuff. CU in development phase and could throw harder once adds strength.

Urena,Jose — SP — Miami

EXP MLB DEBUT: 2015 | H/W: 6-2 195 | FUT: #3 starter | 8D

Thrws R Age 23
2008 FA (DR)

- 92-97 FB ++++
- CU ++++
- SL ++++

Year	Lev	Team	W	L	Sv	IP	K	ERA	WHIP	BF/G	OBA	H%	S%	xERA	Ctl	Dom	Cmd	hr/9	BPV
2011	A-	Jamestown	4	7	0	72	48	4.36	1.43	20.4	267	31	69	3.96	3.6	6.0	1.7	0.5	28
2012	A	Greensboro	9	6	2	138	101	3.39	1.25	20.8	269	31	75	3.85	1.9	6.6	3.5	0.8	85
2013	A+	Jupiter	10	7	0	149	107	3.74	1.19	22.1	260	31	68	3.24	1.7	6.5	3.7	0.5	87
2014	AA	Jacksonville	13	8	0	162	121	3.33	1.14	24.6	253	30	73	3.30	1.6	6.7	4.2	0.8	96

Plus 92-95 mph FB tops out at 97 mph with arm-side run. Improved CU gives him a second plus offering. Breaking ball remains a work in progress but shows potential. Given his awkward delivery, the fact that he walked only 29 suggests there is potential to remain a starter.

Urias,Julio

SP | Los Angeles (N) | EXP MLB DEBUT: 2017 | H/W: 5-11 160 | FUT: #2 starter | 9C

Thrws L Age 18
2012 FA (Mexico)

Velo	Pitch	Grade
92-95	FB	++++
75-81	CB	++++
78-82	CU	++

Year	Lev	Team	W	L	Sv	IP	K	ERA	WHIP	BF/G	OBA	H%	S%	xERA	Ctl	Dom	Cmd	hr/9	BPV
2013	A	Great Lakes	2	0	0	54	67	2.50	1.11	11.8	224	31	82	2.85	2.7	11.1	4.2	0.8	147
2014	A+	Ranch Cuca	2	2	0	87	109	2.37	1.11	13.7	196	29	80	2.14	3.8	11.3	2.9	0.4	117

Small, strong-armed LH continues to dazzle with elite stuff. Attacks hitters with a plus 92-94 mph FB that tops out at 97 mph. Mixes in a outstanding CB with exceptional break and a CU that has potential. Understands how to change speeds and keep hitters off-balance. Did not turn 18 until August.

Valdez,Jose

RP | Detroit | EXP MLB DEBUT: 2015 | H/W: 6-1 200 | FUT: Setup RP | 7D

Thrws R Age 25
2009 FA (DR)

Velo	Pitch	Grade
93-98	FB	++++
83-86	SL	+++
	CU	+

Year	Lev	Team	W	L	Sv	IP	K	ERA	WHIP	BF/G	OBA	H%	S%	xERA	Ctl	Dom	Cmd	hr/9	BPV
2012	Rk	GCL Tigers	0	1	15	22	28	0.82	1.14	3.8	195	31	92	1.79	4.1	11.5	2.8	0.0	114
2013	A	West Michigan	1	1	16	26	35	2.76	1.38	4.1	179	29	78	2.21	6.9	12.1	1.8	0.0	49
2013	A+	Lakeland	1	1	17	23	32	2.74	1.30	4.1	198	31	79	2.61	5.5	12.5	2.3	0.4	95
2014	AA	Erie	2	3	18	57	66	4.11	1.44	5.2	258	35	74	4.25	4.1	10.4	2.5	0.9	95

Strong-armed RP who has spent most of career as closer. All pitches are hard, with electric, lively FB leading the way. Both FB and hard SL serve as out pitches and both enhanced by clean, quick arm. Leaves pitches up and doesn't own offering to retire LHH. Improved control in '14.

Van Orden,Drew

SP | Washington | EXP MLB DEBUT: 2018 | H/W: 6-4 200 | FUT: #4 starter | 7D

Thrws R Age 23
2014 (5) Duke

Velo	Pitch	Grade
88-91	FB	+++
	SL	++
	CU	+

Year	Lev	Team	W	L	Sv	IP	K	ERA	WHIP	BF/G	OBA	H%	S%	xERA	Ctl	Dom	Cmd	hr/9	BPV
2012	NCAA	Duke	0	4	0	34	22	5.82	1.71	6.7	284	36	64	4.91	5.3	8.2	1.6	0.5	23
2013	NCAA	Duke	3	5	0	59	52	6.39	1.69	17.8	298	37	60	5.16	4.4	7.9	1.8	0.6	41
2014	NCAA	Duke	6	5	0	87	91	3.20	1.07	22.6	217	30	68	2.09	2.6	9.4	3.6	0.2	118
2014	Rk	GCL Nationals	0	1	0	5	7	3.60	1.20	10.1	299	46	67	3.31	0.0	12.6		0.0	245
2014	A-	Auburn	2	3	0	41	35	4.39	1.41	17.4	289	35	70	4.59	2.4	7.7	3.2	0.9	91

A big spring at Duke vaulted him into the early rounds, but despite a pro body he's more of a finesse, rather than power, pitcher. Worked at smoothing out his mechanics and learning how to throw downhill. Intelligence and drive to succeed a plus.

Varga,Cameron

SP | Tampa Bay | EXP MLB DEBUT: 2018 | H/W: 6-2 190 | FUT: #3 starter | 8E

Thrws R Age 20
2014 (2) HS (OH)

Velo	Pitch	Grade
88-94	FB	+++
75-79	CB	+++
80-83	CU	++

Year	Lev	Team	W	L	Sv	IP	K	ERA	WHIP	BF/G	OBA	H%	S%	xERA	Ctl	Dom	Cmd	hr/9	BPV
2014	Rk	GCL Devil Rays	2	0	0	14	14	2.55	0.92	10.6	232	32	69	1.72	0.6	8.9	14.0	0.0	162
2014	Rk	Princeton	1	1	0	19	11	4.74	1.74	17.3	327	37	72	5.63	3.3	5.2	1.6	0.5	22

Loose-armed pitcher who has advanced feel for craft. Generates acceptable velocity with easy arm action and could throw harder in time. Has athleticism to repeat mechanics and slot. Throws CB for strikes and can use as chase pitch. Needs to hone CU as it lacks consistency.

Vasquez,Kelvin

SP | Texas | EXP MLB DEBUT: 2017 | H/W: 6-4 195 | FUT: #3 starter | 7D

Thrws R Age 22
2011 FA (DR)

Velo	Pitch	Grade
89-94	FB	+++
81-84	SL	+++
78-82	CU	++

Year	Lev	Team	W	L	Sv	IP	K	ERA	WHIP	BF/G	OBA	H%	S%	xERA	Ctl	Dom	Cmd	hr/9	BPV
2013	A-	Spokane	2	2	0	63	72	2.14	1.27	18.4	205	29	84	2.66	4.8	10.3	2.1	0.4	72
2013	A	Hickory	2	2	0	26	19	6.55	1.88	15.3	296	33	67	6.35	6.2	6.6	1.1	1.4	-32
2014	A	Hickory	3	1	1	51	58	4.39	1.21	17.2	234	33	62	2.79	3.2	10.2	3.2	0.4	116

Tall, thin SP who repeated Low-A and fared much better before ending season in June. Can register Ks with lively FB and knocks out RHH with hard SL. Posted reverse splits despite subpar CU. Improved control, but needs better FB location. Still shows raw pitchability and mixing.

Velasquez,Vincent

SP | Houston | EXP MLB DEBUT: 2016 | H/W: 6-3 200 | FUT: #3 starter | 8C

Thrws R Age 22
2010 (2) HS (CA)

Velo	Pitch	Grade
90-96	FB	++++
75-78	CB	+++
81-84	CU	+++

Year	Lev	Team	W	L	Sv	IP	K	ERA	WHIP	BF/G	OBA	H%	S%	xERA	Ctl	Dom	Cmd	hr/9	BPV
2012	A-	Tri City	4	1	0	45	51	3.38	1.19	20.2	225	31	71	2.69	3.4	10.2	3.0	0.4	109
2013	A	Quad Cities	9	4	3	110	123	3.19	1.12	17.3	225	31	72	2.66	2.7	10.1	3.7	0.6	126
2013	A+	Lancaster	0	2	0	14	19	6.34	1.55	20.7	259	36	60	4.82	5.1	12.0	2.4	1.3	98
2014	Rk	GCL Astros	0	1	0	8	19	2.20	0.85	10.0	178	55	71	0.79	2.2	20.9	9.5	0.0	334
2014	A+	Lancaster	7	4	0	55	72	3.76	1.23	14.9	225	32	73	3.31	3.8	11.8	3.1	1.0	128

Injury-prone SP, but has loads of potential. Missed much of season with groin injury and had elbow surgery in past. Throws hard and owns plus pitch mix to post high K rate. Easy delivery with explosive FB and feel for advanced CU. Exhibits decent control, but can be better with more time.

VerHagen,Drew

SP | Detroit | EXP MLB DEBUT: 2014 | H/W: 6-6 230 | FUT: #4 starter | 7C

Thrws R Age 24
2012 (4) Vanderbilt

Velo	Pitch	Grade
90-95	FB	+++
77-80	CB	++
80-83	CU	++

Year	Lev	Team	W	L	Sv	IP	K	ERA	WHIP	BF/G	OBA	H%	S%	xERA	Ctl	Dom	Cmd	hr/9	BPV
2012	A+	Lakeland	0	3	0	27	17	3.67	1.26	13.8	208	25	68	2.31	4.7	5.7	1.2	0.0	-6
2013	A+	Lakeland	5	3	0	67	35	2.82	1.13	22.1	206	24	73	2.10	3.6	4.7	1.3	0.1	5
2013	AA	Erie	2	5	0	60	40	3.00	1.17	19.9	239	28	75	2.88	2.6	6.0	2.4	0.5	57
2014	AAA	Toledo	6	7	0	110	63	3.68	1.29	23.8	274	31	71	3.63	2.0	5.1	2.5	0.4	56
2014	MLB	Detroit	0	1	0	5	4	5.40	1.60	22.1	262	33	63	3.85	5.4	7.2	1.3	0.0	2

Large-framed SP who ended season early due to bad back. Uses height to pitch downhill and spots sinking FB in lower half of zone. Has flashes of solid CB, but too inconsistent to register Ks. Arm action doesn't provide deception and can slow arm on below average CU.

Vizcaino,Arodys

RP | Atlanta | EXP MLB DEBUT: 2011 | H/W: 6-0 190 | FUT: #3 starter/Setup RP | 8D

Thrws R Age 24
2007 FA (DR)

Velo	Pitch	Grade
89-96	FB	++++
80-83	CB	+++
83-85	CU	++

Year	Lev	Team	W	L	Sv	IP	K	ERA	WHIP	BF/G	OBA	H%	S%	xERA	Ctl	Dom	Cmd	hr/9	BPV
2011	MLB	Atlanta	1	1	0	17	17	4.74	1.46	4.3	249	32	67	3.80	4.7	8.9	1.9	0.5	51
2014	A+	Daytona	0	0	1	9	10	1.00	1.11	3.9	191	28	90	1.70	4.0	10.0	2.5	0.0	90
2014	AA	Tennessee	1	1	1	13	16	2.73	0.76	3.4	158	22	67	1.08	2.0	10.9	5.3	0.7	159
2014	AAA	Iowa	0	0	0	18	16	5.47	1.99	5.1	329	41	71	6.30	5.5	8.0	1.5	0.5	14
2014	MLB	Chi Cubs	0	0	0	5	4	5.40	1.60	4.4	262	28	71	5.54	5.4	7.2	1.3	1.8	2

Managed to appear in 45 games, exclusively in relief, and finally made it back to the majors. When healthy features a plus 93-96 mph FB, an above-avg CB, and an inconsistent CU. FB/CB proved effective in relief. Command can abandon him; was traded back to ATL, who originally drafted him.

Voth,Austin

SP | Washington | EXP MLB DEBUT: 2016 | H/W: 6-1 190 | FUT: #4 starter | 7B

Thrws R Age 22
2013 (5) Washington

Velo	Pitch	Grade
89-92	FB	+++
83-85	SL	+++
	CU	++

Year	Lev	Team	W	L	Sv	IP	K	ERA	WHIP	BF/G	OBA	H%	S%	xERA	Ctl	Dom	Cmd	hr/9	BPV
2013	A-	Auburn	2	0	0	30	42	1.49	0.83	15.7	198	33	80	1.04	1.2	12.5	10.5	0.0	211
2013	A	Hagerstown	1	0	0	10	9	3.53	0.98	19.4	218	29	60	1.70	1.8	7.9	4.5	0.0	113
2014	A	Hagerstown	4	3	0	69	74	2.47	1.05	20.6	207	29	75	1.87	2.9	9.6	3.4	0.1	114
2014	A+	Potomac	2	1	0	37	40	1.45	0.62	21.3	132	18	81	0.29	1.7	9.7	5.7	0.5	146
2014	AA	Harrisburg	1	3	0	19	19	6.60	1.62	17.0	290	34	63	6.06	4.2	9.0	2.1	1.9	65

Fast-mover from 2013 draft worked his way from Low-A to Double-A. Attacks hitters with a lively low-90s FB that he can command at will. Has some deception in delivery, is good athlete and controls running game. Secondaries are still developing; test will be whether he can keep higher level hitters off his fastball.

Wagner,Tyler

SP | Milwaukee | EXP MLB DEBUT: 2016 | H/W: 6-3 195 | FUT: #4 starter | 7C

Thrws R Age 24
2012 (4) Utah

Velo	Pitch	Grade
92-97	FB	++++
85-86	SL	++
	CU	+++

Year	Lev	Team	W	L	Sv	IP	K	ERA	WHIP	BF/G	OBA	H%	S%	xERA	Ctl	Dom	Cmd	hr/9	BPV
2012	NCAA	Utah	2	6	2	42	34	3.63	1.78	8.8	287	36	78	4.86	5.8	7.3	1.3	0.2	-7
2012	Rk	Helena	1	4	0	48	47	7.84	1.76	15.8	317	39	54	6.11	4.1	8.8	2.1	1.1	65
2013	A	Wisconsin	10	8	0	148	116	3.22	1.25	22.3	236	28	75	3.19	3.4	7.0	2.1	0.6	53
2014	A+	Brevard Cnty	13	6	0	150	118	1.86	1.11	23.6	218	26	87	2.60	2.9	7.1	2.5	0.6	68
2014	ind	Brownsville	0	0	0	2	2	13.50	2.00	9.6	347	35	33	10.39	4.5	9.0	2.0	4.5	59

Utah closer was converted to a SP and was impressive, posting a 1.86 ERA. Knows how to pitch and keep hitters off balance. Features a low-90s FB that tops at 95, a hard SL, and a CU that is effective vs. LHH. Keeps the ball down in the zone and getting plenty of groundball outs.

Wahl,Bobby

SP | Oakland | EXP MLB DEBUT: 2016 | H/W: 6-2 210 | FUT: #3 starter/setupRP | 8E

Thrws R Age 23
2013 (5) Mississippi

Velo	Pitch	Grade
88-94	FB	+++
82-84	SL	+++
80-82	CU	+++

Year	Lev	Team	W	L	Sv	IP	K	ERA	WHIP	BF/G	OBA	H%	S%	xERA	Ctl	Dom	Cmd	hr/9	BPV
2013	NCAA	Mississippi	10	0	0	97	78	2.04	1.16	24.2	201	25	83	2.23	4.1	7.2	1.8	0.3	38
2013	Rk	AZL Athletics	0	0	0	1	1	9.00	2.00	4.8	0	0	50	2.18	18.0	9.0	0.5	0.0	-306
2013	A-	Vermont	0	0	2	20	27	4.01	1.29	9.2	260	36	74	4.24	2.7	12.0	4.5	1.3	162
2014	A	Beloit	0	4	4	42	43	5.12	1.54	9.2	279	35	68	4.92	4.1	9.2	2.3	1.1	74
2014	A+	Stockton	0	0	0	10	19	4.41	1.37	4.8	218	38	75	4.26	5.3	16.8	3.2	1.8	177

Big, strong prospect who pitched better out of pen than rotation. Future role still uncertain, but has three solid-average offerings. Throws FB with conviction and nifty CU can be deceptive with nice arm action. Hard SL can miss bats, though lots of effort in delivery and command needs work.

Weaver,Luke
SP | St. Louis | EXP MLB DEBUT: 2017 | H/W: 6-2 170 | FUT: #3 starter | 8D

Thrws R Age 21
2014 (1) Florida State
88-93 FB +++
79-81 CB ++
78-81 CU +++

Year	Lev	Team	W	L	Sv	IP	K	ERA	WHIP	BF/G	OBA	H%	S%	xERA	Ctl	Dom	Cmd	hr/9	BPV
2012	NCAA	Florida State	1	0	1	41	40	5.93	1.51	11.1	262	32	63	4.85	4.6	8.8	1.9	1.3	52
2013	NCAA	Florida State	7	2	0	98	119	2.29	0.99	22.0	220	32	78	2.15	1.7	10.9	6.3	0.5	167
2014	NCAA	Florida State	8	4	0	106	85	2.63	1.05	25.6	227	27	78	2.63	2.0	7.2	3.7	0.7	95
2014	Rk	GCL Cardinals	0	0	0	6	9	0.00	0.67	5.2	191	34	100	0.54	0.0	13.5		0.0	261
2014	A+	Palm Beach	0	1	0	3	3	23.23	4.84	11.9	557	64	50	21.49	11.6	8.7	0.8	2.9	-139

Comes after hitters with a good 88-93 mph FB that hits 96. Keeps the ball down in the zone and gets late action from a high ¾ arm slot. Throws with some effort that results in below-average command, though he does have a quick arm. Mixes in a 79-81 mph SL and a 78-81 mph CU.

Weickel,Walker
SP | San Diego | EXP MLB DEBUT: 2017 | H/W: 6-6 195 | FUT: #3 starter | 7D

Thrws R Age 21
2012 (1-S) HS (FL)
91-94 FB +++
CB ++++
CU ++

Year	Lev	Team	W	L	Sv	IP	K	ERA	WHIP	BF/G	OBA	H%	S%	xERA	Ctl	Dom	Cmd	hr/9	BPV
2012	Rk	AZL Padres	1	3	0	14	12	4.50	1.57	6.8	288	37	68	4.15	3.9	7.7	2.0	0.0	53
2013	A	Fort Wayne	3	6	0	110	82	5.06	1.52	19.9	287	34	66	4.63	3.5	6.7	1.9	0.7	44
2014	Rk	AZL Padres	1	0	0	7	3	1.29	1.00	13.4	202	23	86	1.61	2.6	3.9	1.5	0.0	18
2014	A-	Eugene	0	3	0	34	20	6.09	1.88	22.8	329	37	67	6.34	4.5	5.3	1.2	0.8	-8
2014	A	Fort Wayne	1	8	0	72	39	6.36	1.77	22.1	316	34	64	6.04	4.2	4.9	1.1	1.0	-9

Tall and lean starter who uses height well. Pitches downhill with sinking FB and keeps ball on ground. Could grow into three average offerings, but needs fine-tuning. Lacks deception in delivery and can be inconsistent. Was hit hard giving up an oppBAA well over .300 at both stops.

Wells,Benjamin
SP | Chicago (N) | EXP MLB DEBUT: 2016 | H/W: 6-3 220 | FUT: #4 starter | 7D

Thrws R Age 22
2010 (7) HS (AR)
91-93 FB +++
CB ++
CU ++

Year	Lev	Team	W	L	Sv	IP	K	ERA	WHIP	BF/G	OBA	H%	S%	xERA	Ctl	Dom	Cmd	hr/9	BPV
2012	A	Peoria	3	2	1	44		3.27	1.36	15.3	279	35	73	3.49	2.5	7.4	3.0	0.0	84
2013	A+	Daytona	9	6	0	112	69	3.29	1.21	19.7	233	26	74	3.03	3.2	5.5	1.7	0.6	31
2014	A-	Boise	2	2	0	28	22	3.86	1.50	20.2	255	31	73	3.80	4.8	7.1	1.5	0.3	15
2014	A	Kane County	4	0	0	36	20	2.24	1.39	21.7	197	23	84	2.74	6.2	5.0	0.8	0.2	-61
2014	A+	Daytona	2	4	0	22	18	6.55	2.27	14.0	303	37	69	6.53	9.4	7.4	0.8	0.4	-104

Strong RH uses heavy 90-93 mph sinking FB. Saw action at three different levels, ending the year at High-A. Struggled with control, walking a combined 63 in 86.1 IP and yet managing a 3.86 ERA. Secondary offerings are not advanced. CB and CU both need work, but has clean, repeatable mechanics.

Wells,Nick
SP | Toronto | EXP MLB DEBUT: 2018 | H/W: 6-5 175 | FUT: #3 starter | 8E

Thrws L Age 19
2014 (3) HS (VA)
86-92 FB +++
75-79 CB +++
79-82 CU +

Year	Lev	Team	W	L	Sv	IP	K	ERA	WHIP	BF/G	OBA	H%	S%	xERA	Ctl	Dom	Cmd	hr/9	BPV
2014	Rk	GCL Blue Jays	1	3	0	34	18	5.79	1.61	13.8	313	35	61	4.90	2.9	4.7	1.6	0.3	25

Quick-armed SP who has lengthy development time ahead of him. Has lean frame that projects to more ticks in FB. Has strong delivery that will likely be tweaked to repeat more consistently. Has potential plus CB with nice depth, but rarely uses CU that is in infancy stage. One to watch.

Wetzler,Ben
SP | Miami | EXP MLB DEBUT: 2018 | H/W: 6-1 195 | FUT: #4 starter | 7D

Thrws L Age 23
2014 (9) Oregon State
89-92 FB +++
SL ++
CU +++

Year	Lev	Team	W	L	Sv	IP	K	ERA	WHIP	BF/G	OBA	H%	S%	xERA	Ctl	Dom	Cmd	hr/9	BPV
2011	NCAA	Oregon St.	6	3	1	63	45	4.70	1.36	16.5	279	33	65	4.03	2.4	6.4	2.6	0.6	68
2012	NCAA	Oregon St.	8	2	0	101	75	3.11	1.34	26.3	248	30	75	3.18	3.7	6.7	1.8	0.2	37
2013	NCAA	Oregon St.	10	1	0	96	83	2.25	1.20	24.1	235	30	81	2.73	3.0	7.8	2.6	0.3	77
2014	NCAA	Oregon St.	12	1	0	104	83	0.78	0.77	26.7	143	19	90	0.43	2.7	7.2	2.7	0.1	75
2014	A-	Batavia	0	2	0	39	31	2.98	1.51	15.4	298	35	85	5.21	2.8	7.1	2.6	1.1	72

9th round pick had a solid pro debut, going 0-2 with a 2.98 ERA in the NYPL. Sinking FB tops out at 92 mph, but he complements it well with a plus CU that has good late fade and sink and an inconsistent low-80s SL. Wetzler keeps hitters off-balance and has good FB control and command.

Whalen,Robert
SP | New York (N) | EXP MLB DEBUT: 2017 | H/W: 6-2 200 | FUT: #5 starter/RP | 6C

Thrws R Age 21
2012 (12) HS (FL)
91-93 FB +++
77-79 CB ++++
SL ++
CU ++

Year	Lev	Team	W	L	Sv	IP	K	ERA	WHIP	BF/G	OBA	H%	S%	xERA	Ctl	Dom	Cmd	hr/9	BPV
2012	Rk	Kingsport	0	0	0	1	1	0.00	1.00	3.8	262	35	100	2.32	0.0	9.0		0.0	180
2013	Rk	Kingsport	3	2	0	72	76	1.87	0.93	22.5	197	28	79	1.44	2.1	9.5	4.5	0.1	131
2014	Rk	GCL Mets	0	1	0	7	10	1.29	0.86	8.6	168	29	83	0.78	2.6	12.9	5.0	0.0	180
2014	A	Savannah	9	1	0	62	53	2.03	1.01	21.7	201	26	80	1.86	2.7	7.7	2.8	0.3	82

12th round pick has exceeded expectations. Plus command of sinking FB and CB has keyed success. He also throws developing SL and CU. Pounds strike zone and maintains high GB%. Mixes pitches well, but not much projection left and will struggle to keep Dom as he advances.

Whiting,Boone
SP | St. Louis | EXP MLB DEBUT: 2015 | H/W: 6-1 175 | FUT: #4 starter/Setup RP | 7D

Thrws R Age 25
2010 (18) Centenary
86-91 FB ++
81-83 SL ++
CU ++

Year	Lev	Team	W	L	Sv	IP	K	ERA	WHIP	BF/G	OBA	H%	S%	xERA	Ctl	Dom	Cmd	hr/9	BPV
2012	A	Quad Cities	1	0	0	16	14	0.56	0.50	17.7	134	18	88	0.00	0.6	7.9	14.0	0.0	145
2012	AA	Springfield	0	0	0	12	9	1.50	1.17	23.9	245	31	86	2.54	2.3	6.8	3.0	0.0	79
2013	AA	Springfield	3	2	0	30	34	2.98	1.16	20.0	247	34	76	3.07	2.1	10.1	4.9	0.6	144
2013	AAA	Memphis	5	5	0	105	99	4.11	1.40	21.1	265	33	73	4.25	3.4	8.5	2.5	0.9	78
2014	AAA	Memphis	4	7	0	96	99	4.21	1.46	19.6	261	34	73	4.25	4.1	9.3	2.3	0.8	74

Competes well even without an overpowering FB. High 3/4 delivery and features a 87-91 mph FB that tops out at 92. Also has a decent SL and a good CU that gives him a chance to succeed. Best weapon is that he throws tons of strikes and could help out at the back end of a rotation.

Wieland,Joe
SP | Los Angeles (N) | EXP MLB DEBUT: 2012 | H/W: 6-3 210 | FUT: #3 starter | 7B

Thrws R Age 25
2008 (4) HS (NV)
88-92 FB +++
80-83 CB +++
79-82 CU +++

Year	Lev	Team	W	L	Sv	IP	K	ERA	WHIP	BF/G	OBA	H%	S%	xERA	Ctl	Dom	Cmd	hr/9	BPV
2012	MLB	San Diego	0	4	0	27	24	4.63	1.29	22.3	253	28	70	4.49	3.0	7.9	2.7	1.7	81
2014	Rk	AZL Padres	0	1	0	6	10	3.00	0.67	7.0	151	30	50	0.09	1.5	15.0	10.0	0.0	248
2014	AA	San Antonio	0	1	0	9	6	2.00	1.00	17.2	240	27	88	2.99	1.0	6.0	6.0	1.0	99
2014	AAA	El Paso	2	1	0	23	20	3.49	1.12	22.9	252	32	68	2.86	1.6	7.8	5.0	0.4	116
2014	MLB	San Diego	1	0	0	11	8	7.30	1.89	13.1	338	36	67	8.05	4.1	6.5	1.6	2.4	25

TJS caused him to miss most of '12 and all of '13, and missed more action in '14. When healthy, he has plus control of a nice three-pitch mix. FB sits at 88-92 mph. Has walked only 86 in 476.2 career minor league innings with a 3.27 ERA. Traded to Dodgers as part of the Matt Kemp deal.

Williams,Austen
SP | Washington | EXP MLB DEBUT: 2018 | H/W: 6-3 220 | FUT: #5 starter/RP | 7D

Thrws R Age 22
2014 (6) Texas State
88-91 FB +++
SL ++
CU ++

Year	Lev	Team	W	L	Sv	IP	K	ERA	WHIP	BF/G	OBA	H%	S%	xERA	Ctl	Dom	Cmd	hr/9	BPV
2012	NCAA	Texas State	1	0	1	19	15	5.21	1.42	9.0	309	37	62	4.54	1.4	7.1	5.0	0.5	108
2013	NCAA	Texas State	1	3	1	31	31	3.46	1.25	4.5	221	30	69	2.42	4.0	8.9	2.2	0.0	70
2014	NCAA	Texas State	8	3	0	98	96	3.67	1.19	26.3	241	32	68	2.87	2.7	8.8	3.3	0.4	105
2014	Rk	GCL Nationals	0	0	0	4	1	2.14	1.67	9.4	297	32	86	4.57	4.3	2.1	0.5	0.0	-59
2014	A-	Auburn	4	3	0	38	26	4.71	1.31	17.5	281	33	63	3.83	1.9	6.1	3.3	0.5	77

Big righty gets lots of movement on all his pitches: low-90s fastball with run; 11-to-5 slider, and a developing change-up. Commanded the ball well in short-season, and has prototypical size. Delivery comes with effort, so bullpen may be ultimate destination.

Williams,Devin
SP | Milwaukee | EXP MLB DEBUT: 2017 | H/W: 6-3 165 | FUT: #3 starter | 8D

Thrws R Age 20
2013 (2) HS (MO)
88-95 FB ++++
81-83 CB +++
CU +++

Year	Lev	Team	W	L	Sv	IP	K	ERA	WHIP	BF/G	OBA	H%	S%	xERA	Ctl	Dom	Cmd	hr/9	BPV
2013	Rk	AZL Brewers	1	3	1	34	39	3.42	1.46	11.3	225	33	74	2.99	5.8	10.3	1.8	0.0	46
2014	Rk	Helena	4	7	0	66	66	4.49	1.42	18.7	284	36	69	4.34	2.7	9.0	3.3	0.7	106

Good FB that ranges from 88-95 with the potential for more as he grows into his frame. Complements the FB with a CB and CU that flash plus. Improved mechanics and a more consistent release point led to significant gains in FB command. Does a good job of keeping the ball down in the zone.

Williams,Ronnie
SP | St. Louis | EXP MLB DEBUT: 2019 | H/W: 6-0 170 | FUT: #3 starter | 8E

Thrws R Age 19
2014 (2) HS (FL)
92-95 FB +++
CB ++
CU ++

Year	Lev	Team	W	L	Sv	IP	K	ERA	WHIP	BF/G	OBA	H%	S%	xERA	Ctl	Dom	Cmd	hr/9	BPV
2014	Rk	GCL Cardinals	0	5	1	36	30	4.74	1.33	15.0	277	35	62	3.61	2.2	7.5	3.3	0.2	92

Pounds the strike zone with a plus mid-90s FB that tops out at 98 and showed a good CB in his debut and surprising feel for a CU. Showed good poise and control, walking 9 while striking out 30. Is some effort to his high ¾ delivery, but he has good front-side mechanics and a compact motion.

Williams,Taylor

SP | Milwaukee | EXP MLB DEBUT: 2017 | H/W: 5-11 165 | FUT: #4 starter | 7C

Thrws R Age 23	Year	Lev	Team	W	L	Sv	IP	K	ERA	WHIP	BF/G	OBA	H%	S%	xERA	Ctl	Dom	Cmd	hr/9	BPV
2013 (4) Kent State	2011	NCAA	Washington St	0	1	0	10	4	12.48	3.37	6.2	467	48	63	13.92	8.0	3.6	0.4	1.8	-134
90-94 FB +++	2013	NCAA	Kent State	10	1	0	105	110	2.48	0.96	26.5	219	31	72	1.73	1.5	9.4	6.1	0.1	146
SL +++	2013	Rk	Helena	3	1	0	42	42	4.28	1.40	14.8	261	33	72	4.33	3.6	9.0	2.5	1.1	81
CU ++	2014	A	Wisconsin	8	1	4	107	112	2.36	0.94	18.3	205	28	75	1.77	1.9	9.4	4.9	0.3	135
	2014	A+	Brevard Cnty	1	2	0	25	25	4.30	1.35	21.0	291	35	73	4.97	1.8	9.0	5.0	1.4	131

Short RH had a breakout season in the MWL. Comes after hitters with a low-90s FB. Has good athleticism, but does throw with effort. Uses an above-average SL to great effect vs. RHH and his CU shows nice potential as well. Walked just 28 while striking out 137.

Williams,Trevor

SP | Miami | EXP MLB DEBUT: 2016 | H/W: 6-3 230 | FUT: #4 starter | 7C

Thrws R Age 22	Year	Lev	Team	W	L	Sv	IP	K	ERA	WHIP	BF/G	OBA	H%	S%	xERA	Ctl	Dom	Cmd	hr/9	BPV
2013 (2) Arizona State	2013	Rk	GCL Marlins	0	0	0	2	1	4.50	1.50	8.6	347	39	67	4.95	0.0	4.5		0.0	99
90-95 FB ++++	2013	A-	Batavia	0	2	0	29	20	2.48	1.17	11.6	241	30	76	2.50	2.5	6.2	2.5	0.0	63
77-80 CU ++++	2013	A	Greensboro	0	0	0	3	3	0.00	0.67	10.5	191	27	100	0.59	0.0	9.0		0.0	180
83-85 SL +++	2014	A+	Jupiter	8	6	0	129	90	2.79	1.29	23.1	275	33	78	3.60	2.0	6.3	3.1	0.3	76
CB +++	2014	AA	Jacksonville	0	1	0	15	14	6.00	1.87	23.4	342	44	64	5.74	3.6	8.4	2.3	0.0	72

FB sits in the low-90s and he complements with a plus CU that has good fading action. Also mixes in a SL and CB. None of his offerings are plus but has a good idea of how to set up hitters and gave up just 5 HR in 144 IP. Improved mechanics led to better control and gave up just 29 BB.

Wilson,Tyler

SP | Baltimore | EXP MLB DEBUT: 2015 | H/W: 6-2 185 | FUT: #5 starter | 6B

Thrws R Age 25	Year	Lev	Team	W	L	Sv	IP	K	ERA	WHIP	BF/G	OBA	H%	S%	xERA	Ctl	Dom	Cmd	hr/9	BPV
2011 (10) Virginia	2012	A+	Frederick	7	7	0	111		3.49	1.03	22.5	233	29	70	2.91	1.5	9.2	6.0	1.0	143
87-91 FB +++	2013	A+	Frederick	1	1	0	62	48	4.49	1.32	23.4	246	29	65	3.47	3.6	7.0	1.9	0.6	45
80-82 SL +++	2013	AA	Bowie	7	5	0	89	70	3.84	1.20	22.4	253	28	73	3.95	2.2	7.1	3.2	1.3	85
81-83 CU ++	2014	AA	Bowie	10	5	0	96	91	3.74	1.28	24.6	271	34	73	4.03	2.1	8.5	4.1	0.9	116
	2014	AAA	Norfolk	4	3	0	70	66	3.60	1.17	23.3	236	29	73	3.38	2.7	8.5	3.1	1.0	98

Limited upside SP who has been slow to develop, but is on verge of big leagues. Knows how to pitch and keeps ball down in zone. Doesn't beat himself, but can be hit hard. Moves ball in and out of zone effectively and holds velocity late in games. Repeats clean delivery and throws strikes.

Windle,Tom

SP | Philadelphia | EXP MLB DEBUT: 2016 | H/W: 6-4 215 | FUT: #4 starter | 7C

Thrws L Age 23	Year	Lev	Team	W	L	Sv	IP	K	ERA	WHIP	BF/G	OBA	H%	S%	xERA	Ctl	Dom	Cmd	hr/9	BPV
2013 (2) Minnesota	2011	NCAA	Minnesota	6	2	2	41	35	1.53	1.12	8.5	232	30	87	2.44	2.4	7.7	3.2	0.2	91
90-92 FB +++	2012	NCAA	Minnesota	3	5	1	41	37	3.28	1.29	9.4	237	29	76	3.34	3.7	8.1	2.2	0.7	63
81-84 SL ++	2013	NCAA	Minnesota	6	4	0	92	86	2.15	1.12	25.9	212	28	80	2.16	3.2	8.4	2.6	0.2	82
80-82 CU +++	2013	A	Great Lakes	5	1	0	53	51	2.71	1.32	16.9	250	33	79	3.27	3.4	8.6	2.6	0.3	82
	2014	A+	Ranch Cuca	12	8	0	139	111	4.27	1.37	22.4	273	32	71	4.28	2.8	7.2	2.5	0.9	70

Tall LH continues to show good command and strong pitchability that allows his three-pitch mix to play up. Comes at hitters with a low-90s FB with good sink, an inconsistent SL that shows potential, and a solid avg CU that keeps righties at bay. Generates good downhill plane using his size.

Winkler,Danny

SP | Atlanta | EXP MLB DEBUT: 2016 | H/W: 6-1 200 | FUT: #4 starter | 7C

Thrws R Age 25	Year	Lev	Team	W	L	Sv	IP	K	ERA	WHIP	BF/G	OBA	H%	S%	xERA	Ctl	Dom	Cmd	hr/9	BPV
2011 (20) Central Florida	2011	Rk	Casper	4	3	0	57	65	3.94	1.45	20.3	284	38	75	4.66	3.0	10.2	3.4	0.9	122
89-93 FB +++	2012	A	Asheville	11	10	0	145	136	4.47	1.37	24.3	271	33	69	4.32	2.9	8.4	2.9	1.0	91
80-82 SL ++++	2013	A+	Modesto	12	5	0	130	152	2.97	0.93	22.2	186	24	74	2.16	2.6	10.5	4.1	1.0	138
CU ++	2013	AA	Tulsa	1	2	0	26	23	3.09	1.26	21.4	237	28	80	3.62	3.4	7.9	2.3	1.0	67
	2014	AA	Tulsa	5	2	0	70	71	1.41	0.71	20.6	143	18	87	0.79	2.2	9.1	4.2	0.6	123

Short RH attacks hitters with a 91-93 mph FB and a plus SL. Keeps the ball down in the zone and gets swings and misses with SL. Dominated at Double-A, going 5-2 with a 1.41 ERA and 17 BB/71 K before injury hit and he had Tommy John surgery in June. Will miss most of 2015; selected by ATL in Rule 5 draft.

Wiper,Cole

SP | Texas | EXP MLB DEBUT: 2017 | H/W: 6-4 185 | FUT: #4 starter | 7D

Thrws R Age 22	Year	Lev	Team	W	L	Sv	IP	K	ERA	WHIP	BF/G	OBA	H%	S%	xERA	Ctl	Dom	Cmd	hr/9	BPV
2013 (10) Oregon																				
88-93 FB +++																				
77-80 CB +++	2013	NCAA	Oregon	2	1	0	12	4	7.38	2.38	9.1	356	37	68	8.02	7.4	3.0	0.4	0.7	-128
80-83 SL ++	2013	Rk	AZL Rangers	3	1	0	25	26	2.15	1.16	10.0	229	32	79	2.27	2.9	9.3	3.3	0.0	108
82-84 CU ++	2014	A	Hickory	7	8	0	101	96	3.83	1.36	17.6	244	29	76	4.07	4.0	8.6	2.1	1.2	64

Tall, lean SP who wore down at end of season. Inconsistent command hampers decent pitch mix. Has potential for 3 average to plus offerings, led by solid-average FB and sharp SL. CU, though inconsistent, shows flashes of plus. Induces groundballs, but can also hang CB and SL.

Wisler,Matt

SP | San Diego | EXP MLB DEBUT: 2015 | H/W: 6-3 195 | FUT: #3 starter | 8C

Thrws R Age 22	Year	Lev	Team	W	L	Sv	IP	K	ERA	WHIP	BF/G	OBA	H%	S%	xERA	Ctl	Dom	Cmd	hr/9	BPV
2011 (7) HS (OH)	2012	A	Fort Wayne	5	4	0	114	113	2.53	1.08	18.5	228	31	75	2.15	2.2	8.9	4.0	0.1	119
91-94 FB +++	2013	A+	Lake Elsinore	2	1	0	31	28	2.03	0.90	19.2	201	26	78	1.58	1.7	8.1	4.7	0.3	117
82-85 SL +++	2013	AA	San Antonio	8	5	0	105	103	3.00	1.07	20.4	223	29	73	2.54	2.3	8.8	3.8	0.6	114
74-76 CB +++	2014	AA	San Antonio	1	0	0	30	35	2.10	1.07	19.4	235	33	83	2.68	1.8	10.5	5.8	0.6	158
CU ++	2014	AAA	El Paso	9	5	0	116	101	5.03	1.44	22.5	286	33	69	5.15	2.8	7.8	2.8	1.5	84

Tall, athletic starter who continues to evolve into a top prospect. Has feel for pitching by spotting 92-94 mph FB with hard sink, and using two above-avg breaking balls to keep hitters off guard. SL misses bats on any level and CU continues to improve steadily. Struggled when moved up to AAA.

Wittgren,Nick

RP | Miami | EXP MLB DEBUT: 2015 | H/W: 6-2 215 | FUT: Setup RP | 7B

Thrws R Age 23	Year	Lev	Team	W	L	Sv	IP	K	ERA	WHIP	BF/G	OBA	H%	S%	xERA	Ctl	Dom	Cmd	hr/9	BPV
2012 (9) Purdue	2012	A-	Jamestown	0	2	11	24	34	1.49	1.16	5.7	260	41	86	2.65	1.5	12.6	8.5	0.0	205
89-93 FB ++++	2012	A	Greensboro	0	0	2	6	13	0.00	0.33	3.2	56	20	100	0.00	1.5	19.5	13.0	0.0	329
CB +++	2013	A+	Jupiter	2	1	25	54	59	0.83	0.96	4.3	216	30	92	1.77	1.7	9.8	5.9	0.2	150
	2013	AA	Jacksonville	0	0	1	4	4	0.00	0.00	2.8	0	0		0.00	0.0	9.0		0.0	180
	2014	AA	Jacksonville	5	5	20	66	56	3.55	1.32	5.3	282	34	75	4.18	1.9	7.6	4.0	0.8	104

Lacks plus velocity, but attacks hitters with deceptive, low-90s FB and good power CB. Commands both pitches with ease and while he does not overpower hitters, his deceptive, repeatable mechanics have allowed him to be elite in Dom, Ctl, and Cmd. Has logged 46 sv over two seasons at AA.

Wojciechowski,Asher

SP | Houston | EXP MLB DEBUT: 2015 | H/W: 6-4 240 | FUT: #4 starter | 7C

Thrws R Age 26	Year	Lev	Team	W	L	Sv	IP	K	ERA	WHIP	BF/G	OBA	H%	S%	xERA	Ctl	Dom	Cmd	hr/9	BPV
2010 (1-S) The Citadel	2012	A+	Dunedin	7	3	0	93	76	3.58	1.21	20.9	257	32	69	3.08	2.1	7.3	3.5	0.3	93
89-94 FB +++	2012	AA	Corpus Christi	2	2	0	43	34	2.08	1.02	20.7	198	25	77	1.57	2.9	7.1	2.4	0.0	67
80-85 SL +++	2013	AA	Corpus Christi	2	1	1	26	27	2.08	0.92	16.2	188	26	78	1.52	2.4	9.3	3.9	0.3	121
81-84 CU +++	2013	AAA	Oklahoma City	9	7	0	134	104	3.56	1.19	24.4	235	28	71	3.10	3.0	7.0	2.4	0.7	64
	2014	AAA	Oklahoma City	4	4	0	76	59	4.74	1.45	21.6	293	34	70	5.03	2.5	7.0	2.8	1.2	77

Big-framed SP who started late due to bad back, but finished strong. Repeated AAA and was much more hittable. Flyball pitcher who needs to use height and slot more effectively. Spots quality FB to both sides of plate and throws strikes with average SL and CU. Could move to pen.

Wolff,Sam

SP | Texas | EXP MLB DEBUT: 2017 | H/W: 6-1 190 | FUT: #4 starter | 7E

Thrws R Age 23	Year	Lev	Team	W	L	Sv	IP	K	ERA	WHIP	BF/G	OBA	H%	S%	xERA	Ctl	Dom	Cmd	hr/9	BPV
2013 (6) New Mexico	2012	NCAA	New Mexico	1	2	0	45	24	5.58	1.59	16.6	252	28	64	4.28	5.8	4.8	0.8	0.6	-52
91-96 FB +++	2013	NCAA	New Mexico	7	3	0	93	75	2.90	1.32	24.1	243	30	79	3.34	3.8	7.3	1.9	0.5	47
84-87 SL +++	2013	A-	Spokane	3	0	0	16	21	1.12	1.12	6.3	209	33	89	1.91	3.4	11.7	3.5	0.0	139
81-85 CU ++	2013	A	Hickory	1	0	5	13	23	0.00	0.83	4.4	177	36	100	0.78	2.0	15.7	7.7	0.0	245
	2014	A+	Myrtle Beach	9	5	0	120	81	3.37	1.17	20.0	238	27	73	3.11	2.6	6.1	2.3	0.7	56

Small-framed SP who saw massive drop in K rate with equal rise in groundball rate. Added sink to lively FB down in zone and uses as primary offering. Hard SL is average pitch and he needs to stay on top of it. Rudimentary CU can be telegraphed. Needs to add strength and stamina.

Wright,Austin

RP | Philadelphia | EXP MLB DEBUT: 2015 | H/W: 6-4 235 | FUT: reliever | 6B

Thrws L Age 25	Year	Lev	Team	W	L	Sv	IP	K	ERA	WHIP	BF/G	OBA	H%	S%	xERA	Ctl	Dom	Cmd	hr/9	BPV
2011 (8) Mississippi	2011	A	Lakewood	1	2	0	33	41	2.71	1.14	18.8	236	34	78	2.83	2.4	11.1	4.6	0.5	152
91-93 FB +++	2012	A+	Clearwater	11	5	0	147	133	3.49	1.41	23.0	262	33	77	3.98	3.7	8.1	2.2	0.7	65
77-78 CB +++	2013	AA	Reading	6	5	0	94	77	5.93	1.59	15.4	255	29	64	4.91	5.6	7.4	1.3	1.2	-2
82-83 CU ++	2014	Rk	GCL Phillies	0	0	0	1	2	9.00	2.00	4.8	415	71	50	7.40	0.0	18.0		0.0	342
	2014	AA	Reading	2	4	0	48	38	5.06	1.77	6.9	232	27	73	4.77	8.3	7.1	0.9	0.9	-77

Separation he gets from low-90s FB from the left side and the hard-breaking CB is a potent combination in short stints—provided he can command them both. That's been a problem in the past. Gets deception from throwing across his body, but hasn't been able to retire high-minors hitters.

Wright,Mike — SP — Baltimore

EXP MLB DEBUT: 2015 | H/W: 6-6 215 | FUT: #3 starter | 7C

Thrws R Age 25
2011 (3) East Carolina

Velo	Pitch	Grade
90-95	FB	+++
80-83	SL	+++
77-80	CB	++
	CU	+++

Year	Lev	Team	W	L	Sv	IP	K	ERA	WHIP	BF/G	OBA	H%	S%	xERA	Ctl	Dom	Cmd	hr/9	BPV
2012	A+	Frederick	5	2	0	46	35	2.93	1.13	22.8	266	32	76	3.26	1.0	6.8	7.0	0.6	115
2012	AA	Bowie	5	3	0	62	45	4.93	1.42	21.9	288	33	67	4.72	2.5	6.5	2.6	1.0	69
2013	AA	Bowie	11	3	0	143	136	3.27	1.33	22.9	273	35	76	3.86	2.5	8.5	3.5	0.6	106
2013	AAA	Norfolk	0	0	0	6	2	0.00	0.97	23.5	255	28	100	2.21	0.0	2.9		0.0	70
2014	AAA	Norfolk	5	11	0	142	103	4.62	1.41	23.1	284	33	67	4.27	2.6	6.5	2.5	0.6	65

Tall, aggressive SP who finished season hot after poor start. Peppers zone with quality strikes and has found consistency with 3/4 slot and hard, cutting SL. Can be hittable and doesn't miss enough bats to front rotation. Command must be present for success and allows flyballs.

Yamamoto,Jordan — SP — Milwaukee

EXP MLB DEBUT: 2019 | H/W: 6-0 185 | FUT: #4 starter | 7D

Thrws R Age 18
2014 (12) HS (HI)

Velo	Pitch	Grade
92-94	FB	+++
	CB	++
	SL	++
	CU	++

Year	Lev	Team	W	L	Sv	IP	K	ERA	WHIP	BF/G	OBA	H%	S%	xERA	Ctl	Dom	Cmd	hr/9	BPV
2014	Rk	AZL Brewers	0	1	0	21	22	4.67	1.65	9.5	269	33	75	5.25	5.5	9.3	1.7	1.3	37

12th round pick out of Hawaii didn't get as much attention as he should have. Has a good idea of how to pitch and comes after hitters with a good 88-92 mph FB that has late life. Mixes in a SL, CB and CU that all show avg potential. Gets swings-and-misses from the FB/SL combination.

Yarbrough,Ryan — SP — Seattle

EXP MLB DEBUT: 2016 | H/W: 6-5 205 | FUT: #4 starter | 7C

Thrws L Age 23
2014 (4) Old Dominion

Velo	Pitch	Grade
90-94	FB	+++
81-83	SL	++
80-82	CU	++

Year	Lev	Team	W	L	Sv	IP	K	ERA	WHIP	BF/G	OBA	H%	S%	xERA	Ctl	Dom	Cmd	hr/9	BPV
2011	NCAA	Santa Fe CC	0	0	0	17		7.89	1.99	6.3	303	44	56	5.39	6.8	11.1	1.6	0.0	32
2013	NCAA	Old Dominion	4	4	1	82	60	3.28	1.25	19.7	252	30	74	3.25	2.7	6.6	2.4	0.4	62
2014	NCAA	Old Dominion	6	7	0	86	64	4.50	1.31	19.8	288	34	65	3.99	1.6	6.7	4.3	0.5	96
2014	Rk	Pulaski	0	0	1	4	5	0.00	0.50	6.6	81	14	100	0.00	2.3	11.3	5.0	0.0	160
2014	A-	Everett	0	1	0	38	53	1.41	0.76	11.4	188	30	82	0.98	0.9	12.5	13.3	0.2	217

Tall, large prospect with evolving repertoire and potential for more velocity. Throws with excellent angle to plate and hitters bury FB into ground. Throws with clean arm action to get pitch movement. Spots pitches effectively within K zone and needs to improve sweeping SL to advance.

Ybarra,Tyler — RP — Toronto

EXP MLB DEBUT: 2015 | H/W: 6-2 210 | FUT: Setup RP | 6B

Thrws L Age 25
2008 (43) HS (KS)

Velo	Pitch	Grade
90-95	FB	+++
79-81	CB	+++
81-85	SL	++

Year	Lev	Team	W	L	Sv	IP	K	ERA	WHIP	BF/G	OBA	H%	S%	xERA	Ctl	Dom	Cmd	hr/9	BPV
2009	Rk	GCL Blue Jays	2	4	0	20	11	6.72	1.94	6.0	338	38	63	6.32	4.5	4.9	1.1	0.4	-14
2011	Rk	Bluefield	2	0	0	46	54	2.15	1.09	12.8	208	30	81	2.19	3.1	10.6	3.4	0.4	124
2012	A	Lansing	3	2	2	43	57	2.29	1.48	7.1	238	36	85	3.57	5.4	11.9	2.2	0.4	86
2013	A+	Dunedin	2	3	2	55	65	1.96	1.14	5.6	162	25	81	1.45	5.4	10.6	2.0	0.0	64
2014	AA	New Hampshire	4	4	0	53	43	4.42	1.36	5.8	219	24	72	3.96	5.1	7.3	1.4	1.4	12

Tall, strong RP who ended season in July. Owns good FB with late life and counters with CB that can be above average. Limits LHH and could be ideal situational guy. Throws CB in any count and induces weak contact. K rate dropped considerably and has erratic command and control.

Ynoa,Gabriel — SP — New York (N)

EXP MLB DEBUT: 2016 | H/W: 6-2 160 | FUT: #3 starter | 7C

Thrws R Age 21
2010 FA (DR)

Velo	Pitch	Grade
91-93	FB	+++
80-82	CB	++
	CU	++++

Year	Lev	Team	W	L	Sv	IP	K	ERA	WHIP	BF/G	OBA	H%	S%	xERA	Ctl	Dom	Cmd	hr/9	BPV
2011	Rk	Kingsport	0	0	1	8	6	4.50	0.75	14.3	210	11	100	5.27	0.0	6.8		4.5	140
2012	A-	Brooklyn	5	2	0	76	64	2.24	0.93	22.0	221	28	74	1.74	1.2	7.6	6.4	0.1	122
2013	A	Savannah	15	4	0	135	106	2.73	1.03	23.6	244	29	75	2.73	1.1	7.1	6.6	0.6	116
2014	A+	St. Lucie	8	2	0	82	64	3.95	1.32	24.2	291	34	71	4.28	1.4	7.0	4.9	0.8	106
2014	AA	Binghamton	3	2	0	66	42	4.22	1.30	24.8	284	31	71	4.58	1.6	5.7	3.5	1.2	77

Lacks overpowering stuff, but plus-plus control helps everything play up. Solid poise and demeanor; throws strikes from smooth, repeatable delivery. FB velo has inched up and plus CU effective weapon against both LH and RH batters. Development of CB crucial for landing rotation spot.

Ynoa,Michael — RP — Chicago (A)

EXP MLB DEBUT: 2016 | H/W: 6-7 210 | FUT: Setup RP | 7C

Thrws R Age 23
2008 FA (DR)

Velo	Pitch	Grade
90-97	FB	++++
80-83	CB	+++
82-85	CU	++

Year	Lev	Team	W	L	Sv	IP	K	ERA	WHIP	BF/G	OBA	H%	S%	xERA	Ctl	Dom	Cmd	hr/9	BPV
2012	Rk	AZL Athletics	0	1	0	10	6	5.40	2.00	8.0	281	31	74	5.98	8.1	5.4	0.7	0.9	-104
2012	A-	Vermont	1	3	0	20	19	7.13	1.78	11.6	260	32	59	5.10	7.1	8.5	1.2	0.9	-22
2013	A	Beloit	2	1	0	54	48	2.16	1.16	14.4	227	29	83	2.75	3.0	8.0	2.7	0.5	81
2013	A+	Stockton	1	2	1	21	20	7.71	1.90	14.2	280	35	58	5.66	7.3	8.6	1.2	0.9	-24
2014	A+	Stockton	4	2	0	45	64	5.58	1.39	6.1	248	37	60	4.02	4.2	12.7	3.0	1.0	134

Long, lean pitcher who hasn't lived up to lofty expectations. Converted to RP, but has still never pitched above High-A. Posted very high K rate in pen along with reverse splits. Angle to plate is impressive and works off plus FB to set up hard CB. Flyballs and injuries mute upside.

Ysla,Luis — SP — San Francisco

EXP MLB DEBUT: 2017 | H/W: 6-1 185 | FUT: #3 Starter | 8E

Thrws L Age 22
2012 FA (Venezuela)

Velo	Pitch	Grade
90-94	FB	++++
77-80	SL	+++
84-86	CU	+

Year	Lev	Team	W	L	Sv	IP	K	ERA	WHIP	BF/G	OBA	H%	S%	xERA	Ctl	Dom	Cmd	hr/9	BPV
2013	Rk	AZL Giants	4	0	0	51	52	2.65	1.00	16.2	209	29	72	1.80	2.3	9.2	4.0	0.2	121
2014	A	Augusta	6	7	0	121	115	2.45	1.23	20.4	233	30	82	3.08	3.3	8.5	2.6	0.6	82

Athletic LHP turned heads in 1st full season, ramping FB up to 98. Max effort delivery raises questions about future in the rotation. Complements FB with a tight SL, generating Ks, but CU is far behind. Regardless of role, FB-SL combo will play in ML, whether he is a SP or RP depends on the CU and improved Cmd.

Zastryzny,Rob — SP — Chicago (N)

EXP MLB DEBUT: 2016 | H/W: 6-3 205 | FUT: #3 starter | 7C

Thrws L Age 23
2013 (2) Missouri

Velo	Pitch	Grade
90-93	FB	+++
80-83	SL	+++
	CB	++

Year	Lev	Team	W	L	Sv	IP	K	ERA	WHIP	BF/G	OBA	H%	S%	xERA	Ctl	Dom	Cmd	hr/9	BPV
2012	NCAA	Missouri	5	5	0	109	76	3.80	1.28	26.3	262	31	69	3.37	2.6	6.3	2.5	0.3	62
2013	NCAA	Missouri	2	9	0	90	82	3.39	1.30	28.6	268	33	78	4.09	2.4	8.2	3.4	1.0	101
2013	A-	Boise	0	0	0	14	16	3.19	1.35	7.3	274	39	74	3.35	2.6	10.2	4.0	0.0	133
2013	A	Kane County	1	0	0	9	6	0.98	1.41	13.0	258	31	92	3.33	3.9	5.9	1.5	0.0	18
2014	A+	Daytona	4	6	0	110	110	4.66	1.40	20.2	281	36	67	4.36	2.7	9.0	3.3	0.8	107

Isn't overpowering and his FB sits at 90-92 maxing out at 94, but gets swings-and-misses due to ability to change speeds. Also has an average CU and a useable breaking ball. Can leave the ball up but his Cmd gives him the potential to thrive.

Zimmer,Kyle — SP — Kansas City

EXP MLB DEBUT: 2016 | H/W: 6-3 215 | FUT: #1 starter | 9D

Thrws R Age 23
2012 (1) San Francisco

Velo	Pitch	Grade
92-97	FB	++++
80-81	CB	++++
82-84	SL	+++
83-85	CU	+++

Year	Lev	Team	W	L	Sv	IP	K	ERA	WHIP	BF/G	OBA	H%	S%	xERA	Ctl	Dom	Cmd	hr/9	BPV
2012	Rk	AZL Royals	1	0	0	10	13	0.90	0.50	11.1	151	25	80	0.00	0.0	11.7		0.0	229
2012	A	Kane County	2	3	0	29	29	2.47	1.44	20.7	292	38	83	4.15	2.5	8.9	3.6	0.3	112
2013	A+	Wilmington	4	8	0	89	113	4.84	1.24	20.1	241	34	62	3.49	3.1	11.4	3.6	0.9	139
2013	AA	NW Arkansas	2	1	0	18	27	1.98	0.88	16.8	176	27	86	1.85	2.5	13.4	5.4	1.0	192
2014	Rk	Idaho Falls	0	0	0	4	5	2.14	2.14	3.5	297	42	89	5.68	8.6	10.7	1.3	0.0	-21

Tall SP missed most of season with shoulder tightness and eventually underwent surgery in October. Should be ready early in 2015. When healthy, has dominant offerings, highlighted by plus FB and knockout SL. Repeats delivery and arm slot giving him plus command and control.

Ziomek,Kevin — SP — Detroit

EXP MLB DEBUT: 2016 | H/W: 6-3 200 | FUT: #4 starter | 7C

Thrws L Age 23
2013 (2) Vanderbilt

Velo	Pitch	Grade
89-94	FB	+++
80-85	SL	+++
	CU	+++

Year	Lev	Team	W	L	Sv	IP	K	ERA	WHIP	BF/G	OBA	H%	S%	xERA	Ctl	Dom	Cmd	hr/9	BPV
2011	NCAA	Vanderbilt	3	0	1	45	47	1.60	1.09	6.5	206	29	85	2.00	3.2	9.4	2.9	0.2	101
2012	NCAA	Vanderbilt	5	6	0	79	79	5.23	1.49	18.0	262	33	65	4.30	4.4	9.0	2.0	0.8	60
2013	NCAA	Vanderbilt	11	3	0	119	115	2.12	1.00	26.7	191	26	78	1.64	3.0	8.7	2.9	0.2	93
2013	A-	Connecticut	0	1	0	8	3	4.50	1.25	8.1	181	20	60	2.01	5.6	3.4	0.6	0.0	-73
2014	A	West Michigan	10	6	0	123	152	2.27	1.15	21.3	204	30	81	2.29	3.9	11.1	2.9	0.4	113

Athletic SP who led MWL in ERA and 2nd in Ks. Limited oppBA with solid-average pitch mix and crossfire delivery. CU is best secondary offering and features late movement. FB velocity is average, but has decent command of it. SL won't miss many bats, but keeps hitters honest.

Zych,Tony — RP — Chicago (N)

EXP MLB DEBUT: 2016 | H/W: 6-3 190 | FUT: Reliever | 6C

Thrws R Age 24
2011 (4) Louisville

Velo	Pitch	Grade
94-97	FB	++++
83-85	SL	+++

Year	Lev	Team	W	L	Sv	IP	K	ERA	WHIP	BF/G	OBA	H%	S%	xERA	Ctl	Dom	Cmd	hr/9	BPV
2011	A-	Boise	0	0	0	2	2	0.00	0.50	3.3	0	0	100	0.00	4.5	9.0	2.0	0.0	59
2012	A+	Daytona	3	3	6	36	36	3.23	1.08	5.2	239	33	67	2.20	1.7	9.0	5.1	0.0	132
2012	AA	Tennessee	2	1	0	24	28	4.46	1.57	5.3	276	38	70	4.28	4.5	10.4	2.3	0.4	85
2013	AA	Tennessee	5	5	3	56	40	3.05	1.29	4.9	244	29	76	3.13	3.4	6.4	1.9	0.3	43
2014	AA	Tennessee	4	5	2	58	35	5.11	1.60	5.7	314	36	67	5.07	2.8	5.4	1.9	0.5	40

Tall, athletic RP stalled out a AA and took an across-the-board step back. Still has a plus 94-96 mph FB and a good mid-80s SL. Funky low 3/4 delivery gives him deception, but also results in below-avg control and his Dom rate has dropped. Still has the stuff and velo to be an effective reliever.

In his 1985 *Baseball Abstract,* Bill James introduced the concept of major league equivalencies. His assertion was that, with the proper adjustments, a minor leaguer's statistics could be converted to an equivalent major league level performance with a great deal of accuracy.

Because of wide variations in the level of play among different minor leagues, it is difficult to get a true reading on a player's potential. For instance, a .300 batting average achieved in the high-offense Pacific Coast League is not nearly as much of an accomplishment as a similar level in the Eastern League. MLEs normalize these types of variances, for all statistical categories.

The actual MLEs are not projections. They represent how a player's previous performance might look at the major league level. However, the MLE stat line can be used in forecasting future performance in just the same way as a major league stat line would.

The model we use contains a few variations to James' version and updates all of the minor league and ballpark factors. In addition, we designed a module to convert pitching statistics, which is something James did not originally do.

Do MLEs really work?

Used correctly, MLEs are excellent indicators of potential. But just like we cannot take traditional major league statistics at face value, the same goes for MLEs. The underlying measures of base skill—batting eye ratios, pitching command ratios, etc.—are far more accurate in evaluating future talent than raw home runs, batting averages or ERAs.

The charts we present here also provide the unique perspective of looking at up to five years' worth of data. Ironically, the longer the history, the less likely the player is a legitimate prospect—he should have made it to the majors before compiling a long history in AA and/or AAA ball. Of course, the shorter trends are more difficult to read despite them often belonging to players with higher ceilings. But even here we can find small indications of players improving their skills, or struggling, as they rise through more difficult levels of competition. Since players—especially those with any talent—are promoted rapidly through major league systems, a two or three-year scan is often all we get to spot any trends.

Here are some things to look for as you scan these charts:

Target players who...

- spent a full year in AA and then a full year in AAA
- had consistent playing time from one year to the next
- improved their base skills as they were promoted

Raise the warning flag for players who...

- were stuck at a level for multiple seasons, or regressed
- displayed marked changes in playing time from one year to the next
- showed large drops in BPIs from one year to the next

Players are listed on the charts if they spent at least part of 2010-2014 in Triple-A or Double-A and had at least 100 AB or 30 IP within those two levels. Each is listed with the organization with which they finished the season.

Only statistics accumulated in Triple-A and Double-A ball are included (players who split a season are indicated as a/a); Single-A stats are excluded.

Each player's actual AB and IP totals are used as the base for the conversion. However, it is more useful to compare performances using common levels, so rely on the ratios and sabermetric gauges. Complete explanations of these formulas appear in the Glossary.

BATTER	B	Yr	Age	Pos	Lvl	Tm	AB	R	H	D	T	HR	RBI	BB	K	SB	CS	BA	OB	Slg	OPS	bb%	ct%	Eye	PX	SX	RC/G	BPV
Adames,Cristhian	B	13	22	SS	aa	COL	389	36	100	19	2	3	29	27	77	10	7	257	305	337	642	7%	80%	0.35	62	86	2.81	11
		14	23	SS	a/a	COL	475	42	123	19	4	2	36	29	86	8	11	258	301	329	630	6%	82%	0.34	54	77	2.63	8
Adams,Lane	R	13	24	RF	aa	KC	156	23	33	6	1	4	20	14	49	12	0	213	277	333	611	8%	69%	0.28	94	150	2.89	14
		14	25	CF	aa	KC	405	50	94	22	3	8	27	34	95	29	10	232	292	358	650	8%	76%	0.36	97	131	2.84	40
Aguilar,Jesus	R	13	23	1B	aa	CLE	499	49	116	25	0	11	78	41	123	0	1	233	291	352	643	8%	75%	0.33	90	24	2.89	-2
		14	24	1B	aaa	CLE	427	53	111	28	0	14	59	48	113	0	0	260	335	423	758	10%	74%	0.43	131	24	4.14	29
Ahmed,Nick	R	13	23	SS	aa	ARI	487	49	109	21	5	4	39	28	77	22	8	223	265	309	574	5%	84%	0.36	59	134	2.17	37
		14	24	SS	aaa	ARI	407	36	105	22	3	3	30	23	64	9	7	257	297	347	643	5%	84%	0.36	69	87	2.71	32
Aliotti,Anthony	L	12	25	1B	aa	OAK	455	53	109	24	1	7	56	51	155	0	0	238	315	339	654	10%	66%	0.33	88	37	2.98	-33
		13	26	1B	aa	OAK	494	46	127	27	1	9	50	58	155	2	2	257	335	369	704	11%	69%	0.37	96	41	3.54	-13
		14	27	1B	a/a	OAK	409	37	83	22	1	5	32	41	173	1	1	203	275	300	575	9%	58%	0.24	107	43	2.12	-50
Allie,Stetson	R	14	23	1B	aa	PIT	407	44	83	14	0	14	45	50	136	7	7	204	292	340	631	11%	67%	0.37	110	52	2.73	-6
Almora,Albert	R	14	20	CF	aa	CHC	142	15	30	6	2	2	8	2	23	0	1	212	221	313	534	1%	84%	0.07	72	94	1.68	24
Altherr,Aaron	R	14	23	CF	aa	PHI	449	41	92	24	1	11	43	20	125	9	7	204	238	339	577	4%	72%	0.16	109	86	2.05	12
Alvarez,Dariel	R	13	25	RF	aa	BAL	31	1	5.1	0	0	1	1	1	10	0	0	163	182	240	422	2%	67%	0.07	51	6	1.33	-83
		14	26	CF	a/a	BAL	532	52	134	30	2	12	60	15	74	6	6	251	271	380	651	3%	86%	0.20	89	70	2.81	44
Aplin,Andrew	L	14	23	CF	a/a	HOU	452	46	102	12	2	5	48	59	82	19	12	226	314	290	606	12%	82%	0.72	46	87	2.61	15
Arruebarrena,Erisbel	R	14	24	SS	a/a	LA	180	11	38	6	1	1	11	9	67	1	1	209	245	277	522	5%	63%	0.13	64	67	1.78	-67
Asencio,Yeison	R	13	24	RF	aa	SD	291	21	65	12	3	2	26	11	35	2	2	222	250	299	549	4%	88%	0.31	52	72	1.92	25
		14	25	RF	a/a	SD	536	45	121	18	2	10	40	19	83	5	6	226	252	326	578	3%	84%	0.23	67	65	2.27	20
Austin,Tyler	R	13	22	RF	aa	NYY	319	36	75	15	1	6	34	35	85	3	0	236	312	342	655	10%	73%	0.41	84	70	3.09	3
		14	23	RF	aa	NYY	396	44	97	17	3	8	37	29	89	2	2	244	296	366	662	7%	78%	0.33	89	78	3.01	20
Avery,Xavier	L	10	21	8	aa	BAL	107	8	24	5	0	3	14	5	25	8	0	221	257	356	613	5%	76%	0.20	87	91	3.44	14
		11	21	OF	aa	BAL	557	63	137	29	2	4	23	42	163	32	15	245	298	324	622	7%	71%	0.26	60	107	3.32	-21
		12	22	OF	aaa	BAL	390	51	88	12	4	8	31	45	111	20	7	226	306	338	644	10%	72%	0.41	78	124	2.91	-9
		13	23	CF	a/a	SEA	467	59	109	23	3	3	30	42	135	24	9	233	296	309	605	8%	71%	0.31	67	120	2.53	-8
		14	24	LF	aaa	SEA	400	47	89	18	1	6	25	27	109	21	9	223	272	320	593	6%	73%	0.25	82	109	2.38	4
Bandy,Jett	R	13	23	C	aa	LAA	245	22	52	15	1	3	24	12	44	0	1	213	248	325	573	4%	82%	0.26	83	56	1.98	23
		14	24	C	aa	LAA	312	32	68	10	0	11	34	27	72	2	5	219	282	354	636	8%	77%	0.38	95	36	2.79	13
Barnes,Austin	R	13	24	C	aa	MIA	62	8	19	2	2	1	6	10	11	0	0	307	404	431	835	14%	82%	0.90	73	75	5.05	39
		14	25	2B	aa	MIA	284	41	70	17	2	7	32	37	42	6	0	245	333	397	730	12%	85%	0.90	104	99	3.77	79
Barnhart,Tucker	B	12	21	C	aa	CIN	130	9	25	4	1	2	11	10	24	1	1	190	247	278	524	7%	82%	0.41	55	60	1.79	5
		13	22	C	aa	CIN	339	28	83	18	1	3	40	41	63	1	0	245	326	331	656	11%	81%	0.64	66	40	3.02	14
		14	23	C	aaa	CIN	256	13	53	7	2	1	20	20	39	0	1	207	263	261	525	7%	85%	0.50	40	40	1.79	-1
Bethancourt,Christian	R	12	21	C	aa	ATL	268	26	60	5	1	2	23	10	50	7	6	224	251	266	518	3%	81%	0.19	28	82	1.87	-18
		13	22	C	aa	ATL	358	30	92	20	0	10	40	14	64	10	8	256	285	398	683	4%	82%	0.22	97	70	3.15	37
		14	23	C	aaa	ATL	343	24	83	15	1	6	35	10	71	5	1	241	262	339	601	3%	79%	0.14	74	67	2.60	4
Blash,Jabari	R	13	24	RF	aa	SEA	97	12	27	3	0	7	19	17	32	1	1	279	388	541	929	15%	67%	0.53	188	22	6.79	55
		14	25	RF	a/a	SEA	289	34	51	13	1	12	40	30	111	4	4	177	254	345	599	9%	62%	0.27	148	74	2.26	8
Bonifacio,Jorge	R	13	20	RF	aa	KC	93	13	26	7	0	2	16	9	23	2	1	283	348	405	753	9%	75%	0.39	102	59	4.05	19
		14	21	RF	aa	KC	505	40	108	19	4	3	42	41	130	7	3	213	272	285	557	7%	74%	0.31	59	87	2.04	-13
Borenstein,Zach	L	14	24	LF	a/a	ARI	461	41	102	22	4	11	55	29	141	6	8	220	266	357	623	6%	69%	0.21	111	86	2.38	6
Bour,Justin	L	12	24	1B	aa	CHC	506	50	125	31	0	14	86	49	131	3	1	247	314	390	704	9%	74%	0.38	106	42	3.49	14
		13	25	1B	aa	CHC	317	36	63	15	0	14	47	27	73	0	2	200	263	374	638	8%	77%	0.38	118	30	2.66	30
		14	26	1B	aaa	MIA	385	38	92	22	0	10	47	26	69	2	1	239	287	373	660	6%	82%	0.37	97	43	3.02	33
Boyd,Jayce	R	14	24	1B	aa	NYM	413	43	97	17	1	6	42	37	82	1	1	235	297	325	623	8%	80%	0.45	68	51	2.74	9
Brentz,Bryce	R	12	24	OF	a/a	BOS	473	51	126	31	1	13	62	33	150	6	6	267	314	419	734	6%	68%	0.22	123	58	3.71	4
		13	25	RF	aaa	BOS	326	27	75	16	1	12	42	15	98	1	0	229	262	394	656	4%	70%	0.15	124	38	2.97	1
		14	26	LF	aaa	BOS	230	32	48	11	2	9	40	24	67	1	1	210	284	383	666	9%	71%	0.35	132	74	2.91	32
Brett,Ryan	R	13	22	2B	aa	TAM	105	16	22	5	1	2	13	7	16	3	1	211	257	347	603	6%	85%	0.42	87	132	2.45	64
		14	23	2B	aa	TAM	422	51	112	22	5	6	30	19	85	22	8	265	297	385	682	4%	80%	0.22	88	140	3.17	43
Brown,Gary	R	12	24	OF	aa	SF	538	64	135	31	2	6	37	34	99	29	20	250	295	345	640	6%	82%	0.34	70	104	2.61	28
		13	25	CF	aaa	SF	558	52	101	23	4	7	33	22	159	11	13	181	212	278	489	4%	72%	0.14	77	105	1.33	-11
		14	26	CF	aaa	SF	536	56	111	19	4	6	34	23	145	23	24	207	239	288	527	4%	73%	0.16	65	119	1.56	-10
Bruno,Stephen	R	14	24	2B	aa	CHC	384	39	91	23	4	2	31	20	88	4	2	236	274	331	606	5%	77%	0.23	80	95	2.31	13
Bryant,Kris	R	14	22	3B	a/a	CHC	492	91	143	31	1	34	84	68	179	12	4	291	377	562	939	12%	64%	0.38	228	85	6.67	89
Burns,Andy	R	13	23	3B	aa	TOR	265	30	59	18	2	6	24	17	62	9	6	223	270	365	635	6%	76%	0.27	108	106	2.44	38
		14	24	3B	aa	TOR	495	56	113	30	4	13	50	32	113	14	9	228	275	383	658	6%	77%	0.28	117	111	2.67	50
Burns,Billy	B	13	24	CF	WAS		114	21	33	4	0	0	6	15	19	16	2	288	373	320	692	12%	84%	0.82	29	124	4.52	20
		14	25	CF	a/a	OAK	473	51	88	18	2	1	19	37	98	37	7	187	246	238	484	7%	79%	0.38	44	144	1.67	12
Calixte,Orlando	R	13	21	SS	aa	KC	484	48	112	23	4	6	29	34	135	11	12	231	282	334	615	7%	72%	0.25	82	96	2.34	-2
		14	22	SS	aa	KC	374	35	81	14	1	8	30	22	96	7	5	216	260	325	584	6%	74%	0.23	83	74	2.30	-1
Casali,Curt	R	13	25	C	aa	TAM	120	20	39	9	0	4	25	16	22	0	0	324	406	497	903	12%	82%	0.75	123	30	6.41	61
		14	26	C	a/a	TAM	226	14	48	12	0	3	22	34	80	0	0	213	318	308	625	13%	65%	0.43	95	8	2.60	-35
Casteel,Ryan	R	14	23	1B	aa	COL	436	48	114	21	1	14	43	30	96	2	3	261	308	410	719	6%	78%	0.31	107	49	3.71	27
Cecchini,Garin	L	13	22	3B	BOS		240	28	66	14	2	2	22	39	56	6	2	276	378	376	754	14%	77%	0.70	80	98	3.99	31
		14	23	3B	aaa	NYM	407	31	80	15	1	4	34	26	120	7	1	196	245	268	513	6%	71%	0.22	64	72	1.82	-31
Centeno,Juan	L	12	23	C	aa	NYM	281	23	65	9	1	0	28	18	48	1	1	230	276	274	550	6%	83%	0.38	34	56	2.08	-10
		13	24	C	aaa	NYM	236	20	56	8	2	0	21	8	36	1	1	236	262	286	548	3%	85%	0.23	38	67	2.03	-1
		14	25	C	a/a	NYM	256	17	55	7	0	1	16	13	47	1	1	217	255	253	508	5%	82%	0.28	32	37	1.84	-24
Choi,Ji-Man	L	13	22	1B	a/a	SEA	243	24	57	12	4	8	36	28	39	2	2	234	314	400	713	10%	84%	0.71	103	59	3.42	58
		14	23	1B	a/a	SEA	248	32	59	7	1	4	25	28	51	1	2	238	315	326	641	10%	79%	0.55	62	67	2.95	9
Collins,Tyler	L	13	23	LF	aa	DET	466	53	99	26	0	17	62	40	130	3	6	212	274	374	649	8%	72%	0.31	123	46	2.71	19
		14	24	LF	aaa	DET	468	49	107	15	2	14	48	38	126	9	5	230	287	359	646	7%	73%	0.30	95	80	3.00	9

BATTER	B	Yr	Age	Pos	Lvl	Tm	AB	R	H	D	T	HR	RBI	BB	K	SB	CS	BA	OB	Slg	OPS	bb%	ct%	Eye	PX	SX	RC/G	BPV
Colon,Christian	R	11	22	SS	aa	KC	491	51	111	13	2	5	45	33	54	12	8	226	275	291	566	6%	89%	0.62	43	87	2.70	31
		12	23	SS	a/a	KC	290	27	75	9	2	4	24	25	30	9	7	260	318	345	663	8%	90%	0.81	50	79	3.15	40
		13	24	2B	aaa	KC	512	57	124	11	3	9	46	32	62	12	5	242	287	326	613	6%	88%	0.52	49	98	2.84	34
		14	25	SS	a/a	KC	352	41	92	16	0	5	34	22	35	12	5	261	305	353	658	6%	90%	0.64	64	81	3.21	50
Cowart,Kaleb	B	13	21	3B	aa	LAA	498	42	100	18	1	5	37	32	134	12	5	201	249	270	520	6%	73%	0.24	57	80	1.84	-24
		14	22	3B	aa	LAA	435	43	89	16	3	5	48	37	108	23	8	204	266	290	556	8%	75%	0.34	68	121	2.10	9
Cox,Zack	L	11	22	3B	aa	STL	352	35	83	15	0	6	31	19	78	0	1	236	275	331	606	5%	78%	0.25	65	31	3.12	-14
		12	23	3B	a/a	MIA	394	32	86	25	1	7	34	18	101	1	0	219	253	340	593	4%	74%	0.18	94	45	2.26	-3
		13	24	3B	aaa	MIA	288	26	67	14	2	2	24	33	76	2	0	234	312	316	628	10%	74%	0.43	68	68	2.69	-8
		14	25	3B	aaa	MIA	312	26	70	15	2	4	23	19	76	1	0	224	270	329	598	6%	76%	0.25	83	67	2.39	2
Coyle,Sean	R	14	22	2B	aa	BOS	336	50	94	24	1	13	50	31	101	11	1	279	340	470	809	8%	70%	0.30	158	99	4.86	54
Cunningham,Todd	B	12	23	OF	aa	ATL	466	65	130	21	5	2	43	33	58	20	9	279	326	360	686	7%	87%	0.56	53	121	3.39	44
		13	24	CF	aaa	ATL	427	47	98	11	4	2	30	32	72	16	8	229	283	285	568	7%	83%	0.45	38	117	2.24	14
		14	25	CF	aaa	ATL	470	42	111	23	1	6	41	25	96	13	9	235	274	326	600	5%	80%	0.26	72	81	2.37	12
Cuthbert,Cheslor	R	13	21	3B	aa	KC	237	20	46	15	0	4	23	16	52	4	2	196	247	315	563	6%	78%	0.31	93	63	1.96	20
		14	22	3B	a/a	KC	446	36	109	22	1	8	49	34	83	8	4	244	298	354	652	7%	81%	0.42	82	63	2.98	26
Davidson,Matt	R	12	21	3B	aa	ARI	486	65	119	28	2	19	62	54	133	2	4	245	320	428	748	10%	73%	0.40	129	59	3.81	33
		13	22	3B	aaa	ARI	443	35	104	28	2	11	47	29	148	1	0	235	282	385	667	6%	67%	0.19	128	51	2.93	-2
		14	23	3B	aaa	CHW	478	39	78	15	0	15	37	36	189	0	0	164	222	290	512	7%	61%	0.19	112	21	1.76	-46
Decker,Jaff	L	11	21	OF	aa	SD	496	67	95	23	1	13	69	82	168	11	6	192	306	321	627	14%	66%	0.49	83	88	3.46	-12
		12	22	OF	aa	SD	147	23	23	2	2	2	7	33	42	5	2	154	309	236	546	18%	71%	0.78	54	116	1.89	1
		13	23	CF	aaa	SD	350	43	79	17	1	7	27	38	114	3	7	227	302	341	643	10%	67%	0.33	97	57	2.66	-14
		14	24	LF	aaa	PIT	350	30	75	23	1	4	29	36	79	5	7	215	288	319	607	9%	77%	0.46	89	58	2.20	19
Diaz,Elias	R	14	24	C	aa	PIT	359	33	94	18	0	4	39	23	63	2	3	261	307	345	651	6%	83%	0.37	66	38	3.02	8
Dickerson,Alex	L	13	23	RF	aa	PIT	451	48	113	32	2	12	54	21	95	8	3	251	284	413	697	4%	79%	0.22	118	84	3.03	46
		14	24	RF	aa	SD	137	16	37	9	2	2	19	7	34	0	1	273	309	416	726	5%	75%	0.21	113	79	3.41	27
Dickson,O'Koyea	R	14	24	1B	aa	LA	461	50	101	29	2	12	51	26	78	3	7	218	260	366	626	5%	83%	0.33	106	66	2.36	49
Dozier,Hunter	R	14	23	3B	aa	KC	234	26	43	11	0	3	17	25	74	2	2	186	263	270	533	9%	68%	0.33	79	60	1.80	-24
Drury,Brandon	R	14	22	3B	aa	ARI	105	10	29	7	0	3	11	6	20	0	0	274	310	434	744	5%	81%	0.27	118	16	4.02	33
Duffy,Matt	R	14	23	SS	aa	SF	367	43	109	22	3	2	51	34	74	16	4	296	357	392	749	9%	80%	0.46	78	114	4.17	35
Dugan,Kelly	L	13	23	RF	aa	PHI	212	19	48	11	1	8	17	4	62	0	1	228	241	396	637	2%	71%	0.06	126	43	2.63	3
		14	24	RF	aa	PHI	253	32	64	16	1	4	25	21	66	1	0	253	311	368	679	8%	74%	0.32	98	57	3.20	9
Duvall,Adam	R	13	25	3B	aa	SF	385	43	78	19	3	11	41	25	85	1	1	203	251	350	601	6%	78%	0.29	102	78	2.27	31
		14	26	3B	aaa	SF	359	43	81	18	2	15	58	19	101	1	0	226	266	413	678	5%	72%	0.19	140	75	3.10	34
Eibner,Brett	R	13	25	CF	aa	KC	441	56	93	15	9	13	31	40	164	5	3	210	276	372	647	8%	63%	0.24	126	118	2.63	6
		14	26	CF	aaa	KC	274	28	53	11	2	4	18	20	89	3	2	193	247	290	537	7%	67%	0.22	84	89	1.84	-21
Featherston,Taylor	R	14	25	2B	aa	COL	497	51	116	30	4	13	42	28	121	10	7	234	274	390	664	5%	76%	0.23	120	94	2.78	40
Fields,Daniel	L	12	21	OF	aa	DET	106	11	26	4	0	2	6	10	22	7	1	241	309	322	631	9%	80%	0.48	56	83	3.24	8
		13	22	CF	aa	DET	457	57	119	25	6	8	47	36	136	19	8	261	315	394	709	7%	70%	0.27	105	131	3.41	21
		14	23	CF	a/a	DET	302	25	60	11	4	4	26	16	88	7	2	197	236	303	539	5%	71%	0.18	84	116	1.84	-3
Flores,Ramon	L	13	21	LF	aa	NYY	534	67	129	23	4	6	47	67	105	6	6	241	326	332	658	11%	80%	0.64	65	80	2.92	22
		14	22	RF	aaa	NYY	235	23	51	15	2	6	18	26	49	2	2	217	294	377	671	10%	79%	0.52	117	80	2.75	55
Fontana,Nolan	L	14	23	2B	aaa	HOU	229	25	52	18	1	1	20	47	88	4	9	225	356	321	678	17%	62%	0.53	113	57	2.48	-10
Franco,Maikel	R	13	21	3B	aa	PHI	277	36	84	12	1	12	39	8	35	1	2	305	324	492	816	3%	87%	0.22	109	59	5.05	62
		14	22	3B	aaa	PHI	521	49	119	30	3	13	60	23	90	2	1	228	261	372	633	4%	83%	0.26	102	68	2.61	43
Fuentes,Reymond	L	12	21	OF	aa	SD	473	42	87	17	3	3	27	44	152	28	10	184	253	252	505	8%	68%	0.29	56	123	1.68	-28
		13	22	RF	a/a	SD	400	57	113	20	2	5	33	40	96	27	12	282	347	377	724	9%	76%	0.41	75	113	3.86	18
		14	23	CF	a/a	SD	327	38	78	11	4	4	23	23	77	18	3	239	289	330	619	7%	76%	0.30	68	137	2.78	16
Gallo,Joey	L	14	21	3B	aa	TEX	250	36	55	9	0	18	45	30	120	2	0	218	301	478	779	11%	52%	0.25	252	46	4.36	47
Garcia,Greg	L	12	23	SS	aa	STL	412	62	99	17	2	7	39	64	93	8	6	241	343	342	685	13%	77%	0.68	70	84	3.29	20
		13	24	SS	aaa	STL	354	37	81	20	3	2	26	37	80	10	2	228	301	315	616	9%	78%	0.47	71	107	2.52	20
		14	25	2B	a/a	STL	397	45	88	12	2	5	30	31	115	6	6	221	277	300	577	7%	71%	0.26	63	83	2.28	-25
Garcia,Willy	R	14	22	RF	aa	PIT	439	44	102	24	3	12	47	17	153	6	4	232	262	385	647	4%	65%	0.11	133	93	2.66	5
Gonzalez,Erik	R	14	23	SS	aa	CLE	129	17	41	6	2	1	13	6	27	5	1	315	343	406	749	4%	79%	0.21	68	127	4.35	20
Goodwin,Brian	L	12	22	OF	aa	WAS	166	14	34	7	1	4	12	14	52	2	3	203	265	332	597	8%	68%	0.27	98	65	2.21	-11
		13	23	CF	aa	WAS	457	66	104	17	8	8	32	51	129	15	12	227	305	354	659	10%	72%	0.40	91	136	2.67	22
		14	24	CF	aaa	WAS	275	23	51	9	3	3	24	35	104	4	5	186	279	269	547	11%	62%	0.34	76	90	1.83	-39
Gosselin,Phil	R	12	24	2B	aa	ATL	484	45	103	20	2	2	38	38	104	10	5	212	270	278	548	7%	78%	0.37	50	89	1.99	-3
		13	25	2B	a/a	ATL	425	35	93	12	2	2	30	19	82	5	1	218	252	270	522	4%	81%	0.23	39	79	1.95	-12
		14	26	3B	aaa	ATL	378	41	106	24	3	3	22	13	78	4	1	279	304	387	691	3%	79%	0.17	87	94	3.31	25
Gregor,Conrad	L	14	22	1B	aa	HOU	109	11	23	3	1	2	10	10	24	0	1	210	277	323	600	8%	78%	0.43	78	59	2.36	12
Grichuk,Randal	R	13	22	RF	aa	LAA	500	74	116	24	6	18	55	24	100	8	5	231	266	412	678	4%	80%	0.24	117	122	2.91	61
		14	23	LF	aaa	STL	436	53	93	19	1	17	51	20	121	6	6	214	249	378	627	4%	72%	0.17	124	85	2.53	24
Guerrero,Alex	R	14	28	2B	aaa	LA	243	21	57	10	2	8	27	5	58	2	0	233	250	395	645	2%	76%	0.09	114	81	2.84	26
Hager,Jake	R	14	21	SS	aa	TAM	447	34	108	24	4	3	39	24	101	3	4	242	281	333	614	5%	77%	0.24	76	71	2.41	4
Haniger,Mitch	R	14	24	RF	aa	ARI	267	36	62	9	1	8	30	17	50	3	0	233	278	365	642	6%	81%	0.33	88	88	3.03	35
Hanson,Alen	B	13	21	SS	aa	PIT	137	11	32	4	4	1	8	6	27	5	2	231	264	327	592	4%	81%	0.24	59	123	2.15	17
		14	22	SS	aa	PIT	482	48	117	19	8	7	43	22	93	19	12	242	276	360	636	4%	81%	0.24	80	128	2.53	36
Hassan,Alex	R	11	23	OF	aa	BOS	454	54	118	35	1	9	46	55	86	6	2	260	339	399	738	11%	81%	0.63	100	64	5.00	47
		12	24	OF	aaa	BOS	312	32	74	13	0	5	38	44	77	1	1	236	331	331	662	12%	75%	0.58	71	29	3.15	-6
		13	25	RF	aaa	BOS	187	19	53	14	0	3	21	26	57	0	1	283	371	402	773	12%	69%	0.46	109	21	4.24	-2
		14	26	RF	aaa	BOS	408	50	102	30	1	6	41	44	126	2	2	251	324	370	694	10%	69%	0.35	114	52	3.18	5
Hedges,Austin	R	13	21	C	aa	SD	67	3	13	3	0	0	7	5	10	3	1	198	255	235	490	7%	85%	0.51	34	58	1.64	0
		14	22	C	aa	SD	427	26	83	16	2	5	36	19	102	1	3	195	230	276	505	4%	76%	0.19	64	40	1.62	-22

BATTER	B	Yr	Age	Pos	Lvl	Tm	AB	R	H	D	T	HR	RBI	BB	K	SB	CS	BA	OB	Slg	OPS	bb%	ct%	Eye	PX	SX	RC/G	BPV
Herrera,Dilson	R	14	20	2B	aa	NYM	241	39	71	14	2	8	37	22	60	7	4	296	356	473	829	8%	75%	0.37	132	106	4.95	57
Hicks,John	R	13	24	C	aa	SEA	296	35	64	14	1	3	26	19	71	11	4	215	262	300	562	6%	76%	0.26	67	108	2.13	4
		14	25	C	a/a	SEA	290	29	68	10	2	3	33	18	80	5	4	235	280	316	597	6%	72%	0.23	67	87	2.45	-17
Hoying,Jared	L	12	23	OF	aa	TEX	247	31	63	7	3	4	20	14	53	7	5	254	295	347	642	6%	79%	0.27	58	109	2.85	7
		13	24	RF	a/a	TEX	341	37	79	13	7	11	37	15	115	5	3	231	263	403	666	4%	66%	0.13	128	119	2.79	14
		14	25	CF	aaa	TEX	509	56	114	27	5	18	51	27	161	13	8	223	262	404	666	5%	68%	0.16	145	113	2.74	35
Jankowski,Travis	L	14	23	CF	aa	SD	100	11	21	3	1	0	8	6	16	8	2	206	254	255	509	6%	84%	0.39	39	138	1.82	21
Jensen,Kyle	R	12	24	OF	aa	MIA	445	55	87	18	2	17	66	57	184	1	1	197	287	357	645	11%	59%	0.31	135	55	2.81	-17
		13	25	RF	a/a	MIA	447	60	88	28	0	19	63	41	165	5	3	197	265	387	651	8%	63%	0.25	163	68	2.67	22
		14	26	RF	aaa	MIA	497	45	98	23	0	15	59	31	177	1	0	197	245	332	577	6%	64%	0.18	120	34	2.23	-22
Jimenez,A.J.	R	12	22	C	aa	TOR	105	12	25	4	1	2	8	4	15	2	3	237	266	343	609	4%	85%	0.27	64	92	2.26	30
		13	23	C	a/a	TOR	233	22	56	15	0	2	22	13	44	1	3	240	280	337	617	5%	81%	0.29	78	38	2.40	14
		14	24	C	a/a	TOR	313	26	70	20	1	3	30	15	59	2	1	223	259	317	575	5%	81%	0.25	78	55	2.09	14
Johnson,Micah	L	13	23	2B	aa	CHW	21	2	4.5	0	0	0	1	0	5	1	0	212	212	212	425	0%	78%	0.00	0	74	1.61	-62
		14	24	2B	a/a	CHW	419	33	102	16	4	4	31	28	82	15	15	242	290	326	616	6%	80%	0.34	61	94	2.40	13
Kemp,Tony	L	14	23	2B	aa	HOU	233	32	59	10	3	3	16	21	37	10	7	254	317	363	680	8%	84%	0.58	73	125	3.05	51
Kivlehan,Patrick	R	14	25	3B	aa	SEA	377	44	94	21	4	8	50	31	94	7	5	250	307	386	693	8%	75%	0.33	105	99	3.16	31
Kobernus,Jeff	R	12	24	2B	aa	WAS	330	33	82	9	1	1	15	14	63	33	12	247	279	291	570	4%	81%	0.23	32	121	2.42	-4
		13	25	LF	aaa	WAS	371	43	99	16	1	1	26	20	67	31	11	268	305	325	629	5%	82%	0.29	47	124	2.97	14
		14	26	LF	a/a	WAS	230	21	48	11	1	1	18	16	56	12	4	210	263	283	546	7%	76%	0.30	65	101	2.01	1
Kubitza,Kyle	L	14	24	3B	aa	ATL	440	60	113	27	9	6	43	61	156	16	7	258	348	400	748	12%	65%	0.39	128	132	3.61	27
Lamb,Jake	L	14	24	3B	a/a	ARI	392	44	111	35	4	11	59	36	117	1	0	282	343	476	819	8%	70%	0.31	167	79	4.46	57
Lambo,Andrew	L	10	22	8	aa	PIT	272	31	67	11	1	5	29	19	55	1	1	246	296	349	645	7%	80%	0.35	68	59	3.63	6
		11	23	OF	a/a	PIT	437	43	90	25	0	8	46	33	113	4	3	207	263	321	584	7%	74%	0.30	80	54	2.81	-7
		13	25	LF	a/a	PIT	444	51	104	21	3	22	76	32	141	5	1	234	285	446	731	7%	68%	0.23	157	92	3.66	41
		14	26	1B	aaa	PIT	238	31	63	16	1	7	30	15	54	2	2	264	308	431	739	6%	77%	0.28	126	76	3.66	47
Lee,Hak-Ju	L	11	21	SS	aa	TAM	100	12	17	1	3	1	5	8	24	4	2	172	235	272	507	8%	76%	0.35	50	240	2.02	33
		12	22	SS	aa	TAM	475	55	111	13	9	3	30	41	114	30	10	233	294	318	612	8%	76%	0.36	55	147	2.57	10
		13	23	SS	aaa	TAM	45	11	17	3	1	1	6	9	10	5	2	380	485	535	001	17%	77%	0.87	110	147	8.34	75
		14	24	SS	aaa	TAM	315	30	55	8	1	3	19	30	99	10	6	176	248	237	485	9%	69%	0.31	52	94	1.57	-36
Lindor,Francisco	B	13	20	SS	aa	CLE	76	11	20	3	1	1	6	11	8	4	2	259	351	342	693	12%	90%	1.40	52	105	3.42	60
		14	21	SS	a/a	CLE	507	61	125	16	3	9	51	39	108	23	17	247	301	340	641	7%	79%	0.36	66	104	2.82	15
Lindsey,Taylor	L	13	22	2B	aa	LAA	508	59	126	20	5	14	49	40	100	3	4	248	303	388	691	7%	80%	0.40	90	77	3.32	33
		14	23	2B	aaa	SD	441	41	79	13	3	6	29	24	71	4	5	180	222	267	490	5%	84%	0.34	59	87	1.48	21
Liriano,Rymer	R	12	21	OF	aa	SD	183	19	39	8	2	2	16	17	58	8	1	214	281	314	595	8%	69%	0.29	80	119	2.42	-7
		14	23	LF	a/a	SD	433	49	102	24	2	10	46	30	140	14	9	235	285	369	654	7%	68%	0.22	117	99	2.76	9
Machado,Dixon	R	14	22	SS	aa	DET	292	33	78	20	1	4	24	29	38	6	6	267	333	380	713	7%	87%	0.76	85	68	3.37	56
Mahtook,Mikie	R	12	23	OF	aa	TAM	153	14	33	9	1	3	20	9	35	3	3	215	257	343	600	5%	77%	0.25	92	79	2.14	18
		13	24	RF	aa	TAM	511	56	111	26	7	5	54	34	118	20	9	218	266	327	593	6%	77%	0.28	80	135	2.15	26
		14	25	CF	aaa	TAM	489	46	123	28	6	9	56	37	162	15	6	251	304	390	694	7%	67%	0.23	121	113	3.20	14
Marrero,Deven	R	13	23	SS	aa	BOS	72	5	15	0	0	0	4	8	17	5	0	211	285	211	496	9%	76%	0.43	0	76	2.27	-53
		14	24	SS	a/a	BOS	454	51	107	30	2	5	46	35	104	13	9	235	291	339	629	7%	77%	0.34	89	92	2.48	24
Marte,Ketel	B	14	21	SS	a/a	SEA	523	59	140	30	4	3	41	20	89	22	11	267	293	354	647	4%	83%	0.22	70	117	2.82	33
McCann,James	R	12	22	C	aa	DET	220	12	39	11	0	2	15	6	46	2	1	179	202	250	452	3%	79%	0.14	56	43	1.21	-18
		13	23	C	aa	DET	441	40	109	27	1	6	43	24	91	2	3	246	285	355	639	5%	79%	0.26	84	51	2.72	12
		14	24	C	aaa	DET	417	38	107	30	0	5	42	19	98	7	2	258	291	369	660	4%	76%	0.20	98	66	2.98	15
Mejias-Brean,Seth	R	14	23	3B	aa	CIN	226	17	46	6	1	3	17	24	57	1	4	204	281	279	560	10%	75%	0.42	56	52	1.99	-19
Merrifield,Whit	R	13	24	LF	aa	KC	322	24	77	18	5	2	33	17	62	13	8	240	278	345	624	5%	81%	0.27	76	115	2.34	31
		14	25	LF	a/a	KC	483	57	131	35	4	5	35	28	89	12	13	271	311	392	703	6%	82%	0.32	96	95	3.06	45
Mitchell,Jared	L	12	24	OF	a/a	CHW	455	56	96	21	9	10	54	70	209	17	9	210	315	365	681	13%	54%	0.33	142	127	2.86	-4
		13	25	CF	a/a	CHW	300	23	43	7	1	4	18	43	145	13	7	142	250	217	467	13%	52%	0.30	77	100	1.40	-74
		14	26	LF	a/a	CHW	426	48	87	10	3	14	33	47	186	10	14	204	283	342	625	10%	56%	0.25	125	89	2.47	-26
Moncrief,Carlos	L	13	25	RF	aa	CLE	489	55	113	22	4	12	54	39	118	11	8	231	288	365	653	7%	76%	0.33	95	100	2.79	26
		14	26	RF	aaa	CLE	480	47	106	28	2	8	46	27	158	6	4	220	262	341	604	5%	67%	0.17	110	83	2.32	-6
Moran,Colin	L	14	22	3B	aa	HOU	112	9	30	5	0	2	17	7	26	0	1	268	312	359	671	6%	77%	0.27	75	25	3.25	-12
Morban,Julio	L	13	21	RF	aa	SEA	295	43	84	21	4	6	41	25	104	7	2	283	340	441	780	8%	65%	0.24	138	123	4.20	24
		14	22	RF	a/a	SEA	214	18	46	8	1	1	13	13	76	0	1	213	259	272	532	6%	64%	0.18	61	52	1.87	-64
Morris,Hunter	L	12	24	1B	aa	MIL	522	61	140	37	5	24	89	32	137	2	1	268	311	491	802	6%	74%	0.24	154	65	4.35	52
		13	25	1B	aaa	MIL	497	42	102	22	2	19	51	31	146	2	1	206	252	370	622	6%	71%	0.21	121	57	2.56	10
		14	26	1B	a/a	MIL	356	35	82	18	1	9	32	16	95	0	0	231	263	360	624	4%	73%	0.16	103	38	2.67	-3
Moya,Steven	L	14	23	RF	aa	DET	515	58	121	28	3	25	75	16	174	11	5	235	259	446	704	3%	66%	0.09	172	104	3.24	42
Muncy,Max	L	13	23	1B	aa	OAK	172	17	37	10	2	3	18	19	38	0	1	214	292	343	635	10%	78%	0.50	96	61	2.42	28
		14	24	1B	aa	OAK	435	45	97	20	3	5	48	68	105	5	2	223	328	314	641	14%	76%	0.64	73	73	2.78	12
Murphy,J.R.	R	12	21	C	aa	NYY	147	19	31	11	1	4	13	13	34	0	0	212	277	371	649	8%	77%	0.39	115	55	2.59	35
		13	22	C	a/a	NYY	413	52	103	26	0	12	40	41	79	1	1	250	318	399	717	9%	81%	0.52	106	39	3.60	40
		14	23	C	aaa	NYY	179	13	38	8	0	5	21	10	47	0	0	213	254	340	594	5%	74%	0.21	98	13	2.45	-10
Naquin,Tyler	L	13	22	CF	aa	CLE	80	7	15	3	0	1	5	4	25	1	3	193	229	254	483	4%	69%	0.15	54	60	1.29	-51
		14	23	CF	aa	CLE	304	43	83	11	3	3	24	23	82	11	3	274	325	362	686	7%	73%	0.28	69	127	3.53	2
Ngoepe,Gift	B	13	23	SS	aa	PIT	220	23	34	9	1	2	12	21	86	8	1	152	227	234	461	9%	61%	0.25	78	124	1.26	-37
		14	24	2B	aa	PIT	437	41	86	14	6	6	37	35	147	9	9	196	256	295	550	7%	66%	0.24	82	111	1.80	-19
Nicholas,Brett	L	13	25	1B	aa	TEX	506	57	131	23	3	18	73	38	137	2	1	259	311	424	734	7%	73%	0.27	117	58	3.93	18
		14	26	C	aaa	TEX	452	26	99	16	1	7	37	18	132	3	1	219	248	304	553	4%	71%	0.13	71	40	2.15	-38
Nimmo,Brandon	L	14	21	CF	aa	NYM	240	28	47	10	2	5	19	27	62	4	1	198	278	317	595	10%	74%	0.43	90	103	2.29	22
O'Brien,Pete	R	14	24	1B	aa	ARI	287	37	64	13	1	19	42	13	91	0	0	223	256	475	731	4%	68%	0.14	191	44	3.56	49

BATTER	B	Yr	Age	Pos	Lvl	Tm	AB	R	H	D	T	HR	RBI	BB	K	SB	CS	BA	OB	Slg	OPS	bb%	ct%	Eye	PX	SX	RC/G	BPV
Ohlman,Michael	R	14	24	C	aa	BAL	403	29	80	21	1	2	24	31	97	0	0	199	257	267	524	7%	76%	0.32	63	27	1.73	-21
Parker,Kyle	R	13	24	LF	aa	COL	480	54	128	22	3	20	57	31	102	5	7	267	311	450	761	6%	79%	0.30	120	68	4.04	45
		14	25	RF	aaa	COL	502	45	120	26	2	10	44	20	111	2	4	239	268	363	631	4%	78%	0.18	94	60	2.64	14
Pederson,Joc	L	13	21	CF	aa	LA	439	73	114	23	2	20	52	61	123	28	9	260	350	456	806	12%	72%	0.49	142	121	4.81	64
		14	22	CF	aaa	LA	445	67	108	14	2	21	49	61	172	19	15	243	334	423	757	12%	61%	0.35	150	96	4.01	20
Peraza,Jose	R	14	20	2B	aa	ATL	185	30	58	7	3	1	14	6	16	21	9	315	336	391	728	3%	91%	0.36	49	159	3.98	60
Perez,Hernan	R	13	22	2B	a/a	DET	429	40	119	29	2	3	32	14	57	24	8	277	300	376	676	3%	87%	0.24	74	110	3.22	47
		14	23	SS	aaa	DET	547	55	142	29	7	5	42	28	69	17	7	259	295	362	657	5%	87%	0.41	72	116	2.89	54
Perez,Roberto	R	12	24	C	aa	CLE	283	28	55	15	2	1	28	43	74	0	1	193	301	267	568	13%	74%	0.58	63	46	1.89	-12
		13	25	C	a/a	CLE	280	20	47	15	0	1	26	40	99	1	2	166	271	234	505	13%	65%	0.41	72	27	1.46	-48
		14	26	C	aaa	CLE	174	21	43	9	1	6	32	21	62	1	0	249	330	408	737	11%	64%	0.34	140	54	3.91	8
Perkins,Cameron	R	14	24	LF	a/a	PHI	451	31	104	24	3	4	38	25	92	6	7	230	270	323	592	5%	80%	0.27	75	66	2.18	11
Peterson,D.J.	R	14	22	3B	aa	SEA	222	25	51	8	0	9	30	17	58	1	1	229	282	390	672	7%	74%	0.29	115	37	3.26	15
Peterson,Shane	L	10	23	3	aa	OAK	460	49	106	21	3	4	48	47	86	10	2	230	302	315	617	9%	81%	0.55	60	101	3.46	24
		11	23	OF	a/a	OAK	394	45	88	19	3	6	41	37	86	9	2	225	291	332	623	9%	78%	0.43	72	107	3.43	21
		12	24	OF	a/a	OAK	288	46	78	15	3	6	33	50	93	9	7	271	379	409	787	15%	68%	0.54	107	107	4.27	20
		13	25	CF	aaa	OAK	463	47	91	20	1	7	53	53	150	12	2	196	279	291	570	10%	68%	0.35	81	90	2.24	-15
		14	26	CF	aaa	OAK	543	65	128	31	3	6	58	43	171	7	2	236	292	341	633	7%	69%	0.25	97	97	2.65	-2
Pham,Tommy	R	10	23	8	aa	STL	121	15	36	12	1	2	14	14	22	3	2	298	370	463	833	10%	82%	0.64	121	91	6.38	74
		11	23	OF	aa	STL	142	20	33	9	2	3	10	12	45	2	3	234	293	384	677	8%	68%	0.26	98	127	3.59	8
		13	25	CF	a/a	STL	269	24	63	10	5	5	30	20	78	6	5	234	287	357	644	7%	71%	0.25	90	109	2.63	4
		14	26	CF	aaa	STL	346	43	89	13	4	6	30	26	98	14	2	256	309	369	677	7%	72%	0.27	87	128	3.41	11
Pirela,Jose	R	11	22	SS	aa	NYY	468	40	101	18	3	7	36	20	95	7	8	215	248	313	561	4%	80%	0.22	64	81	2.46	5
		12	23	2B	aa	NYY	317	44	83	17	2	7	26	21	53	7	3	263	309	398	707	6%	83%	0.40	86	96	3.52	45
		13	24	2B	a/a	NYY	482	63	118	24	3	9	52	48	71	16	3	244	313	366	679	9%	85%	0.68	80	116	3.29	60
		14	25	2B	aaa	NYY	535	63	136	17	7	8	43	27	87	11	8	254	290	356	647	5%	84%	0.31	67	108	2.87	33
Piscotty,Stephen	R	13	22	RF	aa	STL	184	13	48	8	0	4	18	15	21	5	3	259	314	371	684	7%	89%	0.70	71	50	3.43	43
		14	23	RF	aaa	STL	500	51	120	27	0	6	50	31	69	8	6	241	286	331	617	6%	86%	0.46	69	63	2.60	33
Plawecki,Kevin	R	14	23	C	a/a	NYM	376	38	91	18	0	8	42	20	58	0	0	243	281	353	634	5%	84%	0.34	79	28	2.88	22
Polanco,Jorge	B	14	21	SS	aa	MIN	146	11	38	6	0	1	13	7	30	6	3	258	293	312	605	5%	80%	0.25	47	65	2.68	-12
Pompey,Dalton	B	14	22	CF	a/a	TOR	165	29	49	10	3	3	14	14	31	12	5	296	352	437	789	8%	81%	0.46	101	153	4.28	70
Puello,Cesar	R	13	22	RF	aa	NYM	331	50	93	18	1	13	57	22	96	19	8	282	327	463	790	6%	71%	0.23	135	119	4.54	43
		14	23	LF	aaa	NYM	318	35	59	14	1	4	22	18	87	8	1	187	230	280	510	5%	73%	0.21	79	111	1.71	0
Ramirez,Nick	L	14	25	1B	aa	MIL	490	52	96	18	4	16	61	42	181	1	5	197	260	345	605	8%	63%	0.23	126	62	2.32	-11
Ramos,Henry	B	14	22	RF	aa	BOS	181	21	56	10	2	2	19	9	41	2	4	310	342	408	750	5%	78%	0.22	78	77	3.90	7
Ramsey,James	L	13	24	CF	a/a	STL	350	45	72	9	1	10	32	39	124	6	5	205	286	327	612	10%	65%	0.32	95	87	2.61	-17
		14	25	CF	a/a	CLE	352	49	87	20	1	12	40	33	119	4	2	247	311	411	722	9%	66%	0.27	141	77	3.62	19
Ravelo,Rangel	R	14	22	1B	aa	CHW	476	55	129	32	3	10	50	47	88	8	7	272	337	411	748	9%	82%	0.53	105	75	3.80	53
Realmuto,J.T.	R	13	22	C	aa	MIA	368	35	81	20	3	4	33	31	73	8	1	221	282	321	603	8%	80%	0.43	75	100	2.38	29
		14	23	C	aa	MIA	375	50	97	22	5	5	47	32	66	14	6	259	317	386	704	8%	83%	0.49	91	129	3.29	59
Refsnyder,Rob	R	14	23	2B	a/a	NYY	515	64	144	33	4	12	49	44	118	7	10	279	335	429	764	8%	77%	0.37	115	76	3.90	41
Renfroe,Hunter	R	14	22	LF	aa	SD	224	14	45	10	0	4	19	21	61	2	1	201	269	302	570	8%	73%	0.34	83	32	2.19	-14
Reyes,Elmer	R	14	24	SS	a/a	ATL	417	39	105	28	2	4	39	9	110	4	2	252	268	355	622	2%	74%	0.08	93	80	2.51	-1
Reynolds,Matt	R	14	24	SS	a/a	NYM	478	57	128	16	4	4	40	33	127	13	8	267	314	343	657	6%	74%	0.26	60	105	3.12	-12
Rivera,Yadiel	R	14	22	SS	aa	MIL	183	24	44	8	5	2	10	8	40	4	2	239	271	366	638	4%	78%	0.20	89	137	2.40	35
Rodriguez,Ronny	R	13	21	SS	aa	CLE	468	48	108	23	4	4	40	12	85	9	3	231	251	319	570	3%	82%	0.14	65	110	2.13	20
		14	22	2B	aa	CLE	413	42	83	23	0	4	27	20	102	3	5	202	238	286	524	5%	75%	0.19	75	60	1.66	-10
Rodriguez,Yorman	R	13	21	RF	aa	CIN	262	27	67	14	2	4	28	23	83	4	0	256	315	372	687	8%	68%	0.27	98	86	3.37	-5
		14	22	CF	aa	CIN	450	54	105	18	4	8	31	37	132	9	5	234	292	344	636	8%	71%	0.28	88	103	2.75	1
Rogers,Jason	R	13	25	1B	aa	MIL	481	54	114	22	2	19	68	47	102	5	2	236	305	409	714	9%	79%	0.47	114	70	3.61	48
		14	26	3B	a/a	MIL	493	56	122	25	4	15	59	39	115	4	1	248	303	404	708	7%	77%	0.34	113	84	3.46	39
Roller,Kyle	L	13	25	1B	aa	NYY	443	47	97	20	1	15	55	43	164	0	0	220	288	371	659	9%	63%	0.26	128	32	3.04	-17
		14	26	1B	a/a	NYY	456	56	114	24	2	21	54	43	174	1	0	250	315	450	765	9%	62%	0.25	176	54	4.18	24
Rosario,Eddie	L	13	22	2B	aa	MIN	289	31	74	17	3	3	30	16	72	5	4	254	294	362	656	5%	75%	0.22	87	97	2.76	12
		14	23	CF	aa	MIN	316	32	67	18	3	6	29	13	74	6	4	211	243	341	583	4%	77%	0.18	101	106	2.02	29
Rua,Ryan	R	13	23	3B	aa	TEX	86	16	19	2	1	3	8	6	26	1	0	218	269	356	625	6%	70%	0.23	94	123	2.80	8
		14	24	3B	a/a	TEX	471	47	125	23	2	14	53	37	109	4	6	265	319	413	732	7%	77%	0.34	108	59	3.78	28
Russell,Addison	R	14	20	SS	aa	CHC	241	31	67	13	1	10	35	14	47	4	4	278	317	468	785	5%	80%	0.29	130	72	4.30	60
Saladino,Tyler	R	12	23	SS	a/a	CHW	467	66	99	15	3	4	37	72	123	32	9	211	317	281	598	13%	74%	0.59	52	127	2.59	3
		13	24	SS	aa	CHW	424	39	85	15	1	5	44	45	100	23	9	200	277	274	552	10%	76%	0.45	56	103	2.10	3
		14	25	SS	aaa	CHW	294	27	73	13	2	7	28	19	61	5	1	248	295	375	670	6%	79%	0.32	90	82	3.19	27
Sanchez,Carlos	B	12	20	SS	a/a	CHW	158	19	51	11	1	0	12	10	31	6	5	324	364	401	765	6%	80%	0.31	65	87	4.13	13
		13	21	2B	aaa	CHW	432	41	94	18	1	0	23	26	84	13	8	218	264	267	531	6%	81%	0.31	43	98	1.86	-1
		14	22	2B	aaa	CHW	437	42	108	16	4	6	40	28	97	11	4	248	292	339	632	6%	78%	0.28	68	102	2.84	10
Sanchez,Gary	R	13	21	C	aa	NYY	92	10	21	5	0	2	9	11	17	0	0	232	316	354	670	11%	81%	0.66	89	24	3.09	28
		14	22	C	aa	NYY	429	39	105	17	0	12	53	35	99	1	1	246	303	368	671	8%	77%	0.36	89	26	3.34	4
Santana,Domingo	R	13	21	RF	aa	HOU	416	58	95	21	2	21	51	37	154	10	5	228	292	437	728	8%	63%	0.24	170	97	3.56	35
		14	22	RF	aaa	HOU	443	46	113	23	2	12	59	47	171	4	4	256	328	398	726	10%	61%	0.28	134	62	3.71	-7
Schebler,Scott	L	14	24	LF	aa	LA	489	57	111	19	7	20	51	31	129	7	5	227	273	417	690	6%	74%	0.24	132	110	3.07	47
Seager,Corey	L	14	20	SS	aa	LA	148	21	45	14	2	2	21	7	43	1	1	304	337	455	792	5%	71%	0.17	140	96	4.04	35
Shaffer,Richie	R	14	23	3B	aa	TAM	427	46	82	24	4	14	51	44	135	3	0	191	266	365	632	9%	68%	0.32	142	88	2.49	34
Shaw,Travis	L	12	22	1B	aa	BOS	110	11	24	14	0	2	10	17	36	1	1	222	328	412	740	14%	68%	0.48	174	36	3.02	49
		13	23	1B	aa	BOS	444	44	89	21	3	12	38	58	127	5	3	200	293	341	633	12%	71%	0.46	107	76	2.58	19
		14	24	1B	a/a	BOS	490	62	123	29	2	16	62	44	110	6	3	252	313	415	729	8%	78%	0.40	121	74	3.68	48

BATTER	B	Yr	Age	Pos	Lvl	Tm	AB	R	H	D	T	HR	RBI	BB	K	SB	CS	BA	OB	Slg	OPS	bb%	ct%	Eye	PX	SX	RC/G	BPV
Skole,Matt	L	14	25	1B	aa	WAS	461	39	90	24	1	9	46	50	144	2	1	194	274	309	583	10%	69%	0.35	101	43	2.20	-10
Soler,Jorge	R	14	22	RF	a/a	CHC	175	27	52	18	2	11	39	23	45	0	1	298	379	607	987	12%	74%	0.51	236	62	6.52	129
Souza,Steven	R	13	24	RF	aa	WAS	273	43	72	21	1	12	35	31	84	16	7	265	341	476	817	10%	69%	0.38	168	111	4.56	68
		14	25	RF	aaa	WAS	346	46	102	22	1	13	55	37	86	19	8	293	361	477	838	10%	75%	0.43	138	97	5.18	62
Spangenberg,Cory	L	13	22	2B	aa	SD	287	30	74	8	3	2	17	15	70	16	12	259	294	325	620	5%	75%	0.21	49	118	2.55	-12
		14	23	2B	aa	SD	281	31	81	14	7	2	18	12	75	11	10	290	320	407	727	4%	73%	0.16	91	128	3.22	15
Stamets,Eric	R	14	23	SS	aa	LAA	344	40	73	12	1	3	20	20	69	10	1	211	255	278	533	6%	80%	0.29	52	107	2.07	7
Stassi,Max	R	13	22	C	aa	HOU	289	32	72	18	1	14	48	15	77	1	1	248	286	463	748	5%	73%	0.20	154	50	3.78	44
		14	23	C	aaa	HOU	392	35	81	17	1	7	32	16	119	1	0	208	239	309	548	4%	70%	0.13	86	57	2.00	-26
Story,Trevor	R	14	22	SS	aa	COL	205	23	39	8	1	8	16	22	81	2	1	191	268	355	623	10%	60%	0.27	144	79	2.59	2
Susac,Andrew	R	13	23	C	aa	SF	262	24	56	15	0	8	34	31	77	1	0	213	297	359	656	11%	71%	0.40	116	29	2.92	7
		14	24	C	aaa	SF	213	23	45	7	0	6	21	23	58	0	0	211	286	327	614	10%	73%	0.39	89	24	2.71	-10
Swanner,Will	R	14	23	1B	aa	COL	104	9	27	5	0	3	11	3	36	1	4	260	281	407	688	3%	66%	0.09	125	40	2.86	-17
Sweeney,Darnell	B	14	23	2B	aa	LA	490	63	117	28	3	10	41	53	135	11	18	239	314	370	684	10%	73%	0.40	108	81	2.81	22

PITCHER	Th	Yr	Age	LvL	Org	W	L	G	Sv	IP	H	ER	HR	BB	K	ERA	WHIP	BF/G	OBA	bb/9	k/9	Cmd	hr/9	H%	S%	BPV
Adam,Jason	R	13	22	aa	KC	8	11	26	0	144	171	97	12	52	106	6.04	1.55	24.2	297	3.3	6.6	2.0	0.7	35%	60%	55
		14	23	a/a	MIN	5	9	29	0	121	154	76	9	36	85	5.66	1.58	18.3	312	2.7	6.4	2.4	0.7	36%	63%	60
Adams,Austin	R	11	25	aa	CLE	11	10	26	0	136	176	71	6	67	106	4.72	1.79	24.6	307	4.5	7.0	1.6	0.4	38%	73%	57
		13	27		CLE	3	2	45	4	55	52	18	3	29	60	3.02	1.47	5.2	250	4.8	9.8	2.0	0.5	34%	80%	91
		14	28	aaa	CLE	3	2	42	5	54	54	19	4	17	40	3.08	1.31	5.3	262	2.8	6.7	2.4	0.7	31%	79%	72
Alvarez,R.J.	R	14	23	aa	SD	0	1	38	7	43	32	6.6	0	13	54	1.37	1.03	4.4	207	2.6	11.3	4.3	0.0	32%	85%	172
Anderson,Cody	R	14	24	aa	CLE	4	11	25	0	126	160	88	17	44	68	6.27	1.63	22.4	312	3.1	4.9	1.6	1.2	33%	62%	18
Anderson,Tyler	L	14	25	aa	COL	7	4	23	0	118	115	37	4	44	80	2.82	1.35	21.4	257	3.4	6.1	1.8	0.3	30%	79%	68
Andriese,Matt	R	13	24	a/a	SD	11	7	27	0	135	143	49	4	28	91	3.29	1.27	20.4	274	1.9	6.1	3.3	0.3	32%	73%	96
		14	25	aaa	TAM	11	8	28	0	162	183	84	20	50	107	4.68	1.43	24.6	285	2.8	5.9	2.2	1.1	32%	69%	46
Appel,Mark	R	14	23	aa	HOU	1	2	7	0	39	39	18	2	13	33	4.07	1.31	23.0	260	2.9	7.6	2.6	0.5	32%	68%	89
Armstrong,Shawn	R	13	23	aa	CLE	2	3	30	0	33	35	16	2	19	37	4.33	1.64	4.9	271	5.3	10.0	1.9	0.5	37%	73%	85
		14	24	a/a	CLE	6	2	49	15	56	49	17	4	21	61	2.75	1.25	4.7	236	3.4	9.8	2.8	0.6	32%	80%	107
Asher,Alec	R	14	23	aa	TEX	11	11	28	0	154	165	83	23	34	101	4.84	1.29	22.6	275	2.0	5.9	3.0	1.3	30%	66%	58
Baez,Angel	R	14	23	aa	KC	1	5	35	0	62	67	39	9	29	58	5.62	1.55	7.7	277	4.3	8.4	2.0	1.3	33%	66%	52
Baez,Pedro	R	14	26	a/a	LA	2	1	40	12	42	45	17	4	12	30	3.70	1.34	4.4	273	2.5	6.5	2.6	0.8	32%	74%	72
Banuelos,Manny	L	14	23	a/a	NYY	2	3	21	0	64	62	37	12	30	48	5.16	1.43	12.9	255	4.2	6.8	1.6	1.7	27%	69%	28
Barnes,Matt	R	13	23	a/a	BOS	6	10	25	0	113	135	65	12	49	119	5.15	1.62	20.1	297	3.9	9.4	2.4	1.0	38%	69%	75
		14	24	aaa	BOS	8	9	23	0	128	143	72	9	48	85	5.10	1.50	24.0	285	3.4	6.0	1.8	0.6	33%	65%	52
Barrett,Jake	R	14	23	a/a	ARI	2	2	55	28	55	52	21	3	25	39	3.38	1.39	4.2	248	4.1	6.4	1.5	0.5	29%	76%	61
Bassitt,Chris	R	13	24	aa	CHW	4	2	8	0	48	43	16	3	20	32	3.04	1.33	24.7	242	3.8	6.0	1.6	0.5	28%	78%	59
		14	25	aa	CHW	3	1	6	0	35	30	7.1	2	16	30	1.85	1.33	24.0	237	4.1	7.8	1.9	0.6	29%	89%	75
Beck,Chris	R	14	24	a/a	CHW	6	11	27	0	150	169	65	9	47	73	3.92	1.44	23.7	286	2.8	4.4	1.5	0.6	31%	73%	40
Bedrosian,Cam	R	14	23	a/a	LAA	2	1	38	17	39	16	9.9	1	14	57	2.25	0.76	3.7	123	3.2	13.1	4.0	0.2	22%	69%	188
Berrios,Jose	R	14	20	a/a	MIN	3	5	9	0	44	44	25	2	14	27	5.20	1.33	20.1	263	2.9	5.6	1.9	0.4	30%	58%	64
Berry,Tim	L	14	23	aa	BAL	6	7	23	0	133	137	60	14	44	90	4.02	1.36	24.2	267	3.0	6.1	2.0	0.9	30%	73%	53
Biddle,Jesse	L	13	22	aa	PHI	5	14	27	0	138	111	59	10	77	134	3.86	1.36	21.4	222	5.0	8.7	1.7	0.7	28%	72%	80
		14	23	aa	PHI	3	10	16	0	82	87	53	12	43	69	5.82	1.58	22.7	273	4.7	7.5	1.6	1.3	32%	65%	40
Binford,Christian	R	14	22	a/a	KC	3	3	12	0	58	67	25	7	11	39	3.95	1.33	20.1	290	1.6	6.0	3.7	1.2	32%	74%	77
Blach,Ty	L	14	24	aa	SF	8	8	25	0	141	161	56	7	39	75	3.56	1.41	23.9	288	2.5	4.8	2.0	0.5	32%	75%	53
Black,Corey	R	14	23	aa	CHC	6	7	26	0	124	112	55	14	72	101	3.99	1.48	20.6	243	5.2	7.3	1.4	1.0	28%	76%	50
Blackburn,Clayton	R	14	21	aa	SF	5	6	18	0	93	101	37	1	19	74	3.56	1.29	21.2	278	1.8	7.2	3.9	0.1	35%	70%	123
Blair,Aaron	R	14	22	aa	ARI	4	1	8	0	46	34	12	5	16	39	2.36	1.08	22.6	208	3.0	7.6	2.5	0.9	25%	83%	85
Blazek,Michael	R	11	22	a/a	STL	13	6	26	0	146	156	79	20	65	115	4.91	1.52	24.9	268	4.0	7.1	1.8	1.2	31%	70%	43
		12	23	a/a	STL	5	9	42	0	83	72	43	10	35	70	4.69	1.29	8.2	235	3.8	7.6	2.0	1.1	27%	66%	62
		13	24	a/a	STL	1	2	36	9	46	31	11	1	26	43	2.16	1.24	5.2	194	5.1	8.4	1.7	0.2	26%	82%	96
		14	25	aaa	MIL	4	4	37	1	102	124	56	11	42	73	4.96	1.63	12.3	301	3.7	6.4	1.7	1.0	34%	71%	40
Bonilla,Lisalverto	R	14	24	aaa	TEX	4	2	39	1	75	81	37	10	25	75	4.49	1.42	8.1	278	3.0	9.0	3.0	1.2	34%	71%	82
Boyd,Matt	L	14	23	aa	TOR	1	4	10	0	43	65	41	6	13	38	8.72	1.82	19.8	349	2.8	8.0	2.9	1.3	42%	51%	55
Bradley,Archie	R	13	21	aa	ARI	12	5	21	0	123	111	36	6	60	104	2.62	1.38	24.7	242	4.4	7.6	1.7	0.5	30%	82%	75
		14	22	a/a	ARI	3	7	17	0	79	76	42	2	44	59	4.76	1.53	20.2	255	5.0	6.7	1.3	0.2	31%	66%	65
Bradley,Jed	L	14	24	aa	MIL	5	8	17	0	87	123	53	10	38	61	5.45	1.85	23.9	334	3.9	6.3	1.6	1.0	38%	72%	29
Britton,Drake	L	12	23	aa	BOS	4	7	16	0	85	104	46	3	39	64	4.94	1.69	23.9	303	4.2	6.8	1.6	0.4	36%	69%	58
		13	24	a/a	BOS	7	7	18	0	103	124	55	6	38	70	4.80	1.59	25.1	301	3.4	6.1	1.8	0.5	35%	69%	55
		14	25	aaa	BOS	2	3	45	5	58	95	50	9	40	30	7.74	2.31	6.7	366	6.2	4.6	0.7	1.4	39%	67%	-18
Burawa,Danny	R	14	26	a/a	NYY	3	1	42	4	59	73	39	4	33	58	5.93	1.78	6.5	304	4.9	8.8	1.8	0.6	39%	65%	67
Butler,Eddie	R	14	23	a/a	COL	6	10	19	0	113	129	59	13	35	53	4.65	1.45	25.4	287	2.8	4.2	1.5	1.0	30%	70%	24
Caminero,Arquimedes	R	13	26	a/a	MIA	6	2	43	5	54	43	29	5	25	59	4.76	1.26	5.1	219	4.2	9.7	2.3	0.8	29%	62%	94
		14	27	aaa	MIA	4	1	42	10	63	80	37	6	31	61	5.29	1.75	6.9	310	4.4	8.7	2.0	0.8	39%	70%	62
Campos,Leonel	R	13	26	aa	SD	1	0	26	2	31	17	4	0	17	36	1.04	1.09	4.6	160	5.0	10.4	2.1	0.0	24%	89%	129
		14	27	a/a	SD	2	7	42	1	82	98	59	7	49	88	6.40	1.78	9.0	297	5.4	9.6	1.8	0.8	39%	63%	67
Claudio,Alexander	L	13	21	aa	TEX	1	5	21	0	32	34	14	3	12	25	3.88	1.43	6.4	275	3.3	7.0	2.1	0.8	32%	75%	63
		14	22	a/a	TEX	2	3	10	0	43	41	13	1	4	24	2.65	1.06	16.5	254	0.8	5.0	6.0	0.2	29%	74%	153
Cole,A.J.	R	13	21	aa	WAS	4	2	7	0	45	35	13	3	9	41	2.54	0.96	24.5	213	1.8	8.2	4.5	0.6	27%	76%	138
		14	22	a/a	WAS	13	3	25	0	134	158	49	9	29	93	3.32	1.39	22.6	294	1.9	6.2	3.2	0.6	34%	77%	83
Colome,Alexander	R	11	22	aa	TAM	3	4	9	0	52	43	25	5	26	27	4.25	1.33	24.5	221	4.5	4.7	1.1	0.8	24%	69%	38
		12	23	a/a	TAM	8	4	17	0	92	90	39	3	41	78	3.82	1.43	22.9	258	4.0	7.6	1.9	0.3	32%	72%	80
		13	24	aaa	TAM	4	6	14	0	70	71	27	5	28	61	3.50	1.42	21.3	264	3.6	7.8	2.1	0.6	33%	76%	75
		14	25	aaa	TAM	7	6	15	0	86	100	45	2	31	60	4.68	1.53	24.9	293	3.2	6.3	1.9	0.2	35%	67%	69
Conley,Adam	L	13	23	aa	MIA	11	7	26	0	139	149	65	8	42	117	4.19	1.38	22.4	276	2.7	7.6	2.8	0.5	34%	69%	89
		14	24	aaa	MIA	3	5	12	0	60	70	41	2	25	39	6.12	1.57	22.0	291	3.7	5.9	1.6	0.4	34%	58%	55

PITCHER	Th	Yr	Age	LvL	Org	W	L	G	Sv	IP	H	ER	HR	BB	K	ERA	WHIP	BF/G	OBA	bb/9	k/9	Cmd	hr/9	H%	S%	BPV
Cooney,Tim	L	13	23	aa	STL	7	10	20	0	118	142	53	7	17	105	4.02	1.35	24.7	299	1.3	8.0	6.0	0.5	37%	70%	153
		14	24	aaa	STL	14	6	26	0	158	170	63	18	45	98	3.57	1.36	25.4	276	2.5	5.6	2.2	1.0	30%	77%	48
Corcino,Daniel	R	12	22	aa	CIN	8	8	26	0	143	132	62	12	67	111	3.92	1.39	23.2	245	4.2	7.0	1.6	0.7	29%	73%	60
		13	23	aaa	CIN	7	14	28	0	129	169	110	23	76	78	7.65	1.90	21.7	317	5.3	5.4	1.0	1.6	34%	61%	-4
		14	24	a/a	CIN	10	12	27	0	149	141	79	22	73	102	4.75	1.44	23.5	252	4.4	6.2	1.4	1.3	27%	71%	30
Crick,Kyle	R	14	22	aa	SF	6	7	23	0	90	85	42	6	58	96	4.14	1.58	17.3	250	5.8	9.6	1.7	0.6	33%	74%	79
Darnell,Logan	L	11	22	aa	MIN	1	1	5	0	31	40	19	2	4	17	5.71	1.43	26.7	308	1.1	4.9	4.3	0.7	35%	59%	93
		12	23	aa	MIN	11	12	28	0	156	219	102	20	47	82	5.91	1.70	25.2	332	2.7	4.7	1.7	1.2	36%	67%	18
		13	24	a/a	MIN	10	10	27	0	154	180	62	9	45	98	3.66	1.46	24.4	293	2.7	5.8	2.2	0.5	34%	75%	62
		14	25	aaa	MIN	7	6	23	0	115	131	59	17	51	72	4.61	1.59	22.0	288	4.0	5.6	1.4	1.3	31%	75%	20
Davies,Zach	R	14	21	aa	BAL	10	7	21	0	110	116	46	9	31	94	3.73	1.33	21.7	271	2.5	7.7	3.1	0.7	33%	73%	90
Dayton,Grant	L	13	26	aa	MIA	4	4	30	1	38	42	14	5	14	48	3.26	1.48	5.4	281	3.4	11.3	3.3	1.1	38%	83%	101
		14	27	a/a	MIA	2	3	50	4	72	82	29	9	27	61	3.61	1.52	6.3	289	3.4	7.6	2.2	1.1	34%	80%	56
DeSclafani,Anthony	R	13	23	aa	MIA	5	4	13	0	75	88	36	8	16	56	4.34	1.39	24.3	294	1.9	6.7	3.6	1.0	34%	71%	83
		14	24	a/a	MIA	6	7	20	0	102	103	47	5	31	79	4.10	1.30	21.1	262	2.7	6.9	2.6	0.4	32%	68%	85
Diaz,Jairo	R	14	23	aa	LAA	2	1	27	11	33	35	9.9	2	9.9	41	2.73	1.37	5.1	275	2.7	11.3	4.1	0.6	39%	82%	137
Dominguez,Jose	R	14	24	aaa	LA	1	2	31	10	33	30	10	1	15	33	2.74	1.35	4.5	243	4.0	8.8	2.2	0.2	32%	79%	99
Drake,Oliver	R	11	24	a/a	BAL	3	5	13	0	66	94	48	11	26	40	6.51	1.81	24.0	328	3.5	5.4	1.6	1.4	36%	66%	12
		13	26	aa	BAL	3	0	19	8	31	23	8	1	14	30	2.18	1.19	6.5	208	4.0	8.7	2.1	0.4	27%	83%	99
		14	27	aa	BAL	2	4	50	31	53	50	22	3	18	55	3.84	1.30	4.3	252	3.1	9.3	3.0	0.4	34%	70%	111
Duffey,Tyler	R	14	24	a/a	MIN	10	3	21	0	127	141	66	17	25	81	4.70	1.31	25.0	282	1.8	5.7	3.2	1.2	31%	67%	63
Edwards,C.J.	R	14	23	aa	CHC	1	2	10	0	48	34	15	1	21	39	2.80	1.15	19.0	200	4.0	7.3	1.8	0.2	25%	74%	91
Eickhoff,Jerad	R	14	24	aa	TEX	10	9	27	0	154	156	91	22	56	117	5.31	1.37	24.0	264	3.3	6.8	2.1	1.3	30%	64%	49
Escobar,Edwin	L	13	21	aa	SF	5	4	10	0	54	44	15	1	11	47	2.52	1.03	20.8	225	1.9	7.8	4.1	0.2	29%	75%	136
		14	22	aaa	BOS	3	10	25	0	138	186	94	21	45	99	6.14	1.67	24.8	323	2.9	6.5	2.2	1.3	36%	65%	36
Flynn,Brian	L	12	22	aa	MIA	3	1	9	0	50	63	28	4	15	30	5.01	1.56	24.3	308	2.8	5.4	2.0	0.7	35%	68%	47
		13	23	a/a	MIA	7	12	27	0	161	172	60	10	48	134	3.38	1.37	25.0	275	2.7	7.5	2.8	0.6	34%	76%	86
		14	24	aaa	MIA	8	10	25	0	140	181	64	10	48	85	4.14	1.64	24.9	315	3.1	5.5	1.8	0.7	36%	75%	43
Foltynewicz,Mike	R	13	22	aa	HOU	5	3	23	3	103	82	37	8	51	85	3.18	1.28	18.4	220	4.4	7.4	1.7	0.7	26%	77%	69
		14	23	aaa	HOU	7	7	21	0	103	105	60	10	49	89	5.26	1.50	21.1	265	4.3	7.8	1.8	0.9	32%	65%	61
Frias,Carlos	R	14	25	a/a	LA	10	5	21	0	124	154	59	5	26	65	4.30	1.46	25.2	306	1.9	4.7	2.5	0.4	34%	69%	62
Gagnon,Drew	R	13	23	aa	MIL	4	9	16	0	84	111	66	16	45	51	7.05	1.85	24.5	319	4.8	5.4	1.1	1.7	34%	64%	-3
		14	24	aa	MIL	11	6	28	0	155	157	81	22	65	101	4.74	1.43	23.5	264	3.8	5.9	1.6	1.3	29%	70%	32
Garcia,Yimi	R	13	23	aa	LA	4	6	49	19	60	41	21	10	15	73	3.17	0.92	4.6	194	2.2	10.8	5.0	1.6	24%	76%	140
		14	24	aaa	LA	4	2	47	5	61	57	18	4	15	58	2.62	1.17	5.2	247	2.2	8.5	3.9	0.6	32%	79%	121
Garvin,Grayson	L	14	25	aa	TAM	1	8	20	0	74	87	36	5	15	50	4.33	1.38	15.5	295	1.8	6.0	3.3	0.6	34%	69%	84
Gilmartin,Sean	L	12	22	a/a	ATL	6	10	27	0	157	169	77	15	38	99	4.39	1.32	24.1	276	2.2	5.7	2.6	0.9	31%	68%	62
		13	23	aaa	ATL	3	8	17	0	91	128	69	13	33	57	6.78	1.77	24.5	332	3.3	5.6	1.7	1.2	37%	62%	21
		14	24	a/a	MIN	9	7	26	0	146	170	74	9	45	108	4.56	1.48	24.1	293	2.8	6.7	2.4	0.6	35%	69%	70
Goforth,David	R	13	25	aa	MIL	4	3	20	5	47	39	22	1	20	30	4.33	1.27	9.5	230	3.9	5.8	1.5	0.3	27%	64%	67
		14	26	aa	MIL	5	4	54	27	65	73	34	3	32	38	4.69	1.61	5.3	285	4.4	5.2	1.2	0.4	33%	69%	44
Gonzales,Marco	L	14	22	a/a	STL	7	3	15	0	84	80	28	8	18	73	2.97	1.16	22.4	252	1.9	7.8	4.1	0.8	30%	78%	112
Gonzalez,Alex	R	14	22	aa	TEX	7	4	15	0	73	78	27	4	26	54	3.37	1.41	20.7	273	3.2	6.6	2.1	0.5	33%	76%	70
Gonzalez,Miguel	R	11	27	a/a	BOS	0	6	16	0	52	71	43	6	23	38	7.51	1.83	15.3	321	4.0	6.6	1.7	1.0	38%	58%	36
		12	28	aaa	BAL	3	2	14	1	45	30	12	1	12	39	2.44	0.93	12.0	192	2.4	8.0	3.4	0.3	25%	74%	126
		14	28	a/a	PHI	0	2	23	7	31	25	10	2	19	33	2.92	1.40	5.7	221	5.4	9.7	1.8	0.7	29%	81%	85
Gonzalez,Severino	R	14	22	aa	PHI	9	13	27	0	159	185	90	25	33	101	5.10	1.37	24.6	292	1.9	5.7	3.1	1.4	32%	66%	54
Graham,J.R.	R	12	22	aa	ATL	3	1	9	0	45	40	19	2	17	37	3.85	1.26	20.6	238	3.4	7.4	2.2	0.4	30%	69%	85
		13	23	aa	ATL	1	3	8	0	36	46	21	0	10	24	5.20	1.59	19.7	316	2.6	6.2	2.3	0.0	38%	64%	78
		14	24	aa	ATL	1	5	27	0	71	92	53	2	27	43	6.65	1.66	11.8	313	3.4	5.4	1.6	0.3	36%	56%	50
Graveman,Kendall	R	14	24	a/a	TOR	4	2	7	0	44	51	12	1	7.3	22	2.36	1.31	26.1	288	1.5	4.5	3.0	0.3	32%	82%	80
Gray,Jonathan	R	14	23	aa	COL	10	5	24	0	124	131	74	14	44	89	5.35	1.41	21.9	273	3.2	6.4	2.0	1.0	31%	63%	51
Haley,Justin	R	14	23	aa	BOS	3	2	6	0	38	36	6.4	2	16	28	1.52	1.38	26.3	251	3.9	6.6	1.7	0.5	30%	92%	64
Healy,Tucker	R	14	24	a/a	OAK	1	2	32	4	44	52	28	4	19	47	5.81	1.63	6.1	297	4.0	9.7	2.4	0.9	39%	64%	79
Heaney,Andrew	L	13	22	aa	MIA	4	1	6	0	34	36	14	2	10	21	3.72	1.37	23.5	276	2.7	5.7	2.1	0.6	32%	73%	61
		14	23	a/a	MIA	9	6	24	0	137	130	53	9	35	120	3.48	1.20	23.0	251	2.3	7.9	3.4	0.6	31%	72%	107
Hembree,Heath	R	12	23	aaa	SF	1	1	39	15	38	30	19	2	17	31	4.55	1.24	4.0	218	4.1	7.3	1.8	0.4	27%	61%	81
		13	24	aaa	SF	1	4	54	31	55	55	23	5	14	53	3.75	1.25	4.2	260	2.3	8.6	3.7	0.8	33%	72%	109
		14	25	aaa	BOS	1	4	48	20	46	55	25	6	19	44	4.91	1.62	4.3	299	3.7	8.6	2.3	1.1	37%	72%	62
Heston,Chris	R	12	24	aa	SF	9	8	25	0	149	151	49	2	41	113	2.94	1.29	24.4	264	2.5	6.8	2.7	0.1	33%	76%	97
		13	25	aaa	SF	7	6	19	0	109	134	66	10	41	80	5.46	1.61	25.4	304	3.4	6.6	1.9	0.8	35%	66%	49
		14	26	aaa	SF	12	9	28	0	173	162	63	12	48	99	3.27	1.21	24.9	249	2.5	5.2	2.1	0.6	28%	74%	61

PITCHER	Th	Yr	Age	LvL	Org	W	L	G	Sv	IP	H	ER	HR	BB	K	ERA	WHIP	BF/G	OBA	bb/9	k/9	Cmd	hr/9	H%	S%	BPV
Holland,Neil	R	13	25	aa	WAS	1	4	41	1	51	58	20	3	11	50	3.56	1.35	5.2	287	1.9	8.8	4.6	0.6	37%	74%	128
		14	26	a/a	WAS	7	4	46	1	77	80	34	6	22	49	4.03	1.33	6.9	270	2.6	5.7	2.2	0.7	31%	71%	59
Holmberg,David	L	12	21	aa	ARI	5	5	15	0	95	118	46	9	22	58	4.38	1.48	27.2	307	2.1	5.5	2.6	0.9	34%	72%	55
		13	22	aa	ARI	5	8	26	0	157	166	64	15	51	100	3.69	1.38	25.4	272	2.9	5.7	2.0	0.9	31%	76%	50
		14	23	aaa	CIN	2	6	18	0	93	128	50	4	31	49	4.90	1.72	23.4	329	3.0	4.7	1.6	0.4	37%	70%	38
Hoyt,James	R	13	27	aa	ATL	0	1	22	1	33	22	13	1	15	26	3.48	1.13	5.9	193	4.1	7.3	1.8	0.3	24%	68%	87
		14	28	a/a	ATL	3	3	52	7	60	70	26	6	26	60	3.95	1.62	5.1	295	4.0	9.1	2.3	0.8	38%	77%	74
Hursh,Jason	R	14	23	aa	ATL	11	7	27	0	148	172	69	5	43	72	4.20	1.45	23.4	291	2.6	4.4	1.7	0.3	32%	69%	49
Jackson,Luke	R	14	23	a/a	TEX	9	5	26	1	123	129	86	16	53	105	6.29	1.47	20.4	271	3.8	7.6	2.0	1.2	32%	58%	53
Jaime,Juan	R	14	27	aaa	ATL	1	0	43	18	41	32	19	1	38	50	4.09	1.69	4.3	216	8.2	11.1	1.3	0.2	32%	74%	100
Jensen,Chris	R	14	24	aa	OAK	12	8	26	0	160	166	64	3	63	78	3.58	1.43	26.2	269	3.5	4.4	1.2	0.2	30%	73%	49
Johnson,Brian	L	14	24	aa	BOS	10	2	20	0	118	94	30	7	33	81	2.29	1.08	23.0	221	2.5	6.2	2.4	0.5	26%	81%	84
Johnson,Pierce	R	14	23	aa	CHC	5	4	18	0	92	67	30	8	55	77	2.93	1.33	21.2	207	5.4	7.6	1.4	0.8	25%	81%	64
Jokisch,Eric	L	12	23	aa	CHC	7	2	18	0	105	100	42	8	34	53	3.58	1.28	23.9	252	2.9	4.6	1.6	0.7	27%	73%	44
		13	24	aa	CHC	11	13	27	0	161	167	73	15	56	115	4.09	1.39	25.1	269	3.2	6.4	2.0	0.9	31%	72%	57
		14	25	aaa	CHC	9	10	26	0	158	183	76	13	33	116	4.33	1.36	25.5	290	1.9	6.6	3.5	0.8	34%	69%	88
Jungmann,Taylor	R	13	24	aa	MIL	10	10	26	0	139	141	87	15	79	70	5.59	1.58	23.6	264	5.1	4.5	0.9	1.0	28%	65%	19
		14	25	a/a	MIL	12	10	28	0	154	165	74	14	65	123	4.33	1.50	23.7	276	3.8	7.2	1.9	0.8	33%	72%	59
Karns,Nathan	R	13	26	aa	WAS	10	6	23	0	133	133	61	17	48	119	4.16	1.37	24.2	263	3.3	8.1	2.5	1.1	31%	73%	69
		14	27	aaa	TAM	9	9	27	0	145	177	106	18	67	121	6.59	1.68	24.2	302	4.1	7.5	1.8	1.1	36%	61%	44
Kela,Keone	R	14	21	aa	TEX	2	1	36	5	39	25	9.9	1	28	47	2.30	1.37	4.5	188	6.4	10.9	1.7	0.3	28%	83%	110
Kickham,Mike	L	12	24	aa	SF	11	10	28	0	151	144	67	9	77	115	4.00	1.47	23.1	254	4.6	6.9	1.5	0.5	30%	73%	61
		13	25	aaa	SF	7	7	20	0	111	109	50	6	44	74	4.06	1.38	23.3	259	3.6	6.0	1.7	0.5	30%	70%	59
		14	26	aaa	SF	8	8	27	0	148	182	71	6	60	104	4.28	1.63	24.4	303	3.6	6.3	1.7	0.4	36%	73%	58
Kingham,Nick	R	14	23	a/a	PIT	6	11	26	0	159	152	62	8	47	96	3.51	1.25	24.9	253	2.7	5.4	2.0	0.4	29%	72%	66
Klein,Phil	R	13	24	aa	TEX	5	1	29	0	54	57	22	4	48	60	3.61	1.97	8.9	274	8.1	10.0	1.2	0.7	36%	83%	64
		14	25	a/a	TEX	3	0	33	10	52	26	3.6	0	21	56	0.63	0.91	5.8	151	3.7	9.7	2.6	0.0	22%	92%	138
Knebel,Corey	R	14	23	a/a	TEX	5	1	34	3	45	26	13	3	22	52	2.54	1.07	5.2	169	4.4	10.4	2.3	0.7	23%	79%	112
Lamb,John	L	10	20	aa	KC	2	1	7	0	33	38	21	2	11	24	5.71	1.50	20.8	283	3.1	6.6	2.1	0.5	34%	60%	67
		11	21	aa	KC	1	2	8	0	35	35	12	3	12	18	3.20	1.33	18.6	254	3.0	4.7	1.6	0.7	29%	77%	46
		14	24	aaa	KC	8	10	27	0	138	151	66	17	66	104	4.30	1.57	22.5	279	4.3	6.8	1.6	1.1	32%	76%	40
Leathersich,Jack	L	14	24	a/a	NYM	3	3	48	1	54	46	18	3	25	80	2.97	1.30	4.7	231	4.1	13.3	3.3	0.4	37%	77%	144
Lee,Zach	R	12	21	aa	LA	4	3	13	0	66	75	35	6	20	44	4.74	1.46	21.6	289	2.8	6.1	2.2	0.8	33%	68%	55
		13	22	aa	LA	10	10	28	0	143	152	62	15	36	114	3.94	1.31	21.1	274	2.2	7.2	3.2	0.9	32%	72%	83
		14	23	aaa	LA	7	13	28	0	151	169	75	14	44	83	4.45	1.41	22.8	285	2.6	5.0	1.9	0.8	31%	69%	43
Leon,Arnold	R	12	24	a/a	OAK	4	0	32	1	51	47	12	4	18	41	2.07	1.26	6.5	246	3.1	7.3	2.3	0.6	30%	87%	80
		13	25	a/a	OAK	9	8	25	0	144	188	72	12	24	79	4.50	1.47	24.7	316	1.5	4.9	3.3	0.7	35%	70%	68
		14	26	aaa	OAK	10	7	27	0	145	185	81	10	49	102	5.00	1.62	23.8	311	3.1	6.3	2.1	0.6	36%	69%	55
Liberatore,Adam	L	12	25	a/a	TAM	4	5	49	9	73	82	23	4	28	40	2.86	1.51	6.4	285	3.5	4.9	1.4	0.5	32%	82%	42
		13	26	a/a	TAM	5	3	44	1	62	60	28	1	25	58	4.09	1.37	5.9	254	3.7	8.4	2.3	0.1	33%	68%	98
		14	27	aaa	TAM	6	1	54	4	65	54	16	1	16	68	2.16	1.07	4.7	226	2.2	9.4	4.2	0.2	31%	79%	150
Lively,Ben	R	14	22	aa	CIN	3	6	13	0	72	66	35	8	35	68	4.37	1.40	23.4	246	4.3	8.5	1.9	1.0	30%	71%	66
Lobstein,Kyle	L	12	23	aa	TAM	8	7	27	0	144	154	72	12	66	111	4.50	1.53	23.2	276	4.1	7.0	1.7	0.7	33%	71%	55
		13	24	a/a	DET	13	7	28	0	168	196	77	9	52	117	4.11	1.48	25.7	293	2.8	6.3	2.2	0.5	34%	72%	67
		14	25	aaa	DET	9	11	26	0	146	210	84	11	44	99	5.17	1.74	25.6	338	2.7	6.1	2.3	0.7	39%	70%	50
Lorenzen,Michael	R	14	22	aa	CIN	4	6	24	0	121	123	47	11	42	75	3.53	1.38	21.1	266	3.2	5.6	1.8	0.8	30%	76%	48
Magill,Matt	R	14	25	aaa	LA	7	6	36	0	85	80	42	6	50	57	4.50	1.53	10.2	250	5.3	6.1	1.2	0.7	29%	71%	46
Martin,Cody	R	13	24	a/a	ATL	6	7	29	1	137	145	60	10	60	117	3.98	1.50	20.4	273	4.0	7.7	1.9	0.7	33%	74%	67
		14	25	aaa	ATL	7	8	27	1	156	171	68	17	56	119	3.92	1.45	24.7	280	3.2	6.9	2.1	1.0	32%	76%	56
Martin,Jarret	L	14	25	aa	LA	1	1	46	7	55	37	21	1	44	52	3.38	1.48	5.1	193	7.3	8.6	1.2	0.2	26%	76%	89
Matz,Steven	L	14	23	aa	NYM	6	5	12	0	71	69	18	3	13	61	2.23	1.14	23.5	254	1.6	7.7	4.8	0.4	32%	81%	140
May,Trevor	R	12	23	aa	PHI	10	13	28	0	150	157	94	24	77	129	5.64	1.56	23.4	271	4.6	7.8	1.7	1.4	31%	67%	40
		13	24	aa	MIN	9	9	27	0	152	168	86	13	68	131	5.13	1.56	24.6	282	4.0	7.7	1.9	0.8	34%	67%	62
		14	25	aaa	MIN	8	6	18	0	98	91	40	4	41	75	3.63	1.34	22.7	247	3.7	6.8	1.8	0.4	30%	72%	73
Mayers,Mike	R	14	23	a/a	STL	6	5	14	0	81	97	29	4	23	47	3.26	1.47	24.9	297	2.5	5.2	2.1	0.4	34%	78%	58
Mazzoni,Cory	R	12	23	aa	NYM	5	5	14	0	81	96	42	9	18	46	4.66	1.42	24.4	298	2.0	5.1	2.5	1.0	33%	69%	51
		13	24	aa	NYM	5	3	13	0	66	77	34	4	18	63	4.66	1.43	21.6	292	2.5	8.6	3.5	0.6	37%	67%	105
		14	25	a/a	NYM	7	1	11	0	64	66	30	5	14	50	4.25	1.25	23.7	267	2.0	7.0	3.5	0.7	32%	67%	94
Mejia,Adalberto	L	14	21	aa	SF	7	9	22	0	108	128	61	8	29	72	5.05	1.46	21.0	296	2.4	6.0	2.5	0.6	34%	65%	64
Mercedes,Melvin	R	14	24	aaa	DET	0	3	46	3	60	82	41	9	16	25	6.12	1.62	5.8	324	2.4	3.7	1.5	1.3	33%	64%	4
Meyer,Alex	R	13	23	aa	MIN	4	3	13	0	70	66	28	3	29	70	3.58	1.36	22.5	252	3.7	9.0	2.5	0.4	33%	73%	100
		14	24	aaa	MIN	7	7	27	0	130	138	64	10	66	124	4.42	1.56	21.2	273	4.5	8.6	1.9	0.7	34%	72%	70

PITCHER	Th	Yr	Age	LvL	Org	W	L	G	Sv	IP	H	ER	HR	BB	K	ERA	WHIP	BF/G	OBA	bb/9	k/9	Cmd	hr/9	H%	S%	BPV
Mitchell,Bryan	R	14	23	a/a	NYY	6	7	23	0	103	124	59	13	46	80	5.17	1.65	20.0	300	4.0	7.0	1.7	1.2	35%	71%	38
Montero,Rafael	R	13	23	a/a	NYM	12	7	27	0	155	138	45	5	31	131	2.60	1.09	22.5	239	1.8	7.6	4.3	0.3	30%	76%	133
		14	24	aaa	NYM	6	4	16	0	80	66	26	3	28	69	2.92	1.18	20.0	226	3.2	7.8	2.4	0.4	29%	75%	97
Montgomery,Mark	R	13	23	aaa	NYY	2	3	25	0	40	44	20	6	27	41	4.60	1.77	7.3	281	6.0	9.2	1.5	1.3	35%	77%	48
		14	24	a/a	NYY	2	1	39	4	51	40	15	4	27	42	2.54	1.30	5.4	215	4.7	7.4	1.6	0.7	26%	83%	70
Montgomery,Mike	L	14	25	aaa	TAM	10	5	25	0	126	140	75	10	50	81	5.32	1.50	21.8	282	3.5	5.8	1.6	0.7	32%	64%	47
Morimando,Shawn	L	14	22	aa	CLE	2	6	10	0	56	69	27	2	16	33	4.24	1.50	24.4	302	2.5	5.3	2.1	0.3	35%	70%	61
Moscot,Jon	R	13	22	aa	CIN	2	1	6	0	31	41	15	4	13	25	4.29	1.72	23.5	319	3.6	7.2	2.0	1.2	37%	79%	38
		14	23	a/a	CIN	8	11	28	0	167	176	69	18	48	105	3.74	1.34	24.8	272	2.6	5.6	2.2	1.0	30%	75%	50
Munson,Kevin	R	12	23	aa	ARI	3	5	44	3	53	65	46	4	27	54	7.87	1.73	5.5	302	4.6	9.1	2.0	0.6	39%	51%	73
		13	24	a/a	ARI	2	4	53	14	55	48	29	7	21	55	4.73	1.26	4.2	236	3.5	9.0	2.6	1.1	29%	64%	84
		14	25	aaa	ARI	4	3	56	2	62	53	18	5	20	66	2.65	1.18	4.5	232	2.9	9.5	3.2	0.7	31%	80%	113
Nesbitt,Angel	R	14	24	aa	DET	1	0	24	6	32	22	8.8	3	14	29	2.46	1.14	5.3	196	4.0	8.0	2.0	0.8	24%	83%	80
Nicolino,Justin	L	13	22	aa	MIA	3	2	9	0	45	74	32	2	13	29	6.28	1.92	23.9	365	2.6	5.7	2.2	0.4	42%	65%	48
		14	23	aa	MIA	14	4	28	0	170	182	62	9	20	68	3.29	1.19	24.4	275	1.1	3.6	3.4	0.5	30%	72%	79
Nolin,Sean	L	13	24	a/a	TOR	9	4	20	0	110	119	41	8	35	96	3.37	1.39	23.2	277	2.8	7.8	2.8	0.7	34%	77%	85
		14	25	aaa	TOR	4	6	17	0	87	92	46	8	38	61	4.69	1.48	22.1	271	3.9	6.3	1.6	0.8	31%	69%	49
Norris,Daniel	L	14	21	a/a	TOR	6	2	13	0	58	53	32	8	25	77	4.93	1.33	18.6	243	3.8	11.9	3.1	1.3	34%	66%	105
Northcraft,Aaron	R	13	23	aa	ATL	8	8	26	0	137	148	67	8	53	105	4.40	1.47	22.6	277	3.5	6.9	2.0	0.5	33%	69%	67
		14	24	a/a	ATL	7	10	26	0	130	162	78	8	55	96	5.36	1.67	22.5	306	3.8	6.7	1.8	0.6	36%	67%	54
Ogando,Nefi	R	14	25	aa	PHI	5	1	48	7	56	74	46	7	29	47	7.40	1.84	5.4	320	4.6	7.6	1.6	1.1	38%	59%	38
Okert,Steven	L	14	23	aa	SF	1	0	24	5	33	27	11	3	11	32	3.04	1.13	5.4	222	2.9	8.8	3.0	0.7	28%	75%	105
Olmos,Edgar	L	13	23	aa	MIA	4	2	38	1	50	56	18	1	30	37	3.23	1.72	6.0	283	5.4	6.6	1.2	0.2	34%	80%	58
		14	24	a/a	MIA	3	3	51	3	78	78	38	7	30	49	4.40	1.39	6.4	264	3.4	5.7	1.7	0.9	29%	70%	46
Oramas,Juan Pablo	L	14	24	a/a	SD	10	7	27	0	136	164	68	12	46	101	4.50	1.54	22.0	299	3.0	6.7	2.2	0.8	35%	72%	57
Ortega,Jose	R	11	23	aaa	DET	1	3	33	0	50	72	44	8	27	36	7.93	1.98	7.4	330	4.9	6.5	1.3	1.5	38%	60%	13
		12	24	aaa	DET	5	8	45	1	63	90	49	4	51	54	7.10	2.24	7.1	336	7.3	7.8	1.1	0.6	41%	67%	38
		13	25	aaa	DET	4	3	40	4	48	34	13	2	34	43	2.45	1.42	5.1	201	6.3	8.0	1.3	0.4	26%	84%	76
		14	26	aaa	DET	2	2	43	1	58	62	30	5	38	37	4.63	1.73	6.1	274	6.0	5.7	1.0	0.7	31%	74%	32
Owens,Henry	L	13	21	aa	BOS	3	1	6	0	30	20	7	3	15	40	2.14	1.16	20.1	193	4.4	11.8	2.7	0.9	27%	87%	116
		14	22	a/a	BOS	17	5	26	0	159	140	65	11	59	145	3.67	1.25	24.9	238	3.3	8.2	2.5	0.6	30%	71%	90
Patton,Spencer	R	14	26	aaa	TEX	5	4	49	18	62	49	31	11	26	66	4.46	1.19	5.1	217	3.7	9.6	2.6	1.6	25%	69%	74
Pena,Ariel	R	12	23	aa	MIL	6	8	26	0	147	153	76	22	66	122	4.67	1.50	24.4	270	4.1	7.5	1.8	1.3	31%	73%	44
		13	24	aa	MIL	8	9	27	0	142	139	76	23	86	112	4.82	1.58	23.2	257	5.4	7.1	1.3	1.4	29%	74%	30
		14	25	aaa	MIL	9	8	25	0	128	113	78	15	79	117	5.47	1.50	22.2	237	5.6	8.2	1.5	1.0	29%	64%	57
Petrick,Zach	R	14	25	a/a	STL	9	6	27	1	134	144	66	15	41	78	4.44	1.38	20.8	276	2.7	5.2	1.9	1.0	30%	70%	42
Pike,Tyler	L	14	20	aa	SEA	3	4	13	0	49	60	43	5	30	30	7.83	1.85	17.6	304	5.6	5.6	1.0	0.8	34%	56%	23
Pineyro,Ivan	R	14	23	aa	CHC	0	4	11	0	49	65	34	7	23	35	6.38	1.82	20.5	322	4.3	6.4	1.5	1.4	36%	67%	19
Portillo,Adys	R	12	21	aa	SD	2	5	8	0	35	35	28	3	24	24	7.20	1.69	19.7	262	6.2	6.1	1.0	0.8	30%	56%	35
		14	23	aa	SD	1	4	46	0	56	48	22	2	41	60	3.56	1.61	5.4	236	6.7	9.8	1.5	0.3	32%	77%	87
Purke,Matt	L	14	24	aa	WAS	1	6	8	0	31	46	30	5	16	18	8.48	1.98	18.8	341	4.7	5.1	1.1	1.4	37%	57%	-1
Ramirez,Noe	R	14	25	aa	BOS	2	1	42	18	67	69	21	0	17	45	2.85	1.28	6.6	267	2.3	6.0	2.7	0.0	32%	75%	93
Ranaudo,Anthony	R	12	23	aa	BOS	1	3	9	0	38	50	37	5	28	23	8.88	2.06	20.4	318	6.7	5.4	0.8	1.1	35%	55%	8
		13	24	a/a	BOS	11	5	25	0	140	134	59	11	49	104	3.77	1.30	23.1	253	3.1	6.7	2.1	0.7	30%	72%	68
		14	25	aaa	BOS	14	4	24	0	138	138	53	10	57	89	3.44	1.41	24.3	262	3.7	5.8	1.6	0.7	30%	77%	50
Ray,Robbie	L	13	22	aa	WAS	5	2	11	0	58	63	28	4	19	50	4.38	1.42	22.4	278	3.0	7.8	2.6	0.7	34%	69%	80
		14	23	aaa	DET	7	6	20	0	100	123	57	7	44	61	5.14	1.66	22.5	303	4.0	5.5	1.4	0.6	34%	68%	38
Reed,Chris	L	12	22	aa	LA	0	4	12	0	35	34	21	2	19	25	5.46	1.50	12.7	255	4.8	6.4	1.3	0.5	30%	62%	55
		13	23	aa	LA	4	11	29	0	138	150	74	10	65	91	4.82	1.57	20.8	279	4.3	5.9	1.4	0.7	32%	69%	43
		14	24	a/a	LA	4	11	28	0	158	153	69	13	57	112	3.91	1.33	23.5	256	3.2	6.4	2.0	0.7	30%	72%	62
Riefenhauser,C.J.	L	14	24	aaa	TAM	3	3	39	1	58	48	11	3	24	45	1.71	1.25	6.0	228	3.8	7.0	1.8	0.5	28%	89%	75
Rivero,Armando	R	14	26	a/a	CHC	5	1	49	11	65	52	20	7	30	79	2.73	1.26	5.4	220	4.2	11.0	2.6	0.9	30%	83%	104
Rivero,Felipe	L	14	23	aa	WAS	2	7	10	0	44	48	21	4	16	31	4.26	1.47	18.7	280	3.3	6.4	1.9	0.8	33%	72%	55
Rodriguez,Eduardo	L	13	20	aa	BAL	4	3	11	0	60	57	31	6	23	52	4.72	1.35	22.6	254	3.5	7.8	2.3	0.9	31%	66%	73
		14	21	aa	BOS	6	8	22	0	120	138	59	6	37	93	4.46	1.45	23.3	290	2.7	7.0	2.6	0.5	35%	68%	78
Rodriguez,Joely	L	14	23	aa	PIT	6	11	30	1	134	161	75	8	39	59	5.01	1.49	19.3	299	2.6	3.9	1.5	0.6	32%	66%	33
Rogers,Taylor	R	13	26	aa	SF	5	9	26	1	104	119	65	4	54	56	5.63	1.65	18.0	288	4.6	4.8	1.0	0.3	33%	64%	38
		14	24	aa	MIN	11	6	24	0	145	175	64	4	37	92	3.97	1.46	25.9	299	2.3	5.7	2.5	0.3	35%	71%	73
Romero,Enny	L	14	23	aaa	TAM	5	11	25	0	126	147	75	14	52	101	5.36	1.57	22.1	292	3.7	7.2	2.0	1.0	34%	67%	52
Rucinski,Drew	R	14	26	aa	LAA	10	6	26	0	149	176	69	8	43	112	4.15	1.48	24.6	296	2.6	6.8	2.6	0.5	35%	71%	77
Ryan,Kyle	L	14	23	a/a	DET	10	10	26	0	160	181	80	16	36	80	4.52	1.36	25.7	286	2.0	4.5	2.2	0.9	31%	68%	45

PITCHER	Th	Yr	Age	LvL	Org	W	L	G	Sv	IP	H	ER	HR	BB	K	ERA	WHIP	BF/G	OBA	bb/9	k/9	Cmd	hr/9	H%	S%	BPV
Sadler,Casey	R	13	23	a/a	PIT	11	7	24	0	136	137	57	11	40	58	3.79	1.30	23.4	263	2.7	3.8	1.4	0.7	28%	72%	34
		14	24	aaa	PIT	11	4	21	0	125	137	46	10	23	61	3.31	1.28	24.4	281	1.6	4.4	2.7	0.7	30%	76%	60
Sampson,Adrian	R	14	23	a/a	PIT	11	6	28	0	167	166	58	9	34	88	3.12	1.19	23.9	260	1.8	4.7	2.6	0.5	29%	75%	70
Sanchez,Aaron	R	14	22	a/a	TOR	3	7	22	0	100	102	55	7	57	74	4.90	1.59	20.1	265	5.1	6.6	1.3	0.7	31%	69%	50
Sanchez,Victor	R	14	19	aa	SEA	7	6	23	0	125	133	61	15	30	91	4.38	1.30	22.4	274	2.2	6.5	3.0	1.1	31%	69%	70
Sappington,Mark	R	14	24	aa	LAA	1	4	9	0	43	52	39	2	36	28	8.13	2.05	23.4	300	7.6	5.9	0.8	0.5	35%	57%	33
Selman,Sam	L	14	24	a/a	KC	4	6	33	0	97	100	53	7	56	75	4.93	1.61	13.0	268	5.2	6.9	1.3	0.6	32%	69%	52
Sherfy,Jimmie	R	14	23	aa	ARI	3	1	37	1	38	40	26	5	18	38	6.16	1.52	4.5	270	4.3	8.9	2.1	1.1	34%	60%	65
Shreve,Chasen	L	13	23	aa	ATL	3	1	36	0	43	51	27	1	23	24	5.71	1.74	5.4	299	4.8	5.1	1.1	0.2	34%	64%	41
		14	24	a/a	ATL	5	3	46	9	64	58	22	4	12	74	3.05	1.09	5.4	242	1.7	10.4	6.2	0.6	34%	73%	182
Smith,Carson	R	13	24	aa	SEA	1	3	44	15	50	40	13	1	19	62	2.35	1.17	4.5	221	3.3	11.1	3.3	0.2	33%	79%	141
		14	25	aaa	SEA	1	3	39	10	43	48	14	1	12	38	3.03	1.39	4.6	283	2.5	7.9	3.1	0.2	36%	77%	106
Smith,Kyle	R	14	22	aa	HOU	5	5	21	0	95	99	50	14	24	85	4.69	1.29	18.7	270	2.3	8.1	3.6	1.4	32%	68%	84
Smith,Nate	L	14	23	aa	LAA	5	3	11	0	62	56	25	3	30	57	3.57	1.38	23.8	242	4.3	8.3	1.9	0.5	31%	74%	83
Snodgress,Scott	L	13	24	aa	CHW	11	11	26	0	144	179	101	13	70	77	6.31	1.74	25.2	307	4.4	4.8	1.1	0.8	34%	63%	21
		14	25	a/a	CHW	6	8	29	0	139	155	70	15	61	79	4.54	1.56	21.0	283	4.0	5.1	1.3	1.0	31%	73%	27
Spomer,Kurt	R	14	25	a/a	LAA	4	4	20	0	34	33	10	1	16	11	2.69	1.41	7.3	252	4.1	3.0	0.7	0.2	27%	80%	31
Stephenson,Robert	R	14	21	aa	CIN	7	10	27	0	137	124	80	21	71	126	5.29	1.43	21.5	244	4.7	8.3	1.8	1.4	28%	66%	52
Stilson,John	R	12	22	aa	TOR	2	4	17	1	50	62	34	7	23	39	6.14	1.69	13.3	305	4.1	7.0	1.7	1.3	35%	65%	33
		13	23	a/a	TOR	6	2	35	5	50	45	14	3	15	45	2.59	1.19	5.7	242	2.6	8.1	3.1	0.6	30%	81%	101
		14	24	aaa	TOR	2	0	25	1	34	45	16	3	19	27	4.16	1.88	6.4	319	5.0	7.2	1.4	0.7	38%	78%	44
Stoppelman,Lee	L	13	23	a/a	STL	4	2	40	6	42	26	8	3	16	44	1.61	0.99	4.0	180	3.3	9.3	2.8	0.6	24%	88%	116
		14	24	a/a	STL	1	3	47	4	49	51	32	4	25	47	5.88	1.54	4.6	267	4.6	8.5	1.9	0.8	33%	61%	67
Sulbaran,J.C.	R	14	25	aa	KC	8	10	25	0	127	154	59	12	57	90	4.19	1.66	22.8	300	4.0	6.4	1.6	0.8	35%	76%	42
Syndergaard,Noah	R	13	21	aa	NYM	6	1	11	0	54	48	18	8	11	62	3.04	1.09	19.2	239	1.8	10.3	5.7	1.3	31%	79%	151
		14	22	aaa	NYM	9	7	26	0	133	141	53	8	34	130	3.58	1.32	21.2	273	2.3	8.8	3.8	0.6	35%	73%	116
Thompson,Jake	R	14	20	aa	TEX	4	1	9	0	47	43	19	4	22	44	3.74	1.39	21.8	245	4.3	8.6	2.0	0.7	31%	74%	79
Thompson,Taylor	R	13	26	a/a	CHW	5	4	44	13	66	74	36	3	20	51	4.88	1.41	6.4	283	2.7	6.9	2.6	0.4	34%	64%	82
		14	27	aaa	CHW	3	0	39	7	59	56	16	4	32	54	2.40	1.49	6.5	251	4.9	8.3	1.7	0.5	32%	86%	74
Tropeano,Nick	R	14	24	aaa	HOU	9	5	23	0	125	98	44	11	32	102	3.20	1.04	20.9	218	2.3	7.4	3.2	0.8	26%	72%	100
Turley,Josh	L	14	24	aa	DET	3	4	9	0	50	59	23	8	15	22	4.17	1.49	23.9	295	2.8	4.0	1.4	1.4	30%	77%	7
Urena,Jose	R	14	23	aa	MIA	13	8	26	0	162	173	68	12	29	101	3.78	1.25	25.3	275	1.6	5.6	3.5	0.7	31%	71%	87
Valdez,Jose	R	13	25	aa	SF	3	2	38	0	56	69	34	2	45	43	5.54	2.03	7.2	304	7.2	7.0	1.0	0.2	37%	71%	49
		14	24	aa	DET	2	3	47	18	57	62	29	6	25	53	4.53	1.53	5.3	279	4.0	8.3	2.1	0.9	34%	72%	65
		14	31	a/a	BOS	0	2	24	4	36	52	12	3	13	20	2.96	1.81	6.9	340	3.2	5.1	1.6	0.6	38%	85%	32
Verhagen,Drew	R	13	23	aa	DET	2	5	12	0	60	61	24	3	16	32	3.60	1.29	20.5	265	2.5	4.8	2.0	0.5	30%	72%	58
		14	24	aaa	DET	6	7	19	0	110	138	56	6	26	50	4.56	1.49	25.0	308	2.1	4.1	2.0	0.5	34%	68%	45
Vizcaino,Arodys	R	11	21	a/a	ATL	3	3	17	0	57	56	25	4	17	56	3.90	1.29	14.0	252	2.8	8.9	3.2	0.6	33%	70%	107
		14	24	a/a	CHC	1	1	31	1	32	37	18	2	15	27	4.97	1.61	4.6	290	4.1	7.5	1.8	0.6	35%	68%	62
Whiting,Boone	R	13	24	a/a	STL	8	7	27	0	136	150	63	12	47	109	4.19	1.44	21.5	280	3.1	7.2	2.3	0.8	33%	72%	68
		14	25	aaa	STL	4	7	21	0	97	105	47	8	43	80	4.40	1.53	20.0	279	4.0	7.4	1.9	0.7	34%	72%	61
Wieland,Joe	R	14	24	a/a	SD	2	2	6	0	33	31	10	2	4.5	23	2.87	1.08	21.3	251	1.2	6.2	5.0	0.5	30%	74%	133
Wilson,Tyler	R	13	24	aa	BAL	7	5	16	0	89	99	46	16	23	57	4.59	1.36	23.3	281	2.3	5.8	2.5	1.6	30%	72%	39
		14	25	a/a	BAL	14	8	28	0	167	188	80	21	44	126	4.32	1.39	25.1	286	2.4	6.8	2.9	1.2	33%	72%	65
Winkler,Daniel	R	14	24	aa	COL	5	2	12	0	70	41	15	7	18	55	1.98	0.85	21.4	173	2.4	7.0	3.0	0.9	19%	84%	97
Wisler,Matt	R	14	22	a/a	SD	10	5	28	0	147	155	65	18	36	123	4.01	1.31	21.6	273	2.2	7.6	3.4	1.1	32%	73%	84
Wittgren,Nick	R	14	23	aa	MIA	5	5	52	20	66	82	29	5	14	47	4.02	1.45	5.4	305	1.9	6.4	3.4	0.7	35%	73%	82
Wojciechowski,Asher	R	12	24	aa	HOU	2	2	8	0	44	33	12	0	13	29	2.38	1.05	21.1	209	2.7	5.9	2.2	0.0	26%	75%	94
		13	25	a/a	HOU	11	8	28	1	160	154	69	12	53	110	3.87	1.29	23.5	254	3.0	6.2	2.1	0.7	29%	71%	65
		14	26	aaa	HOU	4	4	15	0	76	101	44	10	21	48	5.22	1.61	22.4	321	2.5	5.7	2.3	1.2	35%	70%	36
Wright,Austin	L	13	24	aa	PHI	6	5	27	0	94	101	68	14	58	64	6.53	1.69	15.8	276	5.5	6.2	1.1	1.3	30%	62%	21
		14	25	aa	PHI	2	4	32	0	48	48	32	6	45	31	5.98	1.94	7.1	261	8.5	5.9	0.7	1.1	29%	70%	21
Wright,Mike	R	12	22	aa	BAL	5	3	12	0	62	79	39	8	16	38	5.68	1.53	22.6	311	2.4	5.5	2.3	1.2	34%	64%	40
		13	23	a/a	BAL	11	3	27	0	150	183	63	11	40	116	3.79	1.48	24.0	301	2.4	6.9	2.9	0.7	36%	75%	77
		14	24	aaa	BAL	5	11	26	0	143	179	83	11	40	85	5.22	1.54	23.9	308	2.6	5.3	2.1	0.7	35%	66%	47
Ybarra,Tyler	L	14	25	aa	TOR	4	4	38	0	53	51	34	10	32	36	5.76	1.57	6.1	256	5.4	6.0	1.1	1.7	27%	67%	12
Ynoa,Gabriel	R	14	21	aa	NYM	3	2	11	0	66	75	29	8	11	38	4.00	1.28	24.7	285	1.4	5.2	3.6	1.1	31%	72%	71
Zych,Tony	R	13	23	aa	CHC	5	5	47	3	56	58	22	2	22	34	3.58	1.42	5.1	268	3.5	5.5	1.6	0.3	31%	74%	57
		14	24	aa	CHC	4	5	45	2	58	86	39	3	19	29	5.97	1.80	6.0	344	2.9	4.5	1.6	0.5	38%	65%	31

This section of the book may be the smallest as far as word count is concerned, but may be the most important, as this is where players' skills and potential are tied together and ranked against their peers. The rankings that follow are divided into long-term potential in the major leagues and shorter-term fantasy value.

HQ100: Lists the top 100 minor league prospects in terms of long-range potential in the major leagues. The overall list is the work of five minor-league analysts at BaseballHQ.com (Rob Gordon, Jeremy Deloney, Brent Hershey, Colby Garrapy and Chris Mallonee). Gordon and Deloney also provide their own personal lists.

ORGANIZATIONAL: Lists the top 15 minor league prospects within each organization in terms of long-range potential in the major leagues.

POSITIONAL: Lists the top 15 prospects, by position, in terms of long-range potential in the major leagues.

TOP POWER: Lists the top 25 prospects that have the potential to hit for power in the major leagues, combining raw power, plate discipline, and at the ability to make their power game-usable.

TOP BA: Lists the top 25 prospects that have the potential to hit for high batting average in the major leagues, combining contact ability, plate discipline, hitting mechanics and strength.

TOP SPEED: Lists the top 25 prospects that have the potential to steal bases in the major leagues, combining raw speed and base-running instincts.

TOP FASTBALL: Lists the top 25 pitchers that have the best fastball, combining velocity and pitch movement.

TOP BREAKING BALL: Lists the top 25 pitchers that have the best breaking ball, combining pitch movement, strikeout potential, and consistency.

2014 TOP FANTASY PROSPECTS: Lists the top 75 minor league prospects that will have the most value to their respective fantasy teams in 2015. This list is ranked in terms of short-term value only.

TOP 100 ARCHIVE: Takes a look back at the top 100 lists from the past eight years.

The rankings in this book are the creation of the minor league department at BaseballHQ.com. While several baseball personnel contributed player information to the book, no opinions were solicited or received in comparing players.

THE HQ100: TOP PROSPECTS OF 2015

#					#			
1	Kris Bryant	3B	CHC		51	Rusney Castillo	OF	BOS
2	Byron Buxton	OF	MIN		52	Sean Manaea	P	KC
3	Carlos Correa	SS	HOU		53	A.J. Cole	P	WAS
4	Addison Russell	SS	CHC		54	Matt Wisler	P	SD
5	Corey Seager	SS	LA		55	Raimel Tapia	OF	COL
6	Francisco Lindor	SS	CLE		56	C.J. Edwards	P	CHC
7	Joc Pederson	OF	LA		57	Dalton Pompey	OF	TOR
8	Miguel Sano	3B	MIN		58	Hunter Renfroe	OF	SD
9	Lucas Giolito	P	WAS		59	Hunter Dozier	3B	KC
10	Joey Gallo	3B	TEX		60	Brandon Nimmo	OF	NYM
11	Dylan Bundy	P	BAL		61	Tim Anderson	SS	CHW
12	Jorge Soler	OF	CHC		62	Maikel Franco	3B	PHI
13	Archie Bradley	P	ARI		63	Mike Foltynewicz	P	HOU
14	Julio Urias	P	LA		64	Nick Kingham	P	PIT
15	Jon Gray	P	COL		65	Eddie Butler	P	COL
16	Daniel Norris	P	TOR		66	Steven Matz	P	NYM
17	Carlos Rodon	P	CHW		67	Domingo Santana	OF	HOU
18	Tyler Glasnow	P	PIT		68	Aaron Judge	OF	NYY
19	Noah Syndergaard	P	NYM		69	Daniel Robertson	SS	OAK
20	Blake Swihart	C	BOS		70	Stephen Piscotty	OF	STL
21	Aaron Sanchez	P	TOR		71	Kyle Freeland	P	COL
22	Henry Owens	P	BOS		72	Kevin Plawecki	C	NYM
23	Jameson Taillon	P	PIT		73	Lucas Sims	P	ATL
24	Robert Stephenson	P	CIN		74	Yasmany Tomas	OF	ARI
25	Andrew Heaney	P	LAA		75	Jose Peraza	2B	ATL
26	David Dahl	OF	COL		76	Eduardo Rodriguez	P	BOS
27	Jose Berrios	P	MIN		77	Max Fried	P	ATL
28	Jorge Alfaro	C	TEX		78	Manuel Margot	OF	BOS
29	Hunter Harvey	P	BAL		79	Matt Olson	1B	OAK
30	Alex Meyer	P	MIN		80	Ryan McMahon	3B	COL
31	Kohl Stewart	P	MIN		81	Alex Gonzalez	P	TEX
32	J.P. Crawford	SS	PHI		82	Tyler Beede	P	SF
33	Alex Jackson	OF	SEA		83	Alen Hanson	SS	PIT
34	Jesse Winker	OF	CIN		84	Grant Holmes	P	LA
35	Raul Mondesi	SS	KC		85	Aaron Blair	P	ARI
36	D.J. Peterson	3B	SEA		86	Michael Taylor	OF	WAS
37	Austin Meadows	OF	PIT		87	Trea Turner	SS	SD/WAS
38	Josh Bell	OF	PIT		88	Christian Bethancourt	C	ATL
39	Kyle Crick	P	SF		89	Marco Gonzales	P	STL
40	Luis Severino	P	NYY		90	Michael Conforto	OF	NYM
41	Nick Gordon	SS	MIN		91	Sean Newcomb	P	LAA
42	Kyle Schwarber	OF	CHC		92	Alex Colome	P	TAM
43	Aaron Nola	P	PHI		93	Jeff Hoffman	P	TOR
44	Kyle Zimmer	P	KC		94	Luke Jackson	P	TEX
45	Alex Reyes	P	STL		95	Lewis Brinson	OF	TEX
46	Braden Shipley	P	ARI		96	Willy Adames	SS	TAM
47	Albert Almora	OF	CHC		97	Jake Thompson	P	TEX
48	Clint Frazier	OF	CLE		98	Nick Williams	OF	TEX
49	Tyler Kolek	P	MIA		99	Colin Moran	3B	HOU
50	Mark Appel	P	HOU		100	Bradley Zimmer	OF	CLE

ROB GORDON'S TOP 100

#	Player	Pos	Team	#	Player	Pos	Team
1	Kris Bryant	3B	CHC	51	Jose Peraza	2B	ATL
2	Byron Buxton	OF	MIN	52	Raimel Tapia	OF	COL
3	Carlos Correa	SS	HOU	53	Steven Matz	LHP	NYM
4	Joc Pederson	OF	LA	54	Lucas Sims	RHP	ATL
5	Corey Seager	SS	LA	55	Rusney Castillo	OF	BOS
6	Miguel Sano	3B	MIN	56	Dalton Pompey	OF	TOR
7	Jorge Soler	OF	CHC	57	Kevin Plawecki	C	NYM
8	Joey Gallo	3B	TEX	58	Raul Mondesi	SS	KC
9	Addison Russell	SS	CHC	59	C.J. Edwards	RHP	CHC
10	Lucas Giolito	RHP	WAS	60	Max Fried	LHP	ATL
11	Francisco Lindor	SS	CLE	61	A.J. Cole	RHP	WAS
12	Archie Bradley	RHP	ARI	62	Luis Severino	RHP	NYY
13	Dylan Bundy	RHP	BAL	63	Christian Walker	1B	BAL
14	Julio Urias	LHP	LA	64	Kyle Freeland	LHP	COL
15	Tyler Glasnow	RHP	PIT	65	Matt Wisler	RHP	SD
16	Noah Syndergaard	RHP	NYM	66	Trevor May	RHP	MIN
17	Daniel Norris	LHP	TOR	67	Nick Kingham	RHP	PIT
18	Henry Owens	LHP	BOS	68	Alen Hanson	SS	PIT
19	Jon Gray	RHP	COL	69	Grant Holmes	RHP	LA
20	David Dahl	OF	COL	70	Mike Foltynewicz	RHP	HOU
21	Robert Stephenson	RHP	CIN	71	Marco Gonzales	LHP	STL
22	Blake Swihart	C	BOS	72	Sean Manaea	LHP	KC
23	Carlos Rodon	LHP	CHW	73	Stephen Piscotty	OF	STL
24	Hunter Harvey	RHP	BAL	74	J.P. Crawford	SS	PHI
25	Jameson Taillon	RHP	PIT	75	Christian Bethancourt	C	ATL
26	Jose Berrios	RHP	MIN	76	Michael Conforto	OF	NYM
27	Jorge Alfaro	C	TEX	77	Nick Williams	OF	TEX
28	Aaron Sanchez	RHP	TOR	78	Jose De Leon	RHP	LA
29	Andrew Heaney	LHP	LAA	79	Aaron Blair	RHP	ARI
30	Kyle Schwarber	C/OF	CHC	80	Aaron Judge	OF	NYY
31	Alex Reyes	RHP	STL	81	Mark Appel	RHP	HOU
32	Josh Bell	OF	PIT	82	Colin Moran	3B	HOU
33	Kohl Stewart	RHP	MIN	83	Steven Moya	OF	DET
34	D.J. Peterson	3B	SEA	84	Eddie Butler	RHP	COL
35	Albert Almora	OF	CHC	85	Brandon Drury	3B	ARI
36	Alex Jackson	OF	SEA	86	Billy McKinney	OF	CHC
37	Jesse Winker	OF	CIN	87	Yasmany Tomas	OF	ARI
38	Alex Meyer	RHP	MIN	88	Hunter Renfroe	OF	SD
39	Aaron Nola	RHP	PHI	89	Hunter Dozier	3B	KC
40	Nick Gordon	SS	MIN	90	Trea Turner	SS	SD/WAS
41	Clint Frazier	OF	CLE	91	Tim Anderson	SS	CHW
42	Austin Meadows	OF	PIT	92	Alex Guerrero	2B	LA
43	Domingo Santana	OF	HOU	93	Dominic Smith	1B	NYM
44	Kyle Zimmer	RHP	KC	94	Michael Gettys	OF	SD
45	Tyler Kolek	RHP	MIA	95	Luke Jackson	RHP	TEX
46	Braden Shipley	RHP	ARI	96	Gary Sanchez	C	NYY
47	Maikel Franco	3B	PHI	97	Eduardo Rodriguez	LHP	BOS
48	Brandon Nimmo	OF	NYM	98	Jeff Hoffman	RHP	TOR
49	Kyle Crick	RHP	SF	99	Bradley Zimmer	OF	CLE
50	Ryan McMahon	3B	COL	100	Brandon Finnegan	LHP	KC

JEREMY DELONEY'S TOP 100

#	Player	Pos	Team	#	Player	Pos	Team
1	Byron Buxton	OF	MIN	51	Alex Gonzalez	RHP	TEX
2	Kris Bryant	3B	CHC	52	Nick Gordon	SS	MIN
3	Francisco Lindor	SS	CLE	53	Kohl Stewart	RHP	MIN
4	Corey Seager	SS	LA	54	Alex Reyes	RHP	STL
5	Dylan Bundy	RHP	BAL	55	Sean Manaea	LHP	KC
6	Miguel Sano	3B	MIN	56	Kyle Zimmer	RHP	KC
7	Carlos Correa	SS	HOU	57	Matt Wisler	RHP	SD
8	Addison Russell	SS	CHC	58	Tyler Beede	RHP	SF
9	Joc Pederson	OF	LA	59	Tyler Kolek	RHP	MIA
10	Jon Gray	RHP	COL	60	Jesse Winker	OF	CIN
11	Archie Bradley	RHP	ARI	61	Reese McGuire	C	PIT
12	Carlos Rodon	LHP	CHW	62	Willy Adames	SS	TAM
13	Tyler Glasnow	RHP	PIT	63	Aaron Judge	OF	NYY
14	Lucas Giolito	RHP	WAS	64	Kevin Plawecki	C	NYM
15	Daniel Norris	LHP	TOR	65	Clint Frazier	OF	CLE
16	Henry Owens	LHP	BOS	66	David Dahl	OF	COL
17	Joey Gallo	3B	TEX	67	Aaron Nola	RHP	PHI
18	Robert Stephenson	RHP	CIN	68	Brandon Nimmo	OF	NYM
19	Kyle Crick	RHP	SF	69	A.J. Cole	RHP	WAS
20	Blake Swihart	C	BOS	70	Grant Holmes	RHP	LA
21	Jameson Taillon	RHP	PIT	71	Jorge Alfaro	C	TEX
22	Jorge Soler	OF	CHC	72	Michael Conforto	OF	NYM
23	Aaron Sanchez	RHP	TOR	73	Michael Lorenzen	RHP	CIN
24	Braden Shipley	RHP	ARI	74	Kyle Freeland	LHP	COL
25	Julio Urias	LHP	LA	75	Miguel Almonte	RHP	KC
26	Hunter Renfroe	OF	SD	76	Hunter Harvey	RHP	BAL
27	Luis Severino	RHP	NYY	77	Brandon Finnegan	LHP	KC
28	Alex Jackson	OF	SEA	78	Aaron Blair	RHP	ARI
29	Raul Mondesi	SS	KC	79	Raimel Tapia	OF	COL
30	Andrew Heaney	LHP	LAA	80	Vince Velasquez	RHP	HOU
31	J.P. Crawford	SS	PHI	81	Luke Jackson	RHP	TEX
32	Jose Berrios	RHP	MIN	82	Mark Appel	RHP	HOU
33	Daniel Robertson	SS	OAK	83	Jake Thompson	RHP	TEX
34	Austin Meadows	OF	PIT	84	Billy McKinney	OF	CHC
35	Nick Kingham	RHP	PIT	85	Josh Bell	OF	PIT
36	Eddie Butler	RHP	COL	86	Bradley Zimmer	OF	CLE
37	Alex Meyer	RHP	MIN	87	Jeff Hoffman	RHP	TOR
38	D.J. Peterson	3B	SEA	88	Michael Taylor	OF	WAS
39	Kyle Schwarber	C/OF	CHC	89	Maikel Franco	3B	PHI
40	Hunter Dozier	3B	KC	90	Alen Hanson	SS	PIT
41	Rusney Castillo	OF	BOS	91	Max Pentecost	C	TOR
42	Dalton Pompey	OF	TOR	92	Rob Kaminsky	LHP	STL
43	Noah Syndergaard	RHP	NYM	93	Rafael Montero	RHP	NYM
44	Matt Olson	1B	OAK	94	Brandon Drury	3B	ARI
45	C.J. Edwards	RHP	CHC	95	Lewis Brinson	OF	TEX
46	Albert Almora	OF	CHC	96	Gary Sanchez	C	NYY
47	Mike Foltynewicz	RHP	HOU	97	Ryan McMahon	3B	COL
48	Stephen Piscotty	OF	STL	98	Yasmany Tomas	OF	ARI
49	Tim Anderson	SS	CHW	99	Domingo Santana	OF	HOU
50	Alex Colome	RHP	TAM	100	Steven Matz	LHP	NYM

TOP PROSPECTS BY ORGANIZATION

AL EAST

BALTIMORE ORIOLES
1. Dylan Bundy, RHP
2. Hunter Harvey, RHP
3. Zach Davies, RHP
4. Christian Walker, 1B
5. Tim Berry, LHP
6. Chance Sisco, C
7. Dariel Alvarez, OF
8. Jomar Reyes, 3B
9. Stephen Tarpley, LHP
10. Josh Hart, OF
11. Brian Gonzalez, LHP
12. Mike Wright, RHP
13. Michael Ohlman, C
14. Henry Urrutia, OF
15. Mike Yastrzemski, OF

BOSTON RED SOX
1. Henry Owens, LHP
2. Blake Swihart, C
3. Rusney Castillo, OF
4. Matt Barnes, RHP
5. Brian Johnson, LHP
6. Rafael Devers, 3B
7. Manuel Margot, OF
8. Garin Cecchini, 3B
9. Eduardo Rodriguez, LHP
10. Anthony Ranaudo, RHP
11. Edwin Escobar, LHP
12. Michael Kopech, RHP
13. Michael Chavis, 3B
14. Deven Marrero, SS
15. Trey Ball, LHP

NEW YORK YANKEES
1. Luis Severino, RHP
2. Aaron Judge, OF
3. Ian Clarkin, LHP
4. Gary Sanchez, C
5. Jacob Lindgren, RHP
6. Jorge Mateo, SS
7. Domingo German, RHP
8. Rob Refsnyder, 2B
9. Greg Bird, 1B
10. Eric Jagielo, 3B
11. Luis Torrens, C
12. Bryan Mitchell, RHP
13. Miguel Andujar, 3B
14. Jose Ramirez, RHP
15. Tyler Austin, OF

TAMPA BAY RAYS
1. Alex Colome, RHP
2. Willy Adames, SS
3. Casey Gillaspie, 1B
4. Blake Snell, RHP
5. Enny Romero, LHP
6. Taylor Guerrieri, RHP
7. Steven Souza, OF
8. Brent Honeywell, RHP
9. Ryan Brett, 2B
10. Justin O'Conner, C
11. Mikie Mahtook, OF
12. Nate Karns, RHP
13. Richie Shaffer, 3B
14. Ryne Stanek, RHP
15. Hak-Ju Lee, SS

TORONTO BLUE JAYS
1. Daniel Norris, LHP
2. Aaron Sanchez, RHP
3. Dalton Pompey, OF
4. Jeff Hoffman, RHP
5. Max Pentecost, C
6. Devon Travis, 2B
7. Miguel Castro, RHP
8. Roberto Osuna, RHP
9. Sean Reid-Foley, RHP
10. Dwight Smith, OF
11. Richard Urena, SS
12. Jairo Labourt, LHP
13. Matt Smoral, LHP
14. Matt Dean, 1B
15. Alberto Tirado, RHP

AL CENTRAL

CHICAGO WHITE SOX
1. Carlos Rodon, LHP
2. Tim Anderson, SS
3. Spencer Adams, RHP
4. Francellis Montas, RHP
5. Tyler Danish, RHP
6. Courtney Hawkins, OF
7. Carlos Sanchez, 2B
8. Micah Johnson, 2B
9. Trey Michalczewski, 3B
10. Michael Ynoa, RHP
11. Nolan Sanburn, RHP
12. Matt Davidson, 3B
13. Adam Engel, OF
14. Trayce Thompson, OF
15. Jacob May, OF

CLEVELAND INDIANS
1. Francisco Lindor, SS
2. Clint Frazier, OF
3. Bradley Zimmer, OF
4. Cody Anderson, RHP
5. Bobby Bradley, 1B
6. Tyler Naquin, OF
7. James Ramsey, OF
8. Justus Sheffield, LHP
9. Dylan Baker, RHP
10. Francisco Mejia, C
11. Giovanny Urshela, 3B
12. Austin Adams, RHP
13. Mitch Brown, RHP
14. Jesus Aguilar, 1B
15. Erik Gonzalez, INF

DETROIT TIGERS
1. Derek Hill, OF
2. Steven Moya, OF
3. Buck Farmer, RHP
4. James McCann, C
5. Kevin Ziomek, LHP
6. Hernan Perez, 2B/SS
7. Spencer Turnbull, RHP
8. Melvin Mercedes, RHP
9. Grayson Greiner, C
10. Austin Kubitza, RHP
11. Drew VerHagen, RHP
12. Joe Jimenez, RHP
13. Tyler Collins, OF
14. Javier Betancourt, 2B/SS
15. Dixon Machado, SS

KANSAS CITY ROYALS
1. Raul Mondesi, SS
2. Hunter Dozier, 3B
3. Sean Manaea, LHP
4. Kyle Zimmer, RHP
5. Miguel Almonte, RHP
6. Brandon Finnegan, LHP
7. Foster Griffin, LHP
8. Cheslor Cuthbert, 3B
9. Chase Vallot, C
10. Elier Hernandez, OF
11. Scott Blewett, RHP
12. Christian Binford, RHP
13. Sam Selman, LHP
14. Bubba Starling, OF
15. Jorge Bonifacio, OF

MINNESOTA TWINS
1. Byron Buxton, OF
2. Miguel Sano, 3B
3. Jose Berrios, RHP
4. Alex Meyer, RHP
5. Nick Gordon, SS
6. Kohl Stewart, RHP
7. Lewis Thorpe, LHP
8. Jorge Polanco, INF
9. Trevor May, RHP
10. Eddie Rosario, OF
11. Nick Burdi, RHP
12. Felix Jorge, RHP
13. Stuart Turner, C
14. Stephen Gonsalves, LHP
15. Jason Adam, RHP

AL WEST

HOUSTON ASTROS
1. Carlos Correa, SS
2. Mike Foltynewicz, RHP
3. Vince Velasquez, RHP
4. Mark Appel, RHP
5. Domingo Santana, OF
6. Lance McCullers, RHP
7. Rio Ruiz, 3B
8. Michael Feliz, RHP
9. Colin Moran, 3B
10. Teoscar Hernandez, OF
11. Derek Fisher, OF
12. Brett Phillips, OF
13. Max Stassi, C
14. Josh Hader, LHP
15. Joe Musgrove, RHP

LOS ANGELES ANGELS
1. Andrew Heaney, LHP
2. Sean Newcomb, LHP
3. Cam Bedrosian, RHP
4. Kyle Kubitza, 3B
5. Kaleb Cowart, 3B
6. Nick Tropeano, RHP
7. Joe Gatto, RHP
8. Natanael Delgado, OF
9. Trevor Gott, RHP
10. Alex Yarbrough, 2B
11. Christopher Ellis, RHP
12. Eric Stamets, SS
13. Hunter Green, LHP
14. Erick Salcedo, SS
15. Alfonso Alcantara, RHP

OAKLAND ATHLETICS
1. Daniel Robertson, SS
2. Matt Olson, 1B
3. R.J. Alvarez, RHP
4. Matt Chapman, 3B
5. Renato Nunez, 3B
6. Franklin Barreto, SS
7. Dillon Overton, LHP
8. Chad Pinder, 2B/SS
9. Chris Bassitt, RHP
10. Sean Nolin, LHP
11. Raul Alcantara, RHP
12. Dylan Covey, RHP
13. Jaycob Brugman, OF
14. Tucker Healy, RHP
15. Bobby Wahl, RHP

SEATTLE MARINERS
1. Alex Jackson, OF
2. D.J. Peterson, 3B
3. Gabby Guerrero, OF
4. Patrick Kivlehan, 3B
5. Edwin Diaz, RHP
6. Victor Sanchez, RHP
7. Austin Wilson, OF
8. Carson Smith, RHP
9. Luiz Gohara, LHP
10. Tyler O'Neill, OF
11. Ketel Marte, SS
12. Danny Hultzen, LHP
13. Ryan Yarbrough, LHP
14. Austin Cousino, OF
15. Tyler Marlette, C

TEXAS RANGERS
1. Joey Gallo, 3B
2. Alex Gonzalez, RHP
3. Jorge Alfaro, C
4. Luke Jackson, RHP
5. Jake Thompson, RHP
6. Lewis Brinson, OF
7. Luis Ortiz, RHP
8. Nomar Mazara, OF
9. Ryan Rua, 3B
10. Nick Williams, OF
11. Travis Demeritte, 2B
12. Alec Asher, RHP
13. Corey Knebel, RHP
14. Jairo Beras, OF
15. Keone Kela, RHP

TOP PROSPECTS BY ORGANIZATION

NL EAST

ATLANTA BRAVES
1. Jose Peraza, 2B
2. Lucas Sims, RHP
3. Christian Bethancourt, C
4. Braxton Davidson, OF
5. Ozhaino Albies, SS
6. Ricardo Sanchez, LHP
7. Jason Hursh, RHP
8. Mallex Smith, OF
9. Max Fried, LHP
10. Garrett Fulenchek, RHP
11. Tyrell Jenkins, RHP
12. Alec Grosser, RHP
13. Mauricio Cabrera, RHP
14. Cody Martin, RHP
15. Dustin Peterson, 3B

MIAMI MARLINS
1. Tyler Kolek, RHP
2. J.T. Realmuto, C
3. Justin Nicolino, LHP
4. Avery Romero, 2B
5. Jose Urena, RHP
6. Trevor Williams, RHP
7. Brian Anderson, 2B
8. Jarlin Garcia, LHP
9. Isael Soto, OF
10. Justin Twine, SS
11. Michael Mader, LHP
12. Nick Wittgren, RHP
13. Kendry Flores, RHP
14. Adam Conley, LHP
15. Austin Dean, OF

NEW YORK METS
1. Noah Syndergaard, RHP
2. Dilson Herrera, 2B
3. Brandon Nimmo, OF
4. Steven Matz, LHP
5. Kevin Plawecki, C
6. Michael Conforto, OF
7. Amed Rosario, SS
8. Rafael Montero, RHP
9. Dominic Smith, 1B
10. Gavin Cecchini, SS
11. Marcos Molina, RHP
12. Cesar Puello, OF
13. Michael Fulmer, RHP
14. Cory Mazzoni, RHP
15. Milton Ramos, SS

PHILADELPHIA PHILLIES
1. J.P. Crawford, SS
2. Maikel Franco, 3B
3. Aaron Nola, RHP
4. Zach Eflin, RHP
5. Roman Quinn, OF
6. Ben Lively, RHP
7. Jesse Biddle, LHP
8. Aaron Brown, OF
9. Carlos Tocci, OF
10. Dylan Cozens, OF
11. Matt Imhof, LHP
12. Miguel Alfredo Gonzalez, RHP
13. Kelly Dugan, OF
14. Yoel Mecias, LHP
15. Tom Windle, LHP

WASHINGTON NATIONALS
1. Lucas Giolito, RHP
2. A.J. Cole, RHP
3. Trea Turner, SS*
4. Erick Fedde, RHP
5. Joe Ross, RHP
6. Reynaldo Lopez, RHP
7. Michael Taylor, OF
8. Nick Pivetta, RHP
9. Wilmer Difo, SS
10. Rafael Bautista, OF
11. Brian Goodwin, OF
12. Jake Johansen, RHP
13. Jakson Reetz, C
14. Drew Ward, 3B
15. Matt Skole, 1B

NL CENTRAL

CHICAGO CUBS
1. Kris Bryant, 3B
2. Jorge Soler, OF
3. Addison Russell, SS
4. Kyle Schwarber, C/OF
5. Albert Almora, OF
6. C.J. Edwards, RHP
7. Billy McKinney, OF
8. Pierce Johnson, RHP
9. Dan Vogelbach, 1B
10. Gleyber Torres, SS
11. Eloy Jimenez, OF
12. Victor Caratini, C
13. Jake Stinnett, RHP
14. Gioskar Amaya, 2B
15. Carson Sands, LHP

CINCINNATI REDS
1. Robert Stephenson, RHP
2. Jesse Winker, OF
3. Nick Travieso, RHP
4. Michael Lorenzen, RHP
5. Yorman Rodriguez, OF
6. Anthony DeSclafani, RHP
7. Alex Blandino, SS
8. Amir Garrett, LHP
9. Raisel Iglesias, RHP
10. Phillip Ervin, OF
11. Nick Howard, RHP
12. Jonathan Crawford, RHP
13. Aristides Aquino, OF
14. Tanner Rahier, 3B
15. Kyle Waldrop, OF

MILWAUKEE BREWERS
1. Tyrone Taylor, OF
2. Orlando Arcia, SS
3. Monte Harrison, OF
4. Kodi Medeiros, LHP
5. Clint Coulter, C
6. Jake Gatewood, SS
7. Devin Williams, RHP
8. Gilbert Lara, SS
9. Taylor Jungmann, RHP
10. Taylor Williams, RHP
11. Tyler Wagner, RHP
12. Victor Roache, OF
13. Jorge Lopez, RHP
14. Michael Reed, OF
15. Kyle Wren, OF

PITTSBURGH PIRATES
1. Tyler Glasnow, RHP
2. Jameson Taillon, RHP
3. Josh Bell, OF
4. Austin Meadows, OF
5. Nick Kingham, RHP
6. Alen Hanson, SS
7. Harold Ramirez, OF
8. Reese McGuire, C
9. Cole Tucker, SS
10. JaCoby Jones, SS
11. Mitch Keller, RHP
12. Willy Garcia, OF
13. Luis Heredia, RHP
14. Trey Supak, RHP
15. Wyatt Mathisen, 3B

ST. LOUIS CARDINALS
1. Alex Reyes, RHP
2. Marco Gonzales, LHP
3. Stephen Piscotty, OF
4. Rob Kaminsky, LHP
5. Jack Flaherty, RHP
6. Randal Grichuk, OF
7. Luke Weaver, RHP
8. Tim Cooney, LHP
9. Charlie Tilson, OF
10. Sam Tuivailala, RHP
11. Magneuris Sierra, OF
12. Edmundo Sosa, SS
13. Carson Kelly, C
14. Juan Herrera, SS
15. Ronnie Williams, RHP

NL WEST

ARIZONA DIAMONDBACKS
1. Archie Bradley, RHP
2. Braden Shipley, RHP
3. Aaron Blair, RHP
4. Brandon Drury, 3B
5. Jake Lamb, 3B
6. Touki Toussaint, RHP
7. Robbie Ray, LHP
8. Pete O'Brien, C/1B
9. Jake Barrett, RHP
10. Nick Ahmed, SS
11. Cody Reed, LHP
12. Matt Railey, OF
13. Mitch Haniger, OF
14. Domingo Leyba, 2B
15. Sergio Alcantara, SS

COLORADO ROCKIES
1. Jon Gray, RHP
2. David Dahl, OF
3. Ryan McMahon, 3B
4. Raimel Tapia, OF
5. Kyle Freeland, LHP
6. Eddie Butler, RHP
7. Rosell Herrera, SS/3B
8. Trevor Story, SS
9. Forrest Wall, 2B
10. Tom Murphy, C
11. Tyler Anderson, LHP
12. Kyle Parker, OF
13. Dom Nunez, C
14. Max George, SS
15. Jose Briceno, C

LOS ANGELES DODGERS
1. Joc Pederson, OF
2. Corey Seager, SS
3. Julio Urias, LHP
4. Grant Holmes, RHP
5. Jose De Leon, RHP
6. Alex Guerrero, 2B
7. Alex Verdugo, OF
8. Chris Anderson, RHP
9. Chris Reed, LHP
10. Zach Lee, RHP
11. Scott Schebler, OF
12. Pedro Baez, RHP
13. Darnell Sweeney, INF
14. Yimi Garcia, RHP
15. Julian Leon, C

SAN DIEGO PADRES
1. Matt Wisler, RHP
2. Hunter Renfroe, OF
3. Trea Turner, SS*
4. Michael Gettys, OF
5. Austin Hedges, C
6. Rymer Liriano, OF
7. Casey Kelly, RHP
8. Taylor Lindsey, 2B
9. Jose Rondon, SS
10. Cory Spangenberg, 2B
11. Alex Dickerson, OF
12. Tayron Guerrero, RHP
13. Franchy Cordero, SS
14. Gabriel Quintana, 3B
15. Jordan Paroubeck, OF

SAN FRANCISCO GIANTS
1. Kyle Crick, RHP
2. Tyler Beede, RHP
3. Keury Mella, RHP
4. Andrew Susac, C
5. Christian Arroyo, SS
6. Clayton Blackburn, RHP
7. Mac Williamson, OF
8. Adalberto Mejia, LHP
9. Chris Stratton, RHP
10. Ty Blach, LHP
11. Aramis Garcia, C
12. Luis Ysla, LHP
13. Kendry Flores, RHP
14. Johneshwy Fargas, OF
15. Martin Agosta, RHP

*Due to the unique situation where Trea Turner was revealed as the PTBL in a December trade from the Padres to the Nationals but not technically eligible to be dealt until June, we have decided to include him on both teams' top 15 lists.

TOP PROSPECTS BY POSITION

CATCHER
1. Blake Swihart, BOS
2. Jorge Alfaro, TEX
3. Kevin Plawecki, NYM
4. Christian Bethancourt, ATL
5. Austin Hedges, SD
6. Reese McGuire, PIT
7. Gary Sanchez, NYY
8. Chance Sisco, BAL
9. Max Pentecost, TOR
10. Luis Torrens, NYY
11. Andrew Susac, SF
12. J.T. Realmuto, MIA
13. James McCann, DET
14. Clint Coulter, MIL
15. Justin O'Conner ,TAM

FIRST BASEMEN
1. Matt Olson, OAK
2. Christian Walker, BAL
3. Dominic Smith, NYM
4. Dan Vogelbach, CHC
5. Matt Skole, WAS
6. Peter O'Brien, ARI
7. Casey Gillaspie, TAM
8. Bobby Bradley, CLE
9. Matt Dean, TOR
10. Greg Bird, NYY
11. Daniel Palka, ARI
12. Travis Shaw, BOS
13. A.J. Reed, HOU
14. Jesus Aguilar, CLE
15. Sam Travis, BOS

SECOND BASEMEN
1. Jose Peraza, ATL
2. DIlson Herrera, NYM
3. Avery Romero, MIA
4. Alex Guerrero, LA
5. Devon Travis, TOR
6. Taylor Lindsey, SD
7. Rob Refsnyder, NYY
8. Forrest Wall, COL
9. Ryan Brett, TAM
10. Kean Wong, TAM
11. Travis Demeritte, TEX
12. Andrew Pullin, PHI
13. Carlos Sanchez, CHW
14. Cory Spangenberg, SD
15. Gioskar Amaya, CHC

SHORTSTOP
1. Carlos Correa, HOU
2. Addison Russell, CHC
3. Corey Seager, LA
4. Francisco Lindor, CLE
5. J.P. Crawford, PHI
6. Raul Mondesi, KC
7. Nick Gordon, MIN
8. Tim Anderson, CHW
9. Daniel Robertson, OAK
10. Alen Hanson, PIT
11. Trea Turner, SD/WAS
12. Willy Adames, TAM
13. Franklin Barreto, OAK
14. Jorge Mateo, NYY
15. Wilmer Difo, WAS

THIRD BASEMEN
1. Kris Bryant, CHC
2. Miguel Sano, MIN
3. Joey Gallo, TEX
4. D.J. Peterson, SEA
5. Hunter Dozier, KC
6. Maikel Franco, PHI
7. Ryan McMahon, COL
8. Colin Moran, HOU
9. Rio Ruiz, HOU
10. Rafael Devers, BOS
11. Brandon Drury, ARI
12. Jake Lamb, ARI
13. Garin Cecchini, BOS
14. Kyle Kubitza, LAA
15. Renato Nunez, OAK

OUTFIELDERS
1. Byron Buxton, MIN
2. Joc Pederson, LA
3. Jorge Soler, CHC
4. David Dahl, COL
5. Alex Jackson, SEA
6. Jesse Winker, CIN
7. Austin Meadows, PIT
8. Josh Bell, PIT
9. Kyle Schwarber, CHC
10. Albert Almora, CHC
11. Clint Frazier, CLE
12. Rusney Castillo, BOS
13. Raimel Tapia, COL
14. Dalton Pompey, TOR
15. Hunter Renfroe, SD
16. Brandon Nimmo, NYM
17. Domingo Santana, HOU
18. Aaron Judge, NYY
19. Stephen Piscotty, STL
20. Yasmany Tomas, ARI
21. Manuel Margot, BOS
22. Michael Taylor, WAS
23. Michael Conforto, NYM
24. Lewis Brinson, TEX
25. Nick Williams, TEX
26. Bradley Zimmer, CLE
27. Billy McKinney, CHC
28. Steven Moya, DET
29. Eddie Rosario, MIN
30. Michael Gettys, SD
31. Gabby Guerrero, SEA
32. Derek Hill, DET
33. Tyrone Taylor, MIL
34. Rymer Liriano, SD
35. Randal Grichuk, STL
36. Steven Souza, TAM
37. Rafael Bautista, WAS
38. Aaron Altherr, PHI
39. Alex Verdugo, LA
40. Dylan Cozens, PHI
41. Dwight Smith, TOR
42. Mikie Mahtook, TAM
43. Nomar Mazara, TEX
44. Tyler Naquin, CLE
45. Monte Harrison, MIL

STARTING PITCHERS
1. Lucas Giolito, WAS
2. Dylan Bundy, BAL
3. Archie Bradley, ARI
4. Julio Urias, LA
5. Jon Gray, COL
6. Daniel Norris, TOR
7. Carlos Rodon, CHW
8. Tyler Glasnow, PIT
9. Noah Syndergaard, NYM
10. Aaron Sanchez, TOR
11. Henry Owens, BOS
12. Jameson Taillon, PIT
13. Robert Stephenson, CIN
14. Andrew Heaney, LAA
15. Jose Berrios, MIN
16. Hunter Harvey, BAL
17. Alex Meyer, MIN
18. Kohl Stewart, MIN
19. Kyle Crick, SF
20. Luis Severino, NYY
21. Aaron Nola, PHI
22. Kyle Zimmer, KC
23. Alex Reyes, STL
24. Braden Shipley, ARI
25. Tyler Kolek, MIA
26. Mark Appel, HOU
27. Sean Manaea, KC
28. A.J. Cole, WAS
29. Matt Wisler, SD
30. C.J. Edwards, CHC
31. Mike Foltynewicz, HOU
32. Nick Kingham, PIT
33. Eddie Butler, COL
34. Steven Matz, NYM
35. Kyle Freeland, COL
36. Lucas Sims, ATL
37. Eduardo Rodriguez, BOS
38. Max Fried, ATL
39. Alex Gonzalez, TEX
40. Tyler Beede, SF
41. Grant Holmes, LA
42. Aaron Blair, ARI
43. Marco Gonzales, STL
44. Sean Newcomb, LAA
45. Alex Colome, TAM
46. Jeff Hoffman, TOR
47. Luke Jackson, TEX
48. Jake Thompson, TEX
49. Brandon Finnegan, KC
50. Trevor May, MIN
51. Vince Velasquez, HOU
52. Jose De Leon, LA
53. Michael Lorenzen, CIN
54. Miguel Almonte, KC
55. Reynaldo Lopez, WAS
56. Touki Toussaint, ARI
57. Francellis Montas, CHW
58. Joe Ross, WAS
59. Rob Kaminsky, STL
60. Lance McCullers, HOU

61. Rafael Montero, NYM
62. Spencer Adams, CHW
63. Taylor Guerrieri, TAM
64. Erick Fedde, WAS
65. Nick Travieso, CIN
66. Justin Nicolino, MIA
67. Keury Mella, SF
68. Miguel Castro, TOR
69. Matt Barnes, BOS
70. Brian Johnson, BOS
71. Anthony DeSclafani, CIN
72. Jose Urena, MIA
73. Roberto Osuna, TOR
74. Jack Flaherty, STL
75. Michael Feliz, HOU

RELIEF PITCHERS
1. R.J. Alvarez, OAK
2. Armando Rivero, CHC
3. Jacob Lindgren, NYY
4. Nick Burdi, MIN
5. Derek Law, SF
6. Victor Araujo, LA
7. Cam Bedrosian, LAA
8. Carson Smith, SEA
9. Raisel Iglesias, CIN
10. Jake Barrett, ARI
11. Corey Knebel, TEX
12. Trevor Gott, LAA
13. Colby Suggs, MIA
14. Scott Oberg, COL
15. Tayron Guerrero, SD

TOP PROSPECTS BY SKILLS

2015 TOP FANTASY IMPACT

TOP POWER

Joey Gallo, 3B, TEX
Kris Bryant, 3B, CHC
Miguel Sano, 3B, MIN
Dan Vogelbach, 1B, CHC
Joc Pederson, OF, LA
Kyle Schwarber, C/OF, CHC
Matt Olson, 1B, OAK
Jorge Soler, OF, CHC
Steven Moya, OF, DET
Aaron Judge, OF, NYY
Ryan McMahon, 3B, COL
Alex Jackson, OF, SEA
Domingo Santana, OF, HOU
Gary Sanchez, C, NYY
Adam Brett Walker, OF, MIN
Renato Nunez, 3B, OAK
Casey Gillaspie, 1B, TAM
Josh Bell, OF, PIT
Brandon Drury, 3B, ARI
Victor Roache, OF, MIL
David Dahl, OF, COL
Austin Meadows, OF, PIT
Hunter Renfroe, OF, SD
D.J. Peterson, 3B, SEA
Nomar Mazara, OF, TEX

TOP BA

Kris Bryant, 3B, CHC
David Dahl, OF, COL
Byron Buxton, OF, MIN
Francisco Lindor, SS, CLE
Carlos Correa, SS, HOU
J.P. Crawford, SS, PHI
Kyle Schwarber, C/OF, CHC
Joc Pederson, OF, LA
Forrest Wall, 2B, COL
Colin Moran, 3B, HOU
Austin Meadows, OF, PIT
Addison Russell, SS, CHC
Daniel Robertson, SS, OAK
Blake Swihart, C, BOS
Jorge Soler, OF, CHC
D.J. Peterson, 3B, SEA
Avery Romero, 2B, MIA
Garin Cecchini, 3B, BOS
Devon Travis, 2B, TOR
Christian Arroyo, SS, SF
Franklin Barreto, SS, OAK
Rob Refsnyder, 2B, NYY
Nick Gordon, SS, MIN
Dalton Pompey, OF, TOR
Rusney Castillo, OF, BOS

TOP SPEED

Byron Buxton, OF, MIN
Mallex Smith, OF, ATL
Rafael Bautista, OF, WAS
Manuel Margot, OF, BOS
Brian Goodwin, OF, WAS
D.J. Davis, OF, TOR
Kyle Wren, OF, MIL
Delino DeShields, OF, TEX
Raimel Tapia, OF, COL
Micah Johnson, 2B, CHW
Billy Burns, OF, OAK
Tony Kemp, 2B, HOU
Roemon Fields, OF, TOR
Alen Hanson, SS, PIT
Dalton Pompey, OF, TOR
Monte Harrison, OF, MIL
Wilmer Difo, SS, WAS
Michael O'Neill, OF, NYY
Lane Adams, OF, KC
Travis Jankowski, OF, SD
Jacob May, OF, CHW
Jesus Solorzano, OF, MIA
Andrew Toles, OF, TAM
Austin Wates, OF, MIA
Rymer Liriano, OF, SD

TOP FASTBALL

Lucas Giolito, RHP, WAS
Alex Meyer, RHP, MIN
Jon Gray, RHP, COL
Tyler Glasnow, RHP, PIT
Kyle Crick, RHP, SF
Carlos Rodon, LHP, CHW
Tyler Kolek, RHP, MIA
Erick Fedde, RHP, WAS
Dylan Bundy, RHP, BAL
Jameson Taillon, RHP, PIT
Brandon Finnegan, LHP, KC
Daniel Norris, LHP, TOR
Archie Bradley, RHP, ARI
Jose Berrios, RHP, MIN
Mike Foltynewicz, RHP, HOU
Sean Manaea, LHP, KC
Aaron Sanchez, RHP, TOR
Kyle Zimmer, RHP, KC
Alex Reyes, RHP, STL
Francellis Montas, RHP, CHW
Touki Toussaint, RHP, ARI
C.J. Edwards, RHP, CHC
Kyle Freeland, LHP, COL
Julio Urias, LHP, LA
Luis Severino, RHP, NYY

TOP BREAKING BALL

Carlos Rodon, LHP, CHW
Lucas Giolito, RHP, WAS
Jameson Taillon, RHP, PIT
Aaron Sanchez, RHP, TOR
Andrew Heaney, LHP, LAA
Jon Gray, RHP, COL
Dylan Bundy, RHP, BAL
Daniel Norris, LHP, TOR
Archie Bradley, RHP, ARI
Nate Karns, RHP, TAM
Kyle Zimmer, RHP, KC
Jacob Lindgren, LHP, NYY
Rob Kaminsky, LHP, STL

Jake Thompson, RHP, TEX
Justin Nicolino, LHP, MIA
Mark Appel, RHP, HOU
Alex Meyer, RHP, MIN
Jose Urena, RHP, MIA
C.J. Edwards, RHP, CHC
Julio Urias, LHP, LA
Chris Anderson, RHP, LA
Alex Gonzalez, RHP, TEX
Anthony DeSclafani, RHP, CIN
Hunter Harvey, RHP, BAL
Lance McCullers, RHP, HOU
Touki Toussaint, RHP, ARI

1 Kris Bryant (3B, CHC)
2 Jorge Soler (OF, CHC)
3 Joc Pederson (OF, LA)
4 Aaron Sanchez (RHP, TOR)
5 Archie Bradley (RHP, ARI)
6 Dylan Bundy (RHP, BAL)
7 Noah Syndergaard (RHP, NYM)
8 Francisco Lindor (SS, CLE)
9 Andrew Heaney (LHP, LAA)
10 Maikel Franco (3B, PHI)
11 Jameson Taillon (RHP, PIT)
12 Carlos Rodon (LHP, CHW)
13 Daniel Norris (LHP, TOR)
14 Alex Guerrero (2B, LA)
15 Joey Gallo (3B, TEX)
16 Marco Gonzales (LHP, STL)
17 Alex Meyer (RHP, MIN)
18 Jose Berrios (RHP, MIN)
19 Anthony Ranaudo (RHP, BOS)
20 Jake Lamb (3B, ARI)
21 Randall Grichuk (OF, STL)
22 Henry Owens (LHP, BOS)
23 Rafael Montero (RHP, NYM)
24 Rymer Liriano (OF, SD)
25 Jonathan Gray (RHP, COL)
26 Trevor May (RHP, MIN)
27 Matt Barnes (RHP, BOS)
28 Robbie Ray (LHP, ARI)
29 Michael Taylor (OF, WAS)
30 Aaron Nola (RHP, PHI)
31 Edwin Escobar (LHP, BOS)
32 Blake Swihart (C, BOS)
33 Addison Russell (SS, CHC)
34 Byron Buxton (OF, MIN)
35 Stephen Piscotty (OF, STL)
36 Domingo Santana (OF, HOU)
37 Rusney Castillo (OF, BOS)
38 Cory Spangenberg (2B, SD)

39 Nick Kingham (RHP, PIT)
40 Mike Foltynewicz (RHP, HOU)
41 Kevin Plawecki (C, NYM)
42 Miguel Sano (3B, MIN)
43 D.J. Peterson (3B, SEA)
44 Carlos Correa (SS, HOU)
45 Tim Cooney (RHP, STL)
46 Eddie Butler (RHP, COL)
47 Luis Sardinas (SS, TEX)
48 C.J. Edwards (RHP, CHC)
49 A.J. Cole (RHP, WAS)
50 Chris Reed (LHP, LA)
51 Matt Wisler (RHP, SD)
52 Jorge Alfaro (C, TEX)
53 Kyle Crick (RHP, SF)
54 Brandon Nimmo (OF, NYM)
55 Kyle Zimmer (RHP, KC)
56 Corey Seager (SS, LA)
57 Kyle Parker (OF, COL)
58 Travis Shaw (1B, BOS)
59 Steven Moya (OF, DET)
60 Micah Johnson (2B, CHW)
61 Christian Bethancourt (C, ATL)
62 Clayton Blackburn (RHP, SF)
63 Luis Severino (RHP, NYY)
64 Kyle Schwarber (C, CHC)
65 Eddie Rosario (2B, MIN)
66 Mark Appel (RHP, HOU)
67 Brian Johnson (LHP, BOS)
68 James Ramsey (OF, CLE)
69 Eduardo Rodriguez (LHP, BOS)
70 Robert Stephenson (RHP, CIN)
71 Robert Refsnyder (2B, NYY)
72 James McCann (C, DET)
73 Dalton Pompey (OF, TOR)
74 Gary Sanchez (C, NYY)
75 Nick Tropeano (RHP, LAA)

TOP 100 PROSPECTS ARCHIVE

2014

1. Byron Buxton (OF, MIN)
2. Oscar Taveras (OF, STL)
3. Xander Bogaerts (SS, BOS)
4. Taijuan Walker (RHP, SEA)
5. Miguel Sano (3B, MIN)
6. Francisco Lindor (SS, CLE)
7. Javier Baez (SS, CHC)
8. Archie Bradley (RHP, ARI)
9. Carlos Correa (SS, HOU)
10. Gregory Polanco (OF, PIT)

11. Addison Russell (SS, OAK)
12. Jameson Taillon (RHP, PIT)
13. Kris Bryant (3B, CHC)
14. Dylan Bundy (RHP, BAL)
15. George Springer (OF, HOU)
16. Nick Castellanos (3B, DET)
17. Noah Syndergaard (RHP, NYM)
18. Kevin Gausman (RHP, BAL)
19. Carlos Martinez (RHP, STL)
20. Robert Stephenson (RHP, CIN)

21. Yordano Ventura (RHP, KC)
22. Jonathan Gray (RHP, COL)
23. Kyle Zimmer (RHP, KC)
24. Albert Almora (OF, CHC)
25. Mark Appel (RHP, HOU)
26. Aaron Sanchez (RHP, TOR)
27. Travis d'Arnaud (C, NYM)
28. Kyle Crick (RHP, SF)
29. Joc Pederson (OF, LA)
30. Alex Meyer (RHP, MIN)

31. Garin Cecchini (3B, BOS)
32. Jorge Soler (OF, CHC)
33. Jonathan Singleton (1B, HOU)
34. Maikel Franco (3B, PHI)
35. Lucas Giolito (RHP, WAS)
36. Eddie Butler (RHP, COL)
37. Andrew Heaney (LHP, MIA)
38. Jackie Bradley (OF, BOS)
39. Taylor Guerrieri (RHP, TAM)
40. Corey Seager (SS, LA)

41. Adalberto Mondesi (SS, KC)
42. Billy Hamilton (OF, CIN)
43. Clint Frazier (OF, CLE)
44. Tyler Glasnow (RHP, PIT)
45. Kolten Wong (2B, STL)
46. Henry Owens (LHP, BOS)
47. Gary Sanchez (C, NYY)
48. Jorge Alfaro (C, TEX)
49. Austin Meadows (OF, PIT)
50. Austin Hedges (C, SD)

51. Alen Hanson (SS, PIT)
52. Marcus Stroman (RHP, TOR)
53. Kohl Stewart (RHP, MIN)
54. Max Fried (LHP, SD)
55. Jake Odorizzi (RHP, TAM)
56. Michael Choice (OF, TEX)
57. C.J. Edwards (RHP, CHC)
58. Trevor Bauer (RHP, CLE)
59. Julio Urias (LHP, LA)
60. Jake Marisnick (OF, MIA)

61. Jesse Biddle (LHP, PHI)
62. Eddie Rosario (2B, MIN)
63. Lucas Sims (RHP, ATL)
64. Lance McCullers (RHP, HOU)
65. A.J. Cole (RHP, WAS)
66. Rougned Odor (2B, TEX)
67. Colin Moran (3B, MIA)
68. Mike Foltynewicz (RHP, HOU)
69. Allen Webster (RHP, BOS)
70. Chris Owings (SS, ARI)

71. Eduardo Rodriguez (LHP, BAL)
72. Miguel Almonte (RHP, KC)
73. Blake Swihart (C, BOS)
74. Jose Abreu (1B, CHW)
75. Zach Lee (RHP, LA)
76. Danny Hultzen (LHP, SEA)
77. Matt Wisler (RHP, SD)
78. Matt Barnes (RHP, BOS)
79. James Paxton (LHP, SEA)
80. Rosell Herrera (SS, COL)

81. Erik Johnson (RHP, CHW)
82. David Dahl (OF, COL)
83. Hak-Ju Lee (SS, TAM)
84. D.J. Peterson (3B, SEA)
85. Luke Jackson (RHP, TEX)
86. Delino DeShields (OF, HOU)
87. Brian Goodwin (OF, WAS)
88. Hunter Dozier (SS, KC)
89. Matt Davidson (3B, CHW)
90. Anthony Ranaudo (RHP, BOS)

91. Jimmy Nelson (RHP, MIL)
92. Bubba Starling (OF, KC)
93. Christian Bethancourt (C, ATL)
94. Courtney Hawkins (OF, CHW)
95. Domingo Santana (OF, HOU)
96. Kaleb Cowart (3B, LAA)
97. Jose Berrios (RHP, MIN)
98. Braden Shipley (RHP, ARI)
99. Justin Nicolino (LHP, MIA)
100. Alex Colome (RHP, TAM)

2013

1. Jurickson Profar (SS, TEX)
2. Dylan Bundy (RHP, BAL)
3. Wil Myers (OF, TAM)
4. Gerrit Cole (RHP, PIT)
5. Oscar Taveras (OF, STL)
6. Taijuan Walker (RHP, SEA)
7. Trevor Bauer (RHP, CLE)
8. Jose Fernandez (RHP, MIA)
9. Travis d'Arnaud (C, NYM)
10. Miguel Sano (3B, MIN)

11. Zack Wheeler (RHP, NYM)
12. Christian Yelich (OF, MIA)
13. Tyler Skaggs (LHP, ARI)
14. Francisco Lindor (SS, CLE)
15. Javier Baez (SS, CHC)
16. Shelby Miller (RHP, STL)
17. Nick Castellanos (OF, DET)
18. Xander Bogaerts (SS, BOS)
19. Jameson Taillon (RHP, PIT)
20. Danny Hultzen (LHP, SEA)

21. Jonathan Singleton (1B, HOU)
22. Mike Zunino (C, SEA)
23. Billy Hamilton (OF, CIN)
24. Anthony Rendon (3B, WAS)
25. Mike Olt (3B, TEX)
26. Byron Buxton (OF, MIN)
27. Nolan Arenado (3B, COL)
28. Carlos Correa (SS, HOU)
29. Archie Bradley (RHP, ARI)
30. Julio Teheran (RHP, ATL)

31. Matt Barnes (RHP, BOS)
32. Gary Sanchez (C, NYY)
33. Jackie Bradley (OF, BOS)
34. Carlos Martinez (RHP, STL)
35. Bubba Starling (OF, KC)
36. Jake Odorizzi (RHP, TAM)
37. Jedd Gyorko (3B, SD)
38. Alen Hanson (SS, PIT)
39. George Springer (OF, HOU)
40. Nick Franklin (2B, SEA)

41. Aaron Sanchez (RHP, TOR)
42. Albert Almora (OF, CHC)
43. Kaleb Cowart (3B, LAA)
44. Taylor Guerrieri (RHP, TAM)
45. Kyle Zimmer (RHP, KC)
46. Noah Syndergaard (RHP, NYM)
47. Kolten Wong (2B, STL)
48. Tyler Austin (OF, NYY)
49. James Paxton (LHP, SEA)
50. Rymer Liriano (OF, SD)

51. Jake Marisnick (OF, MIA)
52. Trevor Story (SS, COL)
53. Kevin Gausman (RHP, BAL)
54. Trevor Rosenthal (RHP, STL)
55. Alex Meyer (RHP, MIN)
56. Jorge Soler (OF, CHC)
57. Matt Davidson (3B, ARI)
58. Brett Jackson (OF, CHC)
59. Michael Choice (OF, OAK)
60. David Dahl (OF, COL)

61. Mason Williams (OF, NYY)
62. Robert Stephenson (RHP, CIN)
63. Chris Archer (RHP, TAM)
64. Oswaldo Arcia (OF, MIN)
65. Zach Lee (RHP, LA)
66. Tony Cingrani (LHP, CIN)
67. Jesse Biddle (LHP, PHI)
68. Gregory Polanco (OF, PIT)
69. Addison Russell (SS, OAK)
70. Robbie Erlin (RHP, SD)

71. Courtney Hawkins (OF, CHW)
72. Brian Goodwin (OF, WAS)
73. Martin Perez (LHP, TEX)
74. Luis Heredia (RHP, PIT)
75. Yasiel Puig (OF, LA)
76. Wilmer Flores (3B, NYM)
77. Justin Nicolino (LHP, MIA)
78. Max Fried (LHP, SD)
79. Adam Eaton (OF, ARI)
80. Gary Brown (OF, SF)

81. Casey Kelly (RHP, SD)
82. Lucas Giolito (RHP, WAS)
83. Wily Peralta (RHP, MIL)
84. Michael Wacha (RHP, STL)
85. Austin Hedges (C, SD)
86. Kyle Gibson (RHP, MIN)
87. Hak-Ju Lee (SS, TAM)
88. Dan Straily (RHP, OAK)
89. Kyle Crick (RHP, SF)
90. Avisail Garcia (OF, DET)

91. Cody Buckel (RHP, TEX)
92. Tyler Thornburg (RHP, MIL)
93. Allen Webster (RHP, BOS)
94. Jarred Cosart (RHP, HOU)
95. Bruce Rondon (RHP, DET)
96. Delino DeShields (2B, HOU)
97. A.J. Cole (RHP, OAK)
98. Manny Banuelos (LHP, NYY)
99. Yordano Ventura (RHP, KC)
100. Trevor May (RHP, MIN)

TOP 100 PROSPECTS ARCHIVE

2012

1. Bryce Harper (OF, WAS)
2. Matt Moore (LHP, TAM)
3. Mike Trout (OF, LAA)
4. Julio Teheran (RHP, ATL)
5. Jesus Montero (C, NYY)
6. Jurickson Profar (SS, TEX)
7. Manny Machado (SS, BAL)
8. Gerrit Cole (RHP, PIT)
9. Devin Mesoraco (C, CIN)
10. Wil Myers (OF, KC)

11. Miguel Sano (3B, MIN)
12. Jacob Turner (RHP, DET)
13. Anthony Rendon (3B, WAS)
14. Trevor Bauer (RHP, ARI)
15. Nolan Arenado (3B , COL)
16. Jameson Taillon (RHP, PIT)
17. Shelby Miller (RHP, STL)
18. Dylan Bundy (RHP, BAL)
19. Brett Jackson (OF, CHC)
20. Drew Pomeranz (LHP, COL)

21. Martin Perez (LHP, TEX)
22. Yonder Alonso (1B, SD)
23. Taijuan Walker (RHP, SEA)
24. Danny Hultzen (LHP, SEA)
25. Gary Brown (OF, SF)
26. Anthony Rizzo (1B, CHC)
27. Bubba Starling (OF, KC)
28. Travis d'Arnaud (C, TOR)
29. Mike Montgomery (LHP, KC)
30. Jake Odorizzi (RHP, KC)

31. Hak-Ju Lee (SS, TAM)
32. Jonathan Singleton (1B, HOU)
33. Garrett Richards (RHP, LAA)
34. Manny Banuelos (LHP, NYY)
35. James Paxton (LHP, SEA)
36. Jarrod Parker (RHP, OAK)
37. Carlos Martinez (RHP, STL)
38. Jake Marisnick (OF, TOR)
39. Yasmani Grandal (C, SD)
40. Trevor May (RHP, PHI)

41. Gary Sanchez (C, NYY)
42. Mike Olt (3B, TEX)
43. Wilin Rosario (C, COL)
44. John Lamb (LHP, KC)
45. Francisco Lindor (SS, CLE)
46. Dellin Betances (RHP, NYY)
47. Michael Choice (OF, OAK)
48. Arodys Vizcaino (RHP, ATL)
49. Trayvon Robinson (OF, SEA)
50. Matt Harvey (RHP, NYM)

51. Will Middlebrooks (3B, BOS)
52. Jedd Gyorko (3B, SD)
53. Randall Delgado (RHP, ATL)
54. Zack Wheeler (RHP, NYM)
55. Zach Lee (RHP, LA)
56. Tyler Skaggs (LHP, ARI)
57. Nick Castellanos (3B, DET)
58. Robbie Erlin (LHP, SD)
59. Christian Yelich (OF, MIA)
60. Anthony Gose (OF, TOR)

61. Addison Reed (RHP, CHW)
62. Javier Baez (SS, CHC)
63. Starling Marte (OF, PIT)
64. Kaleb Cowart (3B, LAA)
65. George Springer (OF, HOU)
66. Jarred Cosart (RHP, HOU)
67. Jean Segura (2B, LAA)
68. Kolten Wong (2B, STL)
69. Nick Franklin (SS, SEA)
70. Alex Torres (RHP, TAM)

71. Rymer Liriano (OF, SD)
72. Josh Bell (OF, PIT)
73. Leonys Martin (OF, TEX)
74. Joe Wieland (RHP, SD)
75. Joe Benson (OF, MIN)
76. Wily Peralta (RHP, MIL)
77. Tim Wheeler (OF, COL)
78. Oscar Taveras (OF, STL)
79. Xander Bogaerts (SS, BOS)
80. Archie Bradley (RHP, ARI)

81. Kyle Gibson (RHP, MIN)
82. Allen Webster (RHP, LA)
83. C.J. Cron (1B, LAA)
84. Grant Green (OF, OAK)
85. Brad Peacock (RHP, OAK)
86. Chris Dwyer (LHP, KC)
87. Billy Hamilton (SS, CIN)
88. A.J. Cole (RHP, OAK)
89. Aaron Hicks (OF, MIN)
90. Noah Syndergaard (RHP, TOR)

91. Tyrell Jenkins (RHP, STL)
92. Anthony Ranaudo (RHP, BOS)
93. Jed Bradley (LHP, MIL)
94. Nathan Eovaldi (RHP, LA)
95. Andrelton Simmons (SS, ATL)
96. Taylor Guerrieri (RHP, TAM)
97. Cheslor Cuthbert (3B, KC)
98. Edward Salcedo (3B, ATL)
99. Domingo Santana, OF, HOU)
100. Jesse Biddle (LHP, PHI)

2011

1. Bryce Harper (OF, WAS)
2. Domonic Brown (OF, PHI)
3. Jesus Montero (C, NYY)
4. Mike Trout (OF, LAA)
5. Jeremy Hellickson (RHP, TAM)
6. Aroldis Chapman (LHP, CIN)
7. Eric Hosmer (1B, KC)
8. Dustin Ackley (2B, SEA)
9. Desmond Jennings (OF, TAM)
10. Julio Teheran (RHP, ATL)

11. Mike Moustakas (3B, KC)
12. Brandon Belt (1B, SF)
13. Freddie Freeman (1B, ATL)
14. Michael Pineda (RHP, SEA)
15. Matt Moore (LHP, TAM)
16. Mike Montgomery (LHP, KC)
17. Brett Jackson (OF, CHC)
18. Nick Franklin (SS, SEA)
19. Jameson Taillon (RHP, PIT)
20. Jacob Turner (RHP, DET)

21. Shelby Miller (RHP, STL)
22. Martin Perez (LHP, TEX)
23. Wil Myers (C, KC)
24. Kyle Gibson (RHP, MIN)
25. Lonnie Chisenhall (3B, CLE)
26. Tyler Matzek (LHP, COL)
27. Brett Lawrie (2B, TOR)
28. Yonder Alonso (1B, CIN)
29. Jarrod Parker (RHP, ARI)
30. Jonathan Singleton (1B, PHI)

31. Tanner Scheppers (RHP,TEX)
32. Kyle Drabek (RHP, TOR)
33. Jason Knapp (RHP, CLE)
34. Manny Banuelos (LHP, NYY)
35. Alex White (RHP, CLE)
36. Jason Kipnis (2B, CLE)
37. Wilin Rosario (C, COL)
38. Manny Machado (SS, BAL)
39. Chris Sale (LHP, CHW)
40. Devin Mesoraco (C, CIN)

41. Tyler Chatwood (RHP, LAA)
42. John Lamb (LHP, KC)
43. Danny Duffy (LHP, KC)
44. Trevor May (RHP, PHI)
45. Mike Minor (LHP, ATL)
46. Jarred Cosart (RHP, PHI)
47. Tony Sanchez (C, PIT)
48. Brody Colvin (RHP, PHI)
49. Zach Britton (LHP, BAL)
50. Dee Gordon (SS, LA)

51. Miguel Sano (3B, MIN)
52. Grant Green (SS, OAK)
53. Danny Espinosa (SS, WAS)
54. Simon Castro (RHP, SD)
55. Derek Norris (C, WAS)
56. Chris Archer (RHP, CHC)
57. Jurickson Profar (SS, TEX)
58. Zack Cox (3B, STL)
59. Billy Hamilton (2B, CIN)
60. Gary Sanchez (C, NYY)

61. Zach Lee (RHP, LA)
62. Drew Pomeranz (LHP, CLE)
63. Randall Delgado (RHP, ATL)
64. Michael Choice (OF, OAK)
65. Nick Weglarz (OF, CLE)
66. Nolan Arenado (3B, COL)
67. Chris Carter (1B/OF, OAK)
68. Arodys Vizcaino (RHP, ATL)
69. Trey McNutt (RHP, CHC)
70. Dellin Betances (RHP, NYY)

71. Aaron Hicks (OF, MIN)
72. Aaron Crow (RHP, KC)
73. Jake McGee (LHP, TAM)
74. Lars Anderson (1B, BOS)
75. Fabio Martinez (RHP, LAA)
76. Ben Revere (OF, MIN)
77. Jordan Lyles (RHP, HOU)
78. Casey Kelly (RHP, SD)
79. Trayvon Robinson (OF, LA)
80. Craig Kimbrel (RHP, ATL)

81. Jose Iglesias (SS, BOS)
82. Garrett Richards (RHP, LAA)
83. Allen Webster (RHP, LA)
84. Chris Dwyer (LHP, KC)
85. Alex Colome (RHP, TAM)
86. Zack Wheeler (RHP, SF)
87. Andy Oliver (LHP, DET)
88. Andrew Brackman (RHP,NYY)
89. Wilmer Flores (SS, NYM)
90. Christian Friedrich (LHP, COL)

91. Anthony Ranaudo (RHP, BOS)
92. Aaron Miller (LHP, LA)
93. Matt Harvey (RHP, NYM)
94. Mark Rogers (RHP, MIL)
95. Jean Segura (2B, LAA)
96. Hank Conger (C, LAA)
97. J.P. Arencibia (C, TOR)
98. Matt Dominguez (3B, FLA)
99. Jerry Sands (1B, LA)
100. Nick Castellanos (3B, DET)

TOP 100 PROSPECTS ARCHIVE

2010

1. Stephen Strasburg (RHP, WAS)
2. Jason Heyward (OF, ATL)
3. Jesus Montero (C, NYY)
4. Buster Posey (C, SF)
5. Justin Smoak (1B, TEX)
6. Pedro Alvarez (3B, PIT)
7. Carlos Santana (C, CLE)
8. Desmond Jennings (OF, TAM)
9. Brian Matusz (LHP, BAL)
10. Neftali Feliz (RHP, TEX)

11. Brett Wallace (3B, TOR)
12. Mike Stanton (OF. FLA)
13. M. Bumgarner (LHP, SF)
14. J. Hellickson (RHP, TAM)
15. Dustin Ackley (1B/OF, SEA)
16. Aroldis Chapman (LHP, CIN)
17. Yonder Alonso (1B, CIN)
18. Alcides Escobar (SS, MIL)
19. Brett Lawrie (2B, MIL)
20. Starlin Castro (SS, CHC)

21. Logan Morrison (1B, FLA)
22. Mike Montgomery (LHP, KC)
23. Domonic Brown (OF, PHI)
24. Josh Vitters (3B, CHC)
25. R. Westmoreland (OF, BOS)
26. Todd Frazier (3B/OF, CIN)
27. Eric Hosmer (1B, KC)
28. Freddie Freeman (1B, ATL)
29. Derek Norris (C, WAS)
30. Martin Perez (LHP, TEX)

31. Wade Davis (RHP, TAM)
32. Trevor Reckling (LHP, LAA)
33. Jordan Walden (RHP, LAA)
34. Mat Gamel (3B, MIL)
35. Tyler Flowers (C, CHW)
36. T. Scheppers (RHP, TEX)
37. Casey Crosby (LHP, DET)
38. Austin Jackson (OF, DET)
39. Devaris Gordon (SS, LA)
40. Kyle Drabek (RHP, TOR)

41. Ben Revere (OF, MIN)
42. Michael Taylor (OF, OAK)
43. Jacob Turner (RHP, DET)
44. Tim Beckham (SS, TAM)
45. Carlos Triunfel (SS, SEA)
46. Aaron Crow (RHP, KC)
47. Matt Moore (LHP, TAM)
48. Jarrod Parker (RHP, ARI)
49. F. Martinez (OF, NYM)
50. C. Friedrich (LHP, COL)

51. Jenrry Mejia (RHP, NYM)
52. Tyler Matzek (LHP, COL)
53. Brett Jackson (OF, CHC)
54. Aaron Hicks (OF, MIN)
55. Jhoulys Chacin (RHP, COL)
56. Josh Bell (3B, BAL)
57. Brandon Allen (1B, ARI)
58. Chris Carter (1B, OAK)
59. Jason Knapp (RHP, CLE)
60. Danny Duffy (LHP, KC)

61. Tim Alderson (RHP, PIT)
62. Matt Dominguez (3B, FLA)
63. Mike Moustakas (3B, KC)
64. Jake Arrieta (RHP, BAL)
65. Carlos Carrasco (RHP, CLE)
66. Wilmer Flores (SS, NYM)
67. Drew Storen (RHP, WAS)
68. Lonnie Chisenhall (3B, CLE)
69. Aaron Poreda (LHP, SD)
70. A. Cashner (RHP, CHC)

71. Tony Sanchez (C, PIT)
72. Julio Teheran (RHP, ATL)
73. Jose Tabata (OF, PIT)
74. Jason Castro (C, HOU)
75. Casey Kelly (RHP, BOS)
76. Alex White (RHP, CLE)
77. Jay Jackson (RHP, CHC)
78. Dan Hudson (RHP, CHW)
79. Brandon Erbe (RHP, BAL)
80. Zack Wheeler (RHP, SF)

81. Shelby Miller (RHP, STL)
82. Jordan Lyles (RHP, HOU)
83. Simon Castro (RHP, SD)
84. Aaron Miller (LHP, LA)
85. Michael Ynoa (RHP, OAK)
86. Ethan Martin (RHP, LA)
87. Scott Elbert (LHP, LA)
88. Nick Weglarz (OF, CLE)
89. Donavan Tate (OF, SD)
90. Jordan Danks (OF, CHW)

91. Hector Rondon (RHP, CLE)
92. Chris Heisey (OF, CIN)
93. Kyle Gibson (RHP, MIN)
94. Mike Leake (RHP, CIN)
95. Mike Trout (OF, LAA)
96. Jake McGee (LHP, TAM)
97. Chad James (LHP, FLA)
98. C. Bethancourt (C, NYY)
99. Miguel Sano (SS, MIN)
100. Noel Arguelles (LHP, KC)

2009

1. Matt Wieters (C, BAL)
2. David Price (LHP, TAM)
3. Rick Porcello (RHP, DET)
4. Colby Rasmus (OF, STL)
5. Madison Bumgarner (LHP, SF)
6. Neftali Feliz (RHP, TEX)
7. Jason Heyward (OF, ATL)
8. Andrew McCutchen (OF, PIT)
9. Pedro Alvarez (3B, PIT)
10. Cameron Maybin (OF, FLA)

11. Trevor Cahill (RHP, OAK)
12. Mike Moustakas (3B/SS, KC)
13. Jordan Zimmermann (RHP, WAS)
14. Travis Snider (OF, TOR)
15. Tim Beckham (SS, TAM)
16. Eric Hosmer (1B, KC)
17. Tommy Hanson (RHP, ATL)
18. Dexter Fowler (OF, COL)
19. Brett Anderson (LHP, OAK)
20. Carlos Triunfel (SS/2B, SEA)

21. Buster Posey (C, SF)
22. Chris Tillman (RHP, BAL)
23. Brian Matusz (LHP, BAL)
24. Justin Smoak (1B, TEX)
25. Jarrod Parker (RHP, ARI)
26. Derek Holland (LHP, TEX)
27. Lars Anderson (1B, BOS)
28. Michael Inoa (RHP, OAK)
29. Mike Stanton (OF, FLA)
30. Taylor Teagarden (C, TEX)

31. Gordon Beckham (SS, CHW)
32. Brett Wallace (3B, STL)
33. Matt LaPorta (OF, CLE)
34. Jordan Schafer (OF, ATL)
35. Carlos Santana (C, CLE)
36. Aaron Hicks (OF, MIN)
37. Adam Miller (RHP, CLE)
38. Elvis Andrus (SS, TEX)
39. Alcides Escobar (SS, MIL)
40. Wade Davis (RHP, TAM)

41. Austin Jackson (OF, NYY)
42. Jesus Montero (C, NYY)
43. Tim Alderson (RHP, SF)
44. Jhoulys Chacin (RHP, COL)
45. Phillippe Aumont (RHP, SEA)
46. James McDonald (RHP, LA)
47. Reid Brignac (SS, TAM)
48. Desmond Jennings (OF, TAM)
49. Fernando Martinez (OF, NYM)
50. JP Arencibia (C, TOR)

51. Wilmer Flores (SS, NYM)
52. Brett Cecil (LHP, TOR)
53. Aaron Poreda (LHP, CHW)
54. Jeremy Jeffress (RHP, MIL)
55. Michael Main (RHP, TEX)
56. Josh Vitters (3B, CHC)
57. Mat Gamel (3B, MIL)
58. Yonder Alonso (1B, CIN)
59. Gio Gonzalez (LHP, OAK)
60. Michael Bowden (RHP, BOS)

61. Angel Villalona (1B, SF)
62. Carlos Carrasco (RHP, PHI)
63. Jake Arrieta (RHP, BAL)
64. Jordan Walden (RHP, LAA)
65. Freddie Freeman (1B, ATL)
66. Logan Morrison (1B, FLA)
67. Shooter Hunt (RHP, MIN)
68. Junichi Tazawa (RHP, BOS)
69. Nick Adenhart (RHP, LAA)
70. Jose Tabata (OF, PIT)

71. Adrian Cardenas (SS/2B, OAK)
72. Chris Carter (3B/OF, OAK)
73. Ben Revere (OF, MIN)
74. Josh Reddick (OF, BOS)
75. Jeremy Hellickson (RHP, TAM)
76. Justin Jackson (SS, TOR)
77. Wilson Ramos (C, MIN)
78. Jason Castro (C, HOU)
79. Julio Borbon (OF, TEX)
80. Tyler Flowers (C, CHW)

81. Gorkys Hernandez (OF, ATL)
82. Neftali Soto (3B, CIN)
83. Henry Rodriguez (RHP, OAK)
84. Dan Duffy (LHP, KC)
85. Daniel Cortes (RHP, KC)
86. Dayan Viciedo (3B, CHW)
87. Matt Dominguez (3B, FLA)
88. Jordan Danks (OF, CHW)
89. Chris Coghlan (2B, FLA)
90. Brian Bogusevic (OF, HOU)

91. Ryan Tucker (RHP, FLA)
92. Jonathon Niese (LHP, NYM)
93. Martin Perez (LHP, TEX)
94. James Simmons (RHP, OAK)
95. Nick Weglarz (OF/1B, CLE)
96. Daniel Bard (RHP, BOS)
97. Yamaico Navarro (SS, BOS)
98. Jose Ceda (RHP, FLA)
99. Jeff Samardzija (RHP, CHC)
100. Jason Donald (SS, PHI)

TOP 100 PROSPECTS ARCHIVE

2008

1. Jay Bruce (OF, CIN)
2. Evan Longoria (3B, TAM)
3. Clay Buchholz (RHP, BOS)
4. Clayton Kershaw (LHP, LAD)
5. Joba Chamberlain (RHP, NYY)
6. Colby Rasmus (OF, STL)
7. Cameron Maybin (OF, FLA)
8. Homer Bailey (RHP, CIN)
9. David Price (LHP, TAM)
10. Andrew McCutchen (OF, PIT)

11. Brandon Wood (3B/SS, LAA)
12. Matt Wieters (C, BAL)
13. Jacoby Ellsbury (OF, BOS)
14. Travis Snider (OF, TOR)
15. Reid Brignac (SS, TAM)
16. Jacob McGee (LHP, TAM)
17. Wade Davis (RHP, TAM)
18. Adam Miller (RHP, CLE)
19. Rick Porcello (RHP, DET)
20. Franklin Morales (LHP, COL)

21. Carlos Triunfel (SS, SEA)
22. Andy LaRoche (3B/OF, LAD)
23. Jordan Schafer (OF, ATL)
24. Kosuke Fukodome (OF, CHC)
25. Jose Tabata (OF, NYY)
26. Carlos Gonzalez (OF, OAK)
27. Joey Votto (1B/OF, CIN)
28. Daric Barton (1B, OAK)
29. Angel Villalona (3B, SF)
30. Eric Hurley (RHP, TEX)

31. Nick Adenhart (RHP, LAA)
32. Fernando Martinez (OF, NYM)
33. Ross Detwiler (LHP, WAS)
34. Johnny Cueto (RHP, CIN)
35. Chris Marrero (OF, WAS)
36. Jason Heyward (OF, ATL)
37. Mike Moustakas (SS, KC)
38. Elvis Andrus (SS, TEX)
39. Taylor Teagarden (C, TEX)
40. Ian Kennedy (RHP, NYY)

41. Kasey Kiker (LHP, TEX)
42. Scott Elbert (LHP, LAD)
43. Justin Masterson (RHP, BOS)
44. Max Scherzer (RHP, ARI)
45. Brandon Jones (OF, ATL)
46. Josh Vitters (3B, CHC)
47. Jarrod Parker (RHP, ARI)
48. Matt Antonelli (2B, SD)
49. Gio Gonzalez (LHP, CHW)
50. Ian Stewart (3B, COL)

51. Chase Headley (3B, SD)
52. Anthony Swarzak (RHP, MIN)
53. Jair Jurrjens (RHP, DET)
54. Billy Rowell (3B, BAL)
55. Jeff Clement (C, SEA)
56. Tyler Colvin (OF, CHC)
57. Neil Walker (3B, PIT)
58. Geovany Soto (C/1B, CHC)
59. Steven Pearce (1B/OF, PIT)
60. Fautino de los Santos (RHP, CHW)

61. Manny Parra (LHP, MIL)
62. Matt LaPorta (OF, MIL)
63. Austin Jackson (OF, NYY)
64. Carlos Carrasco (RHP, PHI)
65. Jed Lowrie (SS/2B, BOS)
66. Deolis Guerra (RHP, NYM)
67. Jonathon Meloan (RHP, LAD)
68. Chin-Lung Hu (SS, LAD)
69. Blake Beaven (RHP, TEX)
70. Michael Main (RHP, TEX)

71. Gorkys Hernandez (OF, ATL)
72. Jeff Niemann (RHP, TAM)
73. Desmond Jennings (OF, TAM)
74. Radhames Liz (RHP, BAL)
75. Chuck Lofgren (LHP, CLE)
76. Luke Hochevar (RHP, KC)
77. Brent Lillibridge (SS, ATL)
78. Jaime Garcia (LHP, STL)
79. Bryan Anderson (C, STL)
80. Troy Patton (LHP, BAL)

81. Nolan Reimold (OF, BAL)
82. Matt Latos (RHP, SD)
83. Tommy Hanson (RHP, ATL)
84. Aaron Poreda (LHP, CHW)
85. Cole Rohrbough (LHP, ATL)
86. Lars Anderson (1B, BOS)
87. Chris Volstad (RHP, FLA)
88. Henry Sosa (RHP, SF)
89. Madison Bumgarner (LHP, SF)
90. Michael Bowden (RHP, BOS)

91. Hank Conger (C, LAA)
92. JR Towles (C, HOU)
93. Greg Reynolds (RHP, COL)
94. Adrian Cardenas (2B/SS, PHI)
95. Chris Nelson (SS, COL)
96. Ryan Kalish (OF, BOS)
97. Dexter Fowler (OF, COL)
98. James McDonald (RHP, LAD)
99. Beau Mills (3B/1B, CLE)
100. Michael Burgess (OF, WAS)

2007

1. Delmon Young (OF, TAM)
2. Alex Gordon (3B, KC)
3. Daisuke Matsuzaka (RHP, BOS)
4. Justin Upton (OF, ARI)
5. Homer Bailey (RHP, CIN)
6. Philip Hughes (RHP, NYY)
7. Brandon Wood (SS, LAA)
8. Jay Bruce (OF, CIN)
9. Billy Butler (OF, KC)
10. Cameron Maybin (OF, DET)

11. Andrew McCutchen (OF, PIT)
12. Troy Tulowitzki (SS, COL)
13. Evan Longoria (3B, TAM)
14. Jose Tabata (OF, NYY)
15. Reid Brignac (SS, TAM)
16. Chris Young (OF, ARI)
17. Adam Miller (RHP, CLE)
18. Mike Pelfrey (RHP, NYM)
19. Carlos Gonzalez (OF, ARI)
20. Tim Lincecum (RHP, SF)

21. Andy LaRoche (3B, LAD)
22. Fernando Martinez (OF, NYM)
23. Yovani Gallardo (RHP, MIL)
24. Colby Rasmus (OF, STL)
25. Ryan Braun (3B, MIL)
26. Scott Elbert (LHP, LAD)
27. Nick Adenhart (RHP, LAA)
28. Andrew Miller (LHP, DET)
29. Billy Rowell (3B, BAL)
30. John Danks (LHP, CHW)

31. Luke Hochevar (RHP, KC)
32. Erick Aybar (SS, LAA)
33. Jacoby Ellsbury (OF, BOS)
34. Eric Hurley (RHP, TEX)
35. Ian Stewart (3B, COL)
36. Clay Buchholz (RHP, BOS)
37. Elvis Andrus (SS, ATL)
38. Jason Hirsh (RHP, COL)
39. Hunter Pence (OF, HOU)
40. Franklin Morales (LHP, COL)

41. Adam Lind (OF, TOR)
42. Travis Snider (OF, TOR)
43. Jeff Niemann (RHP, TAM)
44. Clayton Kershaw (LHP, LAD)
45. James Loney (1B, LAD)
46. Chris Iannetta (C, COL)
47. Elijah Dukes (OF, TAM)
48. Chuck Lofgren (LHP, CLE)
49. Joey Votto (1B, CIN)
50. Jacob McGee (LHP, TAM)

51. Adam Jones (OF, SEA)
52. Brad Lincoln (RHP, PIT)
53. Brian Barton (OF, CLE)
54. Will Inman (RHP, MIL)
55. Wade Davis (RHP, TAM)
56. Donald Veal (LHP, CHC)
57. Michael Bowden (RHP, BOS)
58. Ryan Sweeney (OF, CHW)
59. Josh Fields (3B, CHW)
60. Jarrod Saltalamacchia (C, ATL)

61. Felix Pie (OF, CHC)
62. Brandon Erbe (RHP, BAL)
63. Giovanny Gonzalez (LHP, CHW)
64. Trevor Crowe (OF, CLE)
65. Travis Buck (OF, OAK)
66. Daric Barton (1B, OAK)
67. Kevin Kouzmanoff (3B, SD)
68. Jeff Clement (C, SEA)
69. Neil Walker (C, PIT)
70. Troy Patton (LHP, HOU)

71. Brandon Morrow (RHP, SEA)
72. Dustin Pedroia (2B, BOS)
73. Blake DeWitt (2B, LAD)
74. Carlos Carrasco (RHP, PHI)
75. Jonathon Meloan (RHP, LAD)
76. Hank Conger (C, LAA)
77. Sean Rodriguez (SS, LAA)
78. Humberto Sanchez (RHP, NYY)
79. Phil Humber (RHP, NYM)
80. Edinson Volquez (RHP, TEX)

81. Dustin Nippert (RHP, ARI)
82. Anthony Swarzak (RHP, MIN)
83. Chris Parmalee (OF/1B, MIN)
84. Ubaldo Jimenez (RHP, COL)
85. Dexter Fowler (OF, COL)
86. Drew Stubbs (OF, CIN)
87. Miguel Montero (C, ARI)
88. Carlos Gomez (OF, NYM)
89. Kevin Slowey (RHP, MIN)
90. Nolan Reimold (OF, BAL)

91. Daniel Bard (RHP, BOS)
92. Chris Nelson (SS, COL)
93. Cedric Hunter (OF, SD)
94. Angel Villanoa (3B, SF)
95. Jamie Garcia (LHP, STL)
96. Travis Wood (LHP, CIN)
97. Cesar Carillo (RHP, SD)
98. Pedro Beato (RHP, BAL)
99. Joba Chamberlain (RHP, NYY)
100. Kei Igawa (LHP, NYY)

AVG: Batting Average (see also BA)

BA: Batting Average (see also AVG)

Base Performance Indicator (BPI): A statistical formula that measures an isolated aspect of a player's situation-independent raw skill or a gauge that helps capture the effects of random chance has on a skill. Although there are many such formulas, there are only a few that we are referring to when the term is used in this book. For pitchers, our BPI's are control (bb%), dominance (k/9), command (k/bb), opposition on base average (OOB), ground/line/fly ratios (G/L/F), and expected ERA (xERA). Random chance is measured witih the hit rate (H%) and strand rate (S%).

*Base Performance Value (BPV): A single value that describes a pitcher's overall raw skill level. This is more useful than any traditional statistical gauge to track performance trends and project future statistical output. The BPV formula combines and weights several BPIs:

(Dominance Rate x 6) + (Command ratio x 21) – Opposition HR Rate x 30) – ((Opp. Batting Average - .275) x 200)

The formula combines the individual raw skills of power, command, the ability to keep batters from reaching base, and the ability to prevent long hits, all characteristics that are unaffected by most external team factors. In tandem with a pitcher's strand rate, it provides a complete picture of the elements that contribute to a pitcher's ERA, and therefore serves as an accurate tool to project likely changes in ERA. **BENCHMARKS:** We generally consider a BPV of 50 to be the minimum level required for long-term success. The elite of bullpen aces will have BPV's in the excess of 100 and it is rare for these stoppers to enjoy long-term success with consistent levels under 75.

Batters Faced per Game *(Craig Wright)*

((IP x 2.82) + H + BB) / G

A measure of pitcher usage and one of the leading indicators for potential pitcher burnout.

Batting Average (BA, or AVG)

(H/AB)

Ratio of hits to at-bats, though it is a poor evaluative measure of hitting performance. It neglects the offensive value of the base on balls and assumes that all hits are created equal.

Batting Eye (Eye)

(Walks / Strikeouts)

A measure of a player's strike zone judgment, the raw ability to distinguish between balls and strikes. **BENCHMARKS:** The best hitters have eye ratios over 1.00 (indicating more walks than strikeouts) and are the most likely to be among a league's .300 hitters. At the other end of the scale are ratios

less than 0.50, which represent batters who likely also have lower BAs.

bb%: Walk rate (hitters)

bb/9: Opposition Walks per 9 IP

BF/Gm: Batters Faced Per Game

BPI: Base Performance Indicator

*BPV: Base Performance Value

Cmd: Command ratio

Command Ratio (Cmd)

(Strikeouts / Walks)

This is a measure of a pitcher's raw ability to get the ball over the plate. There is no more fundamental a skill than this, and so it is accurately used as a leading indicator to project future rises and falls in other gauges, such as ERA. Command is one of the best gauges to use to evaluate minor league performance. It is a prime component of a pitcher's base performance value. **BENCHMARKS:** Baseball's upper echelon of command pitchers will have ratios in excess of 3.0. Pitchers with ratios under 1.0 — indicating that they walk more batters than they strike out — have virtually no potential for long term success. If you make no other changes in your approach to drafting a pitching staff, limiting your focus to only pitchers with a command ratio of 2.0 or better will substantially improve your odds of success.

Contact Rate (ct%)

((AB - K) / AB)

Measures a batter's ability to get wood on the ball and hit it into the field of play. BENCHMARK: Those batters with the best contact skill will have levels of 90% or better. The hackers of society will have levels of 75% or less.

Control Rate (bb/9), or Opposition Walks per Game

BB Allowed x 9 / IP

Measures how many walks a pitcher allows per game equivalent. **BENCHMARK:** The best pitchers will have bb/9 levels of 3.0 or less.

ct%: Contact rate

Ctl: Control Rate

Dom: Dominance Rate

Dominance Rate (k/9), or Opposition Strikeouts per Game

(K Allowed x 9 / IP)

Measures how many strikeouts a pitcher allows per game equivalent. **BENCHMARK:** The best pitchers will have k/9 levels of 6.0 or higher.

*Expected Earned Run Average (*Gill and Reeve*)

(.575 x H [per 9 IP]) + (.94 x HR [per 9 IP]) + (.28 x BB [per 9 IP]) - (.01 x K [per 9 IP]) - Normalizing Factor

"xERA represents the expected ERA of the pitcher based on a normal distribution of his statistics. It is not influenced by situation-dependent factors." xERA erases the inequity between starters' and relievers' ERA's, eliminating the effect that a pitcher's success or failure has on another pitcher's ERA.

Similar to other gauges, the accuracy of this formula changes with the level of competition from one season to the next. The normalizing factor allows us to better approximate a pitcher's actual ERA. This value is usually somewhere around 2.77 and varies by league and year. **BENCHMARKS:** In general, xERA's should approximate a pitcher's ERA fairly closely. However, those pitchers who have large variances between the two gauges are candidates for further analysis.

Extra-Base Hit Rate (X/H)

(2B + 3B + HR) / Hits

X/H is a measure of power and can be used along with a player's slugging percentage and isolated power to gauge a player's ability to drive the ball. **BENCHMARKS:** Players with above average power will post X/H of greater than 38% and players with moderate power will post X/H of 30% or greater. Weak hitters with below average power will have a X/H level of less than 20%.

Eye: Batting Eye

h%: Hit rate (batters)

H%: Hits Allowed per Balls in Play (pitchers)

Hit Rate (h% or H%)

(H—HR) / (AB – HR - K)

The percent of balls hit into the field of play that fall for hits.

hr/9: Opposition Home Runs per 9 IP

ISO: Isolated Power

Isolated Power (ISO)

(Slugging Percentage - Batting Average)

Isolated Power is a measurement of power skill. Subtracting a player's BA from his SLG, we are essentially pulling out all the singles and single bases from the formula. What remains are the extra-base hits. ISO is not an absolute measurement as it assumes that two doubles is worth one home run, which certainly is not the case, but is another statistic that is a good measurement of raw power. **BENCHMARKS:** The game's top sluggers will tend to have ISO levels over .200. Weak hitters will be under .100.

k/9: Dominance rate (opposition strikeouts per 9 IP)

Major League Equivalency (*Bill James*)

A formula that converts a player's minor or foreign league statistics into a comparable performance in the major leagues. These are not projections, but conversions of current performance.

Contains adjustments for the level of play in individual leagues and teams. Works best with Triple-A stats, not quite as well with Double-A stats, and hardly at all with the lower levels. Foreign conversions are still a work in process. James' original formula only addressed batting. Our research has devised conversion formulas for pitchers, however, their best use comes when looking at BPI's, not traditional stats.

MLE: Major League Equivalency

OBP: On Base Percentage (batters)

OBA: Opposition Batting Average (pitchers)

On Base Percentage (OBP)

(H + BB) / (AB + BB)

Addressing one of the two deficiencies in BA, OBP gives value to those events that get batters on base, but are not hits. By adding walks (and often, hit batsmen) into the basic batting average formula, we have a better gauge of a batter's ability to reach base safely. An OBP of .350 can be read as "this batter gets on base 35% of the time."

Why this is a more important gauge than batting average? When a run is scored, there is no distinction made as to how that runner reached base. So, two thirds of the time—about how often a batter comes to the plate with the bases empty—a walk really is as good as a hit. **BENCHMARKS:** We all know what a .300 hitter is, but what represents "good" for OBP? That comparable level would likely be .400, with .275 representing the level of futility.

On Base Plus Slugging Percentage (OPS): A simple sum of the two gauges, it is considered as one of the better evaluators of overall performance. OPS combines the two basic elements of offensive production — the ability to get on base (OBP) and the ability to advance baserunners (SLG). **BENCHMARKS:** The game's top batters will have OPS levels over .900. The worst batters will have levels under .600.

Opposition Batting Average (OBA)

(Hits Allowed / ((IP x 2.82) + Hits Allowed))

A close approximation of the batting average achieved by opposing batters against a particular pitcher. **BENCHMARKS:** The converse of the benchmark for batters, the best pitchers will have levels under .250; the worst pitchers levels over .300.

Opposition Home Runs per Game (hr/9)

(HR Allowed x 9 / IP)

Measures how many home runs a pitcher allows per game equivalent. **BENCHMARK:** The best pitchers will have hr/9 levels of under 1.0.

Opposition On Base Average (OOB)

(Hits Allowed + BB) / ((IP x 2.82) + H + BB)

A close approximation of the on base average achieved by opposing batters against a particular pitcher. **BENCHMARK:** The best pitchers will have levels under .300; the worst pitchers levels over .375.

Opposition Strikeouts per Game: See Dominance Rate.

Opposition Walks per Game: See Control Rate.

OPS: On Base Plus Slugging Percentage

RC: Runs Created

RC/G: Runs Created Per Game

Runs Created *(Bill James)*

(H + BB - CS) x (Total bases + (.55 x SB)) / (AB + BB)

A formula that converts all offensive events into a total of runs scored. As calculated for individual teams, the result approximates a club's actual run total with great accuracy.

Runs Created Per Game *(Bill James)*

Runs Created / ((AB - H + CS) / 25.5)

RC expressed on a per-game basis might be considered the hypothetical ERA compiled against a particular batter. **BENCHMARKS:** Few players surpass the level of a 10.00 RC/G in any given season, but any level over 7.50 can still be considered very good. At the bottom are levels below 3.00.

S%: Strand Rate

Save: There are six events that need to occur in order for a pitcher to post a single save...

1. The starting pitcher and middle relievers must pitch well.
2. The offense must score enough runs.
3. It must be a reasonably close game.
4. The manager must choose to put the pitcher in for a save opportunity.
5. The pitcher must pitch well and hold the lead.
6. The manager must let him finish the game.

Of these six events, only one is within the control of the relief pitcher. As such, projecting saves for a reliever has little to do with skill and a lot to do with opportunity. However, pitchers with excellent skills sets may create opportunity for themselves.

Situation Independent: Describing a statistical gauge that measures performance apart from the context of team, ballpark, or other outside variables. Strikeouts and Walks, inasmuch as they are unaffected by the performance of a batter's surrounding team, are considered situation independent stats.

Conversely, RBIs are situation dependent because individual performance varies greatly by the performance of other batters on the team (you can't drive in runs if there is nobody on base). Similarly, pitching wins are as much a measure of the success of a pitcher as they are a measure of the success of the offense and defense performing behind that pitcher, and are therefore a poor measure of pitching performance alone.

Situation independent gauges are important for us to be able to separate a player's contribution to his team and isolate his performance so that we may judge it on its own merits.

Slg: Slugging Percentage

Slugging Percentage (Slg)

(Singles + (2 x Doubles) + (3 x Triples) + (4 x HR)) / AB

A measure of the total number of bases accumulated per at bat. It is a misnomer; it is not a true measure of a batter's slugging ability because it includes singles. SLG also assumes that each type of hit has proportionately increasing value (i.e. a double is twice as valuable as a single, etc.) which is not true. **BENCHMARKS:** The top batters will have levels over .500. The bottom batters will have levels under .300.

Strand Rate (S%)

(H + BB - ER) / (H + BB - HR)

Measures the percentage of allowed runners a pitcher strands, which incorporates both individual pitcher skill and bullpen effectiveness. **BENCHMARKS:** The most adept at stranding runners will have S% levels over 75%. Once a pitcher's S% starts dropping down below 65%, he's going to have problems with his ERA. Those pitchers with strand rates over 80% will have artificially low ERAs, which will be prone to relapse.

Strikeouts per Game: See Opposition Strikeouts per game.

Walks + Hits per Innings Pitched (WHIP): The number of baserunners a pitcher allows per inning. **BENCHMARKS:** Usually, a WHIP of under 1.20 is considered top level and over 1.50 is indicative of poor performance. Levels under 1.00 — allowing fewer runners than IP — represent extraordinary performance and are rarely maintained over time.

Walk rate (bb%)

(BB / (AB + BB))

A measure of a batter's eye and plate patience. BENCHMARKS: The best batters will have levels of over 10%. Those with the least plate patience will have levels of 5% or less.

Walks per Game: See Opposition Walks per Game.

WHIP: Walks + Hits per Innings Pitched

Wins: There are five events that need to occur in order for a pitcher to post a single win...

1. He must pitch well, allowing few runs.
2. The offense must score enough runs.
3. The defense must successfully field all batted balls.
4. The bullpen must hold the lead.
5. The manager must leave the pitcher in for 5 innings, and not remove him if the team is still behind.

X/H: Extra-base Hit Rate

*xERA: Expected ERA

* Asterisked formulas have updated versions in the Baseball Forecaster. *However, those updates include statistics like Ground Ball Rate, Fly Ball Rate or Line Drive Rate, for which we do not have reliable data for minor leaguers. So we use the previous version of those formulas, as listed here, for the players in this book.*

TEAM AFFILIATIONS

TEAM	ORG	LEAGUE	LEV	TEAM	ORG	LEAGUE	LEV
Aberdeen	BAL	New York-Penn League	SS	Connecticut	DET	New York-Penn League	SS
Akron	CLE	Eastern League	AA	Corpus Christi	HOU	Texas League	AA
Albuquerque	COL	Pacific Coast League	AAA	Danville	ATL	Appalachian League	Rk
Altoona	PIT	Eastern League	AA	Dayton	CIN	Midwest League	A-
Arkansas	LAA	Texas League	AA	Daytona	CIN	Florida State League	A+
Asheville	COL	South Atlantic League	A-	Delmarva	BAL	South Atlantic League	A-
Auburn	WAS	New York-Penn League	SS	Dunedin	TOR	Florida State League	A+
Augusta	SF	South Atlantic League	A-	Durham	TAM	International League	AAA
AZL Angels	LAA	Arizona League	Rk	El Paso	SD	Pacific Coast League	AAA
AZL Athletics	OAK	Arizona League	Rk	Elizabethton	MIN	Appalachian League	Rk
AZL Brewers	MIL	Arizona League	Rk	Erie	DET	Eastern League	AA
AZL Cubs	CHC	Arizona League	Rk	Eugene	CHC	Northwest League	SS
AZL Diamondbacks	ARI	Arizona League	Rk	Everett	SEA	Northwest League	SS
AZL Dodgers	LAD	Arizona League	Rk	Fort Myers	MIN	Florida State League	A+
AZL Giants	SF	Arizona League	Rk	Fort Wayne	SD	Midwest League	A-
AZL Indians	CLE	Arizona League	Rk	Frederick	BAL	Carolina League	A+
AZL Mariners	SEA	Arizona League	Rk	Fresno	HOU	Pacific Coast League	AAA
AZL Padres	SD	Arizona League	Rk	Frisco	TEX	Texas League	AA
AZL Rangers	TEX	Arizona League	Rk	GCL Astros	HOU	Gulf Coast League	Rk
AZL Reds	CIN	Arizona League	Rk	GCL Blue Jays	TOR	Gulf Coast League	Rk
AZL White Sox	CHW	Arizona League	Rk	GCL Braves	ATL	Gulf Coast League	Rk
Bakersfield	SEA	California League	A+	GCL Cardinals	STL	Gulf Coast League	Rk
Batavia	MIA	New York-Penn League	SS	GCL Marlins	MIA	Gulf Coast League	Rk
Beloit	OAK	Midwest League	A-	GCL Mets	NYM	Gulf Coast League	Rk
Billings	CIN	Pioneer League	Rk	GCL Nationals	WAS	Gulf Coast League	Rk
Binghamton	NYM	Eastern League	AA	GCL Orioles	BAL	Gulf Coast League	Rk
Birmingham	CHW	Southern League	AA	GCL Phillies	PHI	Gulf Coast League	Rk
Bluefield	TOR	Appalachian League	Rk	GCL Pirates	PIT	Gulf Coast League	Rk
Boise	COL	Northwest League	SS	GCL Rays	TAM	Gulf Coast League	Rk
Bowie	BAL	Eastern League	AA	GCL Red Sox	BOS	Gulf Coast League	Rk
Bowling Green	TAM	Midwest League	A-	GCL Tigers	DET	Gulf Coast League	Rk
Bradenton	PIT	Florida State League	A+	GCL Twins	MIN	Gulf Coast League	Rk
Brevard County	MIL	Florida State League	A+	GCL Yankees 1	NYY	Gulf Coast League	Rk
Bristol	PIT	Appalachian League	Rk	GCL Yankees 2	NYY	Gulf Coast League	Rk
Brooklyn	NYM	New York-Penn League	SS	Grand Junction	COL	Pioneer League	Rk
Buffalo	TOR	International League	AAA	Great Falls	CHW	Pioneer League	Rk
Burlington	KC	Appalachian League	Rk	Great Lakes	LAD	Midwest League	A-
Burlington	LAA	Midwest League	A-	Greeneville	HOU	Appalachian League	Rk
Carolina	ATL	Carolina League	A+	Greensboro	MIA	South Atlantic League	A-
Cedar Rapids	MIN	Midwest League	A-	Greenville	BOS	South Atlantic League	A-
Charleston	NYY	South Atlantic League	A-	Gwinnett	ATL	International League	AAA
Charlotte	CHW	International League	AAA	Hagerstown	WAS	South Atlantic League	A-
Charlotte	TAM	Florida State League	A+	Harrisburg	WAS	Eastern League	AA
Chattanooga	MIN	Southern League	AA	Helena	MIL	Pioneer League	Rk
Clearwater	PHI	Florida State League	A+	Hickory	TEX	South Atlantic League	A-
Clinton	SEA	Midwest League	A-	High Desert	TEX	California League	A+
Colorado Springs	MIL	Pacific Coast League	AAA	Hillsboro	ARI	Northwest League	SS
Columbus	CLE	International League	AAA	Hudson Valley	TAM	New York-Penn League	SS

TEAM	ORG	LEAGUE	LEV	TEAM	ORG	LEAGUE	LEV
Huntsville	MIL	Southern League	AA	Portland	BOS	Eastern League	AA
Idaho Falls	KC	Pioneer League	Rk	Potomac	WAS	Carolina League	A+
Indianapolis	PIT	International League	AAA	Princeton	TAM	Appalachian League	Rk
Inland Empire	LAA	California League	A+	Pulaski	NYY	Appalachian League	Rk
Iowa	CHC	Pacific Coast League	AAA	Quad Cities	HOU	Midwest League	A-
Jackson	SEA	Southern League	AA	Rancho Cucamonga	LAD	California League	A+
Jacksonville	MIA	Southern League	AA	Reading	PHI	Eastern League	AA
Jamestown	PIT	New York-Penn League	SS	Reno	ARI	Pacific Coast League	AAA
Johnson City	STL	Appalachian League	Rk	Richmond	SF	Eastern League	AA
Jupiter	MIA	Florida State League	A+	Rochester	MIN	International League	AAA
Kane County	ARI	Midwest League	A-	Rome	ATL	South Atlantic League	A-
Kannapolis	CHW	South Atlantic League	A-	Round Rock	TEX	Pacific Coast League	AAA
Kingsport	NYM	Appalachian League	Rk	Sacramento	SF	Pacific Coast League	AAA
Lake County	CLE	Midwest League	A-	Salem	BOS	Carolina League	A+
Lake Elsinore	SD	California League	A+	Salem-Keizer	SF	Northwest League	SS
Lakeland	DET	Florida State League	A+	Salt Lake	LAA	Pacific Coast League	AAA
Lakewood	PHi	South Atlantic League	A-	San Antonio	SD	Texas League	AA
Lancaster	HOU	California League	A+	San Jose	SF	California League	A+
Lansing	TOR	Midwest League	A-	Savannah	NYM	South Atlantic League	A-
Las Vegas	NYM	Pacific Coast League	AAA	Scranton/Wilkes-Barre		NYY	Inter-
Lehigh Valley	PHI	International League	AAA	national League	AAA		
Lexington	KC	South Atlantic League	A-	South Bend	CHC	Midwest League	A-
Louisville	CIN	International League	AAA	Spokane	TEX	Northwest League	SS
Lowell	BOS	New York-Penn League	SS	Springfield	STL	Texas League	AA
Lynchburg	CLE	Carolina League	A+	St. Lucie	NYM	Florida State League	A+
Mahoning Valley	CLE	New York-Penn League	SS	State College	STL	New York-Penn League	SS
Memphis	STL	Pacific Coast League	AAA	Staten Island	NYY	New York-Penn League	SS
Midland	OAK	Texas League	AA	Stockton	OAK	California League	A+
Mississippi	ATL	Southern League	AA	Syracuse	WAS	International League	AAA
Missoula	ARI	Pioneer League	Rk	Tacoma	SEA	Pacific Coast League	AAA
Mobile	ARI	Southern League	AA	Tampa	NYY	Florida State League	A+
Modesto	COL	California League	A+	Tennessee	CHC	Southern League	AA
Montgomery	TAM	Southern League	AA	Toledo	DET	International League	AAA
Myrtle Beach	CHC	Carolina League	A+	Trenton	NYY	Eastern League	AA
Nashville	OAK	Pacific Coast League	AAA	Tri-City	HOU	New York-Penn League	SS
New Britain	COL	Eastern League	AA	Tri-City	SD	Northwest League	SS
New Hampshire	TOR	Eastern League	AA	Tulsa	LAD	Texas League	AA
New Orleans	MIA	Pacific Coast League	AAA	Vancouver	TOR	Northwest League	SS
Norfolk	BAL	International League	AAA	Vermont	OAK	New York-Penn League	SS
Northwest Arkansas	KC	Texas League	AA	Visalia	ARI	California League	A+
Ogden	LAD	Pioneer League	Rk	West Michigan	DET	Midwest League	A-
Oklahoma City	LAD	Pacific Coast League	AAA	West Virginia	PIT	South Atlantic League	A-
Omaha	KC	Pacific Coast League	AAA	Williamsport	PHI	New York-Penn League	SS
Orem	LAA	Pioneer League	Rk	Wilmington	KC	Carolina League	A+
Palm Beach	STL	Florida State League	A+	Winston-Salem	CHW	Carolina League	A+
Pawtucket	BOS	International League	AAA	Wisconsin	MIL	Midwest League	A-
Pensacola	CIN	Southern League	AA				
Peoria	STL	Midwest League	A-				

FIRST PITCH 2015
Fantasy Baseball Forums

Read everything you want.
The best advice is live advice.

Get ready for an unforgettable experience— BaseballHQ.com's **First Pitch Forums**. These 3+ hour events are packed full of fantasy baseball talk, interactive activities and fun! Top national baseball analysts disclose competitive secrets unique to 2015: Players to watch, trends to monitor, new strategies to employ and more! Plus, they answer YOUR questions as you look for the edge that will lead to a 2015 championship.

BaseballHQ.com's Ron Shandler, Brent Hershey and Ray Murphy chair the sessions and bring a dynamic energy to every event. They are joined by experts from BaseballHQ.com as well as other sports media sources, such as ESPN.com, MLB.com, Rotowire, FanGraphs, BaseballProspectus, Mastersball, Sirius/XM Radio and more.

Don't forget
First Pitch Arizona:
Nov. 6-8 in Phoenix, at the AFL!

2015 FIRST PITCH FORUM DATES, SITES AND REGISTRATION INFORMATION

Saturday, February 28	CHICAGO
Sunday, March 1	CINCINNATI
Friday, March 6	WASHINGTON DC
Saturday, March 7	NEW YORK
Sunday, March 8	BOSTON
Saturday, March 14	LOS ANGELES
Sunday, March 15	SAN FRANCISCO

NOTE: Schedule is preliminary and subject to change.

For program description and details, visit:

www.firstpitchforums.com

Registration:
$39 per person in advance
$49 per person at the door

Get Baseball Insights Every Single Day.

The *Minor League Baseball Analyst* provides a head-start in evaluating and selecting up-and-coming prospects for your fantasy team. You can maintain that edge all season long.

From spring training to the season's last pitch, **BaseballHQ.com** covers all aspects of what's happening on and off the field—all with the most powerful fantasy slant on the Internet:

- Nationally-renowned baseball analysts.
- MLB news analysis; including anticipating the *next* move.
- Dedicated columns on starting pitching, relievers, batters, and our popular Fact or Fluke? player profiles.
- Minor-league coverage beyond just scouting and lists.
- FAAB targets, starting pitcher reports, strategy articles, daily game resources, call-up profiles and more!

Plus, **BaseballHQ.com** gets personal, with customizable tools and valuable resources:

- Team Stat Tracker and Power Search tools
- Custom Draft Guide for YOUR league's parameters
- Sortable and downloadable stats and projection files
- Subscriber forums, the friendliest on the baseball Internet

Visit **www.baseballhq.com/subscribe**
to lock down your path to a 2015 championship!

Full Season subscription **$89**
(prorated at the time of order; auto-renews each October)

Draft Prep subscription **$39**
(complete access from January through April 30, 2015)

Please read our Terms of service at www.baseballhq.com/terms.html

Minor League Baseball Analyst & BaseballHQ.com: Your season-long championship lineup.